The Editor

MARION L. RUST is Associate Professor of English at the University of Kentucky. She is the author of *Prodigal Daughters: Susanna Rowson's Early American Women.*

A NORTON CRITICAL EDITION

Susanna Rowson

CHARLOTTE TEMPLE

AUTHORITATIVE TEXT

CONTEXTS

CRITICISM

Edited by

MARION L. RUST
UNIVERSITY OF KENTUCKY

W • W • NORTON & COMPANY • *New York* • *London*

W. W. Norton & Company has been independent since its founding in 1923, when William Warder Norton and Mary D. Herter Norton first published lectures delivered at the People's Institute, the adult education division of New York City's Cooper Union. The firm soon expanded its program beyond the Institute, publishing books by celebrated academics from America and abroad. By mid-century, the two major pillars of Norton's publishing program—trade books and college texts—were firmly established. In the 1950s, the Norton family transferred control of the company to its employees, and today—with a staff of four hundred and a comparable number of trade, college, and professional titles published each year—W. W. Norton & Company stands as the largest and oldest publishing house owned wholly by its employees.

Composition by Westchester Book Group
Manufacturing by the Courier Companies—Westford division
Production manager: Eric Pier-Hocking

Library of Congress Cataloging-in-Publication Data

Rowson, Mrs., 1762–1824.
    Charlotte Temple : authoritative text, contexts, criticism / edited by Marion
L. Rust. — 1st ed.
        p. cm. — (A Norton critical edition)
    Includes bibliographical references.
    ISBN 978-0-393-92538-8 (pbk.)
    1. British—New York (State)—New York—Fiction.   2. Illegitimate children—
Fiction.   3. Runaway teenagers—Fiction.   4. Teenage pregnancy—Fiction.
5. New York (N.Y.)—Fiction.   6. Teenage girls—Fiction.   7. Elopement—
Fiction.   8. Seduction—Fiction.   9. Betrayal—Fiction.   10. Soldiers—
Fiction.   11. Rowson, Mrs., 1762–1824. Charlotte Temple.   I. Rust, Marion.
II. Title.
    PS2736.R3C5 2011
    813'.2—dc22   2010007640

W. W. Norton & Company, Inc., 500 Fifth Avenue, New York, N.Y. 10110
www.wwnorton.com
W. W. Norton & Company Ltd., Castle House, 75/76 Wells Street, London
W1T 3QT

1 2 3 4 5 6 7 8 9 0

Contents

Criticism

Illustrations

Introduction

Spoonfuls of Sugar

It's worth remembering that *Charlotte Temple* was originally read for fun. Despite the fact that you may peruse this edition on your way to some form of academic credit, its author, Susanna Rowson, would never have assigned it at the female academy she ran in and around Boston during the first quarter of the nineteenth century. She would have taught history, yes. Geography, definitely. Dancing and piano, even, for those who could afford the extra fee. But not fiction.

To say readers found this book pleasurable enough to read even though they didn't have to, however, is not to say they didn't learn anything from it. Indeed, for a novel reader of Rowson's day, the two—fun and learning—were said to go hand in hand. In late eighteenth-century England, where *Charlotte* was first published, the most common synonym for readerly pleasure was *entertainment*. Almost all novels in this period, as well as essays and other narrative publications, promised to entertain their readers. The word was rarely found on its own, however; instead, it was accompanied by its better half, *instruction*. English novelist Samuel Richardson founds his 1748 novel *Clarissa*, a prototype for *Charlotte Temple*, on just such a balance when he proposes that the foibles of his secondary characters will "entertain and divert; and at the same time both warn and instruct" (see p. 264). Rowson herself introduces a later novel as "instruction . . . blended with amusement" (see p. 360). The idea was that one could do well by doing good: reading a novel provided sensations of well-being that made the learning go down easy, while it warned against bad behavior by spelling out its imagined consequences.

This proposition depended on a model of the mind that kept thought (what instruction made happen) and feelings (to which entertainment appealed) securely cordoned off from one another. If entertainment helped make instruction easier, that was precisely because it maintained its own separate status outside the realm of knowledge. These entities came together in the novel, theoretically at least, only to touch hands briefly and depart. In practice, however, as most of us already know, there is no such neat separation between thought and feeling. The term *sentiment* itself already suggested as much by the mid-eighteenth century, when it meant "a thought or reflection coloured by or proceeding from emotion" (*Oxford English Dictionary*). Conversely, as Michelle Rosaldo argues, emotions themselves can be considered "embodied thoughts" (see p. 313). And the novel was one place where this imbrication became only too clear.

This was especially true of the sentimental novel, of which *Charlotte Temple* is considered a prime example. Sentimental novels both represented characters in the grip of strong emotion and invited readers to respond in kind (the essays in the section "The American Sentimental" elaborate on this definition at some length). At the same time, they attempted to harness these sensations to the production of rational behavior that bettered society. According to the Scottish commonsense philosophy that served as both source and scourge of sentimental novels, it was the benevolent impulse at the heart of each and every person that allowed us to recognize one another's suffering as a first step toward alleviating that suffering. This eighteenth-century emphasis on "sensibility," or a compassionate attentiveness to one's own and other people's state of mind, not only revealed the importance of emotional intimacy to society at large but also illustrated the dangers inherent in human trust (for more on sensibility, see Todd, on p. 280 herein). As Charlotte learned the hard way, not everyone who pretended to have one's best interests at heart really did. How was one to distinguish the selfless from the selfish impulse, in oneself and, perhaps more important, in another person?

For skeptics of the novel in general and the sentimental novel in particular, it exacerbated this danger in at least two ways: one resulting from a dearth of responsiveness, the other from an excess. Regarding the former, readers who spent their time crying over the sorrowful fate of fictional characters might find themselves emotionally exhausted and thereby less inclined to alleviate real suffering, despite its obviously greater claim on the thinking subject. This is what Benjamin Rush warned of in 1787, when he exhorted the students of the Young Ladies' Academy of Philadelphia to read history, travel literature, poetry, and moral essays—anything but British novels, which excited "an abortive sympathy" that "blunts the heart to that which is real."

If on the one hand novels could produce callous, lazy readers who were loathe to lift a finger to assist the less fortunate, at the other extreme, they were thought to create overexcitable readers with poor judgment. Just as sentimental heroines such as Charlotte had a problematic tendency to be drawn to men they knew weren't good for them, readers could not be depended on to avoid in practice the pleasures they rehearsed mentally in a novel, however heinous the consequences might be. This is the fate of Mary Lumley, the character most like Charlotte in Rowson's posthumously published sequel, commonly known as *Lucy Temple*. Because Mary was indulged by her royalty-loving mother in all the light reading she could wish, she demands similarly intense sensations in her everyday life to those she derives from fiction. At the same time, because she has ignored more ennobling fare such as history and advice literature, she possesses little practical knowledge to temper her fantastic expectations. As a result, like the heroines of her beloved novels, she behaves excessively. She is a grouch and a spendthrift, with horrible taste in men. Despite the advice of her adoptive family, she marries a rake, signs over her inheritance to him, and—surprise, surprise—is shortly abandoned.

As the fact that Mary is a character in a novel suggests, novels themselves were continually fighting back against the belief that they must, by their very nature, corrupt. *Charlotte Temple* is full of such defenses, from its claim to be based on fact (and therefore incapable of instilling unrealistic expectations) to its extreme flagging of negative behaviors (not least by a plot that punishes the wicked) to its promise that it is dedicated to the salvation, and not the ruin, of the "hapless fair." But, even if readers were both capable of recognizing bad behavior and had no intention of imitating it, their very commitment to experiencing folly imaginatively by means of the novel put what Richardson called its "warning" feature in doubt. In fact, experiencing forbidden pleasures was a large part of what kept readers reading. Thus, as Margaret Doody explains, no matter how many prefatory promises authors made, there was no such thing as a truly "exemplary novel": no way to ensure that an author cured, rather than created, hapless readers. This is why Rowson had to downplay her career as a novelist to succeed as the founder of a school (see p. 371).

Had Rowson's school admitted boys, she would probably not have had to go to such lengths. By the same token, it is no coincidence that Rush addressed his lecture on the dangers of the novel to a female academy or that the character ruined by novels in *Lucy Temple* is a girl. For as Doody and many others have argued, novels fell into critical disrepute in the late eighteenth century precisely as they became known as women's work. As more women began to read and write fiction, it began to be imagined as an activity that was both inherently attractive and uniquely threatening to the female sex. This was especially true for women of the expanding middle class, who were expected to serve others through their roles as daughters, wives, mothers, and members of the local community. In essence, what this correlation between fiction's increasing "femality" (to quote nineteenth-century author Fanny Fern) and its declining status suggests is that novels were especially perilous to women because they made women less useful. No wonder critics protested. Novels were dangerous, yes: not because they created foolish women but, rather, less tractable ones.

Rowson's sensitivity to, first, the uncomfortable relationship between pleasure and moral instruction and, second, how this discomfort was essential to both the art of the novel and the empowerment of women is evident from her prefatory remarks to *Charlotte Temple*. She hopes to be of service to those who have "neither friends to advise, or understanding to direct them" (*sic;* see p. 5). At first glance, this phrase lines up nicely with the entertain–instruct dyad. Our friends not only make the pleasures of sociability possible—a key aspect of entertainment as perceived in this period—we also belong to these companions through ties of love, envy, affection, anger, compassion, and myriad other emotions. Thus even when we're not out on the town together (not being entertained in the narrow sense of the term), they appeal to our feeling selves, in much the way that novels do. On the other side of Rowson's equation, understanding is precisely that which instruction aims to convey. You must understand what you've read, in order for it to direct your behavior.

Rowson's statement, however, disturbs this apparent opposition in several ways. First of all, the friends whom she mentions "advise"; like the novel itself, they aren't there just to entertain but also to teach us something. Second, *understanding* sounds suspiciously like just such another so-called friend; where he or she advises, it "directs." In other words, it tells you what to do. But isn't knowing what to do a matter of feeling, at least in part? To choose a course of action, one must prefer a particular outcome. And to want a particular outcome is to feel something: desire.

The preface is not the only apparently straightforward declaration in the novel whose meaning becomes more complex on closer inspection. Throughout, *Charlotte Temple* suggests that, for all that defenders of the genre (including Rowson herself) claimed it made entertainment the means to instruction, cognition was as likely to serve emotion as to master it. Charlotte demonstrates the consequences of this complication early in the novel, when she rationalizes her decision to open a letter from Montraville by telling herself she can reseal it afterward to make it look as though it had never been read. As it turns out, such resealing is not as easy as it looks: of a letter, of the virginal body it metonymizes, or of past mistakes that continually intrude themselves upon one's present in the form of misfortune and sorrowful memory.

Charlotte Temple highlights the subversive function of reading in yet another way, one that finally suggests why such a risky business as the novel might be worth the instability it engenders. To understand this, we must take one more look at the author's friendless, ignorant imaginary reader. It's one thing to have one's rational resolve corrupted by desire; but it's quite another not to possess either desire or resolve. And that's the scenario Rowson presents by describing the reader exclusively in terms of what she's missing. Much like Charlotte herself, the figure Rowson imagines has no friends and insufficient understanding. Far from offering more of something a reader already knows to appreciate, the novel describes an abysmal absence and supplies a fundamental lack.

Why should the author describe her potential reader, let alone her protagonist, in such abject terms? One answer emerges from Rowson's own life history. For if this forlorn creature sounds like an orphan, that should come as no surprise. Rowson was only days old when her mother died of complications from childbirth, so she was intimately familiar with the sense of loss and not-knowingness described in *Charlotte Temple*. When she offers to mother the reader, then (an offer that the rest of the novel bears out in the narrator's many comforting asides), she is also in a sense mothering herself. It is in these imagined relationships between text and reader, text and author that we see why Rowson defended novels. However doubtful their educational benefits, she was drawn to them as a surrogate form of intimacy. Whether or not novels taught you anything, they helped alleviate loneliness; and how could that be anything but worthy?

Charlotte Temple performed this task more thoroughly than any other novel of the period, which helps explain its unique popularity among a host of readily available novels that also treated the theme of seduction. More than *The Coquette, The Power of Sympathy, The Story of Margaretta*, or even its own sequel, *Charlotte Temple* virtually embodied friendship, serving less as a set of ideas than a proximate physical being. This can be seen by the fact that almost every affective state in the novel is accompanied by a bodily symptom. Tears are the most frequent: for instance, in the course of a few paragraphs describing the introduction of Charlotte's father, Mr. Temple, to his future wife and her aged father, all three have cause to shed a "pellucid drop." But tears are by no means the only somatic corollary to emotions in the story. Charlotte faints a lot, especially when she's scared. Belcour continually sneers his contempt. Montraville, consumed by guilt, is subject to intermittent "delirium" and continual "fits of melancholy." Even atonement has its embodiment, in the form of the soon-to-be-orphaned infant whom Charlotte hands over to her father at the end of the novel. Whatever *Charlotte Temple* did or failed to do for the reader's cognitive processes, then, it continually played the role of a distraught friend, whose every gesture invites one in reply. Ultimately, it is the reader who fulfills the novel's project of embodiment, providing proof of the book's humanity with his or her own tears, clenched fists, and sighs.

If *Charlotte*'s historic appeal can be explained in part by its claim on the reader's own body as the register of human intimacy, it also achieved something quite different, having to do with the sheer number of readily available roles it describes. In other words, Rowson did not expect her actual readership to consist of a plethora of motherless daughters. Rather, just as in mothering herself she plays two roles, the reader is invited to a range of possibilities. And just as she knew what it was to be the reader she described, we are free to identify with the concerned parent-narrator she addresses directly in the story: or indeed, the dissatisfied "Sir" who finds the whole thing improbable. The tale could even have appealed to a skeptical reader, whose amusement at such histrionics signaled his or her own sophistication. Most likely, these and a host of other responses occurred simultaneously and continued to overlap throughout the reading process.

In its dual appeal to soulful intimacy and theatrical self-modulation, *Charlotte Temple* provided the ultimate challenge to those who would treat the novel as either glorified advice book or unwise indiscretion. Unlike, say, John Gregory's *A Father's Legacy to His Daughters*, a popular advice book of the period, *Charlotte Temple* provides too many possibilities to allow the reader to determine a proper course of action, despite its outspoken intent to get readers to do the right thing. Like any novel worth its salt, this one provided relief from the pressure to choose one behavioral alternative over another, even as it made clear (especially for women of Charlotte's age and station) the limited options available. Figuring out how early American readers found relief within a story of female misery is to me the most important lesson the book can teach. This Norton Critical Edition provides materials to make that endeavor possible.

A Life's Work

Set in England, published in London, and devoured in a country it depicted as mercenary and heartless, *Charlotte Temple*'s enthusiastic reception in the postrevolutionary United States is as surprising as it is significant. Rowson reciprocated the affection, displaying an unexpected fondness for the nation that bested her country of origin while she was still a teenager. In a letter to a close relative written in 1795, shortly after her return to the United States, she described herself as an "Englishwoman" with "an unaccountable affection for America." By 1814, she could call America her own. Recalling her childhood on the outskirts of Boston, she wrote:

> [M]y own native land is not more dear to me than is my foster country, America. If I drew my first breath in Britain; it was

here I began to feel the value of life, here my ideas first expanded, here I first sipped at the fountain of knowledge; and here my heart first glowed with those exquisitely delightful sensations, friendship and gratitude (p. 364 herein).

This was also the country that took her family's property and sent them packing back to England, penniless, during the American Revolution, on the basis of her father's employ as a British naval officer. Rowson's failure to mention this fact, however, is not merely a sign of Christian charity. Rather, her outspoken patriotism on her second immigration to the United States reflects flexible national allegiances that allowed her to flourish as a public figure in both nations. Her success can be measured in *Charlotte Temple*'s lasting love affair with its "foster country."

The currents linking Rowson's British and American careers make her most-successful publication an exemplary transatlantic text, even if it is not an exemplary novel, as discussed in the last section of this volume. Why should the rubric of the transatlantic, which considers cultural artifacts on one side of the Atlantic Ocean as inextricably related to their counterparts on the other side, matter to our understanding of this author, this novel, or the readers who made it famous? To me, transatlanticism is important because it denies the notion of singularity as it pertains to identity, whether of persons, objects, or nations. As such, it insists on the continued acknowledgment of even those influences that do not predominate in our inevitably skewed self-depictions and the exchanges of power that they document and shape. As the product of warring nations with allegiances to both, Rowson was particularly adept at both remembering the vanquished and assuaging the victorious. This grants her unusual accuracy as a chronicler of her era.

Rowson's transatlantic sensibilities as reflected in her dual national identity also allowed for an unprecedented commitment to female self-determination in her own life if not always that of her heroines. The author describes her citizenship as a complex and shifting state, one informed by conscious reflection ("ideas" and "knowledge") rather than the mere accident of birthplace. As such, she uses it to surpass constraints normally incumbent on her sex. In contrast, Charlotte's fatal flaw is precisely the absence of similar confidence in her ability to reconcile conflicting sensations so as to influence her life's course under challenging circumstances.

Susanna Rowson was not a tall woman. Observers described her as rather small and round, with a gift for dressing her "inelegant and clumsy form" to advantage in "stylish and tasteful . . . dress," often stripes or black silk. Being short, she tended to associate height with power. How else explain the fact that Charlotte literally shrinks over the course of the novel, than by her declining social stature? She begins her eponymous tale "tall" and "elegant." By the end of the novel, pregnant, homeless, and alone, she has ceded her influence over her lover to a richer woman from a better family—and with it her statuesque appearance. For "Julia Franklin was the very reverse of Charlotte Temple: she was tall."

The most obvious explanation for Charlotte's unlikely shrinkage is authorial forgetfulness of the same kind that makes the novel's male arch-villain, Belcour, utter the phrase "whining, pining" twice in two pages. Hastily composing her novel in order to receive a flat fee from London publisher William Lane in 1791, Rowson probably simply never noticed such inconsequential incongruities. We know she wrote one of her plays, *Slaves in Algiers*, in two months; why would she spend longer on an anonymous publication that everyone knew was going to be light reading by the mere fact that it issued from Minerva Press, infamous for what English essayist Charles Lamb called its "scanty" fare? (Lamb considered Lane a "lesser wit" and, in a comment that indicates how closely the novel's denigration was linked to its feminization, held him largely responsible for "those scanty intellectual viands of the whole female reading public.")

The novel's inconsistencies speak not only to Rowson's proclivities as an artist but also to the demands of the English literary marketplace, where the novel was first published, and the American, where it had its biggest success (for more on the novel's first American publication, see p. 183). Like everyone else in the novel business, the Minerva Press claimed (in a statement at the front of *Charlotte*) that its books would "improve the understanding," even as its "study shall be to please, as this will equally add to our interest as reflect to our honor." The extent to which interest trumped honor, however, is clear from another line of the "Appeal," which offers potential authors £500 per "literary production." As Lane bought novels in lots to cater to an ever-expanding "female reading public," *Charlotte* kept company with myriad anonymous Minerva "productions," from *Phantoms of the Cloister; or, the Mysterious Manuscript* (1795), to *Nobility Run Mad; or Raymond and His Three Wives* (1802). From its English distribution in new circulating libraries catering primarily to working-class women, to its 1867 release as one of "Munro's 10-cent novels," *Charlotte Temple* appealed to a popular audience for whom a flair for the dramatic was valued over exactitude.

The positive qualities the novel attributes to female height can also be seen as a response to the gender politics that informed these markets. Put simply, Rowson associated height with masculinity, and masculinity with power. This association would have been familiar to her from her earliest days growing up in a colonial American naval town surrounded by enlisted men. She would soon come to succeed in a variety of activities that required her either to assume traditionally male duties (such as supporting her father's family) or to please male superiors who could help (such as the Prince of Wales, who is said to have offered her family financial assistance on the basis of her precocious charm). Experiences like these would have familiarized her with masculinity as both a way of being she could approximate (as when she wrote anonymous poems that displayed classical expertise typically available only to men) and an external force she could shape to her benefit (as when she flirted with male readers in *Charlotte Temple*).

Charlotte herself, of course, did none of these things. In contrast with her creator, Charlotte's career emphasized the dangers associated with extreme femininity as it was conceived of during this period. Reckless infatuation, misplaced trust, excessive deference to the wishes of others and, finally, unwanted pregnancy characterize her fate. Only women who successfully negotiated their ascribed gender characteristics so as to maximize their own (implicitly masculine) authority stayed tall: women like Julia Franklin, who managed to hold her suitor's interest precisely by maintaining her own "independent fortune" in both a financial and an emotional sense, whereas Charlotte sacrificed hers to the desires of her lover and the wiles of an evil friend.

Rowson, then, despite her own motherless state, small stature, and unstable financial status, was no Charlotte. The following brief account of her life emphasizes the conditions that inspired and shaped this dissimilarity. It attempts to do justice to three aspects of her experience on both sides of the Atlantic: her emotional and financial insecurity; the active role played in the earliest professional fields open to women—teaching and authorship—to relieve that insecurity; and the reliance placed on her, obscured by many early biographers, by the two most documented men in her life, her father and her husband.

Rowson was born in 1762 in the garrison town of Portsmouth, England, one fourth of a large naval station whose population consisted of "sailors, naval officers, and dockyard workers." Her father, William Haswell, was a lieutenant in the British navy. Her mother, Susanna Musgrave Haswell, about whom almost nothing is known, died within days of her birth. This early loss had important repercussions not only for *Charlotte Temple* but also in Rowson's other fiction, where mothers are a yearned-for and immaculate, though rarely an intimate, presence.

Susanna's father came to America as collector of royal customs soon after her birth, leaving her in England under the care of a nurse

while he settled in Nantasket, about nine miles from Boston. There
he met and married Rachel Woodward, the daughter of a successful merchant, with whom he was to have three sons.* In 1766, he
returned to England to pick up his daughter and her nurse, and the
family embarked for New England. The journey itself lasted twelve
weeks and almost resulted in the starvation of those on board, before
ending in a shipwreck off the coast of Boston. Like the heroine of her
semiautobiographical novel, *Trials of the Human Heart*, Susanna
indicates that she was rescued by having a rope tied around her waist
and being lowered over the ship's side "like a bundle of straw." Again,
her early life can be seen to have thematic repercussions on her
work, where sailing and its attendant disasters figure prominently
in such novels as *Rebecca* and *Trials of the Human Heart* as well as in
several verses. In her own way, Charlotte too finds crossing the Atlantic risky: it is "on board of the ship" between Portsmouth, England,
and New York—"a tedious and tempestuous passage" if ever there
was one—that she has sex with her seducer, Lieutenant Montraville,
while her letters home, unbeknownst to her, are tossed overboard. In
their own demonstration of the hold the ocean held over the family,
Rowson's half-brothers all became naval officers. By 1767, the family
was back in Nantasket.

There, under the aegis of her father, whom literary biographer
Patricia Parker calls "a jovial man who enjoyed storytelling and jests,"
Susanna flourished in a wide circle of genteel acquaintance, including the revolutionary statesman and orator James Otis Jr. (he is said
to have called her "his little pupil"). But jovial or not, as an officer
of the British Royal Navy Susanna's father found himself increasingly unwelcome as revolutionary tensions increased, while he
remained unwilling to take the required oath of allegiance to the
revolutionary cause. In 1777, when Susanna was fifteen, his property
was confiscated, and he was detained as a prisoner of war. The entire
family was forced fourteen miles inland to Abington, and then twelve
miles south to Halifax. In 1778, the family, now destitute and with
William in poor health, was sent back to England as part of a prisoner exchange.

At this point, Susanna became the family's primary breadwinner (her song lyrics for London theatrical productions may have
been her first literary creations). Her father, unable to continue his
service to the Royal Navy, spent the following years in futile petitions to the British government to recoup his financial losses. Literary biographer Dorothy Weil attributes his inability to the

---

* If the fictional reference in *Lucy Temple* is any indication, Susanna and her stepmother
enjoyed an amicable, if not a close, relationship: "though she experienced not the most
tender affection, yet Aura Melville found in her all the care and solicitude of a mother."

"physical and psychological effects of his detention." One can only wonder what psychological effects such detention had on Susanna herself.

Rowson helped support her family until her marriage in 1786 to hardware merchant William Rowson. In the same year, her first novel, *Victoria*, was published. Among the motives behind Susanna's marriage, Parker includes the desire for "economic support." Rather than release her from her financial obligations, however, Susanna's marriage essentially widened the circle of her male dependents, for her husband relied on her to make ends meet. Bibliographer R. W. Vail writes of him: "Mr. Rowson, though something of a musician, seems to have been a person of no particular ability or ambition. Though he appears now and then in the story of Mrs. Rowson's life, he is always very much in the background." In addition to supporting her husband, Susanna also raised William's son from outside the marriage, William Jr. They corresponded when he was an adult, and it has been suggested that her sea shanty "The Little Sailor Boy" was written with him in mind.

However forgiving a spouse she may have been, Rowson's unusual relationships with her father and her husband, both of whom depended on her economically for much of their lives, is reflected in ambivalent portrayals of father figures throughout her work. It must be emphasized that she went to great lengths to honor domestic patriarchs such as Charlotte's own father, who arrives at her dying bedside in time to forgive her and accept her infant daughter. Scholar Nina Baym notes that among all the woman-authored dialogue texts she studied from between 1790 and 1860, Rowson's *Biblical Dialogues* was the only one "with a father present." Even Lieutenant Montraville, Charlotte Temple's weak-willed seducer and the absent father to her daughter Lucy, redeems himself in the sequel, *Lucy Temple*, where he prevents his daughter's incestuous marriage while continuing to heartily repent past misdeeds. In the novel that followed *Charlotte Temple*'s American publication, *Trials of the Human Heart*, Rowson even resorts to mistaken identity to salvage her protagonist's faith in fatherhood, as she discovers that the cruel and neglectful man she had once called "Father" was an impostor. Nevertheless, the sheer number of weak, duplicitous, or downright dastardly male characters in her literary compositions (see, for example, "Verses to a Libertine" on p. 376 herein), along with a corresponding dearth of morally upstanding self-sufficient types, suggests that she recognized and at times resented her supposed caretakers' relative inadequacy to the task, even as she excelled in the role left vacant by their inability or unwillingness.

Whatever his flaws, William Rowson, who sang, acted, and played trumpet in the Royal Horse Guards, did introduce his wife to the world of public entertainment. Along with William's sister, the couple performed in Edinburgh and other British cities in the winter of 1792–93, until comedian and theatrical manager Thomas Wignell asked them to join his New Theatre, about to be opened in Philadelphia. In 1793, Susanna returned with her husband to what was now the United States, on a three-year engagement with Wignell's theater. Arriving in Philadelphia only to find it evacuated in the midst of a yellow fever epidemic, the New Theatre opened its season in Annapolis. There, Rowson embarked on a moderately well-received career of stage acting. During this period, she also began a long-term working relationship with Alexander Reinagle, an admired composer and cofounder of the New Theatre, with whom she collaborated on musical dramas and songs. In 1794, the company returned to Philadelphia's Chestnut Street Theater for one successful season, and then to Baltimore for two. In 1796, she left for Boston's Federal Street Theater, where the bouncer was paid a higher weekly salary than any actor or musician.

Rowson's career was soon to take a turn that offered greater opportunities for social advancement, when in November of 1797 she opened the Young Ladies' Academy in Boston. In 1800, she moved the school to Medford, and then to Newton, both nearby suburbs, before returning it to Boston in 1807. The Young Ladies' Academy was an immediate success. According to Rowson's friend and first memoirist Samuel Knapp, it went from one to about one hundred pupils in less than a year. It also gained Rowson the respectability that acting and authorship never had, as indicated by her membership in several of Boston's leading social organizations. Rowson served as president of the Boston Fatherless and Widow's Society and by 1816 was also a member of the Prayer Book and Tract Society, whose first anniversary she celebrated in an ode and a hymn. She ran the Young Ladies' Academy until shortly before her death, March 2, 1824.

Throughout this somewhat nomadic and financially insecure life, Rowson continued to publish. While still in England, she published eight works (and the majority of her fiction), including four novels, a picaresque tale, a rhymed critique of the contemporary theater scene, a book of poems, and a series of edifying sketches for young ladies. Arriving in the United States, she continued with an American edition of *Charlotte* (1794) and the four-volume *Trials of the Human Heart* (1795). A historical novel followed in which she professed to have made her last attempt at fiction, *Reuben and Rachel: or Tales of Old Times* (1798). The last novel printed during her lifetime was *Sarah: or, the Exemplary Wife* (1813). (This appeared in serial form as *Sincerity* in the *Boston Weekly Magazine* in 1803–04.) Between 1794 and 1796, Rowson also wrote a number of plays, of which two are at least partially extant: *Slaves in Algiers; or, A Struggle for Freedom* (1794) and *The Volunteers*. In addition, she published a collection of her poems and songs as *Miscellaneous Poems* in 1804.

After establishing herself as the founder of a female academy, Rowson modified her work to suit her new public role. First came *An Abridgment of Universal Geography* (1805), a geography text-book largely based on the work of the famous American geographer Jedidiah Morse. Over the next two decades she continued to produce textbooks, mainly for use in her own school: a *Spelling Dictionary* (1807), *A Present for Young Ladies* (1811), *Youth's First Step in Geography* (1818), and finally *Biblical Dialogues between a Father and His Family* (1822) and *Exercises in History, Chronology, and Biography* (1822). Between 1807 and 1818, Rowson also contributed articles, verses, and fiction to the *Boston Weekly Magazine* (which she may also have edited), the *Boston Magazine*, the *Monthly Anthology, or Magazine of Polite Literature*, and the *New England Galaxy*. Four years after her death, the sequel to *Charlotte Temple* was published from an undated manuscript: *Charlotte's Daughter; or, The Three Orphans* (1828), generally known as *Lucy Temple*.

How to Use This Book

As this overview of Rowson's publishing career indicates, by the time she returned to the United States at the age of thirty-one, she had published at least eight books. *Charlotte* did not stand out from this list in any obvious way. It was one of three novels published by William Lane (along with *Mentoria* and *Rebecca*); one of two published anonymously (the other was *The Test of Honour*); one of four to be reviewed in the London *Critical Review*. Today, only one known copy of the English publication of *Charlotte* survives. Had the book never been republished in the United States, it would probably not be much read or studied today; nor would its author, who began to receive renewed critical attention in the 1970s largely on the basis of this work.

Why, then, are we reading it now? The answer is partly that lots of other people have before us, stretching back to the earliest years of the nation. For as we know, everything changed when the book traveled across the Atlantic Ocean: on being published in the United States, it became a best-seller and remained in print continuously until the Civil War (the frontispiece of an 1860 edition appears on p. 99). And yet to ignore either the book's less successful initial London publication or its author's British heritage is to miss a great deal. Whether we call *Charlotte Temple* an English or an American book depends entirely on how, if at all, one defines a novel's nationality: by its author's birthplace, its place of composition, its setting, its primary readership, its representativeness of a particular cultural moment, or even whether the course it's taught in counts toward one's American or English requirements for the English major.

To my mind, then, there is no single right answer to the question of the book's nationality, and the question itself is somewhat beside the point. What does matter is that we recognize the interdependence of the two cultures at the time of the novel's first American appearance. (To a lesser extent, this is true of other non-English-speaking European nations as well; the novel was translated into German, for instance, in Philadelphia, in 1861.) The United States and England not only had a language and a recent war in common; they also both participated in a host of imperialist mercantile endeavors, from the African slave trade to importing the clothing and foodstuffs celebrated in "America, Commerce & Freedom" (see "The Sailor's Landlady," p. 385), to the ventures off the coast of North Africa that inspired Rowson's play *Slaves in Algiers* and a host of other American publications (see p. 402). Finally, the United States loved Charlotte at least in part precisely because both she and her author were British. Americans continued to look to England not only for the manufactured items they didn't yet produce in volume, including novels, but, more important, for the standards of taste these items both satisfied and symbolized. Like Charlotte, then, one reason Rowson was so popular in the United States is that she had the cachet of being, and sounding, English during a period when U.S. residents were as anxious about their cultural status as they were proud of their political independence.

The worst mistake we can make, then, is to call this an American novel and then retroactively impose all sorts of qualities onto it that weren't in existence at the time, such as a secure sense of national identity as distinct from the mother country. When the temptation to commit this faux pas occurs, one need simply attend to the fact that most of the book is set in England or that all the worst things that happen to Charlotte happen after her arrival in New York. At the same time, there's no denying that something made Americans want to read this book more than the British did. This distinction suggests that tastes were not identical on the two continents.

To provide access to the text that the most people read, this Norton Critical Edition is based on the first American edition of *Charlotte*. But a great deal of supplementary material in this volume is dedicated to helping us parse out the novel's overlapping British and U.S. contexts. Readers interested in their relationship will want to attend first to Camryn Hansen's fascinating essay "A Changing Tale of Truth? *Charlotte Temple* and Textual History," which overturns much received wisdom on the circumstances surrounding the novel's American publication. As Hansen demonstrates in her study of

Rowson's relationship with the novel's first American publisher, Mathew Carey, the author had far more to do with the book's first American publication than previously assumed. One chapter of the first British edition is also excerpted here to allow for firsthand collation, the detailed comparison of texts. Janet Todd's classic analysis of sensibility helps us come to terms with the British literary and cultural traditions that inform *Charlotte Temple*; so do the preface to Samuel Richardson's *Clarissa*, a review of the London edition of *Charlotte*, and an excerpt from Rowson's first published novel, *Victoria*. Nancy Armstrong shows how American sentimental novels emphasized the importance of "remaining English in North America"; Blythe Forcey describes what happened to the British epistolary tradition in the United States; and Ruth Bloch demonstrates how virtue, once a classic feature of exemplary British manhood, was feminized in the early years of the republic. Finally, a host of materials help flesh out the diverse gender, class, geographic, and political makeup of *Charlotte*'s early American readership, from Cathy Davidson's examination of how and in what form various individuals got hold of Rowson's novel, to William Gilmore's analysis of how reading was taught and Linda Kerber's discussion of what female readers chose to read once they knew how. Those curious about what exactly these readers were seeing and how that changed over the course of the nineteenth century can turn to a selection of later frontispieces and covers, which range from 1812 to 1867.

As the earlier discussion of the novel's place within both transatlantic and early national culture suggests, this volume is meant to allow readers to form connections between widely spaced supplementary readings. It presents materials in two categories: contexts and criticism. Within "Contexts," there are four subcategories: "Women in Early America," "Reading in Early America," "The American Sentimental," and "Selections from Rowson's Writing." Each grouping presents a range of complementary perspectives on the topic in question. At the same time, new topics emerge when one ignores the categorical organization presented here. Anyone interested in the history of novel reading would benefit not only from discussions of the subject contained in "Reading in Early America" but also from Rowson's prefaces to her novels, in which she defends her choice of genre and subject, contained in "Selections from Rowson's Writing." A study of female education might include both Benjamin Rush's "Thoughts Upon Female Education" and the sketches performed at Rowson's school. Accounts of Rowson's life appear not only in the works of her earliest memoirists, Samuel Knapp and Elias Nason, but also in the autobiographical excerpt from *Rebecca*. Armstrong's essay "Why Daughters Die: The Racial Logic of American Sentimentalism" sheds new light both on the excerpt from Rowson's

Reuben & Rachel featuring an interracial love triangle and on the depiction of Charlotte's surviving daughter in *Charlotte's Daughter*. Finally (though the list is nowhere near exhausted), those with an interest in how early national readers conceived of female agency could begin with Judith Sargent Murray's two polemics, continue with Eliza Wharton's contrasting self-assessments from the beginning and end of Hannah Foster's novel *The Coquette*, review Rowson's own satirical call for women's "supreme dominion" in the epilogue to *Slaves in Algiers*, and conclude with Jane Tompkins's attack on a masculinist literary tradition that has denied "Susanna Rowson, Father of the American Novel" her rightful place in the history of American letters.

Just as this edition benefits from being read across the grain, it attempts to present a variety of *Charlotte Temple* criticism that gains significance from being read as a multifaceted, interactive entity. Twentieth-century literary historian Leslie Fiedler's diatribe against the sentimental tradition and its effeminization of a properly masculine American literary tradition sounds suspiciously familiar once one has encountered Rowson contemporary William Cobbett's even more strident detraction. It meets its just rebuke, meanwhile, in Joanne Dobson's "formalist methodology." Elizabeth Barnes and Julia Stern's discussions of the novel were published concurrently, yet one sees the novel "seducing" readers into an "intimate relationship with patriarchal authority," whereas the other argues that it begins to "enfranchise a post-Revolutionary community linked by claims of universal compassion."

Finally, some critics question the notion of a single community, especially one linked by grief, as it pertains to the novel at all. At some point, virtually all of these critics (including myself) note that *Charlotte Temple*'s American readers designed her a grave in New York's Trinity Churchyard, seeming testament to the seriousness of their attachment. But as Lauren Coats describes (and as the newspaper excerpts she discusses show), they were as likely to visit to show off their new clothes as to mourn a fallen woman. And as Larzer Ziff reminds us, their own sexual mores remained decidedly flexible, even as they lamented Charlotte's seduction. If, then, as Anna Mae Duane persuasively argues, the novel's "final focus on a female pregnant body actually vexes the ideal of Lockean self-possession to which the heroines allegedly aspire," it does so to question "whether such ownership is desirable in the first place." Whether viewing the novel as a female "quest romance" or an indictment of aristocratic excess in the service of a developing middle-class patriarchy (see Evans on p. 469 herein), these readings invite us both to appreciate the unprecedented emotional charge that a seduced virgin held for two prior centuries and to remember that she refracted the myriad moods, assumptions, and concerns of a diverse reading public. This ordinary young woman meant, and continues to mean, all things to many people.

Conclusion: Writing Us In

I have suggested that the late-eighteenth-century sentimental novel developed amid equal fascination with and fear of fiction: especially that written by, about, or for women. In response, novels such as *Charlotte Temple* justified their existence by framing themselves as practical aids to the avoidance of unsalutary behaviors, from sloth to sexual depravity to financial extravagance. If *Charlotte Temple* is any indication, they did so to little effect. Their ineptitude as conduct manuals, however, sparked another kind of success. For to exactly the degree that *Charlotte Temple* failed to "save one hapless fair one," it succeeded at creating a reader capable of entertaining opposed truths simultaneously. These ranged from "Charlotte erred/Charlotte was duped," to "it is my responsibility not to turn out like Charlotte/Charlotte was the victim of forces beyond her control," to "I am sad for Charlotte/I enjoy my sadness." As such, it suggested the advantages of, and created the occasion for, a pragmatic and multidimensional view of reality over a univocal, moralistic one. Employing what one student remembered as her uncanny "judgement, or at least . . . knowledge of the taste of her company," Rowson may not have made sense of the world to early readers of *Charlotte Temple*; rather, she helped them cope with the fact that it made little, or at least complicated, sense.

Her efforts paid off in the increasing favor that *Charlotte Temple* found over the course of the nineteenth century, not only with ordinary readers but also with pedagogues, newspaper columnists, political elegists, and others in positions of social and cultural authority. The novel that Rowson most likely would not have let darken the doors of her schoolhouse may not have become assigned reading until late in the twentieth century. But by 1848, it was considered a suitable prize for academic achievement. Catharine Baum found this out when her teacher inscribed a copy of the novel to her: "This book is the property of *Catharine Baum*, as a reward to her: for having gained the head of her class; the greater number of times. Given by B. L. [Shelby?], *her teacher*." (Catharine was proud enough of this trophy that she signed her name, twice, on the next full page.) By 1870, even grown men were not ashamed to admit how much they had loved the book as disobedient young boys. Thus, as scholar Ken Parille observes, Thomas Bailey Aldrich, author of *The Story of a Bad Boy*, includes *Charlotte Temple* among "a motley collection of novels and romances" that his autobiographical protagonist Tom Bailey devours, from Don Quixote to Gil Blas, "all of which I fed upon like a bookworm."

More than a century later, the resourcefulness Rowson displayed in defending novels and their readers might seem a familiar commodity. Charlotte, however, is not. With her timid smile and unassuming disposition, it's easy to forget that this eponymous protagonist has anything to do with us. True, romantic misfortune still exists; but it's rarely fatal. So does gender oppression: in the United States, one need look no further than the discrepancy between how much men and women earn for the same job, the unequal distribution of health care, or the dearth of affordable child care for working mothers. But there's no comparison to what things were like for Charlotte's first female readers. U.S. women can vote, they can own property, they can go out on the street alone without being looked at askance. Today, Charlotte might seem from as distant a world as her future mother, stuck in a tiny apartment in a muslin cap painting a fan mount at the moment her father met her, probably would have to her.

There's at least one area, however, where *Charlotte Temple* remains highly pertinent to readers today, having to do with how the novel makes us think about ourselves as readers. Almost all of us—whether because of our ethnicity, gender, class, body type, religious persuasion, sexual orientation, age, or some other factor—have at one time or another had the experience of not qualifying for the position of implied reader, a term used by literary critics to describe the ideal consumer that a text creates for itself. Around the time of this novel's twentieth-century recovery, many feminist critics described the sense of self-cancellation that results from such an experience, especially as it pertained to gender. Judith Fetterley put the matter succinctly in 1978: "As readers and teachers and scholars, women are taught to think as men, to identify with a male point of view, and to accept as normal and legitimate a male system of values, one of whose central principles is misogyny." And yet despite a narrative's implication that we are incapable of comprehending it, when we come to terms with such a claim we do exactly that. We thereby enter an uncomfortable dual state, erasing ourselves to exist according to the terms of the narrative. At the same time, this can be a deeply empowering condition, for the very fact that we understand that we are not expected to understand proves the fallibility of the text's own assumptions.

Charlotte Temple invites us to remember those reading experiences by providing the opposite extreme. As a generally inexpensive, simply written book addressed to the young, the female, and the newly literate, *Charlotte* directed itself to those who were used to being ignored by authors as the objects, if not the subjects, of meritorious literary discourse. In so doing, it reminded them that this was not a familiar experience. Reawakened by Rowson's insistent, ingratiating address to their existence as readers and hence members of what we now call the public sphere, *Charlotte Temple*'s earliest readers were alerted to the fact that such existence had not always been recognized. That reminder remains pertinent today.

Acknowledgments

Charlotte Temple is about the failure of community, but this edition of the novel could not exist without it. I would like to thank the following individuals and institutions in particular for assisting me in this truly collaborative endeavor. Norton sales representative Lib Triplett happened to drop by my office one afternoon several years ago; half an hour later, we had cooked up the idea for this volume. Norton Editor Carol Bemis took over at that point, demonstrating her well-known patience and expertise from the very start by sending the proposal to Professor Robert Levine and two equally sympathetic and incisive anonymous readers. Norton Assistant Editor Brian Baker began to help me turn the proposal into a book; more recently, I have had the pleasure of bringing this project to completion with his successor, Assistant Editor Rivka Genesen. Graduate student Brynn Jacqueline Harris obtained key permissions agreements. Camryn Hansen provided assistance both practical and intellectual, including the contribution of an essay that corrects the early publication history of the novel. She thanks Jim Green, of the Library Company of Philadelphia, and Professor Melissa Homestead, whom I also owe a debt of gratitude for directing me to the letter from Mathew Carey to Rowson reprinted in this volume. Professors Anna Mae Duane and Lauren Coats also contributed original essays, while Professor Kenneth Parille generously shared research. At the University of Kentucky, colleagues Jeffory Clymer, Peter Kalliney, and Virginia Blum pored over drafts of the introduction. The students in my fall 2008 undergraduate seminar on American Sentimentalism served as test subjects, identifying murky terms in the novel's early chapters and tracking down their meaning for the footnotes. Students Elizabeth J. Oldiges and Robert Wilhelm were especially helpful in this respect. I would also like to thank the University of Virginia Department of Special Collections for maintaining the Rowson archive and making it available for this edition. Finally, I owe the greatest debt to the man who introduced me to *Charlotte Temple*, Professor Jay Fliegelman, 1949–2007.

Note on the Text

The text of *Charlotte Temple* is taken from the first American edition of 1794. The title page of this edition announces that it is "Printed by D. Humphreys, for M. Carey," in Philadelphia. The circumstances surrounding Mathew Carey's publication of the novel are discussed in Camryn Hansen's essay (p. 183). For purposes of comparison, a selection from the first British edition of 1791 is also included (p. 364). Rowson's original spellings have been retained, as has the punctuation unique to the two editions.

The Text of
CHARLOTTE TEMPLE

CHARLOTTE.

A TALE OF TRUTH.

By Mrs. ROWSON,
OF THE NEW THEATRE, PHILADELPHIA;
AUTHOR OF *VICTORIA, THE INQUISITOR,*
FILLE DE CHAMBRE, &c.

IN TWO VOLUMES.

She was her parent's only joy :
They had but one—one darling child.
ROMEO AND JULIET.

Her form was faultlefs, and her mind,
    Untainted yet by art,
Was noble, juft, humane, and kind,
    And virtue warm'd her heart.
But ah ! the cruel fpoiler came——

VOL. I.

PHILADELPHIA:
PRINTED BY D. HUMPHREYS,
FOR M. CAREY, No. 118, MARKET-STREET.
M.DCC.XCIV.

Title page of 1st American edition of *Charlotte. A Tale of Truth.* Special Collections, University of Virginia Library, Charlottesville.

Preface.

For the perusal of the young and thoughtless of the fair sex, this Tale of Truth is designed; and I could wish my fair readers to consider it as not merely the effusion of Fancy, but as a reality. The circumstances on which I have founded this novel were related to me some little time since by an old lady who had personally known Charlotte, though she concealed the real names of the characters, and likewise the place where the unfortunate scenes were acted: yet as it was impossible to offer a relation to the public in such an imperfect slate, I have thrown over the whole a slight veil of fiction, and substituted names and places according to my own fancy. The principal characters in this little tale are now consigned to the silent tomb: it can therefore hurt the feelings of no one; and may, I flatter myself, be of service to some who are so unfortunate as to have neither friends to advise, or understanding to direct them, through the various and unexpected evils that attend a young and unprotected woman in her first entrance into life.

While the tear of compassion still trembled in my eye for the fate of the unhappy Charlotte, I may have children of my own, said I, to whom this recital may be of use, and if to your own children, said Benevolence, why not to the many daughters of Misfortune who, deprived of natural friends, or spoilt by a mistaken education, are thrown on an unfeeling world without the least power to defend themselves from the snares not only of the other sex, but from the more dangerous arts of the profligate[1] of their own.

Sensible as I am that a novel writer, at a time when such a variety of works are ushered into the world under that name, stands but a poor chance for fame in the annals of literature, but conscious that I wrote with a mind anxious for the happiness of that sex whose morals and conduct have so powerful an influence on mankind in general; and convinced that I have not wrote a line that conveys a wrong idea to the head or a corrupt wish to the heart, I shall rest satisfied in the purity of my own intentions, and if I merit not applause, I feel that I dread not censure.

If the following tale should save one hapless fair one from the errors which ruined poor Charlotte, or rescue from impending misery the heart of one anxious parent, I shall feel a much higher gratification in reflecting on this trifling performance, than could possibly result from the applause which might attend the most elegant finished piece of literature whose tendency might deprave the heart or mislead the understanding. *trying to appease critics*

1. Dissolute, decadent.

Charlotte

Chapter I.

A Boarding School.

"Are you for a walk," said Montraville to his companion, as they arose from table; "are you for a walk? or shall we order the chaise and proceed to Portsmouth?"[2] Belcour preferred the former; and they sauntered out to view the town, and to make remarks on the inhabitants, as they returned from church.

Montraville was a Lieutenant in the army: Belcour was his brother officer: they had been to take leave of their friends previous to their departure for America, and were now returning to Portsmouth, where the troops waited orders for embarkation. They had stopped at Chichester[3] to dine; and knowing they had sufficient time to reach the place of destination before dark, and yet allow them a walk, had resolved, it being Sunday afternoon, to take a survey of the Chichester ladies as they returned from their devotions.[4]—

They had gratified their curiosity, and were preparing to return to the inn without honouring any of the belles with particular notice, when Madame Du Pont, at the head of her school, descended from the church. Such an assemblage of youth and innocence naturally attracted the young soldiers: they stopped; and, as the little cavalcade passed, almost involuntarily pulled off their hats. A tall, elegant girl looked at Montraville and blushed: he instantly recollected the features of Charlotte Temple, whom he had once seen and danced with at a ball at Portsmouth. At that time he thought on her only as a very lovely child, she being then only thirteen; but the improvement two years had made in her person, and the blush of recollection which suffused her cheeks as she passed, awakened in his bosom new and pleasing ideas. Vanity led him to think that pleasure at again beholding him might have occasioned the emotion he had witnessed, and the same vanity led him to wish to see her again.

---

2. An island city on the southern coast of England that served as a major naval port. "Chaise": a light carriage for one or two people, generally used for pleasure.
3. A city in Sussex, southern England, with Roman origins.
4. Prayers.

"She is the sweetest girl in the world," said he, as he entered the inn. Belcour stared. "Did you not notice her?" continued Montraville: "she had on a blue bonnet, and with a pair of lovely eyes of the same colour, has contrived to make me feel devilish odd about the heart."

"Pho," said Belcour, "a musket ball from our friends, the Americans, may in less than two months make you feel worse."

"I never think of the future," replied Montraville; "but am determined to make the most of the present, and would willingly compound with any kind Familiar who would inform me who the girl is, and how I might be likely to obtain an interview."

But no kind Familiar at that time appearing, and the chaise which they had ordered, driving up to the door, Montraville and his companion were obliged to take leave of Chichester and its fair inhabitant, and proceed on their journey.

But Charlotte had made too great an impression on his mind to be easily eradicated: having therefore spent three whole days in thinking on her and in endeavouring to form some plan for seeing her, he determined to set off for Chichester, and trust to chance either to favour or frustrate his designs. Arriving at the verge of the town, he dismounted, and sending the servant forward with the horses, proceeded toward the place, where, in the midst of an extensive pleasure ground, stood the mansion which contained the lovely Charlotte Temple. Montraville leaned on a broken gate, and looked earnestly at the house. The wall which surrounded it was high, and perhaps the Arguses who guarded the Hesperian fruit[5] within, were more watchful than those famed of old.

"'Tis a romantic attempt," said he; "and should I even succeed in seeing and conversing with her, it can be productive of no good: I must of necessity leave England in a few days, and probably may never return; why then should I endeavour to engage the affections of this lovely girl, only to leave her a prey to a thousand inquiries, of which at present she has no idea? I will return to Portsmouth and think no more about her."

The evening now was closed; a serene stillness reigned; and the chaste Queen of Night with her silver crescent faintly illuminated the hemisphere. The mind of Montraville was hushed into composure by the serenity of the surrounding objects. "I will think on her no more," said he, and turned with an intention to leave the place; but as he turned, he saw the gate which led to the pleasure grounds

5. Literally, fruit of the west. In Greek mythology, refers to the apples of a tree with golden branches, leaves, and fruit. The Hesperides, daughters of night, guarded this fruit with the help of a dragon. Argus, in Greek mythology, was a hundred-eyed giant; here, a watchful person.

open, and two women come out, who walked arm-in-arm across the field.

"I will at least see who these are," said he. He overtook them, and giving them the compliments of the evening, begged leave to see them into the more frequented parts of the town: but how was he delighted, when, waiting for an answer, he discovered, under the concealment of a large bonnet, the face of Charlotte Temple.

He soon found means to ingratiate himself with her companion, who was a French teacher at the school, and, at parting, slipped a letter he had purposely written, into Charlotte's hand, and five guineas[6] into that of Mademoiselle, who promised she would endeavour to bring her young charge into the field again the next evening.

[handwritten: all too convenient → guilty pleasures!]   *[handwritten: much like Rowson]*

Chapter II.

Domestic Concerns.

[handwritten: critique of wealthy]

Mr. Temple was the youngest son of a nobleman whose fortune was by no means adequate to the antiquity, grandeur, and I may add, pride of the family. He saw his elder brother made completely wretched by marrying a disagreeable woman, whose fortune helped to prop the sinking dignity of the house; and he beheld his sisters legally prostituted to old, decrepit men, whose titles gave them consequence in the eyes of the world, and whose affluence rendered them splendidly miserable. "I will not sacrifice internal happiness for outward shew," said *[handwritten: show]* he: "I will seek Content; and, if I find her in a cottage, will embrace her with as much cordiality as I should if seated on a throne."

Mr. Temple possessed a small estate of about five hundred pounds a year;[7] and with that he resolved to preserve independence, to marry where the feelings of his heart should direct him, and to confine his expenses within the limits of his income. He had a heart open to every generous feeling of humanity, and a hand ready to dispense to those who wanted part of the blessings he enjoyed himself.

As he was universally known to be the friend of the unfortunate, his advice and bounty was frequently solicited; nor was it seldom that he sought out indigent merit, and raised it from obscurity, confining his own expenses within a very narrow compass.

"You are a benevolent fellow," said a young officer to him one day; "and I have a great mind to give you a fine subject to exercise the goodness of your heart upon."

---

6. A unit of British currency.
7. In 1794 (the year of this novel's U.S. publication), £1 British was worth $4.75 in American currency. That $4.75 in 1794 would be worth just under $100 dollars today. So £500 a year would be about $50,000 a year in today's money.

"You cannot oblige me more," said Temple, "than to point out any way by which I can be serviceable to my fellow creatures."

"Come along then," said the young man, "we will go and visit a man who is not in so good a lodging as he deserves; and, were it not that he has an angel with him, who comforts and supports him, he must long since have sunk under his misfortunes." The young man's heart was too full to proceed; and Temple, unwilling to irritate his feelings by making further enquiries, followed him in silence, til they arrived at the Fleet prison.[8]

The officer enquired for Captain Eldridge: a person led them up several pair of dirty stairs, and pointing to a door which led to a miserable, small apartment, said that was the Captain's room, and retired.

The officer, whose name was Blakeney, tapped at the door, and was bid to enter by a voice melodiously soft. He opened the door, and discovered to Temple a scene which rivetted him to the spot with astonishment.

The apartment, though small, and bearing strong marks of poverty, was neat in the extreme. In an arm-chair, his head reclined upon his hand, his eyes fixed on a book which lay open before him, sat an aged man in a Lieutenant's uniform, which, though threadbare, would sooner call a blush of shame into the face of those who could neglect real merit, than cause the hectic of confusion to glow on the cheeks of him who wore it.

Beside him sat a lovely creature busied in painting a fan mount. She was fair as the lily, but sorrow had nipped the rose in her cheek before it was half blown. Her eyes were blue; and her hair, which was light brown, was slightly confined under a plain muslin cap, tied round with a black ribbon; a white linen gown and plain lawn[9] handkerchief composed the remainder of her dress; and in this simple attire, she was more irresistibly charming to such a heart as Temple's, than she would have been, if adorned with all the splendor of a courtly belle.

When they entered, the old man arose from his seat, and shaking Blakeney by the hand with great cordiality, offered Temple his chair; and there being but three in the room, seated himself on the side of his little bed with evident composure.

"This is a strange place," said he to Temple, "to receive visitors of distinction in; but we must fit our feelings to our station. While I am not ashamed to own the cause which brought me here, why should I

---

8. A famous London prison, which by the 18th century was used primarily for debtors (people who owed money they could not pay). Before the mid-19th century, inhabitants of England and America who were unable to pay a debt could be incarcerated (as they still can, in some instances, such as for failure to pay child support). Debtors' prisons varied in the amount of freedom they allowed the debtor. Some, for instance, allowed inmates to receive visitors.
9. Semisheer fabric commonly used for handkerchiefs. "Muslin": a thin cotton fabric.

blush at my situation? Our misfortunes are not our faults; and were it not for that poor girl——"

Here the philosopher was lost in the father. He rose hastily from his seat, and walking toward the window, wiped off a tear which he was afraid would tarnish the cheek of a sailor.

Temple cast his eye on Miss Eldridge: a pellucid[1] drop had stolen from her eyes, and fallen upon a rose she was painting. It blotted and discoloured the flower. "'Tis emblematic," said he mentally: "the rose of youth and health soon fades when watered by the tear of affliction." *overly sentimental*

"My friend Blakeney," said he, addressing the old man, "told me I could be of service to you: be so kind then, dear Sir, as to point out some way in which I can relieve the anxiety of your heart and increase the pleasures of my own."

"My good young man," said Eldridge, "you know not what you offer. While deprived of my liberty I cannot be free from anxiety on my own account; but that is a trifling concern; my anxious thoughts extend to one more dear a thousand times than life: I am a poor weak old man, and must expect in a few years to sink into silence and oblivion; but when I am gone, who will protect that fair bud of innocence from the blasts of adversity, or from the cruel hand of insult and dishonour."

"Oh, my father!" cried Miss Eldridge, tenderly taking his hand, "be not anxious on that account; for daily are my prayers offered to heaven that our lives may terminate at the same instant, and one grave receive us both; for why should I live when deprived of my only friend." *(well I'm not*

Temple was moved even to tears. "You will both live many years," said he, "and I hope see much happiness. Cheerly, my friend, cheerly; these passing clouds of adversity will serve only to make the sunshine of prosperity more pleasing. But we are losing time: you might ere this have told me who were your creditors,[2] what were their demands, and other particulars necessary to your liberation." *oh please.*

"My story is short," said Mr. Eldridge, "but there are some particulars which will wring my heart barely to remember; yet to one whose offers of friendship appear so open and disinterested, I will relate every circumstance that led to my present, painful situation. But my child," continued he, addressing his daughter, "let me prevail on you to take this opportunity, while my friends are with me, to enjoy the benefit of air and exercise. Go, my love; leave me now; to-morrow at your usual hour I will expect you."

1. Transparent. This term suggests not only the visual quality of her tears but also the fact that they offer a clear view into her honest soul. It conveys both clarity and sincerity.
2. Those to whom one owes money.

Miss Eldridge impressed on his check the kiss of filial[3] affection, and obeyed.

Chapter III.

Unexpected Misfortunes.

"My life," said Mr. Eldridge, "till within these few years was marked by no particular circumstance deserving notice. I early embraced the life of a sailor, and have served my King with unremitted ardour for many years. At the age of twenty-five I married an amiable woman; one son, and the girl who just now left us, were the fruits of our union. My boy had genius and spirit. I straitened my little income to give him a liberal education, but the rapid progress he made in his studies amply compensated for the inconvenience. At the academy where he received his education he commenced an acquaintance with a Mr. Lewis, a young man of affluent fortune: as they grew up their intimacy ripened into friendship, and they became almost inseparable companions.

"George chose the profession of a soldier. I had neither friends or money to procure him a commission,[4] and had wished him to embrace a nautical life: but this was repugnant to his wishes, and I ceased to urge him on the subject.

"The friendship subsisting between Lewis and my son was of such a nature as gave him free access to our family; and so specious[5] was his manner that we hesitated not to state to him all our little difficulties in regard to George's future views. He listened to us with attention, and offered to advance any sum necessary for his first setting out.

"I embraced the offer, and gave him my note for the payment of it, but he would not suffer me to mention any stipulated time, as he said I might do it whenever most convenient to myself. About this time my dear Lucy returned from school, and I soon began to imagine Lewis looked at her with eyes of affection. I gave my child a caution to beware of him, and to look on her mother as her friend. She was unaffectedly artless;[6] and when, as I suspected, Lewis made professions of love, she confided in her parents, and assured us her heart was perfectly unbiassed in his favour, and she would chearfully submit to our direction.

your unaffectedly artless

---

3. Pertaining to children's relationships with their parents.
4. I.e., get him appointed as a military officer; allow him to begin his career as a soldier at the rank of officer.
5. Deceptively attractive.
6. Without guile, sincere, innocently expressive.

"I took an early opportunity of questioning him concerning his intentions towards my child: he gave an equivocal answer, and I forbade him the house.

"The next day he sent and demanded payment of his money. It was not in my power to comply with the demand. I requested three days to endeavour to raise it, determining in that time to mortgage my half pay, and live on a small annuity which my wife possessed, rather than be under an obligation to so worthless a man: but this short time was not allowed me; for that evening, as I was sitting down to supper, unsuspicious of danger, an officer entered, and tore me from the embraces of my family.

"My wife had been for some time in a declining state of health: ruin at once so unexpected and inevitable was a stroke she was not prepared to bear, and I saw her faint into the arms of our servant, as I left my own habitation for the comfortless walls of a prison. My poor Lucy, distracted with her fears for us both, sunk on the floor and endeavoured to detain me by her feeble efforts; but in vain; they forced open her arms; she shrieked, and fell prostrate.[7] But pardon me. The horrors of that night unman me. I cannot proceed."

He rose from his seat, and walked several times across the room: at length, attaining more composure, he cried—"What a mere infant I am! Why, Sir, I never felt thus in the day of battle."

"No," said Temple; "but the truly brave soul is tremblingly alive to the feelings of humanity."

"True," replied the old man, (something like satisfaction darting across his features) "and painful as these feelings are, I would not exchange them for that torpor which the stoic mistakes for philosophy. How many exquisite delights should I have passed by unnoticed, but for these keen sensations, this quick sense of happiness or misery? Then let us, my friend, take the cup of life as it is presented to us, tempered by the hand of a wise Providence; be thankful for the good, be patient under the evil, and presume not to enquire why the latter predominates."

"This is true philosophy," said Temple.

"'Tis the only way to reconcile ourselves to the cross events of life," replied he. "But I forget myself. I will not longer intrude on your patience, but proceed in my melancholy tale.

"The very evening that I was taken to prison, my son arrived from Ireland, where he had been some time with his regiment. From the distracted expressions of his mother and sister, he learnt by whom I had been arrested; and, late as it was, flew on the wings of wounded affection, to the house of his false friend, and earnestly enquired the cause of this cruel conduct. With all the calmness of a cool deliber-

7. I.e., fell face downward.

ate villain, he avowed his passion for Lucy; declared her situation in life would not permit him to marry her; but offered to release me immediately, and make any settlement on her, if George would persuade her to live, as he impiously termed it, a life of honour.

"Fired at the insult offered to a man and a soldier, my boy struck the villain, and a challenge ensued. He then went to a coffee-house in the neighbourhood and wrote a long affectionate letter to me, blaming himself severely for having introduced Lewis into the family, or permitted him to confer an obligation, which had brought inevitable ruin on us all. He begged me, whatever might be the event of the ensuing morning, not to suffer regret or unavailing sorrow for his fate, to encrease the anguish of my heart, which he greatly feared was already insupportable.

"This letter was delivered to me early in the morning. It would be vain to attempt describing my feelings on the perusal of it; suffice it to say, that a merciful Providence interposed, and I was for three weeks insensible to miseries almost beyond the strength of human nature to support.

"A fever and strong delirium seized me, and my life was despaired of. At length, nature, overpowered with fatigue, gave way to the salutary power of rest, and a quiet slumber of some hours restored me to reason, though the extreme weakness of my frame prevented my feeling my distress so acutely as I otherways should.

"The first object that struck me on awaking, was Lucy sitting by my bedside; her pale countenance and sable[8] dress prevented my enquiries for poor George: for the letter I had received from him, was the first thing that occurred to my memory. By degrees the rest returned: I recollected being arrested, but could no ways account for being in this apartment, whither they had conveyed me during my illness.

"I was so weak as to be almost unable to speak. I pressed Lucy's hand, and looked earnestly round the apartment in search of another dear object.

"Where is your mother?" said I, faintly.

"The poor girl could not answer: she shook her head in expressive silence; and throwing herself on the bed, folded her arms about me, and burst into tears.

"What! both gone?" said I.

"Both," she replied, endeavouring to restrain her emotions: "but they are happy, no doubt."

Here Mr. Eldridge paused: the recollection of the scene was too painful to permit him to proceed.

8. Black.

Chapter IV.

Change of Fortune.

"It was some days," continued Mr. Eldridge, recovering himself, "before I could venture to enquire the particulars of what had happened during my illness: at length I assumed courage to ask my dear girl how long her mother and brother had been dead: she told me, that the morning after my arrest, George came home early to enquire after his mother's health, staid with them but a few minutes, seemed greatly agitated at parting, but gave them strict charge to keep up their spirits, and hope every thing would turn out for the best. In about two hours after, as they were eating at breakfast, and endeavouring to strike out some plan to attain my liberty, they heard a loud rap at the door, which Lucy running to open, she met the bleeding body of her brother, borne in by two men who had lifted him from a litter, on which they had brought him from the place where he fought. Her poor mother, weakened by illness and the struggles of the preceding night, was not able to support this shock: gasping for breath, her looks wild and haggard, she reached the apartment where they had carried her dying son. She knelt by the bed side; and taking his cold hand, 'my poor boy,' said she, 'I will not be parted from thee: husband! son! both at once lost. Father of mercies, spare me!' She fell into a strong convulsion, and expired in about two hours. In the mean time, a surgeon had dressed George's wounds; but they were in such a situation as to bar the smallest hopes of recovery. He never was sensible from the time he was brought home, and died that evening in the arms of his sister.

"Late as it was when this event took place, my affectionate Lucy insisted on coming to me. 'What must he feel,' said she, 'at our apparent neglect, and how shall I inform him of the afflictions with which it has pleased heaven to visit us?'

"She left the care of the dear departed ones to some neighbours who had kindly come in to comfort and assist her; and on entering the house where I was confined, found me in the situation I have mentioned.

"How she supported herself in these trying moments, I know not: heaven, no doubt, was with her; and her anxiety to preserve the life of one parent in some measure abated her affliction for the loss of the other.

"My circumstances were greatly embarrassed, my acquaintance few, and those few utterly unable to assist me. When my wife and son were committed to their kindred earth, my creditors seized my house and furniture, which not being sufficient to discharge all their demands, detainers were lodged against me. No friend stepped forward to my relief; from the grave of her mother, my beloved Lucy followed an almost dying father to this melancholy place.

"Here we have been nearly a year and a half. My half-pay I have given up to satisfy my creditors, and my child supports me by her industry: sometimes by fine needlework, sometimes by painting. She leaves me every night, and goes to a lodging near the bridge; but returns in the morning, to chear me with her smiles, and bless me by her duteous affection. A lady once offered her an asylum in her family; but she would not leave me. 'We are all the world to each other,' said she. 'I thank God, I have health and spirits to improve the talents with which nature has endowed me; and I trust if I employ them in the support of a beloved parent, I shall not be thought an unprofitable servant. While he lives, I pray for strength to pursue my employment; and when it pleases heaven to take one of us, may it give the survivor resignation to bear the separation as we ought: till then I will never leave him.'

"But where is this inhuman persecutor?" said Temple.

"He has been abroad ever since," replied the old man; "but he has left orders with his lawyer never to give up the note till the utmost farthing[9] is paid."

"And how much is the amount of your debts in all?" said Temple.

"Five hundred pounds," he replied.

Temple started: it was more than he expected. "But something must be done," said he: "that sweet maid must not wear out her life in a prison. I will see you again to-morrow, my friend," said he, shaking Eldridge's hand: "keep up your spirits: light and shade are not more happily blended than are the pleasures and pains of life; and the horrors of the one serve only to increase the splendor of the other."

"You never lost a wife and son," said Eldridge.

"No," replied he, "but I can feel for those that have." Eldridge pressed his hand as they went toward the door, and they parted in silence.

When they got without the walls of the prison, Temple thanked his friend Blakeney for introducing him to so worthy a character; and telling him he had a particular engagement in the city, wished him a good evening.

"And what is to be done for this distressed man," said Temple, as he walked up Ludgate Hill. "Would to heaven I had a fortune that would enable me instantly to discharge his debt: what exquisite transport, to see the expressive eyes of Lucy beaming at once with pleasure for her father's deliverance, and gratitude for her deliverer: but is not my fortune affluence," continued he, "nay superfluous wealth, when compared to the extreme indigence of Eldridge; and what have I done to

9. An English coin worth a quarter of a penny.

deserve ease and plenty, while a brave worthy officer starves in a prison? Three hundred a year is surely sufficient for all my wants and wishes: at any rate Eldridge must be relieved."

When the heart has will, the hands can soon find means to execute a good action.   *blatant instruction*

Temple was a young man, his feelings warm and impetuous; unacquainted with the world, his heart had not been rendered callous by being convinced of its fraud and hypocrisy. He pitied their sufferings, overlooked their faults, thought every bosom as generous as his own, and would chearfully have divided his last guinea with a unfortunate fellow creature.

No wonder, then, that such a man (without waiting a moment for the interference of Madam Prudence) should resolve to raise money sufficient for the relief of Eldridge, by mortgaging part of his fortune.

We will not enquire too minutely into the cause which might actuate him in this instance: suffice it to say, he immediately put the plan in execution; and in three days from the time he first saw the unfortunate Lieutenant, he had the superlative felicity of seeing him at liberty, and receiving an ample reward in the tearful eye and half articulated thanks of the grateful Lucy.   *all too easily*

"And pray, young man," said his father to him one morning, "what are your designs in visiting thus constantly that old man and his daughter?"

Temple was at a loss for a reply: he had never asked himself the question: he hesitated; and his father continued—

"It was not till within these few days that I heard in what manner your acquaintance first commenced, and cannot suppose any thing but attachment to the daughter could carry you such imprudent lengths for the father: it certainly must be her art that drew you in to mortgage part of your fortune."

"Art, Sir!" cried Temple eagerly. "Lucy Eldridge is as free from art as she is from every other error: she is—"

"Everything that is amiable and lovely," said his father, interrupting him ironically: "no doubt in your opinion she is a pattern of excellence for all her sex to follow; but come, Sir, pray tell me what are your designs towards this paragon. I hope you do not intend to complete your folly by marrying her."

"Were my fortune such as would support her according to her merit, I don't know a woman more formed to insure happiness in the married state."

"Then prithee, my dear lad," said his father, "since your rank and fortune are so much beneath what your *Princess* might expect, be so kind as to turn your eyes on Miss Weatherby; who, having only an estate of three thousand a year, is more upon a level with you,

a dose of reality

and whose father yesterday solicited the mighty honour of your alliance. I shall leave you to consider on this offer; and pray remember, that your union with Miss Weatherby will put it in your power to be more liberally the friend of Lucy Eldridge."

The old gentleman walked in a stately manner out of the room; and Temple stood almost petrified with astonishment, contempt, and rage.

[handwritten margin note: exciting turn of plot, some complication to Temple's abundance of virtue.]

Chapter V.

Such Things Are.

Miss Weatherby was the only child of a wealthy man, almost idolized by her parents, flattered by her dependants, and never contradicted even by those who called themselves her friends: I cannot give a better description than by the following lines.

> The lovely maid whose form and face
> Nature has deck'd with ev'ry grace,
> But in whose breast no virtues glow,
> Whose heart ne'er felt another's woe,
> Whose hand ne'er smooth'd the bed of pain,
> Or eas'd the captive's galling chain;
> But like the tulip caught the eye,
> Born just to be admir'd and die;
> When gone, no one regrets its loss,
> Or scarce remembers that it was.

Such was Miss Weatherby: her form lovely as nature could make it, but her mind uncultivated, her heart unfeeling, her passions impetuous, and her brain almost turned with flattery, dissipation, and pleasure; and such was the girl, whom a partial grandfather left independent mistress of the fortune before mentioned.

She had seen Temple frequently; and fancying she could never be happy without him, nor once imagining he could refuse a girl of her beauty and fortune, she prevailed on her fond father to offer the alliance to the old Earl of D——, Mr. Temple's father.

The Earl had received the offer courteously: he thought it a great match for Henry; and was too fashionable a man to suppose a wife could be any impediment to the friendship he professed for Eldridge and his daughter.

Unfortunately for Temple, he thought quite otherwise: the conversation he had just had with his father, discovered to him the situation of his heart; and he found that the most affluent fortune would bring no increase of happiness unless Lucy Eldridge shared it with him;

and the knowledge of the purity of her sentiments, and the integrity of his own heart, made him shudder at the idea his father had started, of marrying a woman for no other reason than because the affluence of her fortune would enable him to injure her by maintaining in splendor the woman to whom his heart was devoted: he therefore resolved to refuse Miss Weatherby, and be the event what it might, offer his heart and hand to Lucy Eldridge.

Full of this determination, he sought his father, declared his resolution, and was commanded never more to appear in his presence. Temple bowed; his heart was too full to permit him to speak; he left the house precipitately, and hastened to relate the cause of his sorrows to his good old friend and his amiable daughter.

In the mean time, the Earl, vexed to the soul that such a fortune should be lost, determined to offer himself a candidate for Miss Weatherby's favour.

What wonderful changes are wrought by that reigning power, ambition! the love-sick girl, when first she heard of Temple's refusal, wept, raved, tore her hair, and vowed to found a protestant nunnery[1] with her fortune; and by commencing abbess,[2] shut herself up from the sight of cruel ungrateful man for ever.

Her father was a man of the world: he suffered this first transport to subside, and then very deliberately unfolded to her the offers of the old Earl, expatiated on the many benefits arising from an elevated title, painted in glowing colours the surprise and vexation of Temple when he should see her figuring as a Countess and his mother-in-law, and begged her to consider well before she made any rash vows.

The *distressed* fair one dried her tears, listened patiently, and at length declared she believed the surest method to revenge the slight put on her by the son, would be to accept the father: so said so done, and in a few days she became the Countess D——.

Temple heard the news with emotion: he had lost his father's favour by avowing his passion for Lucy, and he saw now there was no hope of regaining it: "but he shall not make me miserable," said he. "Lucy and I have no ambitious notions: we can live on three hundred a year for some little time, till the mortgage is paid off, and then we shall have sufficient not only for the comforts but many of the little

1. Two centuries after the disappearance of nunneries from England and despite their association with Catholic heresy, 18th-century female intellectuals from Mary Astell to Mary Wortley Montagu supported their establishment at various times, primarily as a means to educate women and to provide an alternative for women who did not marry. Rowson seems to have been among those who mocked the idea, as Miss Weatherby's entertainment of the concept only emphasizes her ignorance and irreligiosity. See Bridget Hill, "A Refuge from Men: The Idea of the Protestant Nunnery," *Past and Present* 117 (Nov. 1987), 107–30.
2. Head of a convent. "Commencing": beginning.

elegancies of life. We will purchase a little cottage, my Lucy," said
he, "and thither with your reverend father we will retire; we will forget there are such things as splendor, profusion, and dissipation: we
will have some cows, and you shall be queen of the dairy; in a morning, while I look after my garden, you shall take a basket on your
arm, and sally forth to feed your poultry; and as they flutter round
you in token of humble gratitude, your father shall smoke his pipe in
a woodbine[3] alcove, and viewing the serenity of your countenance,
feel such real pleasure dilate his own heart, as shall make him forget
he had ever been unhappy."

Lucy smiled; and Temple saw it was a smile of approbation.[4] He
sought and found a cottage suited to his taste; thither, attended by
Love and Hymen,[5] the happy trio retired; where, during many years
of uninterrupted felicity, they cast not a wish beyond the little boundaries of their own tenement. Plenty, and her handmaid, Prudence,
presided at their board, Hospitality stood at their gate, Peace smiled
on each face, Content reigned in each heart, and Love and Health
strewed roses on their pillows.

Such were the parents of Charlotte Temple, who was the only
pledge of their mutual love, and who, at the earnest entreaty of a
particular friend, was permitted to finish the education her mother
had begun, at Madame Du Pont's school, where we first introduced
her to the acquaintance of the reader.

Chapter VI.

An Intriguing Teacher.

Madame Du Pont was a woman every way calculated to take the care
of young ladies, had that care entirely devolved on herself; but it was
impossible to attend the education of a numerous school without
proper assistants; and those assistants were not always the kind of
people whose conversation and morals were exactly such as parents
of delicacy and refinement would wish a daughter to copy. Among
the teachers at Madame Du Pont's school, was Mademoiselle La
Rue, who added to a pleasing person[6] and insinuating address, a liberal education and the manners of a gentlewoman. She was recommended to the school by a lady whose humanity overstepped the
bounds of discretion: for though she knew Miss La Rue had eloped

---

3. A high-climbing wild plant with fragrant flowers that is native to North America; also
   known as Virginia creeper.
4. Approval.
5. In Greek and Roman mythology, the god of marriage. *and something else*
6. Physical appearance.

fair tale–like plot, rapid issues, quick resolution

from a convent with a young officer, and, on coming to England, had lived with several different men in open defiance of all moral and religious duties; yet, finding her reduced to the most abject want, and believing the penitence which she professed to be sincere, she took her into her own family, and from thence recommended her to Madame Du Pont, as thinking the situation more suitable for a woman of her abilities. But Mademoiselle possessed too much of the spirit of intrigue to remain long without adventures. At church, where she constantly appeared, her person attracted the attention of a young man who was upon a visit at a gentleman's seat in the neighbourhood: she had met him several times clandestinely; and being invited to come out that evening, and eat some fruit and pastry in a summer-house belonging to the gentleman he was visiting, and requested to bring some of the ladies with her, Charlotte being her favourite, was fixed on to accompany her.

The mind of youth eagerly catches at promised pleasure: pure and innocent by nature, it thinks not of the dangers lurking beneath those pleasures, till too late to avoid them: when Mademoiselle asked Charlotte to go with her, she mentioned the gentleman as a relation, and spoke in such high terms of the elegance of his gardens, the sprightliness of his conversation, and the liberality with which he ever entertained his guests, that Charlotte thought only of the pleasure she should enjoy in the visit,—not on the imprudence of going without her governess's knowledge, or of the danger to which she exposed herself in visiting the house of a gay young man of fashion.

Madame Du Pont was gone out for the evening, and the rest of the ladies retired to rest, when Charlotte and the teacher stole out at the back gate, and in crossing the field, were accosted by Montraville, as mentioned in the first chapter.

Charlotte was disappointed in the pleasure she had promised herself from this visit. The levity of the gentlemen and the freedom of their conversation disgusted her. She was astonished at the liberties Mademoiselle permitted them to take; grew thoughtful and uneasy, and heartily wished herself at home again in her own chamber.

Perhaps one cause of that wish might be, an earnest desire to see the contents of the letter which had been put into her hand by Montraville.

Any reader who has the least knowledge of the world, will easily imagine the letter was made up of encomiums[7] on her beauty, and vows of everlasting love and constancy; nor will he be surprised that a heart open to every gentle, generous sentiment, should feel itself

---

7. Formal expressions of praise.

warmed by gratitude for a man who professed to feel so much for her; nor is it improbable but her mind might revert to the agreeable person and martial appearance of Montraville.

In affairs of love, a young heart is never in more danger than when attempted by a handsome young soldier. A man of an indifferent appearance, will, when arrayed in a military habit, shew to advantage; but when beauty of person, elegance of manner, and an easy method of paying compliments, are united to the scarlet coat, smart cockade, and military sash, ah! well-a-day[8] for the poor girl who gazes on him: she is in imminent danger; but if she listens to him with pleasure, 'tis all over with her, and from that moment she has neither eyes nor ears, for any other object.

Now, my dear sober matron, (if a sober matron should deign to turn over these pages, before she trusts them to the eye of a darling daughter,) let me intreat you not to put on a grave face, and throw down the book in a passion and declare 'tis enough to turn the heads of half the girls in England; I do solemnly protest, my dear madam, I mean no more by what I have here advanced, than to ridicule those romantic girls, who foolishly imagine a red coat and silver epaulet[9] constitute the fine gentleman; and should that fine gentleman make half a dozen fine speeches to them, they will imagine themselves so much in love as to fancy it a meritorious action to jump out of a two pair of stairs window, abandon their friends, and trust entirely to the honour of a man, who perhaps hardly knows the meaning of the word, and if he does, will be too much the modern man of refinement, to practice it in their favour.

Gracious heaven! when I think on the miseries that must rend the heart of a doating parent, when he sees the darling of his age at first seduced from his protection, and afterwards abandoned, by the very wretch whose promises of love decoyed her from the paternal roof—when he sees her poor and wretched, her bosom torn between remorse for her crime and love for her vile betrayer—when fancy paints to me the good old man stooping to raise the weeping penitent, while every tear from her eye is numbered by drops from his bleeding heart, my bosom glows with honest indignation, and I wish for power to extirpate[1] those monsters of seduction from the earth.

Oh my dear girls—for to such only am I writing—listen not to the voice of love, unless sanctioned by paternal approbation: be assured, it is now past the days of romance: no woman can be run away with contrary to her own inclination: then kneel down each morning, and

---

8. An exclamation of sorrow comparable to "Alas!" "Cockade": an ornamental ribbon worn as part of a uniform.
9. A decoration on the shoulder of a jacket or coat, especially on a military uniform. In officers' dress, epaulets are usually made of gold or silver braid.
1. Root out, exterminate.

request kind heaven to keep you free from temptation, or, should it please to suffer you to be tried, pray for fortitude to resist the impulse of inclination when it runs counter to the precepts of religion and virtue.

[handwritten margin notes: "incentive enough?" and "arguement doesn't account for their attraction and quick pleasures they offer"]

Chapter VII.

Natural Sense of Propriety Inherent in the Female Bosom.

"I cannot think we have done exactly right in going out this evening, Mademoiselle," said Charlotte, seating herself when she entered her apartment: "nay, I am sure it was not right; for I expected to be very happy, but was sadly disappointed."

"It was your own fault, then," replied Mademoiselle: "for I am sure my cousin omitted nothing that could serve to render the evening agreeable."

"True," said Charlotte: "but I thought the gentlemen were very free in their manner: I wonder you would suffer them to behave as they did."

"Prithee, don't be such a foolish little prude," said the artful woman, affecting anger: "I invited you to go in hopes it would divert you, and be an agreeable change of scene; however, if your delicacy was hurt by the behaviour of the gentlemen, you need not go again; so there let it rest."

"I do not intend to go again," said Charlotte, gravely taking off her bonnet, and beginning to prepare for bed: "I am sure, if Madame Du Pont knew we had been out to-night, she would be very angry; and it is ten to one but she hears of it by some means or other."

"Nay, Miss," said La Rue, "perhaps your mighty sense of propriety may lead you to tell her yourself: and in order to avoid the censure you would incur, should she hear of it by accident, throw the blame on me: but I confess I deserve it: it will be a very kind return for that partiality which led me to prefer you before any of the rest of the ladies; but perhaps it will give you pleasure," continued she, letting fall some hypocritical tears, "to see me deprived of bread, and for an action which by the most rigid could only be esteemed an inadvertency, lose my place and character, and be driven again into the world, where I have already suffered all the evils attendant on poverty."

This was touching Charlotte in the most vulnerable part: she rose from her seat, and taking Mademoiselle's hand—"You know, my dear La Rue," said she, "I love you too well, to do any thing that would injure you in my governess's opinion: I am only sorry we went out this evening."

"I don't believe it, Charlotte," said she, assuming a little vivacity; "for if you had not gone out, you would not have seen the gentleman who met us crossing the field; and I rather think you were pleased with his conversation."

"I had seen him once before," replied Charlotte, "and thought him an agreeable man; and you know one is always pleased to see a person with whom one has passed several chearful hours. But," said she pausing, and drawing the letter from her pocket, while a gentle suffusion of vermillion tinged her neck and face, "he gave me this letter; what shall I do with it?"

"Read it, to be sure," returned Mademoiselle.

"I am afraid I ought not," said Charlotte: "my mother has often told me, I should never read a letter given me by a young man, without first giving it to her."

"Lord bless you, my dear girl," cried the teacher smiling, "have you a mind to be in leading strings all your life time. Prithee² open the letter, read it, and judge for yourself; if you show it your mother, the consequence will be, you will be taken from school, and a strict guard kept over you; so you will stand no chance of ever seeing the smart young officer again."

"I should not like to leave school yet," replied Charlotte, "till I have attained a greater proficiency in my Italian and music. But you can, if you please, Mademoiselle, take the letter back to Montraville, and tell him I wish him well, but cannot, with any propriety, enter into a clandestine correspondence with him." She laid the letter on the table, and began to undress herself.

"Well," said La Rue, "I vow you are an unaccountable girl: have you no curiosity to see the inside now? for my part I could no more let a letter addressed to me lie unopened so long, than I could work miracles: he writes a good hand," continued she, turning the letter, to look at the superscription.

"'Tis well enough," said Charlotte, drawing it towards her.

"He is a genteel young fellow," said La Rue carelessly, folding up her apronat the same time; "but I think he is marked with the small pox."³

"Oh you are greatly mistaken," said Charlotte eagerly; "he has a remarkable clear skin and fine complexion."

"His eyes, if I could judge by what I saw," said La Rue, "are grey and want expression."

2. Please (contraction of *I pray thee*).
3. The only infectious disease among humans known to have been completely eradicated. Smallpox was a serious, often fatal, disease. Its symptoms included blisters, which usually resulted in scarring, primarily on the face. "Genteel": refers both to upper-class status and to polite behavior. Here, La Rue means that Montraville is attractive and has refined manners.

"By no means," replied Charlotte; "they are the most expressive eyes I ever saw."

"Well, child, whether they are grey or black is of no consequence: you have determined not to read his letter; so it is likely you will never either see or hear from him again."

Charlotte took up the letter, and Mademoiselle continued—

"He is most probably going to America; and if ever you should hear any account of him, it may possibly be that he is killed; and though he loved you ever so fervently, though his last breath should be spent in a prayer for your happiness, it can be nothing to you: you can feel nothing for the fate of the man, whose letters you will not open, and whose sufferings you will not alleviate, by permitting him to think you would remember him when absent, and pray for his safety." *La Rue is source of corruption*

Charlotte still held the letter in her hand: her heart swelled at the conclusion of Mademoiselle's speech, and a tear dropped upon the wafer that closed it.

"The wafer is not dry yet," said she, "and sure there can be no great harm—" She hesitated. La Rue was silent. "I may read it, Mademoiselle, and return it afterwards."

"Certainly," replied Mademoiselle.

"At any rate I am determined not to answer it," continued Charlotte, as she opened the letter.

Here let me stop to make one remark, and trust me my very heart aches while I write it; but certain I am, that when once a woman has stifled the sense of shame in her own bosom, when once she has lost sight of the basis on which reputation, honour, every thing that should be dear to the female heart, rests, she grows hardened in guilt, and will spare no pains to bring down innocence and beauty to the shocking level with herself: and this proceeds from that diabolical spirit of envy, which repines[4] at seeing another in the full possession of that respect and esteem which she can no longer hope to enjoy. *basically, you will crumble into worthless*

Mademoiselle eyed the unsuspecting Charlotte, as she perused *being* the letter, with a malignant pleasure. She saw, that the contents had awakened new emotions in her youthful bosom: she encouraged her hopes, calmed her fears, and before they parted for the night, it was determined that she should meet Montraville the ensuing evening.

4. Feels dissatisfied; frets.

Chapter VIII.

Domestic Pleasures Planned.

"I think, my dear," said Mrs. Temple, laying her hand on her husband's arm as they were walking together in the garden, "I think next Wednesday is Charlotte's birth day: now I have formed a little scheme in my own mind, to give her an agreeable surprise; and if you have no objection, we will send for her home on that day." Temple pressed his wife's hand in token of approbation, and she proceeded—"You know the little alcove at the bottom of the garden, of which Charlotte is so fond? I have an inclination to deck this out in a fanciful manner, and invite all her little friends to partake of a collation of fruit, sweetmeats,[5] and other things suitable to the general taste of young guests; and to make it more pleasing to Charlotte, she shall be mistress of the feast, and entertain her visitors in this alcove. I know she will be delighted; and to complete all, they shall have some music, and finish with a dance."

"A very fine plan, indeed," said Temple, smiling; "and you really suppose I will wink at your indulging the girl in this manner? You will quite spoil her, Lucy; indeed you will."

"She is the only child we have," said Mrs. Temple, the whole tenderness of a mother adding animation to her fine countenance; but it was withal[6] tempered so sweetly with the meek affection and submissive duty of the wife, that as she paused expecting her husband's answer, he gazed at her tenderly, and found he was unable to refuse her request.

"She is a good girl," said Temple.

"She is, indeed," replied the fond mother exultingly, "a grateful, affectionate girl; and I am sure will never lose sight of the duty she owes her parents."

"If she does," said he, "she must forget the example set her by the best of mothers."

Mrs. Temple could not reply; but the delightful sensation that dilated her heart sparkled in her intelligent eyes and heightened the vermillion on her cheeks.

Of all the pleasures of which the human mind is sensible, there is none equal to that which warms and expands the bosom, when listening to commendations bestowed on us by a beloved object, and are conscious of having deserved them.

Ye giddy flutterers in the fantastic round of dissipation, who eagerly seek pleasure in the lofty dome, rich treat, and midnight

---

5. Sweets. "Collation": light meal.
6. Nevertheless.

of different species from ♀ ♂

revel—tell me, ye thoughtless daughters of folly, have ye ever found the phantom you have so long sought with such unremitted assiduity? Has she not always eluded your grasp, and when you have reached your hand to take the cup she extends to her deluded votaries, have you not found the long-expected draught strongly tinctured with the bitter dregs of disappointment? <u>I know you have</u>; I see it in the wan cheek, sunk eye, and air of chagrin, which ever mark the children of dissipation. Pleasure is a vain illusion; she draws you on to a thousand follies, errors, and I may say vices, and then leaves you to deplore your thoughtless credulity. *guilt instilling*

Look, my dear friends, at yonder lovely Virgin, arrayed in a white robe devoid of ornament; behold the meekness of her countenance, the modesty of her gait; her handmaids are *Humility, Filial Piety, Conjugal Affection, Industry,* and *Benevolence*; her name is *Content*; she holds in her hand the cup of true felicity, and when once you have formed an intimate acquaintance with these her attendants, nay you must admit them as your bosom friends and chief counsellors, then, whatever may be your situation in life, the meek eyed Virgin will immediately take up her abode with you.

Is poverty your portion?—she will lighten your labours, preside at your frugal board, and watch your quiet slumbers.

Is your state mediocrity?—she will heighten every blessing you enjoy, by informing you how grateful you should be to that bountiful Providence who might have placed you in the most abject situation; and, by teaching you to weigh your blessings against your deserts, show you how much more you receive than you have a right to expect.

Are you possessed of affluence?—what an inexhaustible fund of happiness will she lay before you! To relieve the distressed, redress the injured, in short, to perform all the good works of peace and mercy.

Content, my dear friends, will blunt even the arrows of adversity, so that they cannot materially harm you. She will dwell in the humblest cottage; she will attend you even to a prison. Her parent is Religion; her sisters, Patience and Hope. She will pass with you through life, smoothing the rough paths and tread to earth those thorns which every one must meet with as they journey onward to the appointed goal. She will soften the pains of sickness, continue with you even in the cold gloomy hour of death, and, chearing you with the smiles of her heaven-born sister, Hope, lead you triumphant to a blissfull eternity.

I confess I have rambled strangely from my story: but what of that? if I have been so lucky as to find the road to happiness, why should I be such a niggard[7] as to omit so good an opportunity of pointing

she is really messing w/ us
she rambles on about prudence & virtue while we long to hear what advancements Charlotte makes w/ her admirer

7. Miserly person.

out the way to others. The very basis of true peace of mind is a benevolent wish to see all the world as happy as one's self; and from my soul do I pity the selfish churl,[8] who, remembering the little bickerings of anger, envy, and fifty other disagreeables to which frail mortality is subject, would wish to revenge the affront which pride whispers him he has received. For my own part, I can safely declare, there is not a human being in the universe, whose prosperity I should not rejoice in, and to whose happiness I would not contribute to the utmost limit of my power: and may my offences be no more remembered in the day of general retribution, than as from my soul I forgive every offence or injury received from a fellow creature.

Merciful heaven! who would exchange the rapture of such a reflexion for all the gaudy tinsel which the world calls pleasure!

But to return.—Content dwelt in Mrs. Temple's bosom, and spread a charming animation over her countenance, as her husband led her in, to lay the plan she had formed (for the celebration of Charlotte's birth day,) before Mr. Eldridge.

Chapter IX.

We Know Not What a Day May Bring Forth.

Various were the sensations which agitated the mind of Charlotte, during the day preceding the evening in which she was to meet Montraville. Several times did she almost resolve to go to her governess, show her the letter, and be guided by her advice: but Charlotte had taken one step in the ways of imprudence; and when that is once done, there are always innumerable obstacles to prevent the erring person returning to the path of rectitude: yet these obstacles, however forcible they may appear in general, exist chiefly in imagination.

Charlotte feared the anger of her governess: she loved her mother, and the very idea of incurring her displeasure, gave her the greatest uneasiness: but there was a more forcible reason still remaining: should she show the letter to Madame Du Pont, she must confess the means by which it came into her possession; and what would be the consequence? Mademoiselle would be turned out of doors.

"I must not be ungrateful," said she. "La Rue is very kind to me; besides I can, when I see Montraville, inform him of the impropriety of our continuing to see or correspond with each other, and request him to come no more to Chichester."

8. Rude person or villain.

However prudent Charlotte might be in these resolutions, she certainly did not take a proper method to confirm herself in them. Several times in the course of the day, she indulged herself in reading over the letter, and each time she read it, the contents sunk deeper in her heart. As evening drew near, she caught herself frequently consulting her watch. "I wish this foolish meeting was over," said she, by way of apology to her own heart, "I wish it was over; for when I have seen him, and convinced him my resolution is not to be shaken, I shall feel my mind much easier."

The appointed hour arrived. Charlotte and Mademoiselle eluded the eye of vigilance; and Montraville, who had waited their coming with impatience, received them with rapturous and unbounded acknowledgments for their condescension: he had wisely brought Belcour with him to entertain Mademoiselle, while he enjoyed an uninterrupted conversation with Charlotte.

Belcour was a man whose character might be comprised in a few words; and as he will make some figure in the ensuing pages, I shall here describe him. He possessed a genteel fortune, and had a liberal education; dissipated,[9] thoughtless, and capricious, he paid little regard to the moral duties, and less to religious ones: eager in the pursuit of pleasure, he minded not the miseries he inflicted on others, provided his own wishes, however extravagant, were gratified. Self, darling self, was the idol he worshipped, and to that he would have sacrificed the interest and happiness of all mankind. Such was the friend of Montraville: will not the reader be ready to imagine, that the man who could regard such a character, must be actuated by the same feelings, follow the same pursuits, and be equally unworthy with the person to whom he thus gave his confidence?

But Montraville was a different character: generous in his disposition, liberal in his opinions, and good-natured almost to a fault; yet eager and impetuous in the pursuit of a favorite object, he staid not to reflect on the consequence which might follow the attainment of his wishes; with a mind ever open to conviction, had he been so fortunate as to possess a friend who would have pointed out the cruelty of endeavouring to gain the heart of an innocent artless girl, when he knew it was utterly impossible for him to marry her, and when the gratification of his passion would be unavoidable infamy and misery to her, and a cause of never-ceasing remorse to himself: had these dreadful consequences been placed before him in a proper

---

9. Frivolous; interested only in amusement. "Genteel fortune": i.e., he does not have to work for a living. For the development of a paradoxically "democratic gentility" in the United States, a nation presumably founded on egalitarian principles, see Richard Bushman, *The Refinement of America: Persons, Houses, Cities* (New York: Vintage, 1993), and Catherine Allgor, *Parlor Politics: In Which the Ladies of Washington Help Build a City and a Government* (Charlottesville: University of Virginia, 2000).

light, the humanity of his nature would have urged him to give up the pursuit: but Belcour was not this friend; he rather encouraged the growing passion of Montraville; and being pleased with the vivacity of Mademoiselle, resolved to leave no argument untried, which he thought might prevail on her to be the companion of their intended voyage; and he made no doubt but her example, added to the rhetoric of Montraville, would persuade Charlotte to go with them.

Charlotte had, when she went out to meet Montraville, flattered herself that her resolution was not to be shaken, and that, conscious of the impropriety of her conduct in having a clandestine intercourse with a stranger, she would never repeat the indiscretion.

But alas! poor Charlotte, she knew not the deceitfulness of her own heart, or she would have avoided the trial of her stability.

Montraville was tender, eloquent, ardent, and yet respectful. "Shall I not see you once more," said he, "before I leave England? will you not bless me by an assurance, that when we are divided by a vast expanse of sea I shall not be forgotten?"

Charlotte sighed.

"Why that sigh, my dear Charlotte? could I flatter myself that a fear for my safety, or a wish for my welfare occasioned it, how happy would it make me."

"I shall ever wish you well, Montraville," said she; "but we must meet no more."

"Oh say not so, my lovely girl: reflect, that when I leave my native land, perhaps a few short weeks may terminate my existence; the perils of the ocean—the dangers of war—"

"I can hear no more," said Charlotte in a tremulous voice. "I must leave you."

"Say you will see me once again."

"I dare not," said she.

"Only for one half hour to-morrow evening: 'tis my last request. I shall never trouble you again, Charlotte."

"I know not what to say," cried Charlotte, struggling to draw her hands from him: "let me leave you now."

"And you will come to-morrow," said Montraville.

"Perhaps I may," said she.

"Adieu then. I will live upon that hope till we meet again."

He kissed her hand. She sighed an adieu, and catching hold of Mademoiselle's arm, hastily entered the garden gate.

Chapter X.

When We Have Excited Curiosity, It Is But an Act of Good Nature to Gratify It.

Montraville was the youngest son of a gentleman of fortune, whose family being numerous, he was obliged to bring up his sons to genteel professions, by the exercise of which they might hope to raise themselves into notice.

"My daughters," said he, "have been educated like gentlewomen; and should I die before they are settled, they must have some provision made, to place them above the snares and temptations which vice ever holds out to the elegant, accomplished female, when oppressed by the frowns of poverty and the sting of dependance: my boys, with only moderate incomes, when placed in the church, at the bar, or in the field, may exert their talents, make themselves friends, and raise their fortunes on the basis of merit."

When Montraville chose the profession of arms, his father presented him with a commission, and made him a handsome provision for his private purse. "Now, my boy," said he, "go! seek glory in the field of battle. You have received from me all I shall ever have it in my power to bestow: it is certain I have interest to gain you promotion; but be assured that interest shall never be exerted, unless by your future conduct you deserve it. Remember, therefore, your success in life depends entirely on yourself. There is one thing I think it my duty to caution you against; the precipitancy[1] with which young men frequently rush into matrimonial engagements, and by their thoughtlessness draw a deserving woman into scenes of poverty and distress. A soldier has no business to think of a wife till his rank is such as to place him above the fear of bringing into the world a train of helpless innocents, heirs only to penury[2] and affliction. If, indeed, a woman, whose fortune is sufficient to preserve you in that state of independence I would teach you to prize, should generously bestow herself on a young soldier, whose chief hope of future prosperity depended on his success in the field—if such a woman should offer—every barrier is removed, and I should rejoice in an union which would promise so much felicity. But mark me, boy, if, on the contrary, you rush into a precipitate union with a girl of little or no fortune, take the poor creature from a comfortable home and kind friends, and plunge her into all the evils a narrow income and increasing family can inflict, I will leave you to enjoy the blessed fruits of your rashness; for by all that is

1. Excessive haste.
2. Destitution; helpless poverty.

sacred, neither my interest or fortune shall ever be exerted in your favour. I am serious," continued he, "therefore imprint this conversation on your memory, and let it influence your future conduct. Your happiness will always be dear to me; and I wish to warn you of a rock on which the peace of many an honest fellow has been wrecked; for believe me, the difficulties and dangers of the longest winter campaign are much easier to be borne, than the pangs that would seize your heart, when you beheld the woman of your choice, the children of your affection, involved in penury and distress, and reflected that it was your own folly and precipitancy had been the prime cause of their sufferings."

As this conversation passed but a few hours before Montraville took leave of his father, it was deeply impressed on his mind: when, therefore, Belcour came with him to the place of assignation with Charlotte, he directed him to enquire of the French woman what were Miss Temple's expectations in regard to fortune.

Mademoiselle informed him, that though Charlotte's father possessed a genteel independence, it was by no means probable that he could give his daughter more than a thousand pounds; and in case she did not marry to his liking, it was possible he might not give her a single *sous*;[3] nor did it appear the least likely, that Mr. Temple would agree to her union with a young man on the point of embarking for the seat of war.

Montraville therefore concluded it was impossible he should ever marry Charlotte Temple; and what end he proposed to himself by continuing the acquaintance he had commenced with her, he did not at that moment give himself time to enquire.

Chapter XI.

Conflict of Love and Duty.

Almost a week was now gone, and Charlotte continued every evening to meet Montraville, and in her heart every meeting was resolved to be the last; but alas! when Montraville at parting would earnestly intreat one more interview, that treacherous heart betrayed her; and, forgetful of its resolution, pleaded the cause of the enemy so powerfully, that Charlotte was unable to resist. Another and another meeting succeeded; and so well did Montraville improve each opportunity, that the heedless girl at length confessed no idea could be so painful to her as that of never seeing him again.

"Then we will never be parted," said he.

3. Small French coin.

"Ah, Montraville, replied Charlotte, forcing a smile, "how can it be avoided? My parents would never consent to our union; and even could they be brought to approve it, how should I bear to be separated from my kind, my beloved mother?"

"Then you love your parents more than you do me, Charlotte?"

"I hope I do," said she, blushing and looking down, "I hope my affection for them will ever keep me from infringing the laws of filial duty. So much duty

"Well, Charlotte," said Montraville gravely, and letting go her hand, "since that is the case, I find I have deceived myself with fallacious hopes. I had flattered my fond heart, that I was dearer to Charlotte than any thing in the world beside. I thought that you would for my sake have braved the dangers of the ocean, that you would, by your affection and smiles, have softened the hardships of war, and, had it been my fate to fall, that your tenderness would chear the hour of death, and smooth my passage to another world. But farewell, Charlotte! I see you never loved me. I shall now welcome the friendly ball[4] that deprives me of the sense of my misery."

"Oh stay, unkind Montraville," cried she, catching hold of his arm, as he pretended to leave her, "stay, and to calm your fears, I will here protest that was it not for the fear of giving pain to the best of parents, and returning their kindness with ingratitude, I would follow you through every danger, and, in studying to promote your happiness, insure my own. But I cannot break my mother's heart, Montraville; I must not bring the grey hairs of my doating grand-father with sorrow to the grave, or make my beloved father perhaps curse the hour that gave me birth." She covered her face with her hands, and burst into tears.

"All these distressing scenes, my dear Charlotte," cried Montraville, "are merely the chimeras[5] of a disturbed fancy. Your parents might perhaps grieve at first; but when they heard from your own hand that you was with a man of honour, and that it was to insure your felicity by an union with him, to which you feared they would never have given their assent, that you left their protection, they will, be assured, forgive an error which love alone occasioned, and when we return from America, receive you with open arms and tears of joy."

"Belcour and Mademoiselle heard this last speech, and conceiving it a proper time to throw in their advice and persuasions, approached Charlotte, and so well seconded the entreaties of Montraville, that finding Mademoiselle intended going with Belcour, and feeling her own treacherous heart too much inclined to accompany them, the

4. Bullet from an old-fashioned pistol or musket.
5. Unrealistic creations of the imagination. In Greek mythology, the Chimera was a fire-breathing monster with the head of a lion, the body of a female goat, and the tail of a dragon.

we know

hapless Charlotte, in an evil hour, consented that the next evening they should bring a chaise to the end of the town, and that she would leave her friends, and throw herself entirely on the protection of Montraville. "But should you," said she, looking earnestly at him, her eyes full of tears, "should you, forgetful of your promises, and repenting the engagements you here voluntarily enter into, forsake and leave me on a foreign shore——"

"Judge not so meanly of me," said he. "The moment we reach our place of destination, Hymen shall sanctify our love; and when I shall forget your goodness, may heaven forget me."

"Ah," said Charlotte, leaning on Mademoiselle's arm as they walked up the garden together, "I have forgot all that I ought to have remembered, in consenting to this intended elopement."

"You are a strange girl," said Mademoiselle: "you never know your own mind two minutes at a time. Just now you declared Montraville's happiness was what you prized most in the world; and now I suppose you repent having insured that happiness by agreeing to accompany him abroad."

"Indeed I do repent," replied Charlotte, "from my soul: but while discretion points out the impropriety of my conduct, inclination urges me on to ruin."

"Ruin! fiddlestick!" said Mademoiselle; "am not I going with you? and do I feel any of these qualms?"

"You do not renounce a tender father and mother," said Charlotte.

"But I hazard my dear reputation," replied Mademoiselle, bridling.

"True," replied Charlotte, "but you do not feel what I do." She then bade her good night: but sleep was a stranger to her eyes, and the tear of anguish watered her pillow.

Chapter XII.

> Nature's last, best gift:
> Creature in whom excell'd, whatever could
> To sight or thought be nam'd!
> Holy, divine! good, amiable, and sweet!
> How thou art fall'n!——

When Charlotte left her restless bed, her languid eye and pale cheek discovered to Madame Du Pont the little repose she had tasted.

"My dear child," said the affectionate governess, "what is the cause of the languor so apparent in your frame? Are you not well?"

"Yes, my dear Madam, very well," replied Charlotte, attempting to smile, "but I know not how it was; I could not sleep last night, and my spirits are depressed this morning."

"Come chear up, my love," said the governess; "I believe I have brought a cordial[6] to revive them. I have just received a letter from your good mama, and here is one for yourself."

Charlotte hastily took the letter: it contained these words—

"As to-morrow is the anniversary of the happy day that gave my beloved girl to the anxious wishes of a maternal heart, I have requested your governess to let you come home and spend it with us; and as I know you to be a good affectionate child, and make it your study to improve in those branches of education which you know will give most pleasure to your delighted parents, as a reward for your diligence and attention I have prepared an agreeable surprise for your reception. Your grand-father, eager to embrace the darling of his aged heart, will come in the chaise for you; so hold yourself in readiness to attend him by nine o'clock. Your dear father joins in every tender wish for your health and future felicity, which warms the heart of my dear Charlotte's affectionate mother,

affection justified by the values   L. TEMPLE."
Charlotte possesses

"Gracious heaven!" cried Charlotte, forgetting where she was, and raising her streaming eyes as in earnest supplication.

Madame Du Pont was surprised. "Why these tears, my love?" said she. "Why this seeming agitation? I thought the letter would have rejoiced, instead of distressing you."

"It does rejoice me," replied Charlotte, endeavouring at composure, "but I was praying for merit to deserve the unremitted attentions of the best of parents."

"You do right," said Madame Du Pont, "to ask the assistance of heaven that you may continue to deserve their love. Continue, my dear Charlotte, in the course you have ever pursued, and you will insure at once their happiness and your own."

"Oh!" cried Charlotte, as her governess left her, "I have forfeited both for ever! Yet let me reflect:—the irrevocable step is not yet taken: it is not too late to recede from the brink of a precipice, from which I can only behold the dark abyss of ruin, shame, and remorse!"

She arose from her seat, and flew to the apartment of La Rue. "Oh Mademoiselle!" said she, "I am snatched by a miracle from destruction! This letter has saved me: it has opened my eyes to the folly I was so near committing. I will not go, Mademoiselle; I will not wound the hearts of those dear parents who make my happiness the whole study of their lives."

"Well," said Mademoiselle, "do as you please, Miss; but pray understand that my resolution is taken, and it is not in your power

6. A comforting or exhilarating beverage, often containing alcohol.

to alter it. I shall meet the gentlemen at the appointed hour, and shall not be surprised at any outrage which Montraville may commit, when he finds himself disappointed. Indeed I should not be astonished, was he to come immediately here, and reproach you for your instability in the hearing of the whole school: and what will be the consequence? you will bear the odium of having formed the resolution of eloping, and every girl of spirit will laugh at your want of fortitude to put it in execution, while prudes and fools will load you with reproach and contempt. You will have lost the confidence of your parents, incurred their anger, and the scoffs of the world; and what fruit do you expect to reap from this piece of heroism, (for such no doubt you think it is?) you will have the pleasure to reflect, that you have deceived the man who adores you, and whom in your heart your prefer to all other men, and that you are separated from him for ever."

This eloquent harangue was given with such volubility,[7] that Charlotte could not find an opportunity to interrupt her, or to offer a single word till the whole was finished, and then found her ideas so confused, that she knew not what to say.

At length she determined that she would go with Mademoiselle to the place of assignation, convince Montraville of the necessity of adhering to the resolution of remaining behind; assure him of her affection, and bid him adieu.

Charlotte formed this plan in her mind, and exulted in the certainty of its success. "How shall I rejoice," said she, "in this triumph of reason over inclination, and, when in the arms of my affectionate parents, lift up my soul in gratitude to heaven as I look back on the dangers I have escaped!"

The hour of assignation arrived: Mademoiselle put what money and valuables she possessed in her pocket, and advised Charlotte to do the same; but she refused; "my resolution is fixed," said she; "I will sacrifice love to duty."

Mademoiselle smiled internally; and they proceeded softly down the back stairs and out of the garden gate. Montraville and Belcour were ready to receive them.

"Now," said Montraville, taking Charlotte in his arms, "you are mine for ever."

"No," said she, withdrawing from his embrace, "I am come to take an everlasting farewel."

It would be useless to repeat the conversation that here ensued; suffice it to say, that Montraville used every argument that had formerly been successful, Charlotte's resolution began to waver, and he drew her almost imperceptibly towards the chaise.

7. Fluency. "Harangue": loud, unpleasant expression of protest.

"I cannot go," said she: "cease, dear Montraville, to persuade. I must not: religion, duty, forbid."

"Cruel Charlotte," said he, "if you disappoint my ardent hopes, by all that is sacred, this hand shall put a period to my existence. I cannot—will not live without you."

"Alas! my torn heart!" said Charlotte, "how shall I act?"

"Let me direct you," said Montraville, lifting her into the chaise.

"Oh! my dear forsaken parents!" cried Charlotte.

The chaise drove off. She shrieked, and fainted into the arms of her betrayer.

Chapter XIII.

Cruel Disappointment.

"What pleasure," cried Mr. Eldridge, as he stepped into the chaise to go for his grand-daughter, "what pleasure expands the heart of an old man when he beholds the progeny of a beloved child growing up in every virtue that adorned the minds of her parents. I foolishly thought, some few years since, that every sense of joy was buried in the graves of my dear partner and my son; but my Lucy, by her filial affection, soothed my soul to peace, and this dear Charlotte has twined herself round my heart, and opened such new scenes of delight to my view, that I almost forget I have ever been unhappy."

When the chaise stopped, he alighted with the alacrity[8] of youth; so much do the emotions of the soul influence the body."

It was half past eight o'clock: the ladies were assembled in the school room, and Madame Du Pont was preparing to offer the morning sacrifice of prayer and praise, when it was discovered, that Mademoiselle and Charlotte were missing.

"She is busy, no doubt," said the governess, "in preparing Charlotte for her little excursion; but pleasure should never make us forget our duty to our Creator. Go, one of you, and bid them both attend prayers."

The lady who went to summon them, soon returned, and informed the governess, that the room was locked, and that she had knocked repeatedly, but obtained no answer.

"Good heaven!" cried Madame Du Pont, "this is very strange:" and turning pale with terror, she went hastily to the door, and ordered it to be forced open. The apartment instantly discovered, that no person had been in it the preceding night, the beds appearing

8. Eager speediness.

as though just made. The house was instantly a scene of confusion: the garden, the pleasure grounds were searched to no purpose, every apartment rang with the names of Miss Temple and Mademoiselle; but they were too distant to hear; and every face wore the marks of disappointment.

Mr. Eldridge was sitting in the parlour, eagerly expecting his grand-daughter to descend, ready equipped for her journey: he heard the confusion that reigned in the house; he heard the name of Charlotte frequently repeated. "What can be the matter?" said he, rising and opening the door: "I fear some accident has befallen my dear girl."

The governess entered. The visible agitation of her countenance discovered that something extraordinary had happened.

"Where is Charlotte?" said he, "Why does not my child come to welcome her doating parent?"

"Be composed, my dear Sir," said Madame Du Pont, "do not frighten yourself unnecessarily. She is not in the house at present; but as Mademoiselle is undoubtedly with her, she will speedily return in safety; and I hope they will both be able to account for this unseasonable absence in such a manner as shall remove our present uneasiness."

"Madam," cried the old man, with an angry look, "has my child been accustomed to go out without leave, with no other company or protector than that French woman. Pardon me, Madam, I mean no reflections on your country, but I never did like Mademoiselle La Rue; I think she was a very improper person to be entrusted with the care of such a girl as Charlotte Temple, or to be suffered to take her from under your immediate protection."

"You wrong me, Mr. Eldridge," replied she, "if you suppose I have ever permitted your grand-daughter to go out unless with the other ladies. I would to heaven I could form any probable conjecture concerning her absence this morning, but it is a mystery which her return can alone unravel."

Servants were now dispatched to every place where there was the least hope of hearing any tidings of the fugitives, but in vain. Dreadful were the hours of horrid suspense which Mr. Eldridge passed till twelve o'clock, when that suspense was reduced to a shocking certainty, and every spark of hope which till then they had indulged, was in a moment extinguished.

Mr. Eldridge was preparing, with a heavy heart, to return to his anxiously expecting children, when Madame Du Pont received the following note without either name or date.

"Miss Temple is well, and wishes to relieve the anxiety of her parents, by letting them know she has voluntarily put herself under the protection of a man whose future study shall be to make her happy. Pursuit is needless; the measures taken to avoid discovery are too effectual to be eluded. When she thinks her friends are reconciled to this precipitate step, they may perhaps be informed of her place of residence. Mademoiselle is with her."

As Madame Du Pont read these cruel lines, she turned pale as ashes, her limbs trembled, and she was forced to call for a glass of water. She loved Charlotte truly; and when she reflected on the innocence and gentleness of her disposition, she concluded that it must have been the advice and machinations[9] of La Rue, which led her to this imprudent action; she recollected her agitation at the receipt of her mother's letter, and saw in it the conflict of her mind.

"Does that letter relate to Charlotte?" said Mr. Eldridge, having waited some time in expectation of Madame Du Pont's speaking.

"It does," said she. "Charlotte is well, but cannot return to-day."

"Not return, Madam? where is she? who will detain her from her fond, expecting parents?"

"You distract me with questions, Mr. Eldridge. Indeed I know not where she is, or who has seduced her from her duty."

The whole truth now rushed at once upon Mr. Eldridge's mind. "She has eloped then," said he. "My child is betrayed; the darling, the comfort of my aged heart, is lost. Oh would to heaven I had died but yesterday."

A violent gust of grief in some measure relieved him, and, after several vain attempts, he at length assumed sufficient composure to read the note.

"And how shall I return to my children?" said he: "how approach that mansion, so late the habitation of peace? Alas! my dear Lucy, how will you support these heart-rending tidings? or how shall I be enabled to console you, who need so much consolation myself?"

The old man returned to the chaise, but the light step and chearful countenance were no more; sorrow filled his heart, and guided his motions; he seated himself in the chaise, his venerable head reclined upon his bosom, his hands were folded, his eye fixed on vacancy, and the large drops of sorrow rolled silently down his cheeks. There was a mixture of anguish and resignation depicted in his countenance, as if he would say, henceforth who shall dare to boast his happiness, or even in idea contemplate his treasure, lest, in the very moment his heart is exulting in its own felicity, the object which constitutes that felicity should be torn from him.

9. Dishonest maneuverings (the *ch* can be pronounced as "k" or "sh").

Chapter XIV.

Maternal Sorrow.

Slow and heavy passed the time while the carriage was conveying Mr. Eldridge home; and yet when he came in sight of the house, he wished a longer reprieve from the dreadful task of informing Mr. and Mrs. Temple of their daughter's elopement.

It is easy to judge the anxiety of these affectionate parents, when they found the return of their father delayed so much beyond the expected time. They were now met in the dining parlour, and several of the young people who had been invited were already arrived. Each different part of the company was employed in the same manner, looking out at the windows which faced the road. At length the long-expected chaise appeared. Mrs. Temple ran out to receive and welcome her darling: her young companions flocked round the door, each one eager to give her joy on the return of her birth-day. The door of the chaise was opened: Charlotte was not there. "Where is my child?" cried Mrs. Temple, in breathless agitation.

Mr. Eldridge could not answer: he took hold of his daughter's hand and led her into the house; and sinking on the first chair he came to, burst into tears, and sobbed aloud.

"She is dead," cried Mrs. Temple. "Oh my dear Charlotte!" and clasping her hands in an agony of distress, fell into strong hysterics.

Mr. Temple, who had stood speechless with surprize and fear, now ventured to enquire if indeed his Charlotte was no more. Mr. Eldridge led him into another apartment; and putting the fatal note into his hand, cried—"Bear it like a Christian," and turned from him, endeavouring to suppress his own too visible emotions.

It would be vain to attempt describing what Mr. Temple felt whilst he hastily ran over the dreadful lines: when he had finished, the paper dropt from his unnerved hand. "Gracious heaven!" said he, "could Charlotte act thus?" Neither tear nor sigh escaped him; and he sat the image of mute sorrow, till roused from his stupor by the repeated shrieks of Mrs. Temple. He rose hastily, and rushing into the apartment where she was, folded his arms about her, and saying—"Let us be patient, my dear Lucy," nature relieved his almost bursting heart by a friendly gush of tears.

Should any one, presuming on his own philosophic temper,[1] look with an eye of contempt on the man who could indulge a woman's weakness, let him remember that man was a father, and he will then pity the misery which wrung those drops from a noble, generous heart.

---

1. Calm disposition.

Mrs. Temple beginning to be a little more composed, but still imagining her child was dead, her husband, gently taking her hand, cried—"You are mistaken, my love. Charlotte is not dead."

"Then she is very ill, else why did she not come. But I will go to her: the chaise is still at the door: let me go instantly to the dear girl. If I was ill, she would fly to attend me, to alleviate my sufferings, and chear me with her love."

"Be calm, my dearest Lucy, and I will tell you all," said Mr. Temple. "You must not go, indeed you must not; it will be of no use."

"Temple," said she, assuming a look of firmness and composure, "tell me the truth I beseech you. I cannot bear this dreadful suspense. What misfortune has befallen my child? Let me know the worst, and I will endeavour to bear it as I ought."

"Lucy," replied Mr. Temple, "imagine your daughter alive, and in no danger of death: what misfortune would you then dread?"

"There is one misfortune which is worse than death. But I know my child too well to suspect—"

"Be not too confident, Lucy."

"Oh heavens!" said she, "what horrid images do you start: is it possible she should forget——"

"She has forgot us all, my love; she has preferred the love of a stranger to the affectionate protection of her friends."

"Not eloped?" cried she eagerly.

Mr. Temple was silent.

"You cannot contradict it," said she. "I see my fate in those tearful eyes. Oh Charlotte! Charlotte! how ill have you requited our tenderness! But, Father of Mercies," continued she, sinking on her knees, and raising her streaming eyes and clasped hands to heaven, "this once vouchsafe to hear a fond, a distracted mother's prayer. Oh let thy bounteous Providence watch over and protect the dear thoughtless girl, save her from the miseries which I fear will be her portion, and oh! of thine infinite mercy, make her not a mother, lest she should one day feel what I now suffer."

The last words faultered on her tongue, and she fell fainting into the arms of her husband, who had involuntarily dropped on his knees beside her.

A mother's anguish, when disappointed in her tenderest hopes, none but a mother can conceive. Yet, my dear young readers, I would have you read this scene with attention, and reflect that you may yourselves one day be mothers. Oh my friends, as you value your eternal happiness, wound not, by thoughtless ingratitude, the peace of the mother who bore you: remember the tenderness, the care, the unremitting anxiety with which she has attended to all your wants and wishes from earliest infancy to the present day; behold the mild ray of affectionate applause that beams from her eye on the performance of your duty: listen to her reproofs with silent attention; they proceed from a heart anxious for your future felicity: you must love her; nature, all-powerful nature, has planted the seeds of filial affection in your bosoms.

Then once more read over the sorrows of poor Mrs. Temple, and remember, the mother whom you so dearly love and venerate will feel the same, when you, forgetful of the respect due to your maker and yourself, forsake the paths of virtue for those of vice and folly.

Chapter XV.

Embarkation.

It was with the utmost difficulty that the united efforts of Mademoiselle and Montraville could support Charlotte's spirits during their short ride from Chichester to Portsmouth, where a boat waited to take them immediately on board the ship in which they were to embark for America.

As soon as she became tolerably composed, she entreated pen and ink to write to her parents. This she did in the most affecting, artless manner, entreating their pardon and blessing, and describing the dreadful situation of her mind, the conflict she suffered in endeavouring to conquer this unfortunate attachment, and concluded with saying, her only hope of future comfort consisted in the (perhaps delusive) idea she indulged, of being once more folded in their protecting arms, and hearing the words of peace and pardon from their lips.

The tears streamed incessantly while she was writing, and she was frequently obliged to lay down her pen: but when the task was completed, and she had committed the letter to the care of Montraville to be sent to the post office, she became more calm, and indulging the delightful hope of soon receiving an answer that would seal her pardon, she in some measure assumed her usual chearfulness.

But Montraville knew too well the consequences that must unavoidably ensue, should this letter reach Mr. Temple: he therefore wisely resolved to walk on the deck, tear it in pieces, and commit the fragments to the care of Neptune,[2] who might or might not, as it suited his convenience, convey them on shore.

All Charlotte's hopes and wishes were now centered in one, namely that the fleet might be detained at Spithead[3] till she could receive a letter from her friends: but in this she was disappointed, for the second morning after she went on board, the signal was

2. Roman god of the sea.
3. A favorite anchorage of the British navy just off the coast of southern England.

made, the fleet weighed anchor, and in a few hours (the wind being favourable) they bid adieu to the white cliffs of Albion.[4]

In the mean time every enquiry that could be thought of was made by Mr. and Mrs. Temple; for many days did they indulge the fond hope that she was merely gone off to be married, and that when the indissoluble knot was once tied, she would return with the partner she had chosen, and entreat their blessing and forgiveness.

"And shall we not forgive her?" said Mr. Temple.

"Forgive her!" exclaimed the mother. "Oh yes, whatever be her errors, is she not our child? and though bowed to the earth even with shame and remorse, is it not our duty to raise the poor penitent, and whisper peace and comfort to her desponding soul? would she but return, with rapture would I fold her to my heart, and bury every remembrance of her faults in the dear embrace."

But still day after day passed on, and Charlotte did not appear, nor were any tidings to be heard of her: yet each rising morning was welcomed by some new hope—the evening brought with it disappointment. At length hope was no more; despair usurped her place; and the mansion which was once the mansion of peace, became the habitation of pale, dejected melancholy.

The chearful smile that was wont to adorn the face of Mrs. Temple was fled, and had it not been for the support of unaffected piety, and a consciousness of having ever set before her child the fairest example, she must have sunk under this heavy affliction.

"Since," said she, "the severest scrutiny cannot charge me with any breach of duty to have deserved this severe chastisement, I will bow before the power who inflicts it with humble resignation to his will; nor shall the duty of a wife be totally absorbed in the feelings of the mother; I will endeavour to appear more chearful, and by appearing in some measure to have conquered my own sorrow, alleviate the sufferings of my husband, and rouse him from that torpor into which this misfortune has plunged him. My father too demands my care and attention: I must not, by a selfish indulgence of my own grief, forget the interest those two dear objects take in my happiness or misery: I will wear a smile on my face, though the thorn rankles in my heart; and if by so doing, I in the smallest degree contribute to restore their peace of mind, I shall be amply rewarded for the pain the concealment of my own feelings may occasion.

Thus argued this excellent woman: and in the execution of so laudable a resolution we shall leave her, to follow the fortunes of the hapless victim of imprudence and evil counsellors.

4. This popular phrase combines a poetic nickname for England with a reference to the white cliffs of Dover, the part of England that is closest to the European continent. These cliffs are often the last part of England one sees when departing by ship and the first thing one sees on returning; they serve as a highly charged symbol of nostalgia for an absent home.

Chapter XVI.

Necessary Digression.

On board of the ship in which Charlotte and Mademoiselle were embarked, was an officer of large unincumbered fortune and elevated rank, and whom I shall call Crayton.

He was one of those men, who, having travelled in their youth, pretend to have contracted a peculiar fondness for every thing foreign, and to hold in contempt the productions of their own country; and this affected partiality extended even to the women.

With him therefore the blushing modesty and unaffected simplicity of Charlotte passed unnoticed; but the forward pertness of La Rue, the freedom of her conversation, the elegance of her person, mixed with a certain engaging *je ne sais quoi*,[5] perfectly enchanted him.

The reader no doubt has already developed the character of La Rue: designing, artful, and selfish, she had accepted the devoirs[6] of Belcour because she was heartily weary of the retired life she led at the school, wished to be released from what she deemed a slavery, and to return to that vortex of folly and dissipation which had once plunged her into the deepest misery; but her plan she flattered herself was now better formed: she resolved to put herself under the protection of no man till she had first secured a settlement; but the clandestine manner in which she left Madame Du Pont's prevented her putting this plan in execution, though Belcour solemnly protested he would make her a handsome settlement the moment they arrived at Portsmouth. This he afterwards contrived to evade by a pretended hurry of business; La Rue readily conceiving he never meant to fulfil his promise, determined to change her battery, and attack the heart of Colonel Crayton. She soon discovered the partiality he entertained for her nation; and having imposed on him a feigned tale of distress, representing Belcour as a villain who had seduced her from her friends under promise of marriage, and afterwards betrayed her, pretending great remorse for the errors she had committed, and declaring whatever her affection for Belcour might have been, it was now entirely extinguished, and she wished for nothing more than an opportunity to leave a course of life which her soul abhorred; but she had no friends to apply to, they had all renounced her, and guilt and misery would undoubtedly be her future portion through life.

---

5. *French.* I know not what.
6. Acts expressing courtesy and respect.

Crayton was possessed of many amiable qualities, though the peculiar trait in his character, which we have already mentioned, in a great measure threw a shade over them. He was beloved for his humanity and benevolence by all who knew him, but he was easy and unsuspicious himself, and became a dupe to the artifice of others.

He was, when very young, united to an amiable Parisian lady, and perhaps it was his affection for her that laid the foundation for the partiality he ever retained for the whole nation. He had by her one daughter, who entered into the world but a few hours before her mother left it. This lady was universally beloved and admired, being endowed with all the virtues of her mother, without the weakness of the father: she was married to Major Beauchamp, and was at this time in the same fleet with her father, attending her husband to New-York.

Crayton was melted by the affected contrition and distress of La Rue: he would converse with her for hours, read to her, play cards with her, listen to all her complaints, and promise to protect her to the utmost of his power. La Rue easily saw his character; her sole aim was to awaken a passion in his bosom that might turn out to her advantage, and in this aim she was but too successful, for before the voyage was finished the infatuated Colonel gave her from under his hand a promise of marriage on their arrival at New-York, under forfeiture of five thousand pounds.

And how did our poor Charlotte pass her time during a tedious and tempestuous passage? naturally delicate, the fatigue and sickness which she endured rendered her so weak as to be almost entirely confined to her bed: yet the kindness and attention of Montraville in some measure contributed to alleviate her sufferings, and the hope of hearing from her friends soon after her arrival, kept up her spirits, and cheered many a gloomy hour.

But during the voyage a great revolution took place not only in the fortune of La Rue but in the bosom of Belcour: whilst in pursuit of his amour with Mademoiselle, he had attended little to the interesting, inobtrusive charms of Charlotte, but when, cloyed by possession, and disgusted with the art and dissimulation of one, he beheld the simplicity and gentleness of the other, the contrast became too striking not to fill him at once with surprise and admiration. He frequently conversed with Charlotte; he found her sensible, well informed, but diffident and unassuming. The languor which the fatigue of her body and perturbation of her mind spread over her delicate features, served only in his opinion to render her more lovely: he knew that Montraville did not design to marry her, and he formed a resolution to endeavour to gain her himself whenever Montraville should leave her.

Let not the reader imagine Belcour's designs were honourable. Alas! when once a woman has forgot the respect due to herself, by yielding to the solicitations of illicit love, they lose all their consequence, even in the eyes of the man whose art has betrayed them, and for whose sake they have sacrificed every valuable consideration.

The heedless Fair, who stoops to guilty joys.

A man may pity—but he must despise.

Nay, every libertine will think he has a right to insult her with his licentious[7] passion; and should the unhappy creature shrink from the insolent overture, he will sneeringly taunt her with pretence of modesty.

Chapter XVII.

A Wedding.

On the day before their arrival at New-York, after dinner, Crayton arose from his seat, and placing himself by Mademoiselle, thus addressed the company—

"As we are now nearly arrived at our destined port, I think it but my duty to inform you, my friends, that this lady," (taking her hand,) "has placed herself under my protection. I have seen and severely felt the anguish of her heart, and through every shade which cruelty or malice may throw over her, can discover the most amiable qualities. I thought it but necessary to mention my esteem for her before our disembarkation, as it is my fixed resolution, the morning after we land, to give her an undoubted title to my favour and protection by honourably uniting my fate to hers. I would wish every gentleman here therefore to remember that her honour henceforth is mine, and," continued he, looking at Belcour, "should any man presume to speak in the least disrespectfully of her, I shall not hesitate to pronounce him a scoundrel."

Belcour cast at him a smile of contempt, and bowing profoundly low, wished Mademoiselle much joy in the proposed union; and assuring the Colonel that he need not be in the least apprehensive of any one throwing the least odium on the character of his lady, shook him by the hand with ridiculous gravity, and left the cabin.

The truth was, he was glad to be rid of La Rue, and so he was but freed from her, he cared not who fell a victim to her infamous arts.[8]

The inexperienced Charlotte was astonished at what she heard. She thought La Rue had, like herself, only been urged by the force of

7. Sexually immoral.
8. Cunning.

her attachment to Belcour, to quit her friends, and follow him to the seat of war: how wonderful then, that she should resolve to marry another man. It was certainly extremely wrong. It was indelicate. She mentioned her thoughts to Montraville. He laughed at her simplicity, called her a little ideot, and patting her on the cheek, said she knew nothing of the world. "If the world sanctifies such things, 'tis a very bad world I think," said Charlotte. "Why I always understood they were to have been married when they arrived at New-York. I am sure Mademoiselle told me Belcour promised to marry her."

"Well, and suppose he did?"

"Why, he should be obliged to keep his word I think."

"Well, but I suppose he has changed his mind," said Montraville, "and then you know the case is altered."

Charlotte looked at him attentively for a moment. A full sense of her own situation rushed upon her mind. She burst into tears, and remained silent. Montraville too well understood the cause of her tears. He kissed her cheek, and bidding her not make herself uneasy, unable to bear the silent but keen remonstrance,[9] hastily left her.

The next morning by sun-rise they found themselves at anchor before the city of New-York. A boat was ordered to convey the ladies on shore. Crayton accompanied them; and they were shewn to a house of public entertainment. Scarcely were they seated when the door opened, and the Colonel found himself in the arms of his daughter, who had landed a few minutes before him. The first transport of meeting subsided, Crayton introduced his daughter to Mademoiselle La Rue, as an old friend of her mother's, (for the artful French woman had really made it appear to the credulous Colonel that she was in the same convent with his first wife, and, though much younger, had received many tokens of her esteem and regard.)

"If, Mademoiselle," said Mrs. Beauchamp, "you were the friend of my mother, you must be worthy the esteem of all good hearts."

"Mademoiselle will soon honour our family," said Crayton, "by supplying the place that valuable woman filled: and as you are married, my dear, I think you will not blame—"

"Hush, my dear Sir," replied Mrs. Beauchamp: "I know my duty too well to scrutinize your conduct. Be assured, my dear father, your happiness is mine. I shall rejoice in it, and sincerely love the person who contributes to it. But tell me," continued she, turning to Charlotte, "who is this lovely girl? Is she your sister, Mademoiselle?"

A blush, deep as the glow of the carnation, suffused the cheeks of Charlotte.

9. Statement of grievance; criticism.

"It is a young lady," replied the Colonel, "who came in the same vessel with us from England." He then drew his daughter aside, and told her in a whisper, Charlotte was the mistress of Montraville.

"What a pity!" said Mrs. Beauchamp softly, (casting a most compassionate glance at her.) "But surely her mind is not depraved. The goodness of her heart is depicted in her ingenuous[1] countenance."

Charlotte caught the word pity. "And am I already fallen so low?" said she. A sigh escaped her, and a tear was ready to start, but Montraville appeared, and she checked the rising emotion. Mademoiselle went with the Colonel and his daughter to another apartment. Charlotte remained with Montraville and Belcour. The next morning the Colonel performed his promise, and La Rue became in due form Mrs. Crayton, exulted in her own good fortune, and dared to look with an eye of contempt on the unfortunate but far less guilty Charlotte.

END OF THE FIRST VOLUME.

No way will Rowson Let Mrs. Crayton go w/o dismantling her fortune

1. Innocent, unworldly, and sincere.

CHARLOTTE.
A TALE OF TRUTH.

By Mrs. *ROWSON*,

OF THE NEW THEATRE PHILADELPHIA;
AUTHOR of VICTORIA, THE INQUISITOR, FILLE
DE CHAMBRE, &c.

IN TWO VOLUMES.

She was her parents only joy :
They had but one——one darling child.

ROMEO AND JULIET.

Her form was faultlefs, and her mind,
 Untainted yet by art,
Was nobly, juft, humane, and kind,
 And virtue warm'd her heart.
But ah ! the cruel fpoiler came——

VOL. II.

—SECOND PHILADELPHIA EDITION—
PRINTED FOR MATHEW CAREY,
NO. 118, MARKET-STREET.
OCT. 9—1794.

Title page of volume II of *Charlotte. A Tale of Truth.*
© American Antiquarian Society.

Chapter XVIII.

Reflections.

"And am I indeed fallen so low," said Charlotte, "as to be only pitied? Will the voice of approbation no more meet my ear? and shall I never again possess a friend, whose face will wear a smile of joy whenever I approach? Alas! how thoughtless, how dreadfully imprudent have I been! I know not which is most painful to endure, the sneer of contempt, or the glance of compassion, which is depicted in the various countenances of my own sex: they are both equally humiliating. Ah! my dear parents, could you now see the child of your affections, the daughter whom you so dearly loved, a poor solitary being, without society, here wearing out her heavy hours in deep regret and anguish of heart, no kind friend of her own sex to whom she can unbosom her griefs, no beloved mother, no woman of character will appear in my company, and low as your Charlotte is fallen, she cannot associate with infamy."

These were the painful reflections which occupied the mind of Charlotte. Montraville had placed her in a small house a few miles from New-York: he gave her one female attendant, and supplied her with what money she wanted; but business and pleasure so entirely occupied his time, that he had little to devote to the woman, whom he had brought from all her connections, and robbed of innocence. Sometimes, indeed, he would steal out at the close of evening, and pass a few hours with her; and then so much was she attached to him, that all her sorrows were forgotten while blest with his society: she would enjoy a walk by moonlight, or sit by him in a little arbour at the bottom of the garden, and play on the harp, accompanying it with her plaintive, harmonious voice. But often, very often, did he promise to renew his visits, and, forgetful of his promise, leave her to mourn her disappointment. What painful hours of expectation would she pass! she would sit at a window which looked toward a field he used to cross, counting the minutes, and straining her eyes to catch the first glimpse of his person, till blinded with tears of disappointment, she would lean her head on her hands, and give free vent to her sorrows: then catching at some new hope, she would again renew her watchful position, till the shades of evening enveloped every object in a dusky cloud: she would then renew her complaints, and with a heart bursting with disappointed love, retire to a bed which remorse had strewed with thorns, and court in vain that comforter of weary nature (who seldom visits the unhappy) to come and steep her senses in oblivion.

Who can form an adequate idea of the sorrow that preyed upon the mind of Charlotte? The wife, whose breast glows with affection to her husband, and who in return meets only indifference, can but faintly conceive her anguish. Dreadfully painful is the situation of such a woman, but she has many comforts of which our poor Charlotte was deprived. The duteous, faithful wife, though treated with indifference, has one solid pleasure within her own bosom, she can reflect that she has not deserved neglect—that she has ever fulfilled the duties of her station with the strictest exactness; she may hope, by constant assiduity and unremitted attention, to recall her wanderer, and be doubly happy in his returning affection; she knows he cannot leave her to unite himself to another: he cannot cast her out to poverty and contempt; she looks around her, and sees the smile of friendly welcome, or the tear of affectionate consolation, on the face of every person whom she favours with her esteem; and from all these circumstances she gathers comfort: but the poor girl by thoughtless passion led astray, who, in parting with her honour, has forfeited the esteem of the very man to whom she has sacrificed every thing dear and valuable in life, feels his indifference in the fruit of her own folly, and laments her want of power to recall his lost affection; she knows there is no tie but honour, and that, in a man who has been guilty of seduction, is but very feeble: he may leave her in a moment to shame and want; he may marry and forsake her for ever; and should he, she has no redress, no friendly, soothing companion to pour into her wounded mind the balm of consolation, no benevolent hand to lead her back to the path of rectitude; she has disgraced her friends, forfeited the good opinion of the world, and undone herself; she feels herself a poor solitary being in the midst of surrounding multitudes; shame bows her to the earth, remorse tears her distracted mind, and guilt, poverty, and disease close the dreadful scene: she sinks unnoticed to oblivion. The finger of contempt may point out to some passing daughter of youthful mirth, the humble bed where lies this frail filter of mortality; and will she, in the unbounded gaiety of her heart, exult in her own unblemished fame, and triumph over the silent ashes of the dead? Oh no! has she a heart of sensibility, she will stop, and thus address the unhappy victim of folly—

"Thou had'st thy faults, but sure thy sufferings have expiated them: thy errors brought thee to an early grave; but thou wert a fellow-creature—thou hast been unhappy—then be those errors forgotten."

Then, as she stoops to pluck the noxious weed from off the sod, a tear will fall, and consecrate the spot to Charity.

For ever honoured be the sacred drop of humanity; the angel of mercy shall record its source, and the soul from whence it sprang shall be immortal.

My dear Madam, contract not your brow into a frown of disapprobation. I mean not to extenuate the faults of those unhappy women who fall victims to guilt and folly; but surely, when we reflect how many errors we are ourselves subject to, how many secret faults lie hid in the recesses of our hearts, which we should blush to have brought into open day (and yet those faults require the lenity[2] and pity of a benevolent judge, or awful would be our prospect of futurity) I say, my dear Madam, when we consider this, we surely may pity the faults of others.

Believe me, many an unfortunate female, who has once strayed into the thorny paths of vice, would gladly return to virtue, was any generous friend to endeavour to raise and re-assure her; but alas! it cannot be, you say; the world would deride and scoff. Then let me tell you, Madam, 'tis a very unfeeling world, and does not deserve half the blessings which a bountiful Providence showers upon it.

Oh, thou benevolent giver of all good! how shall we erring mortals dare to look up to thy mercy in the great day of retribution, if we now uncharitably refuse to overlook the errors, or alleviate the miseries, of our fellow-creatures.

Chapter XIX.

A Mistake Discovered.

Julia Franklin was the only child of a man of large property, who, at the age of eighteen, left her independent mistress of an unincumbered[3] income of seven hundred a year; she was a girl of a lively disposition, and humane, susceptible heart: she resided in New-York with an uncle, who loved her too well, and had too high an opinion of her prudence, to scrutinize her actions so much as would have been necessary with many young ladies, who were not blest with her discretion: she was, at the time Montraville arrived at New-York, the life of society, and the universal toast. Montraville was introduced to her by the following accident.

One night when he was upon guard, a dreadful fire broke out near Mr. Franklin's house, which, in a few hours, reduced that and several others to ashes; fortunately no lives were lost, and, by the assiduity of the soldiers, much valuable property was saved from the flames. In the midst of the confusion an old gentleman came up to Montraville, and, putting a small box into his hands, cried—"Keep it, my good Sir, till I come to you again;" and then rushing again into the thickest of the croud, Montraville saw him no more. He waited till the fire was quite extinguished and the mob dispersed; but in vain: the old gentleman did not appear to claim his property; and Montraville, fearing to make any enquiry, lest he should meet with impostors who might lay

2. Mercifulness.
3. I.e., Unencumbered; owned completely, without any portion of it owed to others.

claim, without any legal right, to the box, carried it to his lodgings, and locked it up: he naturally imagined, that the person who committed it to his care knew him, and would, in a day or two, reclaim it; but several weeks passed on, and no enquiry being made, he began to be uneasy, and resolved to examine the contents of the box, and if they were, as he supposed, valuable, to spare no pains to discover, and restore them to the owner. Upon opening it, he found it contained jewels to a large amount, about two hundred pounds in money, and a miniature picture set for a bracelet. On examining the picture, he thought he had somewhere seen features very like it, but could not recollect where. A few days after, being at a public assembly, he saw Miss Franklin, and the likeness was too evident to be mistaken: he enquired among his brother officers if any of them knew her, and found one who was upon terms of intimacy in the family: "then introduce me to her immediately," said he, "for I am certain I can inform her of something which will give her peculiar pleasure."

He was immediately introduced, found she was the owner of the jewels, and was invited to breakfast the next morning in order to their restoration. This whole evening Montraville was honoured with Julia's hand; the lively sallies of her wit, the elegance of her manner, powerfully charmed him: he forgot Charlotte, and indulged himself in saying every thing that was polite and tender to Julia. But on retiring, recollection returned. "What am I about?" said he: "though I cannot marry Charlotte, I cannot be villain enough to forsake her, nor must I dare to trifle with the heart of Julia Franklin. I will return this box," said he, "which has been the source of so much uneasiness already, and in the evening pay a visit to my poor melancholy Charlotte, and endeavour to forget this fascinating Julia."

He arose, dressed himself, and taking the picture out, "I will reserve this from the rest," said he, "and by presenting it to her when she thinks it is lost, enhance the value of the obligation." He repaired to Mr. Franklin's, and found Julia in the breakfast parlour alone.

"How happy am I, Madam," said he, "that being the fortunate instrument of saving these jewels has been the means of procuring me the acquaintance of so amiable a lady. There are the jewels and money all safe."

"But where is the picture, Sir?" said Julia.

"Here, Madam. I would not willingly part with it."

"It is the portrait of my mother," said she, taking it from him: "'tis all that remains." She pressed it to her lips, and a tear trembled in her eyes. Montraville glanced his eye on her grey night gown and black ribbon, and his own feelings prevented a reply.

Julia Franklin was the very reverse of Charlotte Temple: she was tall, elegantly shaped, and possessed much of the air and manner of a woman of fashion; her complexion was a clear brown, enlivened with the glow of health, her eyes, full, black, and sparkling, darted their intelligent glances through long silken lashes; her hair was shining brown, and her features regular and striking; there was an air of innocent gaiety that played about her countenance, where good humour sat triumphant.

"I have been mistaken," said Montraville. "I imagined I loved Charlotte: but alas! I am now too late convinced my attachment to her was merely the impulse of the moment. I fear I have not only entailed[4] lasting misery on that poor girl but also thrown a barrier in the way of my own happiness, which it will be impossible to surmount. I feel I love Julia Franklin with ardour and sincerity; yet, when in her presence, I am sensible of my own inability to offer a heart worthy her acceptance, and remain silent."

Full of these painful thoughts, Montraville walked out to see Charlotte: she saw him approach, and ran out to meet him: she banished from her countenance the air of discontent which ever appeared when he was absent, and met him with a smile of joy.

"I thought you had forgot me, Montraville," said she, "and was very unhappy."

"I shall never forget you, Charlotte," he replied, pressing her hand.

The uncommon gravity of his countenance, and the brevity of his reply, alarmed her.

"You are not well," said she; "your hand is hot; your eyes are heavy; you are very ill."

"I am a villain," said he mentally, as he turned from her to hide his emotions.

"But come," continued she tenderly, "you shall go to bed, and I will sit by, and watch you; you will be better when you have slept."

Montraville was glad to retire, and by pretending sleep, hide the agitation of his mind from her penetrating eye. Charlotte watched by him till a late hour, and then, lying softly down by his side, sunk into a profound sleep, from whence she awoke not till late the next morning.

Chapter XX.

Virtue never appears so amiable as when reaching forth her hand
to raise a fallen sister.
—*Chapter of Accidents.*[5]

When Charlotte awoke, she missed Montraville; but thinking he might have arisen early to enjoy the beauties of the morning, she

---

4. Inflicted; literally, it means to set limits on how property is to be dispersed in one's will.
5. A play by English author Sophia Lee (1750–1824), produced in 1780, and written while she and her father were in debtors' prison.

was preparing to follow him, when casting her eye on the table, she saw a note, and opening it hastily, found these words—

"My dear Charlotte must not be surprised, if she does not see me again for some time: unavoidable business will prevent me that pleasure: be assured I am quite well this morning; and what your fond imagination magnified into illness, was nothing more than fatigue, which a few hours rest has entirely removed. Make yourself happy, and be certain of the unalterable friendship of "Montraville."

"*Friendship!*" said Charlotte emphatically, as she finished the note, "is it come to this at last! Alas! poor, forsaken Charlotte, thy doom is now but too apparent. Montraville is no longer interested in thy happiness; and shame, remorse, and disappointed love will henceforth be thy only attendants."

Though these were the ideas that involuntarily, rushed upon the mind of Charlotte as she perused the fatal note, yet after a few hours had elapsed, the syren[6] Hope again took possession of her bosom, and she flattered herself she could, on a second perusal, discover an air of tenderness in the few lines he had left, which at first had escaped her notice. "He certainly cannot be so base as to leave me," said she, "and in stiling himself my friend does he not promise to protect me. I will not torment myself with these causeless fears; I will place a confidence in his honour; and sure he will not be so unjust as to abuse it."

Just as she had by this manner of reasoning brought her mind to some tolerable degree of composure, she was surprised by a visit from Belcour. The dejection visible in Charlotte's countenance, her swoln eyes and neglected attire, at once told him she was unhappy: he made no doubt but Montraville had, by his coldness, alarmed her suspicions, and was resolved, if possible, to rouse her to jealousy, urge her to reproach him, and by that means occasion a breach between them. "If I can once convince her that she has a rival," said he, "she will listen to my passion if it is only to revenge his slights." Belcour knew but little of the female heart; and what he did know was only of those of loose and dissolute lives. He had no idea that a woman might fall a victim to imprudence, and yet retain so strong a sense of honour, as to reject with horror and contempt every solicitation to a second fault. He never imagined that a gentle, generous female heart, once tenderly attached, when treated with unkindness might break, but would never harbour a thought of revenge.

---

6. I.e., siren; a sea nymph in Greek mythology. Sailors could not resist the lure of the sirens' songs and thus would ground their ships on the rocks in pursuit of the source.

His visit was not long, but before he went he fixed a scorpion in the heart of Charlotte, whose venom embittered every future hour of her life.

We will now return for a moment to Colonel Crayton. He had been three months married, and in that little time had discovered that the conduct of his lady was not so prudent as it ought to have been: but remonstrance was vain; her temper was violent; and to the Colonel's great misfortune he had conceived a sincere affection for her: she saw her own power, and, with the art of a Circe,[7] made every action appear to him in what light she pleased: his acquaintance laughed at his blindness, his friends pitied his infatuation, his amiable daughter, Mrs. Beauchamp, in secret deplored the loss of her father's affection, and grieved that he should be so entirely swayed by an artful, and, she much feared, infamous woman.

Mrs. Beauchamp was mild and engaging; she loved not the hurry and bustle of a city, and had prevailed on her husband to take a house a few miles from New-York. Chance led her into the same neighbourhood with Charlotte; their houses stood within a short space of each other, and their gardens joined: she had not been long in her new habitation before the figure of Charlotte struck her; she recollected her interesting features; she saw the melancholy so conspicuous in her countenance, and her heart bled at the reflection, that perhaps deprived of honour, friends, all that was valuable in life, she was doomed to linger out a wretched existence in a strange land, and sink broken-hearted into an untimely grave. "Would to heaven I could snatch her from so hard a fate," said she; "but the merciless world has barred the doors of compassion against a poor weak girl, who, perhaps, had she one kind friend to raise and reassure her, would gladly return to peace and virtue; nay, even the woman who dares to pity, and endeavour to recall a wandering sister, incurs the sneer of contempt and ridicule, for an action in which even angels are said to rejoice."

The longer Mrs. Beauchamp was a witness to the solitary life Charlotte led, the more she wished to speak to her, and often as she saw her cheeks wet with the tears of anguish, she would say—"Dear sufferer, how gladly would I pour into your heart the balm of consolation, were it not for the fear of derision."

But an accident soon happened which made her resolve to brave even the scoffs of the world, rather than not enjoy the heavenly satisfaction of comforting a desponding fellow-creature.

Mrs. Beauchamp was an early riser. She was one morning walking in the garden, leaning on her husband's arm, when the sound of

7. In Greek mythology, a sorceress who could turn people into beasts.

a harp attracted their notice: they listened attentively, and heard a soft melodious voice distinctly sing the following stanzas:

> Thou glorious orb, supremely bright,
>   Just rising from the sea,
> To chear all nature with thy light,
>   What are thy beams to me?
> In vain thy glories bid me rise,
>   To hail the new-born day,
> Alas! my morning sacrifice
>   Is still to weep and pray.
> For what are nature's charms combin'd,
>   To one, whose weary breast
> Can neither peace nor comfort find,
>   Nor friend whereon to rest?
> Oh! never! never! whilst I live
>   Can my heart's anguish cease:
> Come, friendly death, thy mandate give,
>   And let me be at peace.

" 'Tis poor Charlotte!" said Mrs. Beauchamp, the pellucid drop of humanity stealing down her cheek.

Captain Beauchamp was alarmed at her emotion. "What Charlotte?" said he; "do you know her?"

In the accent of a pitying angel did she disclose to her husband Charlotte's unhappy situation, and the frequent wish she had formed of being serviceable to her. "I fear," continued she, "the poor girl has been basely betrayed; and if I thought you would not blame me, I would pay her a visit, offer her my friendship, and endeavour to restore to her heart that peace she seems to have lost, and so pathetically laments. Who knows, my dear," laying her hand affectionately on his arm, "who knows but she has left some kind, affectionate parents to lament her errors, and would she return, they might with rapture receive the poor penitent, and wash away her faults in tears of joy. Oh! what a glorious reflexion would it be for me could I be the happy instrument of restoring her. Her heart may not be depraved, Beauchamp."

"Exalted woman!" cried Beauchamp, embracing her, "how dost thou rise every moment in my esteem. Follow the impulse of thy generous heart, my Emily. Let prudes and fools censure if they dare, and blame a sensibility they never felt; I will exultingly tell them that the heart that is truly virtuous is ever inclined to pity and forgive the errors of its fellow-creatures."

A beam of exulting joy played round the animated countenance of Mrs. Beauchamp, at these encomiums bestowed on her by a beloved husband, the most delightful sensations pervaded her heart, and, having breakfasted, she prepared to visit Charlotte.

Chapter XXI.

Teach me to feel another's woe,
To hide the fault I see,
That mercy I to others show,
That mercy show to me.
—Pope.[8]

When Mrs. Beauchamp was dressed, she began to feel embarrassed at the thought of beginning an acquaintance with Charlotte, and was distressed how to make the first visit. "I cannot go without some introduction," said she, "it will look so like impertinent curiosity." At length recollecting herself, she stepped into the garden, and gathering a few fine cucumbers, took them in her hand by way of apology for her visit.

A glow of conscious shame vermillioned Charlotte's face as Mrs. Beauchamp entered.

"You will pardon me, Madam," said she, "for not having before paid my respects to so amiable a neighbour; but we English people always keep up that reserve which is the characteristic of our nation wherever we go. I have taken the liberty to bring you a few cucumbers, for I observed you had none in your garden."

Charlotte, though naturally polite and well-bred, was so confused she could hardly speak. Her kind visitor endeavoured to relieve her by not noticing her embarrassment. "I am come, Madam," continued she, "to request you will spend the day with me. I shall be alone; and, as we are both strangers in this country, we may hereafter be extremely happy in each other's friendship."

"Your friendship, Madam," said Charlotte blushing, "is an honour to all who are favoured with it. Little as I have seen of this part of the world, I am no stranger to Mrs. Beauchamp's goodness of heart and known humanity: but my friendship——" She paused, glanced her eye upon her own visible situation, and, spite of her endeavours to suppress them, burst into tears.

Mrs. Beauchamp guessed the source from whence those tears flowed. "You seem unhappy, Madam," said she: "shall I be thought worthy your confidence? will you entrust me with the cause of your sorrow, and rest on my assurances to exert my utmost power to serve you." Charlotte returned a look of gratitude, but could not speak, and Mrs. Beauchamp continued—"My heart was interested in your behalf the first moment I saw you, and I only lament I had not made earlier overtures towards an acquaintance; but I flatter myself you will henceforth consider me as your friend."

8. *The Universal Prayer* (1738), final quatrain (4-line stanza).

"Oh Madam!" cried Charlotte, "I have forfeited the good opinion of all my friends; I have forsaken them, and undone myself."

"Come, come, my dear," said Mrs. Beauchamp, "you must not indulge these gloomy thoughts: you are not I hope so miserable as you imagine yourself: endeavour to be composed, and let me be favoured with your company at dinner, when, if you can bring yourself to think me your friend, and repose a confidence in me, I am ready to convince you it shall not be abused." She then arose, and bade her good morning.

At the dining hour Charlotte repaired to Mrs. Beauchamp's, and during dinner assumed as composed an aspect as possible; but when the cloth was removed, she summoned all her resolution and determined to make Mrs. Beauchamp acquainted with every circumstance preceding her unfortunate elopement, and the earnest desire she had to quit a way of life so repugnant to her feelings.

With the benignant aspect of an angel of mercy did Mrs. Beauchamp listen to the artless tale: she was shocked to the soul to find how large a share La Rue had in the seduction of this amiable girl, and a tear fell, when she reflected so vile a woman was now the wife of her father. When Charlotte had finished, she gave her a little time to collect her scattered spirits, and then asked her if she had never written to her friends.

"Oh yes, Madam," said she, "frequently: but I have broke their hearts: they are either dead or have cast me off for ever, for I have never received a single line from them."

"I rather suspect," said Mrs. Beauchamp, "they have never had your letters: but suppose you were to hear from them, and they were willing to receive you, would you then leave this cruel Montraville, and return to them?"

"Would I!" said Charlotte, clasping her hands; "would not the poor sailor, tost on a tempestuous ocean, threatened every moment with death, gladly return to the shore he had left to trust to its deceitful calmness? Oh, my dear Madam, I would return, though to do it I were obliged to walk barefoot over a burning desart, and beg a scanty pittance of each traveller to support my existence. I would endure it all chearfully, could I but once more see my dear, blessed mother, hear her pronounce my pardon, and bless me before I died; but alas! I shall never see her more; she has blotted the ungrateful Charlotte from her remembrance, and I shall sink to the grave loaded with hers and my father's curse."

Mrs. Beauchamp endeavoured to sooth her. "You shall write to them again," said she, "and I will see that the letter is sent by the first packet that sails for England; in the mean time keep up your spirits, and hope every thing, by daring to deserve it."

She then turned the conversation, and Charlotte having taken a cup of tea, wished her benevolent friend a good evening.

Chapter XXII.

Sorrows of the Heart.

When Charlotte got home she endeavoured to collect her thoughts, and took up a pen in order to address those dear parents, whom, spite of her errors, she still loved with the utmost tenderness, but vain was every effort to write with the least coherence; her tears fell so fast they almost blinded her; and as she proceeded to describe her unhappy situation, she became so agitated that she was obliged to give over the attempt and retire to bed, where, overcome with the fatigue her mind had undergone, she fell into a slumber which greatly refreshed her, and she arose in the morning with spirits more adequate to the painful task she had to perform, and, after several attempts, at length concluded the following letter to her mother—

To Mrs. Temple.
New-York.

"Will my once kind, my ever beloved mother, deign to receive a letter from her guilty, but repentant child? or has she, justly incensed at my ingratitude, driven the unhappy Charlotte from her remembrance? Alas! thou much injured mother! Shouldst' thou even disown me, I dare not complain, because I know I have deserved it: but yet, believe me, guilty as I am, and cruelly as I have disappointed the hopes of the fondest parents, that ever girl had, even in the moment when, forgetful of my duty, I fled from you and happiness, even then I loved you most, and my heart bled at the thought of what you would suffer. Oh! never, never! whilst I have existence, will the agony of that moment be erased from my memory. It seemed like the separation of soul and body. What can I plead in excuse for my conduct? alas! nothing! That I loved my seducer is but too true! yet powerful as that passion is when operating in a young heart glowing with sensibility, it never would have conquered my affection to you, my beloved parents, had I not been encouraged, nay, urged to take the fatally imprudent step, by one of my own sex, who, under the mask of friendship, drew me on to ruin. Yet think not your Charlotte was so soft as to voluntarily rush into a life of infamy; no, my dear mother, deceived by the specious appearance of my betrayer, and every suspicion lulled asleep by the most solemn promises of marriage, I thought not those promises would so easily be forgotten. I never once reflected that the man who could stoop to seduction, would not hesitate to forsake the wretched object of his passion, whenever his capricious heart grew weary of her tenderness. When we arrived at this place, I vainly expected him to fulfil his engagements, but was at last fatally convinced he had never intended to make me his wife, or if he had once thought of it, his mind was now altered. I scorned to claim from his humanity what I could not obtain from his love: I was conscious of having forfeited the only gem that could render me respectable in the eye of the world. I locked my sorrows in my own bosom, and bore my injuries in silence. But how shall I proceed? This man, this cruel Montraville, for whom I sacrificed honour, happiness, and the love of my friends, no longer looks on me with affection, but scorns the credulous[9] girl whom his art has made miserable. Could you see me, my dear parents, without society, without friends, stung with remorse, and (I feel the burning blush of shame die my cheeks while I write it) tortured with the pangs of disappointed love; cut to the soul by the indifference of him, who, having deprived me of every other comfort, no longer thinks it worth his while to sooth the heart where he has planted the thorn of never-ceasing regret. My daily employment is to think of you and weep, to pray for your happiness and deplore my own folly: my nights are scarce more happy, for if by chance I close my weary eyes, and hope some small forgetfulness of sorrow, some little time to pass in sweet oblivion, fancy, still waking, wafts me home to you: I see your beloved forms, I kneel and hear the blessed words of peace and pardon. Extatic joy pervades my soul; I reach my arms to catch your dear embraces; the motion chases the illusive dream; I wake to real misery. At other times I see my father angry and frowning, point to horrid caves, where, on the cold damp ground, in the agonies of death, I see my dear mother and my revered grand-father. I strive to raise you; you push me from you, and shrieking cry—"Charlotte, thou hast murdered me!" Horror and despair tear every tortured nerve; I start, and leave my restless bed, weary and unrefreshed.

"Shocking as these reflexions are, I have yet one more dreadful than the rest. Mother, my dear mother! do not let me quite break your heart when I tell you, in a few months I shall bring into the world an innocent witness of my guilt. Oh my bleeding heart, I shall bring a poor little helpless creature, heir to infamy and shame.

"This alone has urged me once more to address you, to interest you in behalf of this poor unborn, and beg you to extend your protection to the child of lost Charlotte; for my own part I have wrote so often, so frequently have pleaded for forgiveness, and entreated to be received once more beneath the paternal roof, that having received

9. Gullible, easily duped.

no answer, not even one line, I much fear you have cast me from you for ever.

"But sure you cannot refuse to protect my innocent infant: it partakes not of its mother's guilt. Oh my father, oh beloved mother, now do I feel the anguish I inflicted on your hearts recoiling with double force upon my own.

"If my child should be a girl (which heaven forbid) tell her the unhappy fate of her mother, and teach her to avoid my errors; if a boy, teach him to lament my miseries, but tell him not who inflicted them, lest in wishing to revenge his mother's injuries, he should wound the peace of his father.

"And now, dear friends of my soul, kind guardians of my infancy, farewell. I feel I never more must hope to see you; the anguish of my heart strikes at the strings of life, and in a short time I shall be at rest. Oh could I but receive your blessing and forgiveness before I died, it would smooth my passage to the peaceful grave, and be a blessed foretaste of a happy eternity. I beseech you, curse me not, my adored parents, but let a tear of pity and pardon fall to the memory of your lost

Charlotte.

Chapter XXIII.

A Man May Smile, and Smile, and Be a Villain.

While Charlotte was enjoying some small degree of comfort in the consoling friendship of Mrs. Beauchamp, Montraville was advancing rapidly in his affection towards Miss Franklin. Julia was an amiable girl; she saw only the fair side of his character; she possessed an independent fortune, and resolved to be happy with the man of her heart, though his rank and fortune were by no means so exalted as she had a right to expect; she saw the passion which Montraville struggled to conceal; she wondered at his timidity, but imagined the distance fortune had placed between them occasioned his backwardness, and made every advance which strict prudence and a becoming modesty would permit. Montraville saw with pleasure he was not indifferent to her, but a spark of honour which animated his bosom would not suffer him to take advantage of her partiality. He was well acquainted with Charlotte's situation, and he thought there would be a double cruelty in forsaking her at such a time; and to marry Miss Franklin, while honour, humanity, every sacred law, obliged him still to protect and support Charlotte, was a baseness which his soul shuddered at.

He communicated his uneasiness to Belcour: it was the very thing this pretended friend had wished. "And do you really," said he, laughing, "hesitate at marrying the lovely Julia, and becoming master of her fortune, because a little foolish, fond girl chose to leave her friends, and run away with you to America. Dear Montraville, act more like a man of sense; this whining, pining Charlotte, who occasions you so much uneasiness, would have eloped with somebody else if she had not with you."

"Would to heaven," said Montraville, "I had never seen her; my regard for her was but the momentary passion of desire, but I feel I shall love and revere Julia Franklin as long as I live; yet to leave poor Charlotte in her present situation would be cruel beyond description."

"Oh my good sentimental friend," said Belcour, "do you imagine no body has a right to provide for the brat but yourself."

Montraville started. "Sure," said he, "you cannot mean to insinuate that Charlotte is false."

"I don't insinuate it," said Belcour, "I know it."

Montraville turned pale as ashes. "Then there is no faith in woman," said he.

"While I thought you attached to her," said Belcour with an air of indifference, "I never wished to make you uneasy by mentioning her perfidy,[1] but as I know you love and are beloved by Miss Franklin, I was determined not to let these foolish scruples of honour step between you and happiness, or your tenderness for the peace of a perfidious girl prevent your uniting yourself to a woman of honour."

"Good heavens!" said Montraville, "what poignant reflections does a man endure who sees a lovely woman plunged in infamy, and is conscious he was her first seducer; but are you certain of what you say, Belcour?"

"So far," replied he, "that I myself have received advances from her which I would not take advantage of out of regard to you: but hang it, think no more about her. I dined at Franklin's to-day, and Julia bid me seek and bring you to tea: so come along, my lad, make good use of opportunity, and seize the gifts of fortune while they are within your reach."

Montraville was too much agitated to pass a happy evening even in the company of Julia Franklin: he determined to visit Charlotte early the next morning, tax her with her falsehood, and take an everlasting leave of her; but when the morning came, he was commanded on duty, and for six weeks was prevented from putting his design in execution. At length he found an hour to spare, and walked out to spend it with Charlotte: it was near four o'clock in the afternoon when he arrived at her cottage; she was not in the parlour, and without calling the servant he walked up stairs, thinking to find her in her bed room. He

1. Treachery.

opened the door, and the first object that met his eyes was Charlotte asleep on the bed, and Belcour by her side.

"Death and distraction," said he, stamping, "this is too much. Rise, villain, and defend yourself." Belcour sprang from the bed. The noise awoke Charlotte; terrified at the furious appearance of Montraville, and seeing Belcour with him in the chamber, she caught hold of his arm as he stood by the bed-side, and eagerly asked what was the matter.

"Treacherous, infamous girl," said he, "can you ask? How came he here?" pointing to Belcour.

"As heaven is my witness," replied she weeping, "I do not know. I have not seen him for these three weeks."

"Then you confess he sometimes visits you?"

"He came sometimes by your desire."

"'Tis false; I never desired him to come, and you know I did not: but mark me, Charlotte, from this instant our connexion is at an end. Let Belcour, or any other of your favoured lovers, take you and provide for you; I have done with you for ever."

He was then going to leave her; but starting wildly from the bed, she threw herself on her knees before him, protesting her innocence and entreating him not to leave her. "Oh Montraville," said she, "kill me, for pity's sake kill me, but do not doubt my fidelity. Do not leave me in this horrid situation; for the sake of your unborn child, oh! spurn not the wretched mother from you."

"Charlotte," said he, with a firm voice, "I shall take care that neither you nor your child want any thing in the approaching painful hour; but we meet no more." He then endeavoured to raise her from the ground; but in vain; she clung about his knees, entreating him to believe her innocent, and conjuring Belcour to clear up the dreadful mystery.

Belcour cast on Montraville a smile of contempt: it irritated him almost to madness; he broke from the feeble arms of the distressed girl; she shrieked and fell prostrate on the floor.

Montraville instantly left the house and returned hastily to the city.

Chapter XXIV.

Mystery Developed.

Unfortunately for Charlotte, about three weeks before this unhappy rencontre, Captain Beauchamp, being ordered to Rhode-Island, his lady had accompanied him, so that Charlotte was deprived of her friendly advice and consoling society. The afternoon on which Montraville had visited her she had found herself languid and fatigued, and after making a very slight dinner had lain down to endeavour to recruit her exhausted spirits, and, contrary to her expectations, had fallen asleep. She had not long been lain down, when Belcour arrived, for he took every opportunity of visiting her, and striving to awaken her resentment against Montraville. He enquired of the servant where her mistress was, and being told she was asleep, took up a book to amuse himself: having sat a few minutes, he by chance cast his eyes towards the road, and saw Montraville approaching; he instantly conceived the diabolical scheme of ruining the unhappy Charlotte in his opinion for ever; he therefore stole softly upstairs, and laying himself by her side with the greatest precaution, for fear she should awake, was in that situation discovered by his credulous friend.

When Montraville spurned the weeping Charlotte from him, and left her almost distracted with terror and despair, Belcour raised her from the floor, and leading her down stairs, assumed the part of a tender, consoling friend; she listened to the arguments he advanced with apparent composure; but this was only the calm of a moment: the remembrance of Montraville's recent cruelty again rushed upon her mind: she pushed him from her with some violence, and crying— "Leave me, Sir, I beseech you leave me, for much I fear you have been the cause of my fidelity being suspected; go, leave me to the accumulated miseries my own imprudence has brought upon me."

She then left him with precipitation, and retiring to her own apartment, threw herself on the bed, and gave vent to an agony of grief which it is impossible to describe.

It now occurred to Belcour that she might possibly write to Montraville, and endeavour to convince him of her innocence: he was well aware of her pathetic remonstrances, and, sensible of the tenderness of Montraville's heart, resolved to prevent any letters ever reaching him: he therefore called the servant, and, by the powerful persuasion of a bribe, prevailed with her to promise whatever letters her mistress might write should be sent to him. He then left a polite, tender note for Charlotte, and returned to New-York. His first business was to seek Montraville, and endeavour to convince him that what had happened would ultimately tend to his happiness: he found him in his apartment, solitary, pensive, and wrapped in disagreeable reflexions.

"Why how now, whining, pining lover?" said he, clapping him on the shoulder. Montraville started; a momentary flush of resentment crossed his cheek, but instantly gave place to a death-like paleness, occasioned by painful remembrance—remembrance awakened by that monitor, whom, though we may in vain endeavour, we can never entirely silence.

"Belcour," said he, "you have injured me in a tender point."

"Prithee, Jack," replied Belcour, "do not make a serious matter of it: how could I refuse the girl's advances? and thank heaven she is not your wife."

"True," said Montraville; "but she was innocent when I first knew her. It was I seduced her, Belcour. Had it not been for me, she had still been virtuous and happy in the affection and protection of her family."

"Pshaw," replied Belcour, laughing, "if you had not taken advantage of her easy nature, some other would, and where is the difference, pray?"

"I wish I had never seen her," cried he passionately, and starting from his seat. "Oh that cursed French woman," added he with vehemence, "had it not been for her, I might have been happy—" He paused.

"With Julia Franklin," said Belcour. The name, like a sudden spark of electric fire, seemed for a moment to suspend his faculties—for a moment he was transfixed; but recovering, he caught Belcour's hand, and cried—"Stop! stop! I beseech you, name not the lovely Julia and the wretched Montraville in the same breath. I am a seducer, a mean, ungenerous seducer of unsuspecting innocence. I dare not hope that purity like hers would stoop to unite itself with black, premeditated guilt; yet by heavens I swear, Belcour, I thought I loved the lost, abandoned Charlotte till I saw Julia—I thought I never could forsake her; but the heart is deceitful, and I now can plainly discriminate between the impulse of a youthful passion, and the pure flame of disinterested affection."

At that instant Julia Franklin passed the window, leaning on her uncle's arm. She curtseyed as she passed, and, with the bewitching smile of modest chearfulness, cried—"Do you bury yourselves in the house this fine evening, gents?" There was something in the voice! the manner! the look! that was altogether irresistible. "Perhaps she wishes my company," said Montraville mentally, as he snatched up his hat: "if I thought she loved me, I would confess my errors, and trust to her generosity to pity and pardon me." He soon overtook her, and offering her his arm, they sauntered to pleasant but unfrequented walks. Belcour drew Mr. Franklin on one side and entered into a political discourse: they walked faster than the young people, and Belcour by some means contrived entirely to lose sight of them. It was a fine evening in the beginning of autumn; the last remains of day-light faintly streaked the western sky, while the moon, with pale and virgin lustre in the room of gorgeous gold and purple, ornamented the canopy of heaven with silver, fleecy clouds, which now and then half hid her lovely face, and, by partly concealing, heightened every beauty; the zephyrs[2] whispered softly through the trees, which now began to shed their leafy honours; a solemn silence reigned: and to a happy mind an evening such as this would give serenity, and calm, unruffled plea-

2. Gentle winds.

sure; but to Montraville, while it soothed the turbulence of his passions, it brought increase of melancholy reflections. Julia was leaning on his arm: he took her hand in his, and pressing it tenderly, sighed deeply, but continued silent. Julia was embarrassed; she wished to break a silence so unaccountable, but was unable; she loved Montraville, she saw he was unhappy, and wished to know the cause of his uneasiness, but that innate modesty, which nature has implanted in the female breast, prevented her enquiring. "I am bad company, Miss Franklin," said he, at last recollecting himself; but I have met with something to-day that has greatly distressed me, and I cannot shake off the disagreeable impression it has made on my mind."

"I am sorry, she replied, "that you have any cause of inquietude. I am sure if you were as happy as you deserve, and as all your friends wish you—" She hesitated. "And might I," replied he with some animation, "presume to rank the amiable Julia in that number?"

"Certainly," said she, "the service you have rendered me, the knowledge of your worth, all combine to make me esteem you."

"Esteem, my lovely Julia," said he passionately, "is but a poor cold word. I would if I dared, if I thought I merited your attention—but no, I must not—honour forbids. I am beneath your notice, Julia, I am miserable and cannot hope to be otherwise."

"Alas!" said Julia, "I pity you."

"Oh thou condescending charmer," said he, "how that sweet word chears my sad heart. Indeed if you knew all, you would pity; but at the same time I fear you would despise me."

Just then they were again joined by Mr. Franklin and Belcour. It had interrupted an interesting discourse. They found it impossible to converse on indifferent subjects, and proceeded home in silence. At Mr. Franklin's door Montraville again pressed Julia's hand, and faintly articulating "good night," retired to his lodgings dispirited and wretched, from a consciousness that he deserved not the affection, with which he plainly saw he was honoured.

Chapter XXV.

Reception of a Letter.

"And where now is our poor Charlotte?" said Mr. Temple one evening, as the cold blasts of autumn whistled rudely over the heath, and the yellow appearance of the distant wood, spoke the near approach of winter. In vain the chearful fire blazed on the hearth, in vain was he surrounded by all the comforts of life; the parent was still alive in his heart, and when he thought that perhaps his once darling child was ere this exposed to all the miseries of want in a distant land, without a friend to sooth and comfort her, without the benignant look of compassion to chear, or the angelic voice of pity to pour the balm of consolation on her wounded heart; when he thought of this, his whole soul dissolved in tenderness; and while he wiped the tear of anguish from the eye of his patient, uncomplaining Lucy, he struggled to suppress the sympathizing drop that started in his own. "Oh, my poor girl," said Mrs. Temple, "how must she be altered, else surely she would have relieved our agonizing minds by one line to say she lived—to say she had not quite forgot the parents who almost idolized her."

"Gracious heaven," said Mr. Temple, starting from his seat, "who would wish to be a father, to experience the agonizing pangs inflicted on a parent's heart by the ingratitude of a child?" Mrs. Temple wept: her father took her hand; he would have said, "be comforted my child," but the words died on his tongue. The sad silence that ensued was interrupted by a loud rap at the door. In a moment a servant entered with a letter in his hand.

Mrs. Temple took it from him: she cast her eyes upon the super-scription; she knew the writing. "'Tis Charlotte," said she, eagerly breaking the seal, "she has not quite forgot us." But before she had half gone through the contents, a sudden sickness seized her; she grew cold and giddy, and putting it into her husband's hand, she cried—"Read it: I cannot." Mr. Temple attempted to read it aloud, but frequently paused to give vent to his tears. "My poor deluded child," said he, when he had finished.

"Oh, shall we not forgive the dear penitent?" said Mrs. Temple. "We must, we will, my love; she is willing to return, and 'tis our duty to receive her."

"Father of mercy," said Mr. Eldridge, raising his clasped hands, "let me but live once more to see the dear wanderer restored to her afflicted parents, and take me from this world of sorrow whenever it seemeth best to thy wisdom."

"Yes, we will receive her," said Mr. Temple; "we will endeavour to heal her wounded spirit, and speak peace and comfort to her agitated soul. I will write to her to return immediately."

"Oh!" said Mrs. Temple, "I would if possible fly to her, support and chear the dear sufferer in the approaching hour of distress, and tell her how nearly penitence is allied to virtue. Cannot we go and con-duct her home, my love?" continued she, laying her hand on his arm. "My father will surely forgive our absence if we go to bring home his darling."

"You cannot go, my Lucy," said Mr. Temple: "the delicacy of your frame would but poorly sustain the fatigue of a long voyage; but I will go and bring the gentle penitent to your arms: we may still see many years of happiness."

The struggle in the bosom of Mrs. Temple between maternal and conjugal tenderness was long and painful. At length the former triumphed, and she consented that her husband should set forward to New-York by the first opportunity: she wrote to her Charlotte in the tenderest, most consoling manner, and looked forward to the happy hour, when she should again embrace her, with the most animated hope.

Chapter XXVI.

What Might Be Expected.

In the mean time the passion Montraville had conceived for Julia Franklin daily encreased, and he saw evidently how much he was beloved by that amiable girl: he was likewise strongly prepossessed with an idea of Charlotte's perfidy. What wonder then if he gave himself up to the delightful sensation which pervaded his bosom; and finding no obstacle arise to oppose his happiness, he solicited and obtained the hand of Julia. A few days before his marriage he thus addressed Belcour:

"Though Charlotte, by her abandoned conduct, has thrown herself from my protection, I still hold myself bound to support her till relieved from her present condition, and also to provide for the child. I do not intend to see her again, but I will place a sum of money in your hands, which will amply supply her with every convenience; but should she require more, let her have it, and I will see it repaid. I wish I could prevail on the poor deluded girl to return to her friends: she was an only child, and I make no doubt but that they would joyfully receive her; it would shock me greatly to see her henceforth leading a life of infamy, as I should always accuse myself of being the primary cause of all her errors. If she should chuse to remain under your protection, be kind to her, Belcour, I conjure you. Let not satiety[3] prompt you to treat her in such a manner, as may drive her to actions which necessity might urge her to, while her better reason disapproved them: she shall never want a friend while I live, but I never more desire to behold her; her presence would be always painful to me, and a glance from her eye would call the blush of conscious guilt into my cheek.

"I will write a letter to her, which you may deliver when I am gone, as I shall go to St. Eustatia[4] the day after my union with Julia, who will accompany me."

3. The revulsion caused by overindulgence.
4. An island in the West Indies.

Belcour promised to fulfil the request of his friend, though nothing was farther from his intentions, than the least design of delivering the letter, or making Charlotte acquainted with the provision
Montraville had made for her; he was bent on the complete ruin
of the unhappy girl, and supposed, by reducing her to an entire
dependance on him, to bring her by degrees to consent to gratify
his ungenerous passion.

The evening before the day appointed for the nuptials of Montraville and Julia, the former retired early to his apartment; and rumi-
nating on the past scenes of his life, suffered the keenest remorse in
the remembrance of Charlotte's seduction. "Poor girl," said he, "I will
at least write and bid her adieu; I will too endeavour to awaken that
love of virtue in her bosom which her unfortunate attachment to me
has extinguished." He took up the pen and began to write, but words
were denied him. How could he address the woman whom he had
seduced, and whom, though he thought unworthy his tenderness, he
was about to bid adieu for ever? How should he tell her that he was
going to abjure her, to enter into the most indissoluble ties with
another, and that he could not even own the infant which she bore
as his child? Several letters were begun and destroyed: at length he
completed the following:

To Charlotte.

"Though I have taken up my pen to address you, my poor injured
girl, I feel I am inadequate to the task; yet, however painful the
endeavour, I could not resolve upon leaving you for ever without one
kind line to bid you adieu, to tell you how my heart bleeds at the
remembrance of what you was, before you saw the hated Montraville.
Even now imagination paints the scene, when, torn by contending
passions, when, struggling between love and duty, you fainted in my
arms, and I lifted you into the chaise: I see the agony of your mind,
when, recovering, you found yourself on the road to Portsmouth: but
how, my gentle girl, how could you, when so justly impressed with the
value of virtue, how could you, when loving as I thought you loved
me, yield to the solicitations of Belcour?

"Oh Charlotte, conscience tells me it was I, villain that I am, who
first taught you the allurements of guilty pleasure; it was I who
dragged you from the calm repose which innocence and virtue ever
enjoy; and can I, dare I tell you, it was not love prompted to the horrid deed? No, thou dear, fallen angel, believe your repentant Montraville, when he tells you the man who truly loves will never betray
the object of his affection. Adieu, Charlotte: could you still find
charms in a life of unoffending innocence, return to your parents;
you shall never want the means of support both for yourself and
child. Oh! gracious heaven! may that child be entirely free from the
vices of its father and the weakness of its mother.

"To-morrow——but no, I cannot tell you what to-morrow will produce; Belcour will inform you: he also has cash for you, which I beg you will ask for whenever you may want it. Once more adieu: believe me could I hear you was returned to your friends, and enjoying that tranquility of which I have robbed you, I should be as completely happy as even you, in your fondest hours, could wish me, but till then a gloom will obscure the brightest prospects of
MONTRAVILLE."

After he had sealed this letter he threw himself on the bed, and enjoyed a few hours repose. Early in the morning Belcour tapped at his door: he arose hastily, and prepared to meet his Julia at the altar.

"This is the letter to Charlotte," said he, giving it to Belcour: "take it to her when we are gone to Eustatia; and I conjure you, my dear friend, not to use any sophistical[5] arguments to prevent her return to virtue; but should she incline that way, encourage her in the thought, and assist her to put her design in execution.

Chapter XXVII.

> Pensive she mourn'd, and hung her languid head,
> Like a fair lily overcharg'd with dew.

Charlotte had now been left almost three months a prey to her own melancholy reflexions—sad companions indeed; nor did anyone break in upon her solitude but Belcour, who once or twice called to enquire after her health, and tell her he had in vain endeavoured to bring Montraville to hear reason; and once, but only once, was her mind cheared by the receipt of an affectionate letter from Mrs. Beauchamp. Often had she wrote to her perfidious seducer, and with the most persuasive eloquence endeavoured to convince him of her innocence; but these letters were never suffered to reach the hands of Montraville, or they must, though on the very eve of marriage, have prevented his deserting the wretched girl. Real anguish of heart had in a great measure faded her charms, her cheeks were pale from want of rest, and her eyes, by frequent, indeed almost continued weeping, were sunk and heavy. Sometimes a gleam of hope would play about her heart when she thought of her parents— "They cannot surely," she would say, "refuse to forgive me; or should they deny their pardon to me, they will not hate my innocent infant on account of its mother's errors." How often did the poor mourner wish for the consoling presence of the benevolent Mrs. Beauchamp. "If she were here," she would cry, "she would certainly comfort me, and sooth the distraction of my soul."

5. Clever but flawed; deceptive, wily.

She was sitting one afternoon, wrapped in these melancholy reflexions, when she was interrupted by the entrance of Belcour. Great as the alteration was which incessant sorrow had made on her person, she was still interesting, still charming; and the unhallowed flame, which had urged Belcour to plant dissension between her and Montraville, still raged in his bosom: he was determined, if possible, to make her his mistress; nay, he had even conceived the diabolical scheme of taking her to New-York, and making her appear in every public place where it was likely she should meet Montraville, that he might be a witness to his unmanly triumph.

When he entered the room where Charlotte was sitting, he assumed the look of tender, consolatory friendship. "And how does my lovely Charlotte?" said he, taking her hand: "I fear you are not so well as I could wish."

"I am not well, Mr. Belcour," said she, "very far from it; but the pains and infirmities of the body I could easily bear, nay, submit to them with patience, were they not aggravated by the most insupportable anguish of my mind."

"You are not happy, Charlotte," said he, with a look of well-dissembled sorrow.

"Alas!" replied she mournfully, shaking her head, "how can I be happy, deserted and forsaken as I am, without a friend of my own sex to whom I can unburthen my full heart, nay, my fidelity suspected by the very man for whom I have sacrificed every thing valuable in life, for whom I have made myself a poor despised creature, an outcast from society, an object only of contempt and pity."

"You think too meanly of yourself, Miss Temple: there is no one who would dare to treat you with contempt: all who have the pleasure of knowing you must admire and esteem. You are lonely here, my dear girl; give me leave to conduct you to New-York, where the agreeable society of some ladies,[6] to whom I will introduce you, will dispel these sad thoughts, and I shall again see returning chearfulness animate those lovely features."

"Oh never! never!" cried Charlotte, emphatically: "the virtuous part of my sex will scorn me, and I will never associate with infamy. No, Belcour, here let me hide my shame and sorrow, here let me spend my few remaining days in obscurity, unknown and unpitied, here let me die unlamented, and my name sink to oblivion." Here her tears stopped her utterance. Belcour was awed to silence: he dared not interrupt her; and after a moment's pause she proceeded—"I once had conceived the thought of going to New-York to seek out the still dear, though cruel, ungenerous Montraville, to throw myself at his feet, and entreat his compassion; heaven knows, not for myself;

6. I.e., prostitutes.

if I am no longer beloved, I will not be indebted to his pity to redress my injuries, but I would have knelt and entreated him not to forsake my poor unborn—" She could say no more; a crimson glow rushed over her cheeks, and covering her face with her hands, she sobbed aloud.

Something like humanity was awakened in Belcour's breast by this pathetic speech: he arose and walked towards the window; but the selfish passion which had taken possession of his heart, soon stifled these finer emotions; and he thought if Charlotte was once convinced she had no longer any dependance on Montraville, she would more readily throw herself on his protection. Determined, therefore, to inform her of all that had happened, he again resumed his seat; and finding she began to be more composed, enquired if she had ever heard from Montraville since the unfortunate rencontre[7] in her bed chamber.

"Ah no," said she. "I fear I shall never hear from him again."

"I am greatly of your opinion," said Belcour, "for he has been for sometime past greatly attached—"

At the word "attached" a death-like paleness overspread the countenance of Charlotte, but she applied to some hartshorn[8] which stood beside her, and Belcour proceeded.

"He has been for some time past greatly attached to one Miss Franklin, a pleasing lively girl, with a large fortune."

"She may be richer, may be handsomer," cried Charlotte, "but cannot love him so well. Oh may she beware of his art, and not trust him too far as I have done."

"He addresses her publicly," said he, "and it was rumoured they were to be married before he sailed for Eustatia, whither his company is ordered."

"Belcour," said Charlotte, seizing his hand, and gazing at him earnestly, while her pale lips trembled with convulsive agony, "tell me, and tell me truly, I beseech you, do you think he can be such a villain as to marry another woman, and leave me to die with want and misery in a strange land: tell me what you think; I can bear it very well; I will not shrink from this heaviest stroke of fate; I have deserved my afflictions, and I will endeavour to bear them as I ought."

"I fear," said Belcour, "he can be that villain."

"Perhaps," cried she, eagerly interrupting him, "perhaps he is married already: come, let me know the worst," continued she with an affected look of composure: "you need not be afraid, I shall not send the fortunate lady a bowl of poison."

7. Meeting, encounter.
8. Ammonia.

"Well then, my dear girl," said he, deceived by her appearance, "they were married on Thursday, and yesterday morning they sailed for Eustatia."

"Married—gone—say you?" cried she in a distracted accent, "what without a last farewell, without one thought on my unhappy situation! Oh Montraville, may God forgive your perfidy." She shrieked, and Belcour sprang forward just in time to prevent her falling to the floor.

Alarming faintings now succeeded each other, and she was conveyed to her bed, from whence she earnestly prayed she might never more arise. Belcour staid with her that night, and in the morning found her in a high fever. The fits she had been seized with had greatly terrified him; and confined as she now was to a bed of sickness, she was no longer an object of desire: it is true for several days he went constantly to see her, but her pale, emaciated appearance disgusted him: his visits became less frequent; he forgot the solemn charge given him by Montraville; he even forgot the money entrusted to his care; and, the burning blush of indignation and shame tinges my cheek while I write it, this disgrace to humanity and manhood at length forgot even the injured Charlotte; and, attracted by the blooming health of a farmer's daughter, whom he had seen in his frequent excursions to the country, he left the unhappy girl to sink unnoticed to the grave, a prey to sickness, grief, and penury; while he, having triumphed over the virtue of the artless cottager, rioted in all the intemperance of luxury and lawless pleasure.

Chapter XXVIII.

A Trifling Retrospect.

"Bless my heart," cries my young, volatile reader, "I shall never have patience to get through these volumes, there are so many ahs! and ohs! so much fainting, tears, and distress, I am sick to death of the subject." My dear, chearful, innocent girl, for innocent I will suppose you to be, or you would acutely feel the woes of Charlotte, did conscience say, thus might it have been with me, had not Providence interposed to snatch me from destruction: therefore, my lively, innocent girl, I must request your patience: I am writing a tale of truth: I mean to write it to the heart: but if perchance the heart is rendered impenetrable by unbounded prosperity, or a continuance in vice, I expect not my tale to please, nay, I even expect it will be thrown by with disgust. But softly, gentle fair one; I pray you throw it not aside till you have perused the whole; mayhap you may find something therein to repay you for the trouble. Methinks I see a sarcastic smile sit on your countenance—"And what," cry you, "does the conceited author suppose we can gleam from these pages, if Charlotte is held up as an object of terror, to prevent us from falling into guilty errors? does not La Rue triumph in her shame, and by adding art to guilt, obtain the affection of a worthy man, and rise to a station where she is beheld with respect, and chearfully received into all companies. What then is the moral you would inculcate? Would you wish us to think that a deviation from virtue, if covered by art and hypocrisy, is not an object of detestation, but on the contrary shall raise us to fame and honour? while the hapless girl who falls a victim to her too great sensibility, shall be loaded with ignominy and shame?" No, my fair querist,[9] I mean no such thing. Remember the endeavours of the wicked are often suffered to prosper, that in the end their fall may be attended with more bitterness of heart; while the cup of affliction is poured out for wise and salutary ends, and they who are compelled to drain it even to the bitter dregs, often find comfort at the bottom; the tear of penitence blots their offences from the book of fate, and they rise from the heavy, painful trial, purified and fit for a mansion in the kingdom of eternity.

Yes, my young friends, the tear of compassion shall fall for the fate of Charlotte, while the name of La Rue shall be detested and despised. For Charlotte, the soul melts with sympathy; for La Rue, it feels nothing but horror and contempt. But perhaps your gay hearts would rather follow the fortunate Mrs. Crayton through the scenes of pleasure and dissipation in which she was engaged, than listen to the complaints and miseries of Charlotte. I will for once oblige you; I will for once follow her to midnight revels, balls, and scenes of gaiety, for in such was she constantly engaged.

I have said her person was lovely; let us add that she was sur-rounded by splendor and affluence, and he must know but little of the world who can wonder, (however faulty such a woman's con-duct,) at her being followed by the men, and her company courted by the women: in short Mrs. Crayton was the universal favourite; she set the fashions, she was toasted by all the gentlemen, and cop-ied by all the ladies.

Colonel Crayton was a domestic man. Could he be happy with such a woman? impossible! Remonstrance was vain: he might as well have preached to the winds, as endeavour to persuade her from any action, however ridiculous, on which she had set her mind: in short, after a little ineffectual struggle, he gave up the attempt, and left her to follow the bent of her own inclinations: what those were, I think the reader must have seen enough of her character to form a just idea. Among the number who paid their devotions at her shrine,

9. Inquirer; questioner.

she singled one, a young Ensign[1] of mean birth, indifferent education, and weak intellects. How such a man came into the army, we
hardly know to account for, and how he afterwards rose to posts of
honour is likewise strange and wonderful. But fortune is blind, and
so are those too frequently who have the power of dispensing her
favours: else why do we see fools and knaves at the very top of the
wheel, while patient merit sinks to the extreme of the opposite
abyss. But we may form a thousand conjectures on this subject, and
yet never hit on the right. Let us therefore endeavour to deserve her
smiles, and whether we succeed or not, we shall feel more innate
satisfaction, than thousands of those who bask in the sunshine of
her favour unworthily. But to return to Mrs. Crayton: this young
man, whom I shall distinguish by the name of Corydon, was the
reigning favourite of her heart. He escorted her to the play, danced
with her at every ball, and when indisposition prevented her going
out, it was he alone who was permitted to chear the gloomy solitude
to which she was obliged to confine herself. Did she ever think of
poor Charlotte?—if she did, my dear Miss, it was only to laugh at
the poor girl's want of spirit in consenting to be moped up in the
country, while Montraville was enjoying all the pleasures of a gay,
dissipated city. When she heard of his marriage, she smiling said, so
there's an end of Madam Charlotte's hopes. I wonder who will take
her now, or what will become of the little affected prude?

But as you have led to the subject, I think we may as well return
to the distressed Charlotte, and not, like the unfeeling Mrs. Crayton, shut our hearts to the call of humanity.

Chapter XXIX.

We Go Forward Again.

The strength of Charlotte's constitution combated against her disorder, and she began slowly to recover, though she still laboured
under a violent depression of spirits: how must that depression be
encreased, when, upon examining her little store, she found herself
reduced to one solitary guinea, and that during her illness the atten-
dance of an apothecary and nurse, together with many other unavoidable expences, had involved her in debt, from which she saw no
method of extricating herself. As to the faint hope which she had
entertained of hearing from and being relieved by her parents; it
now entirely forsook her, for it was above four months since her letter was dispatched, and she had received no answer: she therefore

---

1. Junior military officer.

imagined that her conduct had either entirely alienated their affection from her, or broken their hearts, and she must never more hope to receive their blessing.

Never did any human being wish for death with greater fervency or with juster cause; yet she had too just a sense of the duties of the christian religion to attempt to put a period to her own existence. "I have but to be patient a little longer," she would cry, "and nature, fatigued and fainting, will throw off this heavy load of mortality, and I shall be released from all my sufferings."

It was one cold stormy day in the latter end of December, as Charlotte sat by a handful of fire, the low state of her finances not allowing her to replenish her stock of fuel, and prudence teaching her to be careful of what she had, when she was surprised by the entrance of a farmer's wife, who, without much ceremony, seated herself, and began this curious harangue.

"I'm come to see if as how you can pay your rent, because as how we hear Captain Montable is gone away, and it's fifty to one if he b'ant killed afore he comes back again; and then, Miss, or Ma'am, or whatever you may be, as I was saying to my husband, where are we to look for our money."

This was a stroke altogether unexpected by Charlotte: she knew so little of the ways of the world that she had never bestowed a thought on the payment for the rent of the house; she knew indeed that she owed a good deal, but this was never reckoned among the others: she was thunder-struck; she hardly knew what answer to make, yet it was absolutely necessary that she should say something; and judging of the gentleness of every female disposition by her own, she thought the best way to interest the woman in her favour would be to tell her candidly to what a situation she was reduced, and how little probability there was of her ever paying any body.

Alas poor Charlotte, how confined was her knowledge of human nature, or she would have been convinced that the only way to insure the friendship and assistance of your surrounding acquaintance is to convince them you do not require it, for when once the petrifying aspect of distress and penury appear, whose qualities, like Medusa's head, can change to stone all that look upon it; when once this Gorgon[2] claims acquaintance with us, the phantom of friendship, that before courted our notice, will vanish into unsubstantial air, and the whole world before us appear a barren waste. Pardon me, ye dear spirits of benevolence, whose benign smiles and chearful-giving hand have strewed sweet flowers on many a thorny path through which my wayward fate forced me to pass; think not,

---

2. In Greek mythology, one of three monstrous women whose glance turned people to stone. Medusa was a Gorgon.

that, in condemning the unfeeling texture of the human heart, I forget the spring from whence flow all the comforts I enjoy: oh no! I look up to you as to bright constellations, gathering new splendours from the surrounding darkness; but ah! whilst I adore the benignant rays that cheared and illumined my heart, I mourn that their influence cannot extend to all the sons and daughters of affliction.

"Indeed, Madam," said poor Charlotte in a tremulous accent, "I am at a loss what to do. Montraville placed me here, and promised to defray all my expenses: but he has forgot his promise, he has forsaken me, and I have no friend who has either power or will to relieve me. Let me hope, as you see my unhappy situation, your charity———"

"Charity," cried the woman impatiently interrupting her, "charity indeed: why, Mistress, charity begins at home, and I have seven children at home, *honest, lawful* children, and it is my duty to keep them; and do you think I will give away my property to a nasty, impudent hussey, to maintain her and her bastard; an I was saying to my husband the other day what will this world come to; honest women are nothing now-a-days, while the harlotings are set up for fine ladies, and look upon us no more nor the dirt they walk upon: but let me tell you, my fine spoken Ma'am, I must have my money; so seeing as how you can't pay it, why you must troop, and leave all your fine gimcracks and fal der ralls³ behind you. I don't ask for no more nor my right, and nobody shall dare for to go for to hinder me of it."

"Oh heavens," cried Charlotte, clasping her hands, "what will become of me?"

"Come on ye!" retorted the unfeeling wretch: "why go to the barracks and work for a morsel of bread; wash and mend the soldiers cloaths, an cook their victuals, and not expect to live in idleness on honest people's means. Oh I wish I could see the day when all such cattle were obliged to work hard and eat little; it's only what they deserve."

"Father of mercy," cried Charlotte, "I acknowledge thy correction just; but prepare me, I beseech thee, for the portion of misery thou may'st please to lay upon me."

"Well," said the woman, "I shall go an tell my husband as how you can't pay; and so d'ye see, Ma'am, get ready to be packing away this very night, for you should not stay another night in this house, though I was sure you would lay in the street."

Charlotte bowed her head in silence; but the anguish of her heart was too great to permit her to articulate a single word.

---

3. I.e., folderols; useless ornaments. "Gimcracks": showy but shoddy and worthless trinkets.

Chapter XXX.

And what is friendship but a name,
A charm that lulls to sleep,
A shade that follows wealth and fame,
But leaves the wretch to weep.[4]

When Charlotte was left to herself, she began to think what course she must take, or to whom she could apply, to prevent her perishing for want, or perhaps that very night falling a victim to the inclemency of the season. After many perplexed thoughts, she at last determined to set out for New-York, and enquire out Mrs. Crayton, from whom she had no doubt but she should obtain immediate relief as soon as her distress was made known; she had no sooner formed this resolution than she resolved immediately to put it in execution: she therefore wrote the following little billet[5] to Mrs. Crayton, thinking if she should have company with her it would be better to send it in than to request to see her.

To Mrs. Crayton.

"Madam,
"When we left our native land, that dear, happy land which now contains all that is dear to the wretched Charlotte, our prospects were the same; we both, pardon me, Madam, if I say, we both too easily followed the impulse of our treacherous hearts, and trusted our happiness on a tempestuous ocean, where mine has been wrecked and lost for ever; you have been more fortunate—you are united to a man of honour and humanity, united by the most sacred ties, respected, esteemed, and admired, and surrounded by innumerable blessings of which I am bereaved, enjoying those pleasures which have fled my bosom never to return; alas! sorrow and deep regret have taken their place. Behold me, Madam, a poor forsaken wanderer, who has no where to lay her weary head, wherewith to supply the wants of nature, or to shield her from the inclemency of the weather. To you I sue, to you I look for pity and relief. I ask not to be received as an intimate or an equal; only for charity's sweet sake receive me into your hospitable mansion, allot me the meanest apartment in it, and let me breath out my soul in prayers for your happiness; I cannot, I feel I cannot long bear up under the accumulated woes that pour in upon me; but oh! my dear Madam, for the love of heaven suffer me not to expire in the street; and when I am at peace, as soon I shall be, extend your compassion to my helpless offspring, should it please heaven that it should survive its unhappy mother. A gleam of joy breaks in on my benighted

---

4. From "The Hermit" (1765), a romantic ballad by English dramatist Oliver Goldsmith.
5. Short note.

soul while I reflect that you cannot, will not refuse your protection to the heart-broken

"CHARLOTTE."

When Charlotte had finished this letter, late as it was in the afternoon, and though the snow began to fall very fast, she tied up a few necessaries which she had prepared against her expected confinement, and terrified lest she should be again exposed to the insults of her barbarous landlady, more dreadful to her wounded spirit than either storm or darkness, she set forward for New-York.

It may be asked by those, who, in a work of this kind, love to cavil[6] at every trifling omission, whether Charlotte did not possess any valuable of which she could have disposed, and by that means have supported herself till Mrs. Beauchamp's return, when she would have been certain of receiving every tender attention which compassion and friendship could dictate: but let me entreat these wise, penetrating gentlemen to reflect, that when Charlotte left England, it was in such haste that there was no time to purchase any thing more than what was wanted for immediate use on the voyage, and after her arrival at New-York, Montraville's affection soon began to decline, so that her whole wardrobe consisted of only necessaries, and as to baubles, with which fond lovers often load their mistresses, she possessed not one, except a plain gold locket of small value, which contained a lock of her mother's hair, and which the greatest extremity of want could not have forced her to part with.

I hope, Sir, your prejudices are now removed in regard to the probability of my story? Oh they are. Well then, with your leave, I will proceed.

The distance from the house which our suffering heroine occupied, to New-York, was not very great, yet the snow fell so fast, and the cold so intense, that, being unable from her situation to walk quick, she found herself almost sinking with cold and fatigue before she reached the town; her garments, which were merely suitable to the summer season, being an undress robe of plain white muslin, were wet through, and a thin black cloak and bonnet, very improper habiliments for such a climate, but poorly defended her from the cold. In this situation she reached the city, and enquired of a foot soldier whom she met, the way to Colonel Crayton's.

"Bless you, my sweet lady," said the soldier with a voice and look of compassion, "I will shew you the way with all my heart; but if you are going to make a petition to Madam Crayton it is all to no purpose I assure you: if you please I will conduct you to Mr. Franklin's; though Miss Julia is married and gone now, yet the old gentleman is very good."

6. Quibble; object without cause.

"Julia Franklin," said Charlotte; "is she not married to Montraville?"

"Yes," replied the soldier, "and may God bless them, for a better
officer never lived, he is so good to us all; and as to Miss Julia, all
the poor folk almost worshipped her."

"Gracious heaven," cried Charlotte, "is Montraville unjust then to
none but me."

The soldier now shewed her Colonel Crayton's door, and, with a
beating heart, she knocked for admission.

Chapter XXXI.

Subject Continued.

When the door was opened, Charlotte, in a voice rendered scarcely
articulate, through cold and the extreme agitation of her mind,
demanded whether Mrs. Crayton was at home. The servant hesitated: he knew that his lady was engaged at a game of picquet[7]
with her dear Corydon, nor could he think she would like to be
disturbed by a person whose appearance spoke her of so little consequence as Charlotte; yet there was something in her countenance that rather interested him in her favour, and he said his
lady was engaged, but if she had any particular message he would
deliver it.

"Take up this letter," said Charlotte: "tell her the unhappy writer
of it waits in her hall for an answer."

The tremulous accent, the tearful eye, must have moved any
heart not composed of adamant.[8] The man took the letter from the
poor suppliant, and hastily ascended the stair case.

"A letter, Madam," said he, presenting it to his lady: "an immediate answer is required."

Mrs. Crayton glanced her eye carelessly over the contents. "What
stuff is this;" cried she haughtily; "have not I told you a thousand
times that I will not be plagued with beggars, and petitions from
people one knows nothing about? Go tell the woman I can't do any
thing in it. I'm sorry, but one can't relieve every body."

The servant bowed, and heavily returned with this chilling message to Charlotte.

"Surely," said she, "Mrs. Crayton has not read my letter. Go, my
good friend, pray go back to her; tell her it is Charlotte Temple who
requests beneath her hospitable roof to find shelter from the inclemency of the season."

7. A card game for two players.
8. Extremely hard stone.

"Prithee, don't plague me, man," cried Mrs. Crayton impatiently, as the servant advanced something in behalf of the unhappy girl. "I tell you I don't know her."

"Not know me," cried Charlotte, rushing into the room, (for she had followed the man up stairs) "not know me, not remember the ruined Charlotte Temple, who, but for you, perhaps might still have been innocent, still have been happy. Oh! La Rue, this is beyond every thing I could have believed possible."

"Upon my honour, Miss," replied the unfeeling woman with the utmost effrontery, "this is a most unaccountable address: it is beyond my comprehension. John," continued she, turning to the servant, "the young woman is certainly out of her senses: do pray take her away, she terrifies me to death."

"Oh God," cried Charlotte, clasping her hands in an agony, "this is too much; what will become of me? but I will not leave you; they shall not tear me from you; here on my knees I conjure you to save me from perishing in the streets; if you really have forgot me, oh for charity's sweet sake this night let me be sheltered from the winter's piercing cold."

The kneeling figure of Charlotte in her affecting situation might have moved the heart of a stoic to compassion, but Mrs. Crayton remained inflexible. In vain did Charlotte recount the time they had known each other at Chichester, in vain mention their being in the same ship, in vain were the names of Montraville and Belcour mentioned. Mrs. Crayton could only say she was sorry for her imprudence, but could not think of having her own reputation endangered by encouraging a woman of that kind in her own house, besides she did not know what trouble and expense she might bring upon her husband by giving shelter to a woman in her situation.

"I can at least die here," said Charlotte, "I feel I cannot long survive this dreadful conflict. Father of mercy, here let me finish my existence." Her agonizing sensations overpowered her, and she fell senseless on the floor.

"Take her away," said Mrs. Crayton, "she will really frighten me into hysterics; take her away I say this instant."

"And where must I take the poor creature?" said the servant with a voice and look of compassion.

"Any where," cried she hastily, "only don't let me ever see her again. I declare she has flurried me so I shan't be myself again this fortnight."

John, assisted by his fellow-servant, raised and carried her down stairs. "Poor soul," said he, "you shall not lay in the street this night. I have a bed and a poor little hovel, where my wife and her little ones rest them, but they shall watch to night, and you shall be sheltered from danger." They placed her in a chair; and the benevolent man, assisted by one of his comrades, carried her to the place where his wife and children lived. A surgeon was sent for: he bled her, she gave signs of returning life, and before the dawn gave birth to a female infant. After this event she lay for some hours in a kind of stupor; and if at any time she spoke, it was with a quickness and incoherence that plainly evinced the total deprivation of her reason.

Chapter XXXII.

Reasons Why and Wherefore.

The reader of sensibility may perhaps be astonished to find Mrs. Crayton could so positively deny any knowledge of Charlotte; it is therefore but just that her conduct should in some measure be accounted for. She had ever been fully sensible of the superiority of Charlotte's sense and virtue; she was conscious that she had never swerved from rectitude, had it not been for her bad precepts and worse example. These were things as yet unknown to her husband, and she wished not to have that part of her conduct exposed to him, as she had great reason to fear she had already lost considerable part of that power she once maintained over him. She trembled whilst Charlotte was in the house, lest the Colonel should return; she perfectly well remembered how much he seemed interested in her favour whilst on their passage from England, and made no doubt, but, should he see her in her present distress, he would offer her an asylum, and protect her to the utmost of his power. In that case she feared the unguarded nature of Charlotte might discover to the Colonel the part she had taken in the unhappy girl's elopement, and she well knew the contrast between her own and Charlotte's conduct would make the former appear in no very respectable light. Had she reflected properly, she would have afforded the poor girl protection; and by enjoining her silence, ensured it by acts of repeated kindness; but vice in general blinds its votaries, and they discover their real characters to the world when they are most studious to preserve appearances.

Just so it happened with Mrs. Crayton: her servants made no scruple of mentioning the cruel conduct of their lady to a poor distressed lunatic who claimed her protection; every one joined in reprobating her inhumanity; nay even Corydon thought she might at least have ordered her to be taken care of, but he dare not even hint it to her, for he lived but in her smiles, and drew from her lavish fondness large sums to support an extravagance to which the state of his own finances was very inadequate; it cannot therefore be supposed that he wished Mrs. Crayton to be very liberal in her bounty to the afflicted suppliant; yet vice had not so entirely seared over his heart, but the sorrows of Charlotte could find a vulnerable part.

Charlotte had now been three days with her humane preservers, but she was totally insensible of every thing: she raved incessantly for Montraville and her father: she was not conscious of being a mother, nor took the least notice of her child except to ask whose it was, and why it was not carried to its parents.

"Oh," said she one day, starting up on hearing the infant cry, "why, why will you keep that child here: I am sure you would not if you knew how hard it was for a mother to be parted from her infant: it is like tearing the cords of life asunder. Oh could you see the horrid sight which I now behold—there—there stands my dear mother, her poor bosom bleeding at every vein, her gentle, affectionate heart torn in a thousand pieces, and all for the loss of a ruined, ungrateful child. Save me——save me——from her frown. I dare not—indeed I dare not speak to her."

Such were the dreadful images that haunted her distracted mind, and nature was sinking fast under the dreadful malady which medicine had no power to remove. The surgeon who attended her was a humane man; he exerted his utmost abilities to save her, but he saw she was in want of many necessaries and comforts, which the poverty of her hospitable host rendered him unable to provide: he therefore determined to make her situation known to some of the officers' ladies, and endeavour to make a collection for her relief.

When he returned home, after making this resolution, he found a message from Mrs. Beauchamp, who had just arrived from Rhode-Island, requesting he would call and see one of her children, who was very unwell. "I do not know," said he, as he was hastening to obey the summons, "I do not know a woman to whom I could apply with more hope of success than Mrs. Beauchamp. I will endeavour to interest her in this poor girl's behalf; she wants the soothing balm of friendly consolation: we may perhaps save her; we will try at least.

"And where is she," cried Mrs. Beauchamp when he had prescribed something for the child, and told his little pathetic tale, "where is she, Sir? we will go to her immediately. Heaven forbid that I should be deaf to the calls of humanity. Come we will go this instant." Then seizing the doctor's arm, they sought the habitation that contained the dying Charlotte.

Chapter XXXIII.

Which People Void of Feeling Need Not Read.

When Mrs. Beauchamp entered the apartment of the poor sufferer, she started back with horror. On a wretched bed, without hangings and but poorly supplied with covering, lay the emaciated figure of what still retained the semblance of a lovely woman, though sickness had so altered her features that Mrs. Beauchamp had not the least recollection of her person. In one corner of the room stood a woman washing, and, shivering over a small fire, two healthy but half naked children; the infant was asleep beside its mother, and, on a chair by the bed side, stood a porrenger[9] and wooden spoon, containing a little gruel, and a tea-cup with about two spoonfulls of wine in it. Mrs. Beauchamp had never before beheld such a scene of poverty; she shuddered involuntarily, and exclaiming—"heaven preserve us!" leaned on the back of a chair ready to sink to the earth. The doctor repented having so precipitately brought her into this affecting scene; but there was no time for apologies: Charlotte caught the sound of her voice, and starting almost out of bed, exclaimed—"Angel of peace and mercy, art thou come to deliver me? Oh, I know you are, for whenever you was near me I felt eased of half my sorrows; but you don't know me, nor can I, with all the recollection I am mistress of, remember your name just now, but I know that benevolent countenance, and the softness of that voice which has so often comforted the wretched Charlotte."

Mrs. Beauchamp had, during the time Charlotte was speaking, seated herself on the bed and taken one of her hands; she looked at her attentively, and at the name of Charlotte she perfectly conceived the whole shocking affair. A faint sickness came over her. "Gracious heaven," said she, "is this possible?" and bursting into tears, she reclined the burning head of Charlotte on her own bosom; and folding her arms about her, wept over her in silence. "Oh," said Charlotte, "you are very good to weep thus for me: it is a long time since I shed a tear for myself: my head and heart are both on fire, but these tears of yours seem to cool and refresh it. Oh now I remember you said you would send a letter to my poor father: do you think he ever received it? or perhaps you have brought me an answer: why don't you speak, Madam? Does he say I may go home? Well he is very good; I shall soon be ready."

She then made an effort to get out of bed; but being prevented, her frenzy again returned, and she raved with the greatest wildness and incoherence. Mrs. Beauchamp, finding it was impossible for her to be removed, contented herself with ordering the apartment to be made more comfortable, and procuring a proper nurse for both mother and child; and having learnt the particulars of Charlotte's fruitless application to Mrs. Crayton from honest John, she amply rewarded him for his benevolence, and returned home with a heart oppressed with many painful sensations, but yet rendered easy by the reflexion that she had performed her duty towards a distressed fellow-creature.

9. Small bowl.

Early the next morning she again visited Charlotte, and found her tolerably composed; she called her by name, thanked her for her goodness, and when her child was brought to her, pressed it in her arms, wept over it, and called it the offspring of disobedience. Mrs. Beauchamp was delighted to see her so much amended, and began to hope she might recover, and, spite of her former errors, become an useful and respectable member of society; but the arrival of the doctor put an end to these delusive hopes: he said nature was making her last effort, and a few hours would most probably consign the unhappy girl to her kindred dust.

Being asked how she found herself, she replied—"Why better, much better, doctor. I hope now I have but little more to suffer. I had last night a few hours sleep, and when I awoke recovered the full power of recollection. I am quite sensible of my weakness; I feel I have but little longer to combat with the shafts of affliction. I have an humble confidence in the mercy of him who died to save the world, and trust that my sufferings in this state of mortality, joined to my unfeigned repentance, through his mercy, have blotted my offences from the sight of my offended maker. I have but one care—my poor infant! Father of mercy," continued she, raising her eyes, "of thy infinite goodness, grant that the sins of the parent be not visited on the unoffending child. May those who taught me to despise thy laws be forgiven; lay not my offences to their charge, I beseech thee; and oh! shower the choicest of thy blessings on those whose pity has soothed the afflicted heart, and made easy even the bed of pain and sickness."

She was exhausted by this fervent address to the throne of mercy, and though her lips still moved her voice became inarticulate: she lay for some time as it were in a dose, and then recovering, faintly pressed Mrs. Beauchamp's hand, and requested that a clergyman might be sent for.

On his arrival she joined fervently in the pious office, frequently mentioning her ingratitude to her parents as what lay most heavy at her heart. When she had performed the last solemn duty, and was preparing to lie down, a little bustle on the outside door occasioned Mrs. Beauchamp to open it, and enquire the cause. A man in appearance about forty, presented himself, and asked for Mrs. Beauchamp.

"That is my name, Sir," said she.

"Oh then, my dear Madam," cried he, "tell me where I may find my poor, ruined, but repentant child."

Mrs. Beauchamp was surprised and affected; she knew not what to say; she foresaw the agony this interview would occasion Mr. Temple, who had just arrived in search of his Charlotte, and yet was sensible that the pardon and blessing of her father would soften even the agonies of death to the daughter.

She hesitated. "Tell me, Madam," cried he wildly, "tell me, I beseech thee, does she live? shall I see my darling once again? Perhaps she is in this house. Lead, lead me to her, that I may bless her, and then lie down and die."

The ardent manner in which he uttered these words occasioned him to raise his voice. It caught the ear of Charlotte: she knew the beloved sound: and uttering a loud shriek, she sprang forward as Mr. Temple entered the room. "My adored father." "My long lost child." Nature could support no more, and they both sunk lifeless into the arms of the attendants.

Charlotte was again put into bed, and a few moments restored Mr. Temple: but to describe the agony of his sufferings is past the power of any one, who, though they may readily conceive, cannot delineate the dreadful scene. Every eye gave testimony of what each heart felt—but all were silent.

When Charlotte recovered, she found herself supported in her father's arms. She cast on him a most expressive look, but was unable to speak. A reviving cordial was administered. She then asked, in a low voice, for her child: it was brought to her: she put it in her father's arms. "Protect her," said she, "and bless your dying——"

Unable to finish the sentence, she sunk back on her pillow: her countenance was serenely composed; she regarded her father as he pressed the infant to his breast with a steadfast look; a sudden beam of joy passed across her languid features, she raised her eyes to heaven—and then closed them for ever.

Chapter XXXIV.

Retribution.

In the mean time Montraville having received orders to return to New-York, arrived, and having still some remains of compassionate tenderness for the woman whom he regarded as brought to shame by himself, he went out in search of Belcour, to enquire whether she was safe, and whether the child lived. He found him immersed in dissipation, and could gain no other intelligence than that Charlotte had left him, and that he knew not what was become of her.

"I cannot believe it possible," said Montraville, "that a mind once so pure as Charlotte Temple's, should so suddenly become the mansion of vice. Beware, Belcour," continued he, "beware if you have dared to behave either unjust or dishonourably to that poor girl, your life shall pay the forfeit:——I will revenge her cause."

He immediately went into the country, to the house where he had left Charlotte. It was desolate. After much enquiry he at length found the servant girl who had lived with her. From her he learnt the misery Charlotte had endured from the complicated evils of illness, poverty, and a broken heart, and that she had set out on foot for New-York, on a cold winter's evening; but she could inform him no furthur.

Tortured almost to madness by this shocking account, he returned to the city, but, before he reached it, the evening was drawing to a close. In entering the town he was obliged to pass several little huts, the residence of poor women who supported themselves by washing the cloaths of the officers and soldiers. It was nearly dark: he heard from a neighbouring steeple a solemn toll that seemed to say some poor mortal was going to their last mansion: the sound struck on the heart of Montraville, and he involuntarily stopped, when, from one of the houses, he saw the appearance of a funeral. Almost unknowing what he did, he followed at a small distance; and as they let the coffin into the grave, he enquired of a soldier who stood by, and had just brushed off a tear that did honour to his heart, who it was that was just buried. "An please your honour," said the man, "'tis a poor girl that was brought from her friends by a cruel man, who left her when she was big with child, and married another." Montraville stood motionless, and the man proceeded—"I met her myself not a fortnight since one night all wet and cold in the streets; she went to Madam Crayton's, but she would not take her in, and so the poor thing went raving mad." Montraville could bear no more; he struck his hands against his forehead with violence; and exclaiming "poor murdered Charlotte!" ran with precipitation towards the place where they were heaping the earth on her remains. "Hold, hold, one moment," said he. "Close not the grave of the injured Charlotte Temple till I have taken vengeance on her murderer."

"Rash young man," said Mr. Temple," "who art thou that thus disturbest the last mournful rites of the dead, and rudely breakest in upon the grief of an afflicted father."

"If thou art the father of Charlotte Temple," said he, gazing at him with mingled horror and amazement—"if thou art her father—I am Montraville." Then falling on his knees, he continued—"Here is my bosom. I bare it to receive the stroke I merit. Strike—strike now, and save me from the misery of reflexion."

"Alas!" said Mr. Temple," if thou wert the seducer of my child, thy own reflexions be thy punishment. I wrest not the power from the hand of omnipotence. Look on that little heap of earth, there hast thou buried the only joy of a fond father. Look at it often; and may thy heart feel such true sorrow as shall merit the mercy of heaven." He turned from him; and Montraville starting up from the ground, where he had thrown himself, and at that instant remembering the perfidy of Belcour, flew like lightning to his lodgings. Belcour was intoxicated; Montraville impetuous: they fought, and the sword of the latter entered the heart of his adversary. He fell, and expired almost instantly. Montraville had received a slight wound; and overcome with the agitation of his mind and loss of blood, was carried in a state of insensibility to his distracted wife. A dangerous illness and obstinate delirium ensued, during which he raved incessantly for Charlotte: but a strong constitution, and the tender assiduities of Julia, in time overcome the disorder. He recovered; but to the end of his life was subject to severe fits of melancholy, and while he remained at New-York frequently retired to the church-yard, where he would weep over the grave, and regret the untimely fate of the lovely Charlotte Temple.

Chapter XXXV.

Conclusion.

Shortly after the interment of his daughter, Mr. Temple, with his dear little charge and her nurse, set forward for England. It would be impossible to do justice to the meeting scene between him, his Lucy, and her aged father. Every heart of sensibility can easily conceive their feelings. After the first tumult of grief was subsided, Mrs. Temple gave up the chief of her time to her grandchild, and as she grew up and improved, began to almost fancy she again possessed her Charlotte.

It was about ten years after these painful events, that Mr. and Mrs. Temple, having buried their father, were obliged to come to London on particular business, and brought the little Lucy with them. They had been walking one evening, when on their return they found a poor wretch sitting on the steps of the door. She attempted to rise as they approached, but from extreme weakness was unable, and after several fruitless efforts fell back in a fit. Mr. Temple was not one of those men who stand to consider whether by assisting an object in distress they shall not inconvenience themselves, but instigated by the impulse of a noble feeling heart, immediately ordered her to be carried into the house, and proper restoratives applied.

She soon recovered; and fixing her eyes on Mrs. Temple, cried— "You know not, Madam, what you do; you know not whom you are relieving, or you would curse me in the bitterness of your heart. Come not near me, Madam, I shall contaminate you. I am the viper that stung your peace. I am the woman who turned the poor Charlotte out to perish in the street. Heaven have mercy! I see her now," continued she looking at Lucy; "such, such was the fair bud of innocence that my vile arts blasted ere it was half blown."

It was in vain that Mr. and Mrs. Temple intreated her to be composed and to take some refreshment. She only drank half a glass of wine; and then told them that she had been separated from her husband seven years, the chief of which she had passed in riot, dissipation, and vice, till, overtaken by poverty and sickness, she had been reduced to part with every valuable, and thought only of ending her life in a prison; when a benevolent friend paid her debts and released her; but that her illness encreasing, she had no possible means of supporting herself, and her friends were weary of relieving her. "I have fasted," said she, "two days, and last night lay my aching head on the cold pavement: indeed it was but just that I should experience those miseries myself which I had unfeelingly inflicted on others."

Greatly as Mr. Temple had reason to detest Mrs. Crayton, he could not behold her in this distress without some emotions of pity. He gave her shelter that night beneath his hospitable roof, and the next day got her admission into an hospital; where having lingered a few weeks, she died, a striking example that vice, however prosperous in the beginning, in the end leads only to misery and shame.

FINIS

CONTEXTS

CHARLOTTE.

A TALE OF TRUTH.

IN TWO VOLUMES.

She was her parent's only joy;
They had but one——one darling child.
ROMEO AND JULIET.

Her form was faultlefs, and her mind,
Untainted yet by art,
Was noble, juft, humane, and kind,
And virtue warm'd her heart.
But ah! the cruel fpoiler came——

VOL. I.

LONDON:
PRINTED FOR WILLIAM LANE,
AT THE
Minerva,
LEADEN-HALL-STREET.
M.DCC.XCI.

Title page of 1st edition of *Charlotte. A Tale of Truth*.
Special Collections, University of Virginia Library, Charlottesville.

S. Rowson

Portrait of Susanna Haswell Rowson. Special Collections, University of Virginia Library, Charlottesville.

Portrait of Susanna Haswell as a youth. Special Collections, University of Virginia Library, Charlottesville.

Pencil sketch of William Rowson as a young man. Special Collections, University of Virginia Library, Charlottesville.

Portrait of Charlotte Temple, 1842 edition of *Charlotte Temple* (frontispiece). Special Collections, University of Virginia Library, Charlottesville.

Charlotte Temple.

Engraving by C. Tiebout, 1812 edition of *Charlotte Temple*
(frontispiece). Special Collections, University of Virginia Library,
Charlottesville.

LIKENESS OF CHARLOTTE TEMPLE,
(Taken from an Original Portrait.)

Portrait of Charlotte, 1860 edition of *Charlotte Temple* (frontispiece). Special Collections, University of Virginia Library, Charlottesville.

Die schöne und wohlgebildete

Charlotte Temple.

Ein Bericht ihrer Flucht mit

Lieutenant Montroville,

sowie ihres

Unglücklichen Schicksals und ihrer schrecklichen Leiden.

Portrait von Charlotte Temple. (Nach einem Originalgemälde.)

Philadelphia:

Herausgegeben von Barclay und Co., No. 602 Archstraße.

Cover of 1861 Philadelphia edition of *Charlotte Temple* [Die Beklagenswerthe Geschiechter] in German. Special Collections, University of Virginia Library, Charlottesville.

Richter del
J.G.Walker sculp

Temple's benevolence to Eldridge

Vide Page 9

Illustration from excerpt of *Charlotte: A Tale of Truth*, in *The Polite Repository; or, an Amusing Companion*. London, 1791–92. The Bodleian Library.

JUST PUBLISHED,

CHARLOTTE;

OR A

TALE OF TRUTH.

In 2 vols. 12mo.—Price 5s. sewed.

Of Charlotte, the Reviewers have given the following character.

IT may be a Tale of Truth, for it is not unnatural, and it is a tale of real distress—Charlotte, by the artifice of a teacher, recommended to a school, from humanity rather than a conviction of her integrity, or the regularity of her former conduct, is enticed from her governess, and accompanies a young officer to America.—The marriage ceremony, if not forgotten, is postponed, and Charlotte dies a martyr to the inconstancy of her lover, and treachery of his friend.—The situations are artless and affecting —the descriptions natural and pathetic; we should feel for Charlotte if such a person ever existed, who for one error scarcely, perhaps, deserved so severe a punishment. If it is a fiction, poetic justice is not, we think, properly distributed.

London advertisement for *Charlotte Temple* preceding title page of 1794 Philadelphia edition. Special Collections, University of Virginia Library, Charlottesville.

Bill from Susanna Rowson's school, The Young Ladies' Academy, to John Montgomery (1803). Special Collections, University of Virginia Library, Charlottesville.

School reports from the Young Ladies' Academy regarding Mary Montgomery by Susanna Rowson. Special Collections, University of Virginia Library, Charlottesville.

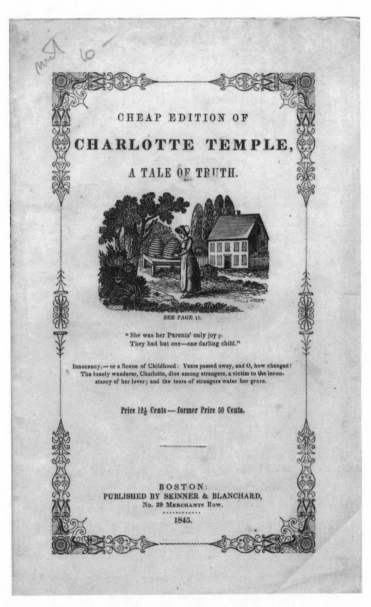

CHEAP EDITION OF

CHARLOTTE TEMPLE,

A TALE OF TRUTH.

SEE PAGE 11.

" She was her Parents' only joy ;
They had but one—one darling child."

Innocency,— or a Scene of Childhood : Years passed away, and O, how changed !
The lonely wanderer, Charlotte, dies among strangers, a victim to the inconstancy of her lover; and the tears of strangers water her grave.

Price 12½ Cents—former Price 50 Cents.

BOSTON:
PUBLISHED BY SKINNER & BLANCHARD,
No. 39 MERCHANTS ROW.
....
1845.

Cheap Edition of *Charlotte Temple. A Tale of Truth* (1845)—cover.
Special Collections, University of Virginia Library, Charlottesville.

Portrait of Charlotte, 1867 edition of *Charlotte Temple*, frontispiece.
Special Collections, University of Virginia Library, Charlottesville.

Women in Early America:
Intellect, Education, Sexuality

BENJAMIN FRANKLIN

[Advice to a Friend upon Choosing a Mistress]†

My dear Friend,   June 25. 1745

I know of no Medicine fit to diminish the violent natural Inclinations you mention; and if I did, I think I should not communicate it to you. Marriage is the proper Remedy. It is the most natural State of Man, and therefore the State in which you are most likely to find solid Happiness. Your Reasons against entering into it at present, appear to me not well-founded. The circumstantial Advantages you have in View by postponing it, are not only uncertain, but they are small in comparison with that of the Thing itself, the being *married and settled*. It is the Man and Woman united that make the compleat human Being. Separate, she wants his Force of Body and Strength of Reason; he, her Softness, Sensibility and acute Discernment. Together they are more likely to succeed in the World. A single Man has not nearly the Value he would have in that State of Union. He is an incomplete Animal. He resembles the odd Half of a Pair of Scissars. If you get a prudent healthy Wife, your Industry in your Profession, with her good Œconomy, will be a Fortune sufficient.

But if you will not take this Counsel, and persist in thinking a Commerce with the Sex inevitable, then I repeat my former Advice, that in all your Amours you should *prefer old Women to young ones*. You call this a Paradox, and demand my Reasons. They are these:

1. Because as they have more Knowledge of the World and their Minds are better stor'd with Observations, their Conversation is more improving and more lastingly agreeable.

2. Because when Women cease to be handsome, they study to be good. To maintain their Influence over Men, they supply the Diminution of Beauty by an Augmentation of Utility. They learn to do a 1000 Services small and great, and are the most tender and useful

† From *The Autobiography of Benjamin Franklin*, edited by Max Farand. © 1949, 1977 Regents of the University of California. Published by the University of California Press.

of all Friends when you are sick. Thus they continue amiable. And hence there is hardly such a thing to be found as an old Woman who is not a good Woman.

3. Because there is no hazard of Children, which irregularly produc'd may be attended with much Inconvenience.

4. Because thro' more Experience, they are more prudent and discreet in conducting an Intrigue to prevent Suspicion. The Commerce with them is therefore safer with regard to your Reputation. And with regard to theirs, if the Affair should happen to be known, considerate People might be rather inclin'd to excuse an old Woman who would kindly take care of a young Man, form his Manners by her good Counsels, and prevent his ruining his Health and Fortune among mercenary Prostitutes.

5. Because in every Animal that walks upright, the Deficiency of the Fluids that fill the Muscles appears first in the highest Part: The Face first grows lank and wrinkled; then the Neck; then the Breast and Arms; the lower Parts continuing to the last as plump as ever: So that covering all above with a Basket, and regarding only what is below the Girdle, it is impossible of two Women to know an old from a young one. And as in the dark all Cats are grey, the Pleasure of corporal Enjoyment with an old Woman is at least equal, and frequently superior, every Knack being by Practice capable of Improvement.

6. Because the Sin is less. The debauching a Virgin may be her Ruin, and make her for Life unhappy.

7. Because the Compunction is less. The having made a young Girl *miserable* may give you frequent bitter Reflections; none of which can attend the making an old Woman *happy*.

8thly and Lastly They are *so grateful!!*

Thus much for my Paradox. But still I advise you to marry directly; being sincerely Your affectionate Friend.

JUDITH SARGENT MURRAY

Desultory Thoughts upon the Utility of Encouraging a Degree of Self Complacency, Especially in Female Bosoms[†]

Self estimation, kept within due bounds,
However oddly the assertion sounds,
May, of the fairest efforts be the root,

[†] This essay was originally published in *The Gentleman and Lady's Town and Country Magazine: or, Repository of Instruction and Entertainment* 6 (October 1784): 251–53.

May yield the embow'ring shade—the mellow fruit;
5   May stimulate to most exalted deeds,
Direct the soul where blooming honor leads;
May give her there, to act a noble part,
To virtuous pleasures yield the willing heart.
Self-estimation will debasement shun,
10   And, in the path of wisdom, joy to run;
An unbecoming act in fears to do,
And still, its exaltation keeps in view.
   "To rev'rence self," a Bard long since directed,
And, on each moral truth HE well reflected;
15   But, lost to conscious worth, to decent pride,
Compass nor helm there is, our course to guide:
Nor may we anchor cast, for rudely tost
In an unfathom'd sea, each motive's lost,
Wildly amid contending waves we're beat,
20   And rocks and quick sands, shoals and depths we meet;
'Till, dash'd in pieces, or, till found'ring, we
One common wreck of all our prospects see!
   Nor, do we mourn, for we were lost to fame,
And never hap'd to reach a tow'ring name;
25   Ne'er taught to "rev'rence self," or to aspire,
Our bosoms never caught ambition's fire;
An indolence of virtue still prevail'd,
Nor the sweet gale of praise was e'er inhal'd;
Rous'd by a new stimulus, no kindling glow.
30   No soothing emulations gentle flow,
We judg'd that nature, not to us inclin'd,
In narrow bounds our progress had confin'd,
And, that our forms, to say the very best,
Only, not frightful, were by all confest.

I think, to teach young minds to aspire, ought to be the ground work of education: many a laudable achievement is lost, from a persuasion that our efforts are unequal to the arduous attainment. Ambition is a noble principle, which properly directed, may be productive of the most valuable consequences. It is amazing to what heights the mind by exertion may tow'r: I would, therefore, have my pupils believe, that every thing in the compass of mortality, was placed within their grasp, and that, the avidity of application, the intenseness of study, were only requisite to endow them with every external grace, and mental accomplishment. Thus I should impel them to progress on, if I could not lead them to the heights I would wish them to attain. It is too common with parents to expatiate in their hearing, upon all the foibles of their children, and to let their virtues pass, in appearance, unregarded: this they do, least they should, (were they to commend) swell their little hearts to pride, and implant in their tender minds, undue conceptions of their own importance. Those, for example, who have the care of a beautiful female, they assiduously guard every avenue, they arrest the stream of due admiration, and endeavour to divest her of all idea of the bounties of nature: what is the consequence? She grows up, and of course mixes with those who are less interested: strangers will be sincere; she encounters the tongue of the flatterer, he will exaggerate, she finds herself possessed of accomplishments which have been studiously concealed from her, she throws the reins upon the neck of fancy, and gives every encomiast[1] full credit for his most extravagant eulogy. Her natural connexions, her home is rendered disagreeable, and she hastes to the scenes, whence arise the sweet perfume of adulation, and when she can obtain the regard due to a merit, which she supposes altogether uncommon. Those who have made her acquainted with the dear secret, she considers as her best friends; and it is more than probable, that she will soon fall a sacrifice to some worthless character, whose interest may lead him to the most hyperbolical lengths in the round of flattery. Now, I should be solicitous that my daughter should possess for me the fondest love, as well as that respect which gives birth to duty; in order to promote this wish of my soul, from my lips she should be accustomed to hear the most pleasing truths, and, as in the course of my instructions, I should doubtless find myself but too often impelled to wound the delicacy of youthful sensibility. I would therefore, be careful to avail myself of this exuberating balance: I would, from the early dawn of reason, address her as a rational being; hence, I apprehend, the most valuable consequences would result: in some such language as this, she might from time to time be accosted. A pleasing form is undoubtedly advantageous, nature, my dear, hath furnished you with an agreeable person, your glass, was I to be silent, would inform you that you are pretty, your appearance will sufficiently recommend you to a stranger, the flatterer will give a more than mortal finishing to every feature; but, it must be your part, my sweet girl, to render yourself worthy respect from higher motives: you must learn "to reverence yourself," that is, your intellectual existence; you must join my efforts, in endeavouring to adorn your mind, for, it is from the proper furnishing of that, you will become indeed a valuable person, you will, as I said, give birth to the most favorable impressions at first sight: but, how mortifying should this be all, if, upon a more extensive knowledge you should be discovered to possess no one mental charm, to be fit only at best, to be hung up as a pleasing picture among the paintings of some spacious

---

1. A person known for giving formal, lavish praise.

hall. The FLATTERER, indeed, will still pursue you, but it will be from interested views, and he will smile at your undoing! Now, then, my best Love, is the time for you to lay in such a fund of useful knowledge, as shall continue, and augment every kind sentiment in regard to you, as shall set you above the snares of the artful betrayer.

Thus, that sweet form, shall serve but as a polished casket, which will contain a most beautiful gem, highly finished, and calculated for advantage, as well as ornament. Was she, I say, habituated thus to reflect, she would be taught to aspire; she would learn to estimate every accomplishment, according to its proper value; and, when the voice of adulation should assail her ear, as she had early been initiated into its true meaning, and from youth been accustomed to the language of praise; her attention would not be captivated, the Siren's song[2] would not borrow the aid of novelty, her young mind would not be enervated or intoxicated, by a delicious surprise, she would possess her soul in serenity, and by that means, rise superior to the deep-laid schemes which, too commonly, encompass the steps of beauty.

Neither should those to whom nature had been parsimonious, be tortured by me with degrading comparisons; every advantage I would expatiate upon, and there are few who possess not some personal charms; I would teach them to gloss over their imperfections, inasmuch as, I do think, an agreeable form, a very necessary introduction to society, and of course it behoves us to render our appearance as pleasing as possible: I would, I must repeat, by all means guard them against a low estimation of self. I would leave no charm undiscovered or unmarked, for the penetrating eye of the pretended admirer, to make unto himself a merit by holding up to her view; thus, I would destroy the weapons of flattery, or render them useless, by leaving not the least room for their operation.

A young lady, growing up with the idea, that she possesses few, or no personal attractions, and that her mental abilities are of an inferior kind, imbibing at the same time, a most melancholy idea of a female, descending down the vale of life in an unprotected state; taught also to regard her character ridiculously contemptible, will, too probably, throw herself away upon the first who approaches her with tenders of love, however indifferent may be her chance for happiness, least if she omits the present day of grace, she may never be so happy as to meet a second offer, and must then inevitably be stigmatized with that dreaded title, an Old Maid, must rank with a class whom she has been accustomed to regard as burthens upon society, and objects whom she might with impunity turn into ridicule! Certainly

2. In general, the term refers to anything that distracts attention from the correct path or action; in classical mythology, the Siren was a sea nymph that lured mariners to destruction with her seductive singing.

love, friendship and esteem, ought to take place of marriage, but, the woman thus circumstanced, will seldom regard these previous requisites to felicity, if she can but insure the honors, which she, in idea, associates with a matrimonial connection—to prevent which great evil, I would early impress under proper regulations, a reverence of self; I would endeavour to rear to worth, and a consciousness thereof: I would be solicitous to inspire the glow of virtue, with that elevation of soul, that dignity, which is ever attendant upon self-approbation, arising from the genuine source of innate rectitude. I must be excused for thus insisting upon my hypothesis, as I am, from observation, persuaded, that many have suffered materially all their life long, from a depression of soul, early inculcated, in compliance to a false maxim, which hath supposed pride would thereby be eradicated. I know there is a contrary extreme, and I would, in almost all cases, prefer the happy medium. However, if these fugitive hints may induce some abler pen to improve thereon, the exemplification will give pleasure to the heart of

CONSTANTIA.

October 22, 1784.

From On the Equality of the Sexes[†]

That minds are not alike, full well I know,
This truth each day's experience will show;
To heights surprising some great spirits soar,
With inborn strength mysterious depths explore;
5   Their eager gaze surveys the path of light,
Confest it stood to Newton's[1] piercing sight.
    Deep science, like a bashful maid retires,
And but the *ardent* breast her worth inspires;
By perseverance the coy fair is won.
10 And Genius, led by Study, wears the crown.
    But some there are who wish not to improve,
Who never can the path of knowledge love,
Whose souls almost with the dull body one,
With anxious care each mental pleasure shun;
15 Weak is the level'd, enervated mind,
And but while here to vegetate design'd.
The torpid spirit mingling with its clod,
Can scarcely boast its origin from God;
Stupidly dull—they move progressing on—

---

† This essay was originally published in *The Massachusetts Magazine; or, Monthly Museum of Knowledge and Rational Entertainment* 2.3–4 (March–April 1790): 132–35, 223–26.
1. Sir Isaac Newton (1642–1727), English philosopher and mathematician.

20 They eat, and drink, and all their work is done.
    While others, emulous of sweet applause,
    Industrious seek for each event a cause,
    Tracing the hidden springs whence knowledge flows,
    Which nature all in beauteous order shows.
25   Yet cannot I their sentiments imbibe,
    Who this distinction to the sex ascribe,
    As if a woman's form must needs enrol,
    A weak, a servile, an inferiour soul;
    And that the guise of man must still proclaim,
30 Greatness of mind, and him, to be the same:
    Yet as the hours revolve fair proofs arise,
    Which the bright wreath of growing fame supplies;
    And in past times some men have *sunk* so *low,*
    That female records nothing *less* can show.
35 But imbecility is still confin'd,
    And by the lordly sex to us consign'd;
    They rob us of the power t'improve,
    And then declare we only trifles love;
    Yet haste the era, when the world shall know,
40 That such distinctions only dwell below;
    The soul unfetter'd, to no sex confin'd,
    Was for the abodes of cloudless day design'd.
        Mean time we emulate their manly fires,
    Though erudition all their thoughts inspires,
45 Yet nature with *equality* imparts,
    And *noble passions,* swell e'en *female hearts.*

Is it upon mature consideration we adopt the idea, that nature is thus partial in her distributions? Is it indeed a fact, that she hath yielded to one half of the human species so unquestionable a mental superiority? I know that to both sexes elevated understandings, and the reverse, are common. But, suffer me to ask, in what the minds of females are so notoriously deficient, or unequal. May not the intellectual powers be ranged under these four heads—imagination, reason, memory and judgment. The province of imagination hath long since been surrendered up to us, and we have been crowned undoubted sovereigns of the regions of fancy. Invention is perhaps the most arduous effort of the mind; this branch of imagination hath been particularly ceded to us, and we have been time out of mind invested with that creative faculty. Observe the variety of fashions (here I bar the contemptuous smile) which distinguish and adorn the female world; how continually are they changing, insomuch that they almost render the wise man's assertion problematical, and we are ready to say, *there is something new under the sun.* Now what a playfulness, what an exuberance of fancy, what strength of inventive imagination, doth this continual variation discover? Again, it hath been observed, that if the turpitude of the conduct of our sex, hath been ever so enormous, so extremely ready are we, that the very first thought presents us with an apology, so plausible, as to produce our actions even in an amiable light. Another instance of our creative powers, is our talent for slander; how ingenious are we at inventive scandal? what a formidable story can we in a moment fabricate merely from the force of a prolifick imagination? how many reputations, in the fertile brain of a female, have been utterly despoiled? how industrious are we at improving a hint? suspicion how easily do we convert into conviction, and conviction, embellished by the power of eloquence, stalks abroad to the surprise and confusion of unsuspecting innocence. Perhaps it will be asked if I furnish these facts as instances of excellency in our sex. Certainly not; but as proofs of a creative faculty, of a lively imagination. Assuredly great activity of mind is thereby discovered, and was this activity properly directed, what beneficial effects would follow. Is the needle and kitchen sufficient to employ the operations of a soul thus organized? I should conceive not. Nay, it is a truth that those very departments leave the intelligent principle vacant, and at liberty for speculation. Are we deficient in reason? we can only reason from what we know, and if an opportunity of acquiring knowledge hath been denied us, the inferiority of our sex cannot fairly be deduced from thence. Memory, I believe, will be allowed us in common, since every one's experience must testify, that a loquacious old woman is as frequently met with, as a communicative old man; their subjects are alike drawn from the fund of other times, and the transactions of their youth, or of maturer life, entertain, or perhaps fatigue you, in the evening of their lives. "But our judgment is not so strong—we do not distinguish so well."—Yet it may be questioned, from what doth this superiority, in this determining faculty of the soul, proceed. May we not trace its source in the difference of education, and continued advantages? Will it be said that the judgment of a male of two years old, is more sage than that of a female's of the same age? I believe the reverse is generally observed to be true. But from that period what partiality! how is the one exalted, and the other depressed, by the contrary modes of education which are adopted! the one is taught to aspire, and the other is early confined and limitted. As their years increase, the sister must be wholly domesticated, while the brother is led by the hand through all the flowery paths of science. Grant that their minds are by nature equal, yet who shall wonder at the *apparent* superiority, if indeed custom becomes *second nature*; nay if it taketh place of nature, and that it doth the experience of each day will evince. At length arrived at womanhood, the uncultivated fair one feels a void, which the employments allotted her are by no means capable of filling. What can she do? to books she may not apply; or if she doth, *to those only of the novel kind,* lest she merit the appellation of a *learned lady;* and what ideas have been affixed to this term, the observation of many can testify. Fashion, scandal, and sometimes what is still more reprehensible, are then called in to her relief; and who can say to what lengths the liberties she takes may proceed. Meantime she herself is most unhappy; she feels the want of a cultivated mind. Is she single, she in vain seeks to fill up time from sexual employments or amusements. Is she united to a person whose soul nature made equal to her own, education hath set him so far above her, that in those entertainments which are productive of such rational felicity, she is not qualified to accompany him. She experiences a mortifying consciousness of inferiority, which embitters every enjoyment. Doth the person to whom her adverse fate hath consigned her, possess a mind incapable of improvement, she is equally wretched, in being so closely connected with an individual whom she cannot but despise. Now, was she permitted the same instructors as her brother, (with an eye however to their particular departments) for the employment of a rational mind an ample field would be opened. In astronomy she might catch a glimpse of the immensity of the Deity, and thence she would form amazing conceptions of the august and supreme Intelligence. In geography she would admire Jehovah in the midst of his benevolence; thus adapting this globe to the various wants and amusements of its inhabitants. In natural philosophy she would adore the infinite majesty of heaven, clothed in condescension; and as she traversed the reptile world, she would hail the goodness of a creating God. A mind, thus filled, would have little room for the trifles with which our sex are, with too much justice, accused of amusing themselves, and they would thus be rendered fit companions for those, who should one day wear them as their crown. Fashions, in their variety, would then give place to conjectures, which might perhaps conduce to the improvement of the literary world; and there would be no leisure for slander or detraction. Reputation would not then be blasted, but serious speculations would occupy the lively imaginations of the sex. Unnecessary visits would be precluded, and that custom would only be indulged by way of relaxation, or to answer the demands of consanguinity and friendship. Females would become discreet, their judgments would be invigorated, and their partners for life being circumspectly chosen, an unhappy Hymen[2] would then be as rare, as is now the reverse.

Will it be urged that those acquirements would supersede our domestick duties? I answer that every requisite in female economy is easily attained; and, with truth I can add, that when once attained, they require no further *mental attention.* Nay, while we are pursu-

---

2. In Greek mythology, the god of marriage.

ing the needle, or the superintendency of the family, I repeat, that our minds are at full liberty for reflection; that imagination may exert itself in full vigor; and that if a just foundation is early laid, our ideas will then be worthy of rational beings. If we were industrious we might easily find time to arrange them upon paper, or should avocations press too hard for such an indulgence, the hours allotted for conversation would at least become more refined and rational. Should it still be vociferated, "Your domestick employments are sufficient"—I would calmly ask, is it reasonable, that a candidate for immortality, for the joys of heaven, an intelligent being, who is to spend an eternity in contemplating the works of Deity, should at present be so degraded, as to be allowed no other ideas, than those which are suggested by the mechanism of a pudding, or the sewing the seams of a garment? Pity that all such censurers of female improvement do not go one step further, and deny their future existence; to be consistent they surely ought.

Yes, ye lordly, ye haughty sex, our souls are by nature *equal* to yours; the same breath of God animates, enlivens, and invigorates us; and that we are not fallen lower than yourselves, let those witness who have greatly towered above the various discouragements by which they have been so heavily oppressed; and though I am unacquainted with the list of celebrated characters on either side, yet from the observations I have made in the contracted circle in which I have moved, I dare confidently believe, that from the commencement of time to the present day, there hath been as many females, as males, who, by the *mere force of natural powers*, have merited the crown of applause; who, *thus unassisted*, have seized the wreath of fame. I know there are who assert, that as the animal powers of the one sex are superiour, of course their mental faculties also must be stronger; thus attributing strength of mind to the transient organization of this earth born tenement. But if this reasoning is just, man must be content to yield the palm to many of the brute creation, since by not a few of his brethren of the field, he is far surpassed in bodily strength. Moreover, was this argument admitted, it would prove too much, for occular demonstration evinceth, that there are many robust masculine ladies, and effeminate gentlemen. Yet I fancy that Mr. Pope,[3] though clogged with an enervated body, and distinguished by a diminutive stature, could nevertheless lay claim to greatness of soul; and perhaps there are many other instances which might be adduced to combat so unphilosophical an opinion. Do we not often see, that when the clay built tabernacle is well nigh dissolved, when it is just ready to mingle with the parent soil, the immortal inhabitant aspires to, and even attaineth heights the most

3. Alexander Pope (1688–1744), English poet.

sublime, and which were before wholly unexplored. Besides, were we to grant that animal strength proved any thing, taking into consideration the accustomed impartiality of nature, we should be induced to imagine, that she had invested the female mind with superiour strength as an equivalent for the bodily powers of man. But waving this however palpable advantage, for *equality only,* we wish to contend.

I am aware that there are many passages in the sacred oracles which seem to give the advantage to the other sex; but I consider all these as wholly metaphorical. Thus David[4] was a man after God's own heart, yet see him enervated by his licentious passions! behold him following Uriah[5] to the death, and shew me wherein could consist the immaculate Being's complacency. Listen to the curses which Job[6] bestoweth upon the day of his nativity, and tell me where is his perfection, where his patience—*literally* it existed not. David and Job were types of him who was to come; and the superiority of man, as exhibited in scripture, being also emblematical, all arguments deduced from thence, of course fall to the ground. The exquisite delicacy of the female mind proclaimeth the exactness of its texture, while its nice sense of honour announceth its innate, its native grandeur. And indeed, in one respect, the preeminence seems to be tacitly allowed us, for after an education which limits and confines, and employments and recreations which naturally tend to enervate the body, and debilitate the mind; after we have from early youth been adorned with ribbons, and other gewgaws, dressed out like the ancient victims previous to a sacrifice, being taught by the care of our parents in collecting the most showy materials that the ornamenting our exteriour ought to be the principal object of our attention; after, I say, fifteen years thus spent, we are introduced into the world, amid the united adulation of every beholder. Praise is sweet to the soul; we are immediately intoxicated by large draughts of flattery, which being plentifully administered, is to the pride of our hearts the most acceptable incense. It is expected that with the other sex we should commence immediate war, and that we should triumph over the machinations of the most artful. We must be constantly upon our guard; prudence and discretion must be our characteristicks; and we must rise superiour to, and obtain a complete victory over those who have been long adding to the native strength of their minds, by an unremitted study of men and books, and who have, moreover,

4. In the Bible, second king of Israel. See 1 Sam. 16:1 to 1 Kings 2:11.
5. In the Bible, one of King David's generals who was executed in order to conceal David's acts of adultery. See 2 Sam. 11:1–25.
6. In the Bible, the example of the suffering saint, whose experiences raise the question of why the religious suffer. See especially Job 42:1–6.

conceived from the loose characters which they have seen portrayed in the extensive variety of their reading, a most contemptible opinion of the sex. Thus unequal, we are, notwithstanding, forced to the combat, and the infamy which is consequent upon the smallest deviation in our conduct, proclaims the high idea which was formed of our native strength; and thus, indirectly at least, is the preference acknowledged to be our due. And if we are allowed an equality of acquirement, let serious studies equally employ our minds, and we will bid our souls arise to equal strength. We will meet upon even ground, the despot man; we will rush with alacrity to the combat, and, crowned by success, we shall then answer the exalted expectations which are formed. Though sensibility, soft compassion, and gentle commiseration, are inmates in the female bosom, yet against every deep laid art, altogether fearless of the event, we will set them in array; for assuredly the wreath of victory will encircle the spotless brow. If we meet an equal, a sensible friend, we will reward him with the hand of amity, and through life we will be assiduous to promote his happiness; but from every deep laid scheme for our ruin, retiring into ourselves, amid the flowery paths of science, we will indulge in all the refined and sentimental pleasures of contemplation. And should it still be urged, that the studies thus insisted upon would interfere with our more peculiar department, I must further reply, that *early hours,* and close application, will do wonders; and to her who is from the first dawn of reason taught to fill up time rationally, both the requisites will be easy. I grant that niggard fortune is too generally unfriendly to the mind; and that much of that valuable treasure, time, is necessarily expended upon the wants of the body; but it should be remembered, that in embarrassed circumstances our companions have as little leisure for literary improvement, as is afforded to us; for most certainly their provident care is at least as requisite as our exertions. Nay, we have even more leisure for sedentary pleasures, as our avocations are more retired, much less laborious, and, as hath been observed, by no means require that avidity of attention which is proper to the employments of the other sex. In high life, or, in other words, where the parties are in possession of affluence, the objection respecting time is wholly obviated, and of course falls to the ground; and it may also be repeated, that many of those hours which are at present swallowed up in fashion and scandal, might be redeemed, were we habituated to useful reflections. But in one respect, O ye arbiters of our fate! we confess that the superiority is indubitably yours; you are by nature formed for our protectors; we pretend not to vie with you in bodily strength; upon this point we will never contend for victory. Shield us then, we beseech you, from external evils, and in return *we* will transact *your* domestick affairs. Yes, *your,* for are you not equally interested in those matters with ourselves? Is not the elegancy of neatness as agreeable to your sight as to ours; is not the well favoured viand equally delightful to your taste; and doth not your sense of hearing suffer as much, from the discordant sounds prevalent in an ill regulated family, produced by the voices of children and many *et ceteras?*

CONSTANTIA.

* * *

ANONYMOUS

A New Bundling Song[†]

*Or a reproof to those young country women, who follow
that reproachful practice, and to their mothers
for upholding them therein.*

> Since bundling very much abounds,
> In many parts in country towns,
> No doubt but some will spurn my song,
> And say I'd better hold my tongue;
> 5   But none I'm sure will take offence,
> Or deem my song impertinence,
> But only those who guilty be,
> And plainly here their pictures see.
>
> Some maidens say, if through the nation,
> 10   Bundling should quite go out of fashion,
> Courtship would lose its sweets; and they
> Could have no fun till wedding day.
> It shan't be so, they rage and storm,
> And country girls in clusters swarm,
> 15   And fly and buz, like angry bees,
> And vow they'll bundle when they please.
>
> Some mothers too, will plead their cause,
> And give their daughters great applause,
> And tell them, 'tis no sin nor shame,
> 20   For we, your mothers, did the same;
> We hope the custom ne'er will alter,
> But wish its enemies a halter.

[†] From Dana Doten, *The Art of Bundling*, 1938, pp. 141–47. According to Doten, the poem
was published in an almanac about 1785.

Dissatisfaction great appeared,
In several places where they've heard
25 Their preacher's bold, aloud disclaim
That bundling is a burning shame;
This too was cause of direful rout
And talked and told of, all about,
That ministers should disapprove
30 Sparks courting in a bed of love,
So justified the custom more,
Than e'er was heard or known before.

The pulpit then it seems must yield,
And female valor take the field,
35 In places where there custom long
Increasing strength has grown so strong;
When mothers herein bear a sway,
And daughters joyfully obey.

And young men highly pleased too,
40 Good Lord! what can't the devil do.
Can this vile practice ne'er be broke?
Is there no way to give a stroke,
To wound it or to strike it dead.
And girls with sparks not go to bed
45 'Twill strike them more than preacher's tongue,
To let the world know what they've done,
And let it be in common fame,
Held up to view a noted shame.

Young miss if this your practice be,
50 I'll teach you now yourself to see:
You plead you're honest, modest too,
But such a plea will never do;
For how can modesty consist,
With shameful practice such as this?
55 I'll give your answer to the life:
"You don't undress, like man and wife,"
That is your plea, I'll freely own,
But whose your bondsmen when alone,
That further rules you will not break,
60 And marriage liberties partake?

Some really do, as I suppose,
Upon design keep on some clothes,
And yet in truth I'm not afraid

For to describe a bundling maid;
65   She'll sometimes say when she lies down,
She can't be cumber'd with a gown,
And that the weather is so warm,
To take it off can be no harm:
The girl it seems had been at strift;
70   For widest bosom to her shift,
She gownless, when the bed they're in,
The spark, nought feels but naked skin.
But she is modest, also chaste,
While only bare from neck to waist,
75   And he of boasted freedom sings,
Of all above her apron strings.
And where such freedoms great are shared,
And further freedoms feebly bar'd,
I leave for others to relate,
80   How long she'll keep her virgin state.

Another pretty lass we'll scan,
That loves to bundle with a man,
For many different ways they take,
Though modest rules they all will break.
85   Some clothes I'll keep on, she will say,
For that has always been my way,
Nor would I be quite naked found,
With spark in bed, for thousand pound.
But petticoats, I've always said,
90   Were never made to wear in bed,
I'll take them off, keep on my gown,
And then I dare defy the town,
To charge me with immodesty,
While I so ever cautious be.
95   The spark was pleased with his maid,
Of apprehension quick he said,
Her witty scheme was keen he swore,
Lying in gown open before.

Another maid when in the dark,
100   Going to bed with her dear spark,
She'll tell him that 'tis rather shocking,
To bundle in with shoes and stockings.
Nor scrupling but she's quite discreet,
Lying with naked legs and feet,
105   With petticoats so thin and short,
That she is scarce the better for't;

But you will say that I'm unfair,
That some who bundle take more care,
For some we may with truth suppose,
110   Bundle in bed with all their clothes.
But bundler's clothes are no defence,
Unruly horses push the fence;
A certain fact I'll now relate,
That's true indeed without debate.
115   A bundling couple went to bed,
With all their clothes from foot to head,
That the defence might seem complete,
Each one was wrapped in a sheet.
But O! this bundling's such a witch,
120   The man of her did catch the itch,
And so provoked was the wretch,
That she of him a bastard catch'd.

Ye bundling misses, don't you blush,
You hang your heads and bid me bush.
125   If you won't tell me how you feel,
I'll ask your sparks, they best can tell.
But it is custom you will say,
And custom always bears the sway,
If I won't take my sparks to bed,
130   A laughing stock I shall be made;
A vulgar custom 'tis, I own,
Admir'd by many a slut and clown,
But 'tis a method of proceeding,
As much abborr'd by those of breeding.

135   You're welcome to the lines I've penn'd,
For they were written by a friend,
Who'll think himself quite well rewarded,
If this vile practice is discarded.

ANONYMOUS

A New Song in Favour of Courting†

Adam at first was form'd of dust,
    As scripture doth record;

† From Dana Doten, *The Art of Bundling*, 1938, pp. 148–53.

And did receive a wife call'd Eve,
    From his Creator Lord.

5 From Adam's side a crooked bride,
    The Lord was pleas'd to form;
Ordained that they in bed might lay
    To keep each other warm.

To court indeed they had no need,
10   She was his wife at first,
And she was made to be his aid,
    Whose origin was dust.

This new made pair full happy were,
    And happy might remained,
15 If his help mate had never ate,
    The fruit that was restrain'd.

Tho' Adam's wife destroyed his life,
    In manner that was awful;
Yet marriage now we all allow
20   To be both just and lawful.

But women must be courted first,
    Because it is the fashion,
And so at times commit great crimes,
    Caus'd by a lustful passion.

25 And now a days there are two ways,
    Which of the two is right,
To lie between sheets sweet and clean,
    Or sit up all the night?

But some suppose bundling in clothes
30   Do heaven sorely vex;
Then let me know which way to go,
    To court the female sex.

Whether they must be huggd or kiss'd
    When sitting by the fire,
35 Or whether they in bed may lay,
    Which doth the Lord require?

But some pretend to recommend
    The sitting up all night;

Courting in chairs as doth appear
40   To them to be most right.

Nature's request is, grant me rest,
    Our bodies seek repose;
Night is the time, and 'tis no crime
    To bundle in your clothes.

45 Since in a bed a man and maid,
    May bundle and be chaste,
It does no good to burn out wood,
    It is a needless waste.

Let coats and gowns be laid aside,
50   And breeches take their flight,
An honest man and woman can
    Lay quiet all the night.

In Genesis no knowledge is
    Of this thing to be got,
55 Whether young men did bundle then,
    Or whether they did not.

The sacred book says wives they took,
    It don't say how they courted,
Whether that they in bed did lay,
60   Or by the fire sported.

But some do hold in times of old,
    That those about to wed,
Spent not the night, nor yet the light
    By fire, or in the bed.

65 They only meant to say they sent
    A man to chuse a bride,
Isaac did so, but let me know
    Of any one beside.

Man don't pretend to trust a friend,
70   To choose him sheep and cows,
Much less a wife which all his life
    He doth expect to house.

Since it doth stand each man in hand,
    To happify his life,

75　　I would advise each to be wise,
　　　　And chuse a prudent wife.

　　　Since bundling is not the thing,
　　　　That judgments will procure,
　　　Go on young men and bundle then,
80　　But keep your bodies pure.

BENJAMIN RUSH

From Thoughts upon Female Education[†]

* * *

The first remark that I shall make upon this subject, is, that female education should be accommodated to the state of society, manners, and government of the country, in which it is conducted.

This remark leads me at once to add, that the education of young ladies, in this country, should be conducted upon principles very different from what it is in Great Britain, and in some respects different from what it was when we were part of a monarchical empire.

There are several circumstances in the situation, employments, and duties of women, in America, which require a peculiar mode of education.

I. The early marriages of our women, by contracting the time allowed for education, renders it necessary to contract its plan, and to confine it chiefly to the more useful branches of literature.

II. The state of property, in America, renders it necessary for the greatest part of our citizens to employ themselves, in different occupations, for the advancement of their fortunes. This cannot be done without the assistance of the female members of the community. They must be the stewards, and guardians of their husbands' property. That education, therefore, will be most proper for our women, which teaches them to discharge the duties of those offices with the most success and reputation.

III. From the numerous avocations to which a professional life exposes gentlemen in America from their families, a principal share of the instruction of children naturally devolves upon the women. It becomes us therefore to prepare them by a suitable education, for the discharge of this most important duty of mothers.

IV. The equal share that every citizen has in the liberty, and the possible share he may have in the government of our country, make

† Philadelphia, 1787. First given as a lecture at the Young Ladies' Academy in Philadelphia. Early American Imprints, Series 1: Evans, no. 20691.

it necessary that our ladies should be qualified to a certain degree by a peculiar and suitable education, to concur in instructing their sons in the principles of liberty and government.

V. In Great Britain the business of servants is a regular occupation; but in America this humble station is the usual retreat of unexpected indigence; hence the servants in this country possess less knowledge and subordination than are required from them; and hence, our ladies are obliged to attend more to the private affairs of their families, than ladies generally do, of the same rank in Great Britain. * * * This circumstance should have great influence upon the nature and extent of female education in America.

The branches of literature most essential for a young lady in this country, appear to be,

I. A knowledge of the English language. She should not only read, but speak and spell it correctly. And to enable her to do this, she should be taught the English grammar, and be frequently examined in applying its rules in common conversation.

II. Pleasure and interest conspire to make the writing of a fair and legible hand, a necessary branch of female education. For this purpose she should be taught not only to shape every letter properly, but to pay the strictest regard to points and capitals.

* * *

III. Some knowledge of figures and bookkeeping is absolutely necessary to qualify a young lady for the duties which await her in this country. There are certain occupations in which she may assist her husband with this knowledge; and should she survive him, and agreeably to the custom of our country be the executrix of his will, she cannot fail of deriving immense advantages from it.

IV. An acquaintance with geography and some instruction in chronology will enable a young lady to read history, biography, and travels, with advantage; and thereby qualify her not only for a general intercourse with the world, but, to be an agreeable companion for a sensible man. To these branches of knowledge may be added, in some instances, a general acquaintance with the first principles of astronomy, and natural philosophy, particularly with such parts of them as are calculated to prevent superstition, by explaining the causes, or obviating the effects of natural evil.

V. Vocal music should never be neglected, in the education of a young lady, in this country. Besides preparing her to join in that part of public worship which consists in psalmody, it will enable her to soothe the cares of domestic life. The distress and vexation of a husband—the noise of a nursery, and, even, the sorrows that will sometimes intrude into her own bosom, may all be relieved by a song, where sound and sentiment unite to act upon the mind. * * *

VI. Dancing is by no means an improper branch of education for an American lady. It promotes health, and renders the figure and motions of the body easy and agreeable. I anticipate the time when the resources of conversation shall be so far multiplied, that the amusement of dancing shall be wholly confined to children. But in our present state of society and knowledge, I conceive it to be an agreeable substitute for the ignoble pleasures of drinking, and gaming, in our assemblies of grown people.

VII. The attention of our young ladies should be directed, as soon as they are prepared for it, to the reading of history—travels—poetry—and moral essays. These studies are accommodated, in a peculiar manner, to the present state of society in America, and when a relish is excited for them, in early life, they subdue that passion for reading novels, which so generally prevails among the fair sex. I cannot dismiss this species of writing and reading without observing, that the subjects of novels are by no means accommodated to our present manners. They hold up *life*, it is true, but it is not as yet *life*, in America. Our passions have not as yet "overstepped the modesty of nature," nor are they "torn to tatters," to use the expressions of the poet, by extravagant love, jealously, ambition, or revenge. As yet the intrigues of a British novel, are as foreign to our manners, as the refinements of Asiatic vice. Let it not be said, that the tales of distress, which fill modern novels, have a tendency to soften the female heart into acts of humanity. The fact is the reverse of this. The abortive sympathy which is excited by the recital of imaginary distress, blunts the heart to that which is real; and, hence, we sometimes see instances of young ladies, who weep away a whole forenoon over the criminal sorrows of a fictitious Charlotte or Werter, turning with disdain at two o'clock from the sight of a beggar, who solicits in feeble accents or signs, a small portion only, of the crumbs which fall from their fathers' tables.

VIII. It will be necessary to connect all these branches of education with regular instruction in the christian religion. For this purpose the principles of the different sects of christians should be taught and explained, and our pupils should early be furnished with some of the most simple arguments in favour of the truth of christianity. A portion of the bible (of late improperly banished from our schools) should be read by them every day, and such questions should be asked, after reading it, as are calculated to imprint upon their minds the interesting stories contained in it.

* * *

IX. If the measures that have been recommended for inspiring our pupils with a sense of religious and moral obligation be adopted, the government of them will be easy and agreeable. I shall only remark under this head, that *strictness* of discipline will always render *severity* unnecessary, and that there will be the most instruction in that school, where there is the most order.

I have said nothing in favour of instrumental music as a branch of female education, because I conceive it is by no means accommodated to the present state of society and manners in America. The price of musical instruments, and the extravagant fees demanded by the teachers of instrumental music, form but a small part of my objections to it.

* * *

I beg leave further to bear a testimony against the practice of making the French language a part of female education in America. In Britain where company and pleasure are the principal business of ladies; where the nursery and the kitchen form no part of their care, and where a daily intercourse is maintained with French-men and other foreigners who speak the French language, a knowledge of it is absolutely necessary. But the case is widely different in this country. Of the many ladies who have applied to this language, how great a proportion of them have been hurried into the cares and duties of a family before they had acquired it; of those who have acquired it, how few have retained it after they were married; and of the few who have retained it, how seldom have they had occasion to speak it, in the course of their lives! It certainly comports more with female delicacy as well as the natural politeness of the French nation, to make it necessary for French-men to learn to speak our language in order to converse with our ladies, than for our ladies to learn their language, in order to converse with them.

Let it not be said in defence of a knowledge of the French language, that many elegant books are written in it. Those of them that are truly valuable, are generally translated; but, if this were not the case, the English language certainly contains many more books of real utility and useful information than can be read, without neglecting other duties, by the daughter, or wife of an American citizen.

It is with reluctance that I object to drawing, as a branch of education for an American lady. To be the mistress of a family is one of the great ends of a woman's being, and while the peculiar state of society in America imposes this station so early, and renders the duties of it so numerous and difficult, I conceive that little time can be spared for the acquisition of this elegant accomplishment.

It is agreeable to observe how differently modern writers, and the inspired author of the proverbs, describe a fine woman. The former confine their praises chiefly to personal charms, and ornamental accomplishments, while the latter celebrates only the virtues of a valuable mistress of a family, and a useful member of society. The one is perfectly acquainted with all the fashionable languages of Europe; the other, "opens her mouth with wisdom" and is perfectly acquainted with all the uses of the needle, the distaff, and the loom. The business of the one, is pleasure; the pleasure of the other, is business. The one is admired abroad; the other is honoured and beloved at home. "Her children arise up and call her blessed, her husband also, and he praiseth her." There is no fame in the world equal to this; nor is there a note in music half so delightful, as the respectful language with which a grateful son or daughter perpetuates the memory of a sensible and affectionate mother.

It should not surprize us that British customs, with respect to female education, have been transplanted into our American schools and families. We see marks of the same incongruity, of time and place, in many other things. We behold our homes accommodated to the climate of Great Britain, by eastern and western directions. We behold our ladies panting in a heat of ninety degrees, under a hat and cushion, which were calculated for the temperature of a British summer. We behold our citizens condemned and punished by a criminal law, which was copied from a country where maturity in corruption renders public executions a part of the amusements of the nation. It is high time to awake from this servility—to study our own character—to examine the age of our country—and to adopt manners in every thing, that shall be accommodated to our state of society, and to the forms of our government. In particular it is incumbent upon us to make ornamental accomplishments, yield to principles and knowledge, in the education of our women.

A philosopher once said "let me make all the ballads of a country and I care not who makes its laws." He might with more propriety have said, let the ladies of a country be educated properly, and they will not only make and administer its laws, but form its manners and character. It would require a lively imagination to describe, or even to comprehend, the happiness of a country, where knowledge and virtue, were generally diffused among the female sex. Our young men would then be restrained from vice by the terror of being banished from their company. The loud laugh, and the malignant smile, at the expence of innocence, or of personal infirmities—the feats of successful mimickry—and the low priced wit, which is borrowed from a misapplication of scripture phrases, would no more be considered as recommendations to the society of the ladies. A double entendre, in their presence, would then exclude a gentleman forever from the company of both sexes, and probably oblige him to seek an asylum from contempt, in a foreign country. The influence of female education would be still more extensive and useful in domestic life. The obligations of gentlemen to qualify themselves by knowledge and industry to discharge the duties of benevolence, would be

encreased by marriage; and the patriot—the hero—and the legisla-
tor, would find the sweetest reward of their toils, in the approbation
and applause of their wives. Children would discover the marks of
maternal prudence and wisdom in every station of life; for it has
been remarked that there have been few great or good men who have
not been blessed with wise and prudent mothers. Cyrus was taught
to revere the gods, by his mother Mandane—Samuel was devoted to
his prophetic office before he was born, by his mother Hannah—
Constantine was rescued from paganism by his mother Constantia—
and Edward the sixth inherited those great and excellent qualities
which made him the delight of the age in which he lived, from his
mother, lady Jane Seymour. Many other instances might be mentioned, if necessary, from ancient and modern history, to establish
the truth of this proposition.

I am not enthusiastical upon the subject of education. In the ordinary course of human affairs, we shall probably too soon follow the
footsteps of the nations of Europe in manners and vices. The first
marks we shall perceive of our declension, will appear among our
women. Their idleness, ignorance and profligacy will be the harbin-
gers of our ruin. Then will the character and performance of a buf-
foon on the theatre, be the subject of more conversation and praise,
than the patriot or the minister of the gospel;—then will our language and pronunciation be enfeebled and corrupted by a flood
of French and Italian words;—then will the history of romantic
amours, be preferred to the immortal writings of Addison, Hawkes-
worth and Johnson;—then will our churches be neglected, and the
name of the supreme being never be called upon, but in profane
exclamations;—then will our Sundays be appropriated, only to
feasts and concerts—and then will begin all that train of domestic
and political calamities——But, I forbear. The prospect is so painful, that I cannot help, silently, imploring the great arbiter of human
affairs, to interpose his almighty goodness, and to deliver us from
these evils, that, at least one spot of the earth may be reserved as
a monument of the effects of good education, in order to shew in
some degree, what our species was, before the fall, and what it shall
be, after its restoration.

*   *   *

* * * To you, therefore,
YOUNG LADIES,
an important problem is committed for solution; and that is, whether
our present plan of education be a wise one, and whether it be calculated to prepare you for the duties of social and domestic life. I know
that the elevation of the female mind, by means of moral, physical
and religious truth, is considered by some men as unfriendly to the
domestic character of a woman. But this is the prejudice of little

minds, and springs from the same spirit which opposes the general diffusion of knowledge among the citizens of our republics. If men believe that ignorance is favorable to the government of the female sex, they are certainly deceived; for a weak and ignorant woman will always be governed with the greatest difficulty. I have sometimes been led to ascribe the invention of ridiculous and expensive fashions in female dress, entirely to the gentlemen, in order to divert the ladies from improving their minds, and thereby to secure a more arbitrary and unlimited authority over them. It will be in your power, LADIES, to correct the mistakes and practice of our sex upon these subjects, by demonstrating, that the female temper can only be governed by reason, and that the cultivation of reason in women, is alike friendly to the order of nature, and to private as well as public happiness.

MARY WOLLSTONECRAFT

Introduction to
A Vindication of the Rights of Woman[†]

After considering the historic page, and viewing the living world with anxious solicitude, the most melancholy emotions of sorrowful indignation have depressed my spirits, and I have sighed when obliged to confess, that either nature has made a great difference between man and man, or that the civilization which has hitherto taken place in the world has been very partial. I have turned over various books written on the subject of education, and patiently observed the conduct of parents and the management of schools; but what has been the result?—a profound conviction that the neglected education of my fellow-creatures is the grand source of the misery I deplore; and that women, in particular, are rendered weak and wretched by a variety of concurring causes, originating from one hasty conclusion. The conduct and manners of women, in fact, evidently prove that their minds are not in a healthy state; for, like the flowers which are planted in too rich a soil, strength and usefulness are sacrificed to beauty; and the flaunting leaves, after having pleased a fastidious eye, fade, disregarded on the stalk, long before the season when they ought to have arrived at maturity.—One cause of this barren blooming I attribute to a false system of education, gathered from the books written on this subject by men who, considering females rather as women than human creatures, have been more anxious to make them alluring mistresses than affectionate wives and rational mothers; and the understanding of the sex has been so bubbled by this

† Originally published in London in 1792; 1st American edition Philadelphia, 1792. New York: Norton Critical Editions, 2009.

specious homage, that the civilized women of the present century, with a few exceptions, are only anxious to inspire love, when they ought to cherish a nobler ambition, and by their abilities and virtues exact respect.

In a treatise, therefore, on female rights and manners, the works which have been particularly written for their improvement must not be overlooked; especially when it is asserted, in direct terms, that the minds of women are enfeebled by false refinement; that the books of instruction, written by men of genius, have had the same tendency as more frivolous productions; and that, in the true style of Mahometanism, they are treated as a kind of subordinate beings,[1] and not as a part of the human species, when improveable reason is allowed to be the dignified distinction which raises men above the brute creation, and puts a natural sceptre in a feeble hand.

Yet, because I am a woman, I would not lead my readers to suppose that I mean violently to agitate the contested question respecting the equality or inferiority of the sex; but as the subject lies in my way, and I cannot pass it over without subjecting the main tendency of my reasoning to misconstruction, I shall stop a moment to deliver, in a few words, my opinion.—In the government of the physical world it is observable that the female in point of strength is, in general, inferior to the male. This is the law of nature; and it does not appear to be suspended or abrogated in favour of woman. A degree of physical superiority cannot, therefore, be denied—and it is a noble prerogative![2] But not content with this natural pre-eminence, men endeavour to sink us still lower, merely to render us alluring objects for a moment; and women, intoxicated by the adoration which men, under the influence of their senses, pay them, do not seek to obtain a durable interest in their hearts, or to become the friends of the fellow creatures who find amusement in their society.

I am aware of an obvious inference: —from every quarter have I heard exclamations against masculine women; but where are they to be found? If by this appellation men mean to inveigh against their ardour in hunting, shooting, and gaming, I shall most cordially join in the cry; but if it be against the imitation of manly virtues, or, more properly speaking, the attainment of those talents and virtues, the exercise of which ennobles the human character, and which raise females in the scale of animal being, when they are comprehensively termed mankind;—all those who view them with a philo-

---

1. It was a common but mistaken opinion among Europeans that in the Koran, the sacred text of Islam, the Prophet Mohammed taught that women did not have souls and were not permitted an afterlife.
2. First edition reads ". . . the female, in general, is inferior to the male. The male pursues, the female yields—this is the law of nature; and it does not appear to be suspended or abrogated in favour of woman. This physical superiority cannot be denied—and it is noble prerogative!"

sophic eye must, I should think, wish with me, that they may every day grow more and more masculine.

This discussion naturally divides the subject. I shall first consider women in the grand light of human creatures, who, in common with men, are placed on this earth to unfold their faculties; and afterwards I shall more particularly point out their peculiar designation.

I wish also to steer clear of an error which many respectable writers have fallen into; for the instruction which has hitherto been addressed to women, has rather been applicable to *ladies,* if the little indirect advice, that is scattered through Sandford and Merton,[3] be excepted; but, addressing my sex in a firmer tone, I pay particular attention to those in the middle class, because they appear to be in the most natural state.[4] Perhaps the seeds of false-refinement, immorality, and vanity, have ever been shed by the great. Weak, artificial beings, raised above the common wants and affections of their race, in a premature unnatural manner, undermine the very foundation of virtue, and spread corruption through the whole mass of society! As a class of mankind they have the strongest claim to pity; the education of the rich tends to render them vain and helpless, and the unfolding mind is not strengthened by the practice of those duties which dignify the human character.—They only live to amuse themselves, and by the same law which in nature invariably produces certain effects, they soon only afford barren amusement.

But as I purpose taking a separate view of the different ranks of society, and of the moral character of women, in each, this hint is, for the present, sufficient; and I have only alluded to the subject, because it appears to me to be the very essence of an introduction to give a cursory account of the contents of the work it introduces.

My own sex, I hope, will excuse me, if I treat them like rational creatures, instead of flattering their *fascinating* graces, and viewing them as if they were in a state of perpetual childhood, unable to stand alone. I earnestly wish to point out in what true dignity and human happiness consists—I wish to persuade women to endeavour to acquire strength, both of mind and body, and to convince them that the soft phrases, susceptibility of heart, delicacy of sentiment, and refinement of taste, are almost synonymous with epithets of weakness, and that those beings who are only the objects of pity and that kind of love, which has been termed its sister, will soon become objects of contempt.

3. *Sandford and Merton,* by Thomas Day (London, published in three volumes, 1786–89), is the story of Tommy Merton, a spoiled wealthy child, who is befriended by Harry Sandford, a poor but principled lad. Their instruction by the tutor, Mr. Barlow, often includes moral tales, one of which is mentioned approvingly by Wollstonecraft in Chapter III.
4. "Natural" here suggests that the middle classes had not been corrupted by generations of titles, property, and wealth and were thus, as Addison and Steele also asserted, the most educable class.

Dismissing then those pretty feminine phrases, which the men condescendingly use to soften our slavish dependence, and despising that weak elegancy of mind, exquisite sensibility, and sweet docility of manners, supposed to be the sexual characteristics of the weaker vessel, I wish to shew that elegance is inferior to virtue, that the first object of laudable ambition is to obtain a character as a human being, regardless of the distinction of sex; and that secondary views should be brought to this simple touchstone.

This is a rough sketch of my plan; and should I express my conviction with the energetic emotions that I feel whenever I think of the subject, the dictates of experience and reflection will be felt by some of my readers. Animated by this important object, I shall disdain to cull my phrases or polish my style;—I aim at being useful, and sincerity will render me unaffected; for, wishing rather to persuade by the force of my arguments, than dazzle by the elegance of my language, I shall not waste my time in rounding periods,[5] or in fabricating the turgid bombast of artificial feelings, which, coming from the head, never reach the heart.—I shall be employed about things, not words!—and, anxious to render my sex more respectable members of society, I shall try to avoid that flowery diction which has slided from essays into novels, and from novels into familiar letters and conversation.

These pretty superlatives, dropping glibly from the tongue, vitiate the taste, and create a kind of sickly delicacy that turns away from simple unadorned truth; and a deluge of false sentiments and over-stretched feelings, stifling the natural emotions of the heart, render the domestic pleasures insipid, that ought to sweeten the exercise of those severe duties, which educate a rational and immortal being for a nobler field of action.

The education of women has, of late, been more attended to than formerly; yet they are still reckoned a frivolous sex, and ridiculed or pitied by the writers who endeavour by satire or instruction to improve them. It is acknowledged that they spend many of the first years of their lives in acquiring a smattering of accomplishments; meanwhile strength of body and mind are sacrificed to libertine notions of beauty, to the desire of establishing themselves,—the only way women can rise in the world,—by marriage. And this desire making mere animals of them, when they marry they act as such children may be expected to act:—they dress; they paint, and nickname God's creatures.[6]— Surely these weak beings are only fit for a seraglio!—Can they be expected to govern a family with judgment, or take care of the poor babes whom they bring into the world?

---

5. Formulating balanced sentences.
6. Hamlet speaks to Ophelia: "You jig, you amble, and you lisp, and nickname God's creatures, and make your wantonness your ignorance." *Hamlet* 3.1.150.

If then it can be fairly deduced from the present conduct of the sex, from the prevalent fondness for pleasure which takes place of ambition and those nobler passions that open and enlarge the soul; that the instruction which women have hitherto received has only tended, with the constitution of civil society, to render them insignificant objects of desire—mere propagators of fools!—if it can be proved that in aiming to accomplish them, without cultivating their understandings, they are taken out of their sphere of duties, and made ridiculous and useless when the short-lived bloom of beauty is over,[7] I presume that *rational* men will excuse me for endeavouring to persuade them to become more masculine and respectable.

Indeed the word masculine is only a bugbear: there is little reason to fear that women will acquire too much courage or fortitude; for their apparent inferiority with respect to bodily strength, must render them, in some degree, dependent on men in the various relations of life; but why should it be increased by prejudices that give a sex to virtue, and confound simple truths with sensual reveries?

Women are, in fact, so much degraded by mistaken notions of female excellence, that I do not mean to add a paradox when I assert, that this artificial weakness produces a propensity to tyrannize, and gives birth to cunning, the natural opponent of strength, which leads them to play off those contemptible infantine airs that undermine esteem even whilst they excite desire. Let men become more chaste and modest, and if women do not grow wiser in the same ratio, it will be clear that they have weaker understandings. It seems scarcely necessary to say, that I now speak of the sex in general. Many individuals have more sense than their male relatives; and, as nothing preponderates where there is a constant struggle for an equilibrium, without it has[8] naturally more gravity, some women govern their husbands without degrading themselves, because intellect will always govern.

7. "A lively writer, I cannot recollect his name, asks what business women turned of forty have to do in the world?" [Wollstonecraft's note]. Perhaps Wollstonecraft is referring to a passage in Fanny Burney's popular novel *Evelina* spoken by the licentious Lord Merton: "I don't know what the devil a woman lives for after thirty: she is only in other folks' way" (*Evelina* [London and New York, 1958], p. 253).
8. We would probably say, "without its having."

136

ANONYMOUS

Rights of Woman†

[*By a Lady.*]

TUNE—"*God save America.*"

God save each Female's right,
Show to her ravish'd sight
           Woman is Free;
Let Freedom's voice prevail,
5 And draw aside the vail,
Supreme Effulgence hail,
           Sweet Liberty.

Man boasts the noble cause,
Nor yields supine to laws
10   Tyrants ordain:
Let woman have a share,
Nor yield to slavish fear.
Her equal rights declare,
           And well maintain.

15 Come forth with sense array'd,
Nor ever be dismay'd
           To meet the foe,—
Who with assuming hands
Inflict the iron bands,
20 To obey his rash commands,
           And vainly bow.

O let the sacred fire
Of Freedom's voice inspire
           A Female too:—
25 Man makes the cause his own,
And Fame his acts renown,—
Woman thy fears disown,
           Assert thy due.

Think of the cruel chain,
30 Endure no more the pain
           Of slavery:—
Why should a tyrant bind

† Courtesy of the Historical Society of Pennsylvania, Philadelphia.

A cultivated mind,
By Reason well refin'd,
35   Ordained Free.

Why should a woman lie
In base obscurity,
                    Her talents hid;
Has providence assign'd
40   Her soul to be confin'd,
Is not her gentle mind
                    By virtue led?

With this engaging charm,
Where is so much the harm
45   For her to stand,
To join the grand applause
Of truth and equal laws,
Or lend the noble cause,
                    Her feeble band.

50   Let snarling cynics frown,
Their maxims I disown,
                    Their ways detest:—
By man, your tyrant lord,
Females no more be aw'd,
55   Let Freedom's sacred word,
                    Inspire your breast.

Woman aloud rejoice,
Exalt thy feeble voice
                    In chearful strain;
60   See Wolstoncraft, a friend,
Your injur'd rights defend,
Wisdom her steps attend,
                    The cause maintain.

A voice re-echoing round,
65   with joyful accents sound,
                    "Woman be Free;
Assert the noble claim,
All selfish arts disdain;"
Hark how the note proclaim,
70   "Woman is Free!"

SUSANNA ROWSON

Rights of Woman[†]

Read by Miss M. Warner.

While Patriots on wide Philosophic plan,
Declaim upon the wond'rous Rights of Man;
May I presume to speak? and tho' uncommon,
Stand forth the champion of the Rights of Woman.
5 Nay start not gentle sirs, indeed 'tis true
That Woman has her rights as well as you,
And if she's wise, she will assert them too.
If you'll have patience, and your wrath forbear,
In a few words I'll tell you what they are.
10 You know, when Man in Paradise was plac'd,
(Blest garden with eternal verdure grac'd)
In vain for real happiness he tried,
'Till heaven in compassion, from his side
Taking a rib, fair Eve in all her beauty
15 Appear'd; to Adam proffering her duty,
In terms so gentle, sweet, and void of art,
That e'er he thought on't, Adam lost his heart.
Now pray don't think I mean to take Eve's part.
No, she'd no right, 'twas acting very wrong,
20 To listen to the Serpents flattering tongue;
And from her error, her descendant's claim,
A *right* to be tenacious of their fame;
Knowing how easy she was drawn aside,
We claim a right to call up all our pride.
25 Discretion, honor, sense, to our assistance
And keep insiduous flatterers at a distance,
Next we assert our *right*, for 'tis our pride
In all domestic matters to preside;
And on the mystery of raising pies,
30 Compounding stews, and soups, philosophize;
Study the bush, the vine, or brambles fruit,
Into transparent jellies to transmute;
Whip the light syllabub, all froth and show,
White, sweet, and harmless, like a modern beau.

35 Are fathers, brothers, friends; oppressed with care,
We claim *a right* in all their grief to share;

---

† Courtesy of the Historical Society of Pennsylvania, Philadelphia.

Shed balm upon their pillow of repose,
And strip of thorns life's quickly fading rose;
Augmenting to the utmost of our power,
40   The pleasures of the gay or tranquil hour;
While man abroad for happiness may roam,
'Tis ours to make a paradise at home.

Our known exclusive priviledge of beauty
You all allow: and next in filial duty
45   Pre-eminent we stand. The Grecian dame,
Who daily to her father's prison came,
And while maternal fondness wrung her heart,
Forsook the mother's, for the daughter's part.
The fair Virginia, who could not withstand
50   The stroke of death, from a lov'd father's hand;
But meekly yielded, lest the next sad hour
Should give her to the vile Deceiver's pow'r;
The gentle Ruth, whose heart by friendship tried,
Refus'd to quit forlorn Naomi's side,
55   Boldly asserted, and her *right* approved,
To serve the mother of the man she had lov'd.
As 'tis our right, oh! be it still our praise,
To gild the eve of our dear parents days,
Smooth the dread slope which leads to man's last doom,
60   And decorate with grateful love, their tomb.

Next, 'tis our *right* to watch the sick man's bed,
Bathe the swol'n limb, or bind the aching head.
Present each nauseous draught with tenderness,
And hide the anxious tear we can't repress;
65   On tiptoe glide around the darkened room,
And strive by smiles to dissipate its gloom,
Chear, comfort, help them patient to endure,
And mitigate the ills we cannot cure.
We claim undoubted right the tear to dry,
70   Which gushes from afflictions languid eye;
The widow's heart to chear, her wrongs redress,
And be the mother of the parentless;
Snatch them from vice, or poverty's abode,
And dedicate their orphan lives to God.
75   Not by immuring them in gloomy cells,
Where palsied fear, or supersition dwells,
But teaching them the duties of their station,
Guarding their infant minds against temptation,
Learning them by industry how to be
80   Good useful members of society.

These are our rights: those rights who dares dispute
Let him speak now. No answer, what all mute?
But soft, methinks some discontented fair
Cries, "These are duties, miss." Agreed, they are,
85 But know ye not that Woman's proper sphere
Is the domestic walk? To interfere
With politics, divinity, or law,
As much deserved ridicule would draw
On Woman,—as the learned grave divine,
90 Cooking the soup on which he means to dine;
Or solemn Judge the winders at his knee,
Preparing silks to work embroidery.

Domestic duty! Oh how blest are we!
All women are not so, for we are free
95 Those duties to perform, in varied stations,
While the poor woman of the eastern nations,
Shut from society, hard! hard! their case is
Forbid to walk abroad, or shew their faces;
From every care, from thought and duty free,
100 Life lives on listless inactivity.
Live did I say?—no, I'm mistaken there,
'Tis vegitating, like the gay patterre,
Where tulips, roses, pinks, allure the eye;
Expand their beauties, are admir'd, and die.

105 While summon'd to employ life's active pow'rs
How great, how blest, a privilege is ours:
While laudably employ'd, all men respect us,
Oppress'd, we have fathers, brothers to protect us;
And are we Orphans; Orphans never crave
110 In vain, protection from the good and brave,
Then ever let it be our pride ye fair,
To merit their protection love and care,
With useful knowledge be our heads well stor'd,
Whilst in our hearts we every virtue hoard,
115 These *rights* we may assert, and howe'er common,
These, and these only; are the *Rights of Woman*.

OLIVER GOLDSMITH

An Extract[†]

A lover of Gongora sighs for thick lips; a Chinese lover is poetical in praise of thin: In Circasia, a strait nose is thought most consistent with beauty; cross but a mountain which separates it from the Tartars, and there flat noses, tawny skins, and eyes three inches asunder, are all the fashion. In Persia, and some other countries, a man when he marries chooses to have his bride a maid: in the Philipine Islands, if a bridegroom happens to perceive, on the first night, that he is put off with a virgin, the marriage is declared void to all intents and purposes, and the bride sent back with disgrace.

In some parts of the Eastern world, a woman of beauty properly fed up for sale, often amounts to an 100 crowns: in the kingdom of Loango, ladies of the best fashion are sold for a pig; queens, however sell better, and sometimes amount to a cow. In England rich old men, with great bellies, marry girls of eighteen without the hope of increasing the size of their wives. And oh! shame to women, old maids and rich widows often marry boys, for————but in America we manage these things right, we marry young and for love; or partly for the convenience of the thing.

NANCY F. COTT

Sisterhood[‡]

Friendships between women have existed in all ages and cultures. But the diaries and correspondence of New England women suggest that from the late eighteenth through the mid-nineteenth century they invented a newly self-conscious and idealized concept of female friendship. This ideal became a subject of their conversation, reading, reflection, and writing. And in individual relationships women put their new perceptions into effect, making palpable the bonds of womanhood.

More compassion dwelled "within the soul of Woman" than in the soul of man, assumed the clergymen who urged women into Christian benevolence. In fact, a unified set of assumptions about women's

---

† Oliver Goldsmith, *Miscellaneous Works* 452 v. 2, "Letters from a Citizen of the World, to his Friend in the East."

‡ From *The Bonds of Womanhood* (1977), pp. 160–96. Reprinted by permission of Yale University Press.

qualities of "heart" structured all their exhortations regarding women's religious duties. Unitarian Joseph Buckminster used the most succinct phrasing when he said the female sex was "accustomed to feel, oftener than to reason." Others used more elaborate language. The rector of Boston's Episcopalian Trinity Church praised women for possessing "all the milder virtues of humanity," "those endearing sympathies," "a more exquisite sensibility than men." "The God of heaven has more exquisitively [sic] attuned their souls to love, to sympathy and compassion," said the Reverend Daniel Dana of Newburyport.[1]

In identifying women with "the heart" New England ministers followed the emphasis that had been devised during the eighteenth century, when traditional beliefs in many categories of thought were under attack. The placement of new authority in Nature and Reason engendered a kind of pseudo-scientific cataloguing of differences between the sexes. Rather than alter their belief in the subordination of women, "enlightened" thinkers altered, refined (even amplified) their reasons for it, discovering "natural" and "rational" explanations in place of solely God-given ones. "Deference and submission" was woman's part, declared a mid-eighteenth century American commentary on marriage, because of the "superior Degree of Knowledge and Understanding in the Man." The anonymous author claimed, without need to refer to divine command, that "REALLY Nature and the circumstances of human life, seem to design for Man that Superiority, and to invest him with a directing Power in the more difficult and important Affairs of Life."[2] American writers followed the British in converting cultural artifacts into nature's determinants, composing a litany, much-chanted, of the two sexes' qualifications: men were superior in strength and in all of the rational capacities (discernment, judgment, etc.) but women surpassed them in sensibility, grace, tenderness, imagination, compliance—the qualities of "the heart." In a Boston magazine of 1784 an essayist typically described "matrimonial felicity" as the union of complementary souls: "the man all truth, the woman all tenderness; he possessed of cheerful solidity, she of rational gaiety; acknowledging his superior judgment she complies with all his reasonable desires, whilst he, charmed with such repeated instances of superior love, endeavors to suit his requests to her incli-

1. Joseph Buckminster, "A Sermon Preached before the Members of the Boston Female Asylum, Sept. 1810," hand-copied and bound with other printed sermons to the BFA, p. 8, Boston Public Library Rare Book Room, Boston, Mass. Samuel Parker, Charity to Children, Enforced in a Discourse delivered . . . before the Subscribers to the Boston Female Asylum (Boston, 1803), p. 10; Daniel Dana, A Discourse Delivered . . . before the members of the Female Charitable Society of Newburyport (Newburyport, 1804), p. 16.
2. [Mistakenly attributed to Benjamin Franklin], Reflections on Courtship and Marriage (Philadelphia, 1746), p. 31.

nations." These sex-role distinctions were universally employed in the literate Anglo-American world by the late eighteenth century.[3]

In pleas to improve women's lot as well as in rationalization of their subordinate status, the conventional distinctions held. Concluding her now-famous exchange with her husband about women's rights in the "new code of laws" of 1776, Abigail Adams disarmingly warned him, "we [women] have it in our power not only to free ourselves but to subdue our Masters. . . . 'Charm by accepting, by submitting sway. . . .'" Eliza Southgate, even while arguing for more serious female education, assumed that sprightliness, imagination, and pliability were the characteristics of women's minds, profundity and astuteness the characteristics of men's. An "aged matron" who authored a feminist tract in New Haven, Connecticut, in 1801 did not hesitate to declare that women transcended men in the capacities of tenderness, morality, consideration for others, and willingness to forgive.[4]

Literature of the period gave unprecedented attention to sensibility and "improvement of the heart." Frank L. Mott quotes from the *Christian's, Scholar's and Farmer's Magazine* of 1789 a view representative of American magazine literature: "Everyone boasts of having a heart tender and delicate, and even those who know themselves deficient therein, endeavor to persuade others that they possess these qualities." This valuation of the heart at once seemed to raise esteem of women and to justify no change in their assigned role. Excellence in "heart" was their essential and their sufficient

3. *Gentleman's and Lady's Town and Country Magazine* 1 (Sept. 1784): 194. Dr. John Gregory's *A Father's Legacy to His Daughters*, originally published in London in 1774 but quickly, and repeatedly, republished in America, was significant in establishing the contrast between the "hard and masculine spirit" and feminine "softness and sensibility of heart" (p. 20 in edition of London, 1822). The Reverend James Fordyce's *Sermons to Young Women*, first published in England in 1765, and also widely reprinted on this side of the Atlantic, forcefully advised "those masculine women" who wished to participate in politics, commerce, abstract intellectual pursuits, or exercises of strength, to learn that woman's true "empire" had "the heart for its object," and was "secured by meekness and modesty, by soft attraction and virtuous love" (p. 61 in edition of Philadelphia, 1787). Cf. also the suggestion in a woman's letter to the editor of the Boston magazine above, that the two sexes could use their differing strengths to serve one another, "the men elevating our thoughts, and striving to improve our natural geniuses, which are generally too much curbed in education: while we, by a softness natural to us, should smooth the harshness of their tempers, and alleviate all their misfortunes." "Lucia," *Gentleman's and Lady's Town and Country Magazine* 1 (May 1784); 13. On the consistent employment of sex-role distinctions in eighteenth-century British and America writings, see Mary S. Benson, *Women in Eighteenth-Century America* (New York: Columbia University Press, 1935), pp. 37–39. Frank Luther Mott, in *A History of American Magazines, 1741–1785* (Cambridge: Harvard University Press, 1957), pp. 64–65, remarks that essays and poems entitled "Counsel upon Female Virtues" and "Advice to the Fair" became "sickeningly frequent" during the last quarter of the eighteenth century.
4. Abigail Adams to John Adams, May 7, 1776, in Charles Francis Adams, ed., *Familiar Letters of John Adams and his Wife Abigail Adams, During the Revolution* (New York, 1876), p. 169; Eliza Southgate to Moses Porter, June 1801, quoted in Nancy F. Cott, ed., *Root of Bitterness: Documents of the Social History of American Women* (New York: Dutton, 1972), p. 106; *The Female Advocate*, Written by a Lady (New Haven, 1801), pp. 14–17.

endowment. Another magazine contributor acclaimed women for possessing "all the virtues that are founded in the sensibility of the heart. . . . Pity, the attribute of angels, and friendship, the balm of life, delight to dwell in the female breast. What a forlorn, what a savage creature would man be without the meliorating offices of the gentle sex!"[5]

Prescriptions of women's duties and promises of praise for them, both religious and secular, identified women with qualities of heart. There are occasional explicit references to the reign of this attitude in parents' upbringing of daughters, as well. Mary Lee, in a letter to her sister about the latter's children, distinguished the sons' need for book-learning from a daughter's different requirements: "you wish her heart to be more richly cultivated than the head, and this cannot be under any one's tuition so well as yours. A mother alone can do this, I believe." A wealthy Maine lawyer had clear preferences for his teen-aged daughter's education in 1801: "She has enough [intellect], and too much to make her exactly what I wish her to be. I mean only that her thurst [sic] for reading, will probably obstruct the attainment of those amiable, condescending, and endearing manners, without which a woman is, in my estimation, but a poor piece of furniture." Eulogies of women unfailingly focused on their hearts, regardless of their other substantial achievements. An obituary notice for historian and religious controversialist Hannah Adams declared, "Indeed, literary claims are perhaps among the last that . . . present themselves to the minds of her friends. The virtues and excellences of her character, her blameless life, her sensibility, the warmth of her affections, her sincerity and candor, call forth a flow of feeling that cannot be restrained."[6]

The heart's ruling purpose was to express affections, sympathies, consideration and tenderness toward others—in short, to love. Sarah Connell, at eighteen, believed she understood her own character when she confided to her diary, "To love, is necessary to my very existence." The identification of woman with the heart meant that she was defined in *relation to* other persons. "A true woman's heart never grows cold," wrote the female author of *Girlhood and Womanhood*, "even the most isolated of my sex will ever find some object, upon which her affections will expend themselves." Women's appropriate motivation was "affiliation" rather than "achievement" (to borrow psychologist David McClelland's terms); their cardinal

5. Mott, *History of American Magazines*, pp. 42–43; and p. 141, quoting from "The Female Sex," *Literary Magazine* 15 (Jan. 1805).
6. Mary Jackson Lee to Hannah Jackson Lowell, Feb. 27, 1811, in Frances Rollins Morse, ed., *Henry and Mary Lee: Letters and Journals* (Boston: T. Todd, 1926), p. 100; Daniel Davis to James Freeman, Portland, April 18, 1801, in Katherine Minot Channing, ed., *Minot Family Letters 1773–1871* (Shelborn, Mass., privately printed, 1957), p. 97–98; *Memoir of Miss Hannah Adams, written by Herself, with additional notices, by a friend* (Boston: Gray and Bowen, 1832), p. 106.

goal was to establish positive affective relationships.[7] Didactic works on sex-roles and marriage from the late eighteenth through the nineteenth century named a woman's "stations" in life according to her personal relationships as daughter, sister, loved one, wife, and mother, not in terms of her discrete individual status or aims. An 1837 discussion of woman's character and influence on man furnished baroque detail, evidence of the intensification of rhetoric on the subject at the time:

> As a sister, she soothes the troubled heart, chastens and tempers the wild daring of the hurt mind restless with disappointed pride or fired with ambition. As a mistress, she inspires the nobler sentiment of purer love, and the sober purpose of conquering himself for virtue's sake. As a wife, she consoles him in grief, animates him with hope in despair, restrains him in prosperity, cheers him in poverty and trouble, swells the pulsations of his throbbing breast that beats for honorable distinction, and rewards his toils with the undivided homage of a grateful heart. In the important and endearing character of mother, she watches and directs the various impulses of unfledged genius, instills into the tender and susceptible mind the quickening seeds of virtue, fits us to brave dangers in time of peril, and consecrates to truth and virtue the best affections of our nature.[8]

When they privately assessed their own characters, women used the same standard. "My happiness consists in feeling that I deserve the love of my friends," Sarah Connell went on in her diary, "in studying to make their life pass pleasantly, and in cherishing their esteem. I could not exist in a state of indifference. Nature never formed me for it." Nancy Hyde hoped that the students whom she taught in a female academy in Connecticut would be admired for "the excellent qualities of their hearts, and . . . for diffusing around them that happiness, which is the inseparable concomitant of virtue," as well as for their literary accomplishments. Catherine Sedgwick affirmed, even after she achieved fame as a novelist, that her true happiness derived "from the dearest relations of life," and that her "author existence" was "accidental, extraneous & independent of my inner self." Another woman whose literary aims were not so well rewarded as Sedgwick's consoled herself with the thought that "the heart, that is formed for friendship and affection, is in itself an

7. *Diary of Sarah Connell Ayer*, pp. 92–93 (1809); Mrs. A.J. Graves (pseud.), *Girlhood and Womanhood: or, Sketches of my Schoolmates* (Boston, 1844), p. 210. On achievement and affiliation motivation see David McClelland, ed., *Studies in Motivation* (New York: Appleton-Century-Crofts, 1955), and Richard de Charms and Gerald H. Moeller, "Values Expressed in Children's Readers, 1800–1950," *Journal of Abnormal and Social Psychology* 64 (1962): 136–42.
8. *The Discussion: or the Character, Education, Prerogatives, and Moral Influence of Woman* (Boston, 1837), p. 90.

inexhaustible storehouse of happiness, and the true secret of being happy is to love as many of human kind as possible."[9]

In truth, the identification of women with "the heart" was a gloss on the inequality of the sexes. The need for and inspiration of affiliative motives in women derived from their dependent status. "A woman of fine feelings cannot be insensible that *her constitutional condition is secondary and dependent among men*," said the Reverend Amos Chase of Litchfield, Connecticut, in 1791, "nor can she long want conviction that the sure way to avoid any evil consequence . . . is to yield the front of battle to a hardier sex." If women were considered dependent on others (men) for protection and support, self-preservation itself demanded skill in personal relationships. Rousseau's portrayal in *Emile* (1762) was the most unequivocal and influential formulation of this reasoning in the eighteenth century: "Woman, weak as she is . . . perceives and judges the forces at her disposal to supplement her weakness, and those forces are the passions of man. Her own mechanism is more powerful than ours; she has many levers which may set the human heart in motion. She must find a way to make us desire what she cannot achieve unaided . . . without seeming to have any such purpose." Although a feminist such as Mary Wollstonecraft rejected Rousseau's formulation, and other Anglo-Americans—especially Evangelicals, who wished to efface the erotic content of women's influence over men—diluted it, his central meaning resonated through the decades as a description of women's social options and a prescription for their behavior.[1] To identify women with the heart was to imply that they conducted themselves through life by engaging the affections of others. The cultural metonymy by which the nurturant maternal role stood for the whole of woman's experience further confirmed that "heartfelt" caring was woman's characteristic virtue.

Although it was intended to stress the complementary nature of the two sexes while keeping women subordinate, the identification of women with the heart also implied that they would find truly reciprocal interpersonal relationships only with other women. They would find answering sensibilities only among their own sex. The sex-role

9. *Diary of Sarah Connell Ayer*, June 17, 1809, p. 103; *The Writings of Nancy Maria Hyde of Norwich, Conn.* (Norwich, 1816), pp. 150–51; diary of Catherine Maria Sedgwick, Dec. 17, 1835, Sedgwick Collection, Massachusetts Historical Society, Boston, Mass; Luella Case to Sarah Edgarton, Oct. 18, 1839, Hooker Collection, SL.

1. Amos Chase, *On Female Excellence, or a Discourse in which Good Character in Women is Described* (Litchfield, Conn., 1792), p. 12; Jean-Jacques Rousseau, *Emile*, trans. Barbara Foxley (London: J. M. Dent, 1974; orig. 1762), p. 350. For Mary Wollstonecraft's opinions see *A Vindication of the Rights of Women*, ed. Charles W. Hagelman, Jr. (New York: Norton, 1967; orig. 1792), pp. 76–77, 88, 128–129; and on the Evangelicals' de-eroticizing of women's influence over men, Nancy F. Cott, "In the Bonds of Womanhood: Perspectives on Female Experience and Consciousness in New England, 1780–1830" (Ph.D. diss., Brandeis University, 1974), pp. 230–42.

division of the eighteenth century impelled women toward friendship and sisterhood with one another for two corollary reasons. Women characterized by "heart" presumably would seek equivalent sympathies in their friends. And just as women were viewed as inferior to men in rationality, men could not be expected to respond in kind to women's feelings. "Who but a woman can know the heart of a woman?" Daniel Dana put the question in 1804.[2] In their actual friendships women answered him: no one.

One of the few times Esther Edwards Burr, daughter and wife of clergymen, lost her temper so far as to argue with a young minister, was in response to his scorn of women's capacity for friendship. She had a "smart combat" with Mr. Ewing, a tutor at the College of New Jersey, of which Aaron Burr was president, in April 1757. Ewing had criticized a woman friend of hers for being "full of talk about Friendship & Society & Such Stuff" and declared that women should talk about "things that they understood, he did not think women knew what Friendship was, they were hardly capable of anything so cool and rational as friendship." This outraged Esther Burr. Although she had previously admired Ewing, she "retorted Several Severe things upon him before he had time to Speak again" and in an hour of dispute "talked him quite Silent."[3]

Esther Burr had good reason to defend the concept and reality of female friendship. The document that records her argument with Ewing was a letter in journal format to the "Fidelia" she loved, Sarah Prince, who lived in Boston. The two friends had begun to write journals for one another when Esther moved with her husband Aaron Burr from New England to New Jersey. Both women had grown up in large, patriarchal, ministers' families with numerous siblings and relatives. Both married, apparently happily. Yet as Burr's letter-journal reveals, the two considered their ties of friendship as important as, if not more important than, their other ties. "I esteem you one of the best, and in Some respects nerer [sic] than any Sister I have," wrote Burr. "I have not one sister I can write so freely to as to you the sister of my heart."[4]

2. Dana, A Discourse Delivered, p. 18.
3. Journal of Esther Edwards Burr, April 12, 1757, Beinecke Rare Book Library, Yale University. Esther Burr was a daughter of the Reverend Jonathan Edwards of Northampton. I am grateful to Laurie Crumpacker for allowing me to use the typescript of the journal that she and Carol Karlsen, a graduate student of Yale University, had prepared. See also Laurie Crumpacker, "The Journal of Esther Burr addressed to Miss Prince of Boston" (Ph.D. diss., Boston University, 1976).
4. Esther Edwards Burr journal, Oct. 11, 1754; see also April 22, 1756, and passim. In "Two 'Kindred Spirits': Sorority and Family in New England, 1839–1845," New England Quarterly 36 (1963): 23–41, a pioneer recognition of the importance of female friendships in nineteenth-century society, Christopher Lasch and William R. Taylor argued, with emphasis that now seems mistaken, that a "sisterhood of sensibility" arose because of the decline of the large patriarchal family, an increase in geographical mobility, and the desire of women to affirm that they were purer than men.

Burr's relationship with Sarah Prince and her views of the friendship possible between women were symbiotic and mutually intensi-
fying, and compelled her to differ with Ewing. She often dwelled on
the theme of friendship in her letter-journal, alluding to the ideal
while savoring her real (though long-distance) feeling for her "Fidelia." The sending and receipt of journals, together with her faith in
the friendship, steadied her in difficult and lonely circumstances.
The ties of friendship were sacred, Esther Burr believed, and "the
spirit of, & relish for, true friendship" were "God-like." "When I speak
of the *world*, & the things that are in the World, I don't mean friends,"
she wrote, "for *friendship* does not belong to the *world, true friendship*
is first inkindled by a Spark from Heaven."[5]

The Edwardsean canon of the religious affections supplied Esther
Burr with language in which to express her feelings for Sarah Prince.
"Heart," "soul," and "spirit" were involved in what she saw as true
friendship. When Jonathan Edwards had revivified Puritanism as a
"religion of the heart," he made the religious experience of woman
(his wife, Sarah Pierrepont Edwards) the prototype for all conversion.[6] The New Light of the 1740s fostered female religious friendships, by illuminating the "heart," at the same time that it induced
men to approve and share similar religious affections.

Another enduring eighteenth-century friendship, between Susanna
Anthony and Sarah Osborn of Newport, Rhode Island, also illustrates that trend. Both of these women were deeply affected by the
revival preaching of the 1740s Awakening, and both subsequently
became celebrated for piety. They joined in a friendship and correspondence that lasted for four decades. Susanna Anthony's words
suggest the quality of their attachment: "Into your breast, I have
often poured out the joys and sorrows of my soul; and as often found
compassion, tenderness, and sympathy there. . . . O, my dear, my
bosom-friend, I feel my love to you to be without dissimulation,
therefore wish you the same strength and consolation, with my own
soul."[7] Such feelings doubly contradicted the line of argument that
tutor Ewing took against Esther Burr, that women were not capable
of anything so "cool and rational" as friendship. Friendship in the

5. Esther Edwards Burr journal, Jan. 23, 1756, Feb. 15, 1755.
6. See Jonathan Edwards, "Some Thoughts Concerning the Present Revival of Religion in
New England," in *The Works of Jonathan Edwards*, Vol. 4, *The Great Awakening*, ed.
Clarence C. Goen (New Haven: Yale University Press, 1972), esp. part 1, section 5. I am
sincerely indebted to Laurie Crumpacker (see note 12) for a dialogue that has enriched
my knowledge of the Edwards family, Jonathan Edward's conception of the religious
affections, and the connection of the latter with sisterhood in the eighteenth century.
7. *Familiar Letters written by Mrs. Sarah Osborn and Miss Susanna Anthony* (Newport,
R.I.: Mercury Office, 1807), pp. 27, 60. See Samuel Hopkins, ed., *Memoirs of the Life
of Mrs. Sarah Osborn* (Worcester, Mass., 1799), and Hopkins, ed., *The Life and Character of Miss Susanna Anthony . . . consisting chiefly in extracts from her writings* (2d ed.,
Portland, Me., 1810).

cause of Christ was not restricted to the cool and rational but encom-
passed the religious affections, and for women to exercise these
affections was wholly "in character." (Ewing held a minority view in
the dispute, in fact; the other gentleman present sided with Esther
Burr.)

The eighteenth-century emphasis on the religious affections even
created new possibilities for women's religious leadership. Sarah
Osborn, who began in the 1740s to guide a group of young women in
prayer, by the 1760s led scores of "hopeful converts" of many ages,
two races, and both sexes in devotions at her home in Newport. The
effect of the religion of the heart on personal relations was not limited to women, of course. If Sarah Osborn's friendship with Susanna
Anthony stemmed from their religious feelings—Anthony hoped that
their "highest ambition" would be "to join hand in hand, to promote
the cause and interest of our infinitely worthy Redeemer"—so too did
Osborn's friendship with the Reverend Joseph Fish, a mentor of hers,
or Aaron Burr's friendship with Sarah Prince.[8] Both men and women
with religious aims wished to be "tender-hearted." Both men and
women used the same language in recounting their religious experiences in the first Great Awakening; the sex of the writer is not apparent in printed narratives of conversions.[9]

The religion of the heart contributed a language appropriate to,
and an ideal of, female friendship, but alone it did not create "sisters
of the heart." The sisterhood between Esther Burr and Sarah Prince,
certainly, also drew on their concerns for sexual and individual
defense and integrity. Burr once had to resist her temptation to confide in a mutual friend about the journal-letter correspondence
because, she wrote, "I was affraid [sic] she would tell her Man of it,
& *he* knows so much better about matters than *She* that he would
Sertainly make some Ill-natured remarks or other, & So these *Hes*
[sic] shall know nothing about our affairs *untill they are grown as
wise as you & I are*."[1] Her account disclosed certain of her assumptions (confirmed elsewhere in the journal) respecting the marital
relationship, friendship between women, and the relative virtues of
the two. Esther Burr trusted, dearly loved, and revered her husband.
She expected a husband and wife to sustain the "nearest and dearest
Relation." Yet she also recognized that a husband was the "head &
Governor" of his wife. This closest of relations between a man and a

---

8. *Familiar Letters*, p. 60. See also Mary Beth Norton, "'My Resting Reaping Times':
   Sarah Osborn's Defense of Her "Unfeminine" Activities, 1767," *Signs: A Journal of
   Women in Culture and Society*, 1977.
9. This is one of the conclusions of Barbara Leslie Eaton's comparative study of the First
   and the Second Great Awakenings, "Women, Religion and the Family: Revivalism as
   an Indicator of Social Change in Early New England" (Ph.D. diss., University of California, Berkeley, 1974).
1. Esther Edwards Burr journal, Jan. 15, 1756.

woman made the woman subordinate. Without Ewing's contribution, Esther Burr knew that men generally slighted women's intellects and denied knowledge to them, and that husbands could enforce intolerable demands on their wives—although she exempted Aaron Burr from accusation on these counts.[2] Friendships between women, on the contrary, required no such subordination or disparagement of women's capacities.

Esther Burr's exceptional friendship with her Fidelia struck a keynote for subsequent developments. The culture of sensibility of the late eighteenth century proved fertile for female friendships, allowing, in effect, a secular replacement for the religion of the heart which was most in evidence among young women, especially those who read sentimental literature. When Hannah Adams's father lost his fortune during the Revolutionary war, the daughter consoled herself in a circle of "a few dear friends (for novels had taught me to be very romantic,) who were chiefly in indigent circumstances, and like myself had imbibed a taste for reading. . . . Our mutual love of literature, want of fortune, and indifference to the society of those whose minds were wholly uncultivated, served to cement a union between us." Persons who held and acted upon "the highest ideas of friendship," as Adams saw it, "considered their earthly happiness as dependent upon the life of one beloved object, on whose judgment they relied, and in whom they found comfort and support in every difficulty and affliction. . . ."[3]

The diaries and letters of young women of the late eighteenth century (particularly those of the well-to-do, which are the most accessible documents for that period) record extensive social life in which both sexes shared, but also suggest a pattern of reliance on female friendship for emotional expression and security. While Patty Rogers of Exeter, New Hampshire, fluttered with concern over male suitors, she derived her deepest pleasure from her relation to a married woman friend. Friendships between Hannah Emery of Exeter and Mary Carter of Newburyport, and between Susan Kittredge of Andover and Eliza Waite of Salem, around 1790, showed similar division of feelings. The friends engaged in gossip about suitors and assemblies, but made their reciprocal affections, their longings to see one another, and their feelings of loss at parting their major themes. Sarah Connell yearned and sighed "for the presence of *mes chere amies*, Lydia and Emily," when her family moved from Newburyport to Concord, New Hampshire, in 1809, and she immediately pursued similar attachments. After a social call from two female neighbors, she fell into a reverie about the younger of them (who seemed "inter-

2. Esther Edwards Burr journal, Oct. 21, 1756 (quotation); see also April 15, 1755, Dec. 20, 1755, April 12, 1757.
3. *Memoir of Miss Hannah Adams*, pp. 7, 18.

esting, sensible, and cheerful"), and imagined how they would love one another and "ramble" together. Not long after, she fell "quite in love with" a young married woman upon their first meeting. Her greatest satisfaction at this time came from "receiving letters from [her] female friends."[4]

To the point here, in her *Strictures on the Modern System of Female Education* (1799) Hannah More warned against "imprudent and violent friendships" and elaborate correspondences between young women, because she felt that they produced affectation and mutual flattery. In one aspect, epistolary friendships between young women in this period simply defined a mode of discourse. Susan Kittredge began one of her letters to Eliza Waite with the hope that her friend would be "prepared with indulgent candour to listen," explaining that "these lines so expressive of my feelings I have borrow'd from a Magazine. I delight to see flow from another pen the sensations I feel but am unable to express." In another aspect, they showed young women's motive to seek true companions among their own sex. "If I might find one real female friend I would be satisfied," was the thought of newly-wed Peggy Dow when she embarked on an ocean voyage with her husband in 1806.[5]

Eunice Callender of Boston carried on a model epistolary friendship with her country cousin, Sally Ripley of Greenfield, at the beginning of the eighteenth century. In youth the two lived at each other's houses on extended visits, during which they spent all their time together, shared confidences, and even carved their names on "two united trees." Callender called her cousin "the dearest Friend of my heart." She prized their correspondence because it allowed her to "breathe forth the sentiments of my soul," she wrote Ripley. "Oh could you see with what rapture . . . all your epistles are open'd by me . . . then would you acknowledge that *my* Friendship at least equals your own, and yours I believe is as true as pure a flame as ever warmed the breast of any human Creature." Callender weighed their own against the abstract possibility of true friendship and found it not wanting; she had "heard of certain people continuing their most fervent affections for each other until the latest hour of their existence, & such I trust will be ours firm & united to the last."

4. Diary of Patty [or Polly] Rogers, 1785, American Antiquarian Society; correspondence between Hannah Emery (Abbott) and Mary Carter, 1787–91, Cutts Family Manuscripts, EI; correspondence of Eliza Waite and Susan Kittredge, 1786–91, James Duncan Phillips Library, Essex Institute, Salem, Mass.; *Diary of Sarah Connell Ayer,* pp. 92–93, 114, 122. For other evidence of the social life of young women in the late eighteenth century, see diary of Jerusha Leonard, 1791–92, Historic Deerfield Library, Deerfield Mass.; and "Diary of Elizabeth Porter Phelps, 1763–1805," ed. Thomas Eliot Andrews, *NEHGR* 18–22 (1964–68).
5. Hannah More, *Strictures on the Modern System of Female Education* (9th ed., London, 1801), 1:256–57; Susan Kittredge to Betsy Waite, March 24, 1792, EI; Peggy Dow, "Vicissitudes, or the Journey of Life," in Lorenzo Dow, *History of Cosmopolite* (Cincinnati, 1859), p. 613.

In fact, their friendship and correspondence lasted for at least three decades, through Ripley's marriage and widowhood. But, during young womanhood at least, Ripley found an even more intimate friend in Rachel Willard of Greenfield. These two were childhood playmates, and at school "pursued the same studies & the same recreations." They wrote to each other when they were apart, and "each in the friendly bosom of the other, could repose their secret thoughts, in perfect confidence." Upon Willard's sudden death very shortly after her marriage, in 1808, Ripley appeared inconsolable; she could hardly believe that she would "no more behold her lovd [sic] countenance, meeting with the smile of welcome, no more hear her soft voice . . . speaking from the feelings of her heart; . . . to me her loss seems irreparable, I have not a friend on earth, to who [sic] I could so freely communicate my feelings, at any time."[6] Attesting to the strength of their attachment, Ripley gave the name Rachel Willard to her first child, born in 1813.

Sally Ripley's and Rachel Willard's shared education at Dorchester Female Academy added a dimension to their friendship. Willard had attended first, in the summer of 1803, and in the following summer (when Ripley was nineteen) both of them enrolled. Their experience as well as numerous others' suggests that academies for girls propagated friendships better than almost any other institution. A few days after Ripley arrived at the academy she noted, "A number of the Young Ladies formed themselves into a society to be called 'the Band of Sisters.' . . . We . . . are all to live in perfect harmony & friendship & no young Lady belonging to the Society is to speak unkindly to a Sister." Apparently, both the students' parents and their teachers encouraged the sisterly impulse. The aunt and guardian of orphan Mehitable May Dawes wrote to her at school in 1810, when she was fourteen, "be a good girl, and make the utmost use of this very important period of your life. . . . Endeavour to make your Self beloved by your young associates, and be above the little tattle of a boarding school." Lydia Huntley advised the pupils at her academy in Hartford in the 1810s to "consider yourselves as a little band of sisters united for a time in one family with frequent opportunities of retarding or advancing each others enjoyment." Another headmistress early in the century tried, as a former student recalled, "to make us feel that we were a band of sisters, and that in the eye of God we were all equals."[7]

6. Eunice Callender to Sarah Ripley, May 21, 1803, May 26, 1810, Sept. 8, [1808], Oct. 19, 1808, Stearns Collection, Schlesinger Library, Radcliffe College, Cambridge, Mass.; diary of Sarah Ripley Stearns, Nov. 12, 1808, Stearns Collection, SL.
7. Sarah Ripley (Stearns) diary, June 14, 1803, Sept. 19, 1803, May 19, 1804. A. Prescott, Boston, to Mehitable May Dawes, Oct. 7, 1810, May-Goddard Collection, SL; Lydia Huntley, "Letters to the young ladies under her care, Copied by Frances Ann Brace, August 25, 1814," Connecticut Historical Society, Hartford, Conn.; Graves, *Girlhood and Womanhood*, p. 15.

The philosophy of female education that triumphed by 1820 in New England inclined women to see their destiny as a shared one and to look to one another for similar sensibilities and moral support. By providing both convenient circumstances and a justifying ideology, academies promoted sisterhood among women. Even though most individuals spent only a few months at an academy at a time (perhaps only a few months altogether) the experience attuned them to female friendship with a force out of proportion to its duration. Sally Ripley regretted departing from Dorchester since she felt "to many of the young Ladies . . . a degree of attachment which I flatter myself is reciprocal." Similarly, Mary Endicott of Danvers, Massachusetts, hated to be "parted from my dear associates that I have daily conversed with" when she ended a term of school in 1818. "The union which subsisted among us [school companions] bound our hearts with no feeble ties," Sophronia Grout also reflected, after a short period of education in 1822. "Never was a separation so painful I think to any of us as at the close of this school."[8]

When academy education was combined with religious revival the impulse toward female friendship was doubly forceful. The letters surviving from a circle of young women who went to an academy in Hartford, Connecticut, together and shared revival experience there around 1812 are revealing. They corresponded for years after they parted—past the time when several of them married—and continued to reiterate their friendship, their nostalgia for the past, their desires to see one another, and their fears of being forgotten. Not long after their separation Rebeccah Root wrote to Weltha Brown about her depression of spirits and her longing to see their common friend Harriet Whiting, adding, "since our first acquaintance I have felt more at liberty in her company could converse with her more freely than with anyone else, here is Mama but I cannot say any thing to her although the best of Mothers, My sisters feel differently from me therefore cannot participate in my feelings. I often think if I could see you or Harriet a few moments I should feel much more contented." If Brown's correspondence slackened, Root became anxious and fearful that she no longer cared. "My heart often sunk [sic] within me," she confessed, "when I reflected on former joys . . . and past scenes in which we had alike engaged, and professions of friendship which each from each received, and the thought unpleasant as it was often intruded, that Weltha had forgotten her friend; . . . but I would drive it from me as injurious to the character of that friend whom I so dearly love." Another one of this circle acknowledged how female revival meetings had cemented their friendships when she

8. Sarah Ripley diary, Sept. 8, 1804; diary of Mary Endicott, March 3, 1818, EI; diary of Sophronia Grout, May 1822, Pocumtuck Valley Memorial Association Library Collections, HD.

wrote to Weltha Brown, after she moved from Hartford, "I regret very much that we do not have conferences oftener here, they serve to keep the affections warm and make us friendly to each other as well as animated in the glorious cause of Christ."[9]

Intense attachments between women were often rooted in shared or similar experiences of conversion to Christianity. More inclusive than the female academy in its social range, the church was even more instrumental, overall, in shaping female friendships. Two young women who had made public professions of faith along with her at the First Church in Boston in 1796 became Abigail Brackett's best friends. "How much more valuable the friendship founded on Religion," the latter mused in 1802, "—hearts seem as it were to incorporate and become one and indivisible—the deciples [sic] of Jesus are engaged in one common cause—have the same enemies to encounter & the same gracious portions to obtain—they feel bound by sacred obligations to seek others good." Similar feelings lay behind Nancy Meriam's confidence to a friend, "you, Irene, well know my heart, to you I have never been afraid to express my sentiments without reserve, and with you have enjoyed many a pleasing hour of reciprocal friendship. I say reciprocal, I believe it so, and that our friendship is built on a sure foundation Jesus Christ himself being the chief cornerstone." Because they had both professed faith, she did not fear that death would part them. Friends could hope that they would one day be united forever in Heaven. Sophronia Grout, a minister's daughter, was saddened to discover that a friend who had "professed to be on the Lords side on the same day" had to move away. "Her heart is united to mine with the strongest ties," she testified, "Many sweet hours have I spent walking the field and viewing the works of the Almighty and conversing upon the best of subjects with my Julia. . . ." She sustained hope that God would allow them to meet "where we never shall again be parted."[1]

During the Second Great Awakening, religious sisterhood was invested with a self-consciousness about gender that had been absent from a friendship of the earlier revival such as Susanna Anthony's with Sarah Osborn. Women and men narrated their conversion expe-

9. Rebeccah Root to Weltha Brown, Aug. 7, 1815, and 1817 (date uncertain); Almira Eaton, Monson, to Weltha Brown, Hartford, May 7, 1815, Hooker Collection, SL. The Weltha Brown Correspondence in the Hooker Collection includes letters of Almira Eaton, Rebeccah Root (Buell), Eliza Perkins (Gunnell), C. Lloyd, Mary Cogswell, Marcia Hall, and Lucia Hall.
1. Journal of Abigail Brackett Lyman, Oct. 13, 1802, in Helen Roelker Kessler, "The Worlds of Abigail Brackett Lyman" (Master's thesis, Tufts University, 1976), appendix A; see also chap. 1, p. 16, and journal entries of Feb. 3, and 22, March 12 and 30, 1800; Nancy Meriam, Charlton, Mass., to Irene Hartwell, Oxford, Mass., April 16, 1813, Meriam Collection, Worcester Historical Society, Worcester, Mass.; diary of Sophronia Grout, June 15, 1816.

riences in the Second Great Awakening in two different "dialects," in contrast to the case a century earlier, when converts' language was indistinguishable by sex.[2] Because of the sex-segregated forms it took, the religious activism of the revivals accentuated women's conscious-ness of sexual differentiation and of their own sisterhood. Another case in point occurred in the Female Temperance Society of West Bradford, Massachusetts. It was founded by fifteen women who had organized in 1825 for religious self-improvement but then trans-formed their group into a teetotalers society, with a pledge to abstain from alcohol and not to serve it to guests. They gained adherents dur-ing the next five years as they pursued the twofold aim of abstinence and religious conversion among their number. Rather than attempt-ing to reduce intemperance in general, they focused on eliminating *women's* drinking. They took the direct step of sending to women who made "too free use" of liquor a written "remonstrance," which warned of consequences such as illness, loss of reputation, suicidal passion, or an eternity in hell, and then appealed on grounds of female soli-darity: "Do regard your reputation, your influence, the happiness and respectability of your friends—regard the honor and dignity of the female sex."[3]

If Christian sisterhood promised to confute death, in eternity, it also intended to cross earthly barriers of wealth and station. After her conversion Nancy Thompson found her spirits buoyed up by conversations with the hired girl in her family, whom she described as her inferior in "talents, education and circumstances"—"and yet a Christian." Rachel Willard Stearns's religious convictions came to her aid when she had to earn her living, after her father's death. "I thank the Lord for many things," she wrote in her diary in 1835, "first that he has humbled my proud heart, and made me willing to go to Mr Humes, and sew for a girl who once lived as a maid in my grandfather's family, she is now a devoted Christian, and I try to be so, also, and I love her dearly."[4] Ministers stressed, in sponsoring women's charitable and evangelical organizations, that since women were united by their "preeminent susceptibility of heart" and their "correspondent obligations," only they could understand adequately and relieve the needs of members of their sex. "To whom shall the friendless orphan girl repair," asked Daniel Dana, "but to one who knows the feelings, the exigencies, the distresses, the dangers of the sex, and in whom she may hope to find the care and sensibilities of a mother indeed?" Middle-class and upper-class women's founding of

2. See Easton, "Women, Religion and the Family," esp. pp. 12–22, 101–02, 164–74.
3. Record Book of the Female Temperance Society, West Bradford, Mass., 1829–34, EI.
4. "A Short Sketch of the Life of Nancy Thomson [sic]," autobiographical fragment in the diary of Nancy Thompson (Hunt), CHS; diary of Rachel Willard Stearns, Oct. 19, 1835, Stearns Collection, SL.

institutions to aid indigent widows and female orphans involved the idea that women's shared characteristics—epitomized in "heart"—belittled the economic differences among them.[5]

Aware of their alliance on the basis of sex, women friends elicited a new intensity of feeling which, in turn, shaped their concept of friendship. Eliza Chaplin of Salem and Laura Lovell of Bridgewater, Massachusetts, shared a remarkable attachment stretching from 1819, when they were both single, living with parents and siblings and trying to earn support by teaching and handiwork, to 1869, thirty-seven years after Eliza Chaplin's marriage. They were able to visit each other only infrequently. Chaplin indicated the significance of their correspondence as she wrote, in 1820, "when a letter from you was announced, my dear friend, the letter which I had so long, but vainly expected, a tremour pervaded my whole frame. Surely, famishing indigence could scarcely hail food with more delight. I loosed the seal & read its contents with the same eagerness that we may suppose such an individual to partake of a meal." She claimed that she would "have pined like the lover, doomed to a separation from his mistress" without the letters that filled in between their visits, apologizing half-seriously, "if this is romance, romance imparts the most exquisite delight. And never can I desire to be divested of that which savors so much of heaven."[6]

5. Dana, A Discourse Delivered, p. 18 (quotations). Ministers supported these charitable institutions, which were the first to be founded by women, because they feared that the female sex posed a unique threat, as it promised a unique benefit, to society. The Reverend Samuel Stillman, in A Discourse Delivered before the Members of the Boston Female Asylum (Boston, 1801), p. 11, approved that institution's aim to house female orphans because "Such is the delicacy and importance of the female character—such is its influence on society, that it ought to be removed, especially in early life, as far as possible from the very appearance of evil." Thaddeus Harris, in A Discourse, Preached before the Members of the Boston Female Asylum (Boston, 1813), p. 9, was more direct about the threat embodied in female orphans: "there is the utmost reason to apprehend that, instead of being, as their sex should be, the ornament and charm, they will become the scorn and pest of society." The female charitable societies' object, to aid widows and female orphans, itself singled out women from the rest of the population, admitting that women were less competent in self-help than men (and implying, conversely, that able-bodied men who did not succeed at self-help did not deserve any particular sympathy). See Cott, "In the Bonds," pp. 273–80, on these charitable societies.
6. Eliza Chaplin (Nelson), Salem, to Laura Lovell, Bridgewater, Mass., July 27, 1820, June 24, 1821, EI.
   In her path-breaking article, "The Female World of Love and Ritual: Relations between Women in Nineteenth-Century America," Signs: A Journal of Women in Culture and Society 1 (1975):1–29, Carroll Smith-Rosenberg has dealt explicitly with what appears, to twentieth-century minds, to be the paradox of these nineteenth-century friendships, that they were "both sensual and platonic" (p. 4). She argues persuasively that "the twentieth-century tendency to view human love and sexuality within a dichotomized universe of deviance and normality, genitality and platonic love, is alien to the emotions and attitudes of the nineteenth century and fundamentally distorts the nature of these women's emotional interaction" (p. 8), and proposes that in order to fathom nineteenth-century society we must "view sexual and emotional impulses as part of a continuum or spectrum of affect gradations strongly effected [sic] by cultural norms and arrangements, a continuum influenced in part by observed and thus learned behavior" (pp. 28–29). Her perspective is crucial to the understanding of nineteenth-century women's history. I regard the nature and meaning of female friendships as changing

The subject of friendship occupied much of their letters. "Your observation respecting disinterested friendship is certainly very just—" Eliza Chaplin wrote, "my heart fully subscribes to it—for I have met but with a few instances to which I could apply so sacred a name. It cannot be given to those vague unions which are formed only [to] pass away a tedious hour—for in such connexions the sentiments of the heart have no share." Their own friendship was founded on "reciprocal views and feelings." Every one of Laura Lovell's sentiments "[met] with a respond in my heart," Chaplin said. For the mutuality of their views their sex was an implicitly necessary basis, though not a sufficient one. Chaplin often compared Lovell to other women in order to praise her. But their friendship was strongly shaped by preconceptions such as Chaplin revealed in writing that she had "seldom met with individuals of the opposite sex, who have appeared feelingly alive to the beauties of nature." When Lovell wrote about her rejection of a suitor, Chaplin replied that she, too, had never given her heart to an "individual of the other sex"; and added, "*you* my friend possess it—or possess it in common with my father's family." After a period of neglecting her correspondence, Chaplin assured Lovell that she was "not forgotten by that friend who so long has loved you. . . . I always love you, Laura. . . . To you I unfold my whole heart, without apology."[7]

A similar relationship between Luella Case and Sarah Edgarton in the 1830s and 40s originated in their common Universalist religion and literary ambitions. The religious grounding of their friendship was evident in Sarah Edgarton's assurance to her friend that "I love you far too well ever to breathe a word to you that comes not from the soul," and in her comforting hope that their "earthly love" would attain permanence when they ascended to the "heavenly coterie." Luella Case, who was ten years older and of a "darker" cast of mind, hesitated to affirm the reality of true friendship. "I have looked upon friendship, as one of those lovely dreams never meant to be realized on earth, one of the beautiful impossibilities of life, but to be known in the world beyond the grave . . . ," she wrote. "Friendship is something more to be worshipped as an ideal good, than a real, and possible thing, something that *may be*, rather than something *that is*." Yet she verged on admitting that the relationship with Sarah Edgarton fulfilled her criteria; after discovering a poem that the younger woman had written to her, she replied, "words seem

---

rather than stable from the mid-eighteenth through the nineteenth century, however, as I question the "middle-class" basis of her eighteenth-century sources and differ from her assessment of how "generic and unself-conscious" (p. 9), and how far rooted in mother-daughter rather than in peer relationships, such friendships continued to be.

7. Eliza Chaplin to Laura Lovell, April 18, 1819, June 24, 1821, March 13, 1828, June 24, 1821, April 17, 1827.

inadequate to express the sense I feel of your—what shall I say, *friendship?* no, I will rather call it affection, for you know I confessed as one of my weaknesses, an inordinate desire *to be loved.*" Although Luella Case was married and worked off and on with her husband (a journalist and publisher), her model for friendship was female. As a visit from Sarah Edgarton ended, she felt "most lonely," having "no gentle voice to talk with, or read to me, no sweet, beaming, countenance to echo the feelings expressed, none of that gentlest of all sympathies, that of a pure, and true-hearted female. . . ."[8]

What had appeared in the latter part of the eighteenth century in the romantic effusions of adolescent (and mostly upper-class) girls became, by the early part of the nineteenth century, the common experience of middle-class women, youthful or not. In the vast growth of voluntary associations this emotional phenomenon had an institutional expression. "Heart"-felt friendship between women became a way of life.[9]

The character of women's friendships resulted partially from general cultural valuation of "the heart" and emphasis on women's superiority in sensibility. At the same time, the "introspective revolution" broadened ideas about the purpose and content of friendship.[1] Only when individuals recognized and dwelled on private feelings, and deemed them worthy of communication to others, would one seek an intimate to whom she could "unfold her whole heart." In the religious sphere, revivalism had similar kinds of impact, both actual and rhetorical, because it solicited the religious affections and required the individual to search her heart. Revivalism provided unimpeachable justification and circumstances for mutual outpourings of feeling and also identified the flow of affections with the soul, with Heaven, with nonworldly and "disinterested" temperament: exactly the prerogatives of woman's sphere. Non-evangelical Christians, too, adopted the concept that friendship was sacred and separate from "the world." "If you were not my Sister my dear Frances—your friendship—the friendship of a heart so ardent & warm as yours

8. Sarah Edgarton to Luella Case, 1838 or 1839, quoted in A.D. Mayo, ed., *Selections from the Writings of Mrs. Sarah C. Edgarton Mayo, with a Memoir* (Boston, 1850), pp. 32–33; Sarah Edgarton to Luella Case, Jan. 8, 1840; Luella Case, Lowell, Mass., to Sarah Edgarton, Shirley, Mass., Oct. 18, 1839; Luella Case to Sarah Edgarton, "Thursday Morning"; Luella Case, Lowell, to Sarah Edgarton, Nov. 30 [before 1842]; all in Hooker Collection, SL. The article by Lasch and Taylor cited in note 4 is based on the Case-Edgarton correspondence.
9. In "The Female World of Love and Ritual" Carroll Smith-Rosenberg describes in detail the way of life founded on female friendships.
1. Fred Weinstein and Gerald M. Platt, in *The Wish To Be Free: Society, Psyche, and Value Change* (Berkeley: University of California Press, 1969), use the quoted phrase to characterize what is more typically called Romanticism in the late eighteenth and early nineteenth centuries.

would amount to more than all the *world* has ever offered to me," Unitarian Catherine Sedgwick wrote in a solacing letter.[2] The very use of the word *friend* altered. In the eighteenth century women often used "my friends" to refer to their kin. As time went on, the verbal distinction between family members and unrelated friends became clearer. Of the members of the family only the husband continued to be called a "friend," the "nearest" or "best" friend, or "friend and companion."[3] Thus language released "friendship" from blood ties so that it existed purely in elective relationships and became subject to idealization.

Even more important, female friendships assumed a new value in women's lives in this era because relations between *equals*—"peer relationships"—were superseding *hierarchical* relationships as the desired norms of human interaction. In the seventeenth century an ideal of orderly, reciprocal relations between acknowledged superiors and inferiors had guided politics, vocations, and family roles (though perhaps imperfectly). During the eighteenth century it was increasingly eroded. By the post-Revolutionary years the moral justification behind apprentices' service to masters, the people's deference to governors—even children's obedience to parents—was undermined by newer ideals of individual achievement, equal representation, and popular rights. Both the libertarian rhetoric of the American Revolution and the renewed emphasis on the equality of persons before Christ in the religious revivals hastened this process. Myriad voluntary associations in the young republic reaffirmed the decline of deference and its replacement by an activist conception of a polity of peers.[4]

Women's frequent interest in the ideal of friendship and especially in the mutuality of friends' views was a key indication that the peer relationship had arrived (so to speak) as a cultural *desideratum*. Women would value peer relationships among their own sex all the

2. Catherine Sedgwick to [her sister] Frances Watson, March 9, 1831, Sedgwick Collection, Massachusetts Historical Society.
3. The latest usage of "friend" to mean "kin" cited in the *Oxford English Dictionary* is in 1721.
4. On seventeenth-century norms, see Edmund S. Morgan, *The Puritan Family* (rev. ed., New York: Harper Torchbooks, 1966); for changes during the eighteenth-century, especially the later part, see Daniel Scott Smith, "Parental Power and Marriage Patterns—An Analysis of Historical Trends in Hingham, Massachusetts," *Journal of Marriage and the Family* 35 (1973):419–28; Daniel Scott Smith and Michael Hindus, "Premarital Pregnancy in America, 1640–1966," *JIH* 6 (1975):537–71; Philip J. Greven, Jr., *Four Generations* (Ithaca: Cornell University Press, 1970); Edward Burrows and Michael Wallace, "The American Revolution: The Ideology and Psychology of National Liberation," *Perspectives in American History* (1972), pp. 167–302; David Hackett Fischer, "America: A Social History, Vol. 1, The Main Lines of the Subject 1650–1975," unpublished MS draft, 1974, chap. 6, pp. 19–28; Richard D. Brown, "Modernization and the Modern Personality in Early America, 1600–1865," *JIH* 2 (1972):201–28, and "The Emergence of Voluntary Associations in Massachusetts, 1760–1830," *Journal of Voluntary Action Research* 2 (1973):64–73.

more because they were not regarded as peers of men, despite the gains in women's education, religious leadership, and family influence. In innumerable small as well as great ways—from John Adams's compliment to Mrs. Hancock in 1775 that "in large and mixed company she is totally silent as a lady ought to be" to the clearly warmer welcome of a boy's than a girl's birth in the Robert Sedgwick family in the 1820s—it was obvious throughout this period that men and women were not peers.[5] Amidst the weakening of traditional dependency relationships the only hierarchy vociferously maintained (outside of racism) was women's subordination to men, or more specifically, wives' subordination to husbands. In traditional society the subordination and dependency of wives had been one instance of a kind of relationship typical in religious, economic, and political life; but in the early nineteenth century women's ascribed "place" was unique. Women therefore sought and valued peer relationships where they could find them: with other women.

The conventional sex-role distinctions represented more powerful, multiple, and overlapping structures in society at large that encouraged women to view one another as peers *par excellence* because of their shared sexual destiny. While production, exchange, and training for livelihoods moved out of the household, the persistence of married women's occupation there, demanded by their obligation of housekeeping and child care, provided the material basis for separating the qualities of women *as a sex* from those of men. If eighteenth-century "rational" analysis and observation of "nature" had exaggerated the contrast and complementarity between the sexes, early nineteenth century ideology effectively rooted these differences in the characteristic locations of adult women and men, "home" and "world." Religious and secular rhetoric elevated women's household occupations into a sexual vocation, making their typical work-role into their sex-role. Women practicing the domestic vocation perceived it as an experience that united them with other women. The canon of domesticity made motherhood a social and political role that also defined women as a class, and became the prism through which all expectations of and prescriptions for women were refracted. The mainstream of women's education carried these ideas along. Both ideology and practice in reawakened Protestantism confirmed that women had a discrete social, civil, and religious role owing to susceptibilities and responsibilities dictated by gender. Furthermore, evangelical Christianity's championing of the spirit over the flesh, together with its reliance on a female constituency, insinu-

---

5. John Adams to Abigail Adams, Nov. 4, 1775, in C. F. Adams, *Familiar Letters*, p. 121; Elizabeth Ellery Sedgwick, journal of the first years of her child's life, Jan. 1824 and March 1825, Houghton Library, Harvard Univ., Cambridge, Mass.

ated the idea that women's moral nature overcame the physical, free-ing them from carnal passion. Though that notion (so central to nineteenth-century sexual ideology) has frequently been interpreted as oppressive to women, it not only implied women's moral superior-ity but also created proud solidarity among women, and encouraged them to view their own friendships as more honorable than hetero-sexual relationships because they excluded carnality. "I do not believe that men can ever feel so pure an enthusiasm for women as we can feel for one another," wrote Catherine Sedgwick, transported with delight after meeting Fanny Kemble, "—ours is nearest to the love of angels."[6]

A woman discovered among her own sex a world of true peers, in valuing whom she confirmed her own value. In one sense, the female friendships of this period expressed a new individuality on women's part, a willingness and ability to extract themselves from familial definition and to enter into peer relationships as distinct human beings. In another sense, these attachments documented women's construction of a sex-group identity. Women had learned that gender prescribed their talents, needs, outlooks, inclinations; their best chance to escape their stated inferiority in the world of men was on a raft of gender "difference." Female friendships, by upholding such attributes as "heart" as positive qualities, asserted that women were different from but not lesser than—perhaps better than—men.

Women's appreciation of friends of their own sex to whom they could "freely communicate . . . their feelings at any time," or "express . . . their sentiments without reserve," as Sarah Ripley and Nancy Meriam phrased it (and find in return "a sweet, beaming countenance to echo the feelings expressed," in Luella Case's words) reflected the psychological distance placed between the sexes by sex-role typing. Exaggerated sex-role distinctions may have suc-ceeded in making women uncomfortable with men (and vice versa) as often as rendering the two sexes complementary. "I should have been really gratified if a pleasant companion had been with me," wrote a twenty-five-year-old woman patient at a spa, recounting her feelings about dining at a table with forty men, "but as it was I found such beauties in my cup and saucer I look'd at nothing else—how like a fool one acts, and feels, in such a situation, while those high and mighty Lords of the Creation, as they call themselves, will pick their teeth and stare confidently in your face, fast heeding the

6. Catherine Maria Sedgwick diary, May 16, 1834. Cf. Mary Grew's end-of-the-century vindication of her enduring friendship with Mary Burleigh: "Love is spiritual, only pas-sion is sexual." Mary Grew to Isabel Howland, April 27, 1892, quoted in Carroll Smith-Rosenberg, "The Female World of Love and Ritual," p. 27. I have discussed the development of these ideas in "In the Bonds of Womanhood," pp. 217–64, and "Passion-lessness: An Interpretation," unpublished MS.

confusion it occasions." A stagecoach journey with six men as co-passengers prompted similar feelings from another young woman, who wrote to her mother: "the gentlemen were civil, but I was in no enviable situation. I sat in a corner, seldom unclosing my lips excepting when spoken to and that was an unfrequent occurrence. When silence was interrupted by conversation it was upon subjects that ladies are not often consulted about, such as the presidential election, tariff, canals, slave trade, smuggling, &c &c. Some part of the time I felt somewhat more alone, than if alone."[7]

If women were not consulted about wordly events, neither did many men share the feelings closest to women's hearts. Before Catharine Beecher's career in advancing woman's sphere had yet begun, she appraised men's and women's heartfelt needs differently, in the process of deciding whether or not to marry the scholar seeking her hand. To a good friend she wrote, "The truth is Louisa I feel more & more every day that talents learning & good principals [sic] never could make me happy *alone*—I shall need a warm & affectionate heart—& whether I can find it in this case I know not . . . I could not dispense with the little attentions & kindnesses that in domestic life constitute a great share of a womans happiness & which a cold hearted man never could bestow—The more I think of it the more I am sure that I ought to guard my heart from the fascination of genius & the flattery of attentions till I am sure that my happiness is not risqued."[8]

The feminization of religion presents a case in point. How often did women, sincere believers and evangelical activists, have to lament their husbands' failure to join the church or to conform to religious behavior? In how many marriages did this difference in commitment provoke friction—diminution of respect—or despair? In light of the predominance of women among communicants, many must have prayed as did Mrs. Smith of Woodmont, Connecticut, "that the time is not far distant when I shall see my companion my bosom-friend engaged in the same glorious cause. May he be as a guide and example to me and to his children and as an ornament to the church of Christ." If they professed faith during adolescence women might plan to accept none but a man with the same qualification, but not all could succeed. The many besides who joined the church after marriage often regretted their spouses' skepticism or inattention. Sarah Connell Ayer expressed distress at her husband's continuing neglect of his "immortal peace" after fourteen years of marriage.[9]

7. Diary of Abigail May, 1800, May-Goddard Collection, SL (she undoubtedly meant "a pleasant *female* companion"!); Sarah Bradley to Abigail Bradley, Nov. 7, 1828, Bradley-Hyde Collection, SL. Sarah Bradley was about 29 at the time.
8. Catharine Beecher, New London, Conn., to Louisa [Wait], Litchfield, Beecher-Stowe Collection, SL., n.d. but approximately June 1821, when Beecher was 21.
9. Diary of Mrs. S. Smith, Oct. 28, 1821 or 1823, Connecticut State Library, Hartford, Conn.; *Diary of Sarah Connell Ayer,* Oct. 9, 1825, p. 254.

The irony of the situation was that without marriage supplying women with home and children, the central prerequisite of their sex-role disappeared. Nineteenth-century women—even birth control reformers deemed extremists—considered the fate and advancement of women conjoined with those of the home and family (and, necessarily, marriage), not opposed to them.[1] Catherine Sedgwick revealed how deep this belief ran in a diary entry written when she was forty-five (in 1830) and already acclaimed as a novelist. Having never married, she relied on her siblings and their children for emotional support, but wished for something more, as she admitted in a somewhat depressed mood, "Never perhaps was a condition of inferiority & dependence made by the affection of friends more tolerable than mine—Still I hanker after the independence & interests & power of communication of a home of my own."[2] She associated "inferiority and dependence" with her *single* life, despite her public prestige and commercial success, and assumed that "a home of her own"—that is, implicitly, where she was mistress, wife, and mother—would allow "independence and interests and power of communication," when her novels had given her a vaster, and willing, audience.

Catherine Sedgwick may have been taken in by her own sentimentalization of domesticity. (A stronger personal priority prevented her from actually undergoing the "thralldom" of marriage.) But even aside from the rhetorical inflation of woman's power in the home, there was for most women no appealing alternative to marriage in its economic, sexual, and social aspects. The best chance to have both worlds was to balance marriage with conscious sisterly relations. Wives who had female friends or relatives living with them seemed the most contented of women. When Rebeccah Root wrote to Weltha Brown after her marriage and move to upstate New York, she called her husband a "Christian companion & the most tender affectionate friend," yet added, "but I could not bear to live so far from sisters, and by pleading have succeeded in getting Sister Ann with me, & this adds very much to my happiness." Elizabeth Ellery Sedgwick, whose wife-and-motherhood apparently incarnated the ideal of domesticity, described the winter of 1827–28, "in addition to our other pleasures, sister Catherine passed the winter with us. She is the most delightful companion in the world—and her society the greatest treat, that can be enjoyed—Of course she helped to make our domestic circle perfect." Although Luella Case generally balked at her lot during the years of her correspondence with Sarah Edgarton, for the period when she and her husband lived in her

1. Cf. Linda Gordon, "Voluntary Motherhood: The Beginnings of Feminist Birth Control Ideas in the United States," in Mary Hartman and Lois Banner, eds., *Clio's Consciousness Raised* (New York: Harper Torchbooks, 1973).
2. Catherine Sedgwick diary, Aug. 5, 1830. Her use of "friends" to include kin here shows that the usage disappeared only gradually.

sister's household her spirits were "so good," she wrote to Edgarton, "that I cannot by any contrivance of mental incapacity work myself into even a decent fit of the 'blues.'"[3] Women who did not have sisters or peers at home found analogous companionship and support in voluntary associations.[4]

Sisterhood expressed in an affective way the gender identification— the consciousness of "womanhood"—so thickly sown and vigorously cultivated in contemporary social structure and orthodoxy. Women's reliance on each other to confirm their values embodied a new kind of group consciousness, one which could develop into a political consciousness. The "woman question" and the women's rights movement of the nineteenth century were predicated on the appearance of women as a discrete class and on the concomitant group-consciousness of sisterhood. Both the feminists who began to expose and to protest women's oppression in the 1830s and the educators, writers, and social reformers who intended more conservatively to improve women's status took for granted this double-headed assumption. All of them recognized gender as the most important determinant of the shape of their lives. Feminists moved from acknowledging that to sensing the disabilities imposed by gender roles. In the year of the Seneca Falls Convention, for example, Elizabeth Cady Stanton looked toward the achievement of women's rights and declared, "Woman herself must do this work—for woman alone can understand the height, and the depth, the length and the breadth of her own degradation and woe. Man cannot speak for us—because he has been educated to believe that we differ from him so materially, that he cannot judge of our thoughts, feelings and opinions by his own."[5]

If political feminists viewed women's allotment as inequitable and debasing and—perhaps more offensive—imposed on them without their consent, most women were willing to accept a sphere they saw as different but equal. To strengthen women's position within that sphere by reaffirming their powers of moral suasion vis-à-vis men, by improving their educational opportunities, and by enhancing the social role implicit in their child-rearing duties, seemed sufficient reform. The growth of women's schools, publications, and associations during the 1830s showed progress toward these aims. But in

3. Rebeccah Root Buell, Geneseo, N.Y., to Weltha Brown, Hartford, June 24, 1822; Elizabeth Ellery Sedgwick, journal of the first years of her child's life ("sister Catherine" was her husband's sister, Catherine Sedgwick); Luella Case, "Westbrook," to Sarah Edgarton, May 17, 1842.
4. Cf. Carroll Smith-Rosenberg's conclusion in "Beauty, the Beast, and the Militant Woman," AQ 23 (1971):576–77, that New York moral reform activists of the 1830s sought sisterhood, through their association, in order to combat their experience of isolation and status inferiority in their families.
5. Speech at Waterloo Convention, Aug. 2, 1848, Stanton Papers, Library of Congress, quoted in Andrew Sinclair, The Emancipation of the American Woman (New York: Harper and Row, 1965), p. 257.

the same decade, confrontation with voices of incipient feminism (such as those of antislavery speakers Angelina and Sarah Grimké) clarified the fact that the ideology of woman's sphere had inherently limited utility to reform woman's lot.[6] The doctrine restrained women's initiative because of its central distinction between womanly self-abnegation and manly self-assertion. More potently, since it derived from woman's difference from man, and defined women in specifically sexual rather than human terms, it deprived the sexes of their common ground and opened the door to anti-feminist and misogynist philosophies. For the duration of the nineteenth century, nonetheless, most women honored their separate sphere, especially when they had sisterhood to secure it. They had little objective reason and still less subjective cause to envision advancement (or even comfort) outside it.

ANNA MAE DUANE

Pregnancy and the New Birth in
Charlotte Temple and *The Coquette*[†]

Never, I say, had a country so many openings to happiness as this. Her setting out in life, like the rising of a fair morning, was unclouded and promising. Her cause was good. Her principles just and liberal. Her temper serene and firm. Her conduct regulated by the nicest steps, and everything about her wore the mark of honor. It is not every country (perhaps there is not another in the world) that can boast so fair an origin. Even the first settlement of America corresponds with the character of the revolution. Rome, once the proud mistress of the universe, was originally a fair band of ruffians. Plunder and rapine made her rich and her oppression of millions made her great. But America need never be ashamed to tell her birth, nor relate the stages by which she rose to empire.[1]

Thomas Paine's 1783 attempt to imagine the future of infant America in *American Crisis* draws on two heavily circulated metaphors for the new nation—a virtuous young woman and an innocent infant.[2] In Paine's formulation, however, the metaphors clash in provocative

6. See, e.g., the negative responses of moral reformers to Sarah Grimké's *Letters on the Equality of the Sexes and the Condition of Women*, discussed in Carroll Smith-Rosenberg, "Beauty, the Beast, and the Militant Woman," pp. 581–83; and the conflict of opinion between Catharine Beecher and Angelina Grimké evident in the former's *Essay on Slavery and Abolition* and the latter's *Letters to Catharine E. Beecher*.

† Reprinted by permission of the author. Page numbers in brackets refer to this Norton Critical Edition.

1. Thomas Paine, "American Crisis XIII," in *The Rights of Man, Common Sense, and Other Political Writings*, ed. Mark Philip (Oxford and New York: Oxford University Press, 1995), 73. [Originally published 1783].

2. For an excellent analysis of how the female body was deployed in Revolutionary rhetoric, see Shirley Samuels, *Romances of the Republic: Women, the Family and Violence in the Literature of the Early American Nation* (New York: Oxford University Press, 1996).

ways. According to his model, the newly born nation arguably mothers *herself* into being. Invested with the agency of a modest young woman (capable of taking nice steps and wearing a mark of honor), America seems able to bring about her own birth (of which she need not be ashamed, precisely because it was brought about through her own nice steps and honor). Effectively, mother and child are one and the same: the mother's virtues and actions morph imperceptibly into the child whose future will embrace those same virtues. Unable to trace the means through which a fully independent identity can be generated, Paine makes his subject do double duty as both the child and the parent who brings that child into the world, leaving us unsure how to envision the process, or product, of such a "fair origin."

Pregnancy—a precarious state that allows imaginative slippage between private and public; between past and future; and, perhaps most provoking, between self and other—offers one means of solving the rhetorical puzzle Paine provides. After all, only a pregnant woman's body could contain the virtuous mother *and* the prospective child of promising birth within the same space.[3] It should hardly be surprising then, that pregnancy occupies a central role in Susanna Rowson's 1791 *Charlotte Temple* and Hannah Foster's 1797 *The Coquette*, two of the seduction novels that captivated the imagination of an infant nation.

What is perhaps more surprising is that few critics have paid attention to how pregnancy functions in these popular novels. The American seduction novel has traditionally been read either as an allegory for a young nation yearning for independence amid the bonds of sympathy or as an exploration of female agency in a patriarchal society. As critics such as Cathy Davidson, Gillian Brown, and C. Leiren Mower have argued, these texts are deeply concerned with the struggle for a young woman to control the dispensation of her own body in a patriarchal society. But what few critics have noted is that these novels' final focus on a female *pregnant* body actually vexes the ideal of Lockean self-possession to which the heroines allegedly aspire.

Through an exploration of how pregnancy was being reimagined in contemporary political, religious, and scientific discourses, my reading of these texts complicates the critical debate about the novels' depictions of whether, or how, a woman could fully possess her own body. Instead, these novels open onto another debate entirely, about whether such ownership is desirable in the first place. I suggest that pregnancy in these postrevolutionary texts acts as a mediator between two alternating systems of power, one human—in which the body is

---

3. Many thanks to Karen Sánchez-Eppler for the conversation that led me to this observation.

individual property—and the other divine—in which the body is the manifestation of God's will. When we place pregnancy at the center of our analysis of these novels, we find a vacillating investment in Enlightenment thinking and Great Awakening theology that leaves us with a model akin to Paine's wishful, but confused, desire for an unblemished birth for a nation that turned against its colonial mother. Lingering to admonish, and perhaps admire, the dangerous performativity of both the rakes and the heroines who fall prey to them, these novels tap into emerging medical definitions of parturition and Great Awakening notions of the new birth to create a portrait of pregnancy that renders deceptive women utterly transparent. Ultimately, I suggest, pregnancy in these novels reclaims the body as divine property whose domain and actions are beyond individual, rational control.

The emphasis on pregnancy in *Charlotte Temple* and *The Coquette* changes the nature of the battle from *Clarissa's* story of a young woman who rebels against a tyrannical father to a conflict between a deceived—and deceptive—woman and the "truth" her pregnant body will eventually tell. In doing so, Foster and Rowson participate in a transatlantic conversation, exploring the relationship between environment and subjectivity raised by Lockean notions of individual development. The seduction novel, particularly Samuel Richardson's *Clarissa*—a best-seller in the colonies in the pivotal year of 1775 and an undoubted inspiration for Rowson and Foster—provided a key imaginative template for a colonial child wishing to extricate itself from Mother England.[4] One element of the text that lent itself to such a reading was Clarissa's perpetual status as a besieged daughter, rather than as a mother. After all, *Clarissa* merely hints at the possibility that the heroine might be pregnant. While both her seducer and her tyrannous family have their suspicions, Clarissa herself never provides an answer. She orchestrates her own death too quickly and too meticulously for her body to betray the information she wishes to keep private.[5] In both *The Coquette* and *Charlotte Temple*, however, it is the heroines' undeniable pregnancy and disastrous childbearing that drive the plot to its tragic conclusion. In other words, their bodies literalize their individual interior transformation. Their unruly interior becomes increasingly visible, and legible, as the body testifies against the mind's supposed agency.

4. See Jay Fliegelman, *Prodigals to Pilgrims: The American Revolution against Patriarchal Authority* (Cambridge: Cambridge University Press, 1982). Jan Lewis calls *Clarissa* "a political parable with particular lessons for Americans." ("The Republican Wife: Virtue and Seduction in the Early Republic," *William and Mary Quarterly* 44.4 (1987): 693).
5. For an excellent analysis of the implications of Clarissa's possible pregnancy, see Brian McCrea, "Clarissa's Pregnancy and the Fate of Patriarchal Power," *Eighteenth-Century Fiction* 9.2 (1997): 125–48.

Before their pregnancies, the heroines share Lovelace's penchant for performance, often disguising their intentions, or at least their distress, to negotiate the treacherous terrain they must travel. As Jay Fliegelman and others have pointed out, the dangers of performance were particularly acute for those who feared the wayward tendencies of a democratic republic. Without the trappings of birthright to provide an interpretive template for one's body and intentions, the possibility of simply creating a shifting identity through performance was extremely threatening to a nation that many felt could survive only through the unabashed virtue of its citizens.[6] In one of the few analyses that consider pregnancy essential to the early American seduction novel, Fliegelman suggests that the genre seeks to correct the dangerous allure of performance. For him, when the fallen, pregnant heroine of William Hill Brown's 1789 *The Power of Sympathy* runs away and commits suicide in an attempt to escape the "time of explanation," she "reenacts her original sin of believing in an impenetrable private sphere safe from the public eye. The story, like the sin, cannot be hidden in a world where one's face is forever a picture of one's passions."[7] I would point out that the postrevolutionary seduction model in the United States offers such transparency only *after* the heroine becomes pregnant. In both Rowson's and Foster's novels, the drama unfolds precisely *because* the women are so adept at keeping their face from becoming a picture of their passions. Both Eliza and Charlotte are able, at first, to keep their intentions and desire from becoming physically apparent.

As a coquette, Eliza, like her male counterpart the rake, wreaks her damage by cultivating the disparity between her true intentions and the physical and conversational clues she provides to others. Eliza's ability to convince two men of vastly different temperaments that she is a perfect mate testifies to her ability to perform adeptly.[8] Her personal magnetism depends largely on her ability to read the physical cues of others and provide them with the persona they wish to see. She is able to simultaneously encourage the virtuous, if dry, Reverend Boyer through smiles, rational conversation, and promises of friendship, while appearing to Peter Sanford as "the very soul of pleasure."

6. See Caroll Smith-Rosenberg, "Domesticating 'Virtue': Coquettes and Revolutionaries in Young America," in *Literature and the Body: Essays on Populations and Persons*, ed. Elaine Scarry (Baltimore: Johns Hopkins University Press, 1988), 160–84.

7. Jay Fliegelman, *Declaring Independence: Jefferson, Natural Language and the Culture of Performance* (Stanford, CA: Stanford University Press, 1993) 135.

8. My reading of Eliza's feelings differs somewhat from Jeffrey Richards's, who argues that Eliza often betrays her sincerity in her dealings with Boyer and Sanford. I do agree, however, with Richards's larger point that *The Coquette* renders the fallen woman a victim of the irreconcilable tension between social performance and transparent sincerity. Jeffrey H. Richards, "The Politics of Seduction: Theater, Sexuality and National Virtue in the Novels of Hannah Foster," in *Exceptional Spaces: Essays in Performance and History*, ed. Della Pollack (Chapel Hill and London: University of North Carolina Press, 1998), 245.

For the high-living rake, "the highest entertainment receives its great-est charm from her smiles."[9] Eliza's capacity for performance would perhaps, in other circumstances, render her an excellent "female man-ager for the theater," a vocation in which, as she suggests to a friend, she would put forth productions "under much better regulations than at present."[1]

In reality, everyone in Eliza's world is a careful actor. She notes that even the seemingly transparent Reverend Boyer works hard to act the part of the successful suitor:

> I soon perceived that every word, every action, and every look was studied to gain my approbation. As he sat next me at dinner, his assiduity and politeness were pleasing; and as we walked together afterwards, his conversation was improving. Mine was sentimental and sedate; perfectly adapted to the taste of my gallant.[2]

As Jeffrey Richards argues, in Eliza's world, "there is no space in which one can *be* without subjection to exacting standards of what constitutes acceptable performance."[3]

Critics such as Gillian Brown and Carroll Smith-Rosenberg have pointed out that Eliza's physical decline actually begins after Boyer's rebuff, suggesting that Eliza's failing body marks her exit from the performative sphere of courtship and coquetry.[4] Yet while Eliza is deeply affected by the loss of Boyer's attentions, the novel provides ample evidence that she has not yet relinquished her claim to perfor-mance. Once her interest is piqued by Sanford's return, she deftly manipulates the impressions wrought by her changed physical state to disguise her intentions. Writing to Lucy Sumner, Eliza excuses herself from a trip to Boston, a trip that would remove her from San-ford's presence, by alluding to the depression she had physically mani-fested over the past several months. She would find it "painful," she writes, to mix again in company and suggests that the "melancholy reflections" oppressing her were more likely to be dissipated at home than abroad.[5] Eliza is able to exercise her own choice by performing a role based on the perceptions others would have of her symptomatic body. Indeed, after arranging to remain near Sanford, Eliza remains deft enough at subterfuge to carry out an affair with him in her mother's own house for quite some time.

9. Hannah Webster Foster, *The Coquette* (New York: Oxford University Press, 1986), 56. All future citations will be from this edition.
1. Foster, 124.
2. Foster, 12.
3. Richards, 249.
4. See Smith-Rosenberg, "Domesticating 'Virtue,'" and Gillian Brown "Consent, Coquetry and Consequences," *American Literary History* 4 (winter 1997): 625–52.
5. Foster, 125.

Critics have been more likely to read Charlotte Temple as a wholly transparent character. Although she is less practiced than Foster's Eliza, Rowson's Charlotte Temple also produces canny narratives to account for any bodily signs of deception. Facing the school's headmistress after a sleepless night contemplating her imminent elopement with Montraville, Charlotte is not able to maintain her normal composure, but quickly accounts for the pangs of conscience legible in her physiognomy. When Madame Du Pont asks about the "languor so apparent in [her] frame," Charlotte dismisses the inquiry with a smile.[6] In doing so, Charlotte creates a distance between her face and her feelings—a somatic rupture that allows her to make a decision at odds with her guardians' wishes, and, it would seem, her own instincts.

Such skill at masking the signals the body sends could well have been read by an eighteenth-century audience as a product of the girls' "enlightened" upbringing. Both girls are portrayed as models of Lockean childrearing, in which affectionate parents model correct behavior, rather than coerce it through physical punishment. Notably, both Eliza (whose father is dead) and Charlotte (whose father is a model of paternal indulgence) are free from the coercive paternal force that generated much of the conflict in Clarissa. Instead, both Charlotte and Eliza are the product of what Richard Brodhead has deemed the Lockean system of "disciplinary intimacy."[7] Rather than forcing a child to do one's bidding, Lockean-inspired parents must rule by example and by moral suasion. Yet while Locke, and the numerous pedagogues who followed his lead, argued against corporeal punishment, the body was still a vital instrument in his disciplinary toolbox.

For Locke, experience gained through the senses provided the source of both knowledge and morality. Because sensual experience was so incredibly powerful, learning how to modulate one's own response to the body's experience, and the promptings that sprung from such experience, was vital to moral development.[8] In "An Essay Concerning Human Understanding," Locke insists that the ability to mediate consciousness amid sensual experience (both pleasant and unpleasant) is what makes us individual human beings. "[I]f we take wholly away all consciousness of our actions and sensations," Locke writes, "especially of pleasure and pain, and the concernment that accompanies it, it will be hard to know wherein to place personal

---

6. Susanna Rowson, Charlotte Temple, in Charlotte Temple and Lucy Temple, ed. Ann Douglas (New York: Penguin 1991), 46[34].
7. Richard Brodhead, "Sparing the Rod: Discipline and Fiction in Antebellum America," Representations 21 (1988): 67–96.
8. For an excellent analysis of the exploration of science and sensibility in the eighteenth century, see Jessica Riskin, Science and Sensibility: The Sentimental Empiricists of the French Enlightenment (Chicago: University of Chicago, 2002).

identity."[9] Because this concernment that accompanies pleasure and pain is central to identity, I suggest, the ability to carefully distinguish one's consciousness from the pleasure and pain that impinged on it allowed for, indeed demanded, the cultivation of a carefully performed identity. In other words, Locke's concernment, if properly cultivated, should result in behavior and actions that, when appropriate, were rationally detached from the body's inner promptings or outer signals.

Before their pregnancies, the heroines *of The Coquette* and *Charlotte Temple* are able to exist within this dangerous realm of performance, where a discerning mind overrules an emoting body. In fact, both Eliza and Charlotte illustrate a portrait of female subjectivity drawn by another Enlightenment pedagogue—Jean Jacques Rousseau. For women of course, the need to modulate their desires and impulses is more pronounced than for men. Woman, after all, "is made to please and to be subjected." Thus, for Rousseau, she must constantly be aware of the effect she has on others: "she ought to make herself pleasing to man instead of provoking him. Her strength is in her charms; by their means she should compel him to discover his strength and to use it."[1] The skills of a coquette represent the culmination of such a philosophy.

The early lessons in self-control the girls received as children facilitate their later ability to slip through the watchful gaze of female guardians and parents. The Lockean imperative to keep physical sensation at a distance, to maintain dominion over the body, has taught these women, not how to deny their desires, but rather how to disguise the messages the body attempts to transmit. In other words, they have learned to perform the role of virtue that will allow them to elude detection, at least at first. When a child has learned to bear discomfort without flinching and to defer pleasure without visibly pining for it, these novels suggest, she will inevitably become an illegible text that allows no one to discern interior states from exterior signs.

When Charlotte smiles to disguise her sinking heart and Eliza adapts her demeanor to suit her companion, they emblematize Rousseau's portrait of woman as a canny manager of her own often unruly body. As Gillian Brown has argued, Rousseau suggests that *all* women are at pains to distance their exterior performances of modesty from their insatiably desiring bodies.[2] "Why do you consult their mouth when it is not their mouth which ought to speak?" Rousseau

9. John Locke, *An Essay Concerning Human Understanding* 2.11 (Lawrence, KS: Digireads .com Publishing, 2008), 56.
1. Jean-Jacques Rousseau, *Émile, or on Education*, trans. Allan Bloom (New York: Basic, 1979), 385.
2. Brown, "Consent, Coquetry and Consequences," 628–29.

inquires. Instead, a wise observer should discern the truth by observing women's "eyes, their color, their breathing, their fearful manner, and above all, their soft resistance."[3] What a woman says, therefore, is almost always at odds with the signals her body sends.

However, as these novels move toward denouement, they complicate and ultimately refute Rousseau's notion that women's bodies are a source of temptation that demand subterfuge. As the heroines move closer to their fall, it is their own bodies that clamor in protest. And once a woman has "fallen" in these texts, it is the pregnant body that leads her to redemption. Rather than Rousseau's desirous female body requiring the deception of performance, the bodies of these women actually function as the repository of virtue, in conflict with the verbal and physical performances the women enact. Their bodies do not lead them astray; rather, it is their bodies that act as indices of their own uncomfortable consciences. The sleepless night that manifests in Charlotte's physically evident languor has not been produced by her desire for Montraville, but by her inherently virtuous recoiling from the planned elopement. As Marion Rust has argued, "it is in relaxing her sensitivity to her own impulses, not in giving in to them, that Charlotte loses her virginity and then her life."[4] When Eliza Wharton is surprised to find the dry Reverend Boyer in the parlor instead of the charming rake Sanford, she is perplexed by her own physical reaction: "I blushed and stammered; but I know not why; for certain I am, that I neither love nor fear the good man yet, whatever I may do some future day."[5] As her striking depression and decline at his rebuff might suggest, Eliza did indeed feel either love or fear for Boyer—but she was unable, or unwilling to properly interpret the bodily signals that told her so.

The portrait of the female body depicted by these two texts does not endorse an insistence on a disjunction between one's face and one's feelings, but neither does it truly enact the sentimental ethos with which these novels are often associated. Clearly, if characters worked within a fully sentimental framework, wherein, as Karen Sánchez-Eppler suggests, "the self is externally displayed, and the body provides a reliable sign of who one is"[6] or, as Fliegelman has suggested, "one's face is forever the picture of one's passions,"[7] the rakes would never have gotten past the initial meeting. Rather, these texts depict a transition from a modulated detachment from the body to a senti-

3. Rousseau, *Émile*, 385.
4. Marion Rust, "What's Wrong with Charlotte Temple?," *The William and Mary Quarterly* 60.1 (2003): 27[495].
5. Foster, 19.
6. Karen Sánchez-Eppler, "Bodily Bonds: The Intersecting Rhetorics of Feminism and Abolition," *Representations* 24 (1988): 36.
7. See Fliegelman.

mental investment in the body's transparency. Pregnancy, as a means of transforming the heroine's body, operates as the mechanism that articulates the heroines' shift from deceptive and unreadable women into virtual infants whose desires and intentions are perpetually written on their bodies.

These novels' exploration of the mechanics of pregnancy was part of an ongoing conversation in which scientists, doctors, writers, and philosophers struggled with how to understand and implement a theory of human nature in which individual experience, rather than one's place in the great order of things, determined the course of action for a life—or, for that matter, a nation. The understanding of how the fetus was formed was undergoing a revolutionary transformation, in itself not so different from the revolution in thought that insisted that outside influences were responsible for an individual's status, rather than an innate, God-given property. Many were still coming to grips with Harvey's 1651 doctrine of epigenesis, which posited the gradual development of the fetus from unorganized matter. Epigenesis was gradually supplanting the classical doctrine of preformation, in which perfectly formed little humans resided in the wombs of their ancestors, waiting for their ordained time to appear. As critics have suggested, and others have argued, this scientific discovery took over a century to gain full acceptance, at least partly because of the radical threat it posed to notions of a preordained social order in which an all-knowing God has arranged exactly who will appear when, and in which men were the prime movers in regeneration.[8]

As Eve Keller and others have written, the theory of epigenesis challenged the notion of a great chain of being and the patriarchal privilege encoded in that notion. As Keller points out, Harvey's finding that there was no semen in the uterus after intercourse led him to speculate that the embryo was "produced solely by the female" after fertilization.[9] Such a theory threatened notions of the father's role as the prime creative force in generation and, instead, made the female the prime agent in reproduction.[1] As Keller points out, such a finding shares a confluence with Thomas Hobbes's notion of mother-right. In his attempt to discredit the patriarchal notion that children

8. Eve Keller points out that Harvey's theorem defied biblical and political investments in patriarchal power, which insisted that men had the prominent share in the regeneration process. Eve Keller, "Making Up for Losses: The Workings of Gender in William Harvey's *de Generatione animalum*," in *Inventing Maternity: Politics, Science, and Literature, 1650–1865*, ed. Susan Greenfield and Carol Barash (Lexington: University of Kentucky, 1999), 34–56. Ava Chamberlain, "The Immaculate Ovum: Jonathan Edwards and the Construction of the Female Body," *The William and Mary Quarterly* 57.2 (2000): 289–322.
9. Keller, 38.
1. Keller, 39.

owe allegiance to their fathers in perpetuity, Hobbes argues that, because of the certainty of one's maternity (as opposed to paternity) and the vital role mothers play in a child's survival, it is to mothers that children owe their obedience.[2] For Hobbes, however, such maternal power ends abruptly once an individual gains the radical autonomy that is his birthright.

On another register, the theory of epigenesis, with its emphasis on unformed potential, can be read as a biological enactment of Locke's theory that human beings are malleable beings shaped by experience. Because a pregnant woman has the sole power to provide the environment in which the imagined epigenetic fetus unfurls its potential, pregnancy itself emerged as a deeply threatening position to patriarchal privilege. The implications of these evolving notions of pregnancy also raised a host of disturbing implications for those who sought to foster a notion of radical independence and autonomy. After all, when a colonial child felt that its right to independence justified a break from its mother, the question of how much of that child's very nature was created by that same mother was of vital importance.

Charlotte's and Eliza's pregnancies, then, are occurring at a moment when fundamental beliefs about the role of the divine—and, in particular, the patriarchal order endorsed by divinity—in human development were in flux. In the midst of the potentially empowering prospect of a woman's dominion over her own offspring, these novels move instead to reinstate the woman's body as the vessel of divine force. The novels' depiction of the women's pregnancies works through the age-old notion of maternal impression to create a portrait of development in which the body is reinstated as the vessel of divine will. The theory of maternal impression, which harks back to ancient times, took on a particular resonance in light of the gradual acceptance of epigenetic theory. According to this belief, the mother's emotional experiences manifest as a physical imprint on the child's body. In a popular pseudonymous childrearing treatise, *Aristotle's Compleat Masterpiece*, which was republished throughout the eighteenth century, the author expounds on the porous boundary between a mother's mind and an infant's physical composition:

> [T]he imaginative Power, at the time of conception, . . . is of such force, that it stamps a character of the thing imagin'd upon the Child: so that the Children of an Adulteress, by the Mother's Imaginative Power, may have the nearest Resemblance to her own Husband, tho' begotten by another Man. And through this Power of the Imaginative Faculty it was, that a Woman at the

2. Thomas Hobbes, *Leviathan*, ed. C. B. Macpherson (Harmondsworth, Middlesex: Penguin Books, 1968), 254.

time of conception, beholding the Picture of a Blackamoor conceiv'd, and brought forth a Child resembling an Ethiopian.[3]

Maternal impression, as described here, is a decidedly double-edged sword. On one hand, such a model invests women with an incredible amount of power. The savvy adulteress can literally alter the child's body—a body that should provide evidence of her deception—through the force of her thought. The second woman, however, allows her interior to be invaded by outside stimuli, and dooms herself in the process. By her unguardedly "beholding" the portrait of another man at the moment of conception, she allows the portrait's impression to shape the material within her. A similar anxiety surrounding the moment of conception infuses the plot of Laurence Sterne's mid-century novel *Tristam Shandy*, which details the woes of a man who, because of infelicitous circumstances at the moment of conception, was doomed to a life of misfortune.

The *in utero* transubstantiation from the imaginative to the material does not happen only at the moment of conception, however. The *Compleat Masterpiece* relates several cases where a strong impression made on a pregnant woman literally leaves an indelible mark on her offspring. When a "worthy Gentlewoman" passes by a butcher and finds her face splattered with blood, she knows immediately that the child's body would represent a physical memory of the mother's experience. According to the author, she immediately says "[t]hat her Child would have some Blemish on his face: Which proved true; for at the Birth it was found marked with a red Spot."[4]

In one respect, maternal impression provides proof of the mind's power over the body, or to be specific, the power of the mother's mind over the infant's body. For according to this theory, the child's body materializes the immaterial thoughts and feelings of the mother. For instance, Franny Nudelman's astute reading of Nathaniel Hawthorne's *The Scarlet Letter* through the lens of maternal impression suggests that the unruly passion of little Pearl serves as an expression of the ardent mystery of her mother. The child, for Nudelman, acts as a far better agent of discipline than the scarlet letter, whose symbolic indeterminacy has long been celebrated by literary critics. Pearl, unlike the letter, "perfectly reveals her source"—she represents the precise embodiment of Hester's interior state, the literal manifestation of her otherwise unreadable passion and anguish.[5]

---

3. Aristotle (pseud.), *Aristotle's Compleat Masterpiece in Three Parts*, 16th ed. (London: Printed, and Sold by the Booksellers, 1725), 95.
4. Aristotle, 96.
5. Franny Nudelman, "'Emblem and Product of Sin': The Poisoned Child in *The Scarlet Letter* and Domestic Advice Literature," *Yale Journal of Criticism* 10.1 (1997): 194.

The metamorphosis that occurs within Charlotte's and Eliza's bodies ultimately reverses the centuries-old doctrine of maternal impression. In *The Coquette* and *Charlotte Temple*, the unborn fetus enacts an even more compact symbolic economy than what Nudelman describes: rather than acting as a separate entity that reflects the mother's heretofore hidden sinful passions, it acts as a mysterious force within and upon the mother's own body, first to reveal, and then to transform, her shadowy interior. The physical anguish of pregnancy both makes the bearer aware of her own sin and purges her of it. Charlotte refers repeatedly to the developing fetus within her as "innocent," but her pregnancy emerges as a physical manifestation of Charlotte's own guilt. These novels do not merely indicate that pregnancy inevitably renders a woman's interior public—they suggest that the reproductive process actually *alters* that interior itself. And like a guilty conscience, the infant works from within to dispel all subterfuge and to bring the sinner's soul to proper repentance. For Charlotte, the fetus seems to raze the mother from the inside out, causing "the anguish of her heart" to "strike at the strings of life."[6] Her health steadily declines as her pregnancy seems to reassert a direct correlation between interior and exterior states. She is no longer able to conceal the promptings of her body with a hasty story and a smile. "Real anguish of heart," the narrator tells us, "had in a great measure faded her charms, her cheeks were pale from want of rest, and her eyes, by frequent, indeed almost continued weeping, were sunk and heavy."[7] As her body becomes weakened, so does her ability to maintain any shred of artifice. The disjunction between interior and exterior becomes almost perfectly realigned. Put simply, the body first discloses the sin, and then, by inciting remorse, redeems her from it. This process is made possible only through the increasingly visible presence of a fetus, a presence that renders Charlotte, through her physical weakness and vulnerability, increasingly childlike.[8]

Eliza Wharton goes through a similar transformation, perhaps all the more remarkable in light of her previous skill at keeping her intentions from becoming physically legible. In a letter to her mother, written because "the effect of my crime has become too obvious to be longer concealed," Eliza alludes to "the severest pains, both of body and mind."[9] For once, Eliza is not managing her own performance. The pregnancy has rendered her previously deceptive exterior transparent. The sickness of her body perfectly reflects the pangs of

---

6. Rowson, 86[62].
7. Rowson, 103[71].
8. For more on Charlotte as childlike, see Ann Douglas, "Introduction," in *Charlotte Temple* and *Lucy Temple* (New York: Penguin, 1991).
9. Foster, 231.

remorse that torture her. Self-diagnosed with "a confirmed consumption," Eliza dies, along with her infant, after her "conscience is awakened to a conviction of her guilt."[1] Eliza and Charlotte, having enjoyed brief sojourns as consenting agents, capable of keeping their intentions private and unseen, are eventually rendered ciphers—their thoughts, their feelings, and ultimately their bodies subsumed by the power of the fetus.

We cannot fully understand how these women's bodies function as both their chastisement *and* their redemption without engaging the regional voices of the Great Awakening that propounded an alternate vision of the body to those offered by liberal notions of self-ownership or classical republican celebrations of physical self-control. For many of the ministers of the First Great Awakening, one had to allow the body to remain porous to be receptive to the touch of God. New Light Calvinists like George Whitefield expanded on the Puritan insistence that conversion experience was almost always marked by deep suffering and often rendered such suffering in explicitly corporeal terms. As Susan Juster points out, metaphors used to describe the workings of revivalist grace depicted powerful, often painful physical experiences. Believers are subject to "pulsations," "eruptions," "waves," and "fires" that "ignite" and "engulf" them.[2] The experience of intense physical pain and revulsion was in itself an indication that a new spiritual birth was at hand. In a 1728 sermon, Israel Loring insists "[t]here is no bringing a natural man to Christ, til he apprehends himself poor, wretched, blind, naked and miserable, and that he stands in absolute need of him."[3] If an audience member wanted to be saved, Whitefield would have him ask God to "awaken me tho' it be with Thunder, to a sensible feeling of the Corruption of my fallen Nature." To be in the proper state to receive grace, a seeker would have to feel experientially that "I am conceived and born in Sin, my whole Head is sick my whole Heart is faint, from the Crown of my Head to the Sole of my Feet, I am full of Wounds and Bruises and putrifying Sores. And yet I see it not."[4] As Nancy Ruttenberg has discussed, Whitefield was purported to suffer from perpetual vomiting before and after sermons that caused him to physically waste away as part of the kenotic process.[5]

---

1. Foster, 231.
2. Susan Juster, *Disorderly Women: Sexual Politics and Evangelicalism in Revolutionary New England* (Ithaca, N.Y.: Cornell University Press, 1996), 18.
3. Israel Loring, *The Nature and Necessity of the New Birth* (Boston: D. Henchman, 1728), 8.
4. George Whitefield, *The Marks of the New Birth* (Philadelphia: Andrew and William Bradford, 1742), 19.
5. See Nancy Ruttenberg, *Democratic Personality and the Trial of American Authorship* (Stanford, CA: Stanford University Press, 1998), 104–05.

Whitefield's physical ailments notwithstanding, conservative ministers—sharing the era's ambivalent stance toward theatricality—were wary that "the marks of the new birth" could be faked by canny performers. The fact that Whitefield became an object of burlesque parody on the eighteenth-century stage testifies both to how widely recognizable he had become and to the broadly theatrical aspect of his sermons.[6] Even Whitefield himself, in the passage just cited, admits that he cannot "see" the wounded and weakened body that he *feels* so acutely. Although a spiritual transformation could well produce a legible change in the person's physical appearance and behavior, all bodily displays did not necessarily denote a state of grace or virtue within. How to tell the difference between performed spirituality and authentic states of grace was, of course, the great and unsolvable question.

One possible answer can be found in the final pages of the first New England best-seller—Mary Rowlandson's 1682 captivity narrative. In these concluding passages, Rowlandson seeks, and seems to find, reliable evidence of God's personal intervention through her experience of physical suffering during her captivity with the Algonquin Indians:

> Before I knew what affliction meant, I was ready sometimes to wish for it. When I lived in prosperity; having the comforts of the World about me, my Relations by me, and my heart cheerful: and taking little care for anything and yet seeing many (whom I preferred before my self) under many trials and afflictions, in sickness, weakness, poverty, losses, crosses, and cares of the World, I should be sometimes jealous least I have my portion in this life; and that Scripture would come to my mind, *Heb.* 12.6 *For whom the Lord loveth he chasteneth, and scourgeth every Son whom he receiveth.*[7] (emphasis in the original)

The affliction Rowlandson envies here is, first and foremost, the affliction she can "see" in others. As Elaine Scarry argues, much of the Old Testament, which, after all, is dedicated to illustrating God's invisible presence, depends on the wounded and altered body as proof of divine intervention.[8] (Job's many afflictions, and the boils bestowed as part of the ten plagues, are just two examples of the Old Testament God making his presence felt by wounding the body.) Within this framework, affliction functions as evidence that God is

---

6. For more on Whitefield's ambivalent relationship with the stage, see Ruttenberg, 89–91.

7. Mary Rowlandson, "The Sovereignty and Goodness of God," in *Women's Indian Captivity Narratives*, ed. Katherine Derounian-Stodola (New York, Oxford, 1998), 50.

8. Elaine Scarry, *The Body in Pain: The Making and Unmaking of the Word* (New York: Oxford University Press, 1985).

still interested enough in his handiwork to manifest his presence materially.[9]

The other biblical model for God's intervention via the body is, of course, pregnancy. From Abraham's wife, Sarah, who conceives long after she should have been biologically capable, to Mary's miraculously virginal conception, one could trace God's creative force through the generative power of reproduction. As Laura Henigman and others have pointed out, maternity was one of the most powerful metaphors for early New Englanders seeking to describe God's relationship to humankind, a trend that intensified as Christianity moved toward images of God as a benevolent parent, rather than a punitive ruler.[1]

Charlotte's and Eliza's spectacularly painful pregnancies, then, are of a piece with a long tradition in which an altered body denotes God's powerful touch. The Great Awakening's emphasis on the new birth tacitly acknowledged the metaphorical power of pregnancy in revealing miraculous regeneration. However, the emerging rhetoric of the new birth had implications, not just for how one might understand the role of suffering in spiritual transformation, but also for how to understand the material process of human conception, pregnancy, and birth itself. Jonathan Edwards, a man who had spent a good deal of time thinking about the relationship between spiritual and physical transformation, sought to use the concept of the spiritual new birth to ameliorate the evolving—and threatening—concept of an epigenetic fetus.[2] Edwards, struggling with the loss of scientific proof of a great chain of being, fashioned the evolving development of a fetus as an analogy for the process of creating a new creature wrought by Christ, with the heart featuring largely in both terms of the analogy:

> In the conception of an animal and the formation of the embryo, the first thing that appears is the *punctum saliens*, or the heart, which beats as soon as it exists. This is a lively image of the manner of the formation of the new creature. The first thing is a new heart, a new sense and inclination, that is a principle of new life; a principle, that however small, has vigor and power.[3]

---

9. Perry Miller's reading of the jeremiad provides an eloquent articulation of New England ministers' analysis of affliction as affirmation. See Perry Miller, *Errand into the Wilderness* (Boston: Belknap 1956).

1. Laura Henigman, *Coming into Communion: Pastoral Dialogues in Colonial New England* (Albany: SUNY Press, 1999), 14.

2. Jonathan Edwards, *A Treatise Concerning Religious Affections: In Three Parts . . .* (Philadelphia: James Crissy, 1821).

3. Jonathan Edwards, "Images of Divine Things," entry 190, in *Works of Jonathan Edwards*, Volume 2, *Typological Writing*, ed. Mason I. Lowance Jr. with David Watters (New Haven, CT and New York: Yale University Press, 1993), 122.

The heart here does double duty as metaphor and as biological material. By aligning spiritual language with the newest advances in scientific observation, Edwards translates the empirical facts of fetal development into a proof of the power of feeling and the role of grace. This fetal heart welds powerful emotion, salvific grace, and physical change together in one single image.

Edwards also updates the biblical story of God's curse dooming women to suffer in childbirth in order to realign human birth with the painful, but redemptive, process of the new birth. In entry 18 of "Images," Edwards explicitly connects the pain of labor to the pain of spiritual generation: "Women travail and suffer great pains in bringing children [forth], which is to represent the great persecutions and sufferings of the church in bringing forth Christ and [a] type of those spiritual pains that are in the soul when bringing forth Christ."[4] Foster's and Rowson's novels similarly conflate the fetus with redemptive affliction: pregnancy is inseparable from the physical suffering that leads to their pious deaths. It is significant that both women, like the suffering heroines in Puritan captivity narratives and like Whitefield himself, are brought to salvation through their physical pains, pain often rendered in terms that would resonate with readers familiar with conversion experiences. As Rust points out, shortly before her death, "Charlotte descends into a 'phrenzy' that owes much to the evangelical tradition."[5] And as Julia Stern has argued persuasively, Foster creates a heroine who is "at home in the world of emotion, familiar with the sort of fervor that marks the Great Awakening— the repercussions of which are felt in the Connecticut River Valley for decades after its initial eruption."[6]

The Coquette, as several critics have argued, is more critical of religion than *Charlotte Temple* appears to be, yet the willful Eliza seems to have been brought to complete spiritual transformation by her pregnancy, dismantling the strong will that had bedeviled her friends and relatives for most of the narrative. As she nears the end of her pregnancy, her language echoes scripture and the Great Awakening preachers who quoted it. Leaving her mother's house, her words are those of Christ on the Cross, as she momentously declares, "It is finished."[7] In her last exchange with Sanford, Eliza's part of the dialogue could be excerpted from a Whitefield sermon. Whitefield exhorts readers to ask God to "awaken me tho' it be with Thunder, to a sensible feeling of the Corruption of my fallen Nature." Similarly,

4. Jonathan Edwards, "Images of Divine Things," entry 18.
5. Rust, "What's Wrong with Charlotte Temple?" [500].
6. Julia Stern, *The Plight of Feeling; Sympathy and Dissent in the Early American Novel* (Chicago and London: Chicago University Press, 1997), 80.
7. Foster, 148.

Eliza is "awakened to a conviction of [her] guilt" by the painful physical experience of pregnancy.

After exhorting the rake to "add not to the number of those deluded creatures, who will one day rise up in judgment against you, and condemn you," she then softens her manner, and seeks to bring Sanford to an awakening akin to what she has experienced:[8]

> "If I am severe," said she, "it is because I wish to impress your mind with such a sense of your offences against your Maker, your friends, and society in general, as may effect your repentance and amendment. I wish not to be your accuser, but your reformer. On several accounts, I view my own crime in a more aggravated light than yours; but my conscience is awakened to a conviction of my guilt. Yours, I fear, is not. Let me conjure you to return home, and endeavor, by your future kindness and fidelity to your wife, to make her all the amends in your power."[9]

Once disdainful of Reverend Boyer's sanctimonious attempts to control her, Eliza has been utterly remade to the extent that her rhetoric exceeds Boyer's in religiosity. Eliza dies among strangers, but by all reports, her transformative pregnancy has led her to the point at which she can confidently expect a final reward. Her friends take much comfort from what they hear of "the state of her mind, in her last hours."[1]

Charlotte, for her part, reads her own painful pregnancy as the process through which she has bought her own salvation. As she nears death, Charlotte seems surer of herself than at any other point of the novel. "I have an humble confidence," she tells Mrs. Beauchamp, "in the mercy of him who died to save the world, and trust that my sufferings in this state of mortality, joined to my unfeigned repentance, through his mercy, have blotted my offences from the sight of my offended maker."[2] And the novel gives us no reason to think Charlotte's confidence ill-placed. She dies in her father's arms, with a countenance at first "serenely composed" and then illuminated at the moment of passing by a "beam of joy."[3]

If we read these episodes within the framework provided by Great Awakening preaching (as, arguably, many readers did), then these women's deaths are redemptive, rather than tragic. According to this perspective, the worldly, canny female actors who believed they could control the dispensation of their bodies are transformed by the workings of those very bodies into spectacles of sin acknowledged and,

---

8. Foster, 159.
9. Foster, 160.
1. Foster, 168.
2. Rowson, 114[86].
3. Rowson, 127[87].

ultimately, forgiven. Yet unlike Whitefield, the quintessential convert of the mid-to-late eighteenth century, Charlotte and Eliza have no capacity for the personal empowerment and self-aggrandizement that such fusion with the divine seemed to offer. Susan Juster's analysis of female converts in early New England points out that, for women, the job of conversion was to gain a sense of autonomy. For Charlotte and Eliza, however, the result of conversion is not independence, but erasure. While Whitefield was able to emerge from his painful (and seemingly perpetual) conversion experience to lay claim to a personal power he scandalously aligned with Christ's own magnetism, for the women in these novels self-surrender can mean only self-immolation.

To return to Paine's image of America's fair origin once more, I suggest that pregnancy does not actually solve the problem of competing identities that his self-parenting child presents. Rather than providing a figure who can possess both the well-regulated conduct of a republican mother and the absolute innocence of the newborn (or to be more precise, the soon-to-be-born) nation, the disastrous pregnancies of *Charlotte Temple* and *The Coquette* reiterate the conflict so drastically that each possible identity obliterates the other, both literally and figuratively. For Charlotte and Eliza, the mother's new heart, and the "new creature" she is supposedly creating, collapse in on one another.

However, as Cathy Davidson's analysis reminds us, the unwanted pregnancies and deaths in childbirth that figure so prominently in *Charlotte Temple* and *The Coquette* were not simply potent metaphors, but fearful physical realities for women in the postrevolutionary era. Against the backdrop of the very real biological dangers of childbirth that early national women faced and the matrix of male-authored texts in which pregnancy was theorized, these novels provide an extended—and largely unprecedented—female meditation on how pregnancy sabotages a woman's attempt to fully control her body, regardless of whether one believes that controlling the body is a worthy goal. Considered in conjunction with demographic data showing sharply declining fertility rates in the generations following the publication of *The Coquette* and *Charlotte Temple*, we may not be presumptuous in thinking to think that, for the many female readers of these texts, the transcendence these pregnancies appeared to offer was not a sufficient reward for the complete dismantling of agency and individuality that they also seemed to herald.[4]

4. Cathy Davidson, *The Revolution and the Word: The Rise of the Novel in America* (Oxford: Oxford University Press, 2004), 193.

Reading in Early America

CAMRYN HANSEN

A Changing Tale of Truth:
Charlotte Temple's British Roots[†]

In "The Life and Times of *Charlotte Temple*," Cathy Davidson writes that "Mathew Carey's edition of Susanna Rowson's *Charlotte, A Tale of Truth* was, considering the liberties taken with many English novels in their translation to America, a remarkably accurate redaction of the original English version that had been published by William Lane."[1] Such an observation, while no doubt valid from the comparative perspective from which it stems, inadvertently obscures an important fact—namely, that there are quite a few significant differences between the first British and first American editions of Rowson's *Charlotte*.[2] Though perhaps accurate by eighteenth-century printing standards, the Mathew Carey edition nevertheless deviates from the original London edition in nearly four hundred places. While most of the differences consist of altered or added punctuation marks—conventions to which neither authors nor printers in Rowson's era attended as "authentic" parts of the text with the rigor we expect of them today—a number of substantive emendations were made to the British edition of *Charlotte* for its American printing that affect the tone as well as the interpretive potential of the novel. The purpose of this essay is to highlight and briefly contextualize some of these emendations, not only to provide the reader with important (yet relatively unavailable) information about the textual history of *Charlotte Temple*[3] but to lay the groundwork for future

† Reprinted by permission of the author.
1. Cathy Davidson, "The Life and Times of *Charlotte Temple*: A Biography of a Book," in *Reading in America: Literature & Social History* (Baltimore: Johns Hopkins University Press, 1989), 160.
2. See Mrs. Rowson, *Charlotte, A Tale of Truth* (London: Minerva Press, 1791) and Mrs. Rowson, *Charlotte. A Tale of Truth* (Philadelphia: printed by D. Humphreys for Mathew Carey, 1794).
3. The only known complete copy of the first British edition of Rowson's *Charlotte. A Tale of Truth* is currently housed in the Barrett Collection at the University of Virginia. Other partial and/or damaged copies of the British edition also exist at the British Library and at Harvard University's Houghton Library. Contemporary scholarly editions

scholarly inquiry into the historical, sociopolitical, and literary forces that helped convert Rowson's novel from a marginal British work into a celebrated American best-seller.

The most immediately apparent change made to *Charlotte* for its American printing was, as Davidson has noted, the recognition of the author on the title page. In London, William Lane published his edition of the novel anonymously, citing neither Rowson's name nor any of her previously published works under the novel's title. There was also nothing on the British edition's title page to suggest to readers that *Charlotte* had been written by a woman, as identifiers commonly used to signify female authorship of anonymous works, such as "By a Lady," were omitted as well. Mathew Carey's edition, by contrast, not only listed an evidently female "Mrs. Rowson" as *Charlotte*'s author but recognized her as a seasoned author at the same time, citing her publication of *Victoria, The Inquisitor*, and *Fille de Chambre* prominently under her name. Moreover, it identified this Mrs. Rowson as the same tragedian whose artistic talents many Philadelphians would have already experienced in person at the New Theatre—and whose name, in its growing local celebrity, many more would be likely to recognize. By mid-April, 1794, the time of *Charlotte*'s American publication, Mrs. Rowson had been performing regularly in New Theatre productions for several months, and beginning February 1794, her name had begun to appear on a daily basis in local newspaper advertisements for the New Theatre.[4] About a week before *Charlotte*'s release, notices asking for subscribers to *Trials of the Human Heart* (advertised as "An Original Novel" by "Mrs. Rowson, of the New Theatre, Philadelphia, author of Victoria, Inquisitor, Charlotte, Fille de Chambre, &c. &c.") had also begun to run in the local papers.[5] Ads for *Charlotte*, promoting the book as "a New Novel" dedicated "to the Ladies of Philadelphia," soon followed and ran about three times a week for several months after the book's American publication.[6] As a result of this very thorough identification of the author on the title page, a portion of the original 1791 first-person preface that read, "I shall therefore shelter myself from the shafts of criticism under the friendly shade of obscurity" was sensibly removed from the preface included in the first American edition.

---

of *Charlotte Temple*, typically motivated by the novel's great popularity in early America, tend to reprint the first American edition, rather than the first British edition, of the text. To date, the only scholarly edition to ever reprint the British edition of *Charlotte* was published in 1964 (with editors Clara M. and Rudolf Kirk) by North Carolina University Press. This edition is now out of print.

4. See, e.g., *The Philadelphia Gazette and Universal Daily Advertiser*, XI: 1673, February 19, 1794, 3.
5. See, e.g., *The Gazette of the United States*, V: 99, April 7, 1794, 4.
6. See, e.g., *The Gazette of the United States*, V: 117, April 29, 1794, 3.

Another set of important emendations to *Charlotte*'s text occurred in what seems to have been a careful alteration of phrasing and terminology that would have struck a postrevolutionary American audience as politically controversial. Where in Chapter 2, the British edition of the novel describes Lucy Eldridge as being more charming, in her simple attire, than she would have been "if adorned with all the splendor of a birth-night belle," the first American edition compares her charm to that of a "courtly belle." As the birthnight ball was a British celebration commemorating the birthday of the monarch each year, the emended phrasing deftly avoids the association of beauty and goodness with the British crown that was likely to rankle the early American reader. Chapter 6, which the British edition bitingly titled "French Teachers Not Always the Best Women in the World" (*sic*)—France, of course, having played a key role in America's recent independence from England—was renamed the politically neutral "An Intriguing Teacher" for the first American edition. Likewise, where it is "the artful French woman" who in the British edition encourages Charlotte to defy her parents and elope with the rogue soldier Montraville, in the American edition it is merely "the artful woman." The name of the character Blackney was consistently changed to "Blakeney" for the first American edition, conceivably to bypass any racial connotations the former name would be likely to carry in early America. Whereas the first paragraph of the British edition's Chapter 5 reads, with a certain feminist prescience, "I cannot give a better description than by the following lines from a late ingenious female pen," the American edition's opening to Chapter 5 inconspicuously reads, "I cannot give a better description than by the following lines." In what seems to be an unwitting result of this last omission, the four lines of poetry that immediately follow the original phrase were also left out of the American edition. Notably, these lines, "The gay and gaudy morning flowers, / That bloom and die within few hours, / That dying leave no trace behind, / Bring to the deep reflecting mind," were what allowed the poem that appears in the American edition as an ungrammatical construction to be read as a complete sentence.

Despite the above oversight, it seems that in general, there was an effort to increase the grammatical and semantic clarity of *Charlotte*'s text for its American publication. The eighteenth-century status of accidentals notwithstanding, it is impossible to ignore the hundreds of changes that were made to the text's punctuation—particularly since these changes resulted in an American edition that reads at a different pace, and with different emotional effect, than its British predecessor. Commas were added liberally, dividing lengthy sentences into slower, more bite-size phrases, typically several times a page. Compound words and phrases became hyphenated—New-York, sun-rise, arm-chair, grand-father, summer-house, mother-in-law, arm-in-arm, love-sick, well-a-day, etc.—and periods grew into exclamation points at poignant and dramatic moments. Unwieldy or ambiguous grammar was also occasionally altered: in Chapter 6, "A man naturally ordinary, when arrayed in a military habit, will make a tolerable appearance" became "A man of an indifferent appearance, will, when arrayed in a military habit, shew to advantage" for the American edition. The moment in that same chapter when Charlotte opens Montraville's letter, originally described with the ambiguous "she cut the paper round the wafer," appears in the American edition as the palpably clearer "she opened the letter." Outright errors in grammar present in the British edition were also corrected, such as its pervasive use of *it's* to designate the possessive pronoun, or *lead* to denote the past tense of the verb *lead*.

While these kinds of technical emendations arguably enhance the aesthetic of the resulting text, they can also skew the way that we as contemporary readers understand and interpret *Charlotte Temple*, as both an authentic work of art and a historical artifact, if our only exposure to the novel is an isolated copy of the first American edition. Changes as seemingly benign as grammar corrections can have far-reaching effects on the way we construct meaning out of the text, and if we do not stop to question how the American edition came to exist as it does, we may inadvertently assign authorial intention to elements more properly attributable to idiosyncrasies of the edition's manufacture. At one point in Chapter 6, for instance, the British edition's improper use of the plural pronoun *they* as the anaphor of the singular noun *reader* was emended to the singular *he* for the American edition.[7] Though the resulting sentence reads correctly, it also happens to generate an inconsistency in the narrator's pattern of addressing a *female* reader, which appears to have critical significance. The spelling of various words was also systematically altered for the American edition, presumably to make the text conform with printing-house spelling standards: the British *shew* became the more American *show, favourite* became *favorite, encrease* became *increase, entreat* became *intreat,* and so on. While these changes are fairly consistent, there were nonetheless numerous instances in which the text's correctors neglected to make them, and the effect, in the Carey edition, is an appearance of unstandardized spelling in American printing of the era that is, to some extent, historically misleading.

---

7. The first British edition reads: "Any reader who has the least knowledge of the world will easily imagine the letter was made up of encomiums on her beauty, and vows of everlasting love and constancy; nor will *they* be surprised that a heart open to every gentle, generous sentiment, should feel itself warmed by gratitude for a man who professed to feel so much for her, nor is it improbable but her mind might revert to the agreeable person and martial appearance of Montraville" (emphasis added).

The question as to precisely *who* was responsible for making these various changes to Rowson's *Charlotte* has no single or straightforward answer. Because a published work was never the result of a single person's effort but that of a collaborative effort of a team of skilled workers who each had the power to influence (whether purposefully or inadvertently) the form of the printed text, it is difficult to assign agency to any particular change with certainty. Davidson has often implied that responsibility for not only the inception but the subsequent form of the American edition lay uniquely with Mathew Carey, describing him as "one of the most ardent pirates of British and European books" who, ostensibly as a matter of independent course, "quickly perceived the potential readership for Rowson's novel and reprinted it in his own pirated edition soon after he began selling Lane's version in his shop."[8] His "social agenda," she writes, "did not preclude him from copying closely Lane's edition of *Charlotte*. But although he produced a remarkably similar text, Carey made significant additions to the title page of his original American edition." By his insertion of the phrase, "Of the New Theatre, Philadelphia," Davidson argues, Carey "asserted that what he was publishing was an *American* novel."[9]

Evidence from Carey's own records and other primary sources, however, tells a more complicated, sometimes conflicting story. Not only does it suggest that the first American edition of *Charlotte* was actually an *authorized* one but it points to the existence of a substantial business relationship between Carey and Rowson that may have motivated as well as shaped the American publication and marketing of the novel. It is not the case, as Davidson states, that Carey reprinted his edition of *Charlotte* "soon" after beginning to sell the Lane edition in his bookshop. He actually never sold the Lane edition at all; the source that Davidson has cited for this is incorrect.[1] Though the source claims to have found the British edition of *Charlotte* in a 1792 Carey catalog, firsthand examination shows that the book listed in this catalog is not in fact Rowson's *Charlotte*, but almost certainly *The History of Miss Temple*, an entirely different work by A. Rogers.[2] Moreover, two years elapsed between the time

8. Cathy Davidson, Introduction to *Charlotte Temple* (New York: Oxford University Press, 1986), xxxi.
9. Cathy Davidson, "The Life and Times of *Charlotte Temple*: A Biography of a Book," in *Reading in America: Literature & Social History* (Baltimore: Johns Hopkins University Press, 1989), 164–165.
1. See R. W. G. Vail, *Susanna Haswell Rowson, The Author of* Charlotte Temple: *A Bibliographical Study* (Worcester: American Antiquarian Society, 1933).
2. See M. Carey catalog for August–December, 1792. The confusion has arisen because the novel was listed in this catalog as simply "Miss Temple," probably shortening the title of *The History of Miss Temple* in a manner consistent with the rest of the catalog's format. Because *Charlotte. A Tale of Truth* would eventually be renamed *Charlotte Temple* in 1797, the bibliographer Vail seems to have assumed that *Miss Temple* referred to Rowson's novel. In 1792, however, Rowson's novel had yet to be known by any title other than

Carey was supposed to have sold the Lane edition of *Charlotte* and the time he published his own edition in Philadelphia. Notably, it was during these two years that Susanna and William Rowson emigrated from England to begin working at the New Theatre of Philadelphia—the same spot that Carey, particularly "seized with a theatrical mania" in 1793 and 1794, happened to frequent "about twice for every three times the theatre was open."[3] Carey's subsequent production of a set of dramatic criticisms on the plays he had attended prompted William Rowson to personally offer him a paid position as a critic for the New Theatre, which Carey politely declined. Whether or not this particular transaction led to the initial meeting and subsequent business arrangements between Carey and Susanna Rowson, by May 1794 Carey had both printed the first American edition of *Charlotte* and helped facilitate the printing of *Trials of the Human Heart*, a new novel that Rowson herself was then undertaking to publish by subscription. Not only did Carey accept subscription money for this novel at his bookshop (Rowson was also personally accepting money at a location near the New Theatre), but he purchased twenty advance copies of the book—an expense that at the time would have demonstrated enthusiastic patronage on his part. Under Susanna Rowson's advisement, Carey had also contacted William Lane about the possibility of obtaining bulk shipments of novels from the British publisher at an exclusive discount.[4] It is significant that he had also paid Susanna Rowson for the copyright to her soon-to-be best-seller. In May 1794, Carey sent twenty complimentary copies of the newly printed *Charlotte*, a bank check for $20, and a letter to Susanna Rowson expressly designating this check "a small acknowledgement for the copy right of *Charlotte*."[5] The same letter congratulates Rowson for having received about a third of the requisite subscriptions for *Trials of the Human Heart*.

It is clear, given the nature of these transactions, that Rowson played an instrumental role in Carey's decision to publish her work in Philadelphia. One quite plausible scenario is that Rowson and her

---

Charlotte. A Tale of Truth, as it was indeed listed in both the catalogs of Thomas Allen (New York, 1792) and William Blake (Boston, 1793), the only booksellers who seem to have sold this title in the United States before Carey's first American edition of 1794. Notably, the list of works in the 1792 Carey catalog also contains almost no contemporary novels, but predominantly older European editions from the same era as *The History of Miss Temple* (1777).

3. Mathew Carey, *Mathew Carey Autobiography* (New York: Schwab, 1942), 29.
4. Mathew Carey to William Lane, May 28, 1794, Lea & Febiger Papers, Letterbook C: 197, Historical Society of Pennsylvania.
5. Mathew Carey to Mrs. Rowson, May 1, 1794, and May 19, 1794, Lea & Febiger Papers, Letterbook C: 187, 195, HSP. Copyright laws did not require Carey to pay Rowson at all for reprinting her novel, which as a work first published in England claimed no copyright protection in America. Accordingly, Carey could not actually register the copyright for *Charlotte*, thereby protecting his own edition from unauthorized reprinting. His payment to Rowson thus seems to have been more a gesture of respect than a recognition of contractual obligation.

husband arrived in Philadelphia with at least one copy of the first British edition of *Charlotte* and subsequently arranged, perhaps together, to have Carey publish his own edition of it.[6] Of course, support for the theory that Rowson was involved in the process of creating *Charlotte*'s first American edition is not sufficient to demonstrate that any or all of the changes made to her novel's text for its American printing were necessarily a result of her input and/or political agenda. Grammatical and punctuation-related emendations, for instance, are less reasonably attributable to Rowson or even Carey than to Daniel Humphreys, the printer who physically produced the book and would eventually become one of Carey's principal proofreaders—correcting yet another Carey edition of *Charlotte Temple* in 1809. While substantive changes to politically controversial material could have been suggested by Rowson, who incorporated much patriotism into her later writings, they could just as easily have been the work of Carey, whose own popularity as a publisher grew to be inseparable from his politics. In regard, however, to the marketing of Rowson and her novel as "American" by virtue of the author's being "Of the New Theatre, Philadelphia," it is worth noting that the first public appearance of this phrase did not actually occur in Carey's edition of *Charlotte* itself. Rather, it appeared in the newspaper solicitations for *Trials of the Human Heart* subscriptions that preceded the publication of *Charlotte* by a few weeks. As *Trials* was from the outset a work published by Rowson, not Carey, it is plausible that Rowson had as much to do with the content of the advertisement as Carey himself, if not more. The token "Of the New Theatre, Philadelphia" thus seems as likely to have been Rowson's own invention as Carey's.

In this fashion, an alternate history of *Charlotte Temple* emerges. This history is one that would not have presented itself had the contents of the British edition of *Charlotte, A Tale of Truth* not been available for examination. Surprisingly often, an awareness of the changes that occur to texts over time leads one to question the human and historical forces that brought about those changes. In turn, these questions can often lead to surprising historical discoveries that can change the way we think about the past. In the case of *Charlotte Temple*, textual analysis offers a portrait of a Susanna Rowson who played a more active role than previously believed in publishing America's first best-selling novel.

6. The original manuscript of *Charlotte*, currently presumed lost or destroyed, is not likely to have served as the copy text for the first American edition of the novel. Publishers of Carey's era preferred to reissue a text from a printed edition rather than a manuscript for the simple reason that to do so saved time, effort, and money. Similarities between the setting of the two editions, as well as the nature of errors made in the text's resetting, also suggest that the printed British edition, rather than the manuscript, was in fact the copy text for the Carey edition of *Charlotte*.

WILLIAM HILL BROWN

From The Power of Sympathy; or, The Triumph of Nature[†]

Letter XI.

MRS. HOLMES *TO* MYRA.

BELLEVIEW.

I sit down to give you, my dear *Myra*, some account of the visitants of today, and their conversation. We are not always *distinguished* by such company, but perhaps it is sometimes necessary; and as it is a relaxation from thought, it serves to give us more pleasure in returning to the conversation of people of ideas.

Mrs. *Bourn* assumes a higher rank in life than she pretended to seven years ago.—She then walked on foot—she now, by good fortune, rides in a chariot. Placed, however, in a situation with which her education does not altogether comport, she has nothing disagreeable but her over assiduity to please—this is sometimes disgusting, for one cannot feast heartily upon honey: It is an errour which a candid mind easily forgives. She sometimes appears solicitous to display her mental accomplishments, and desirous to improve those of her daughter; but it is merely apparent. Notwithstanding a temporary wish may arise towards the attainment of this point, a habitual vacancy nips it in the bud.

Miss *Bourn* is about the age of fourteen—genteel, with a tolerable share of beauty, but not striking—her dress was elegant, but might have been adjusted to more advantage—not altogether awkward in her manners, nor yet can she be called graceful—she has a peculiar air of *drollery* which takes her by fits, and for this reason, perhaps, does not avail herself of every opportunity of displaying the modesty of her sex—she has seen much company, but instead of polishing her manners, it has only increased her assurance.

Thus much of the characters of our *company*. After some small chat which passed as we took a turn in the garden, we entered the Temple.

"What books would you recommend to put into the hands of my daughter?" said Mrs. *Bourn*, as she walked into the library—"it is a matter of some importance." "It is a matter of *more* importance," answered *Worthy*, "than is generally imagined, for unless a proper selection is made, one would do better never to read at all:—Now, Madam, as much depends on the choice of books, care should be taken not to put those in the way of young persons, which might

---

[†] Boston, 1789. Early American Imprints, Series 1: Evans, no. 21979.

leave on their minds any disagreeable prejudices, or which has a tendency to corrupt their morals."—"As obvious as your remark is,"
added Mr. *Holmes*, "it is evidently overlooked in the common course
of education. We wisely exclude those persons from our conversation, whose characters are bad, whose manners are depraved, or
whose morals are impure; but if they are excluded from an apprehension of contaminating our minds, how much more dangerous is the
company of those books, where the strokes aimed at virtue are
redoubled, and the poison of vice, by repeatedly reading the same
thing, indelibly distains the young mind?"

"We all agree," rejoined *Worthy*, "that it is as great a matter of virtue and prudence to be circumspect in the selection of our books, as
in the choice of our company.—But, Sir, the best things may be subverted to an ill use. Hence we may possibly trace the cause of the ill
tendency of many of the Novels extant."

"Most of the Novels," interrupted my father, "with which our
female libraries are overrun, are built on a foundation not always
placed on strict morality, and in the pursuit of objects not always
probable or praiseworthy.—Novels, not regulated on the chaste principles of true friendship, rational love, and connubial duty, appear to
me totally unfit to form the minds of women, of friends, or of wives."

"But, as most young people read," says Mrs. *Bourn*—"what rule
can be *hit upon* to make study always terminate to advantage?"

"Impossible," cried Miss, "for I read as much as any body, and
though it may afford amusement, while I am employed, I do not
remember a single word, when I lay down the book."

"This confirms what I say of Novels," cried Mr. *Holmes*, addressing
Worthy in a jocular manner, "just calculated to kill time—to attract
the attention of the reader for an hour, but leave not one idea on the
mind."

"I am far from condemning every production in the gross," replied
Worthy; "general satire against any particular class, or order of men,
may be viewed in the same light as a satire against the species—it is
the same with books—If there are corrupt or mortified members, it
is hardly fair to destroy the whole body. Now I grant some Novels
have a bad tendency, yet there are many which contain excellent
sentiments—let these receive their deserved reward—let those be
discountenanced; and if it is impossible "to smite them with an apo-
plexy, there is a moral certainty of their dying of a consumption."——
But, as Mrs. *Bourn* observes, most young persons read, I will
therefore recommend to those who wish to mingle instruction with
entertainment, method and regularity in reading. To *dip* into *any
book* burthens the mind with unnecessary lumber, and may rather be
called a disadvantage, than a benefit—The record of memory is so
scrawled and blotted with imperfect ideas, that not one legible character can be traced."

"Were I to throw my thoughts on this subject," said my good father-in-law, as he began to enter more warmly into the debate—drawing his chair opposite *Worthy*, and raising his hand with a poetical enthusiasm—"Were I to throw my thoughts on this subject into an Allegory, I would describe the human mind as an extensive plain, and knowledge as the river that should water it. If the course of the river be properly directed, the plain will be fertilized and cultivated to advantage; but if books, which are the sources that feed this river, rush into it from every quarter, it will overflow its banks, and the plain will become inundated: When, therefore, knowledge flows on in its proper channel, this extensive and valuable field, the mind, instead of being covered with stagnant waters, is cultivated to the utmost advantage, and blooms luxuriantly into a general efflorescence—for a river properly restricted by high banks, is necessarily progressive."

The old gentleman brought down his hand with great solemnity, and we complimented him on his poetical exertion. "I cannot comprehend the meaning of this matter," said the penetrative Miss *Bourn*. "I will explain it to you, my little dear," said he, with great good nature—"If you read with any design to improve your mind in virtue and every amiable accomplishment, you should be careful to read methodically, which will enable you to form an estimate of the various topicks discussed in company, and to bear a part in all those conversations which belong to your sex—you see, therefore, how necessary general knowledge is—what would you think of a woman advanced in life, who has no other store of knowledge, than what she has obtained from experience?"

"I think she would have a sorry time of it;" answered Miss.

"To prevent it in yourself," said Mrs. *Bourn* to her daughter, "be assiduous to lay in a good stock of this knowledge, while your mind is yet free from prejudice and care."

"How shall I *go to work*, Madam," enquired the delicate daughter.

Mrs. *Bourn* turned towards Mr. *Holmes*, which was hint enough for the good old man to proceed.

"There is a medium to be observed, continued he, in a lady's reading; she is not to receive every thing she finds, even in the best books, as invariable lessons of conduct; in books written in an easy, flowing style, which excel in description and the luxuriance of fancy, the imagination is apt to get heated—she ought, therefore, to discern with an eye of judgment, between the superficial and the penetrating—the elegant and the tawdry—what may be merely amusing, and what may be useful. General reading will not teach her a true knowledge of the world.

"In books she finds recorded the faithfulness of friendship—the constancy of *true love*, and even that honesty is the best policy. If virtue is represented carrying its reward with it, she too easily persuades herself that mankind have adopted this plan: Thus she finds, when, perhaps, it is too late, that she has entertained wrong notions of human nature; that her friends are deceitful—her lovers false—and that men consult interest oftener than honesty.

"A young lady who has imbibed her ideas of the world from desultory reading, and placed confidence in the virtue of others, will bring back disappointment, when she expected gratitude. Unsuspicious of deceit, she is easily deceived—from the purity of her own thoughts, she trusts the faith of mankind, until experience convinces her of her errour—she falls a sacrifice to her credulity, and her only consolation is the simplicity and goodness of her heart.

"The story of Miss *Whitman*[1] is an emphatical illustration of the truth of these observations. An inflated fancy, not restricted by judgment, leads too often to *disappointment* and repentance. Such will be the fate of those who become (to use her own words)

> "Lost in the magick of that sweet employ,
> "To build *gay scenes* and fashion *future joy*.

"With a good heart she possessed a poetical imagination, and an unbounded thirst for novelty; but these airy talents, not counterpoised with judgment, or perhaps serious reflection, instead of adding to her happiness, were the cause of her ruin."

"I conclude from your reasoning," said I, "and it is, besides, my own opinion, that many fine girls have been ruined by reading Novels."

---

1. This young lady was of a reputable family in Connecticut. In her youth she was admired for beauty and good sense. She was a great reader of novels and romances, and having imbibed her ideas of *the characters of men*, from those fallacious sources, became vain and coquetish, and rejected several offers of marriage, in expectation of receiving one more agreeable to her fanciful idea. Disappointed in her *Fairy* hope, and finding her train of admirers less solicitous for the honour of her hand, in proportion as the roses of youth decayed, she was the more easily persuaded to relinquish that *stability* which is the honour and happiness of the sex. The consequences of her amour becoming visible, she acquainted her lover of her situation, and a *husband* was proposed for her, who was to receive a considerable sum for preserving the reputation of the lady; but, having received security for the payment, he immediately withdrew. She then left her friends, and travelled in the stage as far as *Watertown*, where she hired a young man to conduct her in a chaise to *Salem*. Here she wandered alone and friendless, and at length repaired to the *Bell-Tavern*, in *Danvers*, where she was delivered of a lifeless child, and in about a fortnight after (in *July*, 1788) died of a puerperal fever, aged about 35 years.

Before her death she amused herself with reading, writing and needlework, and though in a state of anxiety, preserved a cheerfulness, not so much the effect of insensibility, as of patience and fortitude. She was sensible of her approaching fate, as appears from the following letter, which was written in characters.

"Must I die alone? Shall I never see you more? I know that you will come, but you will come too late: This is, I fear, my last ability. Tears fall so, I know not how to write. Why did you leave me in so much distress? But I will not reproach you: All that was dear I left for you; but do not regret it.—May God forgive in both what was amiss: When I go from hence, I will leave you some way to find me; if I die, will you come and drop a tear over my grave?"

"And I believe," added Mrs. *Bourn*, "we may trace from hence the causes of spleen in many persons advanced in life."

"You mean old maids, Madam," cries the sagacious Miss, "like my aunt *Deborah*—she calls all the men deceitful, and most women, with her, are no better than they should be."

"Well said!" exclaimed *Worthy*, "the recollection of chagrin and former disappointment, sours one's temper and mortifies the heart— disappointment will be more or less severe in proportion as we elevate our expectations; for the most *sanguine tempers* are the soonest discouraged; as the highest building is in the most danger of falling."

"It appears from what I have said," resumed Mr. *Holmes*, "that those books which teach us a knowledge of the world are useful to form the minds of females, and ought therefore to be studied."

I mentioned *Rochefoucault's* maxims.—

"Do they not degrade human nature?" enquired my father.

"This little book," answered *Worthy*, "contains much truth—and those short sketches traced by the hand of judgment, present to us the leading features of mankind." "But," replied my father, "that *interest should assume all shapes*, is a doctrine, which, in my mind, represents a caricature rather than a living picture." "It is the duty of

---

In the following Poem, she, like the dying *Swan*, sings her own Elegy, and it is here added, as a sorrowful instance, how often the best, and most pleasing talents, not accompanied by virtue and prudence, operate the destruction of their possessor.

The description of her unfortunate passion, will remind the critical reader of the famous ode of *Sappho*. In genius and in misfortune, these poetical ladies were similar.

"DISAPPOINTMENT

"With fond impatience all the tedious day
I sigh'd, and wish'd the lingering hours away;
For when bright *Hesper* led the starry train,
My shepherd swore to meet me on the plain;
With eager haste to that dear spot I flew,
And linger'd long, and then with tears withdrew;
Alone, abandon'd to love's tenderest woes,
Down my pale cheeks the tide of sorrow flows;
Dead to all joys that fortune can bestow,
In vain for me her useless bounties flow;
Take back each envied gift, ye pow'rs divine,
And only let me call FIDELIO mine.
"Ah, wretch! what anguish yet thy soul must prove,
Ere thou canst hope to lose thy care in love;
And when FIDELIO meets thy tearful eye,
Pale fear and cold despair his presence fly;
With pensive steps, I sought thy walks again,
And kiss'd thy token on the verdant plain;
With fondest hope, thro' many a blissful bow'r,
We gave the soul to fancy's pleasing pow'r;
Lost in the magick of that sweet employ,
To build gay scenes, and fashion future joy,
We saw mild peace o'er fair *Canäan* rise,
And show'r her blessings from benignant skies;
On airy hills our happy mansion rose,
Built but for joy, no room for future woes;
Sweet as the sleep of innocence, the day,

a painter to produce a likeness," said *Worthy*.—"And a skilful one," cried my father, continuing the metaphor, "will bring the amiable qualities of the heart to light; and throw those which disgrace humanity into the shade." "I doubt," rejoined *Worthy*, "whether this flattery will answer the purpose you aim to accomplish—You entertain a high opinion of *the dignity of human nature*, and are displeased at the author who advances any thing derogatory to that dignity. *Swift*, in speaking of these maxims, in one of his best poems, affirms,

> "They argue no corrupted mind
> In him—the fault is in mankind."

"As I began this subject," added I, "it shall be ended by one observation—As these maxims give us an idea of the manners and characters of men, among whom a young person is soon to appear; and as it is necessary to her security and happiness that she be made acquainted with them—they may be read to advantage."

"There is another medium," said Mr. *Holmes*, assenting to my observation, "to be noticed in the study of a lady—she takes up a book, either for instruction or entertainment; the medium lies in knowing when to put it down. Constant application becomes labour—it sours the temper—gives an air of thoughtfulness, and

---

(By transports measur'd) lightly danc'd away;
To love, to bliss, the union'd soul was given,
And each! too happy, ask'd no brighter heaven.
    "And must the hours in ceaseless anguish roll?
Will no soft sunshine cheer my clouded soul?
Can this dear earth no transient joy supply?
Is it my doom to hope, despair and die?
Oh! come, once more, with soft endearments come,
Burst the cold prison of the sullen tomb;
Through favour'd walks, thy chosen maid attend,
Where well known shades their pleasing branches bend,
Shed the soft poison from thy speaking eye,
And look those raptures lifeless words deny;
Still be, though late, reheard what ne'er could tire,
But, told each eye, fresh pleasures would inspire;
Still hope those scenes which love and fancy drew;
But, drawn a thousand times, were ever new.

    "Can fancy paint, can words express;
Can aught on earth my woes redress;
E'en thy soft smiles can ceaseless prove
Thy truth, thy tenderness and love.
Once thou couldst every bliss inspire,
Transporting JOY, and gay DESIRE:
Now cold DESPAIR her banner rears,
And PLEASURE flies when she appears;
Fond HOPE within my bosom dies,
And AGONY her place supplies;
O, thou! for whose dear sake I bear,
A doom so dreadful, so severe,
May happy fates thy footsteps guide,
And o'er thy *peaceful* hour preside;
Nor let ELIZA's early tomb
Infect thee, with its baleful gloom."

frequently of absence. By *immoderate reading* we hoard up opinions and become insensibly attached to them; this miserly conduct sinks us to affectation, and disgustful pedantry; *conversation* only can remedy this dangerous evil, strengthen the judgment, and make reading really useful. They mutually depend upon, and assist each other.

"A knowledge of history which exhibits to us in one view the rise, progress and decay of nations—which points out the advancement of the mind in society, and the improvements in the arts which adorn human nature, comes with propriety under the notice of a lady. To observe the origin of civilization—the gradual progress of society, and the refinements of manners, policy, morality and religion—to observe the progression of mankind from simplicity to luxury, from luxury to effeminacy, and the gradual steps of the decline of empire, and the dissolution of states and kingdoms, must blend that happy union of instruction and entertainment, which never fails to win our attention to the pursuit of all subjects.

"Poetry claims her due from the ladies. Poetry enlarges and strengthens the mind, refines the taste and improves the judgment. It has been asserted that women have no business with *satire*—now satire is but a branch of poetry. I acknowledge, however, much false wit is sent into the world, under this general title; but no critick with whom I am acquainted ever called satire false wit—for as long as vice and folly continue to predominate in the human heart, the satire will be considered as a useful member of society. I believe *Addison* calls him an auxiliary to the pulpit. Suffer me to enlarge on this *new idea*. Satire is the correction of the vices and follies of the human heart; a woman may, therefore, read it to advantage. What I mean by enforcing this point, is, to impress the minds of females with a principle of self correction; for among all kinds of knowledge which arise from reading, the duty of self knowledge is a very eminent one; and is at the same time, the most useful and important.

Our ordinary intercourse with the world, will present to us in a very clear point of view, the fallacious ideas we sometimes entertain of our own self knowledge.—We are blinded by pride and self love, and will not observe our own imperfections, which we blame with the greatest acrimony in [sic] other people, and seem to detest with the greatest abhorrence; so that it often happens, while we are branding our neighbour for some foible, or vanity, we ourselves are equally guilty.

"Ridiculous as this conduct must appear in the eyes of all judicious people, it is too frequently practiced to escape observation.

"I will drop this piece of morality, with a charge to the fair reader, that whenever she discovers a satire, ridiculing or recriminating the follies or crimes of mankind, that she look into her own heart, and compare the strictures on the conduct of others with her own feelings."

ANONYMOUS

Character and Effects of Modern Novels[†]

When one reflects how easy a matter it is to give a wrong bias to the minds of youth, it is impossible to help being astonished at the remissness of those parents and guardians who suffer their daughters and wards to read, indiscriminately, the multiplicity of novels which are daily published.

It is as incumbent a duty to attend to the books a young lady reads, as to the company the keeps; for if it is allowed, that the frequent bearing of loose conversation naturally prepares the mind for the admittance of vicious ideas, it cannot be denied that books, in which love is the only theme, and intrigues the sole business of the actors, are more dangerous than even bad company; since the recital of lascivious scenes might shock an ear not yet hardened in vice, when the warm representation painted in a novel, and read in the privacy of retirement, cannot fail in exciting desires, and leaving impure traces on the memory.

Novels not only pollute the imaginations of young women, but likewise give them false ideas of life, which too often make them act improperly; owing to the romantic turn of thinking they imbibe from their favourite studies. They read of characters which never existed, and never can exist: and when all the wit and invention of a luxuriant fancy are stretched to paint a young man all perfection in body and mind, it is hardly possible for a girl to avoid falling in love with the phantom, and being out of humour with the piece of plain mortality which she afterwards marries, and finds, to her great disappointment and mortification, does not act like the image her fondness had dressed up to her view.

These authors of novels take great pleasure in making their characters act beyond nature. A young man loves the heroine to distraction: she cannot return his passion: she knows a lady who dies for him, though that lady is certain his heart is devoted to another. The heroine is not satisfied with making the man unhappy, by finding his pursuit hopeless, but she uses her power over him to make him marry the person he cannot love, and with whom he is afterwards miserable. He submits to his hard lot, pleased in having obeyed the commands of the sole arbitress of his fate. In novels, parents are described as cruel and obdurate, thwarting the inclinations of their children; and those children are made to invent numberless ways of

† Appeared in *The Weekly Magazine of Original Essays, Fugitive Pieces, and Interesting Intelligence*, March 10, 1798, p. 184. American Periodicals Series Online.

deceiving the watchful eyes of their real friends, in order to run to their ruin. By reading these books, therefore, young people are taught arts which they never could have dreamed of, and their minds being thus led into a wrong train of thinking, it is no wonder if their maturer age is bent on the pursuit of trifles, if not on vicious indulgencies.

I have heard it said in favour of novels, that there are many good sentiments dispersed in them. I maintain, that good sentiments being found scattered in loose novels, render them the more dangerous, since, when they are mixed with seducing arguments, it requires more discernment than is to be found in youth to separate the evil from the good; they are so nicely blended; and when a young lady finds principles of religion and virtue inculcated in a book, she is naturally thrown off her guard by taking it for granted that such a work can contain no harm: and of course the evil steals imperceptibly into her heart, while she thinks she is reading sterling morality.

ANONYMOUS

Novel Reading, A Cause of Female Depravity[†]

From the Monthly Mirror *for November 1797*

> "The traveller, if he chance to stray,
> May turn uncensur'd to his way;
> Polluted streams again are pure,
> And deepest wounds admit a cure;
> But woman no redemption knows—
> The wounds of honour never close!
> Pity may mourn, but not restore—
> And woman falls to rise no more."

Mr. Editor,
I now begin to hope I shall see good old days come round again— that moderately stiff stays, covered elbows, and concealed bosoms, will soon be prevailing fashions; and, what is of far greater importance, that chastity—pure and spotless CHASTITY!—will once more be the darling attribute of women. Had fashionable depravity been confined to the higher circles of life, I think I should hardly have troubled you with these my sentiments; I should have concluded it the offspring of idleness and voluptuousness, and have despaired of effectually deprecating a vice which not the happy example of conjugal virtue held forth from the throne could discoun-

† *The New England Quarterly Magazine,* April–June 1802, p. 172. American Periodicals Series Online.

tenance. But, like every other fashion, a little day hands it down to *the million*, and woman is now but another name for infamy.

I have been at some trouble to trace to its source this great calamity, in the middling orders of society—for fashion of itself, even if it was introduced by a prince, and his dulcinea's trains were held up by every peeress at court, could never have so unhappily corrupted the female world—and I find those who first made *novel-reading* an indispensible branch in forming the minds of young women, have a great deal to answer for. Without this poison instilled, as it were, into the blood, females in ordinary life would never have been so much the slaves of vice. The plain food, wholesome air, and exercise they enjoy, would have exempted them from the tyranny of lawless passions, and, like their virtuous grandmothers, they would have pointed the finger of shame at the impure and licentious. But those generous sentiments, those liberal opinions, those tender tales abounding with fine feeling, soft ideas, fascinating gentleness, and warm descriptions, have been the ruin of us. A girl with her intellectual powers enervated by such a course of reading, falls an easy prey to the first *boy* who assumes the languishing lover. He has only to stuff a piece of dirty paper into the crevice of her window, full of *thous* and *thees* and *thys* and mellifluous compounds, hyeroglyphically spelled, perhaps, and Miss is not long in finding out that "many waters cannot quench love, neither can the floods drown it;" so as Master is yet in his apprenticeship, and friends would disapprove of an early marriage, they agree to dispense with the ceremony. Nay, even when brooding over a helpless base-born infant, and surrounded by a once respectable and happy family, now dejected and dishonoured, too often does the infatuated fair one take pleasure in the misery she has created, and fancy floods of sorrow *sweetly graceful*, because, forsooth, she is just in the same point of view as the hapless, the distressed, the love-lorn Sappho of some novel or other.

And yet this, bad as it is, is not the worst result of such pernicious reading. It is no uncommon thing for a young lady who has attended her dearest friend to the altar, a few months after a marriage which, perhaps, but for *her*, had been a happy one, to fix her affections on her friend's husband, and by artful blandishments allure him to herself. Be not staggered, moral reader, at the recital! Such serpents are really in existence; such dæmons in the form of women are now too often to be found! Three instances, in as many years, have occurred in the little circle I move in. I have seen two poor disconsolate parents drop into premature graves, miserable victims to their daughter's dishonour, and the peace of several relative families wounded, never to be healed again in this world.

"And was novel-reading the cause of this?" inquires some gentle fair one, who, deprived of such an amusement, could hardly exist; "was novel-reading the foundation of such frail conduct?" I answer yes! It is in that school the poor deluded female imbibes erroneous principles, and from thence pursues a flagrantly vicious line of conduct; it is there she is told that love is involuntary, and that attachments of the heart are decreed by fate. Impious reasoning! As if a Power infinitely wise and beneficent would ordain atrocity! The first idle prepossession, therefore, such a person feels, if it happens to be for the husband of her most intimate friend, instead of calling herself to a severe account for the illegal preference, she sets to work to reconcile it to nature—"There is a fatality in it," argues she; "it is the will of Heaven our souls should be united in the silken bonds of reciprocal love, and there is no striving against fate." This once settled, criminality soon follows; the gentle, the sympathizing, the faithful friend, undauntedly plants a dagger in the bosom of the mother, and ruthlessly tears from the innocent children the parent stem on which their support and comfort depends. And yet this very female has cried, oh how she has cried! over relations of fictitious distress—has railed at hard-hearted fathers, cruel mothers, barbarous uncles, and treacherous friends, till her tongue denied its office, and she sunk beneath the weight of sympathy, for misery far short of *that* she herself is creating.

If good spirits in the other world are sensible of what is done in this, how will the Spartan and Roman dames of antiquity bless themselves that they were not doomed to breathe on earth in the eighteenth century; how will the cheeks of many a British matron be suffused with shame for her polluted descendants! You may think me warm, Mr. Editor, and your readers may think me illiberal; but let me beg of the female part of them to cast their eye into the world for a moment—let them count the disgraceful, and number the dishonoured, and if they do not find reason to blush for expiring virtue, I am content to be reckoned a peevish old maid, or a disappointed old bachelor, as long as I live. *Generosity, liberal judgment*, and *a refined way of thinking*, have done enough for us; for after ages will read in our annals, that when philosophy and humanity were objects of every one's pretension, from the night-man to the minister of state, the rights of nature were never more violated, nor the rights of religion more trampled on. What is refined sophistication; what is lenity, when they tend to corrupt our nature? Surely reprehensible! and as such let them give way to the more severe, but infinitely more beneficial, dictates of truth. Why are we endowed with so noble a power as reason? Why do we boast of a will to control our passions? if we suffer the one to be degraded by a vicious course of life, and the other to abet lascivious enormity.

CHARLES BROCKDEN BROWN

Novel-Reading[†]

I have just been reading a dissertation upon novel-reading, in which the writer says a great many grave and weighty things on the subject, and finally winds up by asserting, that supposing the whole stock of the Novelist's library to amount to one thousand, five hundred of these are void of all judgment, genius and taste, composed without knowledge of the world, or skill in composition; and of the remainder, four hundred and ninety-nine are calculated only to corrupt and deprave the morals. While engaged in pondering on this very comprehensive declaration, who should enter the apartment but Miss D——on a visit to my sister. This lady has an ample fortune, a lively curiosity, studious temper, and, though young and handsome, no lover. She has therefore abundant leisure, and all the means of reading at command. Novels are her favourite performances, and she has collected such a number of these as would enable her to supply the whole stock of a circulating library. As soon as she was seated, I read to her this severe sentence upon novels, and desired her opinion upon the subject.

Pray, said she a little indignant, who is this profound judge? I should like to be acquainted with a man, who knows of the existence, nay, who has, himself, read one thousand novels. I have never been able to collect even the titles of three-fourths of that number, and have spared neither pains nor pence in the attempt.

This number, said I, is merely hypothetical; but why should you suppose him to have read all the thousand?

Because I am charitable enough to suppose him possessed of common justice and common sense; and either of these would hinder him from judging without inquiry, of deciding without knowledge; and especially, would forbid him to pronounce so absolute and so severe a sentence without a careful and extensive examination of the subject.

I doubt much, said I, whether, in this case, he has read very closely or extensively. I am told, that he has little leisure for that kind of reading which the world, in general, has agreed to call mere pastime or amusement, and his taste leads him far away from such a library as yours.

'Tis a pity then, replied the lady, that he did not forbear to judge so severely and so positively. One in ten, that is one hundred in *the thousand* is the least that we novel-readers can allow him as a sample, by which to judge of the rest. If he has read this number

† *The Literary Magazine, and American Register (1803–1807),* March 1804, p. 403. American Periodical Series Online.

impartially and carefully, let him then pronounce judgment, telling us, at the same time, by what shred he has judged of the piece, and then, though we may reject his decision as groundless and absurd, yet we shall not deny his right to deliver an opinion. Without a suitable examination, this surely is a most rash and culpable thing, thus to condemn, as labouring only for corruption and depravity, so great a number of that unfortunate class of men, called authors. Novelists, in general, write for the sake of a subsistence. Their end is not only innocent but laudable, and the means they employ is to gratify that passion of enlightened minds which loves to contemplate human life in the mirror which genius holds up to it.

Those who condemn novels, or fiction, *in the abstract*, (continued the lady) are guilty of shameful absurdity and inconsistency. They are profoundly ignorant of human nature; the brightest of whose properties is to be influenced more by example than by precept: and of human taste; the purest of whose gratifications is to view human characters and events, depicted by a vigorous and enlightened fancy. . . . They condemn every thing which has gained the veneration of the world in all ages. They who condemn novels *as they are actually written*, evince nothing but an early prejudice, which will not permit them to *examine* before they *judge*, or a casual bias in favour of particular pursuits, which always leads a narrow mind to condemn all other reading as frivolous or pernicious.

You are very severe methinks, said I. Are you really willing to maintain that *all* novels are ingenious and beneficial?

That would be the height of the ridiculous, she replied. I love poetry, and revere the poets; but I never dreamed that *all* the verse that ever was written or published is useful and good. I love books, and read not a little; but I do not imagine that *every thing printed* is necessarily full of entertainment or instruction. Neither can I refuse to teach a child to read, because he may possibly light upon something in the form of books trifling or pernicious. It would be just as wise to sew up his mouth, because he may possibly swallow a poisoned berry, or a brass pin: to break both his legs, because he may possibly walk under a penthouse when it is falling. As to prohibit him from reading every thing called a novel, because there are books under that denomination, which may possibly deprave the morals, or vitiate the taste.

But my good friend, said I, you cannot but be aware that your comparisons are out of place. Many serious people prohibit novels altogether, merely because a vast majority of them are bad; because the chances of hurt, from reading them, greatly exceed the chances of benefit.

I deny it, said the zealous lady. A profligate novel is an extreme rarity. To write *immoral* tales, whatever recluse pedants may say, is by no means the road to popularity. In every kind of composition, it is always a small proportion, and the smallest proportion that is excellent. The larger proportion is indifferent or doubtful. The number of good novels, that is to say, novels that may be read with benefit and pleasure by persons of good morals and good taste, is very considerable. It is not true that the rest are particularly deficient in morality. The herd of romance-writers, are, for the most part, goaded by necessity into authorship. They seldom bring to the trade more than a good education, and good intentions; and the deficiency is not in the moral purpose of the work, but in the taste and genius displayed in the execution. If there are many insipid novels, it is because the whole number is very great. The man of taste easily discerns their defects, and lays them aside at the bottom of the first page. Boys and girls, and men and woman [sic] whose judgments are no better than those of boys and girls, read and relish them. The food is suited to the palate, and they derive a pleasure from it which at least is innocent.

The number of good novels, I repeat, is very large. It is not a task of such mighty difficulty, to distinguish them from the still greater number which are trivial or insipid. A list is easily formed, and those who want a guide in the selection may easily find one: and even the trivial and injudicious are not without their use, since there are vast numbers whose judgment and education raise them just high enough to relish these meager tales, and to whom sublimer fictions and austere studies are totally unfit.

They who prate about the influence of novels to unfit us for solid and useful reading, are guilty of a double error: for in the first place, a just and powerful picture of human life in which the connection between vice and misery, and between felicity and virtue is vividly portrayed, is the most solid and useful reading that a moral and social being (exclusive of particular cases and professional engagements) can read; and in the second place, the most trivial and trite of these performances are, to readers of certain ages and intellects, the only books which they will read. If they were not thus employed, they would be employed in a way still more trivial or pernicious. Pray, Crito, what do you think of the matter?

Why, my fair critic, you are a warm and zealous advocate; and, perhaps, defend your cause with a little more eloquence than truth. I cannot but say, however, that my fancy has received more delight, my heart more humanity, and my understanding more instruction from a few novels I could name, than from any other works; and that the merit of a score or two of these is, in my apprehension, so great, that they are the first and principal objects to which I would direct the curiosity of a child or pupil of mine.

I think, however, you assert a little rashly, when you say that a profligate novel is an extreme novelty. I could name half a dozen,

French and English, in a trice, that deserves this character; but all that your cause requires is, that there are a great many specimens of fiction where merit is liable to no exception; that there are the most popular and current works of the kind, and, consequently most likely to fall into the hand of readers who take up books at random: and that guides to a right choice are always to be found.

LINDA KERBER

"We Own That Ladies Sometimes Read": Women's Reading in the Early Republic[†]

> After my Funeral Charges and just Debts are paid, I recommend, give & Bequeath to my Beloved Daughter Idea Strong, my Bibles and inferior, orthodox Treatises on Religion and Morality, or relative or appertaining to vital Piety or practical Godliness, & all other Books, Pamphlets or Manuscripts, except Romances (if any left extant) which I have long since (though not early enough) intentionally consigned or destinated to deserved Oblivion in native Shades of Chaos.
>
> —Will of Jedidiah Strong,
> Litchfield, Connecticut,
> March 31, 1801

The vision of the Republican Mother owed a debt to the Enlightenment and to the Revolution. To the mother's traditional responsibility for maintenance of the household economy, and to the expectation that she be a person of religious faith, were added the obligation that she also be an informed and virtuous citizen. She was to observe the political world with a rational eye, and she was to guide her husband and children in making their way through it. She was to be a teacher as well as a mother.

All agreed that this Republican Mother should be alert and reasonably well acquainted with public affairs. But advice to women on what they should read was accompanied by insistent warnings—of which Jedidiah Strong's is the most extreme—of what not to read.[1] The literary culture of republican America was bifurcated. Men were said to read newspapers and history; women were thought to exercise their weaker intellects on the less demanding fare of fiction and devotional literature. A vigorous proscriptive literature warned of dangers women risked if they persisted in what was said to be their

---

[†] From *Women of the Republic* by Linda K. Kerber. Published for the Omohundro Institute of Early American History and Culture. Copyright © 1980 by the University of North Carolina Press. Used by permission of the publisher and author.

1. Jedidiah Strong's will is on file in the Conn. State Lib., Hartford. Strong was famous for his headstrong temper and his irascibility. His divorce case, which took much of the time of the Connecticut legislature, appears in *Conn. State Recs.*, VII, 206, 282.

taste for frivolous and romantic fiction. Occasionally we even come upon condemnation of reading itself, on the grounds that the new generation of women was being diverted from their proper household tasks. Women made their own responses to this campaign—quietly persisting in their choice of fiction and religious biography, writing romantic fiction that counseled against the loss of self-control, and revising their understanding of housekeeping to make room for their own participation in the world of the imagination.

"Sent the amiable Woodbridge his shirt and with it a letter— What the Consequence will be I know not," confided Polly Rogers to her diary.

> Read in a *sweet novel* the D——r brought me. It affected me so, I could *hardly* read it, and was often obliged to drop the Book to suppress my grief! Went to bed, Lay, and *thot* of the Lovely Woodbridge—shed a *torrent* of tears, at the *Recollection* of past interviews with him! . . . he (Woodbridge) press'd me to his *Bosom* with a *fondness* I thought expressive of approbation *never never* P——y hesitate a *moment* to Let me know if 'tis in my power to make you happy! would you would you no Sir! said I, at the same time kissing his Hand with *trembling* Lips! . . . I flew to my Chamber, & with the *avidity* of a *Lover opened* the Seal and read! sheding tears as I *read*.

By May, "the amiable Woodbridge" had apparently transferred his affections to someone else, and Polly wrote, "O had I *less* sensibility I should not *feel* so much, nor so *severely* my present situation."[2]

As this diary of a young woman in a small western Massachusetts town suggests, reading fiction could play a very important part in a woman's private life and imagination. In the eighteenth century the novel first came into its own as a genre, and the best fiction—*Tom Jones, Clarissa, La Nouvelle Héloïse*—won a large audience. In their substitution of individualized, realistic plots for the traditional plots taken from history and mythology, novels were different from earlier prose fiction. Their abandonment of traditional structure, accompanied by widespread and easy use of quasi-autobiographical detail, resulted, as Ian Watt has put it, in a genre marked by its "defiant . . . assertion of the primacy of individual experience." It was this assertiveness that made the new fiction startling and appealing. The classical unities of place and time were broken by time sequences imitative of human experience. Characters became real people with real names who led lives much like those of their readers.[3]

2. Journal of Polly Rogers, Jan. 10–11, May 14, 1785, Am. Antq. Soc., Worcester, Mass.
3. Ian B. Watt, *The Rise of the Novel: Studies in Defoe, Richardson and Fielding.* (Berkeley, Calif., 1957), 15. This paragraph relies heavily on chap. 2. See also Joseph J. Ellis's shrewd observations in *After the Revolution: Profiles of Early American Culture* (New York, 1979), 94–97.

But women did not always confine their reading to fiction. Surviving lists from booksellers, lending libraries, and diarists indicate clearly that it is impossible to make absolute gender distinctions about the reading audience of any book. Women read *Cato's Letters* and Paley's *Natural Theology*; men read fiction.[4]

Lists alone, however, cannot suggest much about what might be called the psychodynamics of reading. What did novels *mean* to the people who bought or borrowed them? What role did reading play in their imaginative lives? Books were cheaper, and more widely available, for the post-Revolutionary generation than they had been for their parents (although not nearly as easily available as they would be after the invention of better methods of type founding in the 1830s).[5]

For an understanding of the role of reading in one woman's life, we can turn to the revealing diary of Elizabeth Drinker. "It looks as if I spent most of my time reading, which is by no means the case," she wrote in 1795. "A book is soon run over. . . . I believe I may say, without vanity, that I was never an indolent person, or remarkably Bookish, the more so for 5 or 6 years past, than at any other period since I was married, having more leisure [now as a grandmother]— when my Children were young, I seldom read a volume."[6]

Elizabeth Drinker's memory was accurate. Her diary entries are very scanty in the years before the Revolution, and she rarely mentioned a book. During the excitement of the war years, especially during the time her husband was exiled, she kept a careful account of events in which she participated or which she observed, but once Henry Drinker returned she drifted out of the habit of regular entries. When she reached her fifties, the yellow fever epidemic of 1793 sent her back to her diary as a chronicler of the course of the disease, and thereafter book titles appear with great regularity in her journal.

Although she never failed to feel guilty about it, she did read fiction. "Read a romance or novel, which I have not done for a long time

---

4. See, for example, Mary Thomas's Book Catalogue, Isaiah Thomas Papers, Am. Antq. Soc., and the inventory of Mary Ann Woodrow Archbald's library, Archbald Papers, Sophia Smith Collection, Smith College Library, Northampton, Mass. Library loan lists appear in Chester T. Hallenbeck, "A Colonial Reading List from the Union Library of Hatboro, Pennsylvania," *PMHB*, LVI (1932), 289–340; the Salem (Mass.) Social Library, Tapley, *Salem Imprints*, 247; the Brentwood (New Hampshire) social library, 1823, Am. Antq. Soc., Worcester, Mass.; Thomas Bradford's bookstore and library, 1772, Hist. Soc. Pa.

5. Women could be very conscious of the increased availability of books in their own lifetime. In 1836, Margaret Browne wrote to her friend Eliza Quincy, wife of the president of Harvard, that she thought the "increase and circulation of new books" a mixed blessing. "Do you think that either you or I, if we were fourteen years of age, would now become as conversant as we then were with the English classics and poets, which are now reposing in sullen dignity on her bookshelves, while every table is littered with annuals and monthly and weekly journals?" (Eliza Susan Quincy, *Memoir of the Life of Eliza S. M. Quincy* [Boston, 1861], 299).

6. Diary of Elizabeth Drinker, May 22, 1795, Hist. Soc. Pa.

before," she remarked on March 30, 1795. "It was a business I followed in my younger days, not so much as many others, 'tho more
than some others." Even Royall Tyler's *The Contrast*, widely honored
as the first native American play, made her uncomfortable. She
called it "a small ridiculous novel" (meaning, one supposes, that it
was fiction) and felt it necessary to account for her weakness in reading it: "S. Kidd's brother brings them to her, he lives, I believe at a
book shop tho I have read some of them myself, I have been talking
to her against the practice."[7] She thought Ann Radcliffe's *The Italian*
"trash" and could justify Radcliffe's *The Mysteries of Udolpho* only
because she did needlework while her married daughter read the
book aloud: "Molly has been for some days past, at times reading
while we work'd, three romantic vol. intitled The Misteries of
Udolphia—a tremendous tale—but not quite like the old fashion
Gothick stories that I was fond of when young. 'tis seldom I listen to
a romance, nor would I encourage my Children doing much of that
business."[8] But Mrs. Drinker found it hard to stay away. When she
finished reading "a foolish Romance entitled The Haunted priory,"
she made a point of reporting that she had also "finished knitting
a pair large cotton stockings, bound a petticoat and made a batch of
Gingerbread—this I mention to shew that I have not spent the day
reading."[9]

"I read a little of most things." Because she was a serious and committed Quaker, a member of an old and prominent Quaker family,
instructive Quaker tracts and histories appear and reappear in her
diary entries. Although her politics were unambivalently conservative and Federalist, her reading was catholic. She read Thomas Paine
as well as attacks on him; she read criticisms of "Peter Porcupine" as
well as "Porcupine's" attacks on the Federalists. She even perused
the *Confessions* of Jean Jacques Rousseau, remarking, "I like him
not, or his ideas."[1] She ordered "Bolinbroke on the study and use of
History" from the library, but was dismayed to conclude "that it set at
nought the Holy Scriptures." She was even embarrassed that it was
signed out in her name and "sent it back unread."[2]

The sheer volume of Elizabeth Drinker's reading is impressive. In
1796, the year she read Mary Wollstonecraft's *Vindication* and made
her well-known elliptical remark about it, Elizabeth Drinker read a
collection of fifty Cheap Repository tracts and at least twenty-eight
pamphlets on religious and political subjects. She read both sides of
the pamphlet war for and against William Cobbett (three years later

7. *Ibid.*, Mar. 30, 1795, July 26, 1797.
8. *Ibid.*, July 11, 1797, June 20, 1795.
9. *Ibid.*, Feb. 29, 1796.
1. *Ibid.*, end of 1800; Reading list of Elizabeth Drinker, May 6, 1800.
2. Diary of Elizabeth Drinker, July 24, 1800.

she followed the published transcript of the Rush-Cobbett trial). In 1796 she read at least sixteen books in addition to Wollstonecraft's, some in several volumes. Among her selections were Dante's *Inferno*, Erasmus Darwin's *The Botanic Garden* (which she liked very much), and Madame de Genlis's *Adelaide and Theodore*. Though she was no Jacobin, she read six volumes of Wollstonecraft's friend Helen Maria Williams, and several books of poetry, including the sentimental verse of the Della Cruscans. Despite all her embarrassment, Elizabeth Drinker read at least eight novels, including William Godwin's *Caleb Williams*, a book she felt free to like since she as yet knew nothing of the author's politics.

Reading was an integral part of Elizabeth Drinker's daily life, but it was an element about which she always felt self-conscious. She needed to reassure herself and the descendant whom she imagined to be the ultimate reader of her diary that she had not been irresponsible in the amount of time she devoted to reading. She retained from her younger years the sense that there was something inappropriate, even immodest, about fiction. "It may appear strange to some," she wrote, "that an infirm old Woman should begin the year reading romances—'tis a practice I by no means highly approve, yet I trust I have not sined."[3]

Drinker's self-consciousness suggests the impact of the enormous proscriptive literature that counseled everyone, but especially women, against reading novels. Young women were thought to be most vulnerable to the attractions of irresponsibility and passion as depicted in novels, and few observers credited women with a catholicity of tastes and interest approaching Drinker's. "Novels are the favourite, and most dangerous kind of reading, now adopted by the generality of young ladies," thundered Hannah Webster Foster in 1798. "I say dangerous . . . [because they] fill the imagination with ideas which lead to impure desires . . . and a fondness for show and dissipation. . . . They often pervert the judgment, mislead the affections, and blind the understanding." *The American Lady's Preceptor*, a collection of "essays and poetical effusions, designed to direct the female mind," which was widely used in schools, warned that reading novels would encourage self-indulgent "sensibility."[4]

It was assumed that romantic fiction could affect its readers' actual behavior—and for the worse. "Never let my poor Child Read a Novel or Romance," cried the unhappy Elizabeth Gouverneur, divorced by her husband for bearing a child that was not his. "These I am sure helped to [shape] Ideas in my head which perhaps I never should

---

3. *Ibid.*, Jan. 7, 1796. She had just read *The Victim of Magical Illusions*. See also Scott, "Self-Portraits," in Bushman *et al.*, eds., *Uprooted Americans*, 46–55.
4. Hannah Foster, *The Boarding School; Or, Lessons of a Preceptress to Her Pupils . . .* (Boston, 1798), 18; *The American Lady's Preceptor* (Baltimore, 1810), 14–17.

have had, and the person who brought them to me took care to pick out such as would Suit his Purpose."[5] The young William Gaston, lonely in boarding school, wrote to warn his younger sister against romantic novels: "Under those stories, which are thought entertaining, lies a venomous poison. . . . setting aside religion, they never fail to inspire those who read them, with romantic ideas, to give them a disgust for all serious employments." Even Mercy Otis Warren, who wrote her own fiction in the form of plays, warned a niece about to marry that novel reading made for inefficient housewifery: "Throw away no part of your time, in the perusal of . . . the puerile study of romance." John Trumbull versified the fears and dangers.

> We own that Ladies sometimes read,
> And grieve *that* reading is confined
> To books that poison all the mind
> The bluster of romance, that fills
> The head brimfull of purling rills
> And swells the mind with haughty fancies
>
> .   .   .   .
>
>   For while she reads romance, the Fair one
> Fails not to think herself the Heroine
>
> .   .   .   .
>
> Thus *Harriet* reads, and reading really
> Believes herself a young *Pamela*,
> The high-wrought whim, the tender strain
> Elate her mind and turn her brain . . . [6]

Fiction itself warned against fiction. The first step in the seduction of the title character of *Laura* is taken when her suitor, Belfield, provides her with Pope's "Letter of Eloise to Abelard" and copies of romantic novels. Alicia Sheridan LeFanu's *Lucy Osmond* was written "to exemplify the danger attending the early study of works of mere imagination," and the young heroine is early cautioned against novels. *Emily Hamilton* was offered by "A Young Lady of Massachusetts" as "a Novel founded on incidents in real life," and therefore more wholesome than the usual novel, which was frequently "in the highest degree prejudicial to young minds, by giving them wrong ideas of the world, and setting their tastes so high as to occasion a disrelish for those scenes in which they are necessitated to take a

---

5. *Isaac Gouverneur Jr.* v. *Elizabeth Gouverneur*, Chancery No. 41, Mar. 31, 1787, Historical Documents Collection, Queens College, City University of New York. I am indebted to Leo Hershkowitz for this reference.
6. William Gaston to Mrs. Gaston, Jan. 4, 1792, William Gaston Papers, Southern Historical Collection, University of North Carolina, Chapel Hill, N.C.; Mercy Otis Warren to Rebecca Otis, n.d., 1776, Mercy Otis Warren Letterbook, Warren Papers, Mass. Hist. Soc.; John Trumbull, "The Progress of Dulness," in Edwin T. Bowden, ed., *The Satiric Poems of John Trumbull* (Austin, Tex., 1962), 88.

part."[7] The famous Irish novelist Maria Edgeworth wrote an epistolary novel, reprinted in America, in which one sister, Julia, indulges
her taste for romances and acquires "the eager genius, the exquisite
sensibility of enthusiasm" rather than her sister Caroline's "stoical
serenity of philosophy." Julia's preference for romance leads her
directly to the choice of a flashy but unreliable husband, causing her
disappointment in marriage, her separation from her beloved children, and her premature death.[8] It was warnings like these that
Elizabeth Drinker took to heart, and that are reflected in her diary
entries begrudging the time spent on fiction.

When some twenty young women organized the Boston Gleaning
Circle in 1805, they defined it as a self-improvement society. They
met every week to read and discuss "any book favourable to the
improvement of the mind"—by which they meant "Divinity, History,
Geography, Astronomy, Travels Poetry &c but Novels and Romances
are absolutely excluded." The danger of reading novels, these young
women told each other, was that young people "will expect to meet in
life the romantic incidents portrayed by the pen of the Novelist. . . .
[In life,] the roses and thorns are intermixed, but in Novels the
thorns come first, and the roses afterwards." They thought even virtue was too neatly rewarded in fiction, as it often was not on earth,
and so a misleading impression of the instrumentality of good behavior might be given.[9]

These attacks on fiction, it is clear, were in large part attacks on
emotion, on passion, and on sexuality. Even cautionary fiction, like
Charlotte Temple, could be dangerous because it offered details of
seduction in the very act of warning young women to be on their
guard against rakes. The worst books were those that seemed to
endorse the passionate way of life as a course to be emulated. The
very worst example, the one fulminated against most vehemently,
was Julie, Rousseau's *Nouvelle Héloïse*. Had *La Nouvelle Héloïse*
been a typical Sturm und Drang novel, Judith Shklar has observed,
"the heroine would have defied her parents, run off with her lover,
given birth to an illegitimate child, killed the child out of shame, and
then died alone and in misery. The hero would, after similar disasters, have killed himself, or gone mad." But Julie invites her lover to
visit while her own husband is home, she maintains throughout her
love and affection for both men, and all major characters find a

7. [Mrs. Leonara Sansay or Rebecca Rush?], *Laura, By a Lady of Philadelphia* . . . (Philadelphia, 1809), 40–44; Alicia Sheridan LeFanu, *Lucy Osmond* (New York, 1804); [Sukey
Watson], *Emily Hamilton* (Worcester, Mass., 1803), iii–iv.
8. "Letters of Julia and Caroline," reprinted in Edgeworth, *Letters For Literary Ladies*, 5–6.
Similar plot outlines were used by Judith Sargent Murray in *The Gleaner* and Charles
Brockden Brown in *Ormond*.
9. Boston Gleaning Circle, Record Book, Regulation #5, Boston Pub. Lib.; Boston Gleaning Circle, Minute Book, 25, Boston Pub. Lib.

measure of happiness by the novel's close. This ending made Rousseau seem the more dangerous. For the English educator Hannah More, "novel" was a shorthand way of referring to Rousseau, and when she said Rousseau, she was thinking of *La Nouvelle Héloïse*. "Novels . . . are continually shifting their ground, and enlarging their sphere, and are daily becoming vehicles of wider mischief," she complained in *Strictures on the Modern System of Female Education*, published in London in 1799 and in Connecticut in 1801. "Rousseau . . . annihilates the value of chastity, and with pernicious subtlety attempts to make the heroine appear almost more amiable without it."[1]

Julie—her name is sometimes mistranslated as Eloisa—appears and reappears in American fiction as a leitmotif, warning against the pleasures of passion. Martha Read's heroine Monima, browsing in her father's library, comes upon Rousseau's Eloisa, but she is forbidden to read it.[2] In 1802 a Washington, D.C., publisher reprinted an English cautionary novel in which an adulteress reflects: "In the impassioned letters of Heloise, I found sentiments so congenial to my own, that, regardless of the danger of perusing them in my present situation, I could read nothing else: and I was soon so fascinated with the beauties of the style, and the originality of the thoughts, that I considered every doctrine they contained as infallible. . . . like Heloise, [I] persuaded myself that there were moments of happiness for which life and honor would not be too great a sacrifice."[3] As late as 1823, *La Nouvelle Héloïse* was still considered dangerous. From Augusta, Georgia, Henry H. Cumming wrote to his fiancée that he suspected from her last letter that she was secretly reading "the enthusiastic (but unfortunately, *crack-brained*) Rousseau." Although he admired some of Rousseau's work and promised to study it with her in French, he warned that "Julia or the modern Elisa probably contains as many glowing expressions of both sentimental & voluptuous love, and as much immorality as any book in any language."[4]

Historians of American ideas have generally concluded that Rousseau seems to have had relatively little appeal to Americans of his own generation. He was not quoted, for example, in the debates at the Constitutional Convention; major political theorists like Madison, Jefferson, and Adams made little use of his work. *The Social*

1. Judith N. Shklar, *After Utopia: The Decline of Political Faith* (Princeton, N.J., 1957), 29–30; Hannah More, *Strictures on the Modern System of Female Education* (Hartford, Conn., 1801), 25.
2. Martha Read, *Monima; or, The Beggar Girl* (New York, 1802), 367–369.
3. *The Adulteress, or Memoirs of Characters Now Living In The Fashionable World* (Washington, D.C., 1802), 16, 42–48. Another extensive attempt to use a fictional vehicle to condemn Rousseau is *Lucy Osmond*, a British novel republished in New York in 1804.
4. Henry H. Cumming to Julia A. Bryan, May 17, 1823, Hammond-Bryan-Cumming Papers, S. Caroliniana Lib., Univ. S.C., Columbia.

Contract was not widely available in American libraries until well into the nineteenth century, and when influential Americans encountered it, they seem to have found it either perplexing or frightening.[5] But what has been missed in this analysis is the widespread popularity of Rousseau's less theoretical works in America, particularly of *Emile* and *Héloïse*. Each of these books had significant, even revolutionary, things to say about women and their role in society. As we have seen, *Emile*'s Sophie provided the terms for much debate on the appropriate education for women, and she figured in Wollstonecraft's searing attack on Rousseau. *Héloïse*'s celebration of women's passion and instinct prompted an equally intense debate on the nature of women's emotions and the extent to which they could be trusted. There was thus a gender-distinction to be made on the ways Americans used the major works of the European Enlightenment. If *The Social Contract* or *The Spirit of the Laws* were "men's books," *Emile* and *Héloïse* were in some sense women's books. The throngs of second-rate heroines with names like Julia or Eloisa evince the extraordinary appeal of Rousseau's passionate women. The continued attack on romantic fiction for suggesting to young women that they might give free rein to their passions was in some measure a response to Rousseau.

Fiction that taught women to trust their passions was criticized in the picaresque *Female Quixotism*, published in Boston in 1801 and specifically addressed to "all Columbian Young Ladies, who read Novels and Romances."[6] It took as its subject a romantic girl whose head had been turned by the "unrestrained perusal" of fiction. Its author, writing under the possible pseudonym Tabitha Tenney, linked her attack on passion to the need to build virtuous republican citizens.

The heroine, Dorcas Sheldon, has no mother to protect her from reading the novels in her father's large collection of history and fiction. Dorcas's father does not realize that novels that may be harmless when read by men may have a "dangerous tendency to a young inexperienced female mind." Because novels have taught that love is a "violent emotion," Dorcas distrusts her own quiet affection for her first suitor. When his letter of proposal does not come up to the epistolary standard of her favorite novels, she rejects him.[7]

---

5. David Lundberg and Henry F. May, "The Enlightened Reader in America," *American Quarterly*, XXVIII (1976), 285; Paul Merrill Spurlin, *Rousseau in America: 1760–1809* (University, Ala., 1969).
6. [Tabitha Gilman Tenney], *Female Quixotism: Exhibited in the Romantic Opinions and Extravagant Adventures of Dorcasina Sheldon*, I (Boston, 1801), iii. The book is an extended parody of Charlotte Lennox's *The Female Quixote; or the Adventures of Arabella* (London, 1752), which in turn is an extended parody of romantic heroines.
7. [Tenney], *Female Quixotism*, I, 7, 15.

The departure of this young man leaves a series of increasingly unpalatable options. Dorcas's suitors include anti-intellectual men, who disapprove of all reading: "enemies to female improvement, thought a woman had no business with any book but the bible, or perhaps the art of cookery; believing that everything beyond these served only to disqualify her for the duties of domestic life." There finally appears a dashing adventurer, to whose obvious faults she is blinded by her appetite for mystery and romance. She explains away her father's demurrers by reflecting that her favorite heroines had often had cruel and unsympathetic parents. She changes her name to the more poetic "Dorcasina." She hides notes in hollow trees. She does not resist an abduction because she had "frequently read of ladies being forcibly carried off by resolute lovers." In short, she makes a fool of herself. "Oh! those poisonous, those fatal novels!" exclaims her father. "How have they warped your judgment. . . . Would to heaven people could find some better employment, than thus turning the heads of inexperienced females!"[8]

But Dorcas's novels have misled her. The false realism of the pica-resque novel encouraged the unsophisticated girl to conclude that fiction reported life as it might be lived. Although she first came to her novels for entertainment, Dorcas soon finds herself using them as guides to her conduct, and from them she learns hopelessly inap-propriate and artificial forms of behavior. Sure that the only certain guide is emotion and passion, she learns to distrust her own rea-son in the belief that people have no rational control over their relationships.

In a mode more subtle than the didactic essays of Hannah More and Judith Sargent Murray, the tale of Dorcasina suggests what con-temporaries found to criticize in the new fiction. Novels celebrated passion; they suggested that women were well guided by their own emotions. They encouraged people to break out of socially accepted roles, roles thought to be guided by reason. These novels may be understood as examples of the new sensibility that would be labeled romanticism, with which Americans would eventually make their peace. Dorcasina's experiences of romantic love were set against the requirements of the republican enlightenment: rationality and self-control. As Murray argued, the Republic had defined an ideal filled with political implications for woman: she was to be clearheaded and in control of her own emotions so that she could in turn control her husband and her children and thereby guarantee the virtuous behav-ior on which the security of the Republic depended. The Republic did not need emotional women who could easily be manipulated by men for their own gratification or who would lure men away from the

8. *Ibid.*, 17, 129, 171.

path of virtue. Novels seemed to offer approbation for precisely the sort of behavior that political and didactic literature had labeled a danger to the Republic.

Thus the extensive didactic literature critical of women's interest in fiction served an implicit political purpose. It began with a political ideal of what women *ought* to be and attempted to persuade women to emulate one social type—the Roman—at the expense of another—the romantic. It sought to substitute civic virtue for passion. The continued popularity of the criticized fiction, however, suggests that the didactic literature fell on deaf ears. Even so conservative a woman as Elizabeth Drinker read the forbidden genre, though not without embarrassment.

Some demographers have shown that there was a sharp rise in the incidence of premarital pregnancy in the late eighteenth and early nineteenth centuries. This increase in what can easily be called "passionate behavior" accompanied the proscriptive literature against novel reading; in that context, the attacks on romantic fiction may be seen as a response to a perceived rise in deviant sexual behavior. It is not completely clear how this apparent rise in premarital pregnancy ought to be interpreted. It is, however, safe to suggest that it almost certainly is not a mark of increased options and freedom for women; it may well have signified the reverse. At least one historian has suggested that pregnancy may have been a tactic by which young couples pressured parents into allocating property earlier than they otherwise might have, and so may be seen as an emblem of declining prosperity. But the proscriptive moralizers blamed the alleged decline in morality not on economic pressures, but on women who indulged their passions because fictional models had made the previously unthinkable seem possible. Though the demographic record suggests that most of these seduced women ultimately married, the didactic purpose of the cautionary novelists dictated that fictional heroines who were seduced must ultimately also be abandoned.[9]

If women were not to read fiction, what ought they to read? Admonitions against novel reading were characteristically accompanied by the recommendation that women read history instead. Mercy Otis Warren's "rational system" left no time to be "thrown away in the perusal of books that have not a tendency to instill lessons of virtue and science." She thought women ought to read "authentic history, which is now written in a style equally elegant to

---

9. Daniel Scott Smith and Michael S. Hindus, "Premarital Pregnancy in America, 1640–1971: An Overview and Interpretation," *Journal of Interdisciplinary History*, V (1975), 537–570. Nancy Cott has linked the skepticism of passion to the role of evangelical religion and to women's desire to demonstrate their strength in overcoming sexual temptation, a strength that could then be used in support of a claim to increased independence and political autonomy ("Passionlessness: An Interpretation," *Signs*, IV [1979], 219–236).

the many volumes of romance, which in the present age croud upon the public." As Warren's endorsement suggests, there was a double rationale for encouraging the study of history. The entire literate culture agreed that knowledge of history helped develop a sense of social perspective. The classic statement is David Hume's brief essay "Of the Study of History," published in 1741. Hume limits his analysis to a very specific recommendation "to my female readers" of historical study "as an occupation, of all others, the best suited both to their sex and education." Hume contrasted histories with novels, which he believed offered "false representations of mankind." Novels encouraged, he thought, an expectation of human perfection and a belief that love is the primary "passion which governs the male world," rather than the "avarice, ambition, vanity, and a thousand other passions" that in fact regularly overcame love. Women read fiction self-indulgently. Hume urged them to satisfy their passion for intrigue with real plots instead of fictional ones: with Cato's sister and Brutus, rather than Fulvia and Philander. At the same time that history satisfied the taste for excitement and for magnificent spectacles, it was also "a most improving part of knowledge." Much of "what we commonly call erudition . . . is nothing but an acquaintance with historical facts." History, he thought, was an easy way to achieve a reputation as an intellectual, for it "opens the door . . . to most of the sciences" and "extends our experience to all past ages, and to the most distant nations." Nearly a century later, the young women of the Boston Gleaning Circle echoed Hume. "The mind enlarges, its local prejudices subside," they wrote, urging each other to read history. The struggles of the people of the past suggested solutions to private problems and to public dilemmas. The uses made of historical precedent in the political debates of the early Republic are ample evidence of the pervasiveness of this assumption. Counseling women to read history was in part to encourage them to become more involved in the intellectual life of the Republic.[1]

In the endorsement of historical study there was also an appreciation of the narrative value of good history and a lurking hope that a taste for narrative could be more wholesomely satisfied by true tales of life and manners, of kings and queens, of battles and leaders, than by fictional accounts of the emotional struggles of ordinary young women. History seemed "safe" in a way that the sciences, the

1. Mercy Otis Warren to Mary Warren, Nov. 1791, Mercy Otis Warren Letterbook, Warren Papers, 486; David Hume, "Of the Study of History," in *Phil. Works of Hume*, IV, 528–533; Boston Gleaning Circle, Minute Book, 101. For other advice to women to read history, see Noah Webster, "Importance of Female Education," *Am. Mag.* (May 1788), 369; *Wkly. Mag.*, Apr. 7, 1798, Aug. 4, 11, 1798; and Milnor, "On Female Education," *Port Folio*, 3d Ser. (May 1809), 392.

classics, and philosophy were not.[2] It promised learning, but not too
much learning. The essayist who believed that "history and natural
philosophy are alone sufficient to furnish women with an agreeable
kind of study" also recommended that women "avoid all abstract
learning, all difficult researches, which may . . . change the delicacy
in which they excel into pedantic coarseness." Serious mental exercise was thought to be literally dangerous to women. The *Port Folio*,
for example, published the widely reprinted memoir of Elizabeth
Graeme Ferguson, a Philadelphia bluestocking who had translated
Télémaque in order "to relieve and divert her mind" from a broken
engagement. "But this, instead of saving," had the result of "impair-
ing her health." Historical narrative seemed to promise to improve
the mind without exciting the passions. Women were urged to read
history, but not to study it intensely; they might read *The History of
England*, but they were not to think of themselves as Catharine
Macaulays. History was the anti-intellectual's compromise with
higher learning.[3]

The line between the novel and the history, however, was not so
clear. Samuel Richardson's implicit promise that he would report
human experience in accurate detail seems to have had a historical
dimension, and the immense care novelists took to render a setting
accurately suggests an interest historians would share. It is no accident that the subtitle of *Clarissa* is *The History of a Young Lady*. The
novel that purported to be "founded on fact" sought to straddle the
ground between fiction and history. The novel that masqueraded as
"true history" sought to claim the respectability of history and the
appeal of romantic fiction: it could criticize fiction at the same time
that it capitalized on the taste for romance.

One of the most popular of these masquerades was *The Coquette*,
an epistolary novel set in Massachusetts that claimed to be a true
narration of the lives of real people. It was written by Hannah Webster Foster, who had also compiled *The Boarding School*, a popular
textbook of belles lettres for women. *The Coquette* is the history
of Eliza Wharton, a young woman who scorns a virtuous minister
because he seems too serious. She throws herself at a young gentle-

2. Hume felt confident that historians' minds, constrained by reality, were protected against
   poetic or philosophical flights of fancy; good historians would inevitably be defenders of
   virtue. He claimed that even the amoral Machiavelli did not deny the reality of "moral
   distinctions" when he acted primarily as a historian rather than as a philosopher. Historical study had for Hume, as for so many others who wrote on this subject, the added
   advantage that a woman so prepared would be more attractive to men: "A woman may
   behave herself with good manners, and have even some vivacity in her turn of wit; but
   where her mind is so unfurnished, it is impossible her conversation can afford any entertainment to men of sense and reflection" (Hume, "Of History," in *Phil. Works of Hume*, IV,
   531).
3. *American Lady's Preceptor*, 25–26; *Port Folio*, I (1809), 521. For the merger of reading
   history with Republican Motherhood, see John Adams to Abigail Adams 2d (Nabby),
   Aug. 13, 1783, Butterfield *et al.*, eds., *Book of Abigail and John*, 360.

man of uncertain background who is as rakish as it is possible to be in a small New England town. In the end the minister finds another virtuous woman and settles into a happy marriage, while the fallen coquette, who has maintained her romanticism against the advice of mother and friends, is seduced and abandoned. Left to bear her illegitimate child alone in the bedroom of a distant tavern, she dies soon after of exposure and malnutrition.

The twentieth-century reader cannot help noting an uncanny resemblance between the pattern of the fictional Eliza Wharton's life and the progression that Edith Wharton described a century later in *The House of Mirth*. The protagonist first rejects a man who the reader is given to understand is suitable for her, then drifts as a house guest on extended visits through the establishments of the rich, where she is superficially welcomed, but made to know that she does not belong. The dashing men she seeks out wish only to use her; yet she has consciously made herself vulnerable to their irresponsibility. Eliza Wharton finally recognizes that the cause of her ruin "may be found in that unrestrained levity of disposition, that fondness for dissipation and coquetry . . . the delusive dream of sensual gratification."[4] At the very end, she makes a moral choice that results in her death.

Although the tone of the narrative suggests that Eliza is young as well as emotionally immature, a closing footnote identifies her as thirty-seven years old at the time of her death. This detail points to the germ of fact at the core of the fiction. Hannah Foster's novel was indeed a history, loosely based on the life of a distant relative, Elizabeth Whitman.[5] But *The Coquette* only masquerades as history; in fact it is a novel that attempts to teach the reader not to read novels. It offers itself as a permissible indulgence in a mildly wicked form.

4. Samuel Richardson, *Clarissa: Or the History of a Young Lady*, ed. John Angus Burell (New York, 1950); [Foster], *The Coquette*, 221–222.
5. Elizabeth Whitman and the poet Joel Barlow carried on an extended flirtation and correspondence while Barlow was contemplating marriage to another woman. The poet's biographers have trivialized the correspondents' references to each other as husband and wife, but these endearments may signify a physical relationship between the two. "O you are certainly the paragon of Husbands—" Whitman wrote Barlow on Feb. 16, 1779. "Were all married men like you, what a happy world for our Sex!" (BN 435, Baldwin Family Collection, Henry E. Huntington Library, San Marino, Calif.). After Barlow's marriage the letters dwindle. See James Woodress, *A Yankee's Odyssey: The Life of Joel Barlow* (Philadelphia, 1958), 63–64, and Elizabeth Whitman to Joel Barlow, Feb. 9, 16, 1770, Mar. 17, 29, 1770, Apr. 15, 1770, May 12, 1770, June 8, 1770, Baldwin Family Collection, Huntington Library. Caroline Healey Dall's account of the affair in *The Romance of the Association; or, One Last Glimpse of Charlotte Temple and Eliza Wharton: A Curiosity of Literature and Life* shields Whitman's reputation by using the fictional name Foster had used, but identifies the minister as Joseph Buckminster and the seducer as Pierpont Edwards. Dall complained that *The Coquette* smeared Whitman's name and represented the work of a "warm imagination . . . heated by the reading of Richardson's novel" (*The Romance of the Association* . . . [Cambridge, Mass., 1875], 68). For a defense of the men, see Charles Knowles Bolton, *The Elizabeth Whitman Mystery at the Old Bell Tavern in Danvers* (Peabody, Mass., 1912), and Woodress, *Yankee's Odyssey*, 64.

Like others of its genre—*Clarissa, Charlotte Temple*—it offers sexual adventure, but blames the heroine for it. Eliza Wharton loses her control of reality because she misreads her novels.

If one variant of the attack on novel reading was the fear that novels taught women to trust their own passions, another variant was the criticism that fiction wasted women's time. It may be that the increase in leisure reading by women implies that women had increasing amounts of leisure time. But leisure does not happen, it is made. Nothing is more easily manipulated than one's use of time. Within broad limits, leisure is a matter of priorities. If women were in fact reading more, it may not mean that more leisure was *given* to them by increased urban services and industrial inventions, but that they had themselves rearranged their priorities and were *making* time to read. If so, that development would account for the shrill complaint that reading absorbed time that normally would be spent on household tasks and household production. When Mercy Otis Warren warned her niece against fiction, she set her caveat squarely in the context of the use of time in the domestic economy: "As your rank in life has not, nor perhaps ever will set you above an attention to the economy of domestic life; an acquired habit of continual industry will enable you to discharge the duties of prudence, decency and elegance in family affairs, and yet leave you leisure to improve your taste to cultivate your mind, and enlarge your understanding by reading, provided you throw away no part of your time."[6]

It could hardly be denied that "profound or abstruse learning" took long periods of time and concentrated attention—what one writer called "abstraction of mind"—which were thought to be "incompatible with . . . [women's] duties in life, which, though comparatively less important than those of men, are hourly recurring." American women, like British women, were supposed to work to benefit their husbands and families. In the explicitly titled *The Female Guide; or, Thoughts on the Education of That Sex, accomodated to the State of Society, Manners, and Government in the United States*, John Ogden deplored "the increasing luxurious stile of living in America" and complained that women were learning that "it is not genteel to work." He warned his female readers against "the pernicious consequences of that dangerous custom, of spending whole afternoons in company without any work. . . . Idle afternoons are proof of corrupt times, they make bad wives and gay daughters, they make families poor and a country wretched, by circulating scandal and folly, instead of industrious and useful arts, which make us rich and innocent."[7]

6. Mercy Otis Warren to Rebecca Otis, n.d., 1776, Mercy Otis Warren Letterbook, Warren Papers, 57–58.
7. West, *Letters to a Young Lady*, 310; John Ogden, *The Female Guide; or, Thoughts on the Education of That Sex, accomodated to the State of Society, Manners, and Government in the United States* (Concord, N.H., 1793), 34, 39–41.

Stating the popular case against learned women the better to answer it, Maria Edgeworth prepared a "Letter from a Gentleman to his friend, Upon the Birth of a Daughter." The essay, reprinted in America in 1810, cautioned, "I would not expect that my house affairs would be with haste dispatched by a Desdemona, weeping over some unvarnished tale, petrified with some history of horrors . . . at the very time when she should be . . . paying the butcher's bill."[8]

Comments like these were not metaphorical. They reveal that early modern homes were the site of enormous amounts of household production. The romanticization of the home in the nineteenth and twentieth centuries has tended to obscure the economic functions of the home and the housewife, but the steady drone of the spinning wheel and the loom persisted long after industrial development began. Even upper- and middle-class women who lived in cities and towns spent immense amounts of time at work. Elizabeth Drinker began her diary with an account of the work she did between 1757 and 1760, a list covering nearly eight closely written pages. It includes frivolous gifts like braided watchstrings and pincushions, but it also included baby clothes, stockings, and shifts for herself. Long after the Revolution, when she was in her fifties—her children grown and married, her household staffed with both permanent and day-hired servants—she still produced many of the household necessities, "tireing . . . [her] eyes, cutting out Shirts and drawing threads." She measured her days by the rhythms of household production: "To day, like yesterday, only that instead of knitting I was mending stockings." Poorer women worked longer and harder on heavier materials; they made their own mattresses and bed ticking as well as their clothes. Poor relief was often furnished in terms of wool to spin. It seemed a commonsense assumption that women should be constantly busy.[9] A taste for literature—like a taste for dissipation—drew women's attention away from domestic work. In this context, reading of any sort was self-indulgent; it was an assertion of individual choice.

This emphasis on the efficient management of domestic responsibilities, and the notion that domestic work is a woman's *business*, has a curiously modern ring. Alex Inkeles's classic list of the characteristics of the modern personality mentions an acute sense of time and a need for efficiency in using it as leading traits. Mercy Otis Warren suggested this notion privately; Judith Sargent Murray spread it publicly in her writings. Both popularized the home as an efficient

8. Edgeworth, *Letters for Literary Ladies*, 23–24.
9. Diary of Elizabeth Drinker, Mar. 13, 1798, Sept. 14, 1798. See also the detailed accounts of work kept by Ruth Henshaw of Leicester, Mass., beginning in 1801, Ruth Henshaw Bascom Diaries, Am. Antq. Soc. For poor relief furnished as wool for spinning, see Record Book, "Out of Doors Spinners Accounts, 1806–1807," Record Group 35.97, Philadelphia City Archives. Of the 256 recipients, all but a single male weaver were women, reflecting the common occupational segregation. For detailed description of women's work within the New England household, see Cott, *Bonds of Womanhood*, 19–62.

workplace as well as the locale of domestic production, a definition that foreshadows the home economics movement of the early twentieth century. Judith Sargent Murray's "new era in female history" was to be marked by women opposed "to every trivial and unworthy monopolizer of time." She spoke explicitly of "*female administration*" and of the impact efficient housekeepers could have. Her choice of words—"machine," "methodical," "economical"—conveys the sharp edge of her vision of the household. "It would be pleasant to observe the contrast between a family, the females of which were properly methodical, and economical in their distributions and expenditures of time, and one accustomed to leave everything to the moment of necessity. . . . The one is the habitation of tranquillity; it is a well ordered community; it is a complicated machine, the component parts of which are so harmoniously organized, as to produce none but the most concordant sounds. . . . While the other . . . is a restoration of the reign of chaos."[1]

Mercy Otis Warren wrestled valiantly throughout her life with the problem of finding time for writing and reflection while raising four children and maintaining a large, elegant household. At intervals she reflected on these competing claims for female attention and recognized that the answers were not simple. Warren took these issues more seriously than virtually any other woman of her generation. Often the occasion for writing down her thoughts was the marriage or betrothal of a young woman relative or friend, when she would try to describe the new life her correspondent faced.

When she considered the domestic economy, Warren used the quasi-official term "department." She recognized that when a woman married she took on substantial economic responsibilities that resisted rearrangement. "Whatever delight we may have in the use of the pen," Mercy Warren wrote, "however eager we may be in the pursuit of knowledge . . . yet heaven has so ordained the lot of female life that every literary attention, must give place to family avocations." All reading except the Bible, she reported, "must" be postponed "till all matters of economy which belong to her department are promptly adjusted." Warren did not think these responsibilities could be evaded, though she did occasionally describe women as "confined to the narrow circle of domestic cares," and she did indulge herself in a bit of envy of unmarried women who were "free from those constant *interruptions* that necessarily occupy the mind of the wife, the mother and the mistress."

But for the long run Warren counseled a careful allocation of time that would permit the model woman to live in both the world of intellect and the world of domesticity. "A methodical and uniform plan of

1. Murray, *The Gleaner*, III, No. 87, 189, II, No. 35, 6, I, No. 3, 29–30.

conduct, united with an industrious mind" would make a double life possible. She even permitted herself a deprecating comment on women who could not blend both worlds. She was scornful of those "who swim on the surface of pleasure," but she also pitied the woman who "is wholly immersed" in her household "and has *no higher ideas* than those which confine her to the narrow circle of domestic attention." Mercy Otis Warren's vision of the fully domestic woman was not unlike that of Mary Wollstonecraft, who decried those who remained "immured in their families groping in the dark." Warren recognized that ordinary household dynamics encouraged this immersion. "We have one advantage peculiar to ourselves," she wrote bitterly. "We can conceal in the obscure retreat, by our own fireside, the neglect of those mental improvements to which the more domestic animal stands in little *need* of, as it is not necessary for her to leave the retired roof—whereas *man* is generally called out to a full display of his abilities." But if the woman who drowned her mind in domestic detail was shallow and shortsighted, the woman who had "both genius and taste for literary enquiry" but could not "cheerfully leave the pursuit to attend to the daily cares of the prudent housewife" was also to be pitied. Even for Warren, literary pursuits were a form of luxury, and the woman who could not keep their attractions under tight rein was indulging in her own form of folly.[2]

The new attitudes toward housekeeping were reflected in satires in the popular press that suggested that housework was undervalued and should be modernized and made rational. These satires generally were written from the point of view of a woman who desperately seeks to maintain an orderly household, only to be outdone by a selfish, slovenly husband blind to the significance of her work. It may be that the satirical mode freed the writers to be less cautious than usual; certainly the sentiments expressed are sharp and often shrewd. When pursued energetically, housework was shown to be disruptive. "The rage for scouring and cleaning . . . is the vice of the ladies," wrote one satirist. "Mops, pails and brushes . . . Are scepters of control." Men in these caricatures are lazy; they do not care how much disorder they create or how much trouble they give their wives and servants. "The Drone" splatters ink, tracks mud in the house, stashes things on the mantelpiece, conveniently forgets his errands. In Francis Hopkinson's "Nitidia" the husband demolishes the parlor with his scientific experiments, and then expects his wife to prepare a formal dinner for his friends. "Nitidia" refers to her household as her "business" and suggests that it interferes with women's intellectual development; had women time for intellectual matters, surely

---

2. Mercy Otis Warren to the daughter of a deceased friend, n.d., Mercy Otis Warren Letterbook, Warren Papers, 117; Mercy Otis Warren to Abigail Adams, Feb. 1774, *ibid.*, 145.

they would put it to better use than men do. "You hear it echoed from every quarter—My wife cannot make verses, it is true; but she makes an excellent pudding. . . . she can't unravel the intricacies of political economy and federal government; but she can knit charming stockings—and this they call praising a wife, and doing justice to her good character—with much nonsense of the like kind."[3]

Critics thought that instead of reading fiction, women ought to be reading something else (history) or doing something else (household production). But women seem to have persisted in their consumption of fiction; their loyalty to the genre was not undermined.

Only Jane Austen sought to explain this loyalty. Her explanation appeared in 1818 in *Northanger Abbey*. Henry Tilney, his sister Catherine, and their friend Miss Morland are out for a walk. Miss Morland confesses her fondness for popular novels like *The Mysteries of Udolpho*. She is aware that most people would consider history more suitable: "I read it a little as a duty, but it tells me nothing that does not either vex or weary me. The quarrels of popes and kings, with wars or pestilences, in every page; the men all so good for nothing, and hardly any women at all."[4]

The last phrase is the telling one. History promised to teach statecraft, human nature, the management of political affairs. Even the farmer's son, were he ambitious, might be persuaded that historical writing had some personal significance for him. The instrumental argument by which history was justified for boys was inappropriate for girls: women could not be statesmen, they could not preside over legislative assemblies. Even Catharine Macaulay's *History of England* had virtually no women as principal actors, nor, for that matter, did Mercy Otis Warren's *History of the American Revolution*. The best that could be offered girls as a justification for reading history was either the very distant promise that the history they learned could ultimately be taught to their as yet unborn sons, or the argument that history was attractive for its anecdotes and example. If history were reduced to human interest, anecdote, and the idiosyncrasies of individual behavior, it could easily be argued that fiction presented the same material—perhaps better.

If a young woman, or her teacher, acted on the advice of Benjamin Rush or Judith Sargent Murray and took to reading history, she would find very little that was not vulnerable to Jane Austen's criticism. In the years of the early Republic, the only history about

---

3. "On Saturday and abused Cleanliness," *Connecticut Courant* (Hartford), Sept. 1, 1788; "The Drone," *Burlington Advt.*, Feb. 22, 1791; Francis Hopkinson, "Nitidia," ed. Linda K. Kerber, *Signs*, IV (1978), 402–406.
4. Jane Austen, *Northanger Abbey and Persuasion*, ed. John Davie (London, 1971), 97–99.

women consisted of assortments of biographical sketches, many
lacking chronological order and usually lacking interpretative force.
One of the most obvious uses of these compilations was made in
the Philadelphia fund-raising broadside of 1780 which, as shown
earlier, justified itself in part by reference to heroic women of biblical
and historical times. Little was offered to explain the behavior of
the women named in this list extending from Deborah to Catherine
the Great. Other compilers could be more ambitious; the list in
The American Lady's Preceptor was chronologically ordered and more
coherently discussed: Cornelia, Boadicea, Margaret of Anjou, Catherine of Aragon, Anne Boleyn, Marie Antoinette. All except for Elizabeth Graeme Ferguson—who had been conveniently written about
by a friend in a recent issue of the Philadelphia *Port Folio*—were
European.[5]

Judith Sargent Murray's *Gleaner* essays, though they also mar-
shaled scattered examples, were considerably more purposeful. Murray's vision of women's collective past was a history of strength and
fortitude. "Courage," she wrote, "is by no means *exclusively* a masculine virtue." She admired the Spartan women for their "uncommon
firmness." She believed women could be patriots, though she did
think they displayed that patriotism in sacrifice rather than in legis-
lation or fighting. Her interpretation of politics was mildly defensive:
"If the triumphs and attainments of THE SEX, under the various
oppressions with which they have struggled, have been thus splendid, how would they have been augmented, had not ignorant or interested men, after clipping their wings, contrived to erect around them
almost insurmountable barriers." Murray tumbled her historical
examples about, heedless of chronology: Charlotte Corday and Lady
Jane Grey, Jane of Flanders and Margaret of Anjou, Portia, Julia,
Aspasia, Volumnia, Mary Astell and Catharine Macaulay. To name
them was not to provide an analytical history; her purpose was to use
historical data as evidence against the "*idea of the incapability* of
women."[6]

Women's history as a subject of study in America may be said to
have begun with the late eighteenth-century search for a usable past,
begun by compilers of "Ladies' Repositories," ladies' magazines, and
textbooks for girls' schools. Much of their material came from British
and European sources. When literary nationalists complained about
the persistence of European reading materials in America, these
women's books were among the offenders they had in mind. Long

---

5. *The American Lady's Preceptor* had a subtitle: "A compilation of observations, essays, and
   poetical effusions, designed to direct the female mind in a course of pleasing and instructive reading." It was designed as a textbook for female academies: "No volume of selections has been published in this country especially designed for the reading of females."
6. Murray, *The Gleaner*, III, 192, 193, 197, 191.

after political independence had been accomplished, women's reading remained a part of a transatlantic literary culture, of which cultural nationalists like Noah Webster were deeply skeptical. Books reflecting the European class-based social order would, it was feared, give young women a taste of such hierarchies and undermine the effort to build a democratic social order in America. In this sense, imported women's reading seemed unrepublican.

But there were no ready solutions to this problem, even for those who would agree that women ought to pay more attention to works speaking to the American experience. It would be nearly another generation before there were coherent histories of American women available for the female audience. Samuel L. Knapp's *Female Biography* did not appear until 1834, Lydia Maria Child's *Brief History of the Condition of Women* until 1845, Sarah Josepha Hale's *Woman's Record* until 1853. Elizabeth Ellet's great compilation of the activities of women during the Revolution appeared in 1850. Not until the 1840s did Benson Lossing begin the travels that culminated in his *Pictorial Field Book of the Revolution*, which included many accounts of women's deeds.[7]

In the years of the early Republic, very few histories could meet the demands of educators like Rush and Webster, yet refute Jane Austen's criticism that they treated "hardly any women at all" in their pages. When they were available, they were likely to be unsophisticated, even boring. But another sort of history was indeed widely available, one that met general approval and one in which there was no dearth of female heroes: women's confessional tracts, religious autobiographies, accounts of conversion experiences, even, occasionally, funeral sermons delivered in honor of a notable woman and published by her family or her minister. The appeal of these accounts had something in common with the novel, which itself often masqueraded as fictional confession. Among the standard ingredients was the struggle of the heroine against temptation. Her letters to parents and to friends might be included, giving the narrative the coloration of history and the shape of an epistolary novel. Her courtship—sometimes by one man, sometimes by several—was recounted. The saga usually culminated either in a conversion experience or in a triumphant deathbed scene, two public successes for which no woman needed to apologize.

7. Samuel L. Knapp, *Female Biography; containing Notices of Distinguished Women, in Different Nations and Ages* (New York, 1834); L. Maria Child, *Brief History of the Condition of Women . . .*, 2 vols. (Boston, 1845); Sarah Josepha Hale, *Woman's Record; or, Sketches of All Distinguished Women . . .* (New York, 1853); Elizabeth Fries Lummis Ellet, *Domestic History of the American Revolution* (New York, 1850); Benson J. Lossing, *The Pictorial Field Book of the Revolution*, 2 vols. (New York, 1852). The work of Child and Ellet is perceptively discussed in Susan Phinney Conrad, *Perish the Thought: Intellectual Women in Romantic America, 1830–1860* (New York, 1976), 103–122.

The Christian Mourning with Hope is a good example of this genre. It begins with Samuel Worcester's sermon at the funeral of Eleanor Read Emerson in 1808 in Salem, Massachusetts. In this sermon, Mrs. Emerson appears as the model woman; the minister celebrates "the superior endowments of her mind; her quick and clear intelligence, her brilliant imagination, her animating vivacity, her ingenuous disposition, and her engaging social qualities. You knew how admirably she was formed . . . to diffuse a useful and benign influence around her."[8]

The sermon is followed by a lengthy memoir of Mrs. Emerson's life, extracts from her diary, and copies of her letters. While the funeral sermon is composed of glowing generalities, the historical materials introduce us to a woman who had not found her life simple or easy. Her health had been frail from childhood, but her mind was vigorous and her morale evidently high. When she was only fourteen she "commenced her beloved employment of school-keeping." Eleanor Read "kept" school steadily for the next twelve years; she was something of an entrepreneur, traveling to nine different Massachusetts towns in order to establish schools. She developed her own curriculum: reading, spelling, writing, grammar, composition, "religion," plain needlework, and public speaking. This last she considered a serious enterprise, though it was unusual in female schools; her purpose was "to rouse and improve the mind, to form the manners, give energy to the character, and perfect the pupil in the art of reading." She refused to teach painting and embroidery, thinking them "unnecessary." By the time of her death at the early age of thirty-one, she had taught "hundreds of young persons, whose minds she imbued with the rudiments of knowledge."[9]

Throughout her career Eleanor Read considered the state of her soul, attending revival meetings of all sorts, anxiously hoping to be saved. She chose the towns in which she set up schools in part because of her expectations of the ministers or churches there; she introduced "public prayer" in her schools even though she had reason to fear that school prayer "would be deemed ridiculous enthusiasm. . . . Here I began to hesitate. I searched the scriptures, to see, if the injunctions to women, not to speak in the church . . . would not excuse me. . . . But I found nothing. . . . how can I ever describe the conflict in my mind between pride and duty."[1]

8. Samuel Worcester, ed., *The Christian Mourning with Hope. A Sermon, Delivered at Beverly, Nov. 14, 1808, on occasion of the Death of Mrs. Eleanor Emerson, Late Consort of the Rev. Joseph Emerson . . . To which are Annexed Writings of Mrs. Emerson, with a Brief Sketch of her Life* (Boston, 1809), 20.
9. *Ibid.*, 27–28, 21.
1. *Ibid.*, 49–50.

Eleanor Read's world was a small one. Counseled to seek salt air for her health, she went to Salem, where she found the minister Samuel Worcester willing to be the patron for her school. In Salem she met Nancy Eaton, who was living with Worcester's family while she waited to marry another minister, Joseph Emerson. Nancy Eaton was fitting herself to become a minister's wife by living with and observing Worcester's family. The two women became close friends; after Nancy Eaton Emerson's death Eleanor Read married Joseph Emerson, and when Eleanor Read Emerson died, Worcester delivered her funeral sermon.

The two women "discoursed upon the importance of improving the female mind." It is clear that they were sensitive to the public argument about the limits of female intelligence. Eleanor Read reported their conclusions in her journal: "Let the man of real piety carefully examine the origin of the detested sentiment which leads him to consider learning and mental improvement as undesirable in a female. . . . will not the honest christian blush before his God for the unchristian and cruel degradation of the female mind? . . . We expatiated largely on the folly of multitudes of our unthinking sex."[2] Ironically, when Nancy Eaton Emerson died eight months after her marriage, Joseph Emerson blamed her death on the intensity of her studies. "Her bereaved husband is now convinced," wrote their friend Worcester, "that her education was not conducted upon the most judicious plan. While he entertains the same opinion of the capacity of females to understand everything, that man can understand, and also of the importance of improving their minds . . . He is fully of that opinion, that, if females wish to do the greatest possible good, they must not attempt to know every thing; but consent themselves to limit their attention to such pursuits, as are of the greatest moral and practical importance." Emerson thought that every hour that could be taken from "domestic pursuits" ought to be spent "in secret devotion, in religious conversation, in social worship," and in reading "a few of the best histories"—activities preferable to spending time "studying geometry, algebra, or natural philosophy."[3]

The memoir ends with a detailed account of Eleanor Read Emerson's deathbed, her farewells to family and friends, her eloquence in calling on relatives to repent, and, finally, her funeral and burial next to her friend Nancy Eaton Emerson.

When Rush and Webster told women to read history they were thinking of Livy and Tacitus, of Rollin and Macaulay. But the narrative of a life like that of Mrs. Emerson, while generally categorized as a devotional tract, was also a history dealing with themes central

2. *Ibid.*, 72.
3. *Ibid.*, 80n.

to the life experience of women of the post-Revolutionary generation. Eleanor Read, after all, was a girl of respectable family who
developed a career in a relatively new sort of work. She did not
merely "keep school"; she traveled alone to towns where she thought
she could keep it most advantageously. She developed a curriculum
of her own, exercising some originality in the process. She formed a
very close female friendship, and she and her friend seriously considered whether it was appropriate to set bounds on female intellectual-
ity. Under the trappings of a traditional devotional tract is a biography
of an intense young woman who explored more widely than most of
her peers the options open to her community and her generation. A
book like this one must be classified as women's history as well as
religious history.

The novel was the only other widely available form of narrative
that tended to place women at the center. Women were determinedly
present in the fictional "histories" of *Charlotte Temple* or *The
Coquette* as they were not in the public histories written by Rollin or
Macaulay. Even novels that did not name women in their titles—for
example, Charles Brockden Brown's *Alcuin* and *Ormond*—often had
women as central actors. Whether or not these characters came to a
good end, the reader had the opportunity to observe women in physical or emotional crisis, to feel sympathy for heroines in the cautionary tales.

If a woman sought to learn how other women coped with reality,
she had few printed resources other than fiction to which she might
turn. The novel that claimed to be "founded on Fact" smudged the
clear line between fact and fiction, and may well have seemed to its
readers to fulfill some of the functions of narrative history.[4] The
unrealistic elements could be discounted, the elements of truth
sifted out. To deny women access to novels, as Jedidiah Strong had
done, was to deny them access to a rich imagery of what women were
and what they might hope to become.

4. See especially Eliza Foster Cushing's *Yorktown: An Historical Romance* (Boston, 1826),
and *Saratoga; A Tale of the Revolution* (Boston, 1824). For a treatment of novels by and
about women in the 19th century congruent with the interpretation offered here, see
Mary Kelley, "The Sentimentalists: Promise and Betrayal in the Home," *Signs*, IV
(1979), 434–446.

WILLIAM J. GILMORE

From Reading Becomes a Necessity of Life:
Material and Cultural Life in Rural
New England, 1780–1835†

By the mid-1820s, native commentators assessing the progress of American civilization since the Revolution were identifying a new factor as the single most momentous characteristic of the age. It heralded a fourth great revolution, in addition to the American, French, and Industrial Revolutions. Speaking in 1825 when the cornerstone of the Bunker Hill monument was laid, Daniel Webster noted the creation of a new communications environment, terming his era an "age of knowledge" and citing "the general progress of knowledge" throughout Europe and America as one of the most significant events of the 1775–1825 period. Webster observed:

> Such has been the improvement . . . above all, in liberal ideas and the general spirit of the age . . . that the whole world seems changed. [It] peculiarly marks the character of the . . . North Atlantic community of nations [that they make] a common progress like vessels on a common tide, propelled by the gales at different rates, according to their several structures and management, but all moved forward by one mighty current, strong enough to bear onward whatever does not sink beneath it.

The key to this "one mighty current" was the development of a "community of opinions and knowledge amongst men in different nations existing in a degree heretofore unknown." The "Republic of Letters" had greatly expanded, in Webster's view. As a result, in the mid-1820s "a great chord of sentiment and feeling runs through two continents and vibrates over both. . . . Knowledge has, in our time, triumphed, and is triumphing over distance," language barriers, habits, and prejudices. This was the central development of the age: "the diffusion of knowledge, so astonishing in the last half-century."[1]

Webster's assessment of the profound impact of the diffusion of knowledge was extended a year later by Joseph Story in a Phi Beta Kappa discourse delivered less than five miles away, at Cambridge. The happiness "of whole communities" had been affected by "direct or silent changes forced by . . . subtler occurrences . . . into the very structure of society." These "will be read with far deeper emotions in

† From *Reading Becomes a Necessity of Life* by William J. Gilmore. Reprinted by permission of The University of Tennessee Press, Knoxville.
1. Daniel Webster, "The Bunker Hill Monument," in Edwin P. Whipple, ed., *The Great Speeches and Orations of Daniel Webster With an Essay on Daniel Webster as a Master of English Style* (Boston, 1879), 123–35; quotes on 125–27 and 131.

their effects upon future ages" than other historical trends, Story remarked. Chief among the results of these silent changes was the establishment of a new and mighty empire, the empire of public opinion, and "the operation of what Lord Bacon has characterized almost as supreme power, the power of knowledge, working its way to universality, and interposing checks upon government and people, by means gentle and decisive, which have never before been fully felt, and are even now, perhaps, incapable of being fully comprehended."

What subtler occurrences could possibly match the impact of the American Revolution, the conquest of the continent "to the Rocky Mountains," the French Revolution, or the series of revolutions in South America? Essentially there were two, Story contended. Each "has worked deepest in all the [other] changes of the age." First was "the general diffusion of knowledge. This is emphatically the age of reading." It used to be that learning was "the accomplishment of those in the higher orders" and middle classes of society, and that reading was "the privilege of the few"; in this generation it had become "the possession of the many." Reading "now radiates in all directions," chiefly because of the freedom and particularly the "cheapness" of the press. Contributing factors included the spread of schooling, "that liberal commerce, which connects by golden chains the interests of mankind," and the "spirit of inquiry" awakened by Protestantism.

The second subtle occurrence followed from the first. In Story's estimation, the general diffusion of knowledge had created a "universal love and power of reading": books and other print items were eagerly awaited. As a result, "scarcely is a work of real merit dry from the English Press, before it wings its way to both the Indies and America." Keen interest in the latest publications had ushered in a momentous shift in attitudes toward knowledge. "With such a demand for books," Story remarked, and "with such facilities of intercourse, it is no wonder that reading should cease to be a mere luxury, and should be classed among the necessaries of life."[2]

Webster and Story both spoke near Boston, one of the three leading centers of the American book trade in the mid-1820s, and as elite members of eastern Massachusetts' urban society. Were their assessments about the diffusion of print culture accurate? The present investigation concludes that in 1825 their judgments were exact for rural New England, even its most isolated northwestern quadrant.[3]

2. Joseph Story, "Discourse Pronounced at Cambridge Before the Phi Beta Kappa Society, on the Anniversary Celebration, August 31, 1826," in Story, The Miscellaneous Writings, Literary, Critical, Juridical and Political, of Joseph Story, LLD., Now First Collected (Boston, 1835), 3–33; quotes on 3–8, mainly following points of argument.
3. For the apparently different situation in Virginia, see Joseph F. Kett and Patricia A. McClung, "Book Culture in Post-Revolutionary Virginia," PAAS 94, pt. 1 (1984):98–137. On the importance of Boston in the New England book trade, see Rollo Silver, The Boston Book Trade, 1800–1825 (New York, 1949). On the importance of a broad

The half century following the 1783 Peace at Paris marked the first age of mass literacy. An extensive communications network and a new series of cultural forms began to enter the homes of most families. These cultural forms were diffused through books and other reading matter with the expansion of elementary literacy and the continuation of reading activity throughout the life cycle.[4]

* * *

The nation's continued widespread participation in print culture was not assured after the Paris peace treaty that ended the Revolution. True, the habit of reading had become ingrained in many urban and village families, but that had been in response to earthshaking sacred and secular events. It was not inevitable, for example, that novels should gain popularity in the Upper Valley between 1780 and 1830. Although they were the rage among middle-class urban residents of Germany, France, and England by the 1760s, very few were available for purchase, borrowing, or even browsing in Windsor District before the late 1790s. Even interest in events occurring in distant lands was minimal immediately after the Revolution. Between 1784 and early 1787, the leading Upper Valley newspaper, the Windsor *Vermont Journal*, frequently complained that there were too few important events to report. Curiosity about the news reasserted itself during Shays' Rebellion and especially during the Constitutional Convention and the ratification process. But it was the establishment of the federal government in America and the French Revolution that ushered in a long period of sustained interest in both American and transatlantic events. The 1790–1830 period also brought an ever broader and richer selection of reading matter to the attention of Upper Valley residents.[5]

In the rural Western world, a relish for reading and its entertainment, enchantment, and practical value had never previously penetrated very widely. The habit of reading, which spread through virtually the entire population of the Upper Valley between 1780 and 1835, made everyday life in the American Northeast during the Early Republic an utter anomaly. In rural areas beyond the Ameri-

---

international perspective, see Bernard Bailyn, "The Challenge of Modern Historiography," AHR 87 (1982):1–24.

4. For the literature on early communications revolutions, see Elizabeth Eisenstein, *The Printing Press as an Agent of Change: Communications and Cultural Transformation in Early Modern Europe*, 2 vols. (Cambridge, England, 1979), 1:3–159.

5. The first Vermont printed book-length work of fiction, John Filson's *Adventures of Colonel Daniel Boone*, (1793) was preceded by fifteen years of printing and more than 300 other imprints. See Marcus McCorison, *Vermont Imprints, 1778–1820* (Worcester, Mass., 1963), p. 61, no. 264; [First] *Additions and Corrections* (Worcester, Mass., 1968), p. 5; [Second] *Additions and Corrections* (Worcester, 1973); and [Third] *Additions and Corrections to Vermont Imprints, 1778–1820* (Worcester, 1985).

can Northeast, widespread regular reading evolved more gradually during the nineteenth century.[6]

The print vehicles that residents of North Atlantic societies most frequently chose to read in 1730–1830 varied from country to country. In rural northwestern New England, almanacs, broadsides, books, and pamphlets, including the Bible, prayer books, hymnals, psalm books, devotional works, and school-books, were the print vehicles most frequently read in the 1780s. By the late 1790s novels, travel narratives, geographies, and histories had been added to the list. Within another decade rural weekly newspapers had become central in Upper Valley reading. Periodical reading was mostly restricted to quite wealthy families until the 1820s. By contrast, in Germany after 1760, the novel was primary, followed by periodicals and travel books. In France the small book and many varieties of pamphlets were dominant; clandestine publications were a consequential part of reading fare. In Great Britain, books, pamphlets, periodicals, and newspapers were the staples.

The newspaper's rise to prominence heralded a further development in reading. Not only was this most versatile vehicle rich with "knowledge from distant climes" and information about local commerce and culture; it also advertised and shamelessly reprinted material first published elsewhere. Furthermore, newspapers were the most secular of all print forms. Their readers were consequently most likely those whose thirst for knowledge extended to many secular subjects. Very soon, in historical terms—by the second half of the nineteenth century at the latest—a mass culture based on print became prevalent in several other rural areas of the Western world: Scotland, southern England, north and central France, all but southernmost Germany, Sweden, Norway, Finland, and the United States South and West.

The first signs of mass culture were unpredictable in their effects on daily life in the hills and valleys of landlocked rural Vermont and New Hampshire. Change was no longer assimilated slowly, at an almost geological pace, but arrived in rural New England households weekly, with mechanical precision. The expansion of knowledge in fresh, naïve minds fostered great anxiety but also inspired intense curiosity and self-confidence. By the late 1830s this mass culture had given rise to a series of peculiarly American cultural forms. An ideal of intellectual currency as an essential element of "modern life" had

6. In the Upper Valley, nearly two-thirds of all Windsor District families with inventories in 1787–1830 retained family libraries. Members of many other families, at least another 10–15 percent, engaged in reading without retaining a private library. They either did not save or gave away printed materials, including almanacs, pamphlets, broadsides, newspapers, and several categories of books (e.g., novels and children's books). Thus, approximately three-quarters of all families maintained the habit of reading.

even generated a full-fledged critique of the direction being taken by contemporary commercial and early industrial capitalism.

Many cultural leaders, including a host of self-appointed prophets of progress and doom, stepped forward. Joseph Smith found hand-written golden tablets proclaiming a new order of life on earth. William Miller prophesied the end of the world on the basis of calculations made using his Bible. Orestes Brownson predicted many aspects of early industrial society from his vantage point as a rural printer and editor. Horace Greeley and scores of other reformers supported a wide array of small and a few broad-ranging remedies for social ills, including intentional communities and other social experiments. These individuals and groups, together with a much larger share of readers wishing to preserve their traditional values and beliefs, formed the first two widely literate rural generations in the Western world.[7]

* * *

Although reading is often discussed as if it were a skill acquired universally and uniformly, it too has a history.[8] And its intended objectives and its meaning as an act have changed throughout time. Reading can be a strong defender of tradition or an agent of change. The role of reading instruction in instilling a conservative outlook in rural New England children and youth, males and females, is an intricate but essential subject. We must ask, What did reading instruction entail? Specifically, did rural New Englanders see differences among various vehicles of cultural expression—paintings and tavern signs, printed and written matter, music—in the messages carried and the way each mode of expression conveyed its meanings? And was expansion of an individual's fund of knowledge about the world an inevitable concomitant of the alphabet on paper? Reading *might* be a liberating experience, teaching the reader new ways of thinking and feeling, but did it *have* to be? What were the uses of print culture in the lives of people who farmed and grazed? Did differences between men's and women's lives increase or decrease as reading spread? Were changes in patterns of thought and feeling typical and even expected goals of reading?[9]

7. Comparative study of transatlantic populations as they pursued mass literacy and active reading through a long time period offers a central challenge to history. Fundamental change in material and cultural life had differing effects in London and Paris; in the provincial capitols of Great Britain, Germany, France, Sweden, and America; and in the rural countryside areas of each nation. Varying motives and patterns in commerce and culture need to be explored, in the spirit of Bailyn's "Challenge."

8. See Gilmore, "The 'Mystic Chords of Memory': Needs and Opportunities for a History of Reading to 1876" (Paper presented at AAS Conference on the History of the Book, Nov. 1984).

9. Eisenstein, *Printing Press*, 3–159.

Potentially liberating uses of reading were largely ignored by rural New England reading instructors throughout the eighteenth and early nineteenth centuries because these teachers had utter confidence that those who controlled early learning processes controlled the life of the mind. Where anxiety did exist, it was directed toward fiction, especially novels, which were assumed to be both widely read and dangerous. Apart from this assault on fiction, and a small amount of criticism aimed at clandestine and pornographic works, reading was not only tolerated but actively encouraged. Indeed, criticism amounted to a minor, if shrill and persistent, note amid widespread, highly articulated concern with reading. Literacy was promoted as a way of sustaining the new nation in its perilous republican experiment and as a means of insuring individual salvation and a "Bible Commonwealth" by the inculcation of enduring Christian values and behavior. Most secular and religious leaders pursued the linked creation of an enlightened, "informed" citizenry and a phalanx of knowledgeable Christians. Educators agreed that a New World society of Christian republicans could not be sustained without sacred and secular knowledge. Republicanism and Protestantism thrived when literate participants actively engaged in lifelong learning. In the minds of proponents of reading, the twin goals of reading outweighed any fears about the influence that the reading habit might eventually exert on the lower classes; the dominant method of reading instruction in the Early Republic allayed most observers' misgivings until the process had gone too far to stop it. In retrospect it seems clear that institutionalized literacy had, as a major unintended consequence, the creation of a mass culture based on a vast variety of printed and written matter available to men and increasingly to women as well.[1]

As we begin to unravel the complexities of Upper Valley rural life, we must understand not only the material history of communications in early America, emphasizing printing office practices, labor relations, and the economics and technology of the book trade;[2] but also the cultural history of communications, including methods of reading instruction, reading acts, situations, and experiences; and also the history of readers' perceptions of the media of print (and other forms of) communications. Our own era's assumptions are often anachronistic, when applied to the past. Most rural New

1. See the discussion of the push for literacy in Lee Soltow and Edward Stevens, *The Rise of Literacy and the Common School in the United States: A Socioeconomic Analysis to 1870* (Chicago, 1981), 58–66.
2. Rollo Silver is a leading contributor to several of these areas; see his *The Boston Book Trade* and Lawrence Wroth and Rollo Silver, "Book Production and Distribution from the American Revolution to the War Between the States," in *The Book in America: A History of the Making and Selling of Books in the United States*, ed. Hellmut Lehmann-Haupt, 2d. ed. (New York, 1952), 63–136.

Englanders did not make a connection between the messages they received and the particular media involved, whether these were books, periodicals, almanacs, oral discourse, visual objects, dance, instrumental music, singing, writing, or reading. Except within a narrow group of professionals, different media were rarely discussed as embodying distinct modes of expression. In terms of late twentieth century conventions, most rural New Englanders of the day were partially media-blind.[3]

Conservative educators reinforced this trend by stressing the stability and continuity of intellectual traditions worth perpetuating; from their perspective, the goals of citizenship and salvation did not include challenges of whatever form to society's institutions or values. Whichever medium generated a worthwhile idea, the message would emanate from the same broad fund of knowledge— the wisdom of the ages. In retrospect, in the wake of the American Revolution and in view of the radical changes in the diffusion of reading matter then under way throughout the North Atlantic, this attitude appears extremely naïve. Nevertheless it was the dominant opinion. The particular form in which ideas were expressed received little consideration until after 1815, when it was far too late to curb the general thirst for reading and the great variety of reading matter available.

Noah Webster believed that the goal of education was neither personal liberation nor intellectual growth, but the preservation and transmission of the wisdom of the ages. In the hands of the most popular author of reading instruction manuals during the Early Republic, reading acts became a series of elaborate tribalized confirmation rites. From the first learning experiences in home and school, and Dennis Rusche has noted, "imitative learning played an important role in preparing the child for life in a world of fixed forms and ideas."[4] The primary goal of early education was not to instill in the child information about the world or to provoke a challenge to society's basic institutions, but to inaugurate the assimilation of a universe of previous "wisdom." Through about 1825, this educational philosophy prevailed in nearly all Upper Valley schools offering basic education, imparting a peculiar flavor to cultural life in the Early Republic and heightening the tension between tradition and innova-

3. See Walter Ong, *Ramus: Method and the Decay of Dialogue* (Cambridge, Mass., 1958); *The Presence of the Word: Some Prolegomena for Cultural and Religious History*, rev. ed. (Minneapolis, 1981); and *Orality and Literacy: The Technologizing of the Word* (Methuen, 1982). See also Marshall McLuhan, *The Gutenberg Galaxy: The Making of Typographic Man* (Toronto, 1972); and *Understanding Media: The Extensions of Man* (New York, 1964). Some critics of novel reading were pioneers in exploring an important aspect of the relationship between the medium of communication and the messages it contained.

4. Rusche is the most careful student of Webster's educational philosophy; see "An Empire of Reason: A Study of the Writings of Noah Webster" (Ph.D. diss., Univ. of Iowa, 1975), 270.

tion. It was in this context that plans, radical in their effects, were implemented to achieve a profoundly conservative end: the education of all white American women as "Republican mothers."[5]

Webster and his imitators taught boys and girls to read through an extremely conservative technique: the "pronouncing-form method," which was dominant until the mid-1820s. "Oral recitation" was stressed because, as Webster put it, "children learn the language by the ear."[6] Reading instruction was natural, using children's existing ability to talk and listen. Typically, a group of young people ranging in age from five to eighteen years gathered in a single-room district schoolhouse in the Upper Valley, where they began learning to read by sounding out letters, syllables, words, and sentences. The technique formed habits that strongly supported tradition rather than change. In one rural schoolhouse whose instructor was teaching from Webster's speller:

> The schoolmaster would begin by selecting and correctly pronouncing a word from the speller. Then the students, sometimes singly but often in chorus, would respond. Without reference to the text, they would recite the letters of each syllable, pausing to pronounce the syllable, and then . . . proceed to the next syllable, until the whole word had been spelled and pronounced from memory. The schoolmaster with a sharp ear could detect those who had recited poorly or incorrectly. After . . . correction and reprimand, the class would start again with the next word. The whole procedure could take on a rhythm not unlike a chant. Sometimes the recitation would be based on individual competition. Each student vied with the others to see who could . . . stand at the head of the class. For variety the children would be directed to the short reading selections interspersed among the tables. Many of these selections were delightful fables or brief stories about children. . . . Webster believed that this interchange between reciting words and reading easy selections provided enough variety to maintain the interest of the child.[7]

5. See E. Jennifer Monaghan, *A Common Heritage: Noah Webster's Blue Back Speller* (Hamden, Conn., 1983), 31–56 and 196–210; and Rusche, "Empire of Reason," 260–95. Webster's *The American Spelling Book* (Bennington, Vt., 1794) was the most popular book of reading instruction.
6. Webster, *American Spelling Book,* vii. In late Reformation Sweden (c. 1650–1725), the emphasis in reading instruction was on visual and not oral communication. As Egil Johansson puts it, "Learning should pass from what was concrete for the eye, via memory, to a complete understanding and application." Children were taught to "learn to read and see with their own eyes what God bids and commands in His Holy Word." See his *History of Literacy,* quotes on 56–57 and 164. On reading orally in France in the 1760s, see Darnton, "Readers Respond," in *Great Cat Massacre,* 225.
7. Rusche, "The Empire of Reason," 271.

The pronouncing-form mode of reading instruction had several important implications for the history of knowledge and its acquisition and maintenance. First, because people learned to read by speaking aloud, whereby they listened with the mind's ear, the skill was probably acquired far more rapidly than many scholars of reading instruction have assumed.[8] Residents of the Upper Valley were not used to the written word. The achievement of mass literacy for the first generation of future American citizens meant gradually moving beyond the confines of a culture with an inherently oral style of learning about the world. Webster confirmed a longstanding and eminently sensible assumption: reading was "a recreation of the author's conversation," so it should be taught by building on the experience in talking and listening, singing and chanting, that a child brought to school. Precisely because a child's life in the Early Republic was rooted in oral modes of communication, reading instruction began by pronouncing letters, syllables, words, and sentences aloud. It proceeded from the known to the unknown.

Contemporary cultural conditions have not been taken into account by many critics of Webster's modest adaptation of earlier methods of reading instruction. Rusche, however, properly notes that Webster's approach was not just "alphabetic" or, in Jennifer Monaghan's term, a "spelling-for-reading" method. The pronouncing-form method centered on the pronunciation of written words. Webster organized elementary reading instruction "to prepare the child to pronounce correctly any word he might meet in print." Far from being a random collection, in Webster's speller each sound, syllable, and word served as a type, preparing the novice for other, similar-sounding words to be encountered eventually. The link between Webster's speller and his dictionary was that of part to whole, the same relationship that he identified between early education and future cultural participation; the latter was a natural extension of the former.[9]

As boys and girls progressed in reading within Upper Valley homes and district schools, using primers, spellers, and eventually "readers," they repeatedly recited sentences encapsulating conventional wisdom about the world. They early assimilated the helpful wisdom that "reading is talking from a book." Rather than being a wholly new skill, reading started with familiar learning procedures and only gradually added to them. Regarded and taught as a mode of speaking, the habit of reading developed as an extension of the spoken word. As discussed by Rolf Engelsing for Germany and David Hall

---

8. See Monaghan, *A Common Heritage*, 1–90.
9. Rusche, "The Empire of Reason," quotes on 265–66 and 269; also see Monaghan, *A Common Heritage*.

for early America, intensive reading matter and styles of reading represented a continuum with speaking and singing because they were perceived as "an oral activity aimed at a correct rehearsal of an author's speech as set down in written form."[1]

The chief implication of this sort of reading instruction for the cultural history of the Early Republic is not just that oral and reading skills were conflated, but also that the substance of oral and print culture were, from the earliest years of an individual's life, indissolubly linked. The initial fund of knowledge acquired in reading instruction blended easily with information and opinion garnered from talking, listening, singing, and chanting throughout childhood and early youth. As prevailing assumptions about the nature of learning blurred distinctions between modes of cultural expression, they weakened the bases for traditional distinctions between oral and print culture.

The long-term result of such reading instruction was that Upper Valley residents too readily accepted the authority of the printed word, any printed word. Moreover, once an individual became literate and continued the habit of reading, he or she could not easily be restricted to intensive reading styles and traditional subject matter. This was a major unintended consequence of the pronouncing-form method of reading instruction. As their reading tastes began to expand, Upper Valley residents were irresistibly drawn to new knowledge, especially knowledge of current events in the distant world. Beginning in the 1790s, rural weekly newspapers, with their balance of older and newer forms of knowledge, were readily accepted in households far removed from the cities providing so much of the newspaper's content. Regular installments of news from distant parts and information about local commerce ensured that newspapers, of all print media, became the greatest catalyst to cultural and material change throughout rural New England.

As newspapers and other alternative forms of reading matter spread, determined but futile opposition to the diffusion of some forms of new knowledge did coalesce. Supporters of widespread education were among the most outspoken critics of the novel, arguing that it encouraged a new private reading style and so fostered alternatives to the wisdom of the ages, the basic value system underpinning reading instruction. The world depicted in the wisdom of the ages was a known, stable place; the world presented in novels was an invented realm within which the fate of even an ordinary individual might and often did change dramatically. In the novel, chance and

1. Rusche, "The Empire of Reason," 295; Engelsing, "Die Perioden," 112–54; and David Hall, "The Uses of Literacy in New England, 1600–1850," in *Printing and Society in Early America*, ed. William Joyce et al. (Worcester, Mass., 1983), 1–47.

free will actively opposed determinism and eternity. Detractors regarded fiction not as lacking reality but as showcasing false and dangerously enticing alternative realities. Fiction could induce licentiousness and vice. Novels represented potential fissures in the world of wisdom. The reading of novels, as Cathy Davidson argues, was often considered a subversive activity; novels appealed directly to the imagination and thereby, according to their castigators, subverted all the normal structures of authority that governed behavior. The popularity of novels and criticism of them grew in tandem. Rev. Samuel Miller, in his 1803 *Retrospect of the Eighteenth Century*, made the most sweeping attack. Novel reading "dissipated the mind," begat "a dislike to more solid and instructive reading," and excited "a greater fondness for the productions of imagination and fancy than for the sober reasoning of the practical investigations of wisdom." Precisely because the whole point of reading was "the practical investigations of wisdom," novel reading was segregated by its critics from other reading situations and acts.[2]

At least initially in the Early Republic, the prevailing method of instruction inculcated strong habits of conformity in belief. It did so partly by the practice of reading aloud and partly by the blatant attempt at behavioral control that was associated with teaching of elocution in later education. The key assumption of the elocutionists was that reading aloud and public speaking were related processes of reenactment, of talking from a text that recounted an oral discourse. Just as reading was perceived as recreating an author's words in written form, as if he/she were *talking* to the reader, elocution instruction was perceived as guiding the student to recreate the precise emotions of the original speaker. The teacher sought to enhance an accurate recreation of the original oration by training the student to guide the listener to the proper emotional response through display of accurate physical gestures for each emotion conveyed.

In both reading aloud and elocution, the "passions" were to be repressed; only acceptable "emotions" were encouraged. Webster, Blair, Scott, and others engaged in a massive effort to dictate the proper manner of articulating sounds and so to shape audience response to knowledge. Both reading aloud and elocution directed

---

2. On novel reading see Robert Winans, "The Growth of a Novel-Reading Public in Late Eighteenth-Century America," *Early American Lit.* 9 (1975): 267–75: G. Harrison Orians, "Censure of Fiction in American Romances and Magazines, 1789–1810," PMLA 52 (1937):195–214; and Soltow and Stevens, *Rise of Literacy*, 11–22 and 58–88, on types of reading matter advocated generally and in the common school movement after 1834. Davidson kindly allowed me to read several draft chapters of her *Revolution and the Word: The Rise of the Novel in America* (New York, 1986). The Miller quotes are from Orians, p. 200. Throughout this study, unless noted, all quotes have been checked in the original.

the emotions in accordance with the pronouncing-form pedagogical strategy for structuring the intellect; the emphasis remained on learning the wisdom of the ages by ear. Conformity in behavior was the ultimate aim of conformity in reading style. In the Upper Valley, persuading the reader of the author's intended meaning through oral reading retained great popularity through 1830. Reading newspapers aloud was an especially important adaptation of this style of reading to a newly prominent vehicle of communication.[3]

The difficulty with this strategy was that the content of many popular new forms of reading matter undermined this long-term goal. The cultural battle over reading in rural New England had nothing to do with the desirability of making elementary literacy universal; instead the controversy concerned the kinds of knowledge that were acceptable. Small wonder that novelists, and especially early American fiction writers, nearly always contended in their prefaces that their tales were founded on fact, were in fact "histories," and supported traditional morality! Their shrewd stratagem helped secure a vast audience of new readers—youth who had been taught to read partly by reading moral tales and histories.

In the first rural age of reading, the interpenetration of oral and printed cultural forms, along with other cultural forms, was assumed to be almost complete. The learning process in part reflected the way in which readers perceived the mix of media that transmitted knowledge. Upper Valley residents regularly combined and blended several media that we view as distinct and separate. At the same time they defined and described those modes with which they were most familiar.[4]

Daniel Mason of Cavendish, Vermont, was learning to write as a youngster during the 1790s. He was not told by his teacher that the medium of writing was a separate form of expression. Rather, he was instructed to copy again and again the sentence, "A rapid and uniform handwriting is a speaking picture." Mason had mastered the basic cultural skills of talking, listening, and visualizing; writing was taught as a natural extension of these familiar modes. Writing would supplement previously assimilated ways of knowing.[5]

Soon after a pupil had begun spelling, reading, elementary numeracy, and writing—usually within the second month of a district school term—snippets of poetry appeared in reading selections. Most Upper Valley children learned from readers such as *Easy Lessons in*

---

3. See Rusche, "Empire of Reason."
4. See n. 3, p. 234.
5. Mason was later a storekeeper. Daniel Mason, Account Book, 1804–20, Cavendish, Vt. (Manuscripts Collection, VHS). The writing exercises are in the front of the book, and the sentence noted was copied seven times across two facing pages, an exercise book pattern common in district schools because the books were signed and handed in opened up for easy perusal by the teacher.

Reading. In its pages New Englander Joshua Leavitt admonished his audience to "take pains to read the poetry and not to *sing* it." Poetry must be distinguished from the familiar hymns and psalms sung on Sunday. Now the lesson was a more complex one—that not all activities were identical, even if they appeared to be. A poem might resemble a hymn on the printed page, but it differed in that a poem was primarily intended to be read rather than sung. Once again, the instructional method shaped understanding of the communication act by moving from the familiar to the unfamiliar.[6]

Such assumptions about the relationship between one medium and others lasted into adulthood, reinforcing at every step the subtle interpenetration of cultural modes. New England public discourse abounds with examples. For an 1826 meeting of the Franklin Typographical Society, Thomas Green Fessenden, raised in Walpole, New Hampshire, prepared a poem to read. As if he had failed Leavitt's lesson, Fessenden termed it a "hymn" to the art of printing. He then went on to congratulate the assembled group because "the world at length had learn'd to prize, the *art of speaking to the eyes.*" The blending of imagery was further confirmed in Fessenden's statement that printed items were "silent heralds."[7]

By the mid-1820s an alternative whole-word method of reading instruction, the "reading-for-comprehension" method, blossomed. Silent reading, "by the mind's eye" rather than through the mind's ear, quickly gained a first cousin in the mental arithmetic movement. Samuel Goodrich's popular *Child's Arithmetic* urged "teaching beginning arithmetic with tangible objects like counters and bead frames," abandoning the recitation of rules and formulas. The use of concrete objects as an aid in solving problems involving abstract numbers led at more advanced levels to "arithmetic done in the mind, without pencil and paper." Warren Colburn in 1821 termed this method "intellectual arithmetic"; by the late 1820s it was challenging traditional methods in popularity.[8]

As we have seen, then, the habit of reading spread rapidly and reached deeply in rural society because it built on the dominant forms of Upper Valley cultural life. A fairly uniform set of practices introduced male and female readers to the wisdom of the ages. Conservative aims guided a consistent approach that produced solid tra-

---

6. Leavitt, *Easy Lessons in Reading for the Use of Younger Classes in Common Schools* (Watertown, N.Y., 1827), quotes on 14 et passim.
7. Toward evening's end Mr. Metcalf (of Boston) fondly referred to Fessenden's fine poem, reiterating his view that printing was indeed "the art of speaking to the eye." Jefferson Clark, *Address Delivered at the Anniversary Celebration of the Franklin Typographical Society, Jan. 17, 1826* (Boston, 1826), quotes (including poem) on 19 and 22.
8. See Patricia Cline Cohen's intriguing study, *A Calculating People: The Spread of Numeracy in Early America* (Chicago, 1982), 134–41.

ditionalsim in the substance of reading, in reading styles, and in the uses of knowledge. A generation passed before many new readers jettisoned Webster's cultural lenses. Some readers, however, did so almost immediately.

* * *

CATHY N. DAVIDSON

The Life and Times of *Charlotte Temple*: The Biography of a Book[†]

One summer day in 1984, while in residence at the American Antiquarian Society, I called for all copies of all editions of America's first best-selling novel, Susanna Haswell Rowson's *Charlotte, a Tale of Truth* (1791), more commonly known as *Charlotte Temple*. Arranged before me were literally dozens and dozens of *Charlotte Temples*, each one different, each one embodying/reflecting/creating its own history of the book in American culture. For even a quick glance at the assembled volumes affirmed that Charlotte looked different—*was* different—depending upon the dress, the covers and bindings, that she wore. The calf-bound duodecimo destined for the circulating library, the child's size toy book bound for the nursery, the gilt-edged gift book designed for ostentatious display in the middle-class sitting room, the ten-cent story paper marketed for the factory girl, and the contemporary paperback with the scholarly apparatus that signified a university text: each version of Charlotte's story contained its own story about authorship, readership, and publishing in America.

Moreover, the longer I studied the books before me—large and small, ornate and plain—the more I became convinced that what I saw was not just a history of *a* novel but a history of *the* novel as a genre. Concretized by the volumes on the book carts was a new kind of literary history, one that acknowledges that novels are not just texts (as a semiotician might say), not just variant forms of a text (as a bibliographer would use the term), not just plots, characters, metaphors, and images (as the New Critic could point out), not just changing book morphology (as would interest the bibliophile), and not just evolving publishing practices (which should intrigue the historian). On the contrary, the history of the book—and, in this

† From *Reading in America: Literature and Social History*, edited by Cathy Davidson, pp. 157–79. Reprinted with permission of The Johns Hopkins University Press.

case, the history of the novel—entails a combination of all of these diverse elements and requires dialogue among disciplines that do not always speak the same language.

For illustrative purposes, I am focusing on *Charlotte Temple* precisely because it is a text that could be dismissed as "simple," if analyzed by conventional literary methods, but that becomes far more intriguing when viewed as a novel that, more than any other, signaled a new era in the history of the book in America. How was the novel first published, by what methods, and at what expense (to the author, the publisher, the reader)? How did it make its way across the Atlantic to become America's most enduring bestseller? Like the Marquis de Lafayette, who is a hero in America but simply an obscure French soldier buried in an untended grave in Paris and in the footnotes of French history textbooks, *Charlotte Temple* cut a more impressive figure in the land of her adoption than in the land of her birth. One might even ask if *Charlotte Temple* is the same book after a transatlantic crossing. Did success spoil Charlotte Temple? These are provocative questions (not all of them answerable) from which we can begin to see that literature is not just a matter of words but is a complex form of cultural production that has as much to do with national identities, changing economies, new technologies, and developing patterns of work and leisure as it does with symbols and metaphors. As I shall argue in this paper, an overt and covert cultural agenda, an ideological subtext, is encoded in the writing, publishing, reprinting, binding, titling, retitling, pictorializing, advertising, distributing, marketing, selling, buying, reading, interpreting, and, finally, institutionalizing (within literary criticism and historiography) of any text, even (maybe especially) a seemingly simple allegory of female crime and punishment.

I

A comparison of the original American edition of the novel with the first British edition from which it was copied reveals much about the origins of Anglo-American mass publishing.[1] The first American edition, like its English predecessor, is a simple, unassuming, unillustrated, inexpensive duodecimo volume entitled *Charlotte, a Tale of Truth*. It was published in 1794 in Philadelphia by Mathew Carey, former Irish revolutionary turned American Democrat and an ardent champion of social causes ranging from equitable taxation for farm-

---

1. The only known copy of the original British edition of *Charlotte, a Tale of Truth* is in the Barrett Collection at the Alderman Library of the University of Virginia, Charlottesville. I am grateful to the staff at the Alderman Library for making the extensive Rowson collection available to me.

ers and the working class to public charity for the poor, Irish independence, and improved wages for exploited government seamstresses
in Philadelphia who were forced to live and work in horrific conditions.[2] It was singularly appropriate that Mathew Carey should be
the first American publisher of Susanna Rowson's allegory of the
treachery of a British soldier and the subsequent abandonment of a
naive fifteen-year-old schoolgirl in America during the Revolutionary
War, for Carey had immigrated to America in September of 1784,
partly to avoid further imprisonment and prosecution by the British
for publishing an Irish nationalist newspaper, the *Volunteer's Journal*.
No less a personage than the Marquis de Lafayette lent the twenty-
four-year-old immigrant four hundred dollars to set up his printing
operation in the capital of a new nation where he would be rewarded
(not jailed) for his anti-British nationalism.[3]

Mathew Carey went on to become one of the most prosperous
and sagacious publishers of the new Republic. Yet not even Carey
predicted that the novel he printed in a run of a thousand copies (a
typical size for a first edition of a late-eighteenth-century American
novel) would go through over two hundred subsequent editions and
become one of his, and America's, all-time bestsellers.[4] As he wrote
to the author in 1812, "It may afford you great gratification to know
that the sales of *Charlotte Temple* exceed those of any of the most
celebrated novels that ever appeared in England. I think the number disposed of must far exceed 50,000 copies; & the sale still
continues. . . . I have an edition in press of 3000, which I shall sell
at 50 or 60-½ cents each."[5] I hope Susanna Rowson was gratified at
this news of her novel's success, for, with no international copyright laws to protect her work, she received little direct material
reward from the American editions of her novel.

2. See especially Mathew Carey, *Cursory Reflexions on the System of Taxation, Established in the City of Philadelphia; With a Brief Sketch of Its Unequal and Unjust Operation* (Philadelphia, 1806); *Wages of Female Labour* (Philadelphia, 1829); and *Address to
   the Wealthy of the Land, Ladies as Well as Gentlemen, on the Character, Conduct, Situation, and Prospects, of Those Whose Sole Dependence for Subsistence, is on the Labour
   of their Hands* (Philadelphia, 1831).
3. For discussions of Carey, see Earl L. Bradsher, *Mathew Carey: Editor, Author and Publisher* (New York, 1912); James N. Green, *Mathew Carey, Publisher and Patriot* (Philadelphia, 1985); and Kenneth Wyer Rowe, *Mathew Carey: A Study in American
   Economic Development* (Baltimore, Md., 1933).
4. Carey, Account Books, Manuscript Department, American Antiquarian Society,
   Worcester, Mass. (hereafter AAS). See also correspondence and miscellaneous memo-
   randa of Mathew Carey, and the Lea and Febiger Records in the Edward Carey Gardiner
   Collection, Historical Society of Pennsylvania, Philadelphia. See also Eugene L.
   Schwaab, ed., *Mathew Carey Autobiography* (New York, 1942). For a description of most
   of the editions of the novel, see R. W. G. Vail, "Susanna Haswell Rowson, the Author of
   Charlotte Temple: A Bibliographical Study," *Proceedings of the American Antiquarian
   Society* 42 (1932): 47–160.
5. Quoted in Bradsher, *Mathew Carey,* 50. [The entire letter apperars on p. 423 of this
   edition.]

But then Susanna Rowson probably did not earn much for the original English edition of the novel either. In 1790, William Lane advertised that he would pay "a sum, from Five to One Hundred Guineas," for "Manuscripts of Merit." Surviving book contracts suggest that most authors received payments at the lower end of this scale, and many reportedly worked for a mere half-guinea a novel. At such wages, it is small wonder that a number of Lane's authors often wrote mechanically, merely filling out the details of the publisher's outline or else plagiarized from someone else's novel by substituting a new title page and changing the names and a few situations in the plot. Indeed, Rowson's *Mary, or the Test of Honour* (1789), one of only two books to which she never appended her name and a work she never publicly claimed as her own, seems to have been one of Lane's formula novels.[6]

Susanna Rowson, we must remember, wrote before what Michel Foucault has called "the birth of the author," the romantic era's glorification of individual genius and creativity in the service of art. Nor did she write under an older (and primarily European) patronage system. The late eighteenth century, in England and even more so in America, was a time of transition in the publishing world, a time when, as Martha Woodmansee has documented, none of the "requisite legal, economic, and political arrangements and institutions were yet in place to support the large number of writers who came forward."[7] Like most novelists in late-eighteenth-century England and *every* novelist in America before 1820, Rowson was never able to support herself solely by writing novels. That hard economic fact had a tremendous impact on who could afford to write novels, an impact that has not yet been investigated fully by literary historians.[8]

In Rowson's case, the harsh economics of authorship were further exacerbated by her personal situation. She was the breadwinner for herself, her husband, his sister, his sister's children, his illegitimate son, and two adopted children of her own. She managed financially in part because of her prodigious output as a novelist, poet, play-

---

6. For a discussion of author contracts and payments, see the superb biographical-bibliographical study by Dorothy Blakey, *The Minerva Press, 1790–1820* (London, 1939), 72 and 73. See also A. S. Collins, *The Profession of Letters: A Study of the Relation of Author to Patron, Publisher, and Public* (New York, 1929), 44 and 113; and J. M. S. Tompkins, *The Popular Novel in England, 1770–1800* (London, 1932), 9. In her fine new biography, *Susanna Haswell Rowson* (Boston, 1986), Patricia L. Parker documents Rowson's career as a professional writer (see esp. ch. 2).

7. Michel Foucault, "What Is an Author?" in *The Foucault Reader,* ed. Paul Rabinow (New York, 1984), 101–20; and Martha Woodmansee, "The Genius and the Copyright: Economic and Legal Conditions of the Emergence of the 'Author,'" *Eighteenth-Century Studies* 17 (Summer 1984): 443.

8. For a discussion of the relationship between class affiliation and authorship, see William Charvat, *The Profession of Authorship in America, 1800–1870: The Papers of William Charvat,* ed. Matthew J. Bruccoli (Columbus, Ohio, 1968); Robert Escarpit, *The Book Revolution* (London, 1966); and Mary Kelley, *Private Woman, Public Stage: Literary Domesticity in Nineteenth-Century America* (New York, 1984).

wright, essayist, songwriter, and anthologist. Moreover, because the legal and economic rights of eighteenth-century married women were subsumed within their husband's rights, the irresponsible William Rowson received the wages of Susanna's labors, wages, it must be noted, smaller than he (as a male author) would have been likely to receive had he written the books himself. The literary economics of gender, as numerous feminist scholars have noted, further complicate literary history: Susanna Rowson had to supplement her "avocation" as a writer (by social definition, "women writers" were amateurs, even when they wrote to support themselves) with "real" work—as an actress, lecturer, teacher, and founding proprietor of one of early America's foremost women's academies, her Young Ladies' Academy in Massachusetts, an institution over whose operations she exerted full control.[9]

Mathew Carey's edition of Susanna Rowson's *Charlotte, a Tale of Truth* was, considering the liberties taken with many English novels in their translation to America, a remarkably accurate redaction of the original English version that had been published by William Lane at his famous (or infamous) Minerva Press. Here too we can read a story behind the story, for although Carey (unlike his son) was not a major publisher of fiction, he understood the status value of English books for many American readers. Until well into the nineteenth century American publishers pirated popular British novels with great frequency, and often works of American authorship were passed off as English novels and even as Lane novels.[1] Not everyone was impressed by what might be called the Minervizing of early American culture. Reporting to his countrymen on his 1819 journey through America, Englishman Henry Bradshaw Fearon noted,

9. The earliest biography of Rowson is Samuel Lorenzo Knapp's "Memoir," included as a preface to Rowson's posthumously published *Charlotte's Daughter; or, The Three Orphans* (Boston, 1828). The most recent and, all around, the best biography is Parker's *Susanna Haswell Rowson*. Perhaps the most interesting historiographically is Elias Nason's *A Memoir of Mrs. Susanna Rowson, with Elegant and Illustrative Extracts from Her Writings in Prose and Poetry* (Albany, N.Y., 1870). For an eyewitness account of Rowson's activities, see also Myra Montgomery to Mary Ann Means, November 22, 1808, Claude W. Unger Collection, Historical Society of Pennsylvania. For a summary of women's legal and economic status in the new Republic and for evidence that William Rowson collected his wife's wages, see Cathy N. Davidson, *Revolution and the Word: The Rise of the Novel in America* (New York, 1986), ch. 6 and p. 8. For a discussion of the discrepancy between royalties paid to women and men authors, see Hannah Adams's contemporaneous account in *A Memoir of Miss Hannah Adams, Written by Herself* (Boston, 1832).

1. An excellent example of an American publisher attempting to mimic British practices can be seen in George Clark's 1841 (Boston) edition of Tabitha Tenney's popular novel, *Female Quixotism*, originally published as two volumes bound as one by Isaiah Thomas and E. T. Andrews in 1801. Clark actually renumbers the chapters (with little regard to the plot structure of the novel) in order to create a three-volume book on the model of popular British novels of the era. Jay Fliegelman, in *Prodigals and Pilgrims: The American Revolution against Patriarchal Authority, 1750–1800* (New York, 1982), 67–79, recounts the various ways in which *Robinson Crusoe* was reprinted for an American audience.

The *reading* of Americans (for I have not seen in [American] society an approach to what can be called *study*) is English, there being few native writers, and but a small number of these who possess the respect of even their own country men. Our novels and poetry, not excepting those which proceed from the Minerva press, meet with an immediate reprint, and constitute practically the entire American library. . . . Notwithstanding this voluntary national dependence, there are, perhaps, no people, not even excepting the French, who are so vain as the Americans.[2]

The main aspersion here, of course, is directed at American culture (or the lack thereof), the secondary slur at the Minerva Press. With that second slur, Fearon merely echoed the sentiments of many elitist Englishmen. For despite his astonishing success—or because of it—William Lane, with his Minerva Press in Leadenhall Street, was frequently castigated from the pulpit and in the press as a purveyor of cheap (in both senses of that word) books and often blamed for the decline in morals, if not the collapse of civilized society, in the Western world. What most alarmed Lane's detractors was how skillfully he catered to and fostered a new audience for literature, primarily novels. In the derisive summation of one traditionalist, Lane was "a leaden-*headed* dealer in books for the *cheesemongers*."[3]

Viewed from our contemporary vantage point, the extensive and apocalyptic denunciations of fiction in the eighteenth and early nineteenth centuries have a distinctly comical ring. One regularly encounters rampant metaphors of serpents, slavery, seduction, and satanic possession used to dramatize the ostensibly sinister powers of the insidious but increasingly popular literary form. The novel was seen to "mesmerize," "capture," and "tyrannize" a reader's attention and volition. But the contemporary reader can hardly take seriously a denunciation such as the essay "Novel Reading, a Cause of Female Depravity," which describes the sexual fall of a young woman, the "premature graves" to which her parents are brought through her disgrace, and the corollary destruction of "several relative families," all of which disasters follow, as the night the day, from reading fiction.[4]

2. Henry Bradshaw Fearon, *Sketches of America. A Narrative of a Journey of Five Thousand Miles Through the Eastern and Western States of America* (London, 1818), 365–68.

3. For a survey of the censure of fiction in America, see, for example, Jean-Marie Bonnet, *La Critique Littéraire aux Etats-Unis, 1783–1837* (Lyon, 1982); and G. Harrison Orians, "Censure of Fiction in American Romances and Magazines, 1789–1810," *PMLA* 52 (1937): 195–214. The derisive judgment against Lane appeared in *Stuart's Star* (February 16, 1789) and is quoted in Blakey, *Minerva Press*, 14.

4. "Novel Reading, A Cause of Female Depravity," *New England Quarterly* I (1802): 172–74. A headnote indicates that this article was originally published in the (British) *Monthly Mirror* in November 1797.

Yet the apprehensions of the eighteenth century—however baroque their metaphors—may well reflect the magnitude of the cultural changes that social authorities feared and that book entrepreneurs such as Lane in England and Carey in America early anticipated.

What does it *mean* if there is suddenly a massive demand for a literature that is linguistically simple enough to be apprehended by cheesemongers or serving girls, those readers who may have only a minimal education and a low level of literacy? Lane and Carey too understood as keenly as their detractors did that once the publishing industry shifts its primary attention and economy from a limited supply of nonfiction books intended for a specialized (and often elite) audience to a plethora of novels about and for middle- and working-class readers, we have a major shift in the social and political functions of culture. Entertainment, as Raymond Williams has argued, is never a frivolous matter but itself reiterates, in a variety of forms, the hegemonies of the culture.[5] If a hierarchical model of learning (the patriarchal Puritan family presided over by the father reading aloud to his family each night around the dinner table; the same hegemonies reinforced from the pulpit by the minister translating texts for his audience) is replaced by the mostly individualistic activity of perusing novels, the concomitant ideological implications will be as radical as the redistribution of reading power.

Furthermore, as Mikhail Bakhtin has argued, literary styles and genres in themselves embody ideologies. Bakhtin also notes, by way of example, that the novel was initially deemed subversive in every country into which it was introduced, largely because the complex intellectual and emotional activity of reading fiction empowers the hitherto powerless individual, at least imaginatively, by authorizing necessarily private responses to texts that function primarily as repositories for those responses. The distinctive feature of the novel as a genre may not be its formal qualities, its verbal artistry, its realistic or sensational plot lines, nor even its paraphrasable content, but rather the "dialogue" that it enters into with the reader, who in a literal sense is required to "complete" the textual transaction. This active apprehension of text can be psychically liberating for the individual reader in ways that are threatening to those who perceive themselves as the arbiters (or former arbiters) of cultural work. To return to Bakhtin's formulations, "In a novel the individual acquires the ideological and linguistic initiative necessary to change the nature of his own image." Moreover, the novel "has no canon of its

5. Raymond Williams, *The Long Revolution* (New York, 1961), esp. 41–43, 113, and *Keywords: A Vocabulary of Culture and Society* (New York, 1976), 76–82, 145–48, 281–84.

own. It is, by its nature, not canonic. It is plasticity itself. It is a genre that is ever questing, ever examining itself and subjecting its established forms to review," an enterprise that can also encourage the reader to subject other or all established forms of authority to review.[6]

The noncanonical, the plastic, the self-reflexive, and the anti-authoritarian novel (embodying and reflecting its readers) *must* be threatening to the status quo, and it is small wonder that William Lane was vilified by one segment of English society for disseminating, with dazzling efficiency, precisely those kinds of books that seemed to undermine traditional literary and social hegemonies. Lane specialized in "Novels, Tales, Romances, Adventures, &c.," which he distributed through a network of urban and provincial circulating libraries. He not only founded these libraries but supplied their proprietors with a stock of books and "instructions and directions how to plan, systemize, and conduct" an efficient enterprise, a forerunner of the contemporary franchise business venture. Lane also saw novels, his primary stock in trade, as literary peanuts: he knew that it was hard to stop at just one. Leigh Hunt, for example, confessed himself to be a "glutton of novels," and sated his appetite, early in the nineteenth century, on many of the more than seventeen thousand titles available from the Minerva Library on Leadenhall Street.[7] Equally important, by offering annual, semiannual, monthly, weekly, or even book-by-book subscription rates, Lane accommodated those who did not have large disposable incomes—women of all classes, lower- and working-class men, students, and even Romantic poets.

Lane succeeded as a publisher largely by making novels available to a new segment of the reading public that could not afford to buy those books that they wanted to read, but who, through the Minerva Library system, could happily borrow books at a fraction of their purchase price. He also perceived that occasionally his readers became so attached to a particular work that they wanted to own it, to possess it, to make it part of their lives (all that can be implied by book ownership in a society where books are still prized possessions). That too could be arranged, since every Minerva Library doubled as a bookshop. Finally, Lane made his books not only affordable but accessible, often setting up his libraries in such varied establishments as general stores (as was typical also in America), curio shops in seaside resort towns, jewelry shops, fishing-tackle suppliers, hardware stores, tobacconists, and apothecary stores.[8]

6. Mikhail M. Bakhtin, "Epic and Novel," in *The Dialogic Imagination: Four Essays*, ed. and trans. Caryl Emerson and Michael Holquist (Austin, Tex., 1981), 37–39.
7. Leigh Hunt, *Autobiography of Leigh Hunt* (London, 1885), 124; and Blakey, *Minerva Press*, 114.
8. Blakey, *Minerva Press*, 122.

In 1794, no American publisher had yet worked out such an efficient system for disseminating books to all classes of American readers and to various regions of the nation, although Mathew Carey, employing itinerant book peddlers and arranging exchanges with other publishers, certainly had one of the country's most extensive book exchange networks. One of those itinerant book peddlers, the indomitable Mason Locke ("Parson") Weems, was able to get his books out to even small towns in distant parts of the nation. But the differences between the Lane and Carey operations in the 1790s are revealing. For example, bound with the 1791 British edition of *Charlotte* is an advertisement for Lane's "LITERARY MUSEUM, or NOVEL REPOSITORY," which was described as a "Museum of Entertainment, and a Repository of Sciences, Arts, and Polite Literature." Despite that claim, nearly all of the ten thousand books Lane had in stock in 1791 were either novels or novelistic accounts of captivity, travel, or adventure. In contrast, Carey's stock (some imported, some published by Carey) was both considerably smaller and considerably less specialized than Lane's. Carey too bound an advertisement for his shop into his edition of *Charlotte*. Although incomplete, this list is illustrative of Carey's interests as a publisher. It includes just over 280 titles. Among them are tracts by philosophers as diverse as James Beattie, Edmund Burke, and William Godwin; evangelical religious testimonials; sermons; law books; scientific treatises; pedagogical works; advice books; almanacs; feminist books such as Mary Wollstonecraft's *A Vindication of the Rights of Woman*; poetry; classics; biographies; and numerous novels, tales, romances, and adventures on the Minerva model.[9]

One might argue that America was yet too new, too vast, and the population too scattered for a single-minded novel-producing "factory" such as Lane's to be successful here. Or one might argue that Carey felt intimidated by the extensive American censure of fiction, more virulent and persistent here even than in England. But I am inclined to think Carey's varied stock reflected more his personal predilections than the economic and social limitations under which he labored. Consider, for example, that when, in 1804, Hocquet Caritat published the catalogue for his library of fiction in New York City, he could list nearly fifteen hundred titles. Caritat's library, not coincidentally, had direct and reciprocal (if unequal) trade agreements with Lane's Minerva Press.[1] Moreover, as Robert B. Winans has succinctly observed, "The increase in the number of

---

9. See Carey's advertisement, dated Philadelphia, April 17, 1794, bound with his first edition of *Charlotte Temple* (Philadelphia, 1794), n.p.
1. George Raddin, *An Early New York Library of Fiction, with a Checklist of the Fiction of H. Caritat's Circulating Library, No. 1, City Hotel, Broadway, New York, 1804* (New York, 1940).

circulating libraries [in America] was largely the result of the increasing demand for novels; the general growth of the reading public was
caused primarily by the novel."[2] Although my research on this subject is still preliminary, I might also here note that I have located
over forty American libraries that stocked *Charlotte Temple* before
1830. I have found the book listed on surviving library rosters or,
more typically, have discovered a library bookplate within an extant
copy of the novel. Some libraries, especially institutional or social
libraries that catered to a more elite audience, did not stock novels
at all. But thus far, every library roster I have found that includes
novels also lists *Charlotte Temple*.

Mathew Carey published books that could appeal to all classes of
American readers, from the poorest to the most elite, and, like most
urban publishers, he freely mixed in novels or novelistic books with
various nonfictional works. His different social agenda, however,
did not preclude him from copying closely Lane's edition of *Charlotte*. But although he produced a remarkably similar text, Carey
made significant additions to the title page of his original American
edition. First, unlike Lane, he included the author's name on the
title page. Second, by adding a brief attribution, he implies that the
now-identified author is an American: "By Mrs. Rowson, of the New
Theatre, Philadelphia." The author, like the publisher, was a new
immigrant to the new nation, but Rowson's arrival in 1793 preceded
the American imprint of her novel by only one year. Carey nevertheless grants Rowson de facto literary citizenship. He had no way of
knowing that he was publishing a potential bestseller, yet by his
designation he asserted that what he was publishing was an *American* novel.

II

By alluding to Rowson's Philadelphia theater career on its title page,
Carey's edition implicitly raises two theoretical issues worth considering at some length: the historical question of a book-buying public
and the historiographic issue of what constitutes a national literature. Since these are complex issues, I will address them separately,
beginning with the matter of who in the early Republic could afford
to buy books, which were, comparatively speaking, very expensive in
the years before machine-made paper and horse- or steam-powered
presses. Carey sold *Charlotte* for between fifty cents and a dollar

---

2. Robert B. Winans, "Bibliography and the Cultural Historian: Notes on the Eighteenth-
Century Novel," in *Printing and Society in Early America*, ed. William L. Joyce et al.
(Worcester, Mass., 1983), 176.

(depending partly on the bindings and other factors relating to the material condition of the individual book). To put the novel's cost in perspective, it should be remembered that a laborer in Philadelphia in 1794 would be fortunate to earn that much in a day, a serving girl in a week.[3] But by alluding to Rowson's theatrical career, Carey cleverly "target marketed" (to use contemporary advertising jargon) the book for an audience that could afford it. Rowson was a popular character actress and playwright, well known to those upper-class and upper-middle-class Americans who paid as much for a night at the New Theatre as they might pay for a copy of Rowson's novel.[4] Citizens with enough disposable income to spend on culture and entertainment were potential book buyers, something the author-actress, an exceptionally astute businesswoman, also understood.

By describing Mrs. Rowson as "of the New Theatre, Philadelphia," Carey also raised the ideological question of nationality—implicitly supplying an egalitarian answer to Crèvecoeur's famous (and persistent) question, "What is an American?" Crèvecoeur's classic formulation of American identity, published in England by a French immigrant, was reprinted in America by immigrant Mathew Carey in 1793, three years after Crèvecoeur had returned to his native France, where he died, in 1813, at the home of his daughter, America-Francès.[5] As even this ambiguous biographical summation suggests, the whole issue of a national literature has been particularly troubling to American literary historians precisely because it affords no ready answer.[6] Except for the Native Americans, who certainly have not profited by their indigenous status, we are a nation of immigrants exuberantly eager to melt into the homogeneous ideal "American." But what that label means has been a source of anxiety almost since the nation's founding. Indeed, literary historiography has, since

3. U.S. Department of Labor, *History of Wages in the United States from Colonial Times to 1928* (Washington, D.C., 1929), 53, 57, 133–34, 137. These wages are corroborated by many contemporaneous cost accountings, such as those found at the end of the diary of Ethan Allen Greenwood for December 30, 1805, to February 9, 1806, in the Manuscript Department of the AAS.
4. For a discussion of the class affiliations of theatergoers, see Kenneth Silverman, *A Cultural History of the American Revolution* (New York, 1976), esp. 545–46.
5. Michel Guillaume Jean de Crèvecoeur, *Letters From an American Farmer* (London, 1782), letter 3. For a succinct assessment, see John Harmon McElroy, "Michel Guillaume Jean de Crèvecoeur," *Dictionary of Literary Biography*, vol. 3, *American Writers of the Early Republic*, ed. Emory Elliott, 103–7.
6. The inconsistencies in historical claims for an American identity have been analyzed persuasively by William C. Spengemann in "The Earliest American Novel: Aphra Behn's *Oroonoko*," *Nineteenth-Century Fiction* 38 (1984): 384–414, and "What Is American Literature?" *Centennial Review* 22 (1978): 119–38. For the ways in which women have been excluded from the definition of "American," see the perceptive essays by Nina Baym, "Melodramas of Beset Manhood: How Theories of American Fiction Exclude Women Authors," *American Quarterly* 33 (Summer 1981): 123–39; and Annette Kolodny, "The Integrity of Memory: Creating a New Literary History of the United States," *American Literature* 57 (May 1985): 291–307.

the time of the Revolution, been marked by an implicit ideological demand for "national purity," what Moses Coit Tyler, writing in 1878, called a "common national accent," in conflict with—if not in out-right contradiction to—America's rampant heterogeneity.[7]

Nationalist ideologies have especially distinguished the historiography of the novel's rise to cultural respectability and prominence. In the years after the Civil War, literary historians began searching for that mythical creature, the Great American Novel. The very terms of the search acknowledged that, as Nina Baym has demonstrated, the novel had become a relatively respectable literary genre by the mid-nineteenth century.[8] While the new Republic strove for a Great American Epic to embody its aspirations, a hundred years later the Gilded Age sought the Great American Novel. The culture perceived its best fiction to be an apt measure of and metaphor for its status as a nation that was even then beginning to assume international political and economic power.[9] Moreover, one cannot have a Great American Novel without a proper genealogy, and, especially in the 1880s and 1890s, numerous candidates were set forth as the "first American novel." After considerable debate (especially about the notion of national purity), the award was finally conferred on a book of impeccable pedigree, *The Power of Sympathy,* published by the patriot Isaiah Thomas in 1789. This work was written by the native-born William Hill Brown and centered on a quintessentially American seduction story that included, as a subplot, a realistic recounting of a notorious scandal among Boston's aristocracy, with the names only slightly changed to pretend to protect the guilty. It is hard to be more American than that.[1]

But in his edition of Susanna Rowson's novel, Mathew Carey, in one phrase, effectively trivializes any preoccupation with national purity. Unlike subsequent literary genealogists, Carey simply side-stepped the whole question by stating that Rowson was "*of . . .* Philadelphia." However, at least one of Carey's contemporaries was unwilling to accept this ascription. William Cobbett, writing as "Peter Porcupine," denounced Susanna Rowson in a pamphlet enti-tled *A Kick for a Bite* (1795). A scathing attack on all of her work, but mostly on her play *Slaves in Algiers* (1794), Cobbett's diatribe descends into an ad hominem attack on Rowson's feminism, her Democratic politics, *and* her Johnny-come-lately status as an Ameri-

7. Moses Coit Tyler, *A History of American Literature,* 1607–1765, 2 vols. (New York, 1878), I:V.
8. Nina Baym, *Novels, Readers, and Reviewers: Responses to Fiction in Antebellum America* (Ithaca, N.Y., 1984).
9. Herbert Ross Brown, "The Great American Novel," *American Literature* 7 (1935): 1–14.
1. The theoretical issue of literary nationalism in relation to the publication of the first American novel is discussed at length in Davidson, *Revolution and the Word,* 83–109.

can. That Cobbett himself was an immigrant who later returned to England did not keep him from offering up an exclusionary and, I would suggest, perniciously narrow definition of nationality, a subject that Mathew Carey took up in two notably harsh rebuttals of Cobbett (both published in 1799), *A Plumb Pudding for the Humane, Chaste, Valiant, Enlightened Peter Porcupine* and *The Porcupiniad. A Hudibrastic Poem.* Lest it be inferred that Susanna could not speak for herself against such a prickly critic, I hasten to add that in the preface to her *Trials of the Human Heart* (1795), Rowson noted how her "literary world [was] infested with a kind of loathsome reptile," one of which has "crawled over the volumes, which I have had the temerity to submit to the public eye. I say *crawled* over them because I am certain it has never penetrated beyond the title-page of any."[2]

Was Susanna Haswell Rowson American? A bare biography equivocates on that question. Born in England in 1762, she lived in America from 1766 until 1778 and attributed much of her literary education to a family friend, the patriot James Otis, who referred to her as his "little Scholar" and who encouraged her to read Shakespeare and Spenser, Dryden's Virgil, and Pope's Homer before she was ten. With the outbreak of the Revolution, Lieutenant Haswell and his family were returned to England in a prisoner exchange. Yet Susanna retained enough happy memories of those Americans who aided the family in their worst distress to decide, at the age of thirty-one, to return to the country from which she had been exiled at the age of fifteen (the age, of course, at which Charlotte Temple came to America). In 1804, with the naturalization of her husband, Susanna too became legally a citizen of the country that she had psychologically claimed for a decade and to which she referred as "my dear adopted country, America."[3] Four of the novels written after her immigration to America—*Trials of the Human Heart* (1795), *Reuben and Rachel* (1798), *Sarah* (1813), and the posthumously published *Charlotte's Daughter* (1828)—were printed first in America, as were her five pedagogical works, a collection of her poetry, and numerous songs, including "America, Commerce & Freedom," one of the most popular patriotic songs of the new Republic.[4]

Charlotte Temple's national provenance is equally ambiguous. The novel was not a bestseller in England. Lane did not include it in his 1798 prospectus of the most popular works from his press, nor was it

2. Susanna Rowson, *Trials of the Human Heart* (Philadelphia, 1795), p. 357 this edition.
3. Susanna Rowson, *Exercises in History, Chronology, and Biography* (Boston, 1822), preface.
4. For a complete list, with full bibliographical data, see Vail, "Susanna Haswell Rowson," 91–160.

even reprinted in England before 1819.[5] In contrast, Americans read, bought, and loved the book for over a century with an enduring ardor unsurpassed in American literary history. The usual pulpit pronouncement of the nineteenth century was that *Charlotte Temple* had managed to displace the Bible from the bedtables of America.

It was as an American novel that *Charlotte Temple* was read. By the first decade of the nineteenth century, Americans had even created, in Trinity Churchyard in New York City, a "grave" for Charlotte Temple. Until well into the twentieth century, this real grave of a fictional character received far more visitors than the neighboring graves of Alexander Hamilton or Robert Fulton.[6] Despite repeated allegations by historians that the tomb was not authentic, tens of thousands of visitors continued to make a pilgrimage to it for a hundred years. For them, the grave contained the last remains of another immigrant, an English girl seduced by a lieutenant in the British army who promised to marry her once they arrived on American soil. After an arduous ocean crossing (during which, presumably, she lost her virginity), Charlotte was rewarded not with marriage but with abandonment and subsequent death in childbirth while Lieutenant Montraville married a wealthy woman and went off to fight in the Revolutionary War. Is this really an American novel? Perhaps not. But it was printed as one by Carey and read as one by hundreds of thousands of American readers who also, I suspect, read in the devastating denouement of Charlotte's betrayal one of the first and paradigmatic failures of an American dream.

Susanna Rowson never disputed the authenticity of the tombstone erected during her lifetime in a graveyard in New York. Until her death she insisted that *Charlotte, a Tale of Truth* was true, despite the fact that no historical prototype has ever been substantiated.[7] But I would still suggest that the literalization of the novel by myriad American readers has made Charlotte Temple real, just as it had made *Charlotte Temple* American.

Mass culture is often dismissed as commodity, inflicted by a ruling class upon a mindless proletariat, but the ritualistic mourning for Charlotte indicates both the individual intensity of the identification with the heroine for myriad readers as well as the folkloric, communal nature of this experience—the cultural presence of Charlotte Temple is revitalized and concretized by shared, commu-

---

5. Blakey, *Minerva Press,* appendix 4, n.p.
6. "H.S.B.", letter to *New York Evening Post* (September 12, 1903); and "Charlotte Temple's Grave," *New York Daily Tribune* (June 8, 1900). The latter clipping was preserved in a copy of *Charlotte Temple,* Special Collections, Kent State University Library, Kent, Ohio. Special thanks to Kathleen E. Noland for bringing it to my attention.
7. For a biography as fictional as anything Rowson wrote, see novelist Caroline Dall's *The Romance of the Association; or, One Last Glimpse of Charlotte Temple and Eliza Wharton* (Cambridge, Mass., 1875).

nal, cross-generational rituals over a symbolic tomb. Readers flocked to her grave like pilgrims searching for the One True Cross. Readers further signaled their cultural participation in Rowson's novel by leaving (again ritualistically) tokens of themselves: bouquets of flowers, locks of hair, ashes of love letters.

Another indication of the force of *Charlotte Temple* is the misreading it has sustained. Many nineteenth-century descriptions of the novel create a plot that does not appear in Susanna Rowson's originating text. In the familiar misreading (sustained even in present-day accounts), Charlotte sets out, alone and pregnant, in a snowstorm to find Montraville, the faithless lover. The snow whirling madly about her, she collapses only to be saved from certain death by a poor servant who takes her into his hovel where she gives birth to a daughter and then dies among America's underclass, who welcome her with a sympathy and a friendship not found elsewhere in the revolutionary-era America vaguely symbolized in the novel. This popular redaction of Rowson's plot elides events to create a more graphic class allegory than the one Rowson "actually" wrote. More to the point, this invigorated class allegory was ritualistically reenacted (with the culminating snowstorm scene) in a melodrama version popular among the itinerant acting companies that performed in dingy nineteenth-century factory towns.

What I am suggesting is that this novel became a kind of cultural legend with significance beyond that usually ascribed to mass cultural products. This is evident in both the ritual transfiguration of the symbolic, textual Charlotte into the "real" corpse lying in Trinity Churchyard, and at the same time (and this is the classic process in oral, folk culture) the allegorical significance reenacted in readers' everyday lives. This same dual tendency toward literalization and symbolization persists. Even today, at the New-York Historical Society, one can find, filed under Rowson's name, two letters written by Margaret M. Coghlan "who *may* have been the original for Mrs. Rowson's 'Charlotte Temple.'" Margaret Coghlan's diction and her tragic story make a tale as pathetic as the one Rowson tells: "I was married during the American War in Obedience to the Commands of my father ere I had seen fifteen years, to a Captain in the Army, whose barbarous ill usage and abandonment has plunged me into an Abbess [*sic*] of Woe. . . . I have no means of Support and am struggling with more real misery, than I have power to describe."[8] In no objective, historical sense is this Charlotte Temple, who eloped with Montraville without ever consulting the loving parents who could have saved her. A number of other

---

8. Margaret M. Coghlan to Edward P. Livingston, December 28, 1803, Robert R. Livingston Papers, New-York Historical Society.

details in the letter (the political affiliations of the principals, the death of both parents) also suggest a disparity between historical and fictional character.

Nevertheless, the anonymous librarian who cross-listed Margaret Coghlan's letters under "Susanna Rowson" read the truth of her story on a level that transcends mere facticity. For what is essential in the Coghlan "novella" is its quintessential injustice, its disappointed promises, its sense of being betrayed by the liberal and republican ideal that posited a correlation between merit (in a woman, read "virtue") and reward. Charlotte was recognized as just such a victim by even the first reviewer of the novel, who, in London's Critical Review, proclaimed her a "martyr" and protested the severity of the punishment heaped upon her: "We should feel for Charlotte if such a person ever existed, who, for one error, scarcely, perhaps, deserved so severe a punishment. If it is a fiction, poetic justice is not, we think, properly distributed."[9] Mathew Carey felt this public exoneration of a "fallen woman" so important that he tipped it into copies of the first American edition of the novel under the heading "Of Charlotte, the Reviewers have given the following character."[1] For the second edition (published in October of 1794), Carey printed the review on the verso of the title page, a powerful reading directive for an early American interpretive community. Naive, sexually lax, even disobedient, Charlotte Temple was still pitied by reviewers, publishers, and readers who made her into an early American icon—a figura of the seduced female, an embodiment of the interdependent strands of sexual and economic exploitation. Margaret Coghlan becomes Charlotte Temple in the same way that several generations of deceived, distraught, or merely lonely readers—men as well as women, old as well as young, affluent as well as poor—also became Charlotte.

Perhaps because of the pervasiveness of novels (and, no doubt, the more recent incursions into the psyche made by radio and television), we now take for granted those generic and ideological features of the novel that most frightened eighteenth-century social authorities. As they clearly saw, novels encourage identification between reader and character. Moreover, emotional identification subverts moral censure, so much so that the fatal consequence of Charlotte's disobedience and illicit sexuality could be read not as justice delivered but as a tragic metaphor for human pain—for the reader's pain—in all its variety. This transvaluation of value was already present in the first review of Charlotte Temple in the Critical Review, was seconded by Mathew Carey when he reprinted it in his editions of the novel, and

---

9. Critical Review 2d ser., I (1791): 413 this edition.
1. Susanna Rowson, Charlotte, a Tale of Truth (Philadelphia, 1794). The review is affixed to the verso of the front flyleaf.

was echoed, resoundingly, in the hearts and minds of the readers of
the novel who, for a century, left tokens of lost loves upon Charlotte's
grave and who left tender inscriptions and marginalia in copies of
the novel. In the words of an anonymous but representative reader,
written on July 25, 1817, "unfortunate Charlotte" was "fair and sweet
as the Lilly Inosentas / the young lamb folly misled."[2]

Early critics feared the novel for its power to thwart rational moralistic arguments, to subordinate logic to emotion, and to privilege
the "wisdom of the human heart" over the sterner dicta of the head.
The critics feared rightly. Within fictional space-time—the ahistorical, out-of-time dimension of the reading process—there occurs
a transubstantiation wherein the word becomes flesh, the text
becomes the reader, the reader becomes the hero. Through the
intimate, transformative process of reading, *Charlotte Temple* transcends its seemingly formulaic plot to become something much
more than a simple allegory of female crime and punishment.

III

Charlotte Temple enjoyed the longest popularity of any American
novel and was the first fiction in America to signal the novel's rise
to cultural prominence, especially among a new kind of reader
whose tears, for over a century, kept the grass over Charlotte's final
resting place as green as the dollars that passed through many a
publisher's pocket. Mathew Carey, for example, followed his first
American edition of *Charlotte, a Tale of Truth* with many subsequent and, after 1797, retitled versions. Appropriately, just as Carey
had done unto Lane, many American publishers did unto Carey. By
1802, one could read *The History of Charlotte Temple* in a version
by John Babcock of Hartford, Connecticut, or by William W. Morse
of New Haven. One could read a Philadelphia *Charlotte Temple*
published by Peter Stewart or other versions published in Alexan-
dria, Virginia, and New York City.[3]

The way various publishers chose to print, bind, and market this
novel reveals much about the increasing dominance of the novel as
a genre and the many social functions the novel served within the
culture. One *Charlotte Temple* could be repackaged in myriad ways
in order to appeal to different kinds of readers and to perform different kinds of cultural work. Moreover, the external packaging
of the novel—including illustrative front matter—served also to
direct the reader as to how she or he might assess the text therein.
I would therefore suggest that the text *changes* according to how it
is presented or framed by book morphology. In short, although one

2. AAS copy of Carey's 1812 edition, verso of the last page of vol. I.
3. See Vail, "Susanna Haswell Rowson," 93–94.

may not be able to judge a book by its cover, one can read what a given cover signifies.

What do we make, for example, of the editions of *Charlotte Temple* apparently intended for children? In 1811 Samuel Avery produced a toy book *Charlotte Temple* (13 centimeters by 7 centimeters) in a cheap calf binding. An advertisement at the back indicates that Avery also published "School books, bibles, and testaments" as well as "a great variety of juvenile books, which he intends to sell, (wholesale and retail) as cheap as can be Purchased in the United States."[4] Rowson's story of filial disobedience, inept pedagogy, hypocrisy, dishonesty, misogyny, class conflict, and, especially, the tragic consequences of illicit sexuality is transmogrified into a cautionary tale suitable for the nursery. Publishers thus profited from the republican imperative to educate the young for citizenship in the new United States. In keeping with a growing societal reaction against Puritan pedagogical praxis, publishers too saw that education could be tempered with (and encouraged through) entertainment. Through the negative example of poor Charlotte, students could apprehend the need for education not just in religious dogma but also in the ways of the world. By thoroughly involving the reader's emotions in the sad story of the seduction, abandonment, and subsequent death in childbirth of a schoolgirl misled partly by a despicable French teacher, the text also illustrated that women, especially, had to learn to be cautious. Rowson, incidentally, insisted that she intended the book to "advise" the "young and unprotected woman in her first entrance into life" (p. 7), thus setting forth an educational agenda that goes considerably beyond the three R's.

Elaborate mid-nineteenth-century gift book editions, sometimes bound in morocco, often edged and lettered in gilt, made the book suitable for display in any upstanding middle-class home, while story paper versions masqueraded as newspapers in order to take advantage of the low postal rates accorded to the postrevolutionary press and partly circumvent high distribution costs. One story paper edition called itself, on the title page, "CHEAP EDITION OF CHARLOTTE TEMPLE, A TALE OF TRUTH" and boasted a price of twelve and a half cents, a reduction (it claimed) of the normal fifty-cent price.[5] What different class allegories did different readers discover in these varied versions of the same text? Could aspiring middle-class readers hold Charlotte's father accountable for her fall? After all, as the "youngest son of a nobleman, whose fortune was by no means adequate to the antiquity, grandeur, and . . . pride of the family"

---

4. AAS copy of Samuel Avery's 1811 edition.
5. This is in the Skinner and Blanchard (Boston) edition of 1845. An 1877 edition of the novel, published in tabloid format by Norman L. Munro, was "Given Away with Number 211 of the New York Family Story Paper."

(p. 00), Henry Temple had the opportunity to marry the only child of a wealthy man but chose instead to marry for love. Charlotte grew up in a happy home, but her lack of a dowry certainly put her at a disadvantage on the marriage market. The plot device is then inverted in the Montraville family, where the daughters have been provided with enough of a dowry to allow them to attract good husbands, and the sons (Montraville being the youngest of several) have been severely warned against marrying "precipitously," before they are able to support a wife and family (pp 39–41). Montraville thus rejects Charlotte in favor of marriage with a woman who is both virtuous *and* rich. If Rowson wrote a class allegory, the next question must be, *Which* class's allegory? And how are gender and class intertwined in this complex allegory? The case is by no means unequivocal in the text and is further confused by the novel's long history as a bestseller among poor, working-class, middle-class, and even affluent readers. In the words of one of Rowson's early biographers, the novel could be found in the "study of the divine and . . . the workshop of the mechanic," in the "parlor of the accomplished lady and the bedchamber of her waiting-maid."[6]

Robert Escarpit has noted that a book (as opposed to a manuscript) is characterized by a "multiplication of meaning," a public and changing act influenced by material considerations (book morphology and production) and nonmaterial ones (the previous experiences readers bring to their texts).[7] As if to signal their *recreation* of Rowson's text, numerous nineteenth-century publishers again changed the novel's title in ways that served as a reading directive for the book-buying public of that time. These new titles, printed at the height of the popularity of the sentimental novel, acknowledge, at least tacitly, another era in the history of the book in American culture. One now finds such titles as *The Lamentable History of the Beautiful and Accomplished Charlotte Temple, with an Account of her Elopement with Lieutenant Montroville [sic], and her Misfortunes and Painful Sufferings, are Herein Pathetically Depicted.* A version from the 1860s that bears this title also includes an "Original Portrait" of the protagonist as a quintessentially innocent young maiden, sweet and vulnerable, but rather incongruously adorned in the most fashionable couture of the day. Yet this sentimentalized rendition of Charlotte is in striking contrast to an almost simultaneous marketing of her story in highly sensational and even quasi-pornographic terms. An infamous story paper version (which resembles a contemporary tabloid newspaper) pictorializes a more mature and lascivious

---

6. Nason, *Memoir of Mrs. Susanna Rowson*, 50.
7. Robert Escarpit, *Sociology of Literature,* trans. Ernest Pick, 2nd ed. (London, 1971), 55–74.

Charlotte. Although based on a famous Raphael Madonna, this rendition of a smoldering Charlotte is anything but virginal. And lest the reader miss the import of the cover illustration, the printer has emphasized his meaning with an unambiguous banner headline: "The Fastest Girl in New York."[8]

Charlotte, daughter of poverty and innocent victim of masculine (and bourgeois) deception; Charlotte, role model for the learning young; Charlotte, sentimental heroine; Charlotte, seductress: all these Charlotte Temples are evident in nineteenth-century editions even before we turn to the story itself. Book morphology, the title page, dedication, and frontispiece are all texts to be read, texts as significant and as subtle as those found in the pages on which literary scholars have traditionally focused their attention. Similarly, certain texts are chosen by advertisers as the appropriate vehicle from which to sell a product. Take, for example, the Seaside Library pocket edition of *Charlotte Temple* that was published by George Munro early in the 1890s. The book contains an advertisement for Colgate soaps and perfumes, as well as advertisements for Castoria, Beecham's Pills, and a Cactus Blood Cure (a patent medicine touted as a cure for, among other things, consumption). Another ad informs us, "Well Bred, Soon Wed. Girls who use Sapolio are Quickly Married." Yet in the midst of these ads (foreshadowing the contemporary soap opera) is an advertisement for "The Prose Dramas of Henrik Ibsen," the kind of juxtaposition that compromises current critical clichés about elite versus popular culture.

Twentieth-century texts give us still other versions of *Charlotte Temple*. The first scholarly edition of the novel was compiled in 1905 by Francis W. Halsey, who sought to redress the 1,265 errors that he had found in the many popular (but corrupt) versions of the text.[9] So long as textual accuracy is the explicit aim and insofar as a 262-page novel requires a 109-page introduction, we have text about the importance, function, and purpose not only of literature but of literary scholarship as both rigorous discipline and necessary endeavor. Interestingly, Halsey's scholarly edition coincided with the end of *Charlotte Temple's* popularity, and most twentieth-century editions have been aimed at a new audience, a specialized, elite audience of academics, as is confirmed by, for example, a 1964 paperback edition complete with footnotes and other scholarly apparatus. Gone are the sensational or sentimental titles, the extravagant typography, the pictorial representation of the injured—or potentially injurious—

8. Francis W. Halsey, edition of *Charlotte Temple* (New York, 1905), reproduces on pp. xxxv and xxxvi the illustrations from both editions, the first published by Barclay & Co. of Philadelphia about 1860–65 and the second published in New York about 1870, publisher unknown.
9. Ibid., vii.

Charlotte, the advertisements proclaiming cures to the various ailments flesh (especially female flesh) is heir to. Instead, we have an unadorned cover with such descriptive headings as "Masterworks of Literature Series . . . Edited for the Modern Reader"—claims as medicinal, in their own way, as those made for, say, Mrs. Winslow's soothing syrup in many nineteenth-century editions.[1] Unmistakably a classroom text, the 1964 edition seems to proclaim that the text inside will not be much fun to read but, most assuredly, will be good for you. Finally, the most recent edition of the novel (and it happens to be my own) bears the unmistakable stamp of *l'histoire du livre*. This 1986 *Charlotte Temple* proclaims its relationship to its predecessors and views the publishing history and the history of the novel's reception as a paradigm for the evolution of mass culture in the United States.

From Charlotte's long-mourned martyrdom to her present literary "canonization," from the novel's death as a popular novel to its recent resurrection as a literary "masterwork," there is a story in all of these variations on the same story of *Charlotte, a Tale of Truth*. It is to that larger story too that students of literature and history should attend.

1. Clara M. and Rudolf Kirk, eds., *Charlotte Temple* (New Haven, Conn., 1964). The advertisement for Mrs. Winslow's soothing syrup appears in *Charlotte Temple. A Tale of Truth. By Mrs. Susannah Rawson* (sic), published by the F. M. Lupton Publishing Company of New York about 1894–98.

The American Sentimental

SAMUEL RICHARDSON

From Preface to *Clarissa*[†]

The following History is given in a Series of Letters written principally in a double yet separate correspondence;

Between two young Ladies of virtue and honour, bearing an inviolable friendship for each other, and writing not merely for amusement, but upon the most *interesting* subjects; in which every private family, more or less, may find itself concerned: And,

Between two Gentlemen of free lives; one of them glorying in his talents for Stratagem and Invention, and communicating to the other, in confidence, all the secret purposes of an intriguing head and resolute heart.

But here it will be proper to observe, for the sake of such as may apprehend hurt to the morals of Youth, from the more freely written Letters, that the Gentlemen, tho' professed Libertines as to the Female Sex, and making it one of their wicked maxims, to keep no faith with any of the individuals of it, who are thrown into their power, are not, however, either Infidels or Scoffers; nor yet such as think themselves freed from the observance of those other moral duties which bind man to man.

On the contrary, it will be found, in the progress of the Work, that they very often make such reflections upon each other, and each upon himself and his own actions, as reasonable beings *must* make, who disbelieve not a Future State of Rewards and Punishments, and who one day propose to reform—One of them actually reforming, and by that means giving an opportunity to censure the freedoms which fall from the gayer pen and lighter heart of the other.

And yet that other, altho' in unbosoming himself to a select friend, he discover wickedness enough to entitle him to general detestation, preserves a decency, as well in his images, as in his language, which is not always to be found in the works of some of the most celebrated

---

[†] *Clarissa; or, The History of a Young Lady* . . . (London, 1751), vol. 1. Eighteenth Century Collections Online.

modern Writers, whose subjects and characters have less warranted the liberties they have taken.

In the Letters of the two young Ladies, it is presumed will be found not only the highest exercise of a reasonable and *practicable* Friendship, between minds endowed with the noblest principles of Virtue and Religion, but occasionally interspersed, such Delicacy of Sentiments, particularly with regard to the other Sex; such instances of Impartiality, each freely, as a fundamental principle of their friendship, blaming, praising, and setting right the other, as are strongly to be recommended to the observation of the *younger* part (more especially) of the Female Readers.

The principal of these two young Ladies is proposed as an Exemplar to her Sex. Nor is it any objection to her being so, that she is not in all respects a perfect character. It was not only natural, but it was necessary, that she should have some faults, were it only to shew the Reader, how laudably she could mistrust and blame herself, and carry to her own heart, divested of self-partiality, the censure which arose from her own convictions, and that even to the acquittal of those, because revered characters, whom no one else would acquit, and to whose much greater faults her errors were owing, and not to a weak or reproachable heart. As far as is consistent with human frailty, and as far as she could be perfect, considering the people she had to deal with, and those with whom she was inseparably connected, she *is* perfect. To have been impeccable, must have left nothing for the Divine Grace and a Purified State to do, and carried our idea of her from woman to angel. As such is she often esteemed by the man whose *heart* was so corrupt, that he could hardly believe human nature capable of the purity, which, on every trial or temptation, shone out in *hers*.

Besides the four principal persons, several others are introduced, whose Letters are characteristic: And it is presumed that there will be found in some of them, but more especially in those of the chief character among the men, and the second character among the women, such strokes of Gaiety, Fancy, and Humour, as will entertain and divert; and at the same time both warn and instruct.

All the Letters are written while the hearts of the writers must be supposed to be wholly engaged in their subjects (The events at the time generally dubious): So that they abound not only with critical Situations, but with what may be called *instantaneous* Descriptions and Reflections (proper to be brought home to the breast of the youthful Reader); as also with affecting Conversations; many of them written in the dialogue or dramatic way.

"*Much more* lively and affecting," says one of the principal characters, "must be the Style of those who write in the height of a *present* distress; the mind tortured by the pangs of uncertainty (the Events then hidden in the womb of Fate); *than* the dry, narrative, unanimated Style of a person relating difficulties and dangers surmounted, can be; the relater perfectly at ease; and if himself unmoved by his own Story, not likely greatly to affect the Reader."

What will be found to be more particularly aimed at in the following Work, is—To warn the Inconsiderate and Thoughtless of the one Sex, against the base arts and designs of specious Contrivers of the other—To caution Parents against the undue exercise of their natural authority over their Children in the great article of Marriage—To warn Children against preferring a Man of Pleasure to a Man of Probity, upon that dangerous but too commonly-received notion, *That a reformed Rake makes the best Husband*—But above all, To investigate the highest and most important Doctrines not only of Morality, but of Christianity, by shewing them thrown into action in the conduct of the *worthy* characters; while the *unworthy*, who set those Doctrines at defiance, are condignly, and, as may be said, consequentially, punished.

From what has been said, considerate Readers will not enter upon the perusal of the Piece before them, as if it were designed *only* to divert and amuse. It will probably be thought tedious to all such as *dip* into it, expecting a *light Novel*, or *transitory Romance*; and look upon Story in it (interesting as that is generally allowed to be) as its *sole end*, rather than as a vehicle to the Instruction.

* * *

THOMAS JEFFERSON

Head and Heart Letter[†]

To Mrs. Cosway[1]

Paris, October 12, 1786

My Dear Madam,—Having performed the last sad office of handing you into your carriage at the pavillon de St. Denis, and seen the wheels get actually into motion, I turned on my heel & walked, more dead than alive, to the opposite door, where my own was awaiting me. Mr. Danquerville was missing. He was sought for, found, & dragged down stairs. We were crammed into the carriage,

---

† www.pbs.org/jefferson/archives/documents/frame_ih198172.htm
1. Maria Cosway (1760–1838) was an Anglo-Italian artist and musician who entered Thomas Jefferson's social circle while Jefferson was U.S. minister to France (1784–89).

like recruits for the Bastille,[2] & not having soul enough to give orders to the coachman, he presumed Paris our destination, & drove off. After a considerable interval, silence was broken with a "*Je suis vraiment afflige du depart de ces bons gens.*"[3] This was a signal for a mutual confession of distress. We began immediately to talk of Mr. & Mrs. Cosway, of their goodness, their talents, their amiability; & tho we spoke of nothing else, we seemed hardly to have entered into the matter when the coachman announced the rue St. Denis, & that we were opposite Mr. Danquervilles. He insisted on descending there & traversing a short passage to his lodgings. I was carried home. Seated by my fireside, solitary & sad, the following dialogue took place between my Head & my Heart:

HEAD   Well, friend, you seem to be in a pretty trim.

HEART   I am indeed the most wretched of all earthly beings. Overwhelmed with grief, every fibre of my frame distended beyond its natural powers to bear, I would willingly meet whatever catastrophe should leave me no more to feel or to fear.

HEAD   These are the eternal consequences of your warmth & precipitation. This is one of the scrapes into which you are ever leading us. You confess your follies indeed; but still you hug & cherish them; & no reformation can be hoped, where there is no repentance.

HEART   Oh, my friend! This is no moment to upbraid my foibles. I am rent into fragments by the force of my grief! If you have any balm, pour it into my wounds; if none, do not harrow them by new torments. Spare me in this awful moment! At any other I will attend with patience to your admonitions.

HEAD   On the contrary, I never found that the moment of triumph with you was the moment of attention to my admonitions. While suffering under your follies, you may perhaps be made sensible of them, but, the paroxysms over, you fancy it can never return. Harsh therefore as the medicine may be, it is my office to administer it. You will be pleased to remember that when our friend Trumbull used to be telling us of the merits & talents of these good people, I never ceased whispering to you that we had no occasion for new acquaintance; that the greater their merits & talents, the more dangerous their friendship to our tranquillity, because the regret at parting would be greater.

HEART   Accordingly, Sir, this acquaintance was not the consequence of my doings. It was one of your projects which threw us in the way of it. It was you, remember, & not I, who desired the

2. A notorious Paris prison, built in the fourteenth century, which was stormed on July 14, 1789, representing the beginning of the French Revolution.
3. "I am truly afflicted to leave these good people."

meeting at Legrand & Molinos. I never trouble myself with domes nor arches. The Halle aux bleds might have rotted down before I should have gone to see it. But you, forsooth, who are eternally getting us to sleep with your diagrams & crotchets, must go & examine this wonderful piece of architecture. And when you had seen it, oh! It was the most superb thing on earth. What you had seen there was worth all you had yet seen in Paris! I thought so too. But I meant it of the lady & gentleman to whom we had been presented; & not of a parcel of sticks & chips put together in pens. You then, Sir, & not I, have been the cause of the present distress.

HEAD   It would have been happy for you if my diagrams & crotchets had gotten you to sleep on that day, as you are pleased to say they eternally do. My visit to Legrand & Molinos had public utility for its object. A market is to be built in Richmond. What a commodious plan is that of Legrand & Molinos; especially if we put on it the noble dome of the Halle aux bleds. If such a bridge as they shewed us can be thrown across the Schuylkill at Philadelphia, the floating bridges taken up & the navigation of that river opened, what a copious resource will be added, of wood & provisions, to warm & feed the poor of that city? While I was occupied with these objects, you were dilating with your new acquaintances, & contriving how to prevent a separation from them. Every soul of you had an engagement for the day. Yet all these were to be sacrificed, that you might dine together. Lying messengers were to be despatched into every quarter of the city, with apologies for your breach of engagement. You particularly had the effrontery to send word to the Dutchess Danville that, on the moment we were setting out to dine with her, despatches came to hand which required immediate attention. You wanted me to invent a more ingenious excuse; but I knew you were getting into a scrape, & I would have nothing to do with it. Well, after dinner to St. Cloud, from St. Cloud to Ruggieris, from Ruggieri to Krumfoltz, & if the day had been as long as a Lapland summer day, you would still have contrived means among you to have filled it.

HEART   Oh! My dear friend, how you have revived me by recalling to my mind the transactions of that day! How well I remember them all, & that when I came home at night & looked back to the morning, it seemed to have been a month agone. Go on then, like a kind comforter & paint to me the day we went to St. Germains. How beautiful was every object! The Port de Reuilly, the hills along the Seine, the rainbows of the machine of Marly, the terrace of St. Germains, the chateaux, the gardens, the statues of Marly, the pavillon of Lucienne. Recollect too Madrid, Bagatelle, the Kings garden, the Dessert. How grand the idea excited by the remains of such a column! The spiral staircase too was beautiful. Every moment was filled with something agreeable. The wheels of time moved on with a rapidity of which those of our carriage gave but a faint idea. And yet in the evening when one took a retrospect of the day, what a mass of happiness had we travelled over! Retrace all those scenes to me, my good companion, & I will forgive the unkindness with which you were chiding me. The day we went to St. Germains was a little too warm, I think; was it not?

HEAD   Thou art the most incorrigible of all the beings that ever sinned! I reminded you of the follies of the first day, intending to deduce from thence some useful lessons for you, but instead of listening to these, you kindle at the recollection, you retrace the whole series with a fondness which shews you want nothing but the opportunity to act it over again. I often told you during its course that you were imprudently engaging your affections under circumstances that must have cost you a great deal of pain: that the persons indeed were of the greatest merit, possessing good sense, good humour, honest hearts, honest manners, & eminence in a lovely art;[4] that the lady had moreover qualities & accomplishments, belonging to her sex, which might form a chapter apart for her: such as music, modesty, beauty, & that softness of disposition which is the ornament of her sex & charm of ours, but that all these considerations would increase the pang of separation: that their stay here was to be short: that you rack our whole system when you are parted from those you love, complaining that such a separation is worse than death, inasmuch as this ends our sufferings, whereas that only begins them: & that the separation would in this instance be the more severe as you would probably never see them again.

HEART   But they told me they would come back again the next year.

HEAD   But in the meantime see what you suffer: & their return too depends on so many circumstances that if you had a grain of prudence you would not count upon it. Upon the whole it is improbable & therefore you should abandon the idea of ever seeing them again.

HEART   May heaven abandon me if I do!

HEAD   Very well. Suppose then they come back. They are to stay two months, & when these are expired, what is to follow? Perhaps you flatter yourself they may come to America?

HEART   God only knows what is to happen. I see nothing impossible in that supposition. And I see things wonderfully contrived

4. Maria and her husband, Richard Cosway, were both painters.

sometimes to make us happy. Where could they find such objects as in America for the exercise of their enchanting art? especially the lady, who paints landscape so inimitably. She wants only subjects worthy of immortality to render her pencil immortal. The Falling Spring, the Cascade of Niagara, the Passage of the Potowmac through the Blue Mountains, the Natural bridge. It is worth a voyage across the Atlantic to see these objects; much more to paint, and make them, & thereby ourselves, known to all ages. And our own dear Monticello, where has nature spread so rich a mantle under the eye? Mountains, forests, rocks, rivers. With what majesty do we there ride above the storms! How sublime to look down into the workhouse of nature, to see her clouds, hail, snow, rain, thunder, all fabricated at our feet! And the glorious sun when rising as if out of a distant water, just gilding the tops of the mountains, & giving life to all nature? I hope in God no circumstance may ever make either seek an asylum from grief! With what sincere sympathy I would open every cell of my composition to receive the effusion of their woes! I would pour my tears into their wounds: & if a drop of balm could be found on the top of the Cordilleras, or at the remotest sources of the Missouri, I would go thither myself to seek & to bring it. Deeply practised in the school of affliction, the human heart knows no joy which I have not lost, no sorrow of which I have not drunk! Fortune can present no grief of unknown form to me! Who then can so softly bind up the wound of another as he who has felt the same wound himself? But Heaven forbid they should ever know a sorrow! Let us turn over another leaf, for this has distracted me.

HEAD   Well. Let us put this possibility to trial then on another point. When you consider the character which is given of our country by the lying newspapers of London, & their credulous copyers in other countries; when you reflect that all Europe is made to believe we are a lawless banditti, in a state of absolute anarchy, cutting one anothers throats, & plundering without distinction, how can you expect that any reasonable creature would venture among us?

HEART   But you & I know that all this is false: that there is not a country on earth where there is greater tranquillity, where the laws are milder, or better obeyed: where every one is more attentive to his own business, or meddles less with that of others: where strangers are better received, more hospitably treated, & with a more sacred respect.

HEAD   True, you & I know this, but your friends do not know it.

HEART   But they are sensible people who think for themselves. They will ask of impartial foreigners who have been among us, whether they saw or heard on the spot any instances of anarchy. They will judge too that a people occupied as we are in opening rivers, digging navigable canals, making roads, building public schools, establishing academies, erecting busts & statues to our great men, protecting religious freedom, abolishing sanguinary punishments, reforming & improving our laws in general, they will judge I say for themselves whether these are not the occupations of a people at their ease, whether this is not better evidence of our true state than a London newspaper, hired to lie, & from which no truth can ever be extracted but by reversing everything it says.

HEAD   I did not begin this lecture my friend with a view to learn from you what America is doing. Let us return then to our point. I wished to make you sensible how imprudent it is to place your affections, without reserve, on objects you must so soon lose, & whose loss when it comes must cost you such severe pangs. Remember that last night. You knew your friends were to leave Paris to-day. This was enough to throw you into agonies. All night you tossed us from one side of the bed to the other. No sleep, no rest. The poor crippled wrist too, never left one moment in the same position, now up, now down, now here, now there; was it to be wondered at if its pains returned? The Surgeon then was to be called, & to be rated as an ignoramus because he could not divine the cause of this extraordinary change. In fine, my friend, you must mend your manners. This is not a world to live at random in as you do. To avoid those eternal distresses, to which you are forever exposing us, you must learn to look forward before you take a step which may interest our peace. Everything in this world is a matter of calculation. Advance then with caution, the balance in your hand. Put into one scale the pleasures which any object may offer; but put fairly into the other the pains which are to follow, & see which preponderates. The making an acquaintance is not a matter of indifference. When a new one is proposed to you, view it all round. Consider what advantages it presents, & to what inconveniences it may expose you. Do not bite at the bait of pleasure till you know there is no hook beneath it. The art of life is the art of avoiding pain: & he is the best pilot who steers clearest of the rocks & shoals with which he is beset. Pleasure is always before us; but misfortune is at our side: while running after that, this arrests us. The most effectual means of being secure against pain is to retire within ourselves, & to suffice for our own happiness. Those, which depend on ourselves, are the only pleasures a wise man will count on: for nothing is ours which another may deprive us of. Hence the inestimable value of intellectual pleasures. Ever in our power, always leading us to something new, never cloying, we ride serene & sublime above the concerns of this mortal world, contemplating truth & nature, matter & motion, the laws which bind up their existence, & that eternal being who made & bound them up by those laws. Let this be our employ. Leave the bustle & tumult of society to those who have not talents to occupy themselves without them. Friendship is but another name for an alliance with the follies & the misfortunes of others. Our own share of miseries is sufficient: why enter then as volunteers into those of another? Is there so little gall poured into our cup that we must needs help to drink that of our neighbor? A friend dies or leaves us: we feel as if a limb was cut off. He is sick: we must watch over him, & participate of his pains. His fortune is shipwrecked; ours must be laid under contribution. He loses a child, a parent, or a partner: we must mourn the loss as if it were our own.

HEART   And what more sublime delight than to mingle tears with one whom the hand of heaven hath smitten! To watch over the bed of sickness, & to beguile its tedious & its painful moments! To share our bread with one to whom misfortune has left none! This world abounds indeed with misery: to lighten its burthen we must divide it with one another. But let us now try the virtues of your mathematical balance, & as you have put into one scale the burthen of friendship, let me put its comforts into the other. When languishing then under disease, how grateful is the solace of our friends! How are we penetrated with their assiduities & attentions! How much are we supported by their encouragements & kind offices! When heaven has taken from us some object of our love, how sweet is it to have a bosom whereon to recline our heads, & into which we may pour the torrent of our tears! Grief, with such a comfort, is almost a luxury! In a life where we are perpetually exposed to want & accident, yours is a wonderful proposition, to insulate ourselves, to retire from all aid, & to wrap ourselves in the mantle of self-sufficiency! For assuredly nobody will care for him who cares for nobody. But friendship is precious, not only in the shade but in the sunshine of life; & thanks to a benevolent arrangement of things, the greater part of life is sunshine. I will recur for proof to the days we have lately passed. On these indeed the sun shone brightly. How gay did the face of nature appear! Hills, valleys, chateaux, gardens, rivers, every object wore its liveliest hue! Whence did they borrow it? From the presence of our charming companion. They were pleasing, because she seemed pleased. Alone, the scene would have been dull & insipid: the participation of it with her gave it relish. Let the gloomy monk, sequestered from the world, seek unsocial pleasures in the bottom of his cell! Let the sublimated philosopher grasp visionary happiness while pursuing phantoms dressed in the garb of truth! Their supreme wisdom is supreme folly; & they mistake for happiness the mere absence of pain. Had they ever felt the solid pleasure of one generous spasm of the heart, they would exchange for it all the frigid speculations of their lives, which you have been vaunting in such elevated terms. Believe me then my friend, that that is a miserable arithmetic which, could estimate friendship at nothing, or at less than nothing. Respect for you has induced me to enter into this discussion, & to hear principles uttered which I detest & abjure. Respect for myself now obliges me to recall you into the proper limits of your office. When nature assigned us the same habitation, she gave us over it a divided empire. To you she allotted the field of science; to me that of morals. When the circle is to be squared, or the orbit of a comet to be traced; when the arch of greatest strength, or the solid of least resistance is to be investigated, take up the problem; it is yours; nature has given me no cognizance of it. In like manner, in denying to you the feelings of sympathy, of benevolence, of gratitude, of justice, of love, of friendship, she has excluded you from their control. To these she has adapted the mechanism of the heart. Morals were too essential to the happiness of man to be risked on the incertain combinations of the head. She laid their foundation therefore in sentiment, not in science. That she gave to all, as necessary to all: this to a few only, as sufficing with a few. I know indeed that you pretend authority to the sovereign control of our conduct in all its parts: & a respect for your grave laws & maxims, a desire to do what is right, has sometimes induced me to conform to your counsels. A few facts however which I can readily recall to your memory, will suffice to prove to you that nature has not organized you for our moral direction. When the poor wearied soldier whom we overtook at Chickahomony with his pack on his back, begged us to let him get up behind our chariot, you began to calculate that the road was full of soldiers, & that if all should be taken up our horses would fail in their journey. We drove on therefore. But soon becoming sensible you had made me do wrong, that tho we cannot relieve all the distressed we should relieve as many as we can, I turned about to take up the soldier; but he had entered a bye path, & was no more to be found; & from that moment to this I could never find him out to ask his forgiveness. Again, when the poor woman came to ask a charity in Philadelphia, you whispered that she looked like a drunkard, & that half a dollar was enough to give her for the ale-house. Those who want the dispositions to give, easily find

reasons why they ought not to give. When I sought her out afterwards, & did what I should have done at first, you know that she
employed the money immediately towards placing her child at
school. If our country, when pressed with wrongs at the point of
the bayonet, had been governed by its heads instead of its hearts,
where should we have been now? Hanging on a gallows as high
as Hamans.[5] You began to calculate & to compare wealth and
numbers: we threw up a few pulsations of our warmest blood; we
supplied enthusiasm against wealth and numbers; we put our
existence to the hazard when the hazard seemed against us, and
we saved our country: justifying at the same time the ways of
Providence, whose precept is to do always what is right, and
leave the issue to him. In short, my friend, as far as my recollection serves me, I do not know that I ever did a good thing on
your suggestion, or a dirty one without it. I do forever then disclaim your interference in my province. Fill papers as you please
with triangles & squares: try how many ways you can hang &
combine them together. I shall never envy nor control your sublime delights. But leave me to decide when & where friendships
are to be contracted. You say I contract them at random. So you
said the woman at Philadelphia was a drunkard. I receive no one
into my esteem till I know they are worthy of it. Wealth, title,
office, are no recommendations to my friendship. On the contrary great good qualities are requisite to make amends for their
having wealth, title, & office. You confess that in the present
case I could not have made a worthier choice. You only object
that I was so soon to lose them. We are not immortal ourselves,
my friend; how can we expect our enjoyments to be so? We have
no rose without its thorn; no pleasure without alloy. It is the law
of our existence; & we must acquiesce. It is the condition
annexed to all our pleasures, not by us who receive, but by him
who gives them. True, this condition is pressing cruelly on me
at this moment. I feel more fit for death than life. But when
I look back on the pleasures of which it is the consequence, I
am conscious they were worth the price I am paying. Notwithstanding your endeavors too to damp my hopes, I comfort
myself with expectations of their promised return. Hope is
sweeter than despair, & they were too good to mean to deceive
me. In the summer, said the gentleman; but in the spring, said
the lady: & I should love her forever, were it only for that! Know
then, my friend, that I have taken these good people into my
bosom; that I have lodged them in the warmest cell I could find:
that I love them, & will continue to love them through life: that

5. Haman appears in the biblical book of Esther.

if fortune should dispose them on one side the globe, & me on the other, my affections shall pervade its whole mass to reach them. Knowing then my determination, attempt not to disturb it. If you can at any time furnish matter for their amusement, it will be the office of a good neighbor to do it. I will in like manner seize any occasion which may offer to do the like good turn for you with Condorcet, Rittenhouse, Madison, La Cretelle,[6] or any other of those worthy sons of science whom you so justly prize.

I thought this a favorable proposition whereon to rest the issue of the dialogue. So I put an end to it by calling for my night-cap. Methinks I hear you wish to heaven I had called a little sooner, & so spared you the ennui of such a sermon. I did not interrupt them sooner because I was in a mood for hearing sermons. You too were the subject; & on such a thesis I never think the theme long; not even if I am to write it, and that slowly & awkwardly, as now, with the left hand. But that you may not be discouraged from a correspondence which begins so formidably, I will promise you on my honour that my future letters shall be of a reasonable length. I will even agree to express but half my esteem for you, for fear of cloying you with too full a dose. But, on your part, no curtailing. If your letters are as long as the bible, they will appear short to me. Only let them be brimful of affection. I shall read them with the dispositions with which Arlequin, in *Les deux billets*[7] spelt the words "*je taime*," and wished that the whole alphabet had entered into their composition.

HANNAH WEBSTER FOSTER

From The Coquette[†]

Letter V. To Miss Lucy Freeman.

New-Haven.

These bewitching charms of mine have a tendency to keep my mind in a state of perturbation. I am so pestered with these admirers; not that I am so very handsome neither; but I don't know how it is, I am certainly very much the taste of the other sex. Followed, flattered, and caressed; I have cards and compliments in profusion.

---

6. Jefferson mentions four prominent eighteenth-century intellectuals. Nicolas de Condorcet was a liberal French philosopher; David Rittenhouse was an American astronomer; James Madison was an American political philosopher who served as fourth President of the United States; Pierre Louis de Lacretelle was a French politician and writer.

7. *Les Deux Billets* (The Two Tickets): a one-act comedy by Jean-Pierre Claris de Florian, first performed by the Comédie Italienne in 1779, that tells the story of Arlequin.

† *The Coquette; or, The history of Eliza Wharton; a novel; founded on fact* (Boston, 1797). Early American Imprints, Series I: Evans, 1639–1800, no. 32142.

But I must try to be serious; for I have, alas! one serious lover. As I promised you to be particular in my writing, I suppose I must proceed methodically. Yesterday we had a party to dine. Mr. Boyer was of the number. His attention was immediately engrossed; and I soon perceived that every word, every action, and every look was studied to gain my approbation. As he sat next me at dinner, his assiduity and politeness were pleasing; and as we walked together afterwards, his conversation was improving. Mine was sentimental and sedate; perfectly adapted to the taste of my gallant. Nothing, however, was said particularly expressive of his apparent wishes. I studiously avoided every kind of discourse which might lead to this topic. I wish not for a declaration from any one, especially from one whom I could not repulse and do not intend to encourage at present. His conversation, so similar to what I had often heard from a similar character, brought a deceased friend to mind,[1] and rendered me somewhat pensive. I retired directly after supper. Mr. Boyer had just taken leave.

Mrs. Richman came into my chamber as she was passing to her own. Excuse my intrusion, Eliza, said she; I thought I would just step in and ask you if you have passed a pleasant day?

Perfectly so, madam; and I have now retired to protract the enjoyment by recollection. What, my dear, is your opinion of our favorite Mr. Boyer? Declaring him your favorite, madam, is sufficient to render me partial to him. But to be frank, independent of that, I think him an agreeable man. Your heart, I presume, is now free? Yes, and I hope it will long remain so. Your friends, my dear, solicitous for your welfare, wish to see you suitably and agreeably connected. I hope my friends will never again interpose in my concerns of that nature. You, madam, who have ever known my heart, are sensible, that had the Almighty spared life, in a certain instance, I must have sacrificed my own happiness, or incurred their censure. I am young, gay, volatile. A melancholy event has lately extricated me from those shackles, which parental authority had imposed on my mind. Let me then enjoy that freedom which I so highly prize. Let me have opportunity, unbiassed by opinion, to gratify my natural disposition in a participation of those pleasures which youth and innocence afford. Of such pleasures, no one, my dear, would wish to deprive you. But beware, Eliza!—Though strowed with flowers, when contemplated by your lively imagination, it is, after all, a slippery, thorny path. The round of fashionable dissipation is dangerous. A phantom is often pursued, which leaves its deluded votary the real form of wretchedness. She spoke with an emphasis, and taking up her candle, wished me a good night. I had not power to return the compliment. Something seemingly prophetic in her looks and expressions, cast a momentary gloom upon my mind!

---

1. Eliza refers to her recently deceased fiancé.

But I despise those contracted ideas which confine virtue to a cell.
I have no notion of becoming a recluse. Mrs. Richman has ever been
a beloved friend of mine; yet I always thought her rather prudish.
Adieu,

                                             ELIZA WHARTON.

Letter VI. To the Same.

                                                  New Haven.
I had scarcely seated myself at the breakfast table this morning,
when a servant entered with a card of invitation from Major Sanford,
requesting the happiness of my hand this evening, at a ball, given by
Mr. Atkins, about three miles from this. I shewed the billet to Mrs.
Richman, saying, I have not much acquaintance with this gentleman, madam; but I suppose his character sufficiently respectable to
warrant an affirmative answer. He is a gay man, my dear, to say no
more, and such are the companions we wish, when we join a party
avowedly formed for pleasure. I then stepped into my apartment,
wrote an answer, and dispatched the servant. When I returned to the
parlour, something disapprobating appeared in the countenances of
both my friends. I endeavored without seeming to observe, to dissipate it by chit chat; but they were better pleased with each other than
with me; and soon rising, walked into the garden, and left me to
amuse myself alone. My eyes followed them through the window.
Happy pair, said I. Should it ever be my fate to wear the hymenial
chain, may I be thus united! The purest and most ardent affection,
the greatest consonance of taste and disposition, and the most congenial virtue and wishes distinguish this lovely couple. Health and
wealth, with every attendant blessing preside over their favored
dwelling, and shed their benign influence without alloy. The consciousness of exciting their displeasure gave me pain; but I consoled
myself with the idea that it was ill founded.

   They should consider, said I, that they have no satisfaction to look
for beyond each other.

   There every enjoyment is centered; but I am a poor solitary being,
who need some amusement beyond what I can supply myself. The
mind, after being confined at home for a while, sends the imagination abroad in quest of new treasures, and the body may as well
accompany it, for ought I can see.

   General Richman and lady have ever appeared solicitous to promote my happiness since I have resided with them. They have
urged my acceptance of invitations to join parties, though they
have not been much themselves, of late; as Mrs. Richman's present
circumstances render her fond of retirement. What reason can be
assigned for their apparent reluctance to this evening's entertainment is to me incomprehensible; but I shall apply the chymical
powers of friendship and extract the secret from Mrs. Richman

tomorrow if not before. Adieu. I am now summoned to dinner, and after that shall be engaged in preparation till the wished for hour of hilarity and mirth engrosses every faculty of your

ELIZA WHARTON.

* * *

Letter LXXIII. To Miss Julia Granby.

Boston.

A melancholy tale have you unfolded, my dear Julia; and tragic indeed is the concluding scene!

Is she then gone! gone in this most distressing manner! Have I lost my once loved friend; lost her in a way which I could never have conceived to be possible.

Our days of childhood were spent together in the same pursuits, in the same amusements. Our riper years encreased our mutual affection, and maturer judgment most firmly cemented our friendship. Can I then calmly resign her to so severe a fate! Can I bear the idea of her being lost to honor, to fame, and to life! No; she shall still live in the heart of her faithful Lucy; whose experience of her numerous virtues and engaging qualities, has imprinted her image too deeply on the memory to be obliterated. However she may have erred, her sincere repentance is sufficient to restore her to charity.

Your letter gave me the first information of this awful event. I had taken a short excursion into the country, where I had not seen the papers; or if I had, paid little or no attention to them. By your directions I found the distressing narrative of her exit. The poignancy of my grief, and the unavailing lamentations which the intelligence excited, need no delineation. To scenes of this nature, you have been habituted in the mansion of sorrow, where you reside.

How sincerely I sympathize with the bereaved parent of the dear, deceased Eliza, I can feel, but have not power to express. Let it be her consolation, that her child is at rest. The resolution which carried this deluded wanderer thus far from her friends, and supported her through her various trials, is astonishing! Happy would it have been, had she exerted an equal degree of fortitude in repelling the first attacks upon her virtue! But she is no more; and heaven forbid that I should accuse or reproach her!

Yet, in what language shall I express my abhorrence of the monster, whose detestable arts have blasted one of the fairest flowers in creation? I leave him to God, and his own conscience! Already is he exposed in his true colors! Vengeance already begins to overtake him! His sordid mind must now suffer the deprivation of those sensual gratifications, beyond which he is incapable of enjoyment!

Upon your reflecting and steady mind, my dear Julia, I need not inculcate the lessons which may be drawn from this woe-fraught tale; but for the sake of my sex in general, I wish it engraved upon every heart, that virtue alone, independent of the trappings of wealth, the parade of equipage, and the adulation of gallantry, can secure lasting felicity. From the melancholy story of Eliza Wharton, let the American fair learn to reject with disdain every insinuation derogatory to their true dignity and honor. Let them despise, and for ever banish the man, who can glory in the seduction of innocence and the ruin of reputation. To associate, is to approve; to approve, is to be betrayed!

I am, &c.

LUCY SUMNER.

Letter LXXIV. *To Mrs. M. Wharton.*

DEAR MADAM,   *Boston.*

We have paid the last tribute of respect to your beloved daughter. The day after my arrival, Mrs. Sumner proposed that we should visit the sad spot which contains the remains of our once amiable

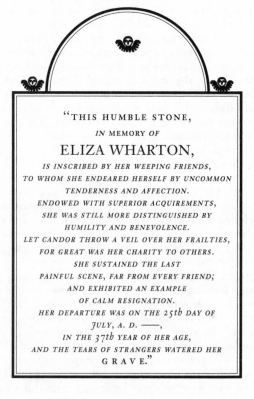

"THIS HUMBLE STONE,

IN MEMORY *OF*

ELIZA WHARTON,

*IS INSCRIBED BY HER WEEPING FRIENDS,
TO WHOM SHE ENDEARED HERSELF BY UNCOMMON
TENDERNESS AND AFFECTION.
ENDOWED WITH SUPERIOR ACQUIREMENTS,
SHE WAS STILL MORE DISTINGUISHED BY
HUMILITY AND BENEVOLENCE.
LET CANDOR THROW A VEIL OVER HER FRAILTIES,
FOR GREAT WAS HER CHARITY TO OTHERS.
SHE SUSTAINED THE LAST
PAINFUL SCENE, FAR FROM EVERY FRIEND;
AND EXHIBITED AN EXAMPLE
OF CALM RESIGNATION.
HER DEPARTURE WAS ON THE 25th DAY OF
JULY, A. D. ——,
IN THE 37th YEAR OF HER AGE,
AND THE TEARS OF STRANGERS WATERED HER
G R A V E.*"

friend. The grave of Eliza Wharton, said she shall not be unbedewed by the tears of friendship.

Yesterday we went accordingly, and were much pleased with the apparent sincerity of the people, in their assurances that every thing in their power had been done to render her situation comfortable. The minutest circumstances were faithfully related; and from the state of her mind, in her last hours, I think much comfort may be derived to her afflicted friends.

We spent a mournful hour, in the place where she is interred, and then returned to the inn, while Mrs. Sumner gave orders for a decent stone to be erected over her grave, with the following inscription:

I hope, madam, that you will derive satisfaction from these exertions of friendship, and that, united to the many other sources of consolation with which you are furnished, they may alleviate your grief; and while they leave the pleasing remembrance of her virtues, add the supporting persuasion, that your Eliza is happy.

I am, &c.

JULIA GRANBY.

JANET TODD

From Sensibility: An Introduction[†]

* * *

The arousal of pathos through conventional situations, stock familial characters and rhetorical devices is the mark of sentimental literature. Such literature buttonholes the reader and demands an emotional, even physical response.

The sentimental work reveals a belief in the appealing and aesthetic quality of virtue, displayed in a naughty world through a vague and potent distress. This distress is rarely deserved and is somehow in the nature of things; in later sentimental works it even overshadows virtue, which may in fact be more manifest in the sympathy of the observer than in the sufferer. The distressed are natural victims, whose misery is demanded by their predicament as defenceless women, aged men, helpless infants or melancholic youths.

The works inhabited by these unfortunates require no deconstructing—although they may affectionately mock aspects of themselves—and they discourage multiple readings. They provoke tears in a way no other literature does. The tears that may be shed at high or heroic tragedy form part of a complex intellectual and

---

† *Sensibility: An Introduction* (London, New York, 1986). Reprinted by permission.

emotional response, but, when sentimental works are accepted and in fashion, they primarily make the reader or watcher cry.

* * *

The sentimental impulse is recurrent in literature. Pathetic and sensationally moving elements involving domestic relationships and distressed virtue exist in the Greek drama of Euripides for example, in medieval morality plays and, most obviously, in the Elizabethan and Jacobean drama of Fletcher, Heywood and Shirley. Pathos resulting from the sudden intrusion of the child-and-parent tie is aroused in Shakespeare's *Antony and Cleopatra* when the asp becomes a baby at the breast and 'sucks the nurse asleep', and in *King Lear* when Lear imagines retreat into a blissful domestic prison with Cordelia. But these pathetic elements remain subordinate to other concerns of plot and character. What is new in the eighteenth century is the centrality of sentiment and pathos.

A further difference from the works of earlier periods derives from the alliance in interests of eighteenth-century literature and moral philosophy. In the early years, philosophy both responded to and created a popular demand for a new set of ideas with which to account for human nature and order society, beyond the explanations given by Christian dogma. Through literature and the popularizations of moral philosophy, sentimental theory and art became extremely widespread in England, touching the perceptions of most literate and semi-literate people.

Sentimentalism entered all literary genres—the novel, essay, poetry and drama. But the cult of sensibility was largely defined by fiction from the 1740s to the 1770s. This fiction initially showed people how to behave, how to express themselves in friendship and how to respond decently to life's experiences. Later, it prided itself more on making its readers weep and in teaching them when and how much to weep. In addition, it delivered the great archetypal victims: the chaste suffering woman, happily rewarded in marriage or elevated into redemptive death, and the sensitive, benevolent man whose feelings are too exquisite for the acquisitiveness, vulgarity and selfishness of his world.

In all forms of sentimental literature, there is an assumption that life and literature are directly linked, not through any notion of a mimetic depiction of reality but through the belief that the literary experience can intimately affect the living one. So literary conventions become a way of life. At the same time literary emotions herald active ones; a theatrical or fictional feeling creates greater virtue in the audience or reader, and a contrived tear foreshadows the spontaneous one of human sympathy. Sentimental literature is exemplary of emotion, teaching its consumers to produce a response equivalent to the one presented in its episodes. It is a kind of pedagogy of seeing and of the physical reaction that this seeing should produce, clarifying when uncontrolled sobs or a single tear should be the rule, or when the inexpressible nature of the feeling should be stressed.

A sentimental work moralizes more than it analyses and emphasis is not on the subtleties of a particular emotional state but on the communication of common feeling from sufferer or watcher to reader or audience. The work may include a constructed sentimental author, but it rarely points back to a particular individual artist whose artistry constitutes his greatness.

The techniques of sentimentalism vary according to genre and time, but most works function through a plot of sudden reversal— * * * whether these are large narrative events like the sudden loss of a newly rediscovered child or the psychological changes when a contrasting mood or thought interrupts a burgeoning emotion. All present these contrasts and the exemplary emotion in tableaux, usually drawing on the notion of the family unit or the reclusive individual; when they occur, the story or argument is arrested so that the author can conventionally intensify the emotion and the reader or spectator may have time physically to respond.

The words in which emotion is described and prescribed are themselves prescribed. Terms such as 'benevolence', 'virtue', 'esteem', 'delicacy', and 'transport' indicate sentimental doctrine and expect a sentimental understanding. The word 'weakness', for example, moves from Johnson's dictionary definition of 'want of judgment . . . foolishness of mind' to suggest a pardonable excess of some quality in which a sentimentalist might have pride, like tenderness or pity. In general, vocabulary in a sentimental work is conventional, repetitive, mannered and overcharged. It is also hyperbolic; a few adjectives such as the eulogistic 'sweet', 'grateful' and 'delicate', and constructions such as 'the best of mothers' do much service, as do the pejoratives, 'cruel' and 'base', and the negatives 'unkind', 'ungenerous' and 'unfeeling', which, as Erik Erämetsä observes in his study of sentimental vocabulary, emphasize the goodness they negate.[1]

The association of nouns and adjectives is predictable—the heart is 'kind', 'honest', 'tender' and 'fond'; feeling is 'melting', 'swelling' or 'overflowing', and sighs and tears are 'pitying' and 'sympathetic'. Adjectives gain intensity through the prefixes 'over', 'ever' and 'all', as in 'all-conquering', and through the adverbs 'vastly' and 'exceedingly', much mocked by Jane Austen's Henry Tilney in *Northanger Abbey*. Terms and structures are repeated to heighten intensity—

---

1. The illustrative nature of Warton's poem is stressed by Louis I. Bredvold, *The Natural History of Sensibility* (Detroit, 1962), p. 57.

'cruel, thrice cruel'—and words come in pairs or triplets, underlining the point and preventing much attention to any individual term: 'griefs and suffering' or 'sincere, honest and open'.

In the sentimental work words are not left to carry a message alone, but are augmented by other heightening devices. Exclamation marks, brackets, italics and capitals pepper and disturb the flow of sentences. At the same time they are shunted into declaring their inadequacy and their subordination to gesture. A physical reaction may, for example, be conveyed through a description which is made deficient or foolish because of the sheer number of words needed to contain what was instantaneous. Or it may be given through typographical devices stressing the absence of words and so the presence of other methods of communication. A work such as Richardson's *Clarissa* is full of lacunae, asterisks, dashes and disturbed or aberrant typography, indicating emotion beyond words, presumably in imitation of the communication of penmanship which the printed novel cannot deliver. In the extreme case of *Tristram Shandy*, black and marbled pages are substituted for verbal descriptions.

Because sensibility is reactive and unstable, the sentimental work of prose or poetry meanders rather than moves logically to its destination. Or it may have no destination at all and pretend to be, or actually be, unfinished. Again this is taken to an extreme in Sterne: in *Tristram Shandy* characters and fictive narrator ride the hobbyhorses of their ideas so hard that the book can never overtake the passing moment; *A Sentimental Journey Through France and Italy by Mr Yorick* breaks off with the clutching hand of the narrator who never sets foot in Italy.

The novels of Richardson, Mackenzie, Sterne and a host of women writers of the late eighteenth century declare themselves fragmented. Gaps are written into the works through the pretence of missing chapters, torn sentences or mutilated letters. The poetry of Gray and Thomson is similarly broken by hiatuses, seeming closures and juxtapositions of conflicting points of view and contrary moods.

The result of these various devices—asterisks, dashes, meandering narrative and fragmentation—is that readers are to some extent prevented from indulging in an identifying fantasy with a character or an author and are forced to respond to the emotion conveyed. At the same time these devices force the literary nature of the work on to the reader by indicating the inadequacy of the medium—language—in which, despite their intrusive presence, most of the business of the work is still transacted.

Terms

The terms 'sentiment', 'sensibility', 'sentimentality', and 'sentimentalism' are counters in eighteenth-century literature and philosophy, sometimes representing precise formulations and sometimes vaguely suggesting emotional qualities. They were at home in the scientific or epistemological treatise and in the familiar letter. Often such terms were used interchangeably. It is possible, however, to extricate 'sentimentalism'. Once employed only pejoratively to suggest affectation and excessive emotional display, it was used by Sir Leslie Stephen in *English Thought in the Eighteenth Century* as 'the name of the mood in which we make a luxury of grief'.[2] More recently the word has come to denote the movement discerned in philosophy, politics and art, based on the belief in or hope of the natural goodness of humanity and manifested in a humanitarian concern for the unfortunate and helpless.

Often in literary criticism 'sentiment' and 'sensibility' are felt to be synonymous, a novel of sentiment differing in no way from a novel of sensibility. But there is, none the less, a useful distinction to be made in historical usage and reference. A 'sentiment' is a moral reflection, a rational opinion usually about the rights and wrongs of human conduct; the early eighteenth-century novel of sentiment is characterized by such generalized reflections. But a 'sentiment' is also a thought, often an elevated one, influenced by emotion, a combining of heart with head or an emotional impulse leading to an opinion or a principle. James Thomson's 'melting sentiments of kindly care', for example, are clearly expressions of a feeling heart as well as a reflecting mind. In this case 'sentiment' comes close to 'sensibility', which also presupposes an emotional susceptibility. After Sterne's novels, it frequently takes the meaning of refined and tender emotion, although the denotation of moral reflection also continues.

'Sensibility' is perhaps the key term of the period. Little used before the mid-eighteenth century, although Addison among others had employed it to suggest delicate emotional and physical susceptibility, it came to denote the faculty of feeling, the capacity for extremely refined emotion and a quickness to display compassion for suffering. Its adjectives tell the tale of its rise and fall. It is 'exquisite' in Addison, 'delicate' in Hume, 'sweet' in Cowper, and 'dear' in Sterne. But as it declines from fashion, it becomes 'acute' in Austen, 'trembling' in Hazlitt, 'mawkish' in Coleridge, and 'sickly' in Byron. In the 1760s and 1770s many poems extol sensibility, while in the 1780s and 1790s book titles such as *Excessive Sensibility* become common.

---

2. François René de Chateaubriand, *Travels in America and Italy* (London, 1828), 1:181.

'Sensibility', an innate sensitiveness or susceptibility revealing itself in a variety of spontaneous activities such as crying, swooning and kneeling, is defined in 1797 by the *Encyclopaedia Britannica* (3rd edn) as 'a nice and delicate perception of pleasure or pain, beauty or deformity', which, as far as it is natural, 'seems to depend upon the organization of the nervous system'. Here it appears physically based, a quality of nerves turning easily to illness and described in contemporary medical treatises in terms of movements within the body.

The cult of sensibility that jangled the nerves of Europe in the mid-eighteenth century is the cultural movement devoted to tear-demanding exhibitions of pathos and unqualified virtue. In literature it was notably expressed in the novels of Sterne, Mackenzie, Rousseau and Goethe, in the melancholic poetry of Young and Gray, in English drama from Steele and Cibber to Cumberland and Kelly, and in French *comédie larmoyante* of Nivelle de la Chaussée. It was also manifested in the religious dread of James Hervey among the 'thickening Shades' of the graveyard, where tender innocence cannot be stained by the world.[3]

In his *L'Homme machine* (1747) La Mettrie associated sexuality and sensibility, seeing the mind and body as different forms of the same substance, and many less systematic thinkers, considering sensibility as moral and physical susceptibility, inevitably found sexuality a component: Tom Jones's robust and Yorick's whimsical sexuality feed into and derive from their sensibility. This was not, however, openly felt to be the case with women, in whom sensibility, when admired, was assumed to imply chastity, and only if denigrated was feared to denote sexuality. As sensibility became more firmly connected with women in the later eighteenth century, it tended to lose the association with sexuality even for men, and the sensibility of the Man of Feeling is physically a matter of tears and gestures, precluding lustiness.

The novel of sentiment of the 1740s and 1750s praises a generous heart and often delays the narrative to philosophize about benevolence; the novel of sensibility, increasingly written from the 1760s onwards, differs slightly in emphasis since it honours above all the capacity for refined feeling. It stops the story to display this feeling in the characters and elicit it in the reader in its physical manifestations of tears and trembling. Such display is justified by the belief that a heightened sense of one's virtue through pity for another is morally improving.

---

3. J. Hector St. John de Crèvecoeur, *Letters from an American Farmer and Sketches of 18th Century America*, ed. Albert E. Stone (New York, 1981), p. 43.

'Sentimentality' came in as a pejorative term in the 1770s when the idea of sensibility was losing ground. It suggested and still suggests debased and affected feeling, an indulgence in and display of emotion for its own sake beyond the stimulus and beyond propriety. In France where 'sensibilité' translated the English sensibility, a new term 'sensiblerie' developed to distinguish sensibility from the debased and self-indulgent quality.

* * *

Although it had its heyday from the 1740s to the late 1770s, the literature of sensibility is not discrete. Sentimental elements increase in importance through Restoration tragedy and early eighteenth-century comedy, and after the 1770s they also inhabit Gothic fiction and Romantic poetry. And yet sentimental literature is distinct from primarily Romantic or Gothic works. If, as Schlegel argues in an early definition, Romanticism includes a depiction of 'emotional matter in an imaginative form', the emphasis on 'imaginative' makes a discrimination, for such individual expression is far from the deliberate clichés of sentimental writing and its common social concern.[4] Gothic fiction, emerging in the 1760s but growing fashionable only in the 1790s, uses sentimental contrasts of virtue and vice or malignancy and distressed worth, but goes far towards sensationalizing and often sexualizing these elements, while it retreats from the didactic aim of sentimental literature.

NANCY ARMSTRONG

From Why Daughters Die: The Racial Logic of American Sentimentalism[†]

Slowly but surely, over the past ten years or so, scholars of English literary history have grown accustomed to the idea that sentimental literature—as exemplified by the novels of Samuel Richardson—systematically rewrote the sexual practices and domestic lives of English people. Scholarship also concedes that the English family so written took on a recognizably modern character. For at least fifty years, furthermore, American literary historians have credited Richardson for the brand of sentimental fiction that became so

4. Schiller, as quoted in McFarland, *Romanticism and the Forms of Ruin*, p. 11.
† From *Yale Journal of Criticism* 7.2 (1992): 1–3, 8–24. © 1992 Yale University and The Johns Hopkins University Press. Reprinted with permission of The Johns Hopkins University Press.

popular during the second half of the eighteenth century on this side of the Atlantic. Indeed, he provides the most obvious link between English authors and readers and their American counterparts. For the sake of argument, let us assume that in order to reproduce their way of life in the colonies, it was necessary for successive generations of English men and women to change the way they conducted sexual relationships as well as the households they made and maintained together. In undergoing these changes, it could then be said, the daily lives of these same English men and women became American. Might we not conclude that sentimental fiction must have changed as well—and changed in a way we must call American?

But scholars rarely so much as glanced in the direction of the sentimental tradition when it came to distinguishing fiction that speaks for English culture on this side of the Atlantic. To understand why the same subject matter that earned Richardson a central place in English literary history should have caused his American counterparts to be excluded out of hand, one can simply turn to the 1917 *Cambridge History of American Literature*. The editors of this history justify their literary preferences by mounting an argument against the anglophilia they attribute to previous editors. They condemn their predecessors for preserving a Restoration comedy and rejecting Bradford's *History of Plymouth*, for prizing a didactic poem in heroic couplets and despising the work of Jonathan Edwards, for relishing the letters of "some third rate English poet" and finding "no gusto" in the correspondence of Benjamin Franklin, or for sending a student to the novels of William Godwin and never directing him to *The Federalist*.[1] The editors of the *Cambridge History* claim that their inclusion of early American writers will "enlarge the spirit of American literary criticism and render it more energetic and masculine."[2] According to the logic laid out in their preface, the kind of masculinity that characterized our colonial forebears simultaneously placed a literary work within an English tradition of letters and identified that work as American. Within this classification system, popular writing could be called literary if it displayed certain traits of masculinity, and feminine writing would be tolerated—even applauded—when it exhibited signs of English literariness. Richardson's novels generally fell into this second category.

Published in 1941, F. O. Matthiessen's *American Renaissance* may have appeared more evenhanded than the *Cambridge History*. But Matthiessen allowed his favorite authors to do the work of gendering

1. William Peterfield Trent, et al., eds. *The Cambridge History of American Literature, Colonial and Revolutionary Literature, Early National Literature: Part I* (New York: G. P. Putnam's Sons, 1917), x.
2. Trent, *Cambridge History*, i:x.

American literature, and they were hardly evenhanded. Nathaniel Hawthorne, for one, made this well-known and oft-quoted equation between women writers and sentimental fiction in the United States: "America is now wholly given over to a damned mob of scribbling women, and I should have no chance of success while the public taste is occupied with their trash—and should be ashamed of myself if I did succeed."[3] Given the sour grapes informing this statement, one has to ask why Matthiessen accepted Hawthorne's view so readily in formulating his account of American literature. More to the point, when Leslie Fiedler came up with his own definition of the great American novel in the 1950s, what could have possessed him to reproduce the same sexual logic? Perhaps most surprising of all is the fact that here we are almost forty years and many scholarly books later, and his *Love and Death in the American Novel* remains one of the most influential studies of the American novel.

This essay is part of a larger project that considers what happened to British sentimentalism when it came to this country. In addressing the problem of how to remain English in North America, the gendered logic of sentimental fiction, or how to get the right man together with the right woman on a permanent basis, had to address the problem of race, or how to distinguish those within the diasporic community from those whose inclusion would cancel out its English identity.[4] In order to explain how, why, and to what effect fiction simultaneously forged and suppressed this link between gender and race, I will turn first to the literary critical debates surrounding Harriet Beecher Stowe's *Uncle Tom's Cabin*. We can observe the historical relationship between gender and race as it generates certain predictable conflicts among various readings of this novel. To show that such conflicts indeed reenact a much earlier cultural logic—a peculiar relationship between gender and race that shapes Stowe's narrative as well—I will turn back to a tradition of colonial writing where these categories first began to stand in for and displace one another as the terms of American identity. In conclusion, I want to investigate the remarkable coincidence between our sudden willingness to call these categories into question and the emergence of an ethnic literature that uses gender to rethink the means by which we all acquire racial identities in the United States.

3. F. O. Mathiessen, *American Renaissance: Art and Expression in the Age of Emerson and Whitman* (New York: Oxford University Press, 1941), x–xi.
4. Doris Sommer has explained how nineteenth-century Latin American novels combined gender with racial proscriptions "to solve the problem of establishing the white man's legitimacy in the New World." "Without a proper genealogy to root them in the Land," she reasons, "the creoles had at least to establish conjugal and then paternity rights, making a *generative* rather than a *genealogical* claim. They had to win America's heart and body so that the fathers could found her and reproduce themselves as cultivated men." See *Foundational Fictions: The National Romances of Latin America* (Berkeley: University of California Press, 1991), 15.

* * *

For nearly a century American literary criticism and scholarship has taken it for granted that sentimental fiction began in England and then came over to this country on the boat with Richardson's stories of seduction. This section of my essay will explain why we must rethink this longstanding assumption if we are going to understand the power of Stowe's sentimental logic. Consider the case of Susanna Rowson's *Charlotte Temple*. Though first written and published in England, it remains one of our most eligible candidates for the first American novel. The heroine commits the very error that Richardson's *Clarissa* told her to avoid: "What risks may poor giddy girls run when they throw themselves out of protection of their natural friends, and into the wide, wide world?"[5] Tossing both her virtue and the chance of a good marriage to the wind, Charlotte runs off to the colonies with a military man. Of course, she comes to a bad end. Mercifully, however, her misfortunes consume little more than two hundred pages. And were this all of poor *Charlotte Temple,* there would be no disputing those critics who read her as a bad imitation of Richardson's Clarissa. In *Clarissa,* a virtuous but desirable young woman manages to stave off many ingenious attempts at seduction, but only by preferring death to dishonor can she ultimately retain the status of a heroine.

In varying this pattern, Rowson becomes a contender for the first American novelist. Just before she dies, Charlotte's father arrives in America to forgive his daughter. Grief-stricken, he decides to take her daughter—his granddaughter—back home to England. Of this fortunate substitution, the novel has these words to say: "After the first tumult of grief subsided, Mrs. Temple gave up the chief of her time to her grand-child, and as she grew up and improved, began to fancy she again possessed Charlotte."[6] The household made of father, mother, and granddaughter may reproduce the structure of the original family made of father, mother, and daughter. But father and granddaughter in fact come from quite different nations. Thus we might pose the problem of being English in America in terms of this question: are you English because you are born of English parents, or are you English because your household is based on the English model? The mission of such a sentimental novel as *Charlotte Temple* is to conceal the gap that emerged between the household and the family in the New World by representing the one as a perfect substitute for the other.

---

5. Samuel Richardson, *Clarissa, or the History of a Young Lady,* ed. Angus Ross (London: Penguin, 1985), 1005.
6. Susanna Rowson, *Charlotte Temple* (New York: Oxford University Press, 1986), 118.

To understand what happened when English sentimentalism took up this particular ideological task, we need to take a new look at colonial American culture. In one of the earliest examples of a specifically colonial genre, an Englishwoman named Mary Rowlandson described the trials she endured as an Indian captive. Embodied in this solitary woman, as I have argued elsewhere, English culture itself seemed to be under assault.[7] As it was cast in a defensive position, however, that culture acquired a form of legitimation peculiarly suited for the colonial situation. English men had to conquer native American men for the sake of English women and their children; colonialism was both a paternal and a patriotic obligation. It is only reasonable to assume that readers who accepted this logic would feel a sense of resolution once Rowlandson was securely in her husband's house and had arranged to buy back both her son and her sister's son from their captors. Indeed, as far as Cotton Mather was concerned, her captivity was over and done with at that moment. His *Magnalia Christi Americana* (1702) tells Rowlandson's story from the husband's point of view: her captivity tested his faith, and her return demonstrated that his faith was stronger than the evils she endured. In telling her own story, however, Rowlandson places a peculiar stress on her daughter's return. The narrator's separation from and reunion with this child mark the beginning and end of her trials in the wilderness, and the family does not become a whole family again until the daughter is restored to them. It is in these marvelous terms that Rowlandson describes the daughter's return: "Thus she traveled three days together, not knowing whither she was going, having nothing to eat or drink but water and green hirtleberries. At last they came into Providence where she was kindly entertained by several of that town. The Indians often said that I should never have her [back for] under twenty pounds. But now the Lord hath brought her in upon free cost and given her to me the second time."[8]

Why call this kind of attention to the daughter's return? Although Rowlandson was clearly obsessed by her need to keep in touch with both God and Boston during her trial in the wilderness, she also felt obliged to frame this experience with the loss and restoration of her daughter. In contrast with the difficulty of recording her emotional life in exile, the task of explaining the relationship between her fate and that of her daughter evidently required very little effort. That we cannot account for what appears to be an almost obligatory link

7. Nancy Armstrong and Leonard Tennenhouse, *The Imaginary Puritan: Literature, Intellectual Labor, and the Origins of Personal Life* (Berkeley: University of California Press, 1992), 196–216.
8. Alden T. Vaughn and Edward W. Clark, eds., *Puritans Among the Indians: Accounts of Captivity and Redemption, 1676–1724* (Cambridge: Harvard University Press, 1981), 73.

between these divergent plots tells us precisely where our own brand of common sense differs from that which Rowlandson could count on from her readers. Let us try to imagine what importance they might have attached to the daughter's fate.

Whenever marriage outside a group threatens that group's ties to the country of its origin, daughters tend to become problematic. There is no question that North America provided such a situation. English people had to develop new courtship practices and marriage rules if they were going to remain English on this side of the Atlantic. Being in the colonies kept them from marrying in the same place and within the same group as their parents had. But since only birth guaranteed the continuity of the English family back in England, any other basis for constituting a household necessarily called into question the English identity of those who had to live by modified cultural rules. Although the very word "creole" inevitably carries connotations of racial impurity for modern readers, this was anything but true for those colonial Europeans to whom the term referred. A creole family distinguished itself and preserved its status as such by marrying only members of the same immigrant or diasporic group.[9] In the early seventeenth century, the English word referred to someone born and naturalized in the Americas but born of pure European or African blood. While "creole" implies that the original may have undergone substantial modifications in the New World, it does not, as the *Oxford English Dictionary* points out, carry any "connotation of colour," much less suggest a mixture of the two. The racialized sense of the term seems to have emerged during the nineteenth century and in American English.

Recognizing that the very concept of Anglo-America contains this contradiction, we can begin to account for the peculiar way in which our fiction deals with daughters. The miraculous return of Rowlandson's daughter is necessary to ensure that she remain her father's. According to narrative tradition, it makes all the difference that he never buys her back from the Indians; if she is truly his, then he is the only one entitled to offer her in exchange. The exclusive nature of the patriarchal prerogative is what makes it possible for Englishness to descend from him to her and through her into the family of another Englishman, thereby preserving the Englishness of the colonial community. When an object is conspicuously removed or somehow manages to remove itself from such a system of exchange, according to anthropologist Annette Weiner, it operates as the special kind of fetish she calls an "inalienable possession."[1] This kind of

9. See, for example, Benedict Anderson, *Imagined Communities: Reflections on the Origin and Spread of Nationalism* (London: Verso, 1991), 41 n1.
1. Annette Weiner, *Inalienable Possessions: The Paradox of Keeping-While-Giving* (Berkeley: University of California Press, 1992).

object is so valuable to the identity of the group that it can neither be taken nor traded away without threatening that group's identity. Daughters who are thus invested with the power of culture-bearers die—often willfully—when they leave the family. Thus we may find them returning through death to their fathers' homes, as Richardson's Clarissa does, or else reborn through their daughters, as in the case of Charlotte Temple. In both novels, the daughter ultimately proves to be the true one when she cannot live outside the family.

The omnipresent anxiety about losing one's English identity gives us reason to believe that this story of the daughter's magical return was written and read with another narrative possibility in mind: a story about going native and starting up a whole new family in the wilderness. Mary Jemison's account of her life among the Senecas, transcribed from her oral testimony in 1823, is such a story. She represents the recessive type of colonial heroine, the daughter who never returned, because she was miraculously chosen to survive among the Indians. Operating according to a different cultural logic than Rowlandson's, Jemison's mother leaves her with these parting words: "Alas, my dear! my heart bleeds at the thoughts of what awaits you; but, if you leave us, remember my child your own name, and the name of your mother and father. Be careful and not forget your English tongue. If you shall have an opportunity, don't try to escape; for if you do they will find and destroy you."[2] Heeding this practical advice, Jemison allows herself to be adopted into a Senecan family, marries, and produces a number of children, all the while helping other captives to survive as she did. She takes particular pride in creating a household under these adverse circumstances: "I live in my own house, and on my own land, with my youngest daughter Polly, who is married to George Chongo, and has three children."[3] Jemison's reward is one that eighteenth-century readers were likely to have considered more appropriate for men than women. She has become the head of a household at the expense of her femininity, and her daughter has married outside the Anglo community, which sets the Jemison family forever apart from "the rich and respectable people, principally from New England," who were beginning "to inhabit the whole country around her."[4] Her ability to reproduce an English household without an English husband distinguishes the members of that household from the creole families who had perpetuated their English identity patrilineally. Although such assimilation flies in the face of sentimental convention, Mary Jemison is

---

2. James E. Seaver, *A Narrative of the Life of Mrs. Mary Jemison*, ed. June Namias (Norman: University of Oklahoma Press, 1992), 69.

3. Seaver, *A Narrative of the Life of Mrs. Mary Jemison*, 158.

4. Seaver, *A Narrative of the Life of Mrs. Mary Jemison*, 54.

nevertheless the heroine of her tale, which consequently exists in direct contradiction with the sentimental paradigm.

The commonplace that men want their daughters pure obviously conceals some questions that we must address with a bit more care * * * in what sense might our national identity have actually depended on the sexual behavior of young English women? how can English identity remain the same when it has to be reproduced outside of England? under these circumstances, isn't the difference between authentic and imitation Englishness destined to collapse? To address these questions, we need to think of the two different captivity narratives I have just described as offering two different theories of social reproduction. According to one, transmission of English culture occurs through the patrilineal family. In this case, the English family is virtually the same thing as English culture in that both depend on the descendants of an English family marrying with their kind. Such a culture abhors a mixture. It prefers a dead daughter to an ethnically impure one. According to the Jemison model, however, English culture is reproduced within the household, and there is nothing pure about it. That is precisely its virtue. No matter who makes up this household or where they come from, it can incorporate, imitate, reenact, parody, or otherwise replicate whatever appears to be most English about the English family. Such a household produces a family peculiar to the settler colonies.[5]

* * *

JOANNE DOBSON

Reclaiming Sentimental Literature[†]

When the fictional Professor William Stearns, self-proclaimed genius and proud author of *History of the Dark Ages*, informs Fanny Fern's writer/protagonist Ruth Hall that "Now and then, there's a gleam of something like reason in your writings, but for the most

---

5. Karen Kupperman, *Providence Island, 1630–1641* (Cambridge: Cambridge University Press, 1993), makes clear that in order for an English colony to succeed, colonists had to have a share in the profits and enjoy ownership of the land, to exercise local control of the military, and to help determine local expenditures and hence have a voice in taxation. But the single most important element was the presence of women. She writes, "Colonial promoters were aware . . . that women were crucial to the long-term success of any English colony." They brought "essential skills of food production" and preparation as well as "clothing production and maintenance," and their presence promised stability and the possibility of social reproduction. She quotes one Virginia planter, "it is not known whether man or woman be more necessary" for the success of the colonial project (158).

† From *American Literature* 69.2 (1997): 263–88. Copyright © 1997, Duke University Press. All rights reserved. Used by permission of the publisher.

part they are unmitigated trash—false in sentiment—unrhetorical in expression,"[1] he enters, in 1855, a debate over the nature and quality of women's sentimental writing whose terms remain little modified today. For many of the critics who have approached American sentimentalism over the past fifty years (and many earlier critics as well), sentimental writing is *inherently* false in sentiment and/or unskilled in expression. It is, quite simply, not *literary*. From mid-twentieth-century New Criticism to the current cultural critique, literary distinctions such as that between individualized, well-crafted, and genuinely moving texts and those that are merely formulaic either do not exist or do not apply to sentimental literature.[2]

In the interests of expanding the critical vocabulary and refining the critical methodologies we bring to American literature in this era of canon expansion, I wish to advocate here a more traditionally literary approach to the influential body of mid-nineteenth-century writing we have come to designate sentimental. Only by understanding how this body of work constructs the literary can we read individual texts as agents operating within a literary field rather than merely as cultural artifacts. Sentimental writing is as varied in quality as other literary modes, and if we approach it solely as a cultural discourse, as the current critique tends to do, we address it only partially. Literary in intention and literary in reception, sentimental fiction and poetry can be more fully addressed if we add to the dominant cultural critique an informed understanding of sentimental literary practice.

It's not that sentimental writing has been ignored.[3] With the accelerating recovery of nineteenth-century women's writing, sentimen-

---

1. Fanny Fern [Sara Parton], *Ruth Hall*, ed. Joyce Warren (New Brunswick: Rutgers Univ. Press, 1986), 166.
2. Twentieth-century scholars—both defenders of sentimentalism (such as Jane Tompkins in *Sensational Designs: The Cultural Work of American Fiction, 1790–1860* [New York: Oxford Univ. Press, 1985]) and its most trenchant critics (such as Ann Douglas in *The Feminization of American Culture* [New York: Avon, 1978])—seem to share a perception of it as a more or less monolithic discourse. * * * The modernist critic in particular, for whom worthwhile literature is alienated, ironic, experimental, fragmented, multivalenced—in a word, difficult—reads in a state of fundamental opposition to the sentimental text, its subject matter, its language, and its philosophical stance. The postmodernist critic, for whom the collapse of the divide between elite and popular culture is a given, has tended to focus on sentimental texts as cultural and political artifacts rather than literary works. And many cultural critics have seen sentimental discourse as politically problematic, complicit in gender, class, and racial oppression. For them, its significance is reduced to its role as a tool of cultural hegemony.

* * *

3. Much traditional criticism of sentimental literature has been scathing and dismissive, as Susan K. Harris points out in *Nineteenth-Century American Women Novelists: Interpretive Strategies* (New York: Cambridge Univ. Press, 1990). Harris sees in canonical literary criticism "a deep-seated revulsion from the feminine" (5). Fred Kaplan, in *Sacred Tears: Sentimentality in Victorian Literature* (Princeton: Princeton Univ. Press,

talism has been approached as a subliterature, as a moral philosophy, and as a hegemonic cultural discourse. But no comprehensive exegesis of sentimentalism, addressing both thematic and stylistic issues, has been attempted. The absence of a literary critique may be due in part to the problematization of the concepts of literature and the literary under the gaze of postmodern critical theory, but it is probably more closely related to the current dominance of cultural criticism. Cultural criticism has added invaluable dimensions to the study of American literature; it has done the necessary work of situating sentimental literature in a complex web of class, race, gender, and economic significance. But the shift to a cultural critique has tended to direct scholars away from the kind of evaluation available in more traditional aesthetic and formalist investigation, since cultural paradigms do not account for distinctions between literary and other forms of cultural expression.

Literature is a specialized discourse, availing itself of distinctive uses of language, genre conventions, and imaginative traditions. In using the word *literature,* I make no a priori judgments about quality. Rather, I mean written texts, fictional or poetic, that announce themselves as literary by being composed in traditional literary modes. While literature participates in cultural discourse, it also, as a product of the interaction of literary convention and individual agency, elaborates upon and often contradicts or transcends a purely cultural imaginary. Yet the critic who wishes to investigate sentimental writing as literature reads in opposition to an entrenched body of commentary compounded of the new cultural practices and the dismissive evaluations of midcentury modernist scholars. The twentieth-century critique of sentimentalism has worked methodologically, ideologically, and institutionally to discourage investigation of sentimental texts as participants in literary traditions, both established and emergent, and as products of individual imagina-

---

1987), considers the possibility that the exaggerated condemnation of sentimentality by literary critics is an anxiety reaction, "a frightened defense against its demands" (41). Robert Solomon, in "In Defense of Sentimentality" (*Philosophy and Literature* 14 [1990]: 304–23), identifies the specific types of "repulsive" emotions, arguing that "the real objection to sentimentality . . . is [the] rejection (or fear) of . . . a certain kind of emotion or sentiment in particular," what he calls the "tender affections" (320). Evidence for the slightly hysterical quality of the critical reaction to sentimental themes and language is so abundant that it almost seems unsporting to point it out. Fred Lewis Pattee's watershed study *The Feminine Fifties* (New York: D. Appleton-Century, 1940) is a case in point. Citing his use of words like "flush," "fervid," "emotionalism," and "explosion," Harris claims that "Pattee's vocabulary quickly reveals that he is repelled by emotional display" (3). The ahistorical exaggeration of Pattee's theorizing compounds that sense of revulsion. "Feeling ruled [the era] from end to end rather than thinking" (4), he begins his study. His conclusion quotes that great misogynist, Ambrose Bierce: "'One cannot be trusted to feel until one has learned to think.' . . . But the great mass of the American readers, for the most part women, did not think at all" (307).

*   *   *

tion, talent, and agency. As David Perkins notes, it is always difficult to break free of the dominant paradigms of literary history: "It takes so much more energy, so much more knowledge and reflection, to disturb the received system than to accept and apply it, that anyone can revise it at only a few points."[4] This essay constitutes an attempt to "disturb the received system" of evaluation by looking at sentimental language and sentimental tropes as they grow out of a loosely organized mid-nineteenth-century sentimental literary practice.

As a body of literary texts, sentimental writing can be seen in a significant number of instances to process a conventional sentimental aesthetics through individual imagination, idiosyncratic personal feeling, and skilled use of language, creating engaging, even compelling fictions and lyrics—as, for example, in works by Alice Cary, Harriet Jacobs, Frances Sargent Osgood, Lydia Sigourney, and Harriet Beecher Stowe, to name a few. Indeed, a number of canonical authors, including Emily Dickinson, Nathaniel Hawthorne, and Herman Melville, can be seen to participate—in often unrecognized ways—in the sentimental literary tradition. In this discussion I intend to step outside the prevailing cultural critique of mid-nineteenth-century American sentimental writing and look primarily at issues of literary accomplishment, at the realization of a set of literary conventions emerging from a shared cultural/aesthetic impetus at a particular historical moment.

For anything resembling an authoritative, evaluated body of texts to develop, sentimental literature must undergo the kind of extensive literary analysis other literary modes, such as American romanticism and realism, have sustained. While I do not wish to impose the restrictions of a traditional scholarly canon on sentimental literature, and it is not my intention here to lay out such a canon, we do need the "canonical" advantage of a secure body of negotiated texts, texts about whose significance some tentative consensus has been reached and whose availability will continue assured. Formalist investigation, currently out of vogue, has always been indispensable to the winnowing process of literary history, but formal "excellence" has conventionally been defined narrowly and used to exclude large bodies of texts from the category of the literary. With insights into the workings of the canon provided by recent reconstructive developments in American literary history, formal analysis can be turned against the process of sexist, racist, and classist exclusion. Employed inclusively—by which I mean taking the trouble to discern and appreciate the particular aesthetic determinants of an individual text—a formal analysis can help provide a fuller under-

---

4. David Perkins, *Is Literary History Possible?* (Baltimore: Johns Hopkins Univ. Press, 1992), 73.

standing of its achievement. As Judith Fetterley argues, "[t]hose of us interested in nineteenth-century American women writers may need to find ways to revitalize modes of criticism no longer fashionable because these modes may represent stages in the process of literary evaluation that we cannot do without."[5]

The traditional formalist methodologies of close reading and thematic study can be, and are, used to develop, support, or enhance cultural readings, but formalist analysis more specifically provides insight into the manner in which the text performs the uniquely aesthetic aspects of its complex task, its mobilizing of language, genre, and individual imagination for the purpose of conveying emotion, insight, and pleasure. A text-based critique focused on close readings and thematic investigations of individual texts in a larger literary and cultural context—similar to that practiced for decades on the more male-identified romanticism and realism—will find that sentimental writing works according to specific and purposeful aesthetic principles toward specific and purposeful literary ends.

"In dealing with genres," Perkins says, "the literary historian must establish a canon (what texts belong to the genre) and a concept."[6] I will leave it to others to continue the work of determining which texts participate in sentimental literary practice, but I would like to propose here an operative concept. Literary sentimentalism, I suggest, is premised on an emotional and philosophical ethos that celebrates human connection, both personal and communal, and acknowledges the shared devastation of affectional loss. It is not a discrete literary category, as the term *genre* might imply, but rather an imaginative orientation characterized by certain themes, stylistic features, and figurative conventions. "There is a ladder to heaven," says Harriet Beecher Stowe in *The Minister's Wooing* (1859), "whose base God has placed in human affections."[7] For Stowe, the most profound of the sentimental apologists, human connection is the genesis, in this life, of the divine. Other writers concur, if not about the "divinity" of affectional relationships, at least about their necessity to a meaningful existence. In a letter to her cousins Fanny and Lou Norcross, Emily Dickinson writes, "Affection is like bread, unnoticed till we starve, and then we dream of it, and sing of it, and paint it" (late 1872).[8] For Stowe and Dickinson, affectional experi-

---

5. Judith Fetterley, "Commentary: Nineteenth-Century American Women Writers and the Politics of Recovery" (*American Literary History* 6 [Fall 1994]: 605).
6. Perkins, 80.
7. Harriet Beecher Stowe, *The Minister's Wooing* (Hartford, Conn.: Stowe-Day Foundation, 1994), 205–06.
8. *The Letters of Emily Dickinson*, ed. Thomas H. Johnson and Theodora Ward, 3 vols. (Cambridge: Harvard Univ. Press, 1958), L379. All Dickinson letters are cited according to Johnson and Ward's numbering.

ence, with its contradictory aspects of fulfillment and constraint, is as essential to human existence as food. As Nina Baym says in *Woman's Fiction*, midcentury women writers "interpreted experience within models of personal relations, . . . not as determined by various memberships, but by various personal interactions."[9] Sentimentalism envisions the self-in-relation; family (not necessarily in the conventional biological sense), intimacy, community, and social responsibility are its primary relational modes.[1] This valorization of affectional connection and commitment is the generative core of sentimental experience as mid-nineteenth-century American writers defined it.

The principal theme of the sentimental text is the desire for bonding, and it is affiliation on the plane of emotion, sympathy, nurturance, or similar moral or spiritual inclination for which sentimental writers and readers yearn. Violation, actual or threatened, of the affectional bond generates the primary tension in the sentimental text and leads to bleak, dispirited, anguished, sometimes outraged, representations of human loss, as well as to idealized portrayals of human connection or divine consolation. In many of the classic men's texts of the era, the ultimate threat to individual existence is contamination of the self by social bonds; in the sentimental vision, the greatest threat is the tragedy of separation, of severed human ties: the death of a child, lost love, failed or disrupted family connections, distorted or unsympathetic community, or the loss of the hope of reunion and/or reconciliation in the hereafter. "Orphaned as we are," says the narrator of Alice Cary's regional tale "The Sisters," "we have need to be kind to each other—ready with loving and helping hands and encouraging words, for the darkness and the silence are hard by where no sweet care can do us any good."[2] It is a collective "we" Cary uses here, and an existential orphanhood to which she refers. The sentimental crisis of consciousness is not so much an anxiety regarding the ultimate nonbeing of the self as it is the certain knowledge of inevitable separation—whether temporal or eternal—from the others who constitute the meaning of one's life.

In light of these thematic characteristics of the sentimental ethos, it becomes possible not only to understand the particular nature of sentimental subject matter but also to begin to elaborate an aesthetics of sentimental literature. Raymond Williams notes that "choice

9. Nina Baym, *Woman's Fiction: A Guide to Novels by and about Women in America, 1820–1870* (Ithaca: Cornell Univ. Press, 1978), 18.
1. I first proposed this definition of sentimentalism in my essay "The American Renaissance Reenvisioned," in *The (Other) American Traditions,* ed. Joyce W. Warren (New Brunswick: Rutgers Univ. Press, 1993), 164–82.
2. Alice Cary, *Clovernook Sketches and Other Stories,* ed. Judith Fetterley (New Brunswick: Rutgers Univ. Press, 1987), 64.

of subject-matter includes real [genre or formal] determinants,"[3] and this is as true of sentimental writing as of any other body of literature. The sentimentalist is concerned, in Lydia Sigourney's words, with "the whole sweet circle of the domestic affections,—the hallowed ministries of women, at the cradle, the hearthstone, and the death-bed."[4] And the "determinants" of these concerns (as well as of other, more public, sentimental interests) mandate a literary idiom designed to further sentimental ends, an idiom whose tropes are designed to elicit feelings of empathy and concern, and whose language, like the language of realism, is intended to communicate meaning with minimal impediment. Such an idiom would prove both familiar and accessible; it would replicate linguistically the relational priorities of the sentimental ethos and facilitate communication with a wide and receptive audience.

From a literary perspective, then, sentimentalism becomes a written imaginative mode defined by a cluster of conventional subjects, themes, characterization modes, narrative and lyric patterns, tropes, tonal qualities, and linguistic patterns focused around relational experience and the consequences of its rupture. We can recognize sentimental literature by its concern with subject matter that privileges affectional ties, and by conventions and tropes designed to convey the primary vision of human connection in a dehumanized world. An emphasis on accessible language, a clear prose style, and familiar lyric and narrative patterns defines an aesthetic whose primary quality of transparency is generated by a valorization of connection, an impulse toward communication with as wide an audience as possible.

When sentimental literature is seen as literary discourse participating in—but not delimited by—a significant body of cultural discourse, it becomes a body of texts we can begin to address with a degree of informed understanding. Operating from a position of familiarity with the sentimental idiom, readers can begin to consider individual texts. As with any other body of writing, sentimental literature is variously realized according to the differing visions, talents, intentions, and aspirations of individual authors. Let me stress that point because, given the critical history of sentimentalism, it seems necessary to clear the ground: sentimental literature can be "good" or "bad." Sentimental texts can be profound or simple, authentic or spurious, sincere or exploitative, strong or weak, radical or conservative, personally empowering or restrictive, well or poorly

---

3. Raymond Williams, *Marxism and Literature* (New York: Oxford Univ. Press, 1977), 185.
4. Lydia H. Sigourney, "An Essay on Her Genius," in *The Works of Mrs. Hemans* (Philadelphia: Lea and Blanchard, 1840), xv; as cited in Cheryl Walker, *Nightingale's Burden: Women Poets and American Culture before 1900* (Bloomington: Indiana Univ. Press, 1982), 24.

written; they can adhere to the strictest limitations of stereotype and formula, or they can elaborate the possibilities of convention in significant ways. An adequate comprehension of the sentimental mode will reveal that—like other forms of expression—it can be used for good or ill, it can be transcendent or degraded. When sentimental conventions are mediated through intelligence, talent, and imagination, and informed with idiosyncratic personal feeling, they can, like any other body of literary conventions, come alive for the reader.

In their handling of sentimental feelings and conventions, strong sentimental writers are just as likely to be agents of their unique visions as are writers in any other mode. A literary critique will offer tools with which to distinguish between the slavishly standardized text and one that plays with conventions in genuinely engaging ways, between the inept versifier and the skilled poet, between the mere technician of language and the uniquely imaginative writer. Further, an approach *combining* cultural and literary considerations will allow us to see specific cultural tensions being worked out within the guidelines offered by a particular genre through the transformative mediation of individual talent and imagination.

A close look at two elements of the sentimental idiom—its use of language and its troping practices—will serve to demonstrate the effectiveness of sentimentalism's rhetoric when it works (and it often does) and the authenticity of its sentiment when it is genuine (as it often is). Both a self-effacing style ("unrhetorical in expression") and conventional, even stereotypical tropes ("false in sentiment") are crucial to effective sentimental literary art. As Mikhail Bakhtin argues in "Discourse in the Novel," sentimental language constitutes "a unitary and authentic language of literature as well as life, one that is adequate to true intentions and true human expression."[5] The language of Lydia Sigourney's poem "Death of an Infant" functions as sentimental language should, as a highly expressive medium appropriate to the conveyance of empathy and consolation, while the pervasive and enduring trope of the sentimental keepsake, as seen in Stowe's *Uncle Tom's Cabin* and *The Minister's Wooing*, Frances Osgood's "The Little Hand," and Harriet Jacobs's *Incidents in the Life of a Slave Girl*, serves as a powerful vehicle for the conveyance of primary affective sentiments.

Although there has been some speculation on the rhetorical use by sentimental writers of "agitated" textual surfaces to convey sincere emotion, I would argue that as most commonly used—as, for

5. M. M. Bakhtin, "Discourse in the Novel," in *The Dialogic Imagination,* ed. Michael Holquist (Austin: Univ. of Texas Press, 1981), 397.

example, by Stowe, Osgood, Cary, Jacobs, and Susan Warner—sentimental language tends to be understated, even self-effacing, focusing not on verbal excesses or flourishes of style but on its function as a communicative medium. Bakhtin notes the tendency of sentimental language to seek transparency; in the sentimental novel, he states, "literary language is brought closer to the conversational norm." While still "literary," it is "opposed both to the unordered and brute heteroglossia of life and to the archaic and conventional high literary genres."[6] A language close "to the conversational norm" is a language that mediates its subject matter without either foregrounding itself or erecting linguistic barriers—such as learned diction, obscure tropes, or experimental uses of language—that impede comprehension. In other words, such a language operates as an apparently transparent medium for the conveyance of its subject matter and affect. In "Death of an Infant," Sigourney employs language whose grammatical regularity, conventional images, and concrete, accessible, "unpoetic" diction provide easy entry to her representation of a dying child.

> Death found strange beauty on that polish'd brow,
> And dash'd it out. There was a tint of rose
> On cheek and lip. He touched the veins with ice,
> And the rose faded.
>   Forth from those blue eyes
> There spake a wishful tenderness, a doubt
> Whether to grieve or sleep, which innocence
> Alone may wear. With ruthless haste he bound
> The silken fringes of those curtaining lids
> For ever.
>   There had been a murmuring sound
> With which the babe would claim its mother's ear,
> Charming her even to tears. The spoiler set
> The seal of silence.
>   But there beam'd a smile,
> So fix'd, so holy, from that cherub brow,
> Death gazed, and left it there. He dar'd not steal
> The signet-ring of Heaven.[7]

"Death of an Infant" is written in the most "conversational" of traditional verse forms, blank verse. Its unrhymed iambic pentameter would have fallen familiarly upon the ears of a populace attuned to the speech of Shakespearean characters in an era when Shakespeare belonged to the popular audience as much as to the cultural

6. Bakhtin, 397.
7. "Death of an Infant" (1827), in *Select Poems by Mrs. L. H. Sigourney* (Philadelphia: A. Hart, 1850), 30–31.

elite. The poem's sentences are complete and, with one exception, composed in the conventional subject-predicate-object order. The exception, the sentence beginning "Forth from those blue eyes / There spake," is also the longest and most complex in the poem, and the only one to contain a manifestly poetic usage, the archaic verb form "spake" for "spoke." Otherwise the diction is standard, concrete, descriptive, accessible.

The poem focuses on the child at the precise moment of passing from life to death. Sigourney sketches the presence of the living child in a few conventionally descriptive lines intended to convey the unwrinkled brow, the healthy glow, the quiet voice, the wistful spirit. It is the last image, the "wishful tenderness" of the blue eyes, that the poem highlights with its departures from "conversational" language: "Forth from those blue eyes / There spake a wishful tenderness, a doubt / Whether to grieve or sleep, which innocence / Alone may wear" (prepositional phrase, predicate, subject). The syntactic transposition, archaic diction, and moderate complexity of the sentence focus attention on the child's subjectivity, its "wishful" desire to live. By its inclusion in the poem's longest section, four full lines and two half-lines, this representation of the child's spirit-filled eyes is coupled with a chilling depiction of Death stitching those eyes permanently shut: "With ruthless haste he bound / The silken fringes of those curtaining lids / For ever." In a poem whose everyday language mediates a painful, but in its era not uncommon, reality, this brief divergence from the poem's self-established idiom functions as a flag, an indicator of intensified emotional significance.

The "conversational" nature of this poem's language—its grammatical regularity, its quotidian diction—is enhanced by the poem's almost total lack of obvious metaphor. The language throughout is conventionally rather than mimetically descriptive: "polished brow," "a tint of rose / On cheek and lip," "silken fringes," "curtaining lids," "cherub brow." In this poem of consolation Sigourney does not show the "brute" and disturbing picture of an actual death. Rather, the poet chooses familiar word pictures that will not give readers pause but will move them smoothly through the descriptive lines leading to the final image, the poem's single manifest metaphor. Through the concentration on conventional images, readers are encouraged to cast a long and "wishfully tender" gaze upon the face of the dying child. Once the image of the child is imprinted, Death's "ruthless haste" registered, and readers sufficiently distressed by the impending separation, Sigourney presents the one conspicuously poetic usage of the poem, her culminating metaphor: "He dared not steal / The signet-ring of Heaven." In this lone metaphor, Heaven's promise of eventual reconciliation bridges the sentimental breach implicit in the deathbed scene. The "wishful tenderness" of affectional desire will be rewarded with reunion in the afterlife.

For Bakhtin, sentimental literary language does exactly what Sigourney does in "Death of an Infant," and does it in exactly the same manner: "[t]he finely detailed descriptions, the . . . deliberateness with which petty secondary everyday details are foregrounded, the tendency of the representation to present itself as an unmediated impression deriving from the object itself and finally a pathos occasioned by helplessness and weakness rather than by heroic strength."[8] A language working toward sentimental ends tends to be subdued as a rhetorical idiom, foregrounding neither itself nor "brute" reality but employing a variety of informal linguistic modalities to render its objects affectively available to a wide readership.

Sentimental tropes, as vehicles for primary affective experience, also call upon the conventional and familiar. When mediated through unique experience and individual talent, familiar metaphoric outlines come to life in powerful and idiosyncratic figures. As Susan K. Harris notes, "[t]he prevailing critical assumption has been that in these [sentimental] novels the baroque metaphors are all rather mindlessly borrowed. Borrowed they are, but very self-consciously; they are used to serve a variety of functions, and, over time, they are revitalized, feminized into figures pregnant with possibility."[9] In the work of sentimental writers, tales of abandoned wives, widows, orphaned children, and separated families; deathbed and graveyard scenes; and fantasies of reunions in heaven are far from being, in their essence, reductive narrative clichés. Rather, they become in the hands of talented writers evocative metaphors for a looming existential threat—the potential devastation of deeply experienced human connections. In addition, these tropes often serve as vehicles for depictions of all-too-common social tragedies and political outrages stemming from the failure of society to care for the disconnected. Thus we see the focus on advocacy for the poor, oppressed, and enslaved. To the sentimental mind motifs of abandonment, orphanhood, and death do not wallow in excessive emotionality; rather, they represent an essential reality and *must* be treated with heightened feeling.

A close investigation of one of sentimentalism's most enduring tropes will highlight the richness of the literature's varying realizations. I have chosen the keepsake tradition because of its centrality to the sentimental imagination and its thematic and emotional complexity. Although keepsake imagery has been employed to vari-

---

8. Bakhtin, 397.
9. Susan K. Harris, "'But is it any *good?*': Evaluating Nineteenth-Century American Women's Fiction," in *The (Other) American Traditions: Nineteenth-Century Women Writers*, ed. Joyce W. Warren (New Brunswick: Rutgers Univ. Press, 1993), 273.

ous ends, I will concentrate here on its primary use, its memorial function, its complex inscription of the nature and quality of affectional memory.

Ann Douglas is on to something when she begins her monumental critical study *The Feminization of American Culture* with a critique of Stowe's treatment of little Eva's curls. While "[h]er adoring Papa and a group of equally adoring slaves in unspeakable grief cluster around her bedside . . . she dispenses Christian wisdom and her own golden locks with profuse generosity." Because Eva, as a character, operates within a dynamic of reader empathy, Douglas finds her an inadequate literary subject: "She does not demand the respect we accord a competitor. She is not extraordinarily gifted. . . . Little Eva's virtue lies partly in her femininity, surely a common enough commodity. And her greatest act is dying, something we all can and must do."[1] A modernist critical antipathy to the feminine and the common blinds Douglas to the significance of Eva's deathbed scene, for here Stowe is working within a dynamic of identification explicitly geared to the feminine and the common. Eva's curls, the keepsakes by which she wishes to be remembered, tap into an enduring tradition in the sentimental imagination; the sentimental keepsake constitutes a vivid symbolic embodiment of the primacy of human connection and the inevitability of human loss. Its use in numerous texts with varying (sometimes contrasting) intentions stems from a body of convention resonant with grief, loss, memory, consolation, and an acknowledgement of the fragility of human life.

Eva's curls play a complex role in *Uncle Tom's Cabin*. Eva *does* "dispense Christian wisdom and her own golden curls with profuse generosity," but this is no cheap thrill or easy consolation. Rather, Eva's generosity is constructed within a cultural and historical context where all too often children *did* die, were snatched incomprehensibly from the arms of helpless families—as Harriet Beecher Stowe knew only too painfully. For Stowe and her sentimental contemporaries, the keepsake, or sentimental artifact, was a potent and multivalenced remembrance, a material object upon which was played out symbolically an all-too-intimate acquaintance with the tragic evanescence of human life.

Emily Dickinson, who left a number of fragmentary manuscript poems as her own memorial keepsake, displays in poem 360 keen insight into the paradoxical memorial function of the sentimental keepsake:

> Death sets a Thing significant
> The Eye had hurried by

---

1. Douglas, 1, 2.

> Except a perished Creature
> Entreat us tenderly

Here Dickinson ponders the meaning of the sentimental relic, the "Thing significant"—in this case literally a sentimental "text":

> A Book I have—a friend gave—
> Whose Pencil—here and there—
> Had notched the place that pleased Him—
> At Rest—His fingers are—
>
> Now—when I read—I read not—
> For interrupting Tears
> Obliterate the Etchings
> Too Costly for Repairs.[2]

The memorial "etchings" of human love are illegible in the face of death. Tears of sorrow and pain blind the eyes that assiduously scrutinize the memento of love, the pencil-marked text left behind by one whose fingers will write no more. The book remains; the one who inscribed upon it a record of what "pleased Him" is irretrievably gone. And the reader/persona pours over the text in a desperate attempt to decipher the "costly" lesson of love and mortality, a lesson ultimately illegible because of those blinding "interrupting Tears." Only sentimental feeling remains, the knowledge of affectional loss, the tears, the ironic durability of the indecipherable keepsake text, the tragic mortality of the "friend."[3]

Variously treated by individual writers, the keepsake tradition could console, stressing, as it does in *Uncle Tom's Cabin*, the assurance of eternal life beyond the otherwise baffling finality of the grave; it could just as easily problematize human affection, as it does in the Dickinson poem, reflecting with bitter irony on the durability of material objects when compared with the tragic impermanence of human lives. Like any other convention, the sentimental keepsake could be used formulaically and reductively, it could be used with simple effectiveness, or it could be used brilliantly and with sensitivity to its most nuanced implications.

Frances Osgood's "The Little Hand" provides an instance of a sentimental text in which the evocation of the transient nature of life and the peril of investing affection in ephemeral human objects is both "true" (in Bakhtin's terms) and moving:

---

2. *The Poems of Emily Dickinson*, ed. Thomas H. Johnson, 3 vols. (Cambridge: Harvard Univ. Press, 1955), P360. All Dickinson poems are cited according to Johnson's numbering.
3. Dickinson focuses on the keepsake in a number of poems, most notably in "In Ebon Box, when years have flown" (P169), and quite bizarrely in "If I may have it, when it's dead" (P577). In the latter the corpse itself becomes the keepsake.

We wandered sadly round the room,—
   We missed the voice's play,
That warbled through our hours of gloom,
   And charmed the cloud away;—

We missed the footstep, loved and light,—
   The tiny, twining hand,—
The quick, arch smile, so wildly bright,—
   The brow, with beauty bland!

We wandered sadly round the room,—
   No relic could we find,
No toy of hers, to sooth our gloom,—
   She left not one behind!

But look! there is a misty trace,
   Faint, undefined and broken,
Of fingers, on the mirror's face,—
   A dear, though simple token!

A cherub hand!—the child we loved
   Had left its impress there,
When first, by young Ambition moved,
   She climbed the easy-chair;—

She saw her own sweet self, and tried
   To touch what seemed to be
So near, so beautiful! and cried,—
   "Why! there's another me!"

Dear hand! though from the mirror's face
   Thy form did soon depart,
I wore its welcome, tender trace,
   Long after, in my heart![4]

Osgood sketches the living presence of the child with a few brief strokes—voice, motion, touch, smile, beauty, and the speaker's emotional response to her. All are defined now negatively, by absence and loss. The speaker searches for a "relic" of the child's presence, a keepsake, to anchor the child in her memory. What she finds is nothing so durable as a material object, but rather a mere "trace," as "faint, undefined and broken" as human life and human relationships. This trace triggers a memory. The child, upon seeing her reflection in a mirror, had announced, "Why! There's another me!"

4. Frances Sargent Osgood, "The Little Hand," in *A Wreath of Wild Flowers from New England* (London: Edward Churton, 1838), 308–09.

The irony of the little girl's discovery is that the reflected child in the mirror is as transient as the smudged handprint on the mirror's face and as unreachable to the living child as the dead child is to the still-living speaker. Like the child, in attempting to touch "what seems to be so near, so beautiful," the speaker fails, finding only its "traces" in memory. Osgood's treatment of the keepsake tradition offers no consolation; it's charming, as Osgood always is, it twists the heart just a little, and in doing so it "works" aesthetically and emotionally, conveying one encounter with the vision of love and loss at the heart of sentimental experience.

Stowe's use of the keepsake is also effective, but more complex in a metaphysical and emotional sense and infused with a trenchant cultural and political critique. Eva wills her curls to the family slaves as redemptive texts. The slaves, she recalls, are not literate and cannot read of God's saving love in the Bible. "O dear! you *can't* read—poor souls!" she cries. Then, "I want to give you something that, when you look at [it], you shall always remember me. I'm going to give all of you a curl of my hair; and when you look at it, think that I loved you and am gone to heaven, and that I want to see you all there."[5] Within this Christian interpretation of the keepsake tradition, Eva's curls become a redeeming remembrance. In remembering their love for Eva, the slaves will be able to read God's redemptive love writ small upon their hearts. Upon the material artifact is inscribed both the human drama of love and loss and the divine drama of love, loss, and redemption. Even those deprived of their hope of salvation by the gross social injustice that keeps them illiterate can learn to read it there.

Yet, lest we postulate too easy a dichotomy between Stowe and Dickinson—the conservative Christian versus the protomodern nihilist—we must take another look at Stowe and the keepsake tradition. In a compelling and beautifully worded meditation on loss in *The Minister's Wooing,* Stowe contemplates with a dark complexity equal to Dickinson's the profound irony of the material relic. Jumping "seamlessly" from a discussion of dressmaking to a meditation on last things, Stowe's narrator says with an air of weary resignation:

> So we go, dear reader,—so long as we have a body and a soul. Two worlds must mingle,—the great and the little, the solemn and the trivial, wreathing in and out, like the grotesque carvings on a Gothic shrine;—only, did we know it rightly, nothing is trivial; since the human soul, with its awful shadow, makes all things sacred. Have not ribbons, cast-off flowers, soiled bits of

5. Harriet Beecher Stowe, *Uncle Tom's Cabin* (1852; reprint, New York: Penguin, 1981), 419.

gauze, trivial, trashy fragments of millinery, sometimes had an awful meaning, a deadly power, when they belonged to one who should wear them no more . . . ? For so sacred and individual is a human being, that, of all the million-peopled earth, no one form ever restores another. The mold of each mortal type is broken at the grave; and never, never, though you look through all the faces on earth, shall the exact form you mourn ever meet your eyes again! You are living your daily life among trifles that one death-stroke may make relics. One false step, one luckless accident, an obstacle on the track of a train, the tangling of the cord in shifting a sail, and the pen-knife, the pen, the papers, the trivial articles of dress and clothing, which to-day you toss idly and jestingly from hand to hand, may become dread memorials of that awful tragedy whose deep abyss ever underlies our common life.[6]

Here Stowe delineates the transience of human life in a meditation both profound and melancholy. As sunny and certain as she may be about Eva's curls as sacred relics, in this passage from a very different novel Stowe broods upon the implications of mortality solely in terms of the tragically irreparable rending of affectional bonds: "never, never, though you look through all the faces on earth." The beloved face is gone and the sentimental artifact, a "trivial, trashy fragment," serves as a reminder that an abyss of death and existential doubt underlies all the fragile certainties of human experience. "The human soul, with its awful shadow," casts its awareness of love and death upon even the most trivial object. With meaning constructed in affectional terms, even committed, hopeful Christians such as Stowe did not skim lightly over the implications of mortality.

For Harriet Jacobs, an enslaved black woman, the memorial function of the keepsake tradition is thoroughly problematized and politicized. As Hazel V. Carby says, "Jacobs used the material circumstances of her life to critique conventional standards of female behavior and to question their relevance and applicability to the experience of black women." If sentimental property figures the primacy of human connection, Linda Brent has no secure hold on either the keepsake tradition or the human bonds it represents. She herself, according to the laws of the land, *is* property and can be severed from her nearest ties at the will of her master. In addition, the sexual "purity" that in the eyes of "respectable" society will render her worthy of sentimental bonds is denied her.

Jacobs is well aware of the affectional connections symbolized by the keepsake object. Indeed, when Linda's uncle Benjamin flees from captivity, Linda gives him a keepsake token. In spite of the ill-

6. Stowe, *The Minister's Wooing*, 650–51.

ness and deprivation that force Benjamin to sell his clothing, he honors the sentiments of that token; as Linda says, he "did not part with a little pin I fastened in his bosom when we parted. It was the most valuable thing I owned, and I thought none more worthy to wear it." Linda herself wears her dead mother's wedding ring. But when Linda tells her grandmother that she is pregnant by her white lover, Aunt Marthy responds by tearing "from [Linda's] fingers [her] mother's wedding ring and her silver thimble." While Linda has entered into the sexual liaison as a nuanced moral strategy to protect herself from rape by her master, her grandmother responds from a moral position unavailable to a slave woman—that of the owner of her own chastity. The keepsake ring, which represents the dead mother's own chastity, embodies a sentimental bond between Linda and her mother that Aunt Marthy feels the young girl no longer deserves.

The perversity of chattel slavery is further figured in Jacobs's recounting of the incident of the silver candelabra. These candelabra are purchased with three hundred dollars borrowed from Linda's grandmother by the grandmother's mistress. The hard-earned money is never repaid, and the valuable candelabra, symbolizing black labor and white betrayal, become keepsakes for the white family. "I presume," says Linda, "they will be handed down in the family, from generation to generation." Linda's own inheritance is one of loss, both of family property and (however briefly) of family affections. Participation in the sentimental ethos renders her at once invested in the keepsake tradition and deeply aware that in slavery she has no ownership rights—not even to "sentimental" property.

For the sentimental writer, the keepsake tradition, like other sentimental conventions, resonates with emotional, metaphysical, and political significance, and its violation is resonantly marked as inhumane. Not merely a self-indulgent token or a silly relic (although in its more reductive usages it may become such), the sentimental keepsake embodies the memory of love, the anguish of separation, the hope of eventual reunion. In the hands of gifted, thoughtful writers, the keepsake tradition inscribed an ethos of human connection and separation personally and politically powerful and sufficiently rich to complicate, and even rival, the long-acknowledged individualist trope of the American isolato.

Historically, blanket condemnations of sentimentalism's "unskilled rhetoric" and "false sentiment" have misunderstood or trivialized its aesthetic purposes and/or focused selectively on exploitative or banal realizations of the tradition. With an awareness of the values and literary practices of the sentimental ethos, critical readers can recognize in accomplished writers the inherent effectiveness of sentimentalism's transparent language and the intrinsic thematic richness of its affectional tropes. Like the keepsake tradition, other sentimental conventions—the orphan, the mother and child, the deathbed scene—when approached with sympathy and a knowledge of the underlying dynamics of the sentimental imagination, can be seen, in the hands of gifted writers, to be infused with individual vision, idiosyncratic insights, and enduring imaginative power. As Suzanne Clark suggests, it is time to "open up" the sentimental and "to recall the variety of traditions, images, tropes, conventions, and ideological implications that modernism reduced to the single, gendered, and awful other."

We respond to literary texts, I suggest, because we feel they have value and meaning for our lives; in Nancy Miller's terms, we find them "plausible."[7] Nineteenth-century sentimentalism is a crucial link between an older philosophical vision in which human relations are by and large infused with religious imperatives, certainties, and consolations, and a modern literary worldview in which human bonds are seriously problematized—tenuous, fleeting, misconstrued. Although sentimental values are certainly not universal—and are not currently intellectually fashionable—I would nonetheless venture to say that they are values by which a considerable number of people continue to live their daily lives. In a world of mortality, of absolute and certain loss—the universal and immutable human condition—a body of literature giving primacy to affectional connections and responsibilities still reflects the dilemmas, anxieties, and tragedies of individual lives.

To reclaim American literary sentimentalism is to restore a particular subject position to literary history and to redress a persistent imbalance in the story we've told ourselves about the American literary past. Informed and flexible conceptual constructs will enable critics to do with sentimentalism the necessary work that literary history has done with other bodies of literature: make comprehensive statements about imaginative and generic similarities, discern subtle distinctions within classes of texts, evaluate the significance of individual texts and the achievement of individual authors, and trace the roots and trajectory of literary change. In other words,

---

7. Nancy Miller, "Emphasis Added: Plots and Plausibilities in Women's Fiction," in *Subject to Change: Reading Feminist Writing* (New York: Columbia Univ. Press, 1988). Miller claims that "[t]he attacks on female plots and plausibilities assume that women writers cannot or will not obey the rules of fiction. It also assumes that the truth devolving from *veri*similitude is male. For sensibility, sensitivity, 'extravagance' . . . are taken to be not merely inferior modalities of production but deviations from some obvious truth" (44). To take sentimentalism seriously enough to investigate it as an integral element of American literary history is to legitimate a realm of human affectional experience unauthorized by the makers of the American literary canon.

appropriate conceptual formulations derived from intensive investigation of the texts and the times will allow critics to talk about sentimentalism as a body of literature within history and culture. Such groundwork would allow critics to read sentimentalism as we read any other mode of imaginative literature whose dominance is now past: carefully, partially, provisionally, and with respect for its otherness. A critic informed about the sentimental project, at least to the degree of being able to recognize sentimental discourse for what it is, is in a position to accept sentimental priorities as a valid subject of literary expression, to assess sentimental literary texts on the basis of individual merit, and to work toward a more comprehensive and representative account of American literary history.

JUNE HOWARD

From What Is Sentimentality?[†]

People talk about sentimentality quite a lot. And they seem to know what they are talking about. The category has had an especially long-standing, conspicuous role in American literary history, and it appears more frequently than ever in current criticism. Cultural studies has foregrounded the way in which we *live* social relations, the inextricable entanglements of subjectivity and power; it is not surprising that sentiment's articulations of feeling and form seem more and more interesting. The term is so charged and pervasive, so plastic, precisely because our reactions to sentimentality are so deeply rooted in our ways of organizing the relation of self and world. I believe that scholarly usages of "sentimentality" are more closely intertwined with everyday meanings of the term than we usually recognize, that they often rely on unexamined and untenable assumptions about the nature of emotion, and that intermittent slides into condemnation or celebration undermine their analytic value.

We need to move on from arguments for and against sentimentality to the task of conceptualizing it as a transdisciplinary object of study. In what follows I discuss investigations of emotions and social life by scholars working separately in fields ranging from neurobiology to anthropology to history. I argue that current work outside the boundary of the humanities can usefully revise our perspective on emotion itself; that the link between sentiment and eighteenth-century notions of sympathy and sensibility should be

† Reprinted by permission of Oxford University Press.

reclaimed; and that we should make a systematic distinction between sentiment and nineteenth-century domestic ideology, and reconstruct the history of their imbrication.

Many readers will agree that it is time for American literary historians to vacate, once and for all, the discourse of judgment that has characterized so much work on sentimentality. The terms of what Laura Wexler calls the "Douglas-Tompkins debate" (9) are familiar: do the popular novels published by women in the mid nineteenth century represent, as argued by Ann Douglas in *The Feminization of American Culture* (1977), a fall from tough-minded, community-oriented Calvinism into "rancid," individualistic emotionalism, the beginnings of a debased mass consumer culture that has swallowed up what was most valuable in American literature and thought (256)? Or do they constitute, as argued by Jane Tompkins in *Sensational Designs: The Cultural Work of American Fiction, 1790–1860* (1985), a complex and effective affirmation of women's power, a grass roots antipatriarchal politics? Douglas and Tompkins both take sentimentality seriously, as do critics following them who have also treated it as culturally powerful and historically resonant. Wexler goes on from her discussion of the critical tradition to analysis of the cultural work of domestic fiction in terms of race as well as gender and class. Richard Brodhead adds a new dimension with his reading of the now-classic novels of Harriet Beecher Stowe and Susan Warner as key documents of a middle-class regime of socialization through coercive love that he calls "disciplinary intimacy." Karen Sánchez-Eppler places women's anti-slavery fiction in rhetorical and political context and produces a striking account of its phenomenology, which I will draw on later. "Reading sentimental fiction is," she writes, "a bodily act," and the way words produce "pulse beats and sobs . . . . radically contracts the distance between narrated events and the moment of their reading, as the feelings in the story are made tangibly present in the flesh of the reader. . . . [T]ears designate a border realm between the story and its reading, since the tears shed by characters initiate an answering moistness in the reader's eye" (100).

* * *

To resist positions "for" and "against" sentimentality, affirming with Lora Romero that "the politics of culture reside in local formulations . . . rather than in some essential and ineluctable political tendency inhering within them" (7–8), is not to say that the form has no specifiable social meanings. Indeed, it is so full of meanings that we cannot escape the debate simply by recognizing it as a closed circle and announcing its end; we need (as Romero suggests) to study its persistence and investigate its terms. Rather than advocate some purification of terminology, I wish to pursue a fairly abstract description of what we are doing when we call something "sentimental." Complex, culturally powerful categories of this sort are invariably conglomerates. Just what sort of mixed bag is sentimentality?

1. Embodied Thoughts

One element never missing from the combinations that constitute "sentimentality" is an association with emotion. In stigmatizing usages, whether vernacular or expert, the emotion involved is characterized as affected and shallow, or as excessive. In Douglas's account, for example, it is both—a suggestion less contradictory than it seems, since counterfeit emotion may be feigned but is more commonly exaggerated. What is at stake is authenticity: the spontaneity, the sincerity, and the legitimacy of an emotion are understood to be the same. This equivalence underpins commentary by defenders as well; Joanne Dobson, for example, argues that sentimental literature can be "an authentic mode of expressing valid human experience" (175).

Habits of mind based on an opposition between manipulated sentiment and genuine emotion are deeply inconsistent with the social constructionism currently prevailing in the humanities. Yet each of us is a layperson as well as an expert, and according to the common sense of the modern world, feelings well up naturally inside individuals—tropes of interiority and self-expression are difficult to resist. Everyday language also has neutral ways of indicating shaped emotion, of course. One can respectably admit that an object is treasured because it reflexively provokes memory and emotion, because it has what we call "sentimental value." Admitting such a sensation always carries the possibility of embarrassment, just as critics who find sentimentality appealing are haunted by its vulnerability to accusations of banality and inauthenticity. What we see in these usages taken together is that "sentiment" and its derivatives indicate a moment when emotion is *recognized* as socially constructed.

A definition offered in a volume endeavoring to bring together sociology and psychology makes an unpejorative distinction between sentiment and emotion that resembles the vernacular usages described above. Steven Gordon writes: "I define a sentiment as a socially constructed pattern of sensations, expressive gestures, and cultural meanings organized around a relationship to a social object, usually another person. . . . Most of a culture's vocabulary of named affective states are sentiments rather than emotions" (566). This formulation does not raise questions of authenticity; in fact, the processes by which culture crafts feelings are precisely what interest

Gordon and others in the relatively new field of the sociology of emotions. Yet the opposition between sentiment and emotion is still correlated with an opposition between the social and the natural. Once again, the argument depends upon a category—emotion—that is left outside the analysis, taken for granted as a fundamental attribute of human beings.

Many anthropologists and psychologists have seen emotion as a natural phenomenon, and they have worked from that assumption whether or not they tried to explain the mechanisms through which nature worked. But over the past 15 years an impressive body of work in and between the two fields has challenged that view, sometimes in terms closely related to cultural studies. One of the most influential texts has been Michelle Z. Rosaldo's early call for "an anthropology of self and feeling," in which she argues that

> feeling is forever given shape through thought and . . . thought is laden with emotional meaning. [W]hat distinguishes thought and affect, differentiating a "cold" cognition from a "hot," is fundamentally a sense of the engagement of the actor's self. Emotions are thoughts somehow "felt" in flushes, pulses, "movements" of our livers, minds, hearts, stomachs, skin. They are *embodied* thoughts, thoughts seeped with the apprehension that "I am involved." (143)

This statement is so powerful because it persuasively addresses not only anthropology, not only social science broadly conceived, but also commonsense understandings of emotion. In Rosaldo's account, the social and the bodily nature of sentimentality characterizes emotion in general.

In their introduction to *Language and the Politics of Emotion* (1990), a collection that demonstrates how quickly anthropologists have moved in the direction Rosaldo suggested, Catherine Lutz and Lila Abu-Lughod describe most anthropological work before 1980 as essentializing, treating emotions as "things internal, irrational, natural." They advocate abandoning the search for "psychobiological" constants underlying locally variable particulars, and functionalist explanations of how different social systems manage emotions, in favor of "contextualizing": analyzing specific social situations to demonstrate how "emotion gets its meaning and force from its location and performance in public discourse" and how social life is affected by emotion discourse (1–2). Their approach challenges naturalizing assumptions and construes emotion as social rather than individual and internal, and brings them very close to the concerns of literary studies. The notion of "discourse," explicated with references to Ferdinand de Saussure and Michel Foucault, is at its center.[1]

In the field of psychology a strong interest in "the cultural factors that contribute to the shaping and the working of human emotions" has emerged, with categories like narrative and "emotion scripts" that point toward the realm of literature figuring prominently (Kitayama and Markus 1). Cultural studies, as an investigation of "the subjective side of social relations," would do well to begin to take heed of such empirical explorations (Johnson 43). Reading (for example) Anna Wierzbicka's account of the affective lexicons of Americans and Poles, learning that in Polish to reply to a compliment by saying "thank you" is potentially offensive (because it treats the remark not as a spontaneous observation but as expressing a desire to please, and therefore might be seen as accusing the speaker of insincerity), can renew one's appreciation of the defamiliarizing power of cross-cultural comparison.

And as social scientists pay more attention to language, humanists may want to reconsider the possibility that components of emotion are "demonstrably hardwired" (Kitayama and Markus 1); Phoebe Ellsworth points out that a comprehensive survey of psychological research yields "abundant evidence for both culturally specific and universal emotional processes" (25). Any experience or examination of the body is mediated by discourse, but that does not mean that literal bodies should be ignored altogether. While anthropologist Arjun Appadurai points out that "emotions have a linguistic life and a public and political status that frequently engender formulaic modes of expression," he also emphasizes that "emotions, unlike other phenomena, appear to have a basis in embodied experience, thus inclining us to see them as rooted in some elementary biophysical repertoire that is both limited and universal" (92).

Some current empirical research into the physiology of mental life is extraordinarily suggestive. For example, in *Descartes' Error: Emotion, Reason, and the Human Brain* (1994), neurologist Anthony Damasio provides a lucid and detailed explanation of how subjectivity can be understood as a "perpetually re-created neurobiological state," with identity depending on the continuous reactivation of two sets of representations: one of memories and one (constantly updated) of body states (100). He shows the brain as continuously responsive,

---

1. Lutz and Abu-Lughod have separately authored important books contributing to the new anthropology of emotion. Their claim that this anthropological work accepts the "psychological orthodoxy" that emotions are "psychobiological processes that respond to cross-cultural environmental differences but retain a robust essence untouched by the social or cultural" (2) should be regarded with some skepticism. Compare Phoebe Ellsworth's account of psychology in the 1960s as dominated by cultural relativism, an orthodoxy that was successfully challenged by the research into universals that is currently being challenged by social constructionism (24–25).

along multiple channels, to neural and chemical signals from various body systems, a kind of "captive audience" (xv) of the body. As Damasio puts it, the "mind is embodied, in the full sense of the term, not just embrained" (118). That self is the ground of all mental activity, and there can be, on Damasio's account, no such thing as selfless or wholly unemotional reason. Feelings, the cognitions most closely linked to body landscapes, are woven into mental activity at every stage. To use Rosaldo's metaphor, some cognitions are cool in comparison with others, but none are at absolute zero. Indeed, Damasio cites clinical and experimental evidence to show that individuals with impaired affect also show impaired decision making; lack of emotion causes people to behave foolishly (52–79).

Congenial as the implications of such research might seem to be for feminist epistemology (for example), only extended interdisciplinary collaboration can build a middle ground on which evidence of such different sorts could be melded. And only on such a landscape can we respond appropriately to work like Paul Ekman's on the cross-cultural recognizability of facial expressions, or Robert Zajonc's on how the action of facial muscles that produce expressions may actually create subjective sensations by altering blood temperatures in the brain (see Ellsworth; Zajonc and McIntosh). Only such collaboration will allow us to avoid either naturalizing by claiming that physiology entails particular experiential or behavioral consequences or rejecting evidence because it conflicts with our social constructionist convictions, so that we can study how physiological processes might enter variably into cultural processes. This prospective intellectual landscape is so hard to imagine partly because such research is rarely available in expositions as accessible to humanists as *Descartes' Error*. It contributes to the difficulty that literary scholarship has, in Neal Oxenhandler's formulation some time ago, "no thoroughgoing affective criticism as such. Although emotive terms serve to locate certain crucially sensitive areas in the reading process, they themselves have never become the locus of a sustained theoretical account" (105).

What are the consequences of these explorations for understanding sentimentality within the horizon of literary and cultural studies? Definitions that rely on judgments of authenticity or inauthenticity are thus decisively undermined. Beyond that, neither the socially constructed nor the bodily nature of sentiment can distinguish it from emotion in general. Rather, expert ascriptions of sentimentality—like vernacular remarks—mark moments when the discursive processes that construct emotion become visible. Many usages of the term are of this order, indicating that the conventionalized quality of some affective response has been noted without implying strong or systematic distinctions among artifacts or situations that evoke emotion. Even this relatively modest clarification has benefits. It moves us out of the terms of the Douglas-Tompkins debate into a less judgmental mode, making it clear that characterizing something as sentimental should open, not close, a conversation. Still, we need to explain why sentimentality should be judged negatively. It is condemned so vehemently in part because its critics feel implicated in it (as Douglas avows she does). Further, the social construction of emotion becomes visible when attitudes about what sensations are appropriate (what sociologist Arlie Russell Hochschild calls "feeling rules") clash. Although not always stigmatized, sentimentality is always suspect; the appearance of the term marks a site where values are contested. We need to examine the nature of that contest, and why a particular range of emotions calls up the term when others do not: horror-movie conventions, however stylized, are rarely described as sentimental. We are left to the task of analyzing a particular set of emotion scripts, in the midst of the ever-widening conversations about the history of emotions and social life.

2. Feeling Right

A comprehensive view of sentiment cannot begin later than the eighteenth century. Critics of earlier generations routinely nodded to the British origins of sentimentalism. More recently, however, many Americanists have neglected the transatlantic and philosophical antecedents of the form. Against the prevailing assumptions of the Douglas-Tompkins debate, I argue that there is a strong relationship between Enlightenment notions of moral sentiments and sympathy and nineteenth- and twentieth-century sentimentalism. Making that link helps us to understand the significance of contemporary usages.

Philosophers like Lord Shaftesbury, Francis Hutcheson, Adam Smith, and Jean-Jacques Rousseau derive benevolence and, ultimately, morality in general from human faculties that dispose us to sympathize with others. For these thinkers, emotions, whether they are innate or produced by Lockean psychology, assume a central place in moral thought—they both lead to and manifest virtue. As contemporary philosopher Charles Taylor puts it, sentiment matters because it is "the touchstone of the morally good. Not because feeling that something is good makes it so . . . [but because] feeling is my way of access into the design of things" (284). The natural goodness of humanity (affirmed with varying degrees of conviction) is visible most directly in our sensations of compassion, and the goodness of God is visible in the implanting of such faculties in humanity.

Taylor's Sources of the Self: The Making of Modern Identity (1989) shows selves as inescapably oriented by the moral sources they acknowledge. It also shows the sense of deeply resonant interiority as fundamental to modern identity. The eighteenth-century moral philosophers occupy an important place in the process by which moral sources are relocated inward. At the same time ordinary life comes to be affirmed as profoundly valuable. The latter view, Taylor points out, is not as obvious as we tend to assume—the record of ancient and medieval thought more often shows some sphere of activity, whether that of the warrior or the philosopher, as intrinsically higher than the everyday. The affirmation sustains what is virtually a moral consensus in the modern world on the values of justice and benevolence: we may not agree about why it is so, or what it would mean to live up to this standard, but we believe that inflicting suffering is wrong and that relieving suffering is good, perhaps even imperative.

The notion of "sentiment" as used in eighteenth-century texts is a crucial element of this modern moral identity. It coordinates complex recognitions of the power of bodily sensations (including emotions), the possibilities of feeling distant from or connected with other human beings, and benevolence as a defining human virtue. A memorable passage from the opening of Smith's *Theory of Moral Sentiments* (1759) binds these elements together to conjure a resolution of the dilemma posed by the increasingly individualist topography of the self:

> As we have no immediate experience of what other men feel, we can form no idea of the manner in which they are affected, but by conceiving what we ourselves should feel in the like situation. Though our brother is upon the rack, as long as we ourselves are at our ease, our sense will never inform us of what he suffers. They never did, and never can, carry us beyond our own person, and it is by the imagination only that we can form any conception of what are his sensations. Neither can that faculty help us to this any other way, than by representing to us what would be our own, if we were in his case. It is the impressions of our own senses only, not those of his, which our imaginations copy. By the imagination we place ourselves in his situation, we conceive ourselves enduring all the same torments, we enter as it were into his body, and become in some measure the same person with him, and thence form some idea of his sensations, and even feel something which, though weaker in degree, is not altogether unlike them. (9)

Smith both recognizes the social and relational character of emotions and focuses on discrete subjectivity, so closely and productively that he is virtually producing the deep interior self. The vicariousness so often criticized in sentimentality is here seen more neutrally as one of its structural elements. The emotion in question is precisely one felt as an identification with another.[2]

The imagination plays a central role in Smith's scenario for sympathy. So it is not surprising that reading was seen as a way to cultivate improving, morally legitimating emotions. Indeed, the extensive English literature of sensibility—Henry Mackenzie's *The Man of Feeling* (1771) is the most programmatic example, but the works of Samuel Richardson and Laurence Sterne are better known—complements the moral philosophers' expositions. Again, it is not surprising that the wide circulation of these narratives provoked the deflating impulse visible in works like Henry Fielding's *Shamela* (1741) and (more complexly) Jane Austen's *Sense and Sensibility* (1811). "Sentimentality" itself originates in the reaction against the elevation of emotional sensitivity to the status of a moral touchstone. Janet Todd tells us that the word "came in as a pejorative term in the 1770's when the idea of sensibility was losing ground"; although the adjective "sentimental" has been used more variously, "by 1800 its use was commonly pejorative" (8, 9). The celebratory and the stigmatizing views of sentiment arise together.

Antisentimentalism has sometimes occluded recognition of the tradition's influence in literature. Yet as Fred Kaplan has shown, the English Victorians continue to draw directly and deeply on moral philosophy; Charles Dickens is sentimental in a much more precise sense than usually acknowledged. Across the Atlantic, Herbert Ross Brown's once-definitive study *The Sentimental Novel in America 1789–1860* (1940) clearly marks the form's philosophical and British roots but treats the connection as dismissively as the novels.[3] Intellectual historians have delineated the profound influence in antebellum America of Smith's inheritors, the Scottish Common Sense philosophers. Certainly some contemporary critics draw on these materials.[4] Most do not; Joanne Dobson's fine recent analysis of the specifically literary qualities of sentimental writing, for example, defines the form in terms of "human connectedness" without ever mentioning moral philosophy. Recovering these connections allows us to read an essay like Laura Wexler's "Tender Violence: Literary Eavesdropping, Domestic Fiction, and Educational Reform"

2. The theatricality of the relations of sympathy in French and English literature of this period has also been anatomized by David Marshall. My thinking here owes much to conversations with Adela Pinch, whose perspective is now available in *Strange Fits of Passion: Epistemologies of Emotion, Hume to Austen* (1996).
3. Making this connection constitutes only a small part of the analysis needed to place any given sentimental fiction in the moment of its production; the fine historical work of Cathy Davidson, essays in *The Culture of Sentiment*, and most recently the work of Elizabeth Barnes offer a multitude of other frameworks for the early American novel.
4. See Philip Fisher, Jay Fliegelman, Gregg Camfield (especially on Stowe's famous injunction to the reader to "feel right"), and Barnes.

(1992) not as a negative assessment of sentimentality but as a contribution to the project of historicizing benevolence.

Only a long, broad view of sentimentality makes it possible to see how many scholars' work contributes to the construction of this object of study, for we are investigating the development of modern subjectivities in their intricate imbrication with belief systems and social structures. Our horizon should include not only Taylor's sources of the self but also Norbert Elias's "civilizing process." Thomas Haskell argues that humanitarianism depends upon a shift in cognitive styles under capitalism. Jean-Christophe Agnew sees the emphasis on "fellow-feeling" as a mark of the distance and potential hostility separating individuals in a world of commodity transactions. Mary Louise Pratt shows sentiment, with its clashing complement science, suturing the self into the new social relations of imperialism. In Peter Hulme's memorable formulation, "Sentimental sympathy began to flow out along the veins of European commerce in search of its victims" (229). On this large landscape, a debate over whether a genre (let alone a novel) is conservative or progressive sounds thin and reductive indeed. The critical edge of the conversation is not lost but redirected to defamiliarize contemporary values like "empathy" as the ritual disavowal of sentimentality never could.

Another consequence of this long view remains to be articulated. So far in this account, sentimentality has been at least as closely linked with men as with women. As subjective and social life are remapped into their modern configurations, emotion is correlated with the private as opposed to the public, and with the feminine as opposed to the masculine. Feminist research over three decades has achieved a rich reconstruction of gender ideologies and women's lives in past eras, and literary critics have drawn on and contributed to that scholarship. But much of it contains an unremarked, confusing elision between sentimentality and domesticity. We have paid little attention to the slippage from Tompkins's "sentimental power" to Mary Kelley's "literary domestics," from Wexler's account of the debate over sentimentality to her subtitle's reference to "domestic fiction." To fail to distinguish the two categories is to become unable to examine the complex historical process that weaves them together. We also need to avoid relying on static and dated conceptions of "separate spheres." Barbara Welter's 1966 essay on the "cult of true womanhood" continues to be cited long after more dynamic accounts have prevailed among historians. The public-private binary can no longer function as an explanation; rather the distinction itself is an important object of analysis. This essay is drawn from a longer study in which I examine the sentimental pedagogy of subjectivity, and

middle-class claims to moral authority, as constitutive elements in
the modern organization of social life into distinct domains.[5] The
domestic sphere is also, of course, the very home of consumer culture, and books are among the commodities that circulate through
that intimate realm. Sentimentality is stigmatized, not only because
it is associated with women, but because the "packaged" quality
of emotion that is so visibly a social construction is a distasteful
reminder that the partition of public and private can never really
separate them.

3. Feeling and Form

How then, on this broad terrain, are we to think about sentimentality in literature, and particularly in American literary history?
I began by affirming the importance of attending to the sheer variety and flexibility of the form (although that is not the task this
essay has undertaken), and I have directed attention to its deployment of the power of sympathy and its embedding in the practice of
domestic reading. We should recognize as well that, in postbellum
America, the literary was often defined *against* sentimentality and
the domestic culture of letters.[6] Prestigious writing gradually and
unevenly became less openly emotional and more ambitiously intellectual, less directly didactic and more conspicuously masculine.
Antisentimentalism is an important part of that story, especially for
literary studies.

Henry James was an articulate spokesman for the reaction against
sentiment. He writes, in an 1867 review, that Rebecca Harding
Davis has made herself "the poet of poor people" but that her material cannot justify her manner:

> She drenches the whole field beforehand with a flood of lach-
> rymose sentimentalism, and riots in the murky vapors which
> rise in consequence of the act. . . . Nothing is more respectable
> on the part of a writer—a novelist—than the intelligent sadness
> which forces itself upon him on the completion of a dramatic
> scheme which is in strict accordance with human life and its
> manifold miseries. But nothing is more trivial than that intel-
> lectual temper which, for ever dissolved in the melting mood,
> goes dripping and trickling over the face of humanity, and wash-
> ing its honest lineaments out of all recognition. . . . Spontaneous

5. The longer version of this essay is part of a work in progress titled "Publishing the Family." It pays particular attention to works by Nancy Armstrong, Mary Ryan, Stuart
Blumin, Karen Halttunen, and Lauren Berlant and discusses the contribution of Jürgen Habermas to understanding the intimate as well as the public sphere.
6. See Richard H. Brodhead, *Cultures of Letters: Scenes of Reading and Writing in
Nineteenth-Century America* (1993), and, for an incisive overview, Brodhead's entry
("Literature and Culture") in *The Columbia Literary History of the United States* (1988).

> pity is an excellent emotion, but there is nothing so hardening as
> to have your pity for ever tickled and stimulated, and nothing so
> debasing as to become an agent between the supply and demand
> of the commodity. (221–22)

We see in this review not only James's youthful vehemence, even
arrogance, but also his sharp recognition of key elements of sentimentality: its association with tears, with humanitarian reform, with
convention and commodification.

   This critique does not in any sense defeat sentimentality (any
more than Fielding's or Austen's did). The form pervasively persists,
beyond this moment and into the present. In the late nineteenth
century its legitimating conventions and capacity for engendering
solidarities were particularly important for writers with minimal
print access, such as the first African-American and Native American
novelists.[7] Complex transformations of those conventions continued; Charles Chesnutt's use of sentimentality in the frame narrative
for *The Conjure Woman* (1899), for example, constitutes a critique
as well as a deployment of the form. Sentimentality remains a powerful element of popular literature, and one can scarcely find a canonical author—including James—who is not drawing on or in dialogue
with the tradition. That continues to be so even when modernism,
with its hostility toward received forms and middle-class culture in
general, intensified the animus against sentimentality.[8]

   Meanwhile the emerging profession of literary scholarship also
defined literature against the domestic and popular and progres-
sively masculinized it—although, given the profound identification
of interiority and literature with the feminine, that masculinization
seems always in need of reassertion. This is not only a matter of
excluding women writers (although, as Paul Lauter among others
has shown, it certainly is that). The whole conceptual landscape of
criticism, particularly the system of genres, is organized according
to gender-inflected values. James wrote against "all those persons,
whether men or women, who pursue literature under the sole guidance of sentimentalism" (222), and in Cleanth Brooks and Robert
Penn Warren's 1946 anthology *Understanding Fiction* (a classic if
forgotten site of New Critical antisentimentalism) the target is not
domestic fiction—those writers have already been excluded from
the table of contents—but the regionalist Bret Harte.

   Brooks and Warren's "Glossary" gives a definition of sentimentality very close to the one with which I began: "Emotional response in

---

7. See, e.g., Richard Yarborough and Susan Bernardin. The phrase "minimal print access"
   is Bernardin's.
8. Suzanne Clark has told this story insightfully, and traced the return of the repressed,
   in *Sentimental Modernism: Women Writers and the Revolution of the Word* (1991).

excess of the occasion; emotional response which has not been prepared for in the story in question" (608). It seems likely that this is
not just an example but a source of the view that sentimental feelings
are simultaneously unreal and overdone; even those who have never
seen the text may have had English teachers—or English teachers
taught by English teachers—influenced by its magisterial pronouncements. Brooks and Warren raise respectful questions about emotion in Dickens ("Is 'The Poor Relation's Story' sentimental? . . .
Does not our acceptance of the story as unsentimental depend, to
some extent at least, on its being grounded firmly in the character?"
[241]) and James Joyce (the story is "Araby"). Harte, on the other
hand, is treated in the vocabulary of pathology used later by Douglas;
about "Tennessee's Partner" they write, "[T]his straining for an emotional effect is one of the surest symptoms that one is dealing with a
case of *sentimentality* (see Glossary)." A sentimental person "weeps at
some trivial occurrence," "lacks a sense of proportion and gets a mor-
bid enjoyment from an emotional debauch for its own sake" (219).
This distaste is in part mapped onto style, in thoroughly gendered
and embodied language (other symptoms are a tendency to "prettify"
language and editorializing, "nudging the reader to respond" [219]),
in part onto characterization.

What Brooks and Warren are most offended by, however, is not
domestic ideology but the story's *failure* to defend family values
when it allows the Partner's loyalty to survive Tennessee's elopement with his wife. Why, they ask, "does Tennessee's Partner forgive Tennessee so easily for the wife-stealing? The matter is never
explained, and we learn nothing of the state of mind which led the
partner to the decision. In other words, Bret Harte has dodged the
real psychological issue of his story" (215). On this masculine literary landscape, the story that provokes their most vehement condemnation focuses on love between men, and it fails to confine
emotion to its proper sphere. The Partner displays the suffering,
sentimental male body that Eve Sedgwick considers "the exemplary
instance of the sentimental" in late-nineteenth- and early-twentieth-
century literature, a character that, by her account, "dramatizes,
embodies for an audience that both desires and cathartically identifies with him, a struggle of masculine identity with emotions or
physical stigmata stereotyped as feminine" (146).[9] Our twentieth-
century usages of sentimentality are routed through not only the
paradoxes of public/private but also the double bind of homo/
heterosexual identity. Both the inseparability of binaries I have

9. I would argue that masculine- and feminine-inflected versions of sentiment coexist for
   much longer than Sedgwick indicates but would agree that the formation she describes
   takes on a particularly vexed power in this period.

already noted and the observable nature of such polemics show that Sedgwick is right in proposing that "there isn't a differentiation to be *made* between sentimentality and its denunciation" (153).

Various tropes have focused sentimental discourses in various periods; Sedgwick's discussion of the sentimental man is complemented by Ann Cvetkovich's study of the suffering woman in Victorian fiction, and I would suggest that the equivalent for our own moment may be the figure of the endangered child. Again, my task here is not developing such specific analyses but delineating a productive conceptual landscape for them.

The view of the form that I am proposing does not generate definitive answers to the question of whether something is sentimental, or not, an inquiry that is in principle unanswerable. Rather, the process by which one creates and evaluates possible responses generates the social meaning of the category. Nor can any account of the form end discussion and produce a consensus for a single definition of sentimentality. We can organize answers to the question "what is sentimentality?" like this. Most broadly—when we call an artifact or gesture sentimental, we are pointing to its use of some established convention to evoke emotion; we mark a moment when the discursive processes that construct emotion become visible. Most commonly—we are recognizing that a trope from the immense repertory of sympathy and domesticity has been deployed; we recognize the presence of at least some fragmentary element of an intellectual and literary tradition. Most narrowly—we are asserting that literary works belong to a genre in which those conventions and tropes are central. But that does not undermine the importance of the recognition that sentimental works consistently engage us in the intricate impasse of the public and private, proclaiming their separation and at the same time demonstrating their inseparability. As emotion, embodied thought that animates cognition with the recognition of the self's engagement; as sympathy, firmly based in the observer's body and imaginatively linking it to another's; as domestic culture, in the peculiar intimacy of the print commodity; sentimentality at the same time locates us in our embodied and particular selves and takes us out of them.

WORKS CITED

Agnew, Jean-Christophe. *Worlds Apart: The Market and the Theater in Anglo-American Thought, 1550–1750.* New York: Cambridge UP, 1986.

Appadurai, Arjun. "Topographies of the Self: Praise and Emotion in Hindu India." Lutz and Abu-Lughod 92–112.

Armstrong, Nancy. *Desire and Domestic Fiction: A Political History of the Novel.* New York: Oxford UP, 1987.

Barnes, Elizabeth. *States of Sympathy: Seduction and Democracy in the American Novel.* New York: Columbia UP, 1997.

Berlant, Lauren. "The Female Complaint." *Social Text* 19/20 (1988): 237–59.

———. "The Female Woman: Fanny Fern and the Form of Sentiment." *American Literary History* 3 (1991): 429–54. Rpt. in Samuels 265–82.

Bernardin, Susan. "On the Meeting Grounds of Sentiment: Alice Callahan's *Wynema* and Foundational Native American Women's Literature." Nineteenth-Century American Women Writers in the Twenty-first Century, Hartford, Connecticut, 1 June 1996.

Blumin, Stuart M. *The Emergence of the Middle Class: Social Experience in the American City, 1760–1900.* Cambridge: Cambridge UP, 1989.

Brodhead, Richard H. *Cultures of Letters: Scenes of Reading and Writing in Nineteenth-Century America.* Chicago: U of Chicago P, 1993.

———. "Literature and Culture." *The Columbia Literary History of the United States.* Ed. Emory Elliott. New York: Columbia UP, 1988. 467–81.

Brooks, Cleanth, Jr., and Robert Penn Warren. *Understanding Fiction.* New York: Crofts, 1946.

Brown, Herbert Ross. *The Sentimental Novel in America 1789–1860.* 1940. New York: Pageant, 1959.

Camfield, Gregg. *Sentimental Twain: Samuel Clemens in the Maze of Moral Philosophy.* Philadelphia: U of Pennsylvania P, 1994.

Clark, Suzanne. *Sentimental Modernism: Women Writers and the Revolution of the Word.* Bloomington: Indiana UP, 1991.

Cvetkovich, Ann. *Mixed Feelings: Feminism, Mass Culture, and Victorian Sensationalism.* New Brunswick: Rutgers UP, 1992.

Damasio, Antonio R. *Descartes' Error: Emotion, Reason and the Human Brain.* New York: Putnam's, 1994.

Davidson, Cathy. *Revolution and the Word: The Rise of the Novel in America.* New York: Oxford UP, 1986.

Dobson, Joanne. "The American Renaissance Reenvisioned." *The (Other) American Traditions: Nineteenth-Century Women Writers.* Ed. Joyce W. Warren. New Brunswick: Rutgers UP, 1994.

———. "Reclaiming Sentimental Literature." *American Literature* 69 (1997): 263–88.

Douglas, Ann. *The Feminization of American Culture.* 1977. New York: Anchor-Doubleday, 1988.

Elias, Norbert. *The Civilizing Process: The History of Manners [and] State Formation and Civilization.* 1939. Trans. Edmund Jephcott. Cambridge: Blackwell, 1994.

Ellsworth, Phoebe C. "Sense, Culture and Sensibility." Kitayama and Markus 23–50.

Fisher, Philip. *Hard Facts: Setting and Form in the American Novel.* New York: Oxford UP, 1987.

Fliegelman, Jay. *Declaring Independence: Jefferson, Natural Language, and the Culture of Performance*. Stanford: Stanford UP, 1993.

Gordon, Steven L. "The Sociology of Sentiments and Emotion." *Social Psychology: Sociological Perspectives*. Ed. Morris Rosenberg and Ralph H. Turner. New York: Basic, 1981. 562–92.

Habermas, Jürgen. *The Structural Transformation of the Public Sphere: An Inquiry into a Category of Bourgeois Society*. 1962. Trans. Thomas Burger and Frederick Lawrence. Cambridge: MIT P, 1989.

Halttunen, Karen. *Confidence Men and Painted Women: A Study of Middle-Class Culture in America, 1830–1870*. New Haven: Yale UP, 1982.

Haskell, Thomas L. "Capitalism and the Origins of the Humanitarian Sensibility, Parts I and II." *American Historical Review* 90 (1985): 339–61, 547–66.

Hochschild, Arlie Russell. *The Managed Heart: Commercialization of Human Feeling*. Berkeley: U of California P, 1983.

Hulme, Peter. *Colonial Encounters: Europe and the Native Caribbean, 1492–1797*. New York: Methuen, 1986.

James, Henry. Rev. of *Waiting for the Verdict,* by Rebecca Harding Davis. *The Nation* 21 Nov. 1867. Rpt. in *Literary Criticism: Essays on Literature; American Writers; English Writers*. Ed. Leon Edel. New York: Library of America, 1984. 218–22.

Johnson, Richard. "What Is Cultural Studies Anyway?" *Social Text* 6 (1987): 38–80.

Kaplan, Fred. *Sacred Tears: Sentimentality in Victorian Literature*. Princeton: Princeton UP, 1987.

Kasson, John F. *Rudeness and Civility: Manners in Nineteenth-Century Urban America*. New York: Hill and Wang, 1990.

Kelley, Mary. *Private Woman, Public Stage: Literary Domesticity in Nineteenth-Century America*. New York: Oxford UP, 1984.

Kitayama, Shinobu, and Hazel Rose Markus, eds. *Emotion and Culture: Empirical Studies of Mutual Influence*. Washington: American Psychological Assoc., 1994.

———. "Introduction to Cultural Psychology and Emotion Research." Kitayama and Markus 1–19.

Lauter, Paul. *Canons and Contexts*. New York: Oxford UP, 1991.

Lutz, Catherine A., and Lila Abu-Lughod, eds. *Language and the Politics of Emotion*. New York: Cambridge UP, 1990.

Marshall, David. *The Surprising Effects of Sympathy: Marivaux, Diderot, Rousseau, and Mary Shelley*. Chicago: U of Chicago P, 1988.

Oxenhandler, Neal. "The Changing Concept of Literary Emotion: A Selective History." *New Literary History* 20 (1988): 105–21.

Pinch, Adela. *Strange Fits of Passion: Epistemologies of Emotion, Hume to Austen*. Stanford: Stanford UP, 1996.

Pratt, Mary Louise. *Imperial Eyes: Travel Writing and Transculturation*. New York: Routledge, 1992.

Romero, Lora. *Home Fronts: Domesticity and Its Critics in the Antebellum United States*. Durham: Duke UP, 1997.

Rosaldo, Michelle Z. "Toward An Anthropology of Self and Feeling." *Culture Theory: Essays on Mind, Self, and Emotion*. Ed. Richard A. Shweder and Robert A. LeVine. New York: Cambridge UP, 1984. 137–57.

Ryan, Mary P. *Cradle of the Middle Class: The Family in Oneida County, New York, 1790–1865*. Cambridge: Cambridge UP, 1981.

Sánchez-Eppler, Karen. *Touching Liberty: Abolition, Feminism, and the Politics of the Body*. Berkeley: U of California P, 1993.

Sedgwick, Eve Kosofsky. *Epistemology of the Closet*. Berkeley: U of California P, 1990.

Smith, Adam. *The Theory of Moral Sentiments*. 1759. Vol. 1 of *The Glasgow Edition of the Works and Correspondence of Adam Smith*. Ed. D. D. Raphael and A. L. Macfie. Oxford: Clarendon P, 1976.

Taylor, Charles. *Sources of the Self: The Making of the Modern Identity*. Cambridge: Harvard UP, 1989.

Todd, Janet. *Sensibility: An Introduction*. New York: Methuen, 1986.

Tompkins, Jane. *Sensational Designs: The Cultural Work of American Fiction 1790–1860*. New York: Oxford UP, 1985.

Welter, Barbara. "The Cult of True Womanhood, 1820–1860." *American Quarterly* 18 (1966): 151–74. Rpt. in *Dimity Convictions: The American Woman in the Nineteenth Century*. Athens: Ohio UP, 1976. 21–41.

Wexler, Laura. "Tender Violence: Literary Eavesdropping, Domestic Fiction, and Educational Reform."

Wierzbicka, Anna. "Emotion, Language, and Cultural Scripts." Kitayama and Markus 133–96.

Yarborough, Richard. Introduction. *Contending Forces: A Romance Illustrative of Negro Life North and South*. By Pauline E. Hopkins. New York: Oxford UP, 1988.

Zajonc, R. B., and Daniel McIntosh. "Emotions Research: Some Promising Questions and Some Questionable Promises." *Psychological Science* 3 (1992): 70–74.

LAUREN COATS

Grave Matters: Susanna Rowson's Sentimental Geographies[†]

Without the infinite dead, the living are but unimportant bits.
—W. E. B. DuBois, *The World and Africa*

Let the whiteness of bones atone to forgetfulness.
—T. S. Eliot, "Ash Wednesday"

I. Generic Tales and Unexceptional American Geography

The plot of Susanna Rowson's wildly popular sentimental novel *Charlotte Temple* most obviously concerns the seduction of its titular character. I argue, however, that the novel takes as its subject and its pedagogical object the education of its readers in geographical knowledge. In other words, this sentimental novel is an exemplary early American geographical primer. Rowson organizes the novel's plot geographically: seduction obtains through the continuing physical removal of Charlotte from her proper place. Young Charlotte's seduction is effected by transporting her across the ocean from England to the colonies on the eve (or in the midst of) the Revolutionary War. Her first "fall" is to trespass beyond her school's grounds without permission to meet her future seducer, Montraville. She then transgresses propriety by joining him in his carriage, which carries her to a ship, which transports her far away from family, home, and nation. Rowson thus correlates Charlotte's moral downfall to a series of geographical dislocations: Charlotte's increasingly marginal identity and increasingly vulnerable position are both metaphorized and materialized in her geographical removes.[1] Indeed, Charlotte's seclusion and dislocation—for instance, when she is isolated in a New York country house—are even integral to the plot of seduction. Only by virtue of this seclusion can her seduction and separation from family transpire.

Despite Rowson's geographical plotting of seduction, few of the landscapes are at all memorable or recognizably specific. For a work so structured by place, the novel contains surprisingly few geographic details. We know there is a cloistered English boarding school at which Charlotte's seduction first is staged, a ship that crosses the Atlantic transporting the seduced Charlotte from Britain to America, an isolated house just outside of New York City, and finally, the

---

† Reprinted by permission of the author.
1. Much like Charlotte's predecessor in peripatetic captivity, Mary Rowlandson, whose eponymous narrative is structured through a series of numbered "removes."

home of poor strangers where Charlotte dies: but none of these sites is drawn in any detail. These places are utterly generic.[2] In this respect, the novel's landscapes mirror the novel's characters. They are, like Charlotte herself, unexceptional.

The obvious connection between place and seduction within the novel has enabled place-based interpretations of it. Specifically, critics tend to interpret the novel as a commentary on the marginalization of women from the new political order of the United States and the recodification of a paternal democratic order through the surveillance of sentimentality.[3] This tendency to interpret Rowson's novel as a narrative about a specific place, namely the United States, provokes cognitive dissonance when read alongside the utterly generic, or unexceptional, worlds of this early American sentimental novel.[4] How can we reconcile the incongruity between the genericness of the sentimental landscapes and the specificity of the U.S. national space? This incongruity is only deepened by Rowson's own transatlantic life, career, and readership, all of which destabilize the U.S. frame of the novel's interpretation. The novel, with its enduring popularity over the decades, has lasted through multiple reconfigurations of U.S. and British nationalism. The nonnational sociospatial forms of the novel come into view when the novel is removed from the single historical moment of the late eighteenth century and the emergence of the United States and instead is read through a hermeneutics of the ongoing historical process of manufacturing place that does not stop with the end of the novel but continues through the spatial practices of its readers.

I have quickly mapped this unexceptional diegetic geography and the place-specific interpretation of the novel as about the emergence of the United States to contrast a particular site that has emerged in response to the novel. The most memorable and distinctive place of *Charlotte Temple* is one that is not in the novel itself. Rather, it is a "real" grave in Trinity Churchyard in New York City. As Cathy Davidson describes in her introduction to the novel, "other

2. Some critics have castigated the novel on precisely these grounds—its shallowness and flatness are read as the marks of Rowson's inferior artistic talent. My argument attempts to relocate the discussion to the realm of the meaning and effect of such flatness, inspired in part by the incontrovertible fact that many people, despite what critics have said ("for what," Davidson reminds us, "do critics know?"), found the novel quite good enough. Susanna Rowson, *Charlotte Temple*, ed. Cathy N. Davidson (New York: Oxford University Press, 1986), xiv. All page references to this novel are hereafter cited parenthetically.
3. For readings of the novel as a text that participates in and responds to the construction of the United States, see Julia A. Stern, *The Plight of Feeling: Sympathy and Dissent in the Early American Novel* (Chicago: University of Chicago Press, 1997), 84. See also Cathy N. Davidson, *Revolution and the Word: The Rise of the Novel in America* (New York: Oxford University Press, 1986).
4. This interpretive tendency is but one strain of the traditional story of American place in which the particularity of the American landscape and the experience thereof breeds the particularity, or exceptionality, of America and especially of the United States.

famous graves in this cemetery, such as those of Alexander Hamilton and Robert Fulton, never attracted as many visitors as did the tomb of Rowson's fictional character" (xiv). In the novel itself, Rowson narrates that the repentant Montraville, who seduced Charlotte and is thus cast as instrumental in her death, "to the end of his life was subject to severe fits of melancholy, and while he remained in New-York frequently retired to the church-yard, where he would weep over the grave, and regret the untimely fate of the lovely Charlotte Temple" (89). Throughout the nineteenth century, readers made the same ritual trip to Charlotte's grave in Trinity Churchyard. This ritual of mourning, enacted by readers who memorialized Charlotte through pilgrimages to her gravesite, instantiates outside the bounds of the novel a "real" place that, I want to suggest, is in productive tension with the placelessness that characterizes the novel's diegetic geographies. How are we to read this grave, whose very particularity seems to counter the repetitive, generic energy that fuels sentimental literature? In this essay I consider what is being memorialized, what place is inscribed, through the practice of visiting the fictional Charlotte Temple's grave. More particularly, I focus on the pilgrimages to Charlotte's grave to think about how unexceptional places can be transformed into sites of exception and exceptionality. The questions I want to raise are why it is that Charlotte's grave has been read as a place that is particularly conducive to such a transformation and whether such a reading is sustainable when the spatial practices of grave visits and the actual site of the grave are made part of the archive.

The places associated with and narrated in *Charlotte Temple*, in their tension between the generic and the exceptional, interrogate the possibilities of representing the unexceptional, the unparticular, the generic. The tension between place and non-place that is the spatial world of *Charlotte Temple* haunts the seemingly straightforward, naturalized-through-convention world of the American sentimental genre and American landscape. I turn to *Charlotte Temple* and the sentimental novel because this genre, particularly this novel, raises the related questions of how to build particularity out of a generic universe and how to locate sites that guarantee representation for those written out of a particular spatial configuration (such as the nation). Whereas the production of generic and national space can obscure the process of its own production by making the process seem natural or inevitable, I argue that *Charlotte Temple* and the ways readers responded spatially to the novel call attention to how place is manufactured out of placelessness.

I first read *Charlotte Temple* as a geographical primer to consider how sentimentality functions as a mode of determining place. I then turn to the pilgrimages to Charlotte's grave to think about the ways in which this empty grave shapes, and at times surpasses, national imaginings. Charlotte Temple's grave marks the presence of an absence, an empty place that, counter to the genealogy of American geographic exceptionalism, suggests that the nation did not always fill the horizon for the subjective or literary experience of the New World. But then, the mechanical reproductions of these hauntings through the various industries that supported the many pilgrimages to Charlotte's grave, which were part of the larger structure of nineteenth-century cult(ure)s of mourning, suggest that Charlotte's ghost is not necessarily a disruptive presence. My essay thus ends by considering what a pilgrimage to a real, (probably) empty grave of a fictional character signifies and what sociospatial form it inscribes.

II. The Pedagogy of Sentimental Cartography

Charlotte Temple, first published in England in 1791 and then in the United States in 1794, appeared at the same time that the literary marketplace witnessed a proliferation of geographical texts. Mathew Carey, who published the novel in the United States, also published some of the first "American" geographies, such as those by the Scotsman William Guthrie, whose various geographies were among the most circulated in the middle to late eighteenth century. Carey reworked Guthrie's textbooks for an American market by having them updated with American content in *American Atlas* (1795). Carey chose Jedidiah Morse, the "father of American geography," to author this updated section, and soon Morse wrote his own American geographies, which were published jointly by Carey and Isaiah Thomas.[5] "[O]nly the Bible and Noah Webster's spelling books," Martin Brückner cites, "were more popular than Morse's geographies" in the late-eighteenth-century United States.[6] Many critics document an explosion of geographical texts in the early national period: from maps to geography textbooks to place names in spellers, the construction of an identifiable U.S. national space became an early national literary project.[7] Rowson herself contributed to this pedagogical and geographical project: two of the six textbooks she authored were geographies.[8] Rowson was also an avid reader of peda-

5. John Rennie Short, *Representing the Republic: Mapping the United States 1600–1900* (London: Reaktion Books, 2001), 97–99 and 116.
6. Martin Brückner, "Lessons in Geography: Maps, Spellers, and Other Grammars of Nationalism in the Early Republic," *American Quarterly* 51.2 (1999): 320.
7. In addition to Martin Brückner and John Rennie Short, see Myra Jehlen, *American Incarnation: The Individual, the Nation, and the Continent* (Cambridge: Harvard University Press, 1986) and Robert Lawson-Peebles, *Landscape and Written Expression in Revolutionary America: The World Turned Upside Down* (New York: Cambridge University Press, 1988).
8. Kay Ferguson Ryals, "America, Romance, and the Fate of the Wandering Woman: The Case of Charlotte Temple," *Women, America, and Movement: Narratives of Relocation,*

gogical geographies, no doubt as part of her activities as the founder of Boston's Young Ladies' Academy in 1797.[9]

Geography was something of a family business for Rowson. Lieutenant John Montresor, Rowson's cousin, served as an engineer in the British army and, in that position, produced multiple maps of the American northeast coast (as did Montresor's father, also an engineer stationed in the British colonies in North America). Montresor was better known to Rowson's readers as a possible model for Rowson's fictional Colonel Montraville—an assertion that has never been proven or disproven by the historical record—but his geographical products have gone unremarked.[1] One of Montresor's maps of New York has been hailed as "one of the most detailed maps of New York region issued during the revolutionary era"[2] and "probably the best overall depiction of the town and environs produced by the British. It is very detailed, and was used and highly regarded, by both sides in the Revolutionary War"[3] (see Figure 1). Against the "accuracy" and "detail" of the Montresor maps, the ostensible unexceptionality of Rowson's geographies seems incongruous and, at first, renders Rowson's own production of place even more generic and seemingly unmappable. However, geographical productions differ in kind from those of Montresor and other cartographers and geographers of the day. *Charlotte Temple* privileges a supplemental geographical knowledge to that contained in contemporary geographical textbooks. Rather than the additive nature of a complement, Rowson's novel maintains the critical quality of a supplement. As a supplement, the novel exposes what falls into the gaps of Montresor's geometric cartographies.

On the surface, geography textbooks and other narratives like the novel share formal similarities because they both depict places

ed. Susan L. Roberson (Columbia: University of Missouri Press, 1998), 104. Rowson's geography textbooks are *An Abridgement of Universal Geography* (1805) and *Youth's First Steps in Geography* (1818). See Patricia L. Parker, *Susanna Rowson* (Boston: Twayne Publishers, 1986), 103–15.

9. Ryals, 103.

1. See Patricia L. Parker's biography, *Susanna Rowson*, for more information on Rowson's family connection to Montresor, esp. 50–52. Parker suspects that Rowson interacted with the Montresors in 1778, when the Haswells and the Montresors both moved back to England from America. It is likely that Rowson was familiar with the cartographic productions of the Montresors. Francis W. Halsey's 1905 edition of *Charlotte Temple* included a partial reprint of one of Montresor's maps in the detailed prefatory materials.

2. Seymour I. Schwartz and Ralph E. Ehrenberg, *The Mapping of America* (New York: Harry N. Abrams, Inc., 1980), 186.

3. *Engineer John Montresor*, The First Foot Guards. Available: footguards.tripod.com/01ABOUT/montresor/000montresor.htm. See also J. B. Harley, Barbara Bartz Petchenik, and Lawrence W. Towner, *Mapping the American Revolutionary War* (Chicago: University of Chicago Press, 1978), and Margaret Beck Pritchard and Henry G. Taliaferro, *Degrees of Latitude: Mapping Colonial America* (Williamsburg, Va., and New York: Colonial Williamsburg Foundation and Harry Abrams, 2002), esp. 28–30 and 212–17.

textually, in what Brückner calls "word maps."[4] The well-established genre of travel and exploration narratives, from Richard Hakluyt's multivolume *The Principal Navigations, Voyages, Traffiques and Discoveries of the English Nation* (1599) to John Filson's *The Discovery, Settlement and Present State of Kentucke* (1784) to William Bartram's *Travels through North and South Carolina, Georgia, East and West Florida* (1794), used words—rather than pictures—to render strange landscapes familiar to their readers. Many of the early geographies contained few maps. For instance Morse's *American Geography*, published in 1789 (the same year as George Washington's inauguration) contained only two.[5] The narrative quality of many late-eighteenth-century geographies suggests that geographical knowledge at this time was not encapsulated within the geometries of the burgeoning map trade. It was not limited to maps but was disseminated and discussed through a variety of mediums.

This formal similarity of Rowson's novel to geographical textbooks and other spatial narratives obscures the qualitative difference between Rowson's geographical insights and those of her fellow geography-minded authors. This difference does not emerge in Rowson's most obviously geographic work: her 1805 textbook, *An Abridgement of Universal Geography*. Indeed, she copied much of this work from Jedediah Morse's *American Geography*.[6] As geographer John Short describes, "the national geographies were full of moral injunctions, social criticism and policy directives," much like novels.[7] Considering her tendency to copy, it is no surprise that Rowson's textbook—like those of her peers—offered prose description of places, moments of moralizing, snippets of history, and colorful comments on inhabitants. Morse's *American Geography*, and thus also Rowson's *Abridgement*, tend to evaluate place. For instance, Morse, a Congregationalist minister, had a severe view of what he saw as the unbridled "licentiousness" of New Orleans, and he made it clear that New England was a model location. Rowson, too, evaluated places. Both geographies proceed methodically through the world, describing in turn each continent and each nation or state therein. Even when assessing the relative value or quality of the places described, the prose tends toward descriptive assertions, such as

4. Martin Brückner, "Geography, Reading, and the World of Novels in the Early Republic," *Early America Re-Explored: New Readings in Colonial, Early National, and Antebellum Culture*, ed. Klaus H. Schmidt and Fritz Fleischmann (New York: Peter Lang, 2000), 389. In this essay, Brückner elucidates the connection between novels and geographies. Although my argument takes its lead from his contention that these texts should be read together and geographically, I differentiate between the spatial sensibilities created in different genres.
5. Short, *Representing the Republic*, 113.
6. Marion Rust, *Prodigal Daughters: Susanna Rowson's Early American Women* (Chapel Hill, N.C.: Omohundro Institute, 2008), 14.
7. Short, *Representing the Republic*, 16.

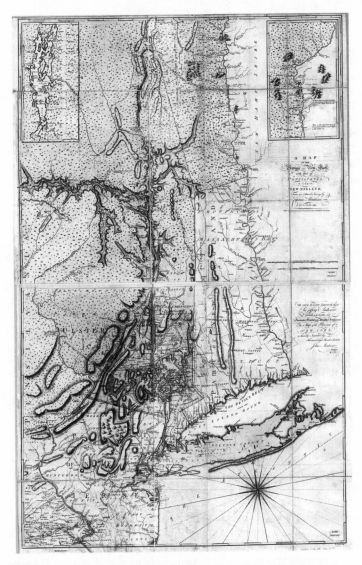

Figure 1. A Map of the Province of New York, with Part of Pensilvania, and New England, from an Actual Survey by Captain Montrésor, Engineer, 1775. P. Andrews, Sculp. American Memory, Library of Congress. Available: hdl.loc.gov/loc.gmd/g3800.ar106702, 7 Sept. 2006. The map was first published in 1775; the copy shown here is a 1777 reprint.

this assessment of Europe: "There are two circumstances which unite to give Europe the superiority over the rest of the world. First, the happy temperature of its climate, no part of it lying within the torrid zone; and secondly, the great variety of its surface."[8] Here, as throughout, Rowson (following Morse) models a climatological assessment of place that naturalizes the hierarchy of places with Europe at the apex. Even when Rowson dwells in greater detail on the defining affects of a population, such as when she describes the Germans as "a frank, honest, hospitable people" known for their "[i]ndustry, application, and perseverance,"[9] such character seems to derive from the physical landscape, as the passages directly preceding this assessment are devoted to describing the physical terrain and natural resources of the country.

Although some geography textbook writers such as Morse included moral claims as part of the geographical information they disseminated, Rowson makes a point to distinguish sentimental understandings as necessary in their own right. Yet her textbooks' dry accounting of the world's terrain and the lack of difference between Rowson's geography textbook and those of her peers complicates her assertion that sentiment is central to her geographical, pedagogical project. Considering, too, that in the late eighteenth and early nineteenth centuries travel narratives influenced by Laurence Sterne's 1765 *A Sentimental Journey through France and Italy* filled the literary marketplace, Rowson's textbook is striking in its lack of sentimentality. But in the preface to *An Abridgement of Universal Geography*, she writes that "I am of opinion that instructors of every kind, particularly those who give their labours publicity, are strictly accountable to the highest of all tribunals, for the sentiments they inculcate. . . . If . . . the minds of the rising generation are not improved by my exertions, I have been studious that their imagination should not be misled, or their judgments perverted, by the dissemination of absurd opinions, or corrupt and pernicious principles." Rowson casts right sentiment, learning to feel properly, as an instrumental form of knowledge that is central to the functioning of "morality, religion, or good government."[1] Unlike Morse, who desires his readers to learn simply what places are bad and what are good, Rowson suggests that sentiment is both ontological and epistemological, a form of knowing and a form of knowledge. Sentimental knowledge of place is a *process* of spatial understanding, rather than something to be learned by rote.

In light of her preface, in which she avers a commitment to a proper sentimental education, what can we make of Rowson's dry,

8. Susanna Rowson, *An Abridgement of Universal Geography Together with Sketches of History Designed for the Use of Schools and Academies in the United States* (Boston: 1805), 15.
9. Rowson, *An Abridgement of Universal Geography*, 64.
1. Rowson, *An Abridgement of Universal Geography*, iv.

largely copied textbook? I would argue the geographical textbook is only one part of Rowson's dedication to the training of women in spatial knowledge, not surprising from a woman who ran the Young Ladies' Academy. The necessity of geographical learning is essential to Rowson, so essential that it is not only disseminated through textbooks but also through the world of the sentimental novel. The sentimental novel functions pedagogically as a necessary supplement to geographical education. Textbooks alone will not situate readers in the world; such reckonings require the pedagogy of the sentimental novel. Rowson's investment in sentimental understanding suggests the power of the sentimental novel to serve as a geographical pedagogy, as instruction in how not only to know about territorial forms but also to overlay them with emotional knowledge of where one belongs in the world.

Rowson, that is, manifests a different spatial sensibility because she supplements geographical knowledge acquired through textbooks with novels like *Charlotte Temple*. The supplemental quality of Rowson's spatial sensibility argues for the necessary inculcation of an affective geography that criticizes rather than complements the study of geometric geography. Rowson's sentimentalization of geography sets her works apart from even the moralizing work of Morse. Mapping places not by longitude or latitude but by affection and sentiment, the novel offers an alternative geography. Sentimental education is necessary to spatial epistemologies because it makes visible an obscured spatial order: one that is not merely about seeing space but about living in it. Rather than the panoptic or bird's-eye view that characterizes most maps of the time, Rowson emphasizes the everyday, on-the-ground vantage point of those who live in and walk through those places shown on maps.[2] The geography that emerges in Rowson's novel is not the clear demarcations that mark boundaries on cartographic productions, such as those on Montresor's map of New York. Rather, her experiential and dynamic cartography charts what effects these boundaries have on those who travel across them and, in so doing, suggests how to negotiate them. That is, Rowson's novel converts geographical knowledge into spatial practice.

Rowson's delineation of a sentimental geography in her novel differentiates her geographical sensibility from those she copied in her textbook by making the accuracy of the geometries of geographical knowledge only one part of her larger geographical project. Rowson's textbook makes clear that she, like Morse, believes that rote knowledge of place matters. Indeed, she frequently had her students at the

2. See Michel de Certeau, *The Practice of Everyday Life*, trans. Steven Rendall (Berkeley: University of California Press, 1988 [1984], esp. "Walking in the City," 92–93.

academy deliver orations on the "principles of nautical navigation."[3] In her novel, however, she makes clear that spatial practice matters, too. *Charlotte Temple* insists that a place as depicted on a map or in a textbook does not represent the different experiences of that place. Montresor's 1767 map of New York was instrumental for the British army's operations in that area (see Figure 2). Rowson's novel poses the question of what good such a map would do for Charlotte: had she had that map in hand, would she have navigated the foreign shore with any better result? Rowson's novel suggests what to do when passing these rationally knowable lines of demarcation and what to do when the rational overlay does not fit the actual spatial experience. Rowson's sentimental, pedagogical geographies are most evidently inscribed through the contrast between Charlotte's position when she arrives in the New World and that of her married neighbor, Mrs. Beauchamp. When Charlotte is removed from her ship cabin to the American shore, Montraville, her seducer, ensconces her in a "small house a few miles from New-York" (50). Charlotte's seclusion forces her dependence on Montraville. Her unnatural alliance with him—that is, her status as *femme couverte*, but without the body of a husband into which to be subsumed—is geographically figured through the ways in which her reclusive situation makes her reliant on Montraville and removes her from other sociospatial networks, such as those of camaraderie and kinship. Charlotte is already a ghostly figure insofar as she has been "incorporated" (to use Sir William Blackstone's definition of the covered woman) into Montraville, because their union is not sanctified by marriage. Blackstone's language emphasizes the problems for those like Charlotte who are incorporated into an absence or a lack rather than into another body. Even before Charlotte's death, then, her incorporation into absence— her dependence on a man who is neither husband nor father—figures her as a ghost in that she becomes invisible within cartographies of womanhood, particularly of virtuous republican womanhood. This paradoxical incorporation, which might be better termed a disincorporation, makes Charlotte's fatal walk to New York read even more like a ghost walk. Charlotte, kicked out of her country house since Montraville (duped by the duplicitous Belcour) has abandoned her and left her penniless, is barely even visible, through a snow that "fell so fast," in her "undress robe of plain white muslin, . . . wet through, and a thin black cloak and bonnet." It is evident that Charlotte's presence is "improper," and this impropriety is rendered in the increasing illegibility of her position in space (80). Charlotte's increasing invisibility suggests that it is not just her pregnancy-out-of-wedlock

3. Ryals, 104.

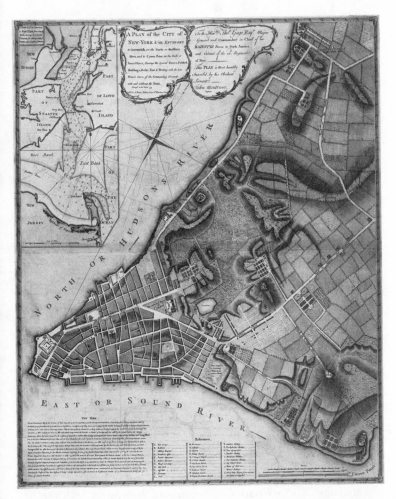

Figure 2. "A Plan of the City of New-York & Its Environs" John Montresor, "A Plan of the City of New-York & Its Environs" (London: A. Dury, c. 1775). *North Ameri[c]an Atlas.* Bethlehem, PA: Special Collections, Lehigh University Libraries. Used with permission of Special Collections, Lehigh University Libraries. This c. 1775 version is a reprint, with some modifications, of one first printed and published in 1767 (the major change is that the printer, perhaps with the hopes of making the map seem current, changed the year that it was surveyed from 1766 to 1775). See W. P. Cumming, "The Montresor-Ratzer-Sauthier Sequence of Maps of New York City, 1766–76." *Imago Mundi* 31 (1979): 55–65.

that shadows her. Rather, Charlotte is invisible because she has left not just the moral but the social path.

Charlotte's snow-covered tracks emphasize the obscurity of her path. As Charlotte disappears into a white void, so does Rowson define Charlotte's place throughout the novel by tropes of absence and illegibility, translating Charlotte's social position into a spatial location. Charlotte lacks any means of social connection: because of both the machinations of blackmailed servants who misdirect her letters and her exile from "proper" society, she cannot participate in traditional circuits of letters and social visits. As Rowson describes, Charlotte is a "poor solitary being in the midst of surrounding multitudes" (51). In contrast to Charlotte's ghostly position, Rowson describes in Mrs. Beauchamp a fully embodied (and "incorporated") woman who is similarly geographically situated. Neighbors, the two both live in country houses just outside of New York, but they inhabit much different sociospatial positions. Mrs. Beauchamp, the "mild and engaging" and eminently proper wife, enjoys her country home; she "loved not the hurry and bustle of a city, and had prevailed on her husband to take a house a few miles from New-York" (56). Unlike Charlotte, she can move about both freely and safely; her continued mobility, conferred by her legitimate, married status, makes her, within this novel at least, not at all the captive that Charlotte is, and her mobility calls attention to the irony that Charlotte's travels across an ocean have culminated not in freedom or expanded geographical horizons, but in confinement. Immobilized, Charlotte spends her time as captive to Montraville because he "had brought [her] from all her connections" (50). Deprived of these connections, her only other option, as we have seen, is a fatal mobility in which she flees her captivity but is lost, alone, and exposed with no safe harbor in sight.

Although the initial geographic similarities between the two women and their country homes may seem to indicate that Mrs. Beauchamp is, like Charlotte, "bound and determined" within the ideological territory of home, family, and femininity, the novel presses the reader to distinguish between the two women.[4] Differ-

---

4. Sentiment, then, here serves to differentiate rather than to associate. Elizabeth Barnes discusses how texts of this time tend to model "affectionate marriage, . . . [that] obscures the violation of democratic principles through models of affinity that would subsume one person's identity in the identity of another." Rowson's application of sentimental geography to recognize rather than elide differences between the two women suggests that this sentimental, differential logic could apply by extrapolation to the "affectionate marriage" of Mr. and Mrs. Beauchamp to differentiate Mrs. from Mr. Beauchamp. See Elizabeth Barnes, States of Sympathy: Seduction and Democracy in the American Novel (New York: Columbia University Press, 1997), 11. The phrase bound and determined echoes Chris Castiglia to emphasize the ways in which genre and gender locate Charlotte. See Chris Castiglia, Bound and Determined: Captivity, Culture-Crossing, and White Womanhood from Mary Rowlandson to Patty Hearst (Chicago: University of Chicago Press, 1996).

entiating along matrimonial lines—Mrs. Beauchamp enjoys the
privilege of a good marriage, Charlotte enjoys not much at all, and
certainly not marriage—underscores their contrásting spatial and
social opportunities despite their geographical proximity.

Rowson uses rhetoric inflected by Christian theology and late-
eighteenth-century matrimonial custom to further differentiate
between these two women. This language fosters knowledge of sentimental geography, knowledge that enables distinction between
people who seem to be in the same geometric geography, such as
Mrs. Beauchamp and Charlotte. The language of sentiment, in other
words, makes visible what cannot be seen on the traditional map.
By marking Charlotte by what cannot be seen, Rowson creates Charlotte as a ghost. In teaching her readers to "see" those differences,
Rowson makes Charlotte's haunted geography visible. Through the
overt presence of the narrator, the novel's pedagogical center, readers learn to differentiate between the "mild and engaging" Mrs.
Beauchamp and the outcast and captive Charlotte, that "poor solitary being, without society" (50). Rowson entwines the language of
geography and sentiment to describe Charlotte's unenviable position:
she is the "wandering sister" whom it is dangerous even to "dare to
pity" (56). Rowson, in order to suggest "an adequate idea of the sorrow
that preyed upon the mind of Charlotte"—and should also haunt
the reader—continuously identifies Charlotte in spatial terms: she
is (again) "a poor solitary being in the midst of surrounding multitudes [whom] shame bows . . . to the earth" (51). In so doing, Rowson suggests that one cannot have adequate geographical knowledge
without the supplement of what I would call affective or sentimental
geographical knowledge. We must know that Charlotte is alone and
that her solitude is cause for sorrow, pity, and mourning.

Thus Rowson's theological rhetoric of "thorny paths" and "errant
ways" allows us not only to differentiate social positions through the
gross calculations, the dead reckonings, of standard geography but
also to make finer distinctions through an understanding of sentimental geographies. The aesthetic form of the sentimental novel,
then, creates affective geographies, differential cartographies that
produce sites of affiliation that do not necessarily coincide with
national cartographies. Through sentiment, we learn to differentiate
between Mrs. Beauchamp's and Charlotte's positions—and, moreover, to denounce the latter. Thus the generic quality that characterizes the places in this sentimental novel inculcates a form of
geographical knowledge—sentimental geography—that emphasizes
social connections, interdependence, and relationality: what we
might think of as boundaries and connections that are analogous to
those that are marked on maps of the world, nations, and colonies,
but are nonetheless invisible in those productions. Charlotte's place

in the world seems to be defined by lack, obscurity, and absence, yet Rowson makes this place visible by drawing attention to the sentimental marks that map it. These marks, as they are recognized by readers and in turn used for readers' own navigations, give Charlotte's ghost a long life.

III. Mourning the Unexceptional American Place

Nothing better illustrates Rowson's geographic lessons than the Trinity Churchyard grave of Charlotte Temple. Although Rowson's interest in training her female academy students in geography strongly suggests that sentimental geographies were of particular use to women, Rowson does not limit the utility of sentimental geography to women alone. Montraville's penitence, expressed spatially through his visits to Charlotte's grave, does double duty as sign of his repentant state and as penitence for his culpability in Charlotte's seduction and death. In short, Rowson suggests that Montraville, too, must learn sentimental geographical knowledge and practice. The importance of Montraville's diegetical mourning raises the question of who learns these sentimental geographies, and with what effects.

If we are to judge Rowson's text as a geographical primer, then by the historical record it is a successful one: throughout the nineteenth century, readers made the same ritual trip to Charlotte's grave in Trinity Churchyard. The spatial practice of visiting the grave makes the textually unexceptional space of Charlotte's death into a particular site of mourning. The Trinity grave not only uncovers the trace of a space that is written out of official maps. Visits to the grave also raise the question of what is at stake—geographically speaking—in the valorization of mourning as an embodied response to the novel and as a particular location produced through it. In other words, what effects does translating the diegetic practice of mourning outside the bounds of the novel and into the "real" world have? Are the spatial practices of readers constrained by the grammar of sentimental geography that Rowson establishes, such that they simply extend her textual spatiality onto physical terrain?[5] Reading the pilgrimages to Charlotte Temple's grave attests to the vibrancy of the ongoing debate about the value and representative-

5. Michel de Certeau writes in "Walking in the City" that spatial grammars, written by those in positions with panoptic views such as urban planners, are the field within which individual spatial iterations are made. This "pedestrian rhetoric" is enabled by the authorizing spatial grammar, but like language itself, there are infinite possibilities of how to arrange the grammar into actual "sentences" of spatial practice. See Certeau, *The Practice of Everyday Life*, esp. 92–93.

ness of her body and the ongoing negotiation of what its placement means.

The regnant critical consensus is that Charlotte Temple's body represents a loss "suffered by the nation."[6] She is made the center of a national project of mourning when those who interpret her absent presence focus attention on her imagined body and fictional grave. Critics such as Eva Cherniavsky and Julia Stern read the grave symbolically as a national site. By their readings, pilgrims to Charlotte's grave mourn the already elided, unexceptional space that is the politically unrepresented female in the formation of the United States. To read Charlotte as emblem of a yet-unfulfilled democracy assumes that each pilgrimage to Charlotte's grave is virtually indistinguishable as the grave timelessly represents this foundational exclusion. This unchanging, ahistorical sameness of Charlotte's symbolic grave allows for the novel to be read as a critique of the United States—in other words, a gendered and more critical version of the Tomb of the Unknown Soldier. Critic Benedict Anderson uses the tomb to see the connection among bodies, territories, and political form. In his formulation, the tomb is "saturated with ghostly *national* imaginings" that are made possible through the soldier's anonymity, or the abstraction of the individual remains and the abstraction of the place of interment.[7] For the unknown soldier, the materiality of the body and the place, in other words, must remain symbolic and divested of particularity. Charlotte's grave complicates these anonymous imaginings because it is a grave that is valued precisely for the particularity of the body it entombs. Critics who read Charlotte's grave as a critical national site draw attention to the particularities of Charlotte's identity—more precisely, her gender. In so doing, they argue that Charlotte's particularity inaugurates a more democratic national vision, because in visiting her grave, this absence at the center of national formation becomes visible. Charlotte's body thus becomes a symbol that embodies the inequalities the emerged from a specific historical moment (the founding of the nation) yet remains itself unchanged over time.

Even as critics attend to the particularity of Charlotte's body when considering her grave, readings of Charlotte's interred body as an allegory for the nation rely on ignoring the particularity and historicity of the grave itself and of visits to it. The history of Charlotte Temple's gravestone problematizes the view that the unrepresented female at the founding of the United States is memorialized and

6. Marc Redfield, "Imagi-Nation: The Imagined Community and the Aesthetics of Mourning," *Diacritics* 29.4 (1999): 68.
7. Benedict Anderson, *Imagined Communities: Reflections on the Origin and Spread of Nationalism*, rev. ed. (New York: Verso, 1991), 9. Emphasis in original.

given life through Charlotte's grave.[8] This view usually presumes
that the grave is a site of mourning. As Stern writes, Charlotte's
grave keeps the foundational national moment open and unfinished:
"mourning becomes melancholia, darkening the dream of democratic transparency in *Charlotte Temple*."[9] To read the grave as melancholic, however, fails to recognize that other affects were displayed
at the grave besides tears and sadness, even if it were just the excited
smiles of interested readers or the curiosity of idle tourists.

What is lost in a reading of Charlotte's grave as only a site to com-
memorate the foundational exclusion of the unrepresented female is
the multiply referential ground of the grave itself that becomes the
object not only of female mourners but of a host of others both
within and without the nation. For, unlike what is assumed by critics
and historians of this site, mourners had a variety of motivations,
expectations, and interpretations that they overlaid on Charlotte's
grave. As Cathy Davidson has shown, contrary to traditional conceptions of the readership of sentimental novels, men and women from
different classes, ages, and literacy levels owned and enjoyed *Charlotte Temple*.[1] So too do reports of visits to Charlotte Temple's grave
reveal a wider demographic than usually acknowledged. In other
words, what has been ignored in interpretations of Charlotte's grave
are the historical particularities of how it has been used and experienced by readers. These particularities challenge assumptions that
she is a national allegory.

My rereading of what Charlotte's grave means builds from my
study of references to Charlotte Temple's grave in newspapers and
journals throughout the nineteenth century. This archive suggests
that the audience for Charlotte's grave is much larger than the group
of bereaved women suggested by many. It includes "thievish boys"
who pilfer her grave marker;[2] a *male* "stranger" who asks in an 1879
newspaper for help in finding the grave;[3] and international and
American tourists, participants in the transnational culture of

8. See especially Ann Douglass and her chapter "The Domestication of Death." *The
   Feminization of American Culture,* rev. ed. (New York: Noonday Press—Farrar, Straus
   and Giroux, 1998), 200–26.
9. Stern, *Plight of Feeling,* 47.
1. *Revolution and the Word.*
2. "New York Correspondence. New York, May 8, 1852," [*Galveston, TX*] *Weekly Journal*
   28 May 1852: 2. *America's Historical Newspapers.* Duke University Libraries. June 13,
   2006. Available: infoweb.newsbank.com/.
3. *The New-Hampshire Patriot and State Gazette,* 2 November 1879: 1. This snippet is one
   of several items of "miscellany." It follows an excerpt taken "from the Ladies' Magazine"
   about a frustrated gentleman detailing his search for a wife, and his difficulty in finding
   a woman to match his ideal; it immediately precedes a report of the jailing of a man for
   arson. As opposed to the "thievish boys," the framing materials in this citation suggest a
   more conventional, disciplinary reading of Charlotte's grave as unifying national paternalism through the sacrifice of women who do not obey its codes. "Miscellany," *New-
   Hampshire Patriot and State Gazette* 2 November 1879. *America's Historical Newspapers.*
   Duke University Libraries. June 13, 2006. Available: infoweb.newsbank.com/.

mourning, who call her the "American Heloise."[4] This wide-ranging audience puts pressure on the received idea that those who mourned Charlotte were uniformly women or even that they uniformly mourned.

In one representative selection from the "New York Correspondence" section of the *Weekly Journal*, published in Galveston, Texas, readers learned about Charlotte Temple's grave along with metropolitan sartorial trends. In the summer of 1852, the article relates, "fashions are extravagantly showy," with "ladies' bonnets . . . small but very gay" and "the *pantaloonery* of the gentlemen . . . exceedingly ostentatious." The column ends with a recounting of the correspondent's visit to Trinity Churchyard and "the celebrated unfortunate" Charlotte Temple's grave.[5] The insertion of this visit within the frame of current fashions and gossip emphasizes the ways in which Charlotte Temple's grave had become a popular tourist site. In this account, the fashion of the grave and the process of visiting it are emphasized over the meaning of that visit. Markedly absent from this article is evidence of Charlotte as a women shaped to critique the nation, especially in ways that modern critics recognize. The author does not suggest that the grave functions as a site of communal mourning for bereaved female readers. Rather, the author dwells, as is evidenced by the affirmation of the novel's popularity, on the style points that adhered to reading the novel and now belong to visiting the grave. The author does not associate Charlotte's grave with tears, sentiment, or the occlusion of women from the United States. A reading of Charlotte's grave as emblematic of a melancholic exclusion must account for the tonal difference apparent in the transformation of Charlotte's grave into a site of celebration. My point is that the depth of melancholy that contemporary critics often attach to the grave does not actually obtain in records of that visit. I believe that developing an archive that includes visits to her grave over time forces us to reconsider the symbolism of that grave and the extent to which we can refashion it into a site of exceptional unexceptionality. As tantalizing as it can be to find in Charlotte's grave the righteous haunting of a class of women disavowed from the nation's founding, the grave itself does not seem stable enough to support such a community.

The current tombstone has no adornments or writing, other than the name "Charlotte Temple." Historical archaeologists such as James Deetz have written extensively on gravestone trends, and

4. A. S. D., "Who Was Charlotte Temple," *[Omaha] Sunday World-Herald* 12 March 1893: 15. *America's Historical Newspapers*. Duke University Libraries. June 13, 2006. Available: infoweb.newsbank.com/. This article appears in a section of the paper particularly geared to female readers, as the section's heading, "THIS IS FOR WOMEN," indicates.

5. "New York Correspondence," 2.

the plain style of Charlotte Temple's grave is not altogether unusual. But what is striking is its lack of any embellishments, such as the death's-heads popular as gravestone designs in the late seventeenth to middle eighteenth century, or the willows and urns more characteristic of early-nineteenth-century gravestones, as well as its lack of dates, titles, or messages.[6] On a practical level, the grave's absolute plainness enables its symbolic power. That Charlotte's body is irretrievable—because no one can agree on her fictionality or historicity—makes it all the more available to symbolic meaning. There is no record (yet found) that specifies when the tombstone appeared, who installed it, or even who is (not) interred beneath it. Trinity Church, one of the oldest churches in New York, which has not moved from its site in lower Manhattan since the early eighteenth century, has maintained archives of births, deaths, and other parish events. Yet, no record exists to give the many curious pilgrims—and critics like myself—further details about the alluring (or "unfortunate") Charlotte because the church's records go back only to 1897, after pilgrimages to Charlotte's grave had already begun. Archivists cannot ascertain whether it is an empty grave dedicated to the fictional character or whether it is the grave of a real woman by the name of Charlotte Temple who has been apocryphally disincorporated so as to remake her into the ghostly, everlasting fictional Charlotte Temple.[7]

One newspaper article comments on Charlotte's historicity not by discussing the novel or the possibility that Rowson based Charlotte on a "real" person but by commenting on "the queer, flat, old tombstone in old Trinity churchyard that is never without a flower." The accompanying engraved image of Charlotte Temple's grave similarly emphasizes that Charlotte's death, and more specifically her grave, contribute much to her historicity and particularity (see Figure 3). Yet at the same time, her fictionality and the grave's emptiness seem to fuel her endless signifying possibility. The Galveston, Texas, column reporting fashions from New York ends with a comment on the physical grave itself. The author describes the construction and look of her gravestone, a plain, "flat marble slab." Its stylistic simplicity is explained by asserting that the grave's embellishment, a "large plate of iron which bore the inscription" had been stolen "by thievish boys, and converted into small change at some old-junk store."[8] The possibility of imagining Charlotte is

6. See James Deetz, *In Small Things Forgotten: An Archaeology of Early American Life*, rev. ed. (New York: Anchor Books-Doubleday, 1996). My thanks to Erik Seeman for his help with the historical chronology of gravestone trends.

7. Conversation with Gwynedd Cannan, Trinity Church archivist, September 1, 2006. In 2008, Cannan hoisted the tombstone, but found no burial chamber beneath. C. J. Hughes, "Buried in the Churchyard: A Good Story, At Least," *NY Times*, December 13, 2008, p. A15.

8. "New York Correspondence," 2.

fueled by her simultaneous absence and presence, emblematized by the particularity of a marker that would give information about the tantalizingly generic Charlotte—if only it were still there.

This ambiguity, represented at the site of the grave by the "missing marker," proved to be an enduring mystery and part of the lore of Charlotte's grave. It is unclear whether there was ever any such plate in the grave. The 1940s history of the churchyard postulates that there was such a marker, indicated by "an oblong depression above the name [that] has been filled in with cement where years ago a metal tablet apparently had been sunk."[9] The existence of this metal marker is evidenced, like Charlotte herself, only in ghostly impressions: a depression in the stone grave marker that still stands today is read as the imprint—or ghostly trace—of the now-missing marker. An 1869 entry in *Appleton's Journal of Science, Literature, and Art* remarks that "The plate placed upon the stone that marks the grave was supposed to be of solid silver, and tempted the cupidity of certain vandals, who . . . succeeded in prying it from the slab. . . . Many years later, some good Samaritan caused the simple name of Charlotte Temple to be cut underneath the excavation. There it may be seen, . . . by anyone who will take the trouble to look through the iron railing."[1] The mysterious plate, which appears as an absent object stolen by robbers, marks the loss of specifics of Charlotte's life and death. Instead of the sedimentation of Charlotte's life in the scripted lines of a tomb, knowing Charlotte requires some "trouble," the trouble of searching for something or someone of which only a trace remains.

The tension between Charlotte as generic character and Charlotte as exceptional individual, capable of inspiring thousands of mournful pilgrimages, similarly models the tension between the exemplarity of a historical figure and the potential to share that exceptionality (one might say to democratize it). But as trips to Charlotte's grave show, the centripetal force of defining Charlotte was not so easy to contain. By the end of the nineteenth century, Charlotte Temple's grave had become part of the official landscape of New York, scripted into urban space as one of multiple spots by which to mark the city's history and developing urban tourism. The first scholarly edition of the novel, published in 1905 and edited by Francis W. Halsey, which elaborated its academic stance in part by correcting more than 1,000 errata from versions published throughout the nineteenth century, signaled the death knell of the novel's popularity.[2] The apotheosis

9. The Reverend John V. Butler, *Churchyards of Trinity Parish in the City of New York* (New York City: Trinity Church Corporation, 1969), 49–50.
1. "Table-Talk," *Appleton's Journal of Science, Literature, and Art* 30 October 1869: 344. *Making of America.* July 7, 2006. Available: name.umdl.umich.edu/acw8433.1-02.031.
2. Susanna Rowson, *Charlotte Temple: A Tale of Truth*, ed. Francis W. Halsey (New York: Funk and Wagnalls, 1905).

GRAVE OF CHARLOTTE TEMPLE, TRINITY
CHURCHYARD, NEW YORK CITY.

Figure 3. Charlotte Temple's grave in Trinity churchyard. From A. S. D.,
"Who Was Charlotte Temple," *Omaha World Herald*, 12 March 1893.

of Charlotte into the official narrative of New York City is signaled
by the inclusion of both a photograph of Charlotte's grave and a
map that plots where Charlotte went in the city, so that anyone can
retrace her footsteps (see Figure 4).

By the opening of the twentieth century, that is, Charlotte's grave
appears not as an exceptional but as a typical site. A 1905 letter sent
to the *New York Times* promises that Charlotte Temple's grave is "not
altogether forgotten amid the roar of Wall Street."[3] Charles Hemstreet's *Nooks & Corners of Old New York* (1899) contained an entry

3. V. M. D., "Not Altogether Forgotten amid the Roar of Wall Street," *New York Times* 19
June 1905: 6. *America's Historical Newspapers*. Duke University Libraries. October 14,
2006. Available: infoweb.newsbank.com/.

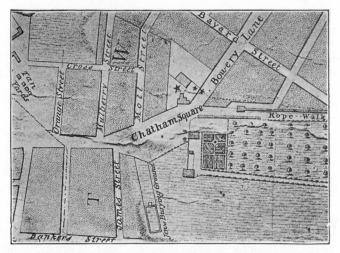

CHARLOTTE HOME IN NEW YORK AS SHOWN ON THE RATZEN MAP OF 1767

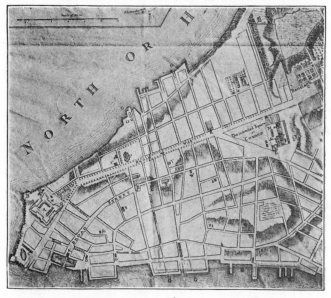

PART OF COL JOHN MONTRESOR'S MAP OF NEW YORK IN 1775
From a copy in the Letter Library

Figure 4. Top: "Charlotte's Home in New York." Bottom: Rowson's cousin's 1775 map of New York. From Halsey's 1905 edition of *Charlotte Temple*. Francis W. Halsey, *Charlotte Temple: A Tale of Truth*, NY: Funk & Wagnalls Co., 1905. Page appears between xlvi–xlvii.

on the "Home of Charlotte Temple," or at least the house where she supposedly died, "within a few steps of the Bowery, on the north side of Pell Street," as well as an entry on her grave. Although the grave increasingly is noted as part of the official New York landscape, especially as evidenced by its inclusion in tour guides, both *Nooks & Corners* and the *Times* letter suggest that this formalizing of Charlotte's presence is nonetheless a precarious exercise. As the letter worries that the grave will be lost in the "roar of Wall Street," so does Hemstreet describe a related kind of loss: Charlotte's grave, he writes, can be seen "each year sinking deeper in the earth."[4] This suggests that the formalizing of Charlotte's presence in the landscape is accompanied and countered by the loss of a clear vision of Charlotte. Whether she is lost in the bustle of the city, clouded by the passing of time, or swallowed up into the ground, Charlotte becomes most absent when she is also most present. This doubleness explains, perhaps, the irony that the imprimatur given by official guides and geometric maps in the early twentieth century heralded the waning interest in Charlotte's grave as a tourist destination.

As Charlotte disappears into the ground, the efforts to define her are but iterations of the ongoing interest in finding the "real" Charlotte from ghostly remnants. Avery Gordon writes that we look for ghosts only out of justice. She calls attention to the ways in which the absent presence of the ghost can mark a loss at the site of embodiment. Gordon explains that a ghost "gives notice not only of itself but also to what it represents. What it represents is usually a loss, sometimes of life, sometimes of a path not taken. From a certain vantage point the ghost also simultaneously represents a future possibility. . . . [T]he ghost is alive, so to speak."[5] She carefully does not name the telos of that future possibility, nor does she align the "radical" potential of the ghost—radical insofar as it keeps the dead alive—with one particular geopolitical and social formation. The history that the ghost represents, as well as the present and future it haunts, are open. This ambivalence must be kept in mind when reading *Charlotte Temple* because the visits to her grave, when taken in their historical contexts and full detail, tend to close down a unilateral vision of her ghostly afterlife. They transform a synchronic tableau into a diachronic spatial practice, whose dynamic reveals a much wider attachment than hitherto imagined. Temporally and spatially flat readings that do not attend to the historical difference and geographic specificity of Charlotte's grave lose the possibility

---

4. Charles Hemstreet, *Nooks and Corners of Old New York* (New York: Charles Scribner's Sons, 1899), 48 and 62–63. *Making of America.* July 7, 2006. Available: name.umdl.umich.edu/ACL7674.0001.001.

5. Avery Gordon, *Ghostly Matters* (Minneapolis: University of Minnesota Press, 1997), 63–64.

of this haunting presence. As an open-ended process, reading Charlotte's grave requires more than attention to the originary moment contained within the novel that describes the grave. To trace the ghost, we must follow Charlotte's remains through the ongoing process of its constitution. Charlotte's grave makes her vulnerable in death as it did in life: for her representativeness and symbolism are not ossified with the extinction of life but reanimated as we continue to pilgrimage to her grave. The diachronic reinvigoration of Charlotte Temple, the constant revivifying that broadcasts that the "ghost is alive," cuts two ways.[6] At the same time that it signals Charlotte's disruptive, haunting presence, it also tends to demystify her, making her not a spectacular and insistent specter, like Toni Morrison's Beloved, but the most benign of friendly ghosts.

To reconstitute carefully the traces of the spatial practices of visiting Charlotte's grave is to fight against the re-erasure of an already elided space, the re-ghosting of the ghost. Critical attention to Charlotte's possibilities and the extension of textual models into spatial practice draw attention to the many possible meanings of Charlotte. To recognize these thwarted—or now ghostly—efforts to make Charlotte *meaningful* is not to ignore what David Harvey calls the power of "permanences." Recognizing the acts of remembering and forgetting required to make Charlotte into an emblem of the nation's exclusions requires full engagement with the process of meaning making. Quite simply, it requires an ethical accountability to Charlotte's ghost, that shape-shifting specter that never ossifies.

6. Gordon, *Ghostly Matters* 64.

The Charlotte Temple tombstone, Trinity Churchyard, New York.
Photograph courtesy of Rivka Genesen.

Selections from Rowson's Writings

To Ladies and Gentlemen,
Patrons of Entertaining Literature[†]

The great encouragement and support our Plan of a LITERARY MUSEUM, or NOVEL REPOSITORY, has received from a generous public, demands the utmost tribute of gratitude; and it is with pleasure announced, that since its commencement Manuscripts have been introduced receiving general approbation. The manner in which we have printed Works committed to our care will better speak our attention and praise than any eulogium of language.

Ladies and Gentlemen, from this specimen of our conduct, will be sure to have the efforts of their genius and productions of their pen introduced to the world in a style of superiority: the printing will be executed with expedition, correctness, accuracy and elegance, and the paper equally correspondent; and we presume to assert that no pains, care, assiduity, or expence, shall be spared to merit the continuance of the approbation we have obtained; and we also affirm, that we have never introduced any subjects but such as are founded on the basis of Virtue, and have tended to improve the understanding and to amend the heart.—Our study shall be to please; as this will equally add to our interest as reflect to our honor.

In addition to this proposal, Authors who wish to derive emolument from their studies, are informed, that five hundred pounds is placed at an eminent bankers, for the sole purpose of purchasing literary productions; and notwithstanding we are now unrivalled in the public estimation, for Novels, Tales, Romances, Adventures, etc. yet, in this undertaking, works of a general nature, whether Originals, Translations, or Compilations, which can entertain or improve the mind, elucidate the sciences, or be of any utility, will find an asylum.

---

† Advertisement for William Lane's Minerva Press that appeared at the front of the first edition of *Charlotte: A Tale of Truth*, 1791.

From the great encrease and general encouragement CIRCULAT-
ING LIBRARIES have received, and which are now established in all
parts of England, Scotland, and Ireland, (an employ both respectable and lucrative), such as are desirous of embarking in that line of
business are informed that books suitable for that purpose are kept
ready bound, in History, Voyages, Novels, Plays, etc. containing from
One Hundred to Five Thousand Volumes, which may be had at a few
days notice, with a catalogue for their subscribers, and instructions
and directions how to plan, systemize, and conduct the same.

Such are the general outlines of this spirited undertaking: a plan
founded on propriety, and sanctioned by the liberal approbation of
the public; and we shall be happy farther to improve the same, so as
to render it the Museum of Entertainment, and a Repository of Sciences, Arts, and Polite Literature.

MINERVA PRINTING OFFICE,
Leadenhall-Street.
[London]

Charlotte. A Tale of Truth.[†]

Chapter VI.

FRENCH TEACHERS NOT ALWAYS THE BEST
WOMEN IN THE WORLD.

Madame Du Pont was a woman every way calculated to take the
care of young ladies, had that care devolved entirely on herself; but
it was impossible to attend the education of a numerous school without proper assistants, and those assistants were not always the kind
of people whose conversation and morals were exactly such as parents of delicacy and refinement could wish a daughter to copy.
Among the teachers at Madame Du Pont's school, was Mademoiselle La Rue, who added to a pleasing person and insinuating
address, a liberal education and the manners of a gentlewoman. She
was recommended to the school by a lady whose humanity overstepped the bounds of discretion: for though she knew Miss La Rue
had eloped from a convent with a young officer, and on coming to
England had lived with several different men in open defiance of all
moral and religious duties, yet finding her reduced to the most
abject want, and believing the penitence which she professed to be
sincere, she took her into her own family, and from thence recommended her to Madame Du Pont, as thinking the situation more
suitable for a woman of her abilities. But Mademoiselle possessed

---

† London. Printed for William Lane, 1791. See also title page of this first British edition
(p. 93) and Hansen, "A Changing Tale of Truth: *Charlotte Temple*'s British Roots" (p. 183).

too much of the spirit of intrigue to remain long without adventures. At church, where she constantly appeared, her person attracted the attention of a young man who was upon a visit at a gentleman's seat in the neighbourhood: she had met him several times clandestinely; and being invited to come out that evening, and eat some fruit and pastry in a summer house belonging to the gentleman he was visiting, and requested to bring some of the ladies with her, Charlotte being her favourite, was fixed on to accompany her.

The mind of youth eagerly catches at promised pleasure: pure and innocent by nature, it thinks not of the dangers lurking beneath those pleasures till too late to avoid them: when Mademoiselle asked Charlotte to go with her, she mentioned the gentleman as a relation, and spoke in such high terms of the elegance of his gardens, the sprightliness of his conversation, and the liberality with which he ever entertained his guests, that Charlotte thought only of the pleasure she should enjoy in the visit,—not on the imprudence of her going without her governess's knowledge, or of the danger to which she exposed herself in visiting the house of a gay young man of fashion.

Madame Du Pont was gone out for the evening, and the rest of the ladies retired to rest, when Charlotte and the teacher stole out at the back gate, and in crossing the field were accosted by Montraville, as mentioned in the first chapter.

Charlotte was disappointed in the pleasure she had promised herself from this visit. The levity of the gentlemen and the freedom of their conversation disgusted her. She was astonished at the liberties Mademoiselle permitted them to take; grew thoughtful and uneasy, and heartily wished herself at home again in her own chamber.

Perhaps one cause of that wish might be an earnest desire to see the contents of the letter which had been put into her hand by Montraville.

Any reader who has the least knowledge of the world will easily imagine the letter was made up of encomiums on her beauty, and vows of everlasting love and constancy; nor will they be surprised that a heart open to every gentle, generous sentiment, should feel itself warmed by gratitude for a man who professed to feel so much for her, nor is it improbable but her mind might revert to the agreeable person and martial appearance of Montraville.

In affairs of love a young heart is never in more danger than when attempted by a handsome young soldier. A man naturally ordinary, when arrayed in a military habit, will make a tolerable appearance; but when beauty of person, elegance of manner, and an easy method of paying compliments, are united to the scarlet coat, smart cockade, and military sash, ah! well a day for the poor girl who gazes on him: she is in imminent danger; but if she listens to him with pleasure, 'tis all over with her, and from that moment she has neither eyes nor ears for any other object.

Now my dear sober matron, (if a sober matron should deign to turn over these pages before she trusts them to the eye of a darling daughter,) let me entreat you not to put on a grave face and throw down the book in a passion and declare 'tis enough to turn the heads of half the girls in England; I do solemnly protest, my dear madam, I mean no more by what I have here advanced than to ridicule those romantic girls who foolishly imagine a red coat and silver epaulet constitute the fine gentleman; and should that fine gentleman make half a dozen fine speeches to them, they will imagine themselves so much in love as to fancy it a meritorious action to jump out of a two pair of stairs window, abandon their friends, and trust entirely to the honour of a man who perhaps hardly knows the meaning of the word, and if he does will be too much the modern man of refinement to practise it in their favour.

Gracious heaven! when I think on the miseries that must rend the heart of a doating parent when he sees the darling of his age at first seduced from his protection, and afterwards abandoned by the very wretch whose promises of love decoyed her from the paternal roof; when he sees her poor and wretched, her bosom torn between remorse for her crime and love for her vile betrayer; when fancy paints to me the good old man stooping to raise the weeping penitent, while every tear from her eye is numbered by drops from his bleeding heart, my bosom glows with honest indignation, and I wish for power to extirpate those monsters of seduction from the earth.

Oh my dear girls, for to such only am I writing, listen not to the voice of love unless sanctioned by paternal approbation: be assured it is now past the days of romance: no woman can be run away with contrary to her own inclination: then kneel down each morning and request kind heaven to keep you free from temptation, or should it please to suffer you to be tried, pray for fortitude to resist the impulse of inclination when it runs counter to the precepts of religion and virtue.

PREFACES

Preface to *Mentoria*;[†]
or, the Young Lady's Friend

Of all the foolish actions a person can commit, I think that of making an apology for a voluntary error, is the most ridiculous; there-

---

[†] *Mentoria; or The young lady's friend.* In two volumes. By Mrs. Rowson, of the New-Theatre, Philadelphia: author of The inquisitor, Fille de chambre, Victoria, Charlotte, &c. &c. Philadelphia, 1794.

fore though I have taken up my pen to write a preface, I am utterly at a loss what to say.

If it is true that "Good wine needs no bush, and a good Play no Epilogue," then must it be equally certain, that a good book requires no preface—and this assertion acknowledged to be true, in what an awkward predicament do I stand, since to publish this Work without a preface, will be tacitly to infer, that it is good and needs no recommendation, and so be deservedly censured as a conceited scribler.

Should I write a preface and condemn the performance, confess it has innumerable faults, and request the reader's pity and patience, I not only prepossess them against it, but acknowledge myself an ideot, for suffering it to meet the public eye, in such an imperfect state. What then am I to say, or how fill up those few pages necessary to be placed at the beginning of a book?

Shall I tell the reader my design in publishing these volumes? I will; It was an anxious desire to see all my dear country-women, as truly amiable as they are universally acknowledged beautiful; it was a wish to convince them that true happiness can never be met with in the temple of dissipation and folly, she flies the glare of fashion, and the midnight revel, and dwells only in the heart conscious of performing its duty, and is the constant companion of those, who, content with the station in which it has pleased Providence to place them, entirely free from envy or malice, make it their whole study to cultivate those amiable virtues which will render them at once beloved, admired, and esteemed, by all who know them.

Whether I have extended this design well or ill, must be hereafter determined, not only by those partial friends, whose kind encouragement prompted me to submit these Pages to the inspection of the Public; but a-well-a-day for me, I must also be judged by some sage critic, who "with spectacles on nose, and pouch by's side," with lengthened visage and contemptuous smile, sits down to review the literary productions of a Woman. He turns over a few pages, and then

> Catching the Author at some that or therefore,
> At once condemns her without why or wherefore.

Then, alas! what may not be my fate? Whose education, as a female, was necessarily circumscribed, whose little knowledge has been simply gleaned from pure nature, and who, on a subject of such importance, write as I feel, with enthusiasm.

I have taken the liberty of placing a Poem at the beginning of the Work, which was published some few years since in the Novel Victoria, and as many Parents utterly forbid their daughters reading any of that species of writing, I thought I should readily be excused for introducing it here.[1]

I must confess, I have neither sufficient conceit or fortitude to enable me to hear, unmoved, the decision of Judicious criticism; yet, conscious that I never wrote a line that would convey a wrong idea to the head, or a corrupt wish to the heart, I sit down satisfied with the purity of my intentions, and leave it to the happy envied class of mortals, who have received a liberal education, to write with that taste and elegance which can only be acquired by a thorough knowledge of the classicks.

Preface to *Trials of the Human Heart*[†]

As a person of sensibility, whom business or necessity, forces into the house of an entire stranger, (especially if that stranger is his superior in genius, education or rank,) experiences a sensation undescribably painful, in being necessiated to announce himself, and explain the intent of his visit: so I feel myself inexpressibly embarrassed and timid, whilst performing the unavoidable task of writing a Preface. It is addressing myself to, and calling up the attention of a multiplicity of strangers; it is introducing not myself indeed, but what is nearly the same thing, the offspring of my imagination, to their notice, and conscious as I am, that it will be perused by those, who are infinitely my superiors, this awkward timidity encreases, to an almost unconquerable degree.

"The works of fiction," says Dr. Johnson, "with which the present generation seems more particularly delighted; are such as exhibit life in its true state, diversified only by accidents that daily happen in the world, and influenced by passions and qualities, which are really to be found in conversing with mankind. In narratives, where historical veracity has no place, I cannot discover why there should not be exhibited a most perfect idea of virtue, not angelical, nor above probability; for what we cannot credit, we shall never imitate; but the highest and purest that humanity can reach, which exer-

---

1. Included here is the first stanza of the poem Rowson refers to in the Preface to *Mentoria* (537).

> I wish not, Anna, to offend,
> But write the language of a friend;
> For tho' my dear from school you're freed,
> You've enter'd on a *task* indeed;
> To act, as you proceed through life,
> As daughter, mother, friend, and wife.

† *Trials of the Human Heart, a novel* (Philadelphia, 1795). Early American Imprints, Series I: Evans, no. 29439.

cised in such trials as the various revolutions of things shall bring upon it, may, by conquering some calamities, and enduring others, teach us what we may hope, and what we can perform."

Upon this plan I have endeavoured to form the "Trials of the Human Heart." My Heroine, though not wholly free from error, (for where shall we find the human being that is so?) I trust is not altogether unworthy imitation. Through various trying situations, as daughter, wife, and mother; I have strove to conduct her with propriety, tempering the weakness of humanity with the patience and fortitude of a Christian, and that dignified pride, which will ever arise from a just sense of the moral virtues.

It is with reluctance I find myself obliged to remark, that the literary world is infested with a kind of loathsome reptile, of the class of non-descripts, for it cannot be ranked with propriety amongst either authors or critics, not possessing the qualifications necessary to form either, and being in itself remarkable for nothing but its noxious qualities: its only aim is to prevent the success of any work of genius; and swelling with envy, should the smallest part of public favour, be conferred on another, spits out its malignant poison, in scurrility and detraction. One of these noisome reptiles, has lately crawled over the volumes, which I have had the temerity to submit to the public eye.[1] I say *crawled over* them, because I am certain it has never penetrated beyond the title-page of any.

Perhaps it would be as well, did I suffer this circumstance to pass unnoticed; the arguments used, I must confess, are unanswerable, being in some parts incomprehensible, and in others of such a nature, that no woman can glance her eye over them, without feeling the blush of offended delicacy crimson her cheek. Yet, as I have been accused of writing in an improper style in my Novel of the "Fille de Chambre," and of expressing sentiments foreign to my heart, in my Comedy of "Slaves in Algiers," I think it necessary to assure the candid and impartial public, that both these assertions are equally false and scandalous.

Though many a leisure hour has been amused, and many a sorrowful one beguiled, whilst giving Fancy the reins, I have applied myself to my pen, it has ever been my pride, that I never yet wrote a line that might tend to mislead the untutored judgment, or corrupt the inexperienced heart; and heaven forbid I should suffer ought to escape my pen, that might call a blush to the cheek of innocence, or deserve a glance of displeasure from the eye of the most rigid moralist.

As to my opinion of the political concerns of America, or my wishes in regard to her welfare, I cannot better explain them, than

---

1. Rowsen refers to William Cobbett, pen name "Peter Porcupine." His critique appears on p. 413.

by giving a slight sketch of my private history, with which, I rather imagine, the *creature* alluded to, is entirely unacquainted.

It was my fate, at a period when memory can scarcely retain the smallest trace of the occurrence, to accompany my father, (Mr. William Haswell, who is a lieutenant in the British navy) to Boston in New England, where he had married a second wife, my mother having lost her life in giving me existence. Blest with a genteel competency, and placed by his rank and education in that sphere of life, where the polite and friendly attentions of the most respectable characters courted our acceptance, and enjoying a constant intercourse with the families of the officers of the British army and navy, then stationary there, eight years of my life glided almost imperceptibly away.

At that time the dissentions between England and America encreased to an alarming degree: my father bore the king's commission, he had taken the oath of allegiance; certain I am that no one who considers the nature of an oath, voluntarily taken, no one who reflects, that previous to this period, he had served thirty years under the British government, will blame him for a strict adherence to principles which were interwoven as it were with his existance. He did adhere to them, the attendant consequence may readily be supposed; his person was confined, his property confiscated.

Then it was that the benevolence and philanthropy, which so eminently distinguish the sons and daughters of Columbia made an indeliable impression on my heart, an impression which neither time or chance can obliterate, for while their political principles obliged them to afflict, the humanity, the Christian like benevolence of their souls, incited them to wipe the tears of sorrow from the eyes of my parents, to mitigate their sufferings, and render those afflictions in some measure supportable. Would to Heaven it was in my power to render their memories as immortal, as my gratitude is unbounded.

Having been detained as a prisoner two years and an half, part of which was spent in *Hingham*, and part in *Abington*; an exchange of prisoners taking place between the British and Americans, my father and his family were sent by cartel to Halifax, from whence we embarked for England. I will not pretend to describe the sorrow I experienced, in being thus separated from the companions of my early years: every wish of my heart was for the welfare and prosperity of a country, which contained such dear, such valuable friends, and the only comfort of which my mind was capable, was indulging in the delightful hope, of being at some future period permitted again to revisit a land so beloved, companions so regretted.

Too young at that time, to have formed any political principles of my own, I may naturally be supposed to have adopted those of my father, but the truth is, that equally attached to either country, the unhappy dissentions affected me in the same manner as a person may be imagined to feel, who having a tender lover, and an affectionate brother who are equally dear to her heart, and by whom she is equally beloved, sees them engaged in a quarrel with, and fighting against each other, when, let whichsoever party conquer, she cannot be supposed insensible to the fate of the vanquished.

During a period of twelve years a variety of a painful circumstances unnecessary here to recount, contributed to deprive me of a decent independence inherited from my paternal grandfather, and at length to bring me back to America, in a very different situation, I must confess, from that in which I left it; but with a heart, still glowing with the same affectionate sensations, and exulting in its evident improvement: the arts are encouraged, manufactures increase, and this happy land bids fair to be in the course of a few years the most flourishing nation in the universe.

Is it then wonderful, that accustomed from the days of childhood, to think of America and its inhabitants with affection, linked to them by many near connections, and sincerely attached to them, from principles of gratitude, that I should offer the most ardent prayers for a continuation of their prosperity, or that feeling the benign influence of the blessings of peace and liberty, here so eminently enjoyed, I should wish that influence extended throughout every nation under heaven.

Before I conclude, I beg leave to say a few words more, concerning my present publication. I am willing to flatter myself, that in offering this novel to the public, I am not preparing for my future life, either shame or repentance. That it is throughout the whole, happily imagined or highly polished, I have not sufficient confidence in my own abilities to warrant; but whatever may be my final sentence from the world in general, I have at least endeavoured to deserve their kindness, nor shall I envy the honours which wit and learning obtain in any other cause, if I may be so happy as to awaken in the bosoms of my youthful readers, a thorough detestation of vice, and a spirited emulation, to embrace and follow the precepts of Piety, Truth and Virtue.

Preface to *Reuben and Rachel*;[†] or, *Tales of Old Times*

Prefaces in general are esteemed of so little consequence, that few persons take the trouble to read them. It is therefore an irksome task to be obliged to write, what will neither call up the attention,

---

† *Reuben and Rachel; or, Tales of Old Times. A Novel.* (Boston, 1798). University of Virginia Library Electronic Text Center: Early American Fiction.

nor interest the feelings of those who may peruse the book; and yet, irksome as the task is, I find myself necessitated to perform it.

I am conscious that some apology ought to be made to the public, for the length of time that has intervened since I first awakened their curiosity by announcing my intention of publishing the present work. In excuse for this tardiness, I must allege several months of ill health, during which time I was incapable of pursuing my favourite amusement of writing; and since my health has been re-established, an avocation of a more serious nature has employed every hour, and almost absorbed every faculty of my mind.

When I first started the idea of writing "*Tales of Old Times*," it was with a fervent wish to awaken in the minds of my young readers, a curiosity that might lead them to the attentive perusal of history in general, but more especially the history of their native country. It has ever been my opinion, that when instruction is blended with amusement, the youthful mind receives and retains it almost involuntarily.

The first volume of the present work was written before I had entered on the arduous (though inexpressibly delightful) task of cultivating the minds and expanding the ideas of the female part of the rising generation. If I was before careful to avoid every expression or sentiment that might mislead the judgment, or corrupt the heart, what was then inclination became now an indispensable duty. And though none of my characters are so very faultless as to occasion the young reader to neglect imitating them at all, because they despair of attaining the same degree of perfection, yet they discover such an innate love of virtue, such a thorough contempt of vice, that the uncontaminated mind will contemplate with pleasure the beauty of the one, and shrink with abhorrence from the deformity of the other.

As a novelist, I think it is more than probable that I have made my last essay.[1] Flattered and encouraged as I am in my present undertaking, in having the education of so many young ladies entrusted to my care by their respectable parents, it shall henceforward be my study conscientiously to discharge the trust reposed in me; and whilst I endeavour to cultivate their taste, and improve their understandings, implant, with the utmost solicitude, in their innocent minds, a love for piety and virtue.

To this end, I shall devote my leisure hours to preparing a set of progressive lessons in reading, for the youth of my own sex; from five years old to ten or twelve; after which period, there are a multiplicity of books, better calculated to forward the great design of education than any my pen could produce.

It is observable, that the generality of books intended for children are written for boys: even Mrs. Barbauld's Lessons, which are the best productions of the kind I ever met with, are addressed to a boy. And

---

1. Attempt.

as for the generality of little books which children are permitted to read, they are such a jumble of inconsistencies, that though they may assist the child to learn to read with propriety, they do not convey one idea to the head that is worth retaining. Mrs. Trimmer, and some few others, are exceptions to this remark, having laboured to correct this false idea, that it was necessary to excite the young mind to the pursuit of learning by tales wonderful and indeed impossible, and have displayed to their view the real wonders and beauties of nature.

For my own sex only I presume to write; and if hereafter one woman should think herself happier or wiser from the fruits of my endeavours, I shall be overpaid for the time or pains bestowed in writing and arranging them.

Preface to *Sarah*[†]

You never read prefaces, you say. Pray oblige me by giving this a slight perusal; it will not detain you long.

The present work made its appearance about eight years since, in the Boston Weekly Magazine; but it was written at snatches of time, and under the pressure of much care and business incident to my profession; consequently was in a degree incorrect. It has now gone through a revision, and is offered to the public as an example of how much the human mind can bear, when supported by conscious rectitude, and whose every impulse is conformable to the strictest integrity and a love of truth. It may be objected that the example will lose its effect, as my heroine is not in the end rewarded for her exemplary patience, virtue, and forbearance: But it was because I wished to avoid every unnatural appearance, that I left Sarah to meet her reward in a better world. Characters of superlative excellence, tried in the furnace of affliction, and at length crowned by wealth, honor, love, friendship, every sublunary good, are to be found abundantly in every novel, but alas! where shall we find them in real life? Such examples therefore, instead of stimulating the young or inexperienced mind to emulate the virtues represented, misleads it by fallacious hopes and expectations which can never be realized; disappointed in the anticipated temporal felicity, where it is discovered that virtue and integrity may be overlooked by the thoughtless and unfeeling; or left to pine in obscurity by the worldly wise, and ostentatiously prudent; it slackens in its endeavour, and concludes the existence of the character portrayed to be as chimerical as the happiness represented as its reward.

[†] *Sarah; or, The Exemplary Wife* (Boston, 1813). University of Virginia Library Electronic Text Center, Early American Fiction.

It may be inquired, "Do I then deny the existence of friendship, generosity, compassion, and that first of Christian virtues, Charity?" Oh no! I should be the most ungrateful of human beings if I did; many have been the instances which I have witnessed of this reality, which, like roses scattered in a wilderness, perfumed and sweetened the journey of life; but in that journey I have also encountered many a thorn, and many a flint, that have lacerated my feelings to the very quick.

Sarah is not a faultless monster; she comes as near perfection as is the lot of humanity; but she was credulous, impetuous, and apt to decide with too much precipitation. Yet under all her misfortunes she is represented as drawing comfort and consolation from a source that is never fallacious, can never be exhausted. She looks up to her heavenly Father with love and confidence, she endeavours to make his laws the rule of her actions, and trusts in his promises for her reward. Who of common reflection but would prefer the death of Sarah, resigned as she was, and upheld by faith and hope, to all the splendors, wealth and honors that were ever heaped upon the heroine in the last pages of a novel? Here let the young voyagers, just entering on the turbulent ocean of life, fix their eyes, and they will find a comforter in disappointment, a support in the heaviest calamity, a safe and sure passport to eternal peace.

Many of the scenes delineated in the following work are drawn from real life; some of them have occurred within my own knowledge; but it was in another hemisphere, and the characters no longer exist. Darnley was a profligate; his crime became his punishment; for surely no life can be pictured so completely wretched as where two persons, knowing from experience the turpitude of each other's heart, are obliged to wear out the last remnant of existence together, in mutual jealousy, hatred and recrimination.

Beware, ye lovely maidens who are now fluttering on the wing of youth and pleasure, how you select a partner for life. Purity of morals and manners in a husband, is absolutely necessary to the happiness of a delicate and virtuous woman. When once the choice is made and fixed beyond revocation, remember patience, forbearance, and in many cases perfect silence, is the only way to secure domestic peace. What, in all marriages? asks some young friend. Why, in truth, there is seldom any so perfectly felicitous, but that instances may occur where patience, forbearance, and silence, may be practised with good effect.

Preface to *Rebecca;*
or, the Fille de Chambre[†]

Introductory Chapter

TO THE SECOND AMERICAN EDITION

Twenty-two years ago, when writing constituted my most pleasurable amusement, when I had few duties to perform and many leisure hours; the following pages were presented to the public. The success of "Charlotte Temple," which had been published two years before, encouraged me to proceed in my favourite employment, and as my reflective turn of mind led me to comment on passing events, and think seriously on circumstances that are treated as ordinary and uninteresting by the generality of the world, I had treasured in my memory from earliest childhood events which I had either been a witness of, an actor in, or received from unimpeachable authority. The latter was the case in respect to "Charlotte;" I had the recital from the lady, whom I introduce under the name of Beauchamp; I was myself personally acquainted with Montraville, and from the most authentic sources could now trace his history from the period of his marriage, till within a very few late years; a history which would tend to prove that retribution treads upon the heels of vice, and that though not always apparent yet even in the midst of splendor and prosperity, conscience stings the guilty, and

"Puts rancles in the vessel of their peace."

Destined very early in life to experience great vicissitudes of fortune, and pass through various scenes on both sides of the Atlantic, I recollected at a more advanced period circumstances which when thrown together in a regular detail, appear to be merely the offspring of fancy; but in the following pages, though Rebecca is a fictitious character, many of the scenes in which she is engaged are sober realities.

The scenes in her father's family previous to her leaving it, those at lord Ossiters, the distress at sea, the subsequent shipwreck; the burning Boston light-house, the death of the poor marine, the imprisonment of the family, the friendship experienced by them in the most distressed circumstances, the removal farther into the country, and exchange to Halifax, are events which really took place between the years 1769 and 1778, though the persons here mentioned as the sufferers are fictitious.

[†] *Rebecca; or, the Fille de Chambre. A Novel.*, 2nd American Edition (Boston, 1814). Library of Congress, Washington, DC.

Dear to memory are the scenes of our early days, though in them the cup of existence was often mingled with the tear of affliction or bitter regrets, yet there are periods when the hiliarity of youth will throw a gleam of sunshine over the darkest moments, to these the mind reverts in more advanced life, and even in its decline will trace with indiscribable pleasure the paths trodden in childhood. When after twenty years absence I revisited the little village of N——— and the town of H——— how impossible it is to delineate my feelings, many of my father's friends were resting in their narrow home, and some also of my young associates had been early removed to the mansion of peace, others were married and surrounded by lovely families. It appeared as if the time of my absence had been annihilated, and I stood again in the midst of my young friends, for such appeared the sons and daughters of those who were little more than boys and girls themselves when I had last seen them. It was a sensation of mingled pain and pleasure; yet certainly the pleasure predominated, and I often regret that it was a sensation which I can never again experience; for alas! Since then, one link and another has fallen from the great chain of life till only a few disolated ones remain, so far removed from each other, that they can never again be united till the awful day when all the families of the peopled earth will stand together in the presence of the most high Judge.

I hope I shall not be thought capable of exaggerating or using the language of romance when describing the scenes which took place during the revolutionary war, nor be suspected of any intentional disrespect in mentioning them, far from my heart is such a design, my own native land is not more dear to me than is my foster country, America. If I drew my first breath in Britain; it was here I began to feel the value of life, here my ideas first expanded, here I first sipped at the fountain of knowledge; and here my heart first glowed with those exquisitely delightful sensations, friendship and gratitude. An army assembled in haste, and under very little discipline, must needs contain some ill regulated and ferocious spirits; besides, at that period, party spirit ran high, and the tempestuous ocean might be as easily argued into order, as party rage when acting on an uninformed and indiscriminate multitude.

When the following pages were first written I had no hope of ever again seeing dear New-England, (though from the hour I left it, to return to it again had been the first wish of my heart) as they were then written they now appear; the language somewhat corrected, but the sentiments the same.

I trust the character of my heroine, Rebecca, is such as every young woman may contemplate with innocence, and imitate with advantage both to herself and those with whom she is connected.

NOVEL EXCERPTS

From Verses to a Libertine[†]

*VERSES addressed by VICTORIA to a young
Gentleman inclined to Libertinism.*

Oh how can man, blest with a reasoning mind,
    Thus from the path of wisdom widely stray;
How to his own contentment be thus blind,
    And rush impetuous down the thorny way?

5 Say, can the sparkling wine, a card or die
    Or the bewitching harlot's wanton smile,
Wipe the big tear from off the grief-swoln eye,
    Or sickness, pain, or misery beguile.

Oh no, tho' wine may numb each keener sense,
10   And for a while take off the edge of grief,
Yet reason would with milder influence,
    Banish despair, and give the mind relief,

Man was for greater, nobler ends design'd,
    Than thus with wine to cloud the immortal soul,
15 'Tis slow but certain poison to the mind,
    That lurks beneath the treacherous flowing bowl.

With caution fly each soul enticing game;
    Gaming has ever been the source of strife,
It serves the boisterous passions to inflame,
20   And oft embitters all the sweets of life.

Shun the gay harlot who with wanton look,
    For the unwary wanderer lays a snare;
Beneath th' alluring bait lies hid the hook,
    And sickness, poverty, and shame are there.

25 If you should have more wealth than you can spend,
    Rather than lose it foolishly at play,
Be to the poor a father and a friend,
    Relieve their wants and chase their grief, away.

[†] *Victoria*, vol. 2, (London, 1786). Reprinted by permission of University of Virginia Department of Special Collections.

If ever time hangs heavy on your hands,
30   Spend it in study; for that use 'twas given,
Study your Great Creator's wise commands,
        Obey them all, and be prepar'd for Heaven.

From The Fille de Chambre[†]

From *Chapter XXIII*

ON THE OTHER SIDE THE ATLANTIC

On the left hand of the entrance of Boston harbour is a beautiful
little peninsula, called N——; it consists of two gradually rising
hills, beautifully diversified with orchards, corn-fields and pasture
land. In the valley is built a little village, consisting of about fifty
houses, the inhabitants of which could just make shift to decently
support a minister, who on a Sunday ascended the pulpit in a rustic
temple, situated by the side of a large piece of water, nearly in the
middle of the village, and taught, to the utmost of his abilities, the
true principles of christianity. The neck of land which joins this
peninsula to the main is extremely narrow, and indeed is sometimes
almost overflown by the tide. On one side it forms a charmingly
picturesque harbour, in which are a variety of small but delightfully
fertile islands, and on the other it is washed by the ocean, to which
it lays open. In this enchanting village stood Mr. Abthorpe's house,
in the midst of a neat and well cultivated garden; and here it was
that, as the spring advanced, our contemplative heroine beheld with
rapture the rapid progress of the infant vegitation; for the earth
seemed hardly released from the fleecy garb of winter, before it
burst forth in the full bloom of vernal pride.

In this agreeable situation Rebecca remained nearly two years,
enjoying as much felicity as she could expect in the friendship of Mr.
and Mrs. Abthorpe and the affection of their amiable daughter. It is
true she sometimes sighed when she thought of Sir George Worthy—
sometimes gazed on his portrait and that of his mother's, till her eyes
overflowing could no longer distinguish them. But these were luxu-
ries, too dangerous to be often indulged, they only served to enervate
her mind, and render her incapable of enjoying the blessings placed
within her reach, and led her to repine at the wise dispensations of
Providence; she therefore exerted her natural good sense to keep
these acute sensibilities within proper restrictions, and by striving to
be happy in her present situation, in a great measure rendered her-

---

[†] *The Fille de Chambre, a novel* (Philadelphia, 1794). Early American Imprints, Series I:
  Evans, no. 27651.

self really so. She had many admirers, and might have entered into matrimonial engagements greatly to her advantage, but she resolutely refused them all, still maintaining towards each that invariable politeness and frankness of demeanor, as at the same moment extinguished their tenderer hopes and yet conciliated their esteem.

* * *

About this time the unhappy breach between Great Britain and her colonies arose to such a height, that it never could be healed, and war, in her most frightful shape, began to stalk over this once happy land. Ere this, the inhabitants of New-England, by their hospitality and primitive simplicity of manners, revived in the mind of our heroine the golden age, so celebrated by poets. Here were no locks or bolts required, for each one, content with his own cot, coveted not the possessions of his neighbour; here should a stranger make his appearance in their little village, though unknown by all, every one was eager to shew him the most civility, inviting him to their houses, and treating him with every delicacy the simplicity of their manner of living afforded.

The only house of entertainment in this village, had scarcely custom sufficient to supply its venerable mistress with the necessaries of life; but she had a garden, a cow, and a few acres of land; the produce of these were sufficient to her wants and wishes, and she would sit in her matted arm chair, in a room whose only beauty was "the white-washed wall, the nicely sanded floor," while the smile of content played about her face, and while she thankfully enjoyed the bounties of heaven, she remembered not that any could be richer or happier than herself.

But when fell discord spread her sable pinions and shook her curling snakes, how soon this blissful prospect was reversed; frighted at the horrid din of arms, hospitality fled her once favourite abode, mutual confidence was no more, and fraternal love gave place to jealousy, dissension, and blind party zeal. The son raised his unhallowed arm against his parent, brothers drenched their weapons in each other's blood, and all was horror and confusion. The terrified inhabitants of N—— left the village and took refuge in the more interior parts of the country, all but Colonel Abthorpe's family, who still remained, though deserted by all their servants; for the Colonel had too high a regard for his royal master to join the cause of his enemies, and it was impossible to join the British troops without relinquishing all his property; he therefore hoped the storm would soon pass over; that some method would be proposed and accepted to conciliate matters, and in the mean time he wished to remain neuter.[1]

---

1. Neutral.

It was a still morning about the latter end of July, when Rebecca, being disturbed by some little rustling at her window, raised her head, and by the faint dawn that just glimmered from the east, discovered armed men placed round the house. Alarmed, she started from her bed and awoke Miss Abthorpe: they threw a few clothes over them and flew to the Colonel's apartment. They were met by Mrs. Abthorpe, who caught her daughter in her arms, and, pointing to the room where they usually slept, cried, "Look Sophia, your poor father."

Miss Abthorpe looked and beheld two soldiers with firelocks, who placed at the door of the apartment, held her father a prisoner.

"Ah, my dear mother," said she, "who are these, and what are they going to do; surely, surely they will not murder us."

"Don't frighten yourself, Miss," said one of the officers, "we do not usually murder such pretty girls."

"But my father," cried she, eagerly, "what do you intend to do with him."

"Set him at liberty again when our expedition is over."

Rebecca now learnt that these were a part of the American army, who had come to N—— in whaleboats, with a design of dragging their boats across the beach before mentioned, and proceeding to the light-house at the entrance of the harbour, intending to destroy it, in order to mislead the expected relief that was coming to Boston which was at that time blockaded: they had before made an unsuccessful attempt to demolish this light-house, and were now come resolved not to leave their work unfinished; accordingly they proceeded as quiet as possible to the beach, almost carried their boats over, and arrived totally unexpected at the little island on which the light-house stood, and which was guarded by a party of marines. A smart skirmish ensued, but the Americans were too numerous to be withstood by so small a party; the whole of which they either killed or took prisoners; and having completed their design, returned to N——, victorious, though in the utmost consternation, for fear of being pursued by boats from the Lively frigate, and other ships that lay in the harbour.

Rebecca was standing at a window as they relanded, the tears streaming down her pale face, and so entirely absorbed in terror that she was inattentive to the surrounding objects. From this state of torpor she was aroused by a deep groan, and raising her eyes, saw two Americans entering the house, bearing between them a wounded marine, whom they laid on the floor, and were preparing to depart, when Mrs. Abthorpe rushed out of the adjoining apartment.

"What are you doing?" said she, "you will not surely leave him here."

"D——n him," cried a wretch, "he is in our way; if he don't die quickly we will kill him."

"Oh, do not kill me!" said the almost expiring soldier; "I am not fit to die."

At this moment Major Tupper entered: Mrs. Abthorpe addressed him in a supplicating accent; "We can procure the poor soul no assistance," said she; "he will perish for want of proper applications to stanch the blood."

"My dear madam," said the Major, "what can we do; we fear pursuit, and must retreat as fast as possible, and should we take him with us, in our hurry and confusion he will perhaps be precipitated into eternity. If we make a safe retreat I will send to morrow." He then departed, and Colonel Abthorpe being now at liberty, turned his thoughts toward the wounded soldier.

He had fainted, a mattress was laid on the ground, and as they all united in endeavouring to remove him upon it, the motion increased the anguish of his wounds and recalled his languid senses.

"Oh, Spare me! do not kill me!" said he looking round with a terrified aspect.

"Be comforted," said the colonel; "you are among friends, who will do all in their power to save your life.

"God will reward you," said he, faintly.

They now examined the wound, and found, from its depth and situation, that a few hours would terminate the existence of the poor sufferer: however they made long bandages of linen, and with pledgets dipped in spirits, endeavoured to stanch the bleeding, but in vain.

"I am very faint," said he.

Rebecca knelt and supported him in her arms, assisted by the weeping Sophia.

"Can I live, think you, Sir?" said he, looking wishfully in the Colonel's face.

"I fear not," was the reply.

"God's will be done," said he; "but I have a long account to settle, and but a short time to do it in. Dear good Christians, pray with me—pray for me. Alas, it is an awful thing to die, and with the weight of murder on my conscience." Here he grew faint again and ceased to speak. A cordial was administered—he revived.

"You see before you, my kind friends," said he, "a most unhappy man, the victim of his own folly. My father is a clergyman in the North of England; I am his only child, and have received from him an education suitable to the station in which he meant to have placed me, which was the church; but, alas, I despised his precepts, and joined myself to a set of the most dissolute companions, with whom I ran into every species of vice and debauchery. By repeated extravagance I involved my poor father, who, no longer able to supply my exhorbitant demands, remonstrated against my way of life;

but I was too much attached to vice to resolve to quit it, and in a fit of desperation, having lost more money than I could pay, I enlisted into a regiment bound for this place. Ah, Sir, I have reason to think my conduct shortened the period of my dear mother's existence, and I have embittered the last hours of a father whom it was my duty to comfort and support. These are heavy clogs upon my departing soul, but he who witnessed the sincerity of my repentance, I trust will compassionate and pardon me."

"No doubt of it," cried Rebecca, whose heart was almost bursting as she listened to the expiring penitent. He looked round, and fixing his eyes on Rebecca and Sophia, "Poor girls," said he, "you are but young, take the advice of a dying sinner, and treasure it in your memories: obey your parents, never forsake them, and shun vicious company, for had I done this it would have been well with me in this evil day."

Rebecca's susceptible heart smote her, she hid her face with her handkerchief, and sighed deeply.

"God for ever bless you, my friends," said he; "I am going, a few pangs more, and all will be over. Oh, may he whose fatal aim took my life have it not remembered against him; may the Father of mercy forgive him as freely as I do."

He then began to repeat the Lord's Prayer, but expired before he could finish it.

"Peace to his repentant spirit," said the Colonel, as he raised his weeping daughter from her knees.

"His poor father," said she, "what would he feel, did he know this."

"He felt more," replied the Colonel, "when the misguided youth forsook the paths of virtue, than he would, could he even behold him now."

The heat at this season of the year is intense, and the Colonel knew the body of the unhappy soldier must that day be consigned to the earth, yet how to make the grave, or how to convey the corpse to it when made were difficulties which he could hardly think it possible to surmount, but sad necessity enforced the attempt; he fixed on a retired spot, just by the side of his garden, and began the melancholy task. Rebecca and Sophia with their delicate hands endeavoured to assist, and by evening they had completed it.

The faint rays of the setting sun just tinged the summit of the highest hill; the sky was serene, and scarce a breeze was heard to move the leaves or russle the smooth surface of the water. Awfully solemn was the silence that reigned through this once cheerful village.

As the Colonel sat pensively considering his situation, and thinking how in the decentest manner possible he could render the last sad duties to the deceased, he saw a small fishing boat, with one man in it, drawing near the shore; he ran hastily down, entreated him to land and assist him in his mournful office.

The body was carefully wrapped in a sheet—it was impossible to obtain a coffin.

"We have no clergyman," said the Colonel, "but the prayers of innocence shall consecrate his grave."

He gave the prayer book to Sophia, she opened it, and with her mother and Rebecca followed the body. She began the service, but her voice faltered, the tears burst forth, she sobbed, and could no longer articulate. The Colonel took it from her; he was a man of undaunted courage in the day of battle, but here even his heart sunk and his voice was tremulous; but he recalled his fortitude and finished the solemn rite in a becoming manner.

"What a day has this been," said Sophia, as they were partaking a little refreshment.

"It has been a heavy day indeed my child," said Mrs. Abthorpe, "but how much heavier would it have been, had the poor departed been related to us by any ties of blood: had he been a father, a husband, or a brother. Think not of the evils we endure, my dear Sophia, but reflect how much more painful our situation might be than it is, and offer up your thanks to your Creator, that our afflictions do not exceed our strength, and that in this solitary place we enjoy health and serenity of mind."

"Ah," said Rebecca, mentally, "I do not enjoy that serenity, for my mother, in affliction, in want, and calling in vain upon her daughter for comfort, is ever present to my imagination."

For several weeks the solitude of Colonel Abthorpe was undisturbed, and Autumn began to advance. He dreaded the approach of Winter, as he knew in that inclement season they would feel the want of many comforts they had been accustomed to enjoy; and shut out from all society, how should they procure sustenance. These reflections made him extremely unhappy. He would gladly have gone to the British troops, but had no possible means of conveying himself and family to them, and his heart revolted from the thought of going to reside with the enemies of his sovereign; however they gave him not the choice, for the latter end of October they dispatched a party, consisting of a captain, lieutenant, and fifty men, who surrounded the house of the defenceless Colonel, making himself, his wife, daughter, and our heroine prisoners, on pretence of his having held correspondence with the enemy. They were conveyed into the country, their house torn to pieces, their furniture destroyed, burnt, or divided among the soldiers, and all their property confiscated.

From Reuben and Rachel[†]

Chapter XIII

ANOTHER VISIT TO SAVAGE HABITATIONS

There had, some little time previous to this event, been several of the Indian chiefs taken prisoners by the Europeans, and it was to this circumstance those, who were taken prisoners by the natives, owed the preservation of their lives, as the savages entertained hopes that by means of these they might procure the liberty of their captured brethren.

Their route lay across the country, and before they had reached their place of destination, a very heavy fall of snow rendered the woods almost impenetrable; but the Indians, inured from their infancy to cold, hunger, every species of hardship, felt little or no inconvenience from the severity of the season, whilst the Europeans sunk under their accumulated sufferings; and of twelve who were taken prisoners, seven died by the way.

Reuben had been slightly wounded, and O'Neil had received a scratch, as he called it, in endeavouring to preserve his master, from the tomahawk of an Indian. But Reuben was by nature intrepid, and O'Neil was callous to every calamity that affected only himself. They mutually comforted and supported each other, and were amongst the few who survived at the end of their wearisome, pedestrian journey.

The morning after their arrival at the Indian settlement, the five surviving captives were presented to the sachem, Wampoogohoon. His wigwam was larger and more commodious than those of his subjects. It was well lined with skins of various wild beasts, and on a kind of throne, covered with the same materials, sat the sachem. At his left hand sat a woman, whose complexion spoke her of European descent, and behind them stood a young female, in appearance about seventeen years old. Her skin was a shade darker than that of the woman's; her eyes were of that kind of dark grey, which may almost be termed blue, and yet, from the shade of long black eyelashes, may sometimes be mistaken for black. Their expression was at once soft and animated, and her dark auburn hair, which did not really curl, but hung in waves down her back and over her shoulders, was ornamented with a few glass beads, and a tuft of scarlet feathers, fancifully arranged, and not entirely devoid of taste. The rest of her dress, though greatly similar to the other women, had a some-

---

† *Reuben and Rachel; or, Tales of Old Times* (1798), vol. 2. University of Virginia Library Electronic Text Center: Early American Fiction.

thing of delicacy, in its formation and method of being put on, that was particularly pleasing to Europeans. Her figure was above the middle size, yet not robust enough to be thought masculine, though every feature glowed with ruddy health, every limb displayed the strength and firmness of her frame. She stood with her right hand leaning on the sachem's shoulder, in her left she held an unbraced bow, and a quiver full of arrows was slung across her back.

Wampoogohoon received the captives with a kind of sullen dignity. He spoke to them in very bad English, but they understood sufficient to comprehend that he mean to detain them till the captured Indians were returned in safety.

During the time he was speaking, Reuben looked attentively at the two women, who from their places, and the universal respect paid them, he concluded were the wife and daughter of the chief. The pensiveness manifest in the countenance of the elder, the beauty and majesty of the younger, awakened in his bosom a wish to be acquainted with their story; for he was certain they were of European extraction, though of what nation he could not determine, as they had neither of them spoke.

At length, when the conference was ended, and the sachem waved his hand for them to depart, his wife arose, and spoke to him in the Mohawk tongue. Reuben perceived, from the soft tone of her voice and her earnest manner, that it was a supplication. He answered, but not with the gentlest accent; she laid her hand on his arm, and repeated her request, in which she was joined by Eumea, his daughter. He looked irresolute for a moment, then seeming to acquiesce in their demands, arose from his seat, and taking his bow and arrows, was followed by his attendants out of the wigwam.

The two interesting females now came forward, and the eldest, whose name was Victoire, addressed our hero in very tolerable French:

"Stranger, I am sorry for your captivity, though my situation amongst these Indians makes me appear your enemy. Yourself and companions are no doubt surprised, to see a person of my complexion so intimately connected with one of theirs; my story may be told in a few words. My mother, a native of France, being of a protestant family, and apprehending persecution, emigrated to this new-found world, in company with her husband, a man of strict piety and principles. Their portion of worldly goods was not large; they purchased a wild, uncultivated spot upon the borders of the Allegany, and by five years of indefatigable labour, rendered their little hut and surrounding garden, together with one field, tolerably comfortable; but just when they began to taste some small degree of happiness, which would scarcely have deserved the name, but by being contrasted with the excess of hardship they had endured in clearing and rendering their little demesne fit for cultivation; then, at the moment when they hoped to reap the reward of their labours, a party of Mohawks came down upon them, rifled and destroyed their dwelling, murdered my father and two little brothers, and carried my wretched mother and myself, then only a year old, into captivity."

Victoire paused; she seemed affected; a tear glistened in the expressive eyes of Eumea. At length the former proceeded:—

"My mother was a convincing proof of the excess of misery the human mind can suffer; she survived the loss of a husband tenderly beloved, and two children. I was her comfort, her stay, which held her to this world; for my sake she bore captivity without murmuring, for my sake she wished and strove to preserve her existence; she lived till I was fourteen years old, and gave me every instruction which memory furnished, for she had no assistance from books. She instilled into my young mind a knowledge and love of a supreme, benignant Being, and taught me to place my whole dependence on him, whose goodness was equal to his power.

"Wampoogohoon was the youngest son of the sachem, who at that time governed this tribe; he offered me his protection. My mother, in a dying state, rather than leave me exposed to insult, advised me to accede to his proposal, and I became his wife. His father and brothers are since dead, and you behold him a chief of the Mohawks. He is not unkind to me, and as the father of my children, I feel an affection for him. Eumea is the only surviving child I have of six; for her sake, I wish for some intercourse with the Europeans, that her mind, which is not a barren soil, may receive the culture of education. To this end, I have requested my husband to permit you to have a wigwam to yourselves, where you may dwell in quiet, till we hear of the safety of those Indians who have been detained by your party. In return, I only request you to exert your abilities to instruct, in your language, customs, manners and religion, my child Eumea."

Saying this, she presented the Indian maid to Reuben, who assured Victoire he would do all in his power to return the obligation she had conferred.

He was then, with his companions, shewn to a habitation that wore a trifling appearance of comfort; in it were three or four bear skins, a quantity of clean dry straw, some dried fish, venison and maize, and without was plenty of fuel.

Here our hero indulged himself in reflection; and often would his thoughts revert to his grandfather, William Dudley, who was for many years in a situation somewhat similar. But Reuben had seen too much of savage men and manners to have a wish to remain amongst them, even though he might have been elevated to the highest seat of dignity.

It was at once a comfort and amusement to Reuben, that he was obliged, for several hours every day, to employ his mind, in order to

cultivate that of his pupil Eumea. He contrived, by boiling the shu-
mak berries, to make a liquid with which he could write on white
birch bark. In this manner, he made an alphabet, which she presently learnt; and seeming to delight in attending to his instructions,
he experienced a double satisfaction in endeavouring to expand and
inform her understanding. She was soon able to read short sentences,
which he composed for her; his hand being generally employed, and
his mind often totally occupied in striving to recollect what might
be of the most service to his lovely scholar, he had little time for
reflection.

O'Neil laboured incessantly to keep their dwelling warm and
tight; and sometimes he went out with his gun, and brought home
some kind of game which served to diversify their scanty repasts;
and often Victoire would accompany her daughter to their wigwam,
and on those occasions generally carried something which they
thought a delicacy, such as noa-cake, omanny, or succatash, viands
composed of maize and dried beans; and thus wore away a very long
and intensely severe winter. Reuben had been a prisoner above six
months, and yet no news had arrived that could raise his hopes of
speedy liberation; and we must leave him amongst these children of
nature, and return to our heroine, whom we left married to Hamden
Auberry, but living in the vicinity of Mary-le-bone, under the assumed
name of Dacres.

*　*　*

From *Chapter Last*

> Where heaven-born Freedom holds her court
> 　Let me erect my humble shed;
> Where all the arts with joy resort,
> 　And Science rears her laurell'd head.

We left Reuben in captivity, employing every leisure moment in
expanding the mind and cultivating the talents of Eumea. In this
manner six weary months passed on, and still no hope of emancipation. At the end of this period, tidings arrived that the Indian chiefs
had been guilty of a breach of the European laws, and in consequence had suffered death. The sachem called a council of his
elders and chieftains, and it was determined that Reuben and his
unhappy companions should on the ensuing morning be bound to
the stake, and suffer those inhuman tortures which none but savages could inflict, and none but savages submit to, without an
endeavour to be avenged of those who inflict them.

Eumea was in the wigwam at the time this horrid sentence was
passed; her heart sunk; there were but a few hours to intervene

before it was to be put in execution. In the dead of night, she entered the wigwam of our hero.

"Englishmen," said she, "awake, get up; danger and death are at hand; haste, quit this place, flee into the woods that skirt the mountains, and the God of the Christians go with you." In a few words she explained to them the necessity of their immediate flight, and directing their steps to a cavern in a hollow glen, she threw her arms round the neck of Reuben, bathed his cheek with her tears, pressed her cold trembling lips to his, and sobbing, Adieu! returned to her restless bed to weep and pray for his safety.

Innumerable were the hardships endured by Reuben and his companions, skulking in caves, or deep woods, feeding on wild fruit, and even glad to make a meal of acorns; terrified by the rustling of the leaves, or the steps of wild though inoffensive animals, natives of the uncultivated tracts through which they were obliged to pass.

After three weeks wearisome journey, they at length arrived at a European settlement; but so reduced through famine and fatigue, that it seemed as though they were only arrived at a place of safety that they might rest from all their cares in death. Even the strength and spirits of O'Neil began to flag, and he bitterly regretted that he was no longer able to cheer, attend and comfort his dear master.

But what was the surprise of Reuben, when, the day after his arrival at this place, he saw Eumea enter the apartment where he was. He raised himself from the bed on which he was reclining, and in a voice that expressed at once surprise and pleasure, exclaimed, "Eumea here! what strange incident!" She stopped him, took hold of his hand, and looking earnestly in his face—

"Is it strange that I should follow you; (said she) were not you my instructor, my more than father, my friend, and was it possible Eumea could stay behind you and live? Do not look angry; I know I have done wrong; for you taught me to love, respect, and never forsake my father and mother. I tried to remember your precepts, I tried to obey your injunctions; but, alas! the silent night was witness to my anguish, and the rising sun could not dry the dew from my eyelids. If I slept, I saw you, listened to you, and was happy. Fleeting joy! that but embittered the moment of awaking! The flowers you had gathered for me the day before you left me, I bound upon my breast next my heart; I have worn them there ever since; they withered and dried, but every day I refresh them with my tears. One morning, just as the day appeared, I arose, took my bow and arrows, and resolved to follow you. My mother was still asleep; I looked at her, I knelt beside her; but I dared not kiss her lest she should awake. I would have prayed, but you had told me that an undutiful child could never be a favourite of our heavenly Father; so I pressed my hands on my heart, which throbbed so loud, it seemed to say,

Oh! God of the Christians, bless my mother! God knows every thought of the heart, and though I dared not pronounce his sacred name with my lips, perhaps its silent petition may be read and answered."

Eumea paused; Reuben would have answered, but he was at a loss what to say. O'Neil, weak and ill as he was, had moved towards her, and sitting at her feet, leaning one hand on her knees, his head rested on it, and his languid eyes were fixed on her face, as he listened to her with profound attention.

"It is my belief," said he, "that God Almighty never turns away from the prayers of an innocent heart; and then to be sure he knows all we want, when we can't speak to ask for even a morsel of bread. Oh! if we were only to have what we deserved, we should find but poor accommodations, in our journey through this world; but you see he was so good as to send people before us, to make every thing comfortable; and all he requires is, that we shall in return make things pleasant and agreeable for them that come after us."

Reuben could not help smiling at O'Neil's morality. Eumea seemed lost in thought, and scarcely to have attended to what he said; but when she found he was silent, she again addressed our hero.

"So you see here I am; but what have I gained by following you? Nothing! for now all that I suffered before for your absence, I now feel on account of my mother. But I will not return. No; I could not support my father's unkindness, and my mother's reproaches, which would be the more painful because mingled with affection. I will follow you, my dear instructor, I will be your handmaid, and love and serve you to the last hour of my life."

"And so will I," said O'Neil, "and I'll well serve you too, my beautiful Indian lady, every day and all the day, and by night too, if so be there be necessity."

"And how did you know that you should find me here?" said Reuben.

"I knew," she replied, "that this was the nearest settlement, and had I not found you here, I should have travelled onward to Philadelphia; and had you not been there, I should have thought you had died by the way, and would have sought you in a better world, the world of spirits."

"You would not, I hope, Eumea, have dared to rush unbidden into eternity?" said Reuben.

"I fear I should," she replied; "for why should we endure life, when the nights are past in anguish, and every day is a day of sorrow? When the wintry blasts howl, when the snow falls, and the frost binds up the lakes: then, when confined to the wigwam, there is no comfort within, but the tempest of the passions rages more furious than the gale that bows the tall cedars, and shakes to the roots the stately oak; why should we not sleep with the insect or the reptile tribes, that pass the dreary season in insensibility? And when the warm southern breeze dissolves the ice, and bids the trees be green, the blossom come; when the blackbird whistles merrily, and the robin begins to dress his plumes; if then nor fragrant blossom, nor cheerful bird, nor flower-speckled field delight the sense, or soothe the tortured soul, were it not better to seek repose in other climes, more suited to our feelings? Or when the deer seeks the deep woods, and pants though lying on the river's brink, when the scorching sun dries the grass and parches up the ground, where is the harm if, plunging in the wave, we quench the fever that consumes us, or from our veins let out the blood, that rushes with such fury through our frame, swelling the heart till it is near to bursting? Or even when the season of corn arrives; when clusters of wild grapes hang on the bending vines; when the berries, blackened by the sun, peep through the half-faded leaves; when the cool, soft breeze of evening, and the sweet air of the morning, affords refreshing slumbers to the eyelids, or uncloses them to pleasing prospects, that, being surveyed, makes the heart dance with joy—Ah! then, if the eyes are dimmed with tears and the heart oppressed with sorrow; is it a sin to seek that happy place where we can neither weep nor suffer more?"

"You have profited but little by my instructions, Eumea," said Reuben, "if you can argue thus."

"I will follow you, then," said she emphatically, "and endeavour to improve."

In about a fortnight, our hero and his companions were enough recovered to continue their journey. It was in vain he entreated Eumea to return to her mother, she persisted in following him. It was without effect that he represented to her, that in accompanying him she would be looked upon with disrespect by the European women; her resolution was taken and was not to be shaken.

*   *   *

About six weeks after this happy meeting, Reuben received the hand of Jessy Oliver. It was a day of festivity. The gates of Mount Pleasant were thrown open, and every visitor made welcome. To add to their mirth, a dance in the evening was to finish the entertainment.

A social meal, dispensed with cheerfulness, and partaken with a true spirit of hilarity, had been just removed, when the parlour door hastily opened, and Eumea entered. Her hair hung loose about her shoulders; her eyes were wild, and her voice broken. She rushed toward Reuben and Jessy, and taking a hand from each, joined them; then pressing them to her bosom, raised her eyes to heaven—

"God of the Christians," said she fervently, "make them forever happy. Wife of Reuben, thou art a happy woman, for thy husband is a man of honour. He saw the weakness of a poor, unprotected Indian maid, he pitied her folly, but took no advantage of it."

Jessy was affected by the simple yet fervent address. Reuben took the hand of Eumea, and would have made her sit down, but she refused.

"No! no!" said she, "Eumea will rest no more, know peace no more. I had raised a deity of my own, built an altar in my bosom, and daily offered the sacrifice of a fond, an affectionate heart; but the days are past, I can worship no longer without a crime. Farewel," said she, enthusiastically clasping her hands, "do not quite forget the poor, poor Eumea!"

She then left the house, and Reuben sent a person to follow and see that she came to no ill. She went home, but continued not long there; a young woman, who from her wild looks and incoherent language imagined her mind to be disordered, endeavoured to detain her, but in vain. About the dusk of the evening she went out, and all inquiry for her was fruitless till three days after, when as Reuben was giving some orders to O'Neil, in that part of his ground that lay on the verge of the Schuylkill, they discovered something floating on the water; the garments bespoke it a woman. Reuben's heart shuddered; they dragged it to the shore; it was the corpse of poor Eumea. Reuben sighed, raised his eyes to heaven, but was silent. Not so O'Neil. He fell on his knees beside the pale corpse, and his honest heart burst in a torrent from his eyes.

"Och! my flower of the forest," said he, "and art thou gone, and was it love that made thee leave us? Beautiful, good, sweetest of savages— O! thy poor O'Neil can pity thee. And what shall he do now thou hast closed thine eyes? Thou hast murdered thy sweet self, and what is there now in the world that he cares for?"

Reuben was struck with the fervency and humility that was at once expressed by O'Neil; for it spoke as plain as words could speak, 'I loved her, but I never dared to tell my love, lest it should offend her.'

Our hero by degrees drew him from the contemplation of the melancholy object, and proper forms being gone through in regard to the body, it was buried in a field near the margin of the river. O'Neil banked up the grave, twisted osier twigs and fenced it round; at the head he planted a weeping willow, and at the foot a wild rose tree. Of a night when his labour was finished, he would visit the spot, sing old ditties, and weep whilst he sung; and though he lived to good old age, O'Neil never knew another love.

* * *

From Charlotte's Daughter[†]

Chapter I

FALSE PRIDE AND UNSOPHISTICATED INNOCENCE

"What are you doing there Lucy?" said Mrs. Cavendish to a lovely girl, about fifteen years old. She was kneeling at the feet of an old man sitting just within the door of a small thatched cottage situated about five miles from Southampton on the coast of Hampshire. "What are you doing there child?" said she, in rather a sharp tone, repeating her question.

"Binding up sergeant Blandford's leg ma'am," said the kind hearted young creature, looking up in the face of the person who spoke to her. At the same time, rising on one knee she rested the lame limb on a stool on which was a soft cushion which this child of benevolence had provided for the old soldier.

"And was there no one but you Miss Blakeney who could perform such an office? You demean yourself strangely." "I did not think it was any degradation," replied Lucy, "to perform an act of kindness to a fellow creature, but I have done now," continued she rising, "and will walk home with you ma'am if you please." She then wished the sergeant a good night, and tying on her bonnet which had been thrown on the floor during her employment, she took Mrs. Cavendish's arm, and they proceeded to the house of the Rector of the village.

"There! Mr. Matthews," exclaimed the lady on entering the parlour, "there! I have brought home Miss Blakeney, and where do you think I found her? and how employed?"

"Where you found her," replied Mr. Matthews, smiling, "I will not pretend to say; for she is a sad rambler, but I dare be bound that you did not find her either foolishly or improperly employed."

"I found her in old Blandford's cottage, swathing up his lame leg." "And how my good madam," inquired Mr. Matthews, "could innocence be better employed, than in administering to the comforts of the defender of his country?"

"Well, well, you always think her right, but we shall hear what my sister says to it. Mrs. Matthews, do you approve of a young lady of rank and fortune making herself familiar with all the beggars and low people in the place?"

"By no means," said the stately Mrs. Matthews, "and I am astonished that Miss Blakeney has not a higher sense of propriety and her own consequence."

---

† *Charlotte's Daughter; or, The Three Orphans. A Sequel to Charlotte Temple* (Boston: Richardson & Lord, 1828). Commonly known as *Lucy Temple.* University of Virginia Library Electronic Text Center: Early American Fiction.

"Dear me, ma'm," interrupted Lucy, "it was to make myself of consequence that I did it; for lady Mary, here at home, says I am nobody, an insignificant Miss Mushroom, but sergeant Blandford calls me his guardian angel, his comforter; and I am sure those are titles of consequence."

"Bless me," said Mrs. Cavendish, "what plebeian ideas the girl has imbibed, it is lucky for you child, that you were so early removed from those people."

"I hope madam," replied Lucy, "you do not mean to say that it was fortunate for me that I was so early deprived of the protection of my dear grandfather? Alas! it was a heavy day for me; he taught me that the only way to become of real consequence, is to be useful to my fellow creatures." Lucy put her hand before her eyes to hide the tears she could not restrain, and courtesying respectfully to Mr. Matthews, his wife and sister, she left the room.

"Well, I protest sister," said Mrs. Cavendish, "that is the most extraordinary girl I ever knew; with a vast number of low ideas and habits, she can sometimes assume the *hauteur* and air of a dutchess. In what a respectful yet independent manner she went out of the room, I must repeat she is a most extraordinary girl."

Mrs. Matthews was too much irritated to reply with calmness, she therefore wisely continued silent. Mr. Matthews was silent from a different cause, and supper being soon after announced, the whole family went into the parlour; Lucy had dried her tears, and with a placid countenance seated herself by her reverend friend, Mr. Matthews. "*You*, I hope, are not angry with me, Sir?" said she with peculiar emphasis. "No my child," he replied, pressing the hand she had laid upon his arm, "No, I am not angry, but my little Lucy must remember that she is now advancing towards womanhood, and that it is not always safe, nor perfectly proper, to be rambling about in the dusk of the evening without a companion."

"Then if you say so sir, I will never do it again; but indeed you do not know how happy my visits make old Mr. Blandford; you know, sir, he is very poor; so Lady Mary would not go with me if I asked her; and he is very lame, so if Aura went with me, she is such a madcap, perhaps she might laugh at him; besides, when I sometimes ask Mrs. Matthews to let her walk with me, she has something for her to do, and cannot spare her."

"Well, my dear," said the kind hearted old gentleman, "when you want to visit him again ask me to go with you." "Oh! you are the best old man in the world," cried Lucy, as rising she put her arms round his neck and kissed him. "There now, there is a specimen of low breeding," said Mrs. Cavendish, "you ought to know, Miss Blakeney, that nothing can be more rude than to call a person old." "I did not mean to offend," said Lucy. "No! I am sure you did not," replied Mr. Matthews, "and so let us eat our supper, for when a man or woman, sister, is turned of sixty they may be termed old, without much exaggeration, or the smallest breach of politeness."

But the reader will perhaps like to be introduced to the several individuals who compose this family.

＊　　＊　　＊

Conclusion

Several years rolled away after the event recorded in the last chapter, without affording any thing worthy the attention of the reader. The persons to whom our narrative relates, were enjoying that calm happiness, which as has frequently been remarked, affords so little matter for history. We must accordingly conclude the story with the incidents of a somewhat later period.

It was the season of the Christmas holidays. Edward and his blooming wife with their two lovely children, were on a visit to his father, and had come to pass an evening at the Rectory. Lady Mary too was there. She had recovered from the wreck of her husband's property enough to support her genteelly, and had found an asylum with her old preceptor and guide, in the only place where she had ever enjoyed any thing like solid happiness.

The Rector, now rapidly declining into the vale of years, afforded a picture of all that is venerable in goodness; his lady retained her placid and amiable virtues, although her activity was gone; and the worthy Mrs. Cavendish, still stately in her carriage, and shrewd and decisive in her remarks, presented no bad counterpart to her milder sister.

Last but not the least interesting of the cheerful group which was now assembled around the fireside of the Rector, was Lucy Blakeney. Her beauty, unimpaired by her early sorrows and preserved by the active and healthful discharge of the duties of benevolence, had now become matured into the fairest model of lovely womanhood. It was not that beauty which may be produced by the exquisite blending of pure tints on the cheek and brow, by fair waving tresses and perfect symmetry of outline—it was the beauty of character and intellect, the beauty that speaks in the eye, informs every gesture and look, and carries to the heart at once the conviction, that in such an one, we behold a lovely work of the Creator, blessed by his own hand and pronounced good.

The Rector was delighted to find the three orphans once more met under his own roof, and apparently enjoying the blessings of this world in such a spirit as gave him no painful apprehensions concerning the future.

"I cannot express to you," he said, "how happy I am to see you all here again once more before my departure. It has long been the desire of my heart. It is accomplished, and I can now leave my blessing with you and depart in peace."

"You cannot enjoy the meeting more highly than we do, I am sure," said Aura, "the return to this spot brings back a thousand tender and delightful associations to my mind, and I regard among the most pleasing circumstances which attend our meeting, the degree of health and enjoyment in which we find all our old friends at the Rectory. But how do all our acquaintances among the cottagers? Is the old sergeant living?"

"He is in excellent health," replied the Rector, "and tells all his old stories with as much animation as ever."

"And your protegés, Lady Mary, the distressed family which you found out," rejoined Aura.

"They are well, and quite a happy industrious family," answered Lady Mary, with a slight blush.

"How goes on the school, Lucy," said Edward, "I regard that as the most effective instrument of benevolent exertion."

"I hope it has effected some good," answered Lucy. "There has been a considerable number from the school who have proved useful and respectable so far; several of the pupils are now married, and others are giving instruction in different parts of the country. A circumstance which has afforded us considerable gratification is, that a pupil, whose merit has raised her to a high station in life, has visited us lately, and presented a handsome donation towards rendering the establishment permanent."

After a short pause in the conversation, Mr. Matthews expressed a wish that they might have some intelligence from their absent friends.

"I have this day received a letter from America," said Edward, taking it from his pocket and looking inquiringly at Lucy.

"I think you may venture to read it to us," said she.

It was from Mrs. Franklin, and informed him that she had purchased a beautiful seat on the banks of the Delaware, and was living there in the enjoyment of all the happiness, which was to be derived from the society of her family and the delightful serenity of nature. One circumstance only had happened since her departure from England to mar this enjoyment, the account of which must be given in her own words.

'My oldest son, your friend—no doubt you have often heard from him. He soon grew tired of the India service, and was at his own desire exchanged into a regiment which had been ordered to join the army in Spain. There, his career was marked with the heroism and generosity which had ever distinguished his character. A young officer is now visiting me, who accompanied him in his last campaign.

He informs me, that my noble son never lost an opportunity either of signalizing himself in action or relieving the distresses of those who suffered the calamities of war.

'In one of the severest battles fought upon the peninsula, it was the fortune of my son to receive a severe wound, while gallantly leading his men to a breach in the walls of a fortified town. The English were repulsed, and a French officer, passing over the field, a few hours after, with a detachment, had the barbarity to order one of his men to fix his bayonet in him. His friend, who was also wounded and lay near him, saw it, but was too helpless himself to raise an arm in his defence.

'The same night, the town was taken by storm. When the English force advanced, the unfortunate officers were both conveyed to safe quarters, and my poor son lived thirty-six hours after the capture of the place. During this time, the story of his inhuman treatment reached the ears of the commander in chief. Fired with indignation, he hastened to the quarters of the wounded officers.

'"Poor Franklin," says his friend, "was lying in the arms of his faithful servant and breathing heavily, when the illustrious Wellington entered the room. It was apparent to all that he had but a few moments to live.

'"Tell me," said the General, "exert but strength enough to describe to me the villain who inflicted that unmanly outrage upon you, and I swear by the honour of a soldier that in one hour his life shall answer it."'

'Never did I see the noble countenance of Franklin assume such an expression of calm magnanimity as when he replied,

'"I am not able to designate him, and if I could do it with certainty, be assured, Sir, that I never would.'"

'These were his last words, and in a few minutes more his spirit fled to a brighter region.'

If there are sorrows which refuse the balm of sympathy, there are also consolations which those around us "can neither give nor take away." Through the remaining years of her life, the orphan daughter of the unfortunate Charlotte Temple evinced the power and efficiency of those exalted principles, which can support the mind under every trial, and the happiness of those pure emotions and lofty aspirations whose objects are raised far above the variable contingencies of time and sense.

In the circle of her friends she seldom alluded to past events; and though no one presumed to invade the sanctuary of her private griefs and recollections, yet all admired the serene composure with which she bore them. Various and comprehensive schemes of benevolence formed the work of her life, and religion shed its holy and healing light over all her paths.

When the summons came, which released her pure spirit from its earthly tenement, and the history of her family was closed with the life of its last representative; those who had witnessed, in her mother's fate, the ruin resulting from once yielding to the seductive influence of passion, acknowledged, in the events of the daughter's life, that benignant power which can bring, out of the most bitter and blighting disappointments, the richest fruits of virtue and happiness.

SONG LYRICS

I Never Will Be Married[†]

Sung by Miss Leary

When I had scarcely told sixteen,
    My flattering tell-tale glass
Told me there seldom could be seen,
    A blyther bonnier lass
5   Full twenty lovers round me bow'd,
    But high my head I carried,
And with a scornful air I vow'd,
    I never wou'd be married.

Young Harry warmly urg'd his suit,
10   And talk'd of wealth in store,
While Jemmy thought to strike me mute,
    And told his conquests o'er,
Each youth a diff'rent ant essay'd,
    And still their arts I parried,
15 Believe me, Sir, I laughing said,
    I never will be married.

Then five revolving summers past,
    While I the tyrant play'd,
Ah! then I fear'd 'twould be at last
20   My fate to die a maid,
Of all the lovers in my train,
    There was but one that tarried,
I thought 'twas time to change my strain,
    And we this morn were married.

† *The Whim of the day (for 1793). Containing an entertaining selection of the choices of approved songs now singing at the Theatres Royal,* Second Edition (London, 1793). Eighteenth Century Collections Online.

The Sailor's Landlady[†]

Words by Mrs. Rowson; Music by Mr. Reinagle.

How blest the life a sailor leads,
    From clime to clime still ranging,
For as the calm the storms succeeds,
    The scene delights by changing.
5 When tempests howl along the main,
    Some object will remind us,
And cheer, with hopes to meet again,
    The friends we left behind us.

CHORUS.

    For, under snug sail, we laugh at the gale;
10   And, tho' landsmen look pale, never heed 'em;
    But toss off the glass, to a favourite lass,
        To America, commerce, and freedom.

And when arriv'd in sight of land,
    Or safe in port rejoicing,
15 Our ship we moor, our sails we hand,
    Whilst out the boat is hoisting.
With chearful hearts the shore we reach;
    Our friends, delighted, greet us;
And tripping lightly o'er the beach,
20   The pretty lasses meet us.

CHORUS.

When the full following bowl enlivens the soul,
    To foot it we merrily lead 'em,
And each bonny lass will drink off her glass,
    To America, commerce, and freedom.

25 Our prizes sold, the chink we share,
    And gladly we receive it;
And when we meet a brother tar
    That wants, we freely give it:
No free-born sailor yet had store,
30   But chearfully would lend it;
And when 'tis gone, to sea for more;
    We earn it, but to spend it.

[†] Philadelphia, 1794. This popular song came to be known as "America, Commerce, & Freedom." Early American Imprints; Series I: Evans, no. 27648.

CHORUS.

Then drink round, my boys; 'tis the first of our joys
    To relieve the distres'd, clothe, and feed 'em;
35 'Tis a duty we share, with the brave and the fair,
    In this land of commerce and freedom.

POEM

Maria. Not a Fiction.[†]

Daughters of vanity, attend;
    Ye sons of riot, hear
The lovely, lost MARIA's end,
    And drop a silent tear.

5   List to the solemn passing bell,
        On the dead silence fall,
    In awful notes that seem to tell,
        This is the end of all.

    MARIA once was young and gay,
10   In beauty's bloom and pride;
    Sweet as the fragrant breath of May,
        And innocent beside.

    Her form was faultless, and her mind,
        Untainted yet by art,
15 Was noble, just, humane and kind,
        And virtue warm'd her heart.

    But ah, the cruel spoiler came,
        Admir'd her charms and youth:
    He feign'd to feel love's pow'rful flame,
20   And vow'd eternal truth.

    Free from disguise herself, she thought
        Her lover as sincere;
    To hide her tenderness ne'er sought,
        But told it without fear.

25 She said she lov'd, one fatal hour;
        The villain, pleas'd to find

---

† Susanna Rowson, *Miscellaneous Poems* (Boston, 1804). American Poetry Full-Text Database, Chadwick Healey, Inc.

The lovely creature in his power;
　　Poison'd her artless mind.

He talk'd of bonds by nature made,
30　　The dearest of all ties;
The heedless girl, by love betray'd,
　　Believ'd his specious lies.

Her honour gone, reduc'd to shame,
　　He leaves the ruin'd fair:
35　Unmanly boaster—blasts her fame,
　　And laughs at her despair.

Her father hear'd the horrid tale;
　　Anger inflam'd his breast;
Repentant pray'rs would nought avail;
40　　All nature was suppress'd.

In vain with tears she bath'd his feet,
　　And vow'd to err no more:
He said her home should be the street,
　　And thrust her from his door.

45　Her sex her miseries insult;
　　Contempt she meets from all;
Some boast their virtue, and exult
　　In poor MARIA's fall.

Wretched, forsaken, and undone;
50　　No friend to take her part,
To teach her future crimes to shun,
　　Or sooth her aching heart;

At first, oh! horrible to name!
　　She's infamous for bread,
55　Till, lost to every sense of shame,
　　She meets it without dread.

Awhile in FOLLY's giddy maze,
　　Thoughtless, her time she spends;
While pleasure seems to wait her days,
60　　And joy each step attends.

But vice soon robb'd her lovely face
　　Of all its wonted bloom,

While black remorse and pale disease
    Her tender frame consume.

65 That bloom she now supplies by art,
    And cheerfulness she feigns;
But still her lacerated heart
    Feels agonizing pains.

Cold blew the wind; descending snow
70   Clad nature all in white;
Maria, now the child of woe,
    Brav'd the tempestuous night.

Passing her vile betrayer's door,
    The sight past scenes recalls:
75 With tears her languid eyes run o'er;
    Low on the ground she falls.

"And must these steps," she weeping cried,
    "Support my aching head?
Oh! would to Heav'n that I had died,
80   Ere innocence was fled.

And thou, false man, who's specious lies
    My easy heart did gain;
Come, see the lost Maria dies,
    Through famine, grief and pain.

85 Oh come, and take my parting sigh,
    And hear me vow to Heaven,
As I forgive thee, so may I,
    Hereafter be forgiven.

But oh, my father! nature sure
90   Might plead within thy breast;
Why didst thou thrust me from thy door?
    Why leave me when distress'd?

Hadst thou but pardon'd my first fault,
    Hadst thou but been my friend,
95 I'd ne'er through grief and shame been brought,
    To this untimely end.

Or had some gen'rous woman strove,
    A fallen wretch to raise,

I now, with gratitude and love,
100   Had liv'd to speak her praise."

A poor man passing, heard her mourn,
    But little was his store;
He thought, to share it, in return
    Just Heav'n would give him more.

105 He gently rais'd her on her feet,
    And led her to his home;
A poor straw bed, and matted seat,
    Were all that grac'd the room.

Some milk with hand humane he brought,
110   And cheer'd the dying fair;
With pious pray'rs to sooth her sought,
    And chas'd away despair.

Bless! bless him, Heav'n! for what he's done!
    For I've no power, she cried:
115 The accent falter'd on her tongue;
    She grasp'd his hand, and died.

DRAMA

From Slaves in Algiers;
or, a Struggle for Freedom[†]

From *Act One*

SCENE ONE

City of Algiers. Apartment at the DEY'S. FETNAH *and* SELIMA.

FETNAH   Well, it's all vastly pretty—the gardens, the house and these fine clothes. I like them very well, but I don't like to be confined.

SELIMA   Yet, surely, you have no reason to complain. Chosen favorite of the Dey, what can you wish for more?

FETNAH   Oh, a great many things. In the first place, I wish for liberty. Why do you talk of my being a favorite? Is the poor bird that

---

† *Slaves in Algiers; or, A struggle for freedom: a play, interspersed with songs, in three acts . . . By Mrs. Rowson. As Performed at the New Theatres, in Philadelphia and Baltimore* (Philadelphia, 1794). Early American Imprints, Series I: Evans, no. 27655.

is confined in a cage (because a favorite with its enslaver) consoled for the loss of freedom? No! Though its prison is of golden
wire, its little heart still pants for liberty. Gladly would it seek the
fields of air, and even perched upon a naked bough, exulting carol
forth its song, nor once regret the splendid house of bondage.

SELIMA Ah! But then our master loves you.

FETNAH What of that? I don't love him.

SELIMA Not love him?

FETNAH No. He is old and ugly; then he wears such tremendous
whiskers. And when he makes love, he looks so grave and stately
that, I declare, if it was not for fear of his huge scimitar, I should
burst out a-laughing in his face.

SELIMA Take care you don't provoke him too far.

FETNAH I don't care how I provoke him, if I can but make him keep
his distance. You know I was brought here only a few days since.
Well, yesterday, as I was amusing myself, looking at the fine things
I saw everywhere about me, who should bolt into the room, but that
great, ugly thing Mustapha. "What do you want?" said I!

"Most beautiful Fetnah," said he, bowing till the tip of his long,
hooked nose almost touched the toe of his slipper, "Most beautiful
Fetnah, our powerful and gracious master, Muley Moloc, sends
me, the humblest of his slaves, to tell you he will condescend to
stop in your apartment tonight, and commands you to receive the
high honor with proper humility."

SELIMA Well—and what answer did you return?

FETNAH Lord, I was so frightened, and so provoked, I hardly know
what I said; but finding the horrid-looking creature didn't move,
at last I told him that if the Dey was determined to come, I supposed he must, for I could not hinder him.

SELIMA And did he come?

FETNAH No, but he made me go to him; and when I went trembling
into the room, he twisted his whiskers and knit his great beetle
brows. "Fetnah," said he, "You abuse my goodness; I have conde-
scended to request you to love me." And then he gave me such a
fierce look, as if he would say, and if you don't love me, I'll cut
your head off.

SELIMA I dare say you were finely frightened.

FETNAH Frightened! I was provoked beyond all patience, and thinking he would certainly kill me one day or other, I thought I might
as well speak my mind, and be dispatched out of the way at once.

SELIMA You make me tremble.

FETNAH So, mustering up as much courage as I could: "Great and
powerful Muley," said I, "I am sensible I am your slave. You took
me from an humble state, placed me in this fine palace, and gave
me these rich clothes. You bought my person of my parents, who

loved gold better than they did their child; but my affections you could not buy. I can't love you."

"How!" cried he, starting from his seat, "How, can't love me?" And he laid his hand upon his scimitar.

SELIMA   Oh, dear! Fetnah!

FETNAH   When I saw the scimitar half drawn, I caught hold of his arm. "Oh, good my lord," said I, "Pray do not kill a poor little girl like me! Send me home again, and bestow your favor on some other, who may think splendor a compensation for the loss of liberty."

"Take her away," said he. "She is beneath my anger."

SELIMA   But how is it, Fetnah, that you have conceived such an aversion to the manners of a country where you were born?

FETNAH   You are mistaken. I was not born in Algiers. I drew my first breath in England. My father, Ben Hassan, as he is now called, was a Jew. I can scarcely remember our arrival here, and have been educated in the Moorish religion, though I always had a natural antipathy to their manners.

SELIMA   Perhaps imbibed from your mother.

FETNAH   No. She has no objection to any of their customs, except that of their having a great many wives at a time. But some few months since, my father, who sends out many corsairs,[1] brought home a female captive to whom I became greatly attached. It was she who nourished in my mind the love of liberty and taught me woman was never formed to be the abject slave of man. Nature made us equal with them and gave us the power to render ourselves superior.

SELIMA   Of what nation was she?

FETNAH   She came from that land where virtue in either sex is the only mark of superiority. She was an American.

SELIMA   Where is she now?

FETNAH   She is still at my father's, waiting the arrival of her ransom, for she is a woman of fortune. And though I can no longer listen to her instructions, her precepts are engraven on my heart. I feel that I was born free, and while I have life, I will struggle to remain so.

Song

I.

> The rose just bursting into bloom,
> Admired where'er 'tis seen,
> Diffuses 'round a rich perfume,
> The garden's pride and queen.

---

1. Pirate ships, especially of the Barbary Pirates. Between 1785 and 1815, these attacked many American ships, seizing vessels and cargoes and taking captives.

When gathered from its native bed,
No longer charms the eye;
Its vivid tints are quickly fled.
'Twill wither, droop, and die.

II.

So woman when by nature dressed,
In charms devoid of art
Can warm the stoic's icy breast,
Can triumph o'er each heart,
Can bid the soul to virtue rise,
To glory prompt the brave,
But sinks oppresed, and drooping dies,
When once she's made a slave. (*Exits.*)

* * *

SCENE SIX

Inside the palace. MULEY MOLOC *and* MUSTAPHA

MULEY MOLOC   Fetnah gone, Zoriana gone . . . and the fair slave Olivia?

MUSTAPHA   All, dread sir.

MULEY MOLOC   Send instantly to the prison of the slave Constant. 'Tis he who has again plotted to rob me of Olivia. (*Exit* MUSTAPHA.) My daughter, too, he has seduced from her duty. But he shall not escape my vengeance.
    Re-enter MUSTAPHA.

MUSTAPHA   Some of the fugitives are overtaken, and wait in chains without.

MULEY MOLOC   Is Zoriana taken?

MUSTAPHA   Your daughter is safe. The old man, too, is taken, but Fetnah and Olivia have escaped.

MULEY MOLOC   Bring in the wretches. (HENRY, CONSTANT, *and several* SLAVES *brought in, chained.*) Rash old man, how have you dared to tempt your fate again? Do you not know the torments that await the Christian who attempts to rob the harem of a Musselman?

CONSTANT   I know you have the power to end my being, but that's a period I more wish than fear.

MULEY MOLOC   Where is Olivia?

CONSTANT   Safe, I hope, beyond your power. Oh, gracious heaven, protect my darling from this tyrant, and let my life pay the dear purchase of her freedom.

MULEY MOLOC   Bear them to the torture. Who and what am I, that a vile slave dares brave me to my face?

HENRY   Hold off! We know that we must die, and we are prepared to meet our fate like men. Impotent, vain boaster, call us not slaves. You are a slave indeed, to rude, ungoverned passion, to pride, to avarice and lawless love. Exhaust your cruelty in finding tortures for us, and we will smiling tell you the blow that ends our lives strikes off our chains and sets our souls at liberty.

MULEY MOLOC   Hence! Take them from my sight. (CAPTIVES *taken off.*) Devise each means of torture. Let them linger months, years, ages, in their misery.

    Enter OLIVIA.

OLIVIA   Stay, Muley, stay. Recall your cruel sentence.

MULEY MOLOC   Olivia here; is it possible?

OLIVIA   I have never left the palace. Those men are innocent. So is your daughter. It is I alone deserve your anger; then on me only let it fall. It was I procured false keys to the apartments; it was I seduced your daughter to our interest. I bribed the guards and with entreaty won the young Christian to attempt to free my father. Then, since I was the cause of their offenses, it is fit my life should pay the forfeiture of theirs.

MULEY MOLOC   Why did you not accompany them?

OLIVIA   Fearing what has happened, I remained, in hopes, by tears and supplications, to move you to forgive my father. Oh, Muley, save his life! Save all his friends, and if you must have blood to appease your vengeance, let me alone be the sacrifice.

MULEY MOLOC (*Aside*). How her softness melts me. (*To* OLIVIA.) Rise, Olivia. You may on easier terms give them both life and freedom.

OLIVIA   No. Here I kneel till you recall your orders. Haste, or it may be too late.

MULEY MOLOC   Mustapha, go bid them delay the execution. (*Exit* MUSTAPHA.)

OLIVIA   Now teach me to secure their lives and freedom, and my last breath shall bless you.

MULEY MOLOC   Renounce your faith. Consent to be my wife. Nay, if you hesitate—

OLIVIA   I do not. Give me but an hour to think.

MULEY MOLOC   Not a moment. Determine instantly. Your answer gives them liberty or death.

OLIVIA   Then I am resolved. Swear to me, by Mohammed—an oath I know you Musselmen never violate—that the moment I become your wife my father and his friends are free.

MULEY   By Mohammed I swear, not only to give them life and freedom, but safe conveyance to their desired home.

OLIVIA   I am satisfied. Now leave me to myself a few short moments, that I may calm my agitated spirits and prepare to meet you in the mosque.

MULEY MOLOC   Henceforth I live but to obey you. (*Exits.*)

OLIVIA   On what a fearful precipice I stand. To go forward is ruin, shame and infamy; to recede is to pronounce sentence of death upon my father and my adored Henry. Oh, insupportable! There is one way, and only one, by which I can fulfill my promise to the Dey, preserve my friends, and not abjure my faith. Source of my being, Thou canst read the heart which Thou hast been pleased to try in the school of adversity. Pardon the weakness of an erring mortal, if, rather than behold a father perish—if, rather than devote his friends to death, I cut the thread of my existence and rush unbidden to Thy presence. Yes, I will to the mosque, perform my promise, preserve the valued lives of those I love, then sink at once into the silent grave and bury all my sorrow in oblivion. (*Exits.*)

SCENE SEVEN

Another apartment. Enter OLIVIA *and* MULEY MOLOC.

MULEY MOLOC   Yes, on my life, they are free. In a few moments they will be here.

OLIVIA   Spare me the trial. For the whole world, I would not see them now; nor would I have them know at what price I have secured their freedom.

Enter HENRY *and* CONSTANT.

CONSTANT   My child—

HENRY   My love—

OLIVIA   My Henry! Oh, my dear father? Pray excuse these tears.

Enter MUSTAPHA.

MUSTAPHA   Great sir, the mosque is prepared, and the priest waits your pleasure.

MULEY MOLOC   Come, my Olivia.

HENRY   The mosque—the priest— What dreadful sacrifice is then intended?

OLIVIA   Be not alarmed. I must needs attend a solemn rite which gratitude requires. Go, my dear father. Dearest Henry, leave me, and be assured when next you see Olivia she will be wholly free.

Enter REBECCA.

REBECCA   Hold for a moment.

MULEY MOLOC   What means this bold intrusion?

REBECCA   Muley, you see before you a woman unused to forms of state, despising titles. I come to offer ransom for six Christian slaves. Waiting your leisure, I was informed a Christian maid, to save her father's life, meant to devote herself a sacrifice to your embraces. I have the means: make your demand of ransom, and set the maid, with those she loves, at liberty.

MULEY MOLOC   Her friends are free already, but for herself she voluntarily remains with me.

REBECCA   Can you, unmoved, behold her anguish? Release her, Muley. Name but the sum that will pay her ransom. 'Tis yours.

MULEY MOLOC   Woman, the wealth of Golconda[2] could not pay her ransom. Can you imagine that I, whose slave she is—I, who could force her obedience to my will and yet gave life and freedom to those Christians to purchase her compliance—would now relinquish her for paltry gold? Contemptible idea. Olivia, I spare you some few moments to your father. Take leave of him, and as you part, remember: his life and liberty depend on you.   (*Exits.*)

REBECCA   Poor girl, what can I do to mitigate your sufferings?

OLIVIA   Nothing. My fate, alas, is fixed. But, generous lady, by what name shall we remember you? What nation are you of?

REBECCA   I am an American; but while I only claim kinship with the afflicted, it is of little consequence where I first drew my breath.

CONSTANT   An American? From what state?

REBECCA   New York is my native place. There did I spend the dear, delightful days of childhood; and there, alas, I drained the cup of deep affliction to the very dregs.

CONSTANT   My heart is strangely interested. Dearest lady, will you impart to us your tale of sorrow, that we may mourn with one who feels so much for us?

REBECCA   Early in life, while my brave countrymen were struggling for their freedom, it was my fate to love and be beloved by a young British officer to whom, though strictly forbid by my father, I was privately married.

CONSTANT   Married! Say you?

REBECCA   My father soon discovered our union. Enraged, he spurned me from him, discarded, cursed me; and for four years I followed my husband's fortune. At length, my father relented; on a sickbed he sent for me to attend him. I went, taking with me an infant son, leaving my husband and a lovely girl, then scarcely three years old. Oh, heavens! What sorrows have I known from that unhappy hour. During my absence the armies met; my husband fell. My daughter was torn from me. What then availed the wealth my dying father had bequeathed me? Long—long did I lose all sense of my misery, and returning reason showed me the world only one universal blank. The voice of my darling boy first called me to myself. For him I strove to mitigate my sorrow; for his dear sake I have endured life.

CONSTANT   Pray proceed.

2. A city of ancient India noted for its diamond trade.

REBECCA   About a year since, I heard a rumor that my husband was still alive. Full of the fond hope of again beholding him, I, with my son, embarked for England; but before we reached the coast we were captured by an Algerine.

CONSTANT   Do you think you should recollect your husband?

REBECCA   I think I should, but fourteen years of deep affliction have impaired my memory and may have changed his features.

CONSTANT   What was his name? Oh, speak it quickly!

REBECCA   His name was Constant; but wherefore—

CONSTANT   It was. It was. Rebecca, don't you know me?

REBECCA   Alas, how you are altered. Oh, Constant, why have you forsaken me so long?

CONSTANT   In the battle you mention, I was indeed severely wounded—nay, left for dead in the field. There my faithful servant found me, when some remaining signs of life encouraged him to attempt my recovery; and by his unremitting care I was at length restored. My first returning thought was fixed on my Rebecca, but after repeated inquiries, all I could hear was that your father was dead and yourself and child removed farther from the seat of war. Soon after, I was told you had fallen a martyr to grief for my supposed loss. But see, my love, our daughter, our dear Olivia. Heaven preserved her to be my comforter.

OLIVIA (*Kneeling and kissing* REBECCA).   My mother, blessed word! Oh, do I live to say I have a mother.

REBECCA   Bless you, my child, my charming, duteous girl; but tell me by what sad chance you became captives.

CONSTANT   After peace was proclaimed with America, my duty called me to India, from whence I returned with a ruined constitution. Being advised to try the air of Lisbon, we sailed for that place, but heaven ordained that here in the land of captivity I should recover a blessing which will amply repay me for all my past sufferings.

    Enter MULEY MOLOC.

MULEY MOLOC   Christians, you trifle with me. Accept your freedom, go in peace, and leave Olivia to perform her promise. For should she waver or draw back, on you I will wreak my vengeance.

REBECCA   Then let your vengeance fall. We will die together; for never shall Olivia, a daughter of Columbia, and a Christian, tarnish her name by apostasy or live the slave of a despotic tyrant.

MULEY MOLOC   Then take your wish. Who's there?

    Enter MUSTAPHA *hastily.*

MUSTAPHA   Arm, mighty sir! The slaves throughout Algiers have mutinied. They bear down all before them. This way they come. They say if all the Christian slaves are not immediately released, they'll raze the city.

REBECCA   Now! Bounteous heaven, protect my darling boy, and aid the cause of freedom!

MULEY MOLOC   Bear them to instant death.

MUSTAPHA   Dread sir, consider.

MULEY MOLOC   Vile, abject slave, obey me and be silent! What, have I power over these Christian dogs, and shall I not exert it? Dispatch, I say! (*Huzza and clash of swords without.*) Why am I not obeyed? (*Clash again; confused noise; several huzza's.*)

AUGUSTUS (*Without*)   Where is my mother? Save, oh, save my mother.

FREDERIC (*Speaking*)   Shut up the palace gates. Secure the guards, and at your peril suffer none to pass.

AUGUSTUS (*Entering*)   Oh, Mother, are you safe?

CONSTANT   Bounteous heaven! And am I then restored to more— much more than life—my Rebecca? My children? Oh, this joy is more than I can bear.

   Enter FREDERIC, FETNAH, SEBASTIAN, BEN HASSAN, SLAVES, &c.

SEBASTIAN   Great and mighty Ottoman, suffer my friends to show you what pretty bracelets these are. Oh, you old dog, we'll give you the bastinado presently.

FREDERIC   Forbear, Sebastian. Muley Moloc, though your power over us is at end, we neither mean to enslave your person, or put a period to your existence. We are free men, and while we assert the rights of men, we dare not infringe the privileges of a fellow creature.

SEBASTIAN   By the law of retaliation, he should be a slave.

REBECCA   By the Christian law, no man should be a slave. It is a word so abject that to speak it dyes the cheek with crimson. Let us assert our own prerogative, be free ourselves, but let us not throw on another's neck the chains we scorn to wear.

SEBASTIAN   But what must we do with this old gentlewoman?

BEN HASSAN   Oh, pray, send me home to Duke's Place.

FREDERIC   Ben Hassan, your avarice, treachery, and cruelty should be severely punished; for, if anyone deserves slavery, it is he who could raise his own fortune on the miseries of others.

BEN HASSAN   Oh, that I was but crying old clothes in the dirtiest alley in London!

FETNAH   So, you'll leave that poor old man behind?

FREDERIC   Yes, we leave him to learn humanity.

FETNAH   Very well. Goodbye, Frederic. Goodbye, dear Rebecca. While my father was rich and had friends, I did not much think about my duty; but now he is poor and forsaken, I know it too well to leave him alone in his affliction.

MULEY MOLOC   Stay, Fetnah. Hassan, stay. I fear from following the steps of my ancestors, I have greatly erred. Teach me, then, you who so well know how to practice what is right, how to amend my faults.

CONSTANT   Open your prison doors. Give freedom to your people. Sink the name of subject in the endearing epithet of fellow citizen. Then you will be loved and reverenced; then will you find, in promoting the happiness of others, you have secured your own.

MULEY   Henceforward, then, I will reject all power but such as my united friends shall think me incapable of abusing. Hassan, you are free. To you, my generous conquerors, what can I say?

HENRY   Nothing, but let your future conduct prove how much you value the welfare of your fellow creatures. Tomorrow we shall leave your capital and return to our native land, where liberty has established her court—where the warlike Eagle extends his glittering pinions in the sunshine of prosperity.

OLIVIA   Long, long, may that prosperity continue. May freedom spread her benign influence through every nation, till the bright Eagle, mixed with the dove and olive branch, waves high, the acknowledged standard of the world.

THE END

Epilogue

WRITTEN AND SPOKEN BY MRS. ROWSON.

PROMPTER (*Behind*).   Come, Mrs. Rowson! Come! Why don't you hurry?

MRS. ROWSON (*Behind*).   Sir I am here—but I'm in such a flurry,
Do let me stop a moment just for breath! (*Enters.*)
Bless me! I'm almost terrified to death.
Yet sure, I had no real cause for fear,
Since none but liberal, generous friends are here.
Say, will you kindly overlook my errors?

You smile. Then to the winds I give my terrors.
Well, ladies, tell me: how d'ye like my play?
"The creature has some sense," methinks you say;
"She says that we should have supreme dominion,
"And in good truth, we're all of her opinion.
"Women were born for universal sway;
"Men to adore, be silent, and obey."

True, ladies: beauteous nature made us fair
To strew sweet roses round the bed of care.
A parent's heart of sorrow to beguile,
Cheer an afflicted husband by a smile.

To bind the truant that's inclined to roam,
Good humor makes a paradise at home.
To raise the fallen, to pity and forgive:
This is our noblest, best prerogative.
By these, pursuing nature's gentle plan,
We hold in silken chains the lordly tyrant man.

But pray, forgive this flippancy. Indeed,
Of all your clemency I stand in need.
To own the truth, the scenes this night displayed
Are only fictions drawn by fancy's aid.
'Tis what I wish. But we have cause to fear
No ray of comfort the sad bosoms cheer
Of many a Christian, shut from light and day,
In bondage languishing their lives away.

Say, you who feel humanity's soft glow,
What rapt'uous joy must the poor captive know,
Who, freed from slavery's ignominious chain,
Views his dear, native land and friends again?

If there's a sense more exquisitely fine,
A joy more elevated, more divine,
'Tis felt by these whose liberal minds conceived
The generous plan by which he was relieved.

When first this glorious universe began,
And heaven to punish disobedient man
Sent to attend him, through life's dreary shade,
Affliction—poor dejected, weeping maid,
Then came Benevolence, by all revered.
He dried the mourner's tears; her heart he cheered.
He wooed her to his breast, made her his own,
And Gratitude appeared, their first-born son.
Since when, the father and the son have joined,
To shed their influence o'er the human mind;
And in the heart where either deign to rest,
Rise transports difficult to be expressed.
Such, as within your generous bosoms glow,
Who feel returned the blessings you bestow.
Oh, ever may you taste those joys divine,
While Gratitude—sweet Gratitude—is mine.

SCHOOL PERFORMANCES

Concluding Address[†]

Read by Miss P. W. Jackson

The human mind, without education, has been compared to the diamond in the mine, the marble in the quarry, and the unshapen block which has never known the artist's forming hand; but it may more aptly be compared to a luxuriant, but wild territory, where the arts of agriculture have never been practised, and of which no one person is the rightful master.

The diamond, continued in its native incrustation; the marble, concealed in its bed of earth; the block, unhewn and shapeless, are, it is true, totally disregarded; their beauty and utility are unknown; but the rich soil, though uncultivated, will spontaneously produce weeds! loathsome, noisome weeds! offensive to the smell, and repugnant to the touch, and fatal to the life of any who should dare to taste. Venomous reptiles twine amongst its entangled foliage; and multitudes of poisonous insects infect every part of the domain. No friendly light beams to direct, no hospitable door opens to receive the fainting weary traveller; all is solitude, desolation, and horror! But let the skillful farmer take possession of it, root up each noxious plant, extirpate the pestiferous race of reptiles, the troublesome insects having no longer a place to harbour in, will perish of themselves. Then let him introduce Agriculture, scattering plenty as he moves, planting and binding up the young trees and herbs, salutary to the life of man, and behold, the wilderness becomes a garden! the ripe and delicious fruits offer an agreeable repast to the traveller; the light in the master's mansion directs his doubtful, benighted steps, and the master himself, at the hospitably opened door, bids him welcome to rest, and refresh his exhausted frame.

So the human mind, left to the wild sallies of uncultivated nature, produces nothing but error; the weeds that spring spontaneous, are Avarice, Pride, unbridled Passion, Sloth, Intemperance, Injustice, Fraud—and a long train of vices, shocking even to remember. The reptiles, are Envy and Malignity—the insects, Vanity and Folly—while Selfishness bars every avenue to Charity, or that benevolence which bids us offer assistance, advice, and consolation to our suffering fellow creatures. But *Education* comes and places Religion as ruler over the domain; she gives to Reason as her viceroy, the reins of government; he roots the Vices out with vigorous hand; the Follies perish, and these pests of society, Envy and Malignity, are trod to

[†] *The Boston Weekly Magazine,* October 29, 1803. American Periodicals Series Online.

annihilation beneath the foot of the sovereign; while Charity, who presides in the heart, the mansions of life, opens every avenue to the social affections, and expands the mind with love, peace, and good will, towards even our enemies.

How deplorable then, is the state of those who are left like the wild territory, to the luxuriant, but erroneous growth of nature; who, uncontroled by the forming hand of Education, know not the beauty of Religion, or the force of Reason. And, how happy are we, my friends and school mates, in being the children of parents, who not only know, and follow the precepts of that comforter of the soul, Religion, but, while anxious that we should cultivate our understandings and store our minds with useful knowledge, are willing that we should blend gracefulness with utility, and not only become serviceable members of society, but accomplished women. Happy indeed! our obligation is so vast, there is scarcely any way to be found in the smallest degree, to return their kindness; there is but one way; let us then embrace it with avidity, and make the most of the opportunity allowed. Perhaps some will tell you, women have little need of cultivated minds; their pretty persons, and a few shewy accomplishments, will gain them admiration. True, and so they will, but will they gain us friends; will they carry us through life; will they enable us to perform with respectability, the important duties, to which, in all human probability, we shall be called?

So far from the education of women being of no consequence, it is of the highest importance to a civilized state. A woman, who is skilled in every useful art, who practises every domestic virtue, who by reading and reflection, has stored her mind with knowledge and learnt from the early practice of self-denial, the difficult task of keeping the impulses of their heart under proper regulation; whose hands are always employed, and whose tongue never uttered a slanderous report; whole ear is shut to the voice of detraction—such a woman may, by her precept and example, inspire her brothers, her husband, or her sons, with such a love of virtue, such just ideas of the true value of civil liberty, and how far a proper exertion of martial ardour may be necessary for its support and defence—that future heroes and statesmen, when arrived at the summit of military or political fame, shall exultingly declare, *it is to my mother I owe this elevation.* She taught me the necessity of application, in order to attain excellence; and how essential order, method, and proper subordination, were to the peace and welfare of society—She taught me how far liberty might go, without overstepping the barrier, and becoming licentiousness. She made me what I am. If so much is in our power, how ungrateful, how wicked would it be to neglect the means of rendering ourselves capable of performing it. We have now an opportunity; it remains with ourselves to improve it. Time flies rapidly. Life, at its longest period, is but a span;—and they who render themselves most useful, make the most of that span. Every hour misemployed or spent in indolence, is lost—and she who has lived *wisely* only twenty years, has had a longer life, than the idiot who has reached nearly the verge of a century.

Mrs. ROWSON has bade me say, she feels how much she is indebted to Miss TUFTS, for the care and attention in the departments committed to her charge; which care she hopes is fully evinced in the writing and manuscript arithmetic exhibited this day. She begs Miss TUFTS to accept her thanks.

To you, my companions, she bids me say, she has many acknowledgments to make for your uniform good behaviour through the season. If there has ever been cause of reproof, she begs you to believe affection prompted it; and that it was ever as painful for her to give, as you to receive it.

She hopes this most respectable audience are satisfied, not only with the performances of the day, but with the proficiency her pupils have made in the various branches of education during the season. She is sensible how much she owes to your encouragement and support, and will be studious to retain that good opinion, which is the pride of a heart, anxious to deserve applause, and grateful for having obtained it.

The Bee—A Fable[†]

Delivered by a Little Miss Nine Years Old.

> Ladies and Gentlemen, will you allow
> A very little girl, who scarce knows how
> To make her curtsey in a proper way,
> To tell a story which she heard one day?
> 5 It chanc'd once on a time, no matter when,
> For all strange things they tell us happen'd then;
> A little Bee on a sun shiny day,
> Crept from the hive, among the flow'rs to play.
> A wise old lab'rer of the hive espied
> 10 His sportive gambols, and thus gravely cried,
> "To work as well as play should be your pride.
> Come learn of me, for wisdom is a treasure,
> And you shall mingle profit with your pleasure.
> Observe this bed of clustring flow'rs, behold
> 15 Their velvet leaves all powder'd o'er with gold,
> And see, within the cups of crimson hue,

[†] Susanna Rowson, *A Present for Young Ladies; containing poems, dialogues, addresses, & c. As recited by the pupils of Mrs. Rowson's Academy, at the annual exhibitions* (Boston, 1811). Chadwyck-Healey American Poetry Database.

The precious drops of rich nectarious dew.
This golden dust, this precious dew collect,
Now in the early morning, nor neglect
20 To bear it to the hive, a valued store,
Against the time when chilling torrents roar,
And Boreas howls, and rains and snows decend,
And bees must on their hoarded stores depend."
Now this young Bee was a good little creature,
25 Had much good sense, industry, and good nature;
She sipp'd the dew, scraped off the golden dust,
That turned to liquid sweets, and in a crust
Composed of this, the ambrosial treasure clos'd;
But as she work'd, a drone who had repos'd
30 For many a morning in a lily's bell,
Addressed her thus; "Poor thing 'tis mighty well,
That you have strength and spirits thus to labour,
I vow you are a valuable neighbour;
To labour thus from morn to eve for others;
35 For trust me little slave I and my brothers,
When we have spent the summer sweetly here,
All winter will regale on your good cheer.
For I'm too delicate, too blythe, too gay,
To waste in toil my summer hours away;
40 I was not form'd for labour, I was made
To rest on thyme beds in the myrtle shade;
I do protest, were I obliged to bear
That yellow dust away, and take such care,
That not a grain is lost; that I should die,
45 Fainting beneath the fervor of the sky.
But you were formed for toil and care by nature,
And are a mighty good industrious creature."
"Winter draws nigh," replies the little Bee,
"And who is wisest we shall quickly see,
50 My friend, who warn'd me to beware in season,
Or yours, who left you in dispite of reason
To bathe in dew, flit over beds of flowers,
Heedless of coming cold, or wintry showers."
When winter came, the little Bee was well,
55 Secure and warm, within her waxen cell.
The drones half starv'd, came shiv'ring to the door,
And forc'd an entrance, they could do no more;
The lab'rers rose, the encroaching tribe drove forth,
To brave the horrors of the frigid north;
60 Shrink in the rigor of a wintry sky,
Lament their idleness, to starve and die.
While the good little Bee, next coming May,

Hail'd the returning sun, alert and gay,
Led forth an infant swarm in health and ease,
65 A bright example unto future bees.
My story's ended; but methinks you say,
Is there no moral, little girl, I pray?
Yes, there's a moral, hear it if you please,
This is the hive, and we're the little bees;
70 Our governess is the adviser sage,
Who fits us for the world's delusive stage,
By pointing out the weeds among the flowers,
By teaching us to use our mental powers;
To shun the former, and with nicest care,
75 Cull from the latter all that's sweet and fair,
Extract their honey, keep their colour bright
To deck the chaplet for a winter's night.
Have we succeeded? judge, you will not wrong us.
I trust we have no idle drones among us;
80 Or is there one or two, how great their shame,
Whilst here, we're striving for the meed of fame,
And catch with transports of exulting joy,
The approbating glance from every eye;
To feel they cannot hope to share our pleasure,
85 To know they slighted wisdom's offered treasure,
To feel that those kind friends, who dearest love them,
Will blush and pity, while they can't approve them
Oh dear, I would not for the richest gem,
That India can produce, feel just like them
90 Nor lose the joy we hope to feel this day,
To hear our friends and patronesses say,
All is done right and well; and truly these
Dear children, are a hive of thriving bees.
And should you thus approve, you'll make of me,
95 A very proud, and happy little Bee.

Dialogue. For Three Young Ladies.[†]

LUCY
'Tis a beautiful morning, come girls let us go
And rumage the shops; there's an elegant show
Of caps, hats, and bonnets; some trim'd with a feather,
Some with flowers, some plain, the whole put together,
Enough to bewitch you; why don't you make haste?

† *A Present for Young Ladies* (Boston, 1811). Chadwyck-Healey American Poetry Database.

MARY

    Because I shan't go; I've no money to waste.
    Mamma has just bought me a hat for the season,
    And a dress for the balls.

LUCY

          Lud child, that's no reason
    For staying at home, when the shops are so full
    Of fashions, of belles and of beaux.—

MARY

        I'm so dull
    Dear sister, to me 'tis no pleasure to fly
    From shop, into shop, without meaning to buy.
    Turning over the goods till they're nearly destroy'd;
    I think that we all may be better employ'd.

ROSA

    I think so indeed, now I have a plan,
    That 'tis better than yours child, deny if you can,
    As we've time on our hands, and the morning is fair;
    Let us walk in the mall, for a little fresh air;
    And when we return, by myself 'tis decreed,
    While two of us work, that the other shall read.

LUCY

    My dear lady Wisdom, now pray condescend,
    To tell us what book you would please recommend.
    Some wise and political treatise perchance,
    On the pride of Old England and power of France;
    Or Bonaparte, wonderful hero, display,
    Holding kingdoms in chains, keeping Europe at bay
    And striding about to decide all disputes,
    Like Woglog the giant in seven league boots.
    Or a juggler at cards, who so dextrous and nice,
    Can turn all his knaves into kings, in a trice.
    So misses your servant; I would not be bound,
    To read such dull stuff for a good hundred pound.

ROSA

    Why Lucy, by this giddy rattle I see,
    You are wiser by far, than your sister and me,
    In political lore; now to me I confess,
    Instruction comes best in a fanciful dress.
    I like a good novel—

LUCY

   Hush child if you do
You must not confess it; your wisdom to shew,
You must rail and look grave, say they're meant to mislead.

MARY

 And say what you will, coz, they are so indeed.

ROSA

 What, all?

MARY

   No; not all; some few we may find
Where piety, learning, and sense are combin'd;
Whose model is nature, whose pictures have art,
To shew life so true, that they better the heart.
But small is the number, while hundreds contain,
A slow subtle poison perverting the brain;
And who through a road wet and miry should wade
To seek for a pearl some rich man had mislaid;
Would surely contract so much soil in the way,
As the price of the jewel would hardly repay.

LUCY

 Oh! mercy! oh mercy! dear girls let me go,
You're so wise, and sententious, so learned, and so
Pedantic; I vow, but it is between friends,
I blush for you both, to my poor fingers ends.

MARY

 I am glad you can blush! but pray let it be known,
You blush some for our faults, but more for your own.
Yet trust me, 'twere better while staying at home,
Read fifty dull novels, than thoughtlessly roam;
Waste your own hours of leisure, and heedless of care
Destroy that for others you cannot repair;
Besides sister Lucy the truth I must tell,
Were there less foreign fashions 'twould be quite as well.

LUCY

 Why Mary, that sentiment comes out so pat,
I believe in my heart you're a strong democrat;
Who would talk of the internal strength of the nation,
Independently great; tho' we've no importation.
Bid us tremble at Britain, who seeks to enslave us;

But honour Napoleon, altho' he dares brave us.
Sell our jewels and plate, and be spare in our diet,
To make up a tribute to keep Woglog quiet.
For should he his seven league boots keep in motion,
Who knows but he'll stride o'er the great Western Ocean.

ROSA

He come! he ask tribute! why Lucy you joke,
Such a measure would age, and mere childhood provoke
To link in a band, place on heav'n their reliance,
And hurt [sic] at the murd'rous usurper defiance.
Of superfluous baubles myself I'd divest,
My food should be coarse, and as coarse I'd be drest,
I'd cheerfully yield my paternal estate,
To defend this lov'd land, from the tyrant I hate
But girl as I am, if 'tis tribute requir'd,
I'd die e'er I'd give him one cent—

MARY

            Most admir'd,
Most excellent patriot, tell me for why
Your voice speaks in thunder, in lightning your eye?
Say where is the nation his power has withstood

ROSA

He stole regal ermine, and stain'd it with blood;
Oh Mary, remember how Louis has died,
That Louis who fought on America's side,
That Louis whose crown now encircles the brows—

LUCY

Of Woglog the giant, as all the world knows.
And which of us three has the power or spirit
To snatch off the crowns or the head? for the merit
Were equal in either.

MARY

            For shame, child, for shame.
I honour Napoleon, I rev'rence his name;
He's superior to all the fam'd heroes of old,
Invincible, noble, intrepid and bold.
As Socrates wise; as the Macedon glorious;
As a lawgiver sage; as a hero victorious.

ROSA

From such sages and heroes heaven save us, I pray—

LUCY

And keep from our shores mighty Woglog away;
For he sets the most dreadful examples in life,
And between you and I, beats and locks up his wife.
Heaven help her, poor soul, she's an empress 'tis true,
But I warrant she's oftentimes pinch'd black and blue.
Her chains, tho' of gold, she may keep for all me,
I'm content to be poor, tho' I may but be free.

MARY

Oh, that's not a point, child, so hard to be carried,
You'll be poor while you live, and be free till you're married.
But get on your bonnets, we'll go if you please,
'Tis folly to talk of such matters as these;
Let kings ask for power, and misers for wealth,
Let us only pray for contentment and health.

ROSA

But health and contentment would cease to be ours,
Should heavenly peace quit America's shores;
Oh! peace! gentle peace! beneath whose benign reign,
Best thrives the rich harvest that gladdens the plain;
Beneath whose auspices fair commerce sails forth,
Brings the gems of the east, and the furs of the north;
The treasures of India, Arabia's perfume,
The pearls of Bassora, the spoils of the loom
Beneficent power, thy pinions expand,
And shed thy best gifts on my dear native land.

LUCY

In this we're united, for this ev'ry day
From demos and despots, I ardently pray,
Some power benign may deliver the nation;
But just now I confess, I've no great inclination
For that, or ought else, on my knees to be dropping;
I want to see fashions; come let's go a shopping.

ROSA

It is better befitting our sex, age and station;
So we'll leave the more arduous cares of the nation—

LUCY

To the wise and magnanimous lords of creation.

CRITICISM

ANONYMOUS

Review of *Charlotte Temple*†

*Of Charlotte, the Reviewers
have given the following character.*

It may be a Tale of Truth, for it is not unnatural, and it is a tale of real distress—Charlotte, by the artifice of a teacher, recommended to a school, from humanity rather than a conviction of her integrity, or the regularity of her former conduct, is enticed from her governess, and accompanies a young officer to America.—The marriage ceremony, if not forgotten, is postponed, and Charlotte dies a martyr to the inconstancy of her lover, and treachery of his friend.—The situations are artless and affecting—the descriptions natural and pathetic; we should feel for Charlotte if such a person ever existed, who for one error scarcely, perhaps, deserved so severe a punishment. If it is a fiction, poetic justice is not, we think, properly distributed.

WILLIAM COBBETT

From Review on the Roman-Drama-Poë-Tic Works of Mrs. S. Rowson, of the New Theatre, Philadelphia.‡

This lady some where mentions "the unbounded marks of approbation," with which her works have been received in this country. Whether this observation from the authoress was dictated by an extreme modesty, or by the overflowings of a grateful heart, is a matter of indifference; the fact, I believe, will not be disputed, and therefore I cannot withold my congratulations on the subject, either from the lady or my countrymen. It is hard to tell which is entitled to most praise on this occasion, she for the possession and exertion of such transcendent abilities, or they for having so judiciously bestowed "their unbounded marks of approbation."

It is the singular good fortune of these States, to be the receptacle of all that is excellent of other nations: they sow and plant, while we gather the fruit. But, as the following elegant lines, on Mrs. White-lock's last year's benefit, express my sentiments on this subject, much better than it can possibly be done in prose, I shall avail myself of their aid.

† *Critical Review*, 2d. ser., I (London, 1791).
‡ Peter Porcupine (pseudonym), *A Kick for a Bite . . . with a critical essay, on the works of Mrs. S. Rowson* (Philadelphia, 1795). Early American Imprints, Series I: Evans, no. 28436.

From Albion's Isle when *genius* takes *her* flight,
'Tis ever sure on these blest shores to light;
Whether by party or by *fancy driven*,
Here sure *it* finds an ever fostering heaven.
Here first *it* breathes invigorating air,
And learns to do whatever *man* should dare;
Here among freemen lifts its *manly* voice
And dreads no ills where all the world rejoice.
Here *Priestley* finds the rest he sought in vain
And *Whitelock* meets applauding *crowds* again.[1]
In these *blest shades* no Lords or Despots sway,
But sons of freedom their own laws obey,
Distress of course is to the land unknown,
And guardian *Science marks it for her own.*

Yes; and these lines are a proof of it. What charming ideas! Genius *driven* by Fancy, all the way from some barn (dubbed with the name of Play-House) to the Land's end in Cornwall; and then taking its flight, like one of Mother Carey's chickens, over the Atlantic Ocean, to America, where it finds a *fostering heaven.* And how artfully has the author (or authoress) managed the personification of *genius!* First it is a *her,* then an *it,* and by-and-by it acts like a *man,* and raises its *manly* voice. An author of ordinary merit would have confined himself to one gender only, or would, at most, have made an hermaphrodite of *genius;* but in a land that "guardian science has marked for her own," that *genius* is not worth a curse, that is not masculine, feminine and neuter, all at once.

If I were to indulge myself in a detail of all the particular beauties, in this little piece, I should never have done; suffice it to say, that it yields to nothing of the kind extant; except perhaps, to some parts of Mrs. Rowson's incomparable Epilogue to that unparalleled play, the *Slaves in Algiers.*

I hope the reader will excuse this digression: in a labyrinth of sweets, it is almost impossible not to lose one's way.

"The necessary conciseness of this article" forbids me to enter into a distinct analysis of each of this lady's performances; I shall, therefore, content myself (and the reader too, I hope) with an extract or two from the *Slaves in Algiers;* which, I think, may be looked upon as a criterion of her style and manner.

The lady asserts the superiority of her sex in the following spirited manner.

---

1. A writer's thus coupling the Reverend Doctor with a Play Actress, may, to some folks, appear as absurd as it would be for a sportsman to couple a crusty old lurcher with a frisking spaniel; but it will be found upon reflection that there is a much nearer affinity between their professions, than one would, at first sight, imagine. [All notes to this selection are Cobbett's own.]

"But some few months since, my father (who sends out many corsairs,) brought home a *female captive*,[2] to whom I became greatly attached; it was she who nourished in my mind the love of liberty, and taught me, woman was never formed to be the abject slave of man. Nature made us equal with them, and gave us the power to render ourselves superior."

This is at once an assertion and a proof. The authoress insists upon the superiority of her sex, and in so doing, she takes care to express herself in such a correct, nervous, and elegant style, as puts her own superiority, at least, out of all manner of doubt. Nor does she confine her ideas to a superiority in the *belles lettres* only, as will appear by the following lines from her epilogue.

> "Women were born for universal sway,
> Men to adore, *be silent*, and *obey*."

Sentiments like these could not be otherwise than well received in a country, where the authority of the wife is so unequivocally acknowledged, that the *reformers* of the *reformed church*, have been obliged (for fear of losing all their custom) to raze the odious word *obey* from their marriage service. I almost wonder they had not imposed it upon the husband; or rather, I wonder they had not dispensed with the ceremony altogether; for most of us know, that in this enlightened age, the work of generation goes hummingly on, whether people are married or not.

I do not know how it is, but I have strange misgivings hanging about my mind, that the whole moral as well as political world is going to experience a revolution. Who knows but our present house of Representatives, for instance, may be succeeded by members of the other sex? What information might not the Democrats and grog-shop politicians expect from their communicative loquacity! I'll engage there would be no secrets then. If the speaker should happen to be with child that would be nothing odd to us, who have so long been accustomed to the sight; and if she should even lie in, during the sessions, her place might be supplied by her aunt or grandmother.

I return from this digression to quote a sentence or two, in which our authoress speaks highly in praise of our alacrity in paying down the ransom for our unfortunate countrymen in Algiers.

"But there are souls to whom the aflicted never cry in vain, who, to dry the widow's tear, or free the captive, would share their last possession.—*Blest spirits of philanthropy*, who inhabit my native land, never will I doubt your friendship, for sure I am, you never will neglect the wretched."

2. Commonly called *a Woman*.

This, you must know, gentle reader, is a figure of speech, that rhetoricians call a *strong hyperbole*, and that plain folks call a *d——d lie*: We will therefore leave it, and come to her versification.

This is an art, in which the lady may be called passing excellent, as I flatter myself the following verses will prove. They are extracted from her Epilogue; where, after having rattled on for some time, with that air solâtre, so natural to her profession, she stops short with,

> "But pray forgive this flippancy—indeed,
> Of all your clemency I stand in need.
> *To own the truth*, the scenes this night display'd,
> Are only *fictions*—drawn by *fancy's* aid.
> *'Tis what I wish*—But we have cause to fear,
> No ray of comfort, the sad *bosoms* cheer,
> Of many *a christian*, shut from *light* and *day*,
> In *bondage*, languishing *their lives* away."

This is a little parterre of beauties.

It was kind of the authoress to tell her gentle audience, that her play was a *fiction*; otherwise they might have gone home in the full belief, that the American prisoners in Algiers had actually conquered the whole country, and taken the Dey prisoner. I confess there was reason to fear that an audience, who had bestowed "unbounded marks of approbation" on such a piece, might fall into this error.

It was not enough to tell them, that the subject of her play was a *fiction*, but she must tell them too, that it was a *fiction* drawn by *fancy's* aid. This was necessary again; for *they* might have thought it was a *fiction*, drawn by the aid of *truth*.

"*'Tis what I wish*."—What do you wish for, my dear lady? Do you wish *that your scenes may be fictions drawn by fancy's aid*? Your words have no other meaning than this; and if you may have another, you have not told us what it is.

Being shut from *light* is the same thing as being shut from *day*, and being shut from day is being *in bondage*; either of these, then, would have been enough, if addressed to an audience of a common capacity.

Many a christian's having a plurality of *bosoms* and *lives*, is an idea, that most assuredly bears in it all the true marks of originality.— The lady tells us somewhere, that she has never read the ancients: so much the better for us; for if she had, she might have met with, "*Prima solaecismi saeditas absit*," and then we had inevitably missed the charming idea, which is here the object of our admiration.[3]

3. May we not, Mr. Reviewer, ascribe several of the beauties, to be found in your composition, to the same cause.
    Memorandum. This note is not to come into print. Take care about this, for heaven's sake.

I would now, reader, indulge you with an extract or two from this amiable authoress's romances; but, as I am rather in haste,[4] I hope it will be sufficient to be observe, that they are, in no respect, inferior to her poetic and "dramatic efforts."

Among the many treasures that the easterly winds have wafted us over, since our political emancipation, I cannot hesitate to declare this lady the most valuable. The inestimable works that she has showered (not to say *poured*, you know) upon us, mend not only our hearts, but, if properly administered, our constitutions also: at least, I can speak for myself. They are my *Materia Medica*, in a literal sense. A liquorish page from the *Fille de Chambre* serves me by way of a philtre, the *Inquisitor* is my opium, and I have ever found the *Slaves in Algiers* a most excellent emetic. As to *Mentoria* and *Charlotte*, it is hardly necessary to say what use they are put to in the chamber of a valetudinarian.

Before we were so happy as to have *a Rowson* amongst us, we were, or seemed to be, ignorant of our real consequence as a nation. We were modest enough to be content with thinking ourselves the only enlightened, virtuous, and happy, people upon earth, without having any pretension to universal dominion; but she, like a second Juno, fires our souls with ambition, shows us our high destiny, bids us "soar aloft, and wave our *acknowledged* standard *o'er the world.*"

After this, it is not astonishing that she should be called the poetess laureate of the Sovereign People of the United States; it is more astonishing that there should be no salary attached to the title; for, I am confident, her dramatic works merit it much more than all the birth-day and new-year odes, ever addressed to her quondam king.

Notwithstanding all this, there are (and I am sorry to say it), some people, who doubt of her sincerity, and who pretend that her sudden conversion to republicanism, ought to make us look upon all her praises as ironical. But these uncandid people do not, or rather will not, recollect, what the miraculous air of America is capable of. I have heard whole cargoes of imported Irish say (and swear too), that, when they came within a few leagues of the coast, they began to feel a sort of regenerative spirit working within them, something like that which is supposed to work in the good honest methodist, when he imagines himself called from the lap-stone to go and hammer the pulpit. However, whether our air do really possess this amazing virtue or not, there are certainly other causes sufficient to work a conversion in any heart, not entirely petrified by the frowns of despotism. Is not the sound of *Liberty*, glorious *Liberty!* heard to ring from one end of the continent to the other? Who dares print a

4. The last Review was kept back nearly three weeks; but, it is hoped, the subscribers will find the great quantity of original matter contained in it (almost a whole page) a sufficient compensation for the want of punctuality.

book or news-paper, without bespangling every page with this dear
word in STARING CHARACTERS? Have not our sign-post daubers
put it into the mouths of all the birds in the air and all the beasts of
the field? What else is heard in the senate, the pulpit, the jail, the
parlour, the kitchen, the cradle? Do not our children squall out *Liberty*, as naturally as kittens mew; and do not their careful, tender,
patriotic parents deck them out in national cockades, and learn
them to sing *"dansons la carmagnole,"* long before they learn them
their A. B. C? In short, is there any thing to be seen, heard, or felt,
but *Liberty*? Is it not through it we live, and move, and have our
being? What great wonder is it then, that she, whose feelings are so
"exquisitely fine," whose soul is like tinder, should catch the "heavenly flame that gilds the life of man?"

Let us reject the ungenerous insinuations of envy and malice; let
us not damp a genius that promises such ample encouragement to
our infant manufactories of ink and paper. That old cynic, Mr. Pea-
chum, has said, that women bring custom to nobody but the hang-
man and the surgeon; and this might, in some measure, be true, if
confined to that vile country, England; but when stretched across
to us, it becomes absolutely false. Here, as Mrs. R. very elegantly
observes, "virtue, heavenly virtue, in *either sex*, is the only mark of
superiority." Under our virgin constellation frailty is unknown, lovers' vows are like the laws of the Medes and Persians, every marriage
ring is equal to the *anneau* of Hans Carval, and even the Green
Room, so long known for the temple of Venus, is here consecrated
to the Goddess of the Silver Bow.

Long may the Theatre thus continue the school of politeness,
innocence, and every virtue. Long may "the Eagle suffer little birds
to sing," and may their melodious caroling never be rendered discordant by the voice of the ominous cuckoo.

*   *   *

JOHN SWANWICK

A Word of Comfort to Mrs. Rowson[†]

It is as criminal for earless pedagogues to be metamorphosed into
critics, as for a scape-gallows to be admitted to the communion
table. Those whipping-post "gnawers" strive to devour publications
as unmercifully as the knife of justice sliced off their "ears," and as

---

[†] *A Rub from Snub . . . addressed to Peter Porcupine* (Philadelphia, 1795). Early American
Imprints, Series I: Evans, no. 29594.

though the gratification of their rancor would palliate for their past disgrace.

Culprits and misanthropists are convertible terms, and when they are afflicted with the itch of criticism, they are literary abortions; because a portion of good nature is an essential ingredient in the formation of every true critic. With what propriety therefore can he, whose delinquency has rendered snarling habitual, attempt an excursion into the fields of criticism? With equal propriety might wolves be the guardians of lambs, or scorpions solicit a soft alliance with harmless doves.

Between criticism and infamy the muses have never decreed an union, and to expose the execrableness of such an union, the heathen mythologists represented the monster *Erichthonius* as the supernatural offspring of Vulcan, when he became enamored of Minerva.

Without any further proem, we will proceed to analize your "*critique* on Mrs. Rowson's works," to see whether your critical talents will bear the test of examination.

This "review" as you term it, appears to be merely an expletive, in order to swell your pamphlet to a more respectable bulk, or something like a short advertisement introduced by printers, in order to complete some column in a news-paper. It is the plainest indication of mental sterility, and seems to have been subjoined, merely because you were destitute of other subject matter: you seemed to be actuated by an impulse similar to that of a blind horse, that luckily stumbles upon tufts of grass while traversing rocky mountains.

If the play of *the slaves in Algiers*, has so much excited your odium, why did you not proclaim war against it after its first exhibition last summer? The reason, I imagine, is sufficiently obvious, and from what information we have derived from your works, we are apt to judge that you were then secluded from an intercourse with the world. You might have been safely immured with some of our *honest* industrious *gentlemen*, who bestow their labor *gratis* to the state, and therefore your time was too precious then to be wasted by *critiques* upon theatrical performances.

The most frivolous and fallacious mode of judging of a commedian's sentiments, is from the language dictated to his characters; and he who would attempt to ascertain an author's principles from the language attributed to his *dramatis personæ*, is the most consummate blockhead that can possibly write. Those palpable fools, who found their decisions upon such principles, are the mere fag-ends of literature, a species of Bedlam lunatics, who excite the admiration of men in their sober senses.

By adopting your rules, I can prove Mrs. Rowson to be an advocate for slavery and murder; I can prove Shakespeare and Otway to have been the greatest villains that every existed: nay, I can prove an absolute absurdity, and that is, that they had all the virtues and vices, perfections, and defects, incident to human nature; that they were demons and angels, and other inconsistencies that could only enter the imagination of boobies.

Upon the same principle, from the speeches of Ben Hassan, one of her characters, you might have scoffed at Mrs. Rowson's grammatical inaccuracy, and in fine, were you to detach particular parts from the discordant colloquies of most plays, you might attribute to authors, the demoniac principles of traitors, robbers, and assassins.

Though she makes Fetnah say "woman was never formed to be the abject slave of man; nature made us equal with them," yet on the contrary, she makes Ben Hassan say, in his soliloquy about Rebecca, "'Tis hard indeed, when masters may not do what they please with their slaves!" and therefore from this last expression, and upon your boobyish principles, you might pronounce Mrs. Rowson to be an advocate for the debasement of her sex. From the ferocity of Muley Moloc, who exclaims "Bear them to torture: who and what am I, that a vile slave dares brave me to my face?" you might suppose the lady to be, not only an abettor of slavery, but one of the fiends of despotism; nay from Muley's charge to Olivia "Renounce your faith," asses might regard her as a Mahometan and not a Christian.

In order to render her assertion of woman's superiority altogether unequivocal as you thought, you adduced this *jou d'esprit* from her epilogue,

> "Women were born for universal sway:
> Men to adore, be silent, and obey."

in order to corroborate your charge, and what does this distitch prove? nothing: It is merely a sally of humor, intended to excite a smile, and not to enforce a conviction of woman's superiority. In all polite circles (with which I presume you have had little intercourse) the superiority is always ascribed to women, when in fact, they may possess an inferiority.

The best criterion by which we may judge of domestic tyranny and brutality, is that machine (I will not say man) who vaunts of an ascendency over women. Let a man's attention to be turned to the various classes of people, and he will observe, that man's deference to women is commensurate with his refinement. But scavengers, oystermen, and the off-scourings of mankind, are ever the most jealous of woman's dominion, and the most strenuous asserters of their own supremacy.

If you have ever been fortunate enough to have a wife, no doubt the scratches of your nails were ever engraved upon her face, and she has ever been the victim of cow-skins and black eyes. If you now happen to be in a state of celibacy, all the lower classes of women, not even excluding negro wenches, ought to be as particularly cautioned against your addresses, as against the approaches of a mad dog.

In consequence of the customs and manners now prevalent in the world, there must be an essential distinction between the sexes, and man's pride and arrogance make him the most ostensible character in our creation; but can you prove that a male education would not qualify a woman for all the duties of a man?

But waving all abstract contemplations, we shall proceed to the consideration of that clause of your works, which you intended as a signal insult to the Americans, and which exhibits such a portrait of unprovoked malice, virulence and falsehood, that even misanthropy would blush in contemplating the picture. Such an attempt to stab the reputation, and to asperse the literary character of a woman, who never gave you any cause of provocation, resembles the indiscriminate fury of desperadoes in the dark, who are unkennelled for the dreary purposes of assassination.

The meanness of your stricture upon the speech of Rebecca, an American woman, is only equalled by the malevolence of your insinuation of the incontinence of a lady elevated beyond the grasp of your calumny; such low suggestions designate you as a cornuto, whose prayers have been dictated by fatal experience. I shall quote this speech together with your *critique* thereon, in order to show the *validity* of your remarks.

'But there are souls to whom the afflicted never cry in vain; who, to dry the widow's tear, or free the captive, would share their last possession. Blest spirits of philanthropy, who inhabit my native land, never will I doubt your friendship, for sure I am you never will neglect the wretched.'

To which you subjoin the following remark:

'THIS, you must know, gentle reader, is a figure of speech, that rhetoricians call a *strong hyperbole*, and that plain folks call a d——d lie.'

The word THIS you intended, no doubt, should refer to the whole speech, and therefore you have denied the existence of charity, friendship and philanthropy, as attributes of the American character, for which libel upon our national dignity, you merit a little salutary correction with a good tough hickory. Caitiffs who experience none of those soft emotions of sensibility, deny the existence of those characteristics of human nature. This *critique* appears to be the ebullition of instinct; a wasp that blunts its puny sting against rocks of adamant, a polish which serves but to make them shine more resplendently. The futility of such animadversions only serves to enhance the value of her works, and your niggardly reprobation of

Mentoria and *Charlottee*, without assigning any reason, is like hanging a man without a trial. Though Zoilous-like, you might say the works of Homer or Shakespear ought to be condemned as victims "in the chamber of a valetudinarian," yet such a sentence would never stamp an odium upon their merit. It is the province of candid criticism to enforce conviction by a display of a writer's defects, but they who found their condemnation merely upon their own caprice, are the despots of criticism and the nuisance of literature.

How callous and lost to sensibility, is the heart that would extort tears from female eyes by such envenomed shafts! I hope the lady has too much fortitude to weep; and that she may not anticipate the stings of future malice, the heroic Snub will ever interpose his shield in her defence, because he regards her as a bright ornament to female science. Though he cannot boast of the pleasure of a personal intimacy with the lady, yet he has derived ineffable satisfaction from the labours of her pen; labours well calculated for the improvement of a heart susceptible of literary refinement.

She must not deem this vindication as officiousness or presumption, but as a candid eulogium to the intrinsic merit of works which we cannot sufficiently applaud.

It will redound to her credit if she connives at the insult; because were she to condescend to expostulate with you, it would inspire you with a fallacious sense of your own importance, and if she resolves to indulge her audience with another epilogue at her next benefit, I would particularly advise her not to mention your name. Let her attend to this injunction, lest her friendly Snub, who intends to be present, may assume the tone of censure, instead of commendation and applause.

You ought to be more cautious and circumspect in discharging your quills, or at least never venture too far from your hole; because, should you provoke the vengeance of Rowson, you would stand no more chance than insects beneath a discharge of thunder-bolts. Whiffets that seize the heels of horses often get their brains kicked out, and men walking bare-footed over hot ashes, are apt to get their toes burnt. I presage that you will not always pass with impunity, and there will be a time when the hand of resentment will twist you from your gloomy receptacle, to be the sport of cudgels and horse-whips.

I shall now dismiss you, and less you may growl again, I shall keep a rod in soak for your future chastisement. But I would advise you to take your departure, lest you may bite the iron of vengeance; fly to your genial climes of despotism, lest the *Sans Culottes* deprive you of your half-pay; depart by stealth, for the empyreum of liberty is too scorching for the mopes of aristocracy, whose necks have been so often trampled on. The natives of one element cannot long exist in another; birds will drown, and fish expire out of water. Slaves disciplined to oppression from their infancy, become so wedded to their yoke that they never acquire a relish for freedom, and fiend-like they vent their sarcasms against the realms of light; they are dismayed like owls that scream at the insufferable brilliance of the sun. Hogs that are dragged from their filth and mire to rooms of golden canopies and costly silks, thirst for their native excrement, as pilgrims do for living streams; and you, Mr. Hedge-Hog, emancipated from the shadow of slavery, dissolve like the ice of Greenland when exposed to Southern skies.

CITIZEN SNUB.

MATHEW CAREY

Letter to S. Rowson, April 23, 1812[†]

S Rowson   April 23, 1812.

Mr. Bliss has shewn me your letter of the 14th of April, which is now before me. I regret extremely that the shortness of my stay in Boston, & the pressure of my business, prevented me from having the pleasure of waiting on you. I was but two days & a half in the town, & every hour of that time was busily occupied in negotiations with the booksellers. I would be sincerely sorry if my failure of calling were to be ascribed to any want of respect or esteem, which would be doing me a great injustice. Of the books & play you want, I do not have a single copy. Should I meet with any of them I shall forward them to you. Of the success of the republication of your works in the form you mention, I am doubtful. Mentoria never was very popular. The sale of Trials of the heart have been slow. Charlotte Temple is by far the most popular, & in my opinion the most useful novel ever published in this country & probably not inferior to any published in England. The Fille de chambre is likewise popular—& the same may be said of Reuben & Rachel. If your object be emolument, I apprehend, that the undertaking w[oul]d not be by any means eligible. If reputation, wh[ich] is a much more laudable motive, be the object, then the only difficulty will be, to induce a bookseller to engage in it. This does not appear to me impracticable, but may soon be reduced to certainty. It w[oul]d not by any means answer me to embark in the business, being at present engaged in various undertakings, which require my whole capital & all my exertions.

It must afford you great gratification to know that the sales of Charlotte Temple exceed those of the most celebrated novels that

† Reprinted courtesy of the Historical Society of Pennsylvania, Philadelphia.

ever appeared in England. I think the number disposed of must far exceed 50,000 copies; & the sale still continues. There has lately been published an edition at Hartford, of as I am informed 5000 copies, as a chap book—& I have an edition in the press of 3000, which I shall sell at 50 or 62 ½ cents.

SAMUEL L. KNAPP

From Memoir[†]

The incidents of Mrs. Rowson's life were such as peculiarly to fit her for the task of a novelist. Her pursuits were not less suited to render her productions in this department of literature, eminently useful to those, for whose benefit they seem to have been particularly intended, the young of her own sex.

* * *

No writer of fiction has enjoyed a greater popularity in this country than Mrs. Rowson. Of "Charlotte Temple" upwards of twenty-five thousand copies were sold in a short time after its appearance, and three sets of stereotype plates are at present sending forth their interminable series of editions, in different parts of the country. Several of her other novels have gone through many editions.

If we were required to point out a single circumstance to which more than all others this remarkable success is to be attributed, we should say it was that of her delineations being drawn directly from nature. Next to this, the easy familiarity of her style and the uniformly moral tendency of her works, have furnished the readiest passports to the favour of the American people. She cannot be pronounced a consummate artist, nor did her education furnish the requisite qualifications of a highly finished writer. Novel writing as an art, she seems to have considered a secondary object. Her main design was to instruct the opening minds and elevate the moral character of her own sex. Fiction was one of the instruments which she employed for this laudable purpose. In using it, she drew practical maxims of conduct from the results of every day experience. Such a plan hardly admitted of extraordinary exhibitions of what is technically called *power*. Her pictures have been criticised for being tame. Admitting that they are occasionally so, it results from the nature of her designs and her subjects. A critic might as well find fault with

---

† This memoir was originally published in *Charlotte's Daughter, or The Three Orphans* (Boston, 1828), a posthumous novel by Rowson commonly known as *Lucy Temple*. Whitefish, MT: Kessinger Publishing, 2004.

one of the quiet landscapes of Doughty for not exhibiting the savage grandeur and sublimity of Salvator Rosa, as object to Mrs. Rowson's delineations of domestic life for a want of strength and energy. She was, however, by no means deficient in spirited representations of character, when the occasion required them. Her pathetic passages will be found to justify this observation.

* * *

Still she has none of the tricks of practised authorship. There is no straining for effect, nor laboured extravagance of expression in any of her performances. On the contrary her style is perfectly simple, perspicuous and unaffected. She seems to have given herself up to "nature's teachings," and in so doing, she frequently accomplished what art and refinement labour in vain to effect. There is a naiveté in her female characters, an unconscious disclosure of their little foibles, which is never to be found except in the delineations of female writers, who draw from nature; for these nicer traits lie beyond the observation of writers of the other sex.

In her pathetic passages we are struck with a natural eloquence, which never fails to reach the hearts of her readers; and it is perhaps in these passages that her genius exerts its highest efforts. When brought into circumstances of distress, her characters assume a new dignity; the deeper springs of feeling are opened; and its expression bursts forth with an energy, of which while reading her more calm delineations, we had hardly suspected the writer to be capable.

In this abandonment of herself to nature, if we may be allowed the expression, Mrs. Rowson was certainly far in advance of the popular writers of fiction of her day; for, it must be recollected that except the present publication, all her novels were given to the world before the great reform in this department of literature had been effected by the commanding genius of Scott. She wrote in the time of Radcliffe and her imitators; in the very atmosphere of the Della Cruscan school; and some of her works actually issued from the Minerva Press, although it is difficult to tell what could entitle them to such a distinction.

It is no trifling merit, that she should have drawn her characters and incidents directly from the life, when it was the prevailing fashion of writers of fiction to riot exclusively in the regions of fancy; nor is it less to her praise, that in an age of false sentiment and meretricious style, she should have relied for success on the unpretending qualities of good sense, pure morality, and unaffected piety.

We shall conclude this memoir with a notice of Mrs. Rowson's personal character, from the pen of one who was favoured with her intimate acquaintance.

"Mrs. Rowson was singularly fitted for a teacher. Such intelligence as she possessed, was then rare among those who took upon themselves the task of forming the characters, and enlightening the minds of young females. To her scholars she was easy and accessible, but not too familiar. Her manners were dignified, without distance or affectation. Her method of governing the school was strict, cautious and precise, without severity, suspicion or capriciousness. She watched the progress of sentiment, as well as of knowledge in the minds of her pupils, and taught them that they might fully confide in her judgment; and when their imaginations reflected the hues of life, she struggled to give a just direction to the bright colours, that they might not fall to dazzle or enchant, when there was but little reason or stability of purpose to oppose the delirium. A guide to the female mind in this dangerous hour, is a friend that can never be forgotten. Many have ability "to wake the fancy," but few have power, by the same means, "to mend the heart," particularly the female heart, when the character is passing from girlish frivolity, to sentiment, susceptibility and passion. She did not chill by austerity, "the genial current of the soul," but taught it to flow in the channels of correct feeling, taste, virtue and religion. Many dames, perhaps, who have the care of female youth, can boast of bringing forward as fine scholars as Mrs. Rowson, but few can show so many excellent wives and exemplary mothers—and this is the proudest criterion of the worth of instruction that can be offered to the world. Many educated by her care might with justice say—

"My soul, first kindled by thy bright example, To noble thought and generous emulation, Now but reflects those beams that flow'd from thee."

"Few men were ever great whose mothers were not intelligent and virtuous—first impressions often stamp the future character. Education, for every purpose, is further advanced in the nursery than is generally imagined.

"Mrs. Rowson was a model of industry. By a judicious arrangement of her time, she found opportunities to visit her friends, attend to her pupils, and to write large volumes for amusement and instruction; and yet never seemed hurried or overwhelmed with cares or labours.—Method gave harmony to her avocations, and if she suffered, it was not perceived; if she was weary or exhausted, it was not known to those around her. This was the more wonderful, as she was for a great portion of her life, a valetudinarian. She was an economist of the closest calculation, in every arrangement of her school, or household affairs. The mere good, industrious housewife, learned something more of her duty, and added to her stock of culinary information at every visit she paid this patron of industry and economy. The science and skill of the kitchen were as familiar to her as works of taste, and if she ever seemed proud of any acquirement, it was of the knowledge of housewifery.

"Mrs. Rowson was an admirable conversationist. There was nothing affected or pedantic in her manner, at the same time that there was nothing trite or common-place. In colloquial intercourse she rather followed than led, although at home in most subjects—interesting to the learned or accomplished. She was firm, at all times, in her opinions, but modest in support of them. She reasoned with eloquence, and skill, but seldom pushed her remarks in the form of debate. She was patient in the protracted communion of opposing thoughts, but shrunk at once from the war of words. Bland and gentle, she pursued her course of thinking fairly, and astutely to perfect victory, but her opponent never felt in her presence the mortification of a defeat.

"She was truly a mother in Israel—to her charities there was no end. Not only 'apportioned maids' and apprenticed orphans blessed her bounty, but many, cast helpless on the world, found in her the affection, tenderness and care of a parent. Her charities were not the whim of a benevolent moment, but such as suffer long and are kind, and which reach to the extent of the necessity. The widow and fatherless will remember her affectionate efforts in their behalf—she was President of a society for their relief, and for many years, her purse, pen and powers of solicitation, were always at their service; and the cold winds of winter, and the shattered hovel, and the children of want, have been witnesses to the zeal and judgment she has shown in their cause, and could also declare how often she stole silently to places, where misery watched and wept, to bring consolation and comfort.

"Mrs. Rowson possessed a most affectionate disposition— too often the sad concomitant of genius. There are times when the pulses of a susceptible heart cannot be checked by reason, nor soothed by religious hopes—the ills of the world crowd upon its surface, until it bleeds and breaks. There will always be some evils in our path, however circumspectly we may travel. No one can stay in this sad world, until the common age of man, without numbering more dear friends among the dead, than he finds among the living. A strong and fervid imagination, after years spent in labouring to paint the bow upon the dark surrounding clouds of life, but finding the lively tints fade away as fast as they are drawn, often grows weary of thinking on the business of existence, and fixing an upward gaze on another world, stands abstracted from this, until the curtain falls and the drama is closed forever."

ELIAS NASON

From A Memoir of Mrs. Susanna Rowson[†]

Chapter VII.

* * *

* * * Criticise [*Charlotle Temple*] as we may, the people after all
will read it, weep over it and enjoy it. It appeals to the tenderest
sentiments of the human heart, and sweeps across the chords of
feeling as the evening breeze across the strings of the Æolian harp.
It exhibits passages of beautiful description, as the one commencing; "It was a fine evening in the beginning of autumn;" of tender
pathos, as the visit of Mr. Temple to Fleet prison, the sorrows of a
mother, and the death of Charlotte; of moral sublimity, as the agonizing struggles of a wounded conscience. The character of an
intriguing, heartless teacher is well portrayed in that of Madam De
la Rue, and that of a fiendish libertine in that of Belcour. * * *

The plot of the story is as simple and as natural as Boileau himself could desire; the denouement comes in just at the right time
and place; and the reader's interest is enchained, as by magic, to
the very last syllable of the book. * * *

Charlotte Temple is a literary curiosity. Twenty-five thousand copies[1] were sold within a few years after its publication, and editions
almost innumerable have appeared both in England and America.
During the first quarter of the present century, this little book
distanced in popular favor, Horace Walpole's *Castle of Otranto*;
Henry Mackenzie's *Man of Feeling*; Ann Radcliffe's *Romance of
the Forest*, published 1791; Regina Maria Roche's *Children of the
Abbey*; Frances Burney's celebrated *Evelina*; and every other competitor in the field; and it was not until the *Great Wizard of the
North* began to enchain our attention, that the pathetic history of
Charlotte Temple found a rival in the hearts of the people; and even
now it is more than probable that a greater number of persons could
be found in American who have perused this book, than *Waverley*
itself.

[†] 1870. By permission of the University of Virginia Department of Special Collections.
1. "The most popular of her works was *Charlotte Temple, a Tale of Truth,* over which thousands have 'sighed and wept, and sighed again,' which had the most extensive sale of any
   work of the kind that had been published in this country, twenty-five thousand copies having been sold in a few years."—*Personal Memoirs of Joseph T. Buckingham*, vol. 1, p. 82.

   "The tears of many thousand rulers have borne ample testimony to the power and
   pathos of this work."—*Memoir of Mrs. Rowson*, by Samuel L. Knapp, Esq., prefixed to
   Charlotte's Daughter.

It has stolen its way alike into the study of the divine and into the workshop of the mechanic; into the parlor of the accomplished lady and the bedchamber of her waiting maid; into the log-hut on the extreme border of modern civilization and into the forecastle of the whale ship on the lonely ocean. It has been read by the grey-bearded professor after his "divine Plato;" by the beardless clerk after balancing his accounts at night; by the traveler waiting for the next conveyance at the village inn; by the school girl stealthfully in her seat at school. It has beguiled the woodman in his hut at night in the deep solitudes of the silent forest; it has cheated the farmer's son of many an hour while poring over its fascinating pages, seated on the broken spinning wheel in the old attic; it has drawn tears from the miner's eye in the dim twilight of his subterranean dwelling; it has unlocked the secret sympathies of the veteran soldier in his tent before the day of battle.

A great warm loving heart guided the fingers which portrayed the picture, and that is power; and ply the rules of rhetoric as we may, the people feel the power and they acknowledge it. The common mind of the common people is after all the true arbiter of the merit of the works of genius. * * *

* * *

LARZER ZIFF

From Gaining Confidence†

* * * Charlotte Temple *and Real Property* * * *

Protestant tradition located identity in the soul. The relationship of an individual to other individuals as manifested in behavior was a matter of appearance, while reality resided in an inner condition invisible to all but the deity. To be sure, negative signs such as licentious behavior or the profession of heretical opinions were fairly reliable indices of a depraved soul, but their reverse, moral conduct and the profession of orthodox belief, were, it was recognized, not entirely reliable indications of a saved condition. Piety would necessarily result in morality, but morality could be simulated for worldly ends and was not thus a sure sign of piety. The reality that counted was internal, not a matter of appearance.

In a society such as Puritan New England, which rewarded acknowledged believers with civic and economic privileges, the

† From *Writing in the New Nation* (1991), pp. 54–59, 71–75. Reprinted by permission of Yale University Press.

temptation to feign the signs of salvation was great, and, it was assumed, some did so successfully in the visible world. Accordingly, Protestant culture was acutely sensitive to its vulnerability to hypocrisy. Spenser's arch villain, Archimago, is the master of hypocrisy; Milton's Satan succeeds in entering paradise because not even angels can detect hypocrisy.

By the middle decades of the eighteenth century, however, emphasis had shifted, and increasingly in Protestant America social conduct was taken as an adequate sign of individual virtue and individual virtue, in turn, taken as an adequate sign of the sanctity of the soul. Independence, republican government, and the volatile range of economic opportunities in the new nation accelerated the process that led one political and religious conservative to the following observation at the time of Jefferson's presidency:

> In established society, influence is chiefly the result of personal character, seen and known through the period in which the character is formed and the conduct by which it is displayed. In such society, notwithstanding the corruption of the present world, a man of worth and wisdom will, unless prevented by particular circumstances, be almost always more respectfully regarded than persons destitute of these characteristics, and will have a superior efficacy in the affairs of those around him. But in a state of society recently begun, influence is chiefly gained by those who directly seek it; and these in almost all instances are the ardent and bustling. Such men make bold pretensions to qualities which they do not possess, clamor everywhere about liberty and rights, are patriots of course, and jealous of the encroachments of those in power, thrum over incessantly the importance of public economy, stigmatize every just and honorable public expenditure, arraign the integrity of those whose wisdom is undisputed, and the wisdom of those whose integrity cannot be questioned, and profess universally the very principles and feelings of him with whom they are conversing.[1]

In "established society" persons were known over a period of years, but in the new society in which upward social mobility was frequently pursued through movement into growing cities or onto new lands, persons were known principally by what they represented themselves as being. Whatever its theological import, hypocrisy was no longer a grave social concern. By the same token, with conduct no longer grounded in grace and personality no longer "seen and known through the period in which the character is formed and the

---

1. Timothy Dwight, *Travels in New England and New York*, ed. Barbara Miller Solomon (Cambridge, Mass., 1969) 2: 329.

conduct by which it is displayed," vulnerability to duplicity became a consuming social concern. Almost every novel or personal narrative in English written from the mid-eighteenth through the early nineteenth century has at least one major episode of deception, confidence misplaced in a seeming friend, and many make such deceptions the dominant theme. Archimago and Satan who preyed on souls were replaced by the human deceivers who preyed on the property of men and the chastity of women.

The period's most popular literary entertainment, the novel of seduction, strikingly embodies society's pervasive suspicion that deceit is latent in every relationship. The novel throve on the theme of the fatal consequences of seduction while, in point of fact, seduction itself posed little threat in an America in which there was a steady rise in premarital intercourse from the beginning of the eighteenth century to a peak at around 1800 when as many as one in every three brides was pregnant at the time of her marriage. As the historian James Henratta has pointed out, "this alteration in sexual behavior did not endanger the traditional nuclear family (since conception was followed by marriage and not by illegitimate birth)."[2] The popularity of the novel of seduction in America does not, then, stem from the applicability of its explicit message. Beneath its detailing of the threat to traditional standards of female conduct another concern was at stake, one for which sexual misconduct served as an attractive dramatic vehicle. This was a concern with the destructive consequences of a discrepancy between what another represented himself as and the self he truly was, an anxiety about the ease with which persons could be separated from property in a mobile society in which traditional guides to an individual's worth were unavailable or inapplicable so that self-representation had to be accepted as the self. Too often circumstances revealed a difference only after the damage had been done.

It is no accident that novels that centered upon the seduced and abandoned woman almost always also included at least one man, usually her father, who had been driven to financial ruin through signing a note for a false friend. Although peripheral to the main narrative and detachable from it in formal terms, the bankruptcy subplot sounded the theme of trust betrayed and social identity destroyed which was more fully enacted in the plot of sexual seduction. Additionally, of course, it underlined the message that chastity was negotiable property. The disaster that awaited the seduced maiden who failed to secure marriage in exchange for her virginity was paralleled by the ruin that awaited her father when he failed to

2. James A. Henratta, *The Evolution of American Society* (New York, 1973), p. 133.

secure collateral from the seeming friend for whom he signed a note.

Henry Fielding's Tom Jones left the West Country and journeyed to London across a landscape he had never before encountered. Time and again as strangers sought to estimate him they did so in terms of his obvious membership in an upper class, a condition about which they were not easily fooled since their entire lives— whether they were strumpets, publicans, or gentlefolk—had been shaped by their awareness of class, and their welfare was keyed to their ability to locate strangers in its terms. Moreover, far as he might have been from home, Tom was rarely in any community that had not heard of the family in which he was raised, and once this was known, he, as it were, was known.

In America, however, even before independence and markedly after it, such signs did not serve. While classes did exist, class structure did not play so defining a role. Upward social mobility was valued and its achievement was tied in good part to geographical mobility. The way up was to get out into an area long on resources and short on manpower. Although one did not necessarily leave home in order to escape being known, one usually did venture into a society in which family provided little clue to identity and where, if one wished, it was possible to invent background even as one attempted to create a foreground. Benjamin Franklin rose socially to stand before kings, and to do so he also ran away from his family to another province to live among those who had no way of measuring who he was save by how he represented himself. Charles Brockden Brown's fictional Arthur Mervyn, a lad from the country wandering in the city, is only who he says he is, and those who befriend and employ him accept him on these terms and then allow his behavior to speak for him.

Because of its chronic need for manpower as well as its attachment to the doctrine of equality, the society in which such figures moved permitted a stranger some initial acceptance into it on his own terms rather than those of family or class. Moreover, such self-representations, abstractions from the immanent selves known to all in a community where one had lived from birth, were paralleled by what was, in Henratta's words, "the increasing predominance of personal wealth (in the form of cash, mortgages, loans, and movable goods) over landed property."[3] We remember the young Franklin's commercial foothold in Philadelphia was secured by his collecting a note for a friend and using the capital for his own ends without authorization (albeit he eventually repaid the "borrowed" amount).

3. Ibid.

Analogously, in Brown's novels, *Arthur Mervyn* (1799) and *Edgar Huntly* (1799), the dominant theme of the questionable reliability of self-representation is played out in plots that also contain seemingly superfluous episodes concerned with the wealth to be acquired from the mere cashing of a note by its possessor regardless of whose labor or property gave that note its monetary value.

To examine the theme of deceitful appearances in American writings of the turn of the century is, however, to discern that its powerful hold on the imagination does not stem simply from a dread of it, but from the mixture of that dread with a fascination at the capacity of appearance to convert itself into the truth of social reality. Representation—personal, commercial, political—could deceive in that it falsified what it purported to represent, but it could also be seen as not so much opposed to or measurable by an immanent world apart from it as it was constitutive of that world.

*   *   *

Many, perhaps most, of the novels of the period, whether English or American, followed the Richardsonian pattern and centered on the theme of the disasters that followed from seduction. The seducers are archetypical confidence men, but it would seem a distortion to relate the popular appeal of the theme of a virgin's ruin to the advent of the paper-based economy that brought increasing power to the middle class did these novels not, as they do, contextualize the central seduction with economic details. A strong example is provided by *Charlotte Temple* (1791; first American edition, 1794) which, indeed, in the career of its author and the history of its reception also exemplifies the mutual attraction that existed between its themes and the unarticulated anxieties of American society.[4] Susanna Rowson wrote the novel in her native England before imitating her central characters in moving to the United States in 1793. There she continued to write while working first as a professional actress and then for the last twenty-five years of her life (she died in 1824) as headmistress of the young ladies' academy she had founded. Meanwhile, *Charlotte Temple* entered upon a career that saw it become the most frequently published novel of nineteenth-century America with over two hundred editions. In it, the heroine, Charlotte, is persuaded to leave her boarding school in England and accompany her wooer, Montraville, to America where he will serve in the British army. She assumes he will marry her, but he abandons her in her pregnancy and she dies shortly after giving birth to a daughter.

4. *Memoirs of the Notorious Stephen Burroughs of New Hampshire* (New York, 1924), p. 48.

In her preface, Rowson says she wrote "with a mind anxious for the happiness of that sex whose morals and conduct have a powerful influence on mankind in general," a conventional but not necessarily insincere disclaimer common to novelists of the genre (p. 5). It also establishes a physical fact, female virginity, as an undeniable reality against which appearance can be measured. In the world of the seduction novel, unlike that of commerce, appearance and reality cannot be reversed—chaste behavior cannot restore lost chastity. The everyday reality of the eighteenth-century American reader in which, as was noted, probably one in three women was pregnant before her marriage gave contrary evidence: although in point of physical fact virginity once lost could never be regained, more broadly speaking a moral, socially useful life was available to the "fallen" woman even as it was available to a man who had misconducted himself earlier in life. But the seduction novel is notorious for its insistent hounding of its heroine to death even while, at the same time, it assumes the privilege of standing beside the deathbed and weeping. Why?

The economic details with which such novels abound suggest that the answer resides in the assignment of the role of lost immanence to women by a society that yearned for an absolute behind the appearances that seemed to have replaced it in all transactions. Women were put into the position of embodying the quality of a fixed reality that had disappeared from the everyday world of getting a living; their chastity figured in the plot as a determinate value in a world in which the worth of most things was indeterminate. The novel of seduction typically concerns itself with a negative example; the woman cannot preserve the true value she represents and as a result dies. The repetition of such negative examples in popular novels suggests indulgence in nostalgia for a world that is no longer rather than an obsession with female chastity.

Charlotte Temple's father was the younger son of an earl, and his brother, who would inherit the title, married for money to prop the sinking wealth of their ancient family. Temple had also seen "his sisters legally prostituted to old decrepid men" toward the same end. In a society in which portable wealth had overwhelmed landedness he nevertheless vowed to keep the old ways and seek what he called "content" (p. 9). Accordingly, he rejected a marriage to a wealthy woman arranged by his father, who then banished him from the family seat; he married for love, and, for a time, found contentment in a rural cottage with his Lucy.

This Lucy was the daughter of Eldridge, a respectable retired army officer whose tale within the larger tale mirrors its theme. Eldridge unsuspectingly accepted a generous loan from a man named Lewis in order to assist his son's career, only to learn that Lewis expected Lucy

Eldridge to become his mistress in exchange. Eldridge, that is, had unwittingly borrowed with his daughter's virginity as collateral. When he learned of Lewis's design he spurned it, and Lewis then foreclosed, sending Eldridge off to debtors prison. Temple, hearing of the plight of a worthy man who was a stranger to him, visited him in prison and out of sheer benevolence to mankind in general redeemed Eldridge's note at the cost of a good portion of his already straitened income. Made wary by Lewis's behavior, Eldridge suspected Temple of a similar design on Lucy's virtue, but Temple replied that although in the course of his acquaintance with the Eldridges he had come to love Lucy and wished to marry her, his redemption of Eldridge's debt was unconditional. Happily, Lucy also loved him and they married, but this exemplary true-love marriage, the only one in the novel, is, nevertheless, also accompanied by a financial transaction.

Charlotte is the only child of Lucy and Temple. Montraville, her seducer, is, as Temple had been, forbidden by his father to marry unless he marries wealth. Without even the modest income of Temple, the only way he can possess Charlotte is as his mistress, since his financial well-being depends upon his remaining available for marriage to an heiress. Accordingly, he promises Charlotte marriage in order to possess her and once he has succeeded makes some trifling accommodation for her and moves on to marry wealth. The one positive example standing against the vicious marriages and liaisons that abound in the novel is that of Lucy and Temple, but not only does their marriage involve a financial transaction but that marriage can be happily sustained only in a retreat from society that proves, finally, to be temporary when the wider world in the person of Montraville tests it.

It is significant that while the men in *Charlotte Temple* plan and operate on the basis of their ability to represent themselves credibly, Charlotte, around whom the action swirls, is not permitted such an augmentation of her character.[5] She represents nothing beyond her virginity; her real self and her apparent self are identical; when she loses her virtue there is no Charlotte left over. Late in the novel she attempts to represent her position by sending letters home to her family from America, but they are intercepted by the villainous Belcour and never reach their destination. This interception, a minor piece of plot machinery, symbolizes a larger if buried theme, that of Charlotte's inability to construct a self-narrative that in organizing her experience for her permits her to assimilate and survive it. She is blocked from entering the world of representation and held to being only her chastity; once that is lost she has reached her end.

5. William Godwin, *Caleb Williams* (London, 1970), p. 326.

Rowson appears to recognize the conflict between the ideology of female immanence she preaches and the realities of her reader's world because she offers contrasting messages when she speaks directly to her reader. From within the tale she talks, for example, to those whom she expects to be impatient with the triumphs of vice and defeats of virtue: "Remember, the endeavours of the wicked are often suffered to prosper, that in the end their fall may be attended with more bitterness of heart; while the cup of affliction is poured out for wise and salutary ends," the principal one of which is a mansion in the kingdom of eternity (p. 75). But from a position a step farther outside the plot and a step closer inside the reader's everyday world, she offers skeptical advice very much in the vein of Poor Richard's empirical observations: "the only way to ensure the friendship and assistance of your surrounding acquaintances is to convince them you do not require it" (p. 77).

The imbalance between the values enforced by the emotional pattern of the plot and the shrewd practical advice the author offers from outside it suggests that the context of the novel of seduction was coming close to overwhelming its text of lost chastity. Society's shift from real to personal (that is, represented) property and the unsettling of the values previously attached to a distinction between reality and appearance compromised, if indeed they did not dominate, the simple story of innocence betrayed.

* * *

BLYTHE FORCEY

Charlotte Temple and the End of Epistolarity[†]

One of the few universally acknowledged truths of modern literary studies is that the roots of the British and, by extension, American novel can be traced to the epistolary form. What has not been adequately explained, however, is why the effective lifespan of this form was nearly as brief as those of its typically benighted heroines. I propose that the epistolary novel could not survive as a dominant form because, in the fast-changing, polyglot world of late eighteenth-century Anglo-America, it fell victim to the same forces of seduction and betrayal that its heroines were unable to avoid. *Charlotte Temple*, with a traditional Richardsonian plot and an authoritative, unifying

† From *American Literature* 63.2 (1997): 225–41. Copyright © 1997, Duke University Press. All rights reserved. Used by permission of the publisher.

narrative voice, exposes the forces that combined to render the epistolary novel obsolete.

I

In 1794, when *Charlotte Temple* emerged as America's first publishing sensation, the new nation was changing and growing at an unprecedented rate.[1] New York City, for example, more than doubled its population in the forty years between 1749 and 1789.[2] Even though over seventy-five percent of the white population was of English, Scotch, or Irish origin, and most were Protestant, the community did not feel homogeneous or stable. This majority was highly mobile and various, a significant portion of it was made up of recent immigrants, and it was constantly blended with other groups. The remaining white twenty-five percent was a dynamic blend of mostly German, French, Dutch, and Spanish. Also present, and even more volatile, was a large minority of Black slaves, indentured servants, and Native Americans. New people were arriving in the cities each day from Europe and the surrounding rural communities. Some of these new people stayed for a while, some moved on. Most of the people who did stay in the cities had only known a rural way of life, and a majority of them had been born in Europe.

Of this diverse and disoriented population, the actual readers were usually young and at least as likely to be female as male. As one commentator points out, "because of the high mortality rate during the Revolutionary War and the population explosion in its aftermath, by the first decades of the nineteenth century, a full two-thirds of the white population of America was under the age of twenty-four. Furthermore, because of the increasing attention to childhood education in the later part of the eighteenth century, young people, especially women, tended to be more literate than old people."[3]

However, even those early American readers who were anything but innocent young girls could have found much to identify with in *Charlotte Temple*. The revolution just over, a new government laboring to gain support and control, and all foundations seemingly left behind, fears of chaos, rootlessness, and abandonment

---

1. *Charlotte Temple* was first published in England as *Charlotte: A Tale of Truth* (1791). Though some copies of the English edition were immediately distributed in America, it was not widely available or widely known there until it was published in Philadelphia by Mathew Carey in 1794.
2. John Tebbel, *A History of Book Publishing in the United States* (New York: Bowker, 1972), I, 83.
3. Cathy N. Davidson, *Revolution and the Word: The Rise of the Novel in America* (New York: Oxford Univ. Press, 1986), p. 112.

dominated.[4] Most potential readers, even those seemingly least likely to identify with Charlotte Temple—battle-scarred old soldiers, jaded prostitutes, sophisticated society matrons, successful merchants, or ambitious young entrepreneurs—would still have been affected by the pervasive sense of "homelessness." The general mood was one of distrust, alienation, and isolation, which was exaggerated by a nostalgic idealization of a supposedly stable, communal, and cooperative colonial or European past.[5]

Thus, the anonymity and volatility of the New World created many new freedoms and, along with them, many new problems. No longer could all Americans know their neighbors; class boundaries were blurred; channels of authority shifted; and, as a result, the force of community could not be relied upon to provide effective social control. Without a recognizable common community, correspondence between individuals could not be assumed; coming from many different places, people did not necessarily speak in the same idiom; misreading of even the simplest exchanges became very possible, and an individual could not anticipate the rules on which a social encounter would be based.[6] Neither the ways nor the words of the Old World appeared to work in their original form. For most early Americans, the passage from Old World to New had brought on many unexpected and frightening changes to which they were struggling to adapt. *Charlotte Temple* could be read by the American reader as a parable of this very struggle, as it is a tale of a crossing that tears Charlotte Temple from her "mother country" and brings her to a New World where homelessness and foreignness define the conditions of her life.

II

With its warm, motherly narrator, *Charlotte Temple* tells a terrifying cautionary tale in a way that comfortably allows readers to approach and acknowledge their feelings of homelessness and rootlessness without ever feeling lost or abandoned. It conforms, externally, to "the commonest of all plots of the eighteenth-century Gothic novel," which, according to Marilyn Butler, "involves a frail protagonist in terrible danger." The result "is a nightmare, and perhaps the reason for its potent appeal is that it enables the reader to live vicariously

4. Everett Emerson, "The Cultural Context of the American Revolution," in *American Literature, 1764–1789: The Revolutionary Years*, ed. Everett Emerson (Madison: Univ. of Wisconsin Press, 1977), p. 4.
5. Gary B. Nash, *Red, White, and Black: The Peoples of Early America* (Englewood Cliffs, N. J.: Prentice-Hall, 1982), p. 212.
6. Alexander Cowie, *The Rise of the American Novel* (New York: American Book Co., 1948), p. 1. Cowie tells us, in fact, that "speech varied so sharply in different parts of the country that at the time of the First Continental Congress members had difficulty in understanding each other."

through nightmare. . . . Facing up to one's fears is emotionally satis-
fying. Besides, there is something comforting, again almost magical,
in anticipating the worst. It is a common intuition that the known
evil never comes."[7] Early American readers were able, as they read
this novel, to live through a nightmare of dislocation, alienation, and
abandonment that mapped their worst fears. But, guided by the careful and caring narrative of Mrs. Rowson, they emerged safe and
unscathed, with all troubling ambiguities and terrors temporarily put
to rest.

The motherly character of Rowson's narrative voice is evident from
her first addresses to the reader. In her preface, she states that it is
"for the perusal of the young and thoughtless of the fair sex, [that]
this Tale of Truth is designed."[8] She expresses her desire to be "of
use . . . to the many daughters of Misfortune who, deprived of natural friends, or spoilt by mistaken education, are thrown on an unfeeling world without the least power to defend themselves from the
snares not only of the other sex, but from the more dangerous arts of
the profligate of their own" (p. 5). Thus she offers, quite explicitly, to
stand in for those "natural friends" that the reader might have lost
and to protect them from the horrors of the world.

Lacking the support of such narrative guidance, the epistolary
novel could not make the successful crossing to the New World. As
Richardson once said, the epistolary novel was addressed to an imaginary "country reader," a person who shared a common (albeit idealized) culture with the writer: a stable rural culture governed by a
fixed and well-understood set of common rules.[9] In her excellent
study of epistolarity, Janet Gurkin Altman states that "the epistolary
form is unique in making the reader (narratee) almost as important
an agent in the narrative as the writer (narrator). . . . The letter is by
definition . . . the result of a union of writer and reader."[1] She goes
on to say that "for the external reader, reading an epistolary novel is
very much like reading over the shoulder of another character whose
own readings—and misreadings—must enter into our experience of
the work."[2] This implies that for readers to "narrate" an epistolary
novel properly, they must have a reasonably thorough understanding
of the sorts of characters over whose shoulders they are figuratively
peering.

7. *Romantics, Rebels, and Reactionaries: English Literature and Its Background, 1760–
1830.* (New York: Oxford Univ. Press, 1981), p. 29.
8. Susanna Rowson, *Charlotte Temple*, ed. Cathy N. Davidson (1791; New York: Oxford
Univ. Press, 1986), p. 5. All further references to this work will be included parenthetically in the text.
9. As quoted by William M. Sale in his introduction to *Pamela* (1740; New York: Norton,
1958), p. v.
1. *Epistolarity: Approaches to a Form* (Columbus: Ohio State Univ. Press, 1982), p. 88.
2. Altman, p. 111.

The epistolary novel thus assumes not only correspondence between the writers within the novel but also a correspondence between the writer of the novel and its readers. Readers of an epistolary novel must function as their own narrators. The author's narrative role is more like that of an editor. Authors exercise narrative control in the composition and presentation of the letters but then assume that readers will read the letters correctly and, unaided, will understand the underlying purpose or message. Writers of epistolary novels trust that they know their readers and that their readers know them; for the form to work properly, they must correspond.

As the eighteenth century drew to a close, writers for the Anglo-American market could no longer sustain this assumption. Knowing that they were writing in a time of rapid transition and for many possible audiences (rural/urban, British/American, naive/worldly, male/female, moral/amoral), they could no longer trust readers to interpret on their own. Even Samuel Richardson must have realized this when faced with the varied readings of *Pamela* and *Clarissa*. The existence of *Shamela* (1741), Fielding's satirical "re-reading" of *Pamela*, and of the many other spoofs and re-writings of epistolary novels that proliferated at the time, highlights the facility with which a "narrator-less" novel could be reinterpreted according to the predilections of the current reader.[3] Though these problems were already beginning to lead to the decline of the epistolary form in Britain, they became immediately significant in the volatile and polyglot market of early America.

The openness of epistolary novels to reinterpretation could be even more problematic with novels written by women, about women, and for women. As Ruth Perry suggests, the lack of boundaries in an epistolary novel can be equated with the lack of boundaries that traditionally surround a woman's person and allow her to be molded to fit others' needs rather than her own. In an epistolary novel, the audience is allowed direct access to a woman's consciousness: "Reading the letters written and intended for other eyes is the most reprehensible invasion of privacy and consciousness in epistolary fiction. There are overtones of sexual invasion . . . in the intercepting or 'violating' of another's words."[4] Without the protective boundaries established by a controlling narrative presence, the epistolary novel leaves the female protagonist exposed, vulnerable, and even invisible.

If Rowson had not intervened, Charlotte's simple, quiet voice could easily have been misread or ignored. Most readers would have found the persuasive, self-justifying speeches of her seducers at least as

---

3. Martin C. Battestin in his introduction to Henry Fielding, *Joseph Andrews and Shamela* (1742 and 1741; Boston: Houghton Mifflin, 1961), p. vii.
4. *Women, Letters, and the Novel* (New York: AMS Press, 1980), p. 130.

compelling. Charlotte would have been unfairly represented and her story misconstrued. Rowson's narrative intervention thus addresses the inherent contradiction of a tale of seduction and betrayal told through letters alone. Letters, so open to misreading and abuse themselves, cannot possibly suffice to tell a story of a young girl subject to the same sort of misinterpretation and misrepresentation; Rowson, seeking to protect those "daughters of misfortune" most likely to benefit from Charlotte's experience, must intervene to ensure that her message is effectively delivered.

Linda S. Kauffman, in her study of amorous epistolary discourse, has also shown how the critical and literary response to epistolary novels (and collections of letters) by women illustrates this very point. Without a "guardian" narrator, readers can interpret letters in any way that fits comfortably with their preconceived notions.[5] According to Kauffman, modern readers have continued to re-interpret epistolary novels and collections of letters quite freely and easily. Without the guidance of a controlling narrator, it appears that readers can, often irrefutably, choose to "narrate" the text in a way that fits with their preconceived expectations.

Thus, Rowson, thinking explicitly about a young woman who had been seduced, abused, misrepresented, and abandoned, understandably rejected the epistolary form. Instead, she entered the novel herself and introduced the narrator as a character in her own right. A warm, motherly presence, this narrator acts as an editor, moralizer, translator, and guide for her young readers. Rowson eschewed the role of mere passive compiler of letters and, in the process, ensured that Charlotte Temple's voice was not misconstrued or erased.

III

Rowson guides the reader through the tale much as an ideal mother would guide her child through difficult passages of life. Her narrative voice is unselfish, affectionate, gently admonitory, helpful, teacherly, and attentive. From the opening passages of the text, she creates a homey atmosphere that is never saccharine or idealized. She does not hide unpleasant realities or try to soften their impact on the reader. Warm, comfortable, and nurturing, yet intelligent, honest, and pragmatic, she provides an implicit example of the proper way to mother as she exhibits the disastrous effects of improper mothering on young Charlotte.

In the preface she addresses her two primary audiences as she expresses her altruistic and didactic intent: "If the following tale should save one hapless fair one from the errors which ruined poor

5. *Discourses of Desire: Gender, Genre, and Epistolary Fictions* (Ithaca: Cornell Univ. Press, 1986), p. 314.

Charlotte, or rescue from impending misery the heart of one anxious parent, I shall feel a much higher gratification in reflecting on
this trifling performance, than could possibly result from the
applause which might attend the most elegant finished piece of literature whose tendency might deprave the heart or mislead the
understanding" (p. 5). She speaks, thus, to young girls and their
parents, and has placed herself in the position of a "parental supplement" of sorts. This novel will help young girls who have not got
enough help from their parents, will help parents who do not know
how to help their daughters, and will help anyone else who needs
guidance and support in an uncertain world.

Even with the primary didactic intent, however, "teacherly" narrative digressions do not dominate the novel. The story moves at a
lively pace, and the authorial incursions seem to appear only at
moments where proper interpretation of a scene might be in question. Usually, narrative intrusions are brief and to the point, and they
often explicitly address the reader most likely to have misread the
passage or scene. However, at several points, Rowson intervenes
more extensively. Significantly, these more forceful interventions
usually occur when a potentially damaging letter has been delivered.
Rowson replaces the text of the letter with an interpretive passage
that neutralizes its potentially negative effect.

The first such intervention occurs when Charlotte receives her
initial letter from Montraville, the man who is to be her seducer.
Rowson does not include the text of the letter but, rather, informs us
that "any reader who has the least knowledge of the world, will easily
imagine the letter was made up of encomiums on [Charlotte's]
beauty, and vows of everlasting love and constancy" (p. 21). Rowson
thus re-aligns the reader's potential identification with Charlotte
through a distancing ironic stance—reducing a passionate letter (the
mainstay of the epistolary tradition) to an almost ironic cliché. Rowson goes on to point out, however, that Charlotte, who does not have
the least knowledge of the world, would respond to such a letter with
"a heart open to every gentle, generous sentiment, [which felt] itself
warmed by gratitude for a man who professed to feel so much for her"
(p. 21–22). And in case a young reader, perhaps just as innocent as
Charlotte, had missed the irony behind these statements, she goes on
to warn her explicitly that "in affairs of love, a young heart is never in
more danger than when attempted by a handsome young soldier . . .
ah! well-a-day for the poor girl who gazes on him: she is in imminent
danger; but if she listens to him with pleasure, 'tis all over with her,
and from that moment she has neither eyes nor ears for any other
object" (p. 22).

Next, realizing that in spite of her admonitions, she might have
worried mothers by referring at all to the potential attractions of a

handsome soldier, Rowson shifts narrative attention: "Now, my dear sober matron, (if a sober matron should deign to turn over these pages, before she trusts them to the eye of a darling daughter,) let me intreat you not to put on a grave face and throw down the book in a passion and declare 'tis enough to turn the heads of half the girls in England; I do solemnly protest, my dear madam, I mean no more by what I have here advanced than to ridicule those romantic girls, who foolishly imagine a red coat and silver epaulet constitute a fine gentleman" (p. 22). As Alexander Cowie points out, such reassurance may well have been needed for many readers. Although the value of didactic novels was not disputed, "there were those who felt that the moral lessons might be learned at too great peril. Tender readers might be singed if they witnessed at too close range the blaze of passion which consumed the frail characters of a novel. The serpent of evil, if studied too intently, might claim a new victim in the observer. To be wholly innocuous a novel must recommend virtue without even describing vice."[6] Rowson effectively uses her narrative voice to avoid this dilemma. Not only does she erase the text of the letter, along with its possible misinterpretations and temptations, she also replaces it with specific moral lessons for each of the readers it might have negatively affected.

After addressing the innocent young maiden and the sober matron, she becomes even more emotional as she imagines the feelings of the fathers of young girls like Charlotte: "Gracious heaven! when I think on the miseries that must rend the heart of a doating parent, when he sees the darling of his age at first seduced from his protection, and afterwards abandoned, by the very wretch whose promises of love decoyed her from the paternal roof . . . when fancy paints to me the good old man stooping to raise the weeping penitent, while every tear from her eye is numbered by drops from his bleeding heart, my bosom glows with honest indignation, and I wish for power to extirpate these monsters of seduction from the earth" (pp. 22).

Finally, the nearly two pages of narrative incursion that follow the delivery of the letter are concluded with another strong plea to "my dear girls—for to such only am I writing—listen not to the voice of love, unless sanctioned by paternal approbation: be assured, it is now past the days of romance: no woman can be run away with contrary to her own inclination: then kneel down each morning, and request kind heaven to keep you free from temptation, or, should it please to suffer you to be tried, pray for fortitude to resist the impulse of inclination when it runs counter to the precepts of religion and virtue" (p. 22–23).

6. Cowie, p. 17.

I have quoted extensively from this first narrative intervention, for it is, in form, tone, and audiences addressed, typical of those that follow (though it is much longer than most). A difficult moment has been reached in the text—one that, in epistolary novels of seduction and betrayal, could only have been handled by including the letter. In *Charlotte Temple*, the text of the actual letter is omitted, along with the potential romantic excitement and danger it might provide, and is replaced, strategically, with the narrator's clear-cut moral guidelines. This reveals one of the most serious problems of the epistolary form. As all characters, even the villains, are allowed to "speak for themselves" through the inclusion of their letters, they each have an opportunity to attract the sympathy and identification of the reader. Wayne Booth has shown that in any novel, "a prolonged intimate view of a character works against our capacity for judgment."[7] Further, he has pointed out that this effect is intensified by the unmediated intimate contact provided in the epistolary form. For, "unlike our reaction to villains presented only from the outside, [in *Clarissa*] our feeling is a combination of natural detestation and natural fellow feeling; bad as [Lovelace] is, he is made of the same stuff we are."[8] Rowson uses her narrative role to counteract this effect. She fills the space that the potentially seductive letter would occupy with thoughtful and persuasive addresses to all who could be affected (in various ways) by such a letter, thus ensuring that each of these potential readers will respond to it appropriately.

Charlotte, essentially virtuous even though naive, *does* know that she should not read this letter: "my mother has often told me, I should never read a letter given me by a young man, without first giving it to her" (p. 24). Rowson, by omitting the letter and replacing it with sensible motherly admonitions, has thus performed the duty of a good mother. We must assume that if Charlotte had given her mother the letter before she read it, the mother, like Rowson, would have destroyed it and replaced it with a moral lecture. Disaster probably would have been averted. Charlotte does not give her mother the letter, however. After Mlle. La Rue, her persuasive and self-interested French teacher, convinces her to overcome her many moral scruples, Charlotte eventually opens it and reads it. Thus, explicitly, begins her fall.

Although none of the "evil letters" written by Montraville is included in the text, "virtuous letters" occasionally are. For example, just as Charlotte is about to elope with Montraville, she is nearly prevented by a loving letter from her mother asking her to come home to celebrate her sixteenth birthday. This letter, the entire text of which

7. *The Rhetoric of Fiction*, 2nd ed. (Chicago: Univ. of Chicago Press, 1983), p. 322.
8. *Rhetoric*, p. 323.

is included, has a powerful effect on the extremely torn and confused Charlotte. As she puts it, "I am snatched by a miracle from destruction! This letter has saved me: it has opened my eyes to the folly I was so near committing. I will not go. . . . How shall I rejoice . . . when in the arms of my affectionate parents . . . I look back on the dangers I have escaped" (p. 35).

Nevertheless, the "miracle" of the letter cannot be sustained in the face of the immediate persuasion of Mlle. La Rue and Montraville. They have the advantage of direct address. Rowson again does not include the actual text of the final seduction, for, as she puts it, "it would be useless to reprint the conversation that here ensued; suffice it to say, that Montraville used every argument that had formerly been successful, Charlotte's resolution began to waver, and he drew her almost imperceptibly towards the chaise" (p. 36). Drawn into the chaise, Charlotte "shrieked" as it drove off, "and fainted into the arms of her betrayer" (p. 37). This physical collapse effectively illustrates the total collapse of Charlotte's will to resist. Montraville's persuasion has proven stronger than the force of a letter from Charlotte's mother.

Rowson, trying to help young girls who might find themselves in situations like Charlotte's, has thus shrewdly chosen to enter the narrative with direct addresses to the reader. In a world where a lover's strongest assaults often occur outside of letters and can prove even more powerful than a letter from a virtuous and caring mother, a novelist who genuinely wishes to combat such forces must allow her own persuasive voice to enter the narrative in order to compete successfully with the written and spoken appeals of a verbally sophisticated would-be seducer.

Although Rowson uses her narrative voice most often to warn her readers about the specific risks of seduction and betrayal, she also, at times, offers more general passages about ways to achieve happiness in life. In one such passage of almost two pages, addressed to "ye giddy flutterers in the fantastic round of dissipation," she proposes that the way to happiness is "worshipping content": "Content, my dear friends, will blunt even the arrows of adversity. . . . She will pass with you through life, smoothing the rough paths . . . and, chearing you with smiles of her heaven-born-sister, Hope, lead you triumphant to blissful eternity" (pp. 26–27). The rhetoric is nearly biblical, and the intent appears stronger than mere didacticism; it can be better described as evangelical. Thus, Rowson also uses her narrative prerogative to guide her readers to a happier life by teaching them the lessons she has learned from her own experience of the world.

And aware, apparently, that such a lengthy digression might seem intrusive, Rowson follows it with an explicit justification of her motherly narrative intent: "I confess I have rambled strangely from my story: but what of that? If I have been so lucky as to find the road to happiness, why should I . . . omit so good an opportunity of pointing out the way to others. The very basis of true peace of mind is a benevolent wish to see all the world as happy as one's self. . . . For my own part, I can safely declare, there is not a human being in the universe, whose prosperity I should not rejoice in, and to whose happiness I would not contribute to the utmost limit of my power" (p. 27–28).

Rowson's narrative role is thus three-fold. First, she acts to protect Charlotte from misrepresentation and erasure. She enters the narrative to tell Charlotte's story, since if this were an epistolary novel without an active narrator Charlotte's experience would have been seriously distorted or even obscured. Second, she intervenes to protect and guide the reader at difficult, confusing, or dangerous moments of the tale. At such moments, her narration ensures that each potential reader understands the text properly and does not entertain any damaging misconceptions. And, third, she includes passages of explicit advice and guidance. Such passages are intended to inform, improve, and enrich the lives of her readers in ways that extend far beyond the lessons to be learned from Charlotte's tragic tale.

IV

Taken together, Rowson's narrative incursions provide an authoritative unifying voice which gives structure and guidance to the reader. An epistolary novel can have no such unifying voice; inherently multi-vocal, its linguistic duplicity resists the explicit direction and control possible in the narrated form. As in real life, the characters who speak most persuasively, frequently, and emphatically are at least as likely to be heard as characters who speak most truthfully, virtuously, and morally.

Intriguingly, multi-vocality in the novel becomes an explicit metaphor for duplicity. Charlotte's fate is effected largely—and not coincidentally—by a French teacher. Indeed, all three of the novel's villains are French, at least in name: La Rue, Montraville, and Belcour. Partly, this might hark back to the fact that Rousseau, with such epistolary novels as *La Nouvelle Héloise* (1761), was considered the great novelistic "seducer" of the eighteenth century. It also confirms the general British impression of the profligate French. But, more specifically, it reflects the conservative, xenophobic mood of 1790s Britain and the general fear of rebellious "contamination" by French Revolutionaries. Butler has shown that much of late-eighteenth-century British literature was influenced by Francophobia.[9] This anti-French strain in English and American literature

9. Butler, pp. 53–56.

rested not only on a horror of the French Revolution but also on the idea that the French, through their vaunted verbal arts, could seduce even the sane into hysterical behavior. Were *Charlotte Temple* to be "translated" into an epistolary novel, the immediate effect would be entire dominance of the multilingual "foreign" voices of the villains at the expense of Charlotte's voice. Rowson, with her domestic and very British voice of reason, retains control of the narrative, guards, supports, and amplifies Charlotte's voice, and ensures that this erasure does not occur.

Such intervention is badly needed as, in the hands of her worldly seducers, Charlotte cannot communicate her will. Although this incapacity is illustrated graphically through her inability to ensure the delivery of her letters, it also occurs on an interpersonal level. Raised in idyllic patriarchal seclusion and trained to be trusting, obedient, and virtuous, the painfully naive Charlotte cannot speak or understand the language of the new world she has entered. Her language has no effect on La Rue, Montraville, Belcour, or, eventually, herself. The simple, open, pastoral idiom provided by her parents cannot withstand the force of worldly persuasion. And, because she is unable to adapt to the requirements of her new situation by learning to speak, or even reliably understand, the idiom of her captors, she becomes effectively mute.

La Rue, Montraville, and Belcour, on the other hand, are multilingual—they know Charlotte's morally pure language even though they do not adhere to the principles that underlie it. With self-serving and hypocritical appeals for help and compassion, they transparently play on her exaggerated sensibility whenever she feels qualms or tries to escape. Charlotte cannot resist or even question such pleas. As she is entirely honorable, cynicism is impossible for her. Without imagination or initiative, she accepts their histrionic banalities as if they were the genuine outpourings of the heart, for that is the only language she knows how to speak or understand.

This underscores the necessity of a narrator to "translate" such utterances. If this were an epistolary novel, naive readers might, along with Charlotte, unwittingly be seduced by the deceptive blandishments of the verbally sophisticated foreign villains. Readers as innocent as Charlotte would be just as unable to distinguish between heartfelt truths and the self-serving lies of a seducer. Rowson teaches not only the conventional message that young ladies should avoid dangerous seducers but also, most significantly, how to recognize them.

This added guidance would have been especially significant to early Americans. In the bustling, multicultural, multilingual new world, survival depended on the ability to learn to be one's own best guide. Rowson emphasizes that readers must learn to distinguish between honesty and dishonesty by themselves. Charlotte's fate is explicitly tied to her inability to learn to make such distinctions. Her credulous attachment to her betrayers persists in spite of overwhelming evidence that they might not have her best interests at heart.

For the perfidy of the villains goes beyond their insincere words. Their irreverence for honest spoken language extends to an equally dangerous irreverence for the written word aptly illustrated by the name of the arch-villain, Belcour. Belcour means "elegant/fashionable/handsome seducer" and could not better describe the man who is to emerge as the most thoroughly malevolent character in the tale. However, *cour* is a word rich in meanings, including courtier, rogue, pursuer, philanderer, and, also, significantly, runner, messenger, or letter carrier.

Indeed, Charlotte's letters are constantly being destroyed. Although she writes many letters to her parents, begging them to rescue her, her seducers confiscate all but one before they can be delivered. When she "throw[s] herself entirely on the protection of Montraville" (p. 34), Charlotte loses her ability to direct her writings; her identity is entirely obscured behind his. Not only does her maladapted language render her dumb, it also effectively renders her illiterate. Without the power of voice or pen, Charlotte has no control over her situation or the narrative. Thus, without the intercession of the narrator, she would have been almost entirely effaced. If this tale were presented in epistolary form, it would be told by Charlotte's self-justifying and persuasive seducers. Rowson, by actively narrating the novel, retains and protects Charlotte's voice and tells a story that could not have been properly or fairly told through the letters delivered during its course.

Letter writing becomes futile the moment Charlotte boards the ship that will take her to America. While they are still in the harbor, waiting for favorable winds in order to depart, Charlotte decides to write her parents to explain her decision "in the most affecting, artless manner, entreating their pardon and blessing, and describing the dreadful situation of her mind" (p. 42). Charlotte becomes reconciled to the voyage after she "had committed the letter to the care of Montraville to be sent to the post office" (p. 42). She cannot conceive of his action, which is "to walk on the deck, tear it in pieces, and commit the fragments to the care of Neptune, who might or might not, as it suited his convenience, convey them on shore" (p. 42).

Charlotte, an entire believer in the sanctity of letter writing, never imagines that her letters have not been delivered. Even as she becomes more worldly about certain things, the possibility that her letters are not being sent does not cross her mind. In the world she has been educated to believe in, the destruction or misdirection of letters would be unthinkable. Letters were treated as nearly sacred objects. They were the primary method of communication between respectable middle-class women. As Ruth Perry points out, "letters were an important line of communication with the outside world in this time when women lived rather cloistered lives. Women generally stayed at home writing letters which were at once a way of being involved with the world and of keeping it at a respectable arm's length. Correspondence became the medium for weaving the social fabric of family and friendships in letters of invitation, acceptance, news, condolence, and congratulations."[1]

Thus, Belcour and Montraville reveal the instability of the established social order as they violate the sanctity of the letter. Their disregard of traditional conventions destroys the mutual trust that allows the epistolary novel to be read as it should, a properly naive young maiden to remain virtuous, or early Americans to rely on the traditions and customs of their past. In a world where miscommunication, seduction, and even revolution are possible, the epistolary novel is no longer viable. Further, its openness to misinterpretation and abuse makes it an especially inappropriate form for the traditional Richardsonian tale of the seduction and betrayal of a virtuous young girl.

V

A solution to this problem is suggested when Charlotte finally manages to deliver successfully one letter with the help of another woman. Mrs. Beauchamp, her country neighbor, mails the letter that, after over a year, finally reaches Charlotte's parents. Although Mrs. Beauchamp, like the villains, has a French name, she is an American, and she is honorable. This suggests that the answer lies not in xenophobic and naive retreat but in enlightened multilingualism. Mrs. Beauchamp is both worldly *and* honorable. She immediately understands how Charlotte has been duped and, in spite of Charlotte's now dubious social status, responds with a genuine desire to help. Very significantly, this also suggests that women must work together and help each other, that they cannot throw themselves entirely on the protection of men if they wish to maintain any reliable networks of communication. Women (and men) who wished to survive and thrive in the "foreign" and multilingual environment of the New World thus needed to create new and imaginative ways to communicate effectively with each other and the world. The narrated novel could be used to serve this purpose.

1. Perry, p. 69.

After *Charlotte Temple*, the American audience continued to favor the narrated novel. In fact, the epistolary novel never acquired much of a foothold in the New World. Rowson's authoritatively maternal narrative style can thus be seen to mark the beginning of a trend which was to become a powerful force in American literature. The extraordinary success of the "domestic" novels of the nineteenth century—a time when the United States was continuing to change and expand at a phenomenal rate—can be linked to the continuing need for reliable guidance and to the effectiveness of the solution Rowson proposed. Thus, as Rowson's most popular novel marked the end of epistolarity, it also heralded the emergence of the American domestic novel, a form uniquely suited to address the needs of a young nation.

JANE TOMPKINS

Susanna Rowson, Father of the American Novel[†]

The point I have to make in this essay is so simple and obvious that I have trouble believing it myself. It is that by any normal, reasonable standard, the title "father of the American novel" or, alternately, "first American man of letters," should have gone not to Charles Brockden Brown, who has always held it (Brown is referred to variously as "father of the American novel,"[1] "the first of our novelists,"[2] "our first professional author,"[3] "the first of our writers to make a profession of literature,"[4] "the first professional man of letters in America,"[5] "the first American to make authorship his sole career,"[6] "the first American writer to devote himself wholly to a literary career"[7]) but to a person named Susanna Rowson, who wrote at the same time Brown did, whose literary production far exceeded his, whose influence on American culture was incompara-

---

† Reprinted by permission of the author.
1. Harry R. Warfel, *Charles Brockden Brown: American Gothic Novelist* (Gainesville: University of Florida Press, 1949), ix.
2. Evert A. Duyckinck and George L. Duyckinck, eds., *Cyclopedia of American Literature: Embracing Personal and Critical Notices of Authors and Selections from Their Writings from the Earliest Period to the Present Day* (New York: Charles Scribner, 1855), 1:586.
3. F. O. Matthiessen, *American Renaissance: Art and Expression in the Age of Emerson and Whitman* (London: Oxford University Press, 1941), 202.
4. Robert E. Spiller, Willard Thorp, Thomas H. Johnson, Henry Seidel Canby, eds., *Literary History of the United States* (New York: Macmillan, 1948), 1:181.
5. Fred Lewis Pattee, ed., *Century Readings for a Course in American Literature*, 3rd ed. (New York: Century, 1926), 168.
6. William Peterfield Trent, John Erskine, Stuart P. Sherman, Carl Van Doren, eds., *The Cambridge History of American Literature* (New York: G. P. Putnam's Sons, 1917), 1:287.
7. Darrel Abel, ed., *American Literature* (Great Neck, N.Y.: Barron's Educational Series, 1963), 1:294.

bly greater, and whose name was misspelled in the MLA program the year I gave the paper from which this essay derives.

If you have never heard of Rowson, do not feel bad. She is not someone you were supposed to have studied for your Ph.D. orals; nor have people who write for *Critical Inquiry* and *Representations* been dropping her name lately. She wasn't the father of the American novel; I am going to talk about why.

One reason is that the terminology of literary history is made for describing men, not women. One has never heard the phrase "mother of the American novel" (or the British novel or the Russian novel). Novels do not have mothers; nor do literary traditions of any sort, at least none that I know of. There is no mother of the Renaissance pastoral, or of the German theater, or of the Portuguese epic. We speak of masterpieces and masterworks and "Masters of Modern Drama." And whether or not sex is specified overtly, the general terms we use to refer to people in the field of literature always designate men, not women. Words like "author," "artist," "creator," "poet," and "genius" automatically evoke a male image, even though women are commonly known to have been authors, artists, creators, poets, and, albeit rarely, geniuses (women do not as a rule get that accolade). It follows then that if, when we say "author," we mean a man, literary genealogies will be patrilineal. Especially so in a country that has a political father (George Washington) and a spiritual father (the male Christian god), but no political or spiritual mothers. Such a country *must* have a father, not a mother, for its literature as well. I say this in order to assert that the sex of our literary progenitor was scripted from the start. No matter what the facts were.

Now let us look at the facts. If, taking into account the number, variety, and influence of their words, you compare the careers of Susanna Rowson and Charles Brockden Brown, there is no escaping the conclusion that Rowson is the more important and substantial figure by a considerable margin. Although she is known chiefly as the author of *Charlotte Temple,* one of the all-time bestsellers in our literature and by far the most popular novel of its period, Susanna Rowson published seven other novels, two sets of fictional sketches, seven theatrical works, two collections of poetry, six pedagogical works, many occasional pieces and song lyrics, and contributed to two periodicals. Her writing career spanned the thirty-six years betwen 1786 and 1822. Of the works she produced besides *Charlotte Temple,* several were very popular in her own day: the sequel to *Charlotte Temple, Charlotte's Daughter,* was published in over thirty editions; *The Fille de Chambre,* another of her novels, sold extremely well, as did *Reuben and Rachel; Trials of the Human Heart,* a four-volume novel, had a large number of socially prominent subscribers; *Slaves in Algiers* was popular as a theatrical stock piece; and the song

"America, Commerce, and Freedom" was still recognized as popular in the 1820s.

On the other hand, with the exception of a few essays published in 1789, Charles Brockden Brown's literary production is confined to a three-year period, 1798 to 1801, during which he published a dialogue on the rights of women, and six novels. From then on he devoted himself to editing a magazine and wrote four political pamphlets. Whether or not we count the nonliterary productions of these authors, the contrast in their output is remarkable. Its nature can be gauged by some comments Evert and George Duyckinck make in their account of Brown in the *Cyclopedia of American Literature*.[8] The Duyckincks convey, with obvious relish, the image of a man, passionate, intense, introverted, and plagued by ill health (Brown died of consumption). As part of this picture they mention several unpublished or uncompleted works he had embarked on at various times in his life: sketches for three epic poems on the model of Virgil and Homer, a geography (geography, they say, was Brown's great love), and a history of Rome under the Antonines. Brown had also written two acts of a tragedy, according to *The Cambridge History of American Literature*, but, told that the play wouldn't act, he burned the manuscript and kept the ashes in a snuffbox.[9] When you turn to the entry for Susanna Rowson in the Duyckincks' encyclopedia, you find that she actually published translations of Virgil and Horace and wrote two geography textbooks, one history textbook, and seven works for the theater, all of which were performed and one of which became part of the period's standard repertory.[1] The contrast here between the doer and the dreamer, money in the bank and ashes in the snuffbox, the published and the unpublished, the read and the unread only adds to the overall contrast between a woman who worked hard at writing over a period of more than three decades, stuck to her work through thick and thin, and exerted an extraordinary influence over the public imagination through one bestseller and several other very popular works, and a man who, in a burst of creativity, wrote six novels in a very short period, grew discouraged, and then turned his mind to other tasks. The question then is, if Rowson outproduces Brown, and outsells him, and has a much greater impact on American society, why don't we have a mother of the American novel instead of a father?

There are several ways of answering this question, one of which I touched on earlier, having to do with sexual attitudes. I will return to that in a moment, but first let me take up some more conservative

---

8. Duyckinck, *Cyclopedia*, 586–591.
9. Trent, et al. *Cambridge History*, 292.
1. Duyckinck, *Cyclopedia*, 502–504.

suggestions for why Rowson didn't get the job. The first two reasons are technical. One is that although Rowson did write a great deal of imaginative literature, she did not devote herself solely to a literary career, and that is why the title went to Charles Brockden Brown. (Rowson began work as a governess to support herself and her parents, married, went on the stage with her husband, whose business had failed, and eventually founded a school for young ladies. She wrote throughout her adult life as a way of supplementing her income.) This would be a powerful argument were it not for the fact that Charles Brockden Brown started out studying for the law, edited a magazine, wrote his novels, went back to editing, and then from 1801 to 1806 became an active partner with his brothers in the mercantile firm of James Brown and Company; when the firm dissolved, he "continued until his death to conduct a small retail business alone, selling pots and pans by day and editorializing by night." [2] In view of these facts, it would be quite easy to argue, if one wanted to (although I do not), that Rowson had never actually engaged in business but had followed exclusively professional callings—teaching, acting, and writing—and that therefore hers was the better claim.

The second technical difficulty is that Rowson was not born in the United States. But this objection is, precisely, technical. Rowson is considered an American author by all of the literary historians who write about her; her Americanness, as far as I know, has never been in dispute. It becomes an issue only if you want to deny her importance on other grounds.

There are other grounds. Someone will say, why not cut through all this patriarchal-attitudes-and-cultural-influence stuff and admit what everybody knows: that *Charlotte Temple* is a sentimental tearjerker, that Brown's first four novels are fascinating works of fiction, the beginning of an important tradition in American writing (in the nineteenth-century, Poe and Hawthorne, in the twentieth, Faulkner), and that all this talk about numbers of works written and length of career is just substituting quantity for quality. Brown was a truly interesting writer and Rowson was not and that is why he is the father of the American novel.

Why not admit all this? Because it isn't true. *Charlotte Temple* was interesting to tens, perhaps hundreds, of thousands of people for an extraordinarily long period of time. Between 1794 and 1860 it went through 160 *known* editions. It exercised such power over the minds of its readers that in 1905, more than a hundred years after its publication, people were still visiting the heroine's supposed tomb in Trinity churchyard in New York. On the other hand, if you count three

2. David Lee Clark, *Charles Brockden Brown: Pioneer Voice of America* (Durham, N.C.: Duke University Press, 1952), 216.

French translations, Charles Brockden Brown's most successful novel, *Wieland,* went through thirteen editions before 1860. Yet the number of articles and reviews written on Brown in this period is greater than the number written on Rowson by a factor of almost thirteen to one. To say that *Charlotte Temple* is not interesting and that *Wieland* is is simply not to *count* the interest shown by a certain sector of the population. It is to define "interest" as that which attracts only a small group of literati. Moreover, to say that the value or quality of a work has nothing to do with considerations such as commercial success or the lack of it, or the size and character of its readership, is simply to ignore the data of literary history.

Facts about popularity, number of editions, and the inverse ratio of critical interest in a book to the book's popular success are not extrinsic to questions of literary merit, they are constitutive of it. They determine the way a text is identified, labeled, and transmitted to future generations; they determine whether an author will be seen as a literary ancestor or not. In the next few paragraphs I want to sketch in what I see as the determinants of the critical, as opposed to popular, success, in the cases of Susanna Rowson and Charles Brockden Brown. I want to suggest that the answer to the question why, given her superior productivity and influence, Rowson did not become the first professional author in America, is that given the class structure, given the gender system, given the economic hierarchy, given the relationship of literature to all of these, and given a complex set of interrelated cultural attitudes, for the author of *Charlotte Temple* to have become an important literary figure was not simply an impossibility, it was literally unimaginable. "Why wasn't Susanna Rowson the mother of the American novel?" is a stupid question. Not because *Charlotte Temple* is a trashy book, but because, given the nature of American culture since the late eighteenth century, it could never have been seen as anything else by the people whose opinions counted.

These are the people who write literary histories, and in their portraits of Brown and Rowson you can see the entrenched habits of thought and standards of evaluation that produced the story of early American fiction we have now. The portrait of Brown that emerges from these histories reflects what we might call the "ashes-in-the-snuffbox" view of him that makes Brown out to be a sort of brilliant romantic failure. "Few have failed of 'greatness' by so narrow a margin," says the *Literary History of the United States,*[3] summing up a chorus of similar pronouncements made before and since. Although as editor first of *The Literary Magazine and American Register* and then of *The American Register, or General Repository of History, Poli-*

3. Spiller et al., *Literary History,* 181.

tics, and Science, he wrote quite a bit of literary criticism, lengthy historical surveys, and reports on recently published books at home and abroad, these solid accomplishments tend to be glossed over by the people who created the role of first professional man-of-letters. They like their Brown pale and distraught, the victim of "tortured nerves" and author of unfinished or unpublished works. They admire him for his passionate though brief dedication to imaginative literature at a time when no one else (allegedly) was writing fiction, and they like to picture him struggling to reach a disapproving, puritanical public. But Brown's commercial failure only adds luster to his reputation. The Duyckincks say, "We are not aware that the author ever derived any pecuniary advantage" from the novels, and William Peterfield Trent observes that despite their legendary status "new editions were not called for."[4] While it is true that in Brown's lifetime there were no new editions, by the time Trent wrote there had been almost a score.[5] His ignoring this is evidence of the general rule that commercial failure *is* success where literary distinction is concerned, for the subtext of such remarks is that only the discriminating few were able to appreciate Brown's peculiar genius. The fact that this genius was also failed, in the opinion of the critics, only enhances his attractiveness as a literary forebear. Here is a representative statement of the "flawed genius" position: "His novels are all structurally weak. The best of them, it must be admitted, are among the most seriously flawed."[6] But "overriding the major flaws are strong virtues which clearly reveal the undeniable genius of the author."[7] What is notable about these pronouncements is how clearly they show that Brown's "genius" exists not so much in spite of as because of its flaws. Accompanying this irresistible cliché is always an intimation that the present critic alone understands the special character of Brown's art. "Brown has been underestimated: he had powers that approached genius. . . . He had a creative imagination. . . . He had, more than this, the power to project his reader into the inner life of his characters; . . . he had poetic vision."[8] Literary portraits of Brown reflect an image of the artist as a tragic, sensitive, misunderstood "failure" so predictably and so often that one cannot help wondering why literary critics and their audiences needed this image so badly. Whatever other functions it serves, however, it clearly separates the sheep from the goats where taste and sensibility are concerned. Those who

4. Duyckinck, *Cyclopedia,* 590; Trent, *Cambridge History,* 292.
5. Sydney J. Krause and Jane Nieset, "A Census of the Works of Charles Brockden Brown," *The Serif. Kent State University Library Quarterly* 3 (December 1966): 27–55.
6. Donald A. Ringe, *Charles Brockden Brown,* Twayne's United States Author Series, ed. Sylvia E. Bowman, no. 98 (New York: Twayne, 1966), 138.
7. Ibid., 140.
8. Charles Brockden Brown, *Wieland,* ed. Fred Lewis Pattee (New York, 1926), Introduction, xiv; quoted in Clark, *Charles Brockden Brown,* 316.

appreciate Brown appreciate passion, intellect, and genius; they look beyond the superficial faults that mislead others; they see the tortured nerves, the inner life, the poetic vision. And they are few and far between. The way this kind of portrait creates a special group of highly perceptive readers, a chosen few who alone understand genius, provides a clue as to why the author of *Charlotte Temple* could never have been taken seriously by the literary establishment.

If Charles Brockden Brown won critical success through commercial and artistic failure, Susanna Rowson, whose popular fame as a novelist was unequaled until Stowe wrote *Uncle Tom's Cabin,* won critical failure through popular success. Yet even to speak of her as a critical failure is to exaggerate her importance, because it implies that she had been at some point a *candidate* for critical success. It is quite clear that this was never the case. Although *Charlotte Temple* had gone through most of its 160 editions before the Duyckincks wrote, they were so little impressed with Rowson's fame that they didn't even bother to write an original entry for her in their *Cyclopedia* but reprinted an obituary from the *Boston Gazette* which they had found in the appendix to something called Moore's Historical Collections for 1824. In 1824, the year of Rowson's death, and over thirty years before the Duyckincks wrote, it appears that *Charlotte Temple*'s enormous sales garnered it small respect; the author of the obituary refers to it dismissively as "a popular little romance."[9] The ensuing description is worth attending to, because it expresses what became the general attitude toward this novel among literary people from that time forward.

> Of the latter [*Charlotte Temple*] twenty-five thousand copies were sold in a few years. It is a tale of seduction, the story of a young girl brought over to America by a British officer and deserted, and being written in a melodramatic style has drawn tears from the public freely as any similar production on the stage. It is still a popular classic at the cheap book-stall and with traveling chapmen.[1]

This description, which seems neutral enough, combines all the ways in which *Charlotte Temple* has been devalued in American criticism. The apparently factual account, delivered offhand and deadpan, places the novel automatically beyond the pale of literature and writes it off without even trying. First of all, the novel's cheapness and general availability set it at a discount. Because it cost practically nothing, it is worth practically nothing, the equation of

9. Duyckinck, *Cyclopedia,* 502.
1. Ibid.

monetary value with literary value being unstated but assumed. Second, it is read by the wrong class of people—those who buy at cheap bookstalls and from traveling chapmen; hence, it is associated with readers who are at the bottom of the socioeconomic ladder, low social status and lack of literary taste being tacitly equated. (The tacit nature of these assumptions testifies to their strength; it is because they don't have to be argued that they can remain undeclared.) Third, its contents aren't nice. It is "a tale of seduction," and the moral degradation of the heroine lines up with the cheapness of the price and the socially undesirable character of the readers to reinforce an image of debased value, of something that has been cheapened by being made too accessible, too common. More than a hint of prostitution hangs about descriptions of this book—its easy availability becomes conflated with the heroine's easy virtue, the social status of its readers with the social status of unwed mothers, the low price with low behavior, so that the subject matter of the book and the object itself seem to merge and the book becomes a female thing that is passed from hand to hand for the purpose of illicit arousal.[2] Thus, the negative aesthetic judgment that arrives at the end is inevitable: inevitable and integrally related to the attitudes toward sex, social class, and economic status that subtend the preceding description. The terms of the judgment—tears and melodrama—are identifiable as an inferior, feminine form of response to literature, one that is implicitly contrasted to a superior male rationality and implicitly linked to the poorly controlled instincts of a proletarian readership. There is even a tiny hint of politically subversive behavior in the reference to the unruly feelings the novel provokes "freely as any similar production on the stage." The novel, in a word, is vulgar: loved by the *vulgus*, the crowd, and therefore bad.

The female-male, vulgar-genteel opposition established by the contrast between Rowson and Brown, as literary history has constituted them, perfectly illustrates Pierre Bourdieu's notion that art works function to define and maintain hierarchical social distinctions within a culture. Indeed, the oxymoronic term "popular classic" that the *Boston Gazette* uses to describe *Charlotte Temple* flags the work as something valued by the lower classes and therefore automatically excluded from consideration as a real classic. One might almost say that in order for Brown to be seen as the founder of our novelistic tradition, there had to be a Rowson to define his exclusiveness and distinction by contrast to her commonness, in both

---

2. See Susanna Haswell Rowson, *Charlotte Temple: A Tale of Truth*, ed. Francis W. Halsey (New York: Funk & Wagnalls, 1905), Introduction, xxxv–xxxvi.

senses of the term. In fact William Peterfield Trent, in concluding his discussion of Rowson and the other "amiable ladies" who were her contemporaries, says, "Thus early did the American novel acquire the permanent background of neutral domestic fiction against which the notable figures stand out in contrast."[3] The "father of the American novel"—tragic, conflicted, failed, unappreciated except by a few—depends for his profile and his status upon his opposite number, the popular female novelist loved by the unwashed millions, whose vulgarity and debasement ratify and enable his preeminence.

The places assigned to discussions of Brown and Rowson in the literary histories tend to support this claim. These authors are assigned to separate spheres not only in the literary hierarchy but also in the volumes that "record" it; so complete is their segregation that although they were published at exactly the same time and shared at least one common element—seduction—they are never mentioned in the same paragraph, much less the same breath. This separation, which now we take for granted, goes with ways of thinking about gender, social class, and political and economic structures, all of which are inseparable from the way we think about literature. There is nothing natural or inevitable about any of these ways of thinking, but they are so ingrained and so intertwined that statements that challenge their authority—such as that Susanna Rowson should by rights be known as America's first professional author— seem not only counterintuitive, but absurd.

What is the upshot of all this? It is that, as members of the academy, we have for too long been the purveyors of a literary tradition to whose social and ideological bases we no longer subscribe. It means that when we teach early American fiction, it is time we stopped behaving as if Charles Brockden Brown were the only pebble on the beach. As Cathy Davidson demonstrates, the late eighteenth century produced an extremely varied and interesting array of novelists, many of them women, whose works performed a crucial role in shaping American culture.[4] The present genealogy of American novelists, which begins with Brown and proceeds to Cooper, Irving, Hawthorne, Melville, Twain, James, and on down the line, must be revised, because it rests on a set of values that are not worth giving our lives for.

3. Trent et al., *Cambridge History*, 285.
4. Cathy N. Davidson, ed., *Reading in America: Literature and Social History* (Baltimore: The Johns Hopkins University Press, 1989). Since this essay was written, Cathy Davidson's *Revolution and the Word* (New York: Oxford University Press, 1986) has reconstituted American literary history of the Revolutionary and post-Revolutionary period, giving Susanna Rowson and her contemporaries their proper place in the record.

GARETH EVANS

Rakes, Coquettes and Republican Patriarchs: Class, Gender and Nation in Early American Sentimental Fiction[†]

A number of recent studies underline the novel's role in the formation and consolidation of American middle-class identity (Brodhead 1991; Davidson 1986; Hansen 1991a, 1991b; Lewis 1987). However, when these studies turn to assess the politics of sentimental novels such as William Hill Brown's *The Power of Sympathy* ([1789] 1969), Hannah Webster Foster's *The Coquette* ([1794] 1986), and Susanna Rowson's *Charlotte Temple* ([1797] 1986), they either deny sentimental fiction's particular role in middle-class development (Davidson 1986),[1] or fail to elaborate on Ian Watt's claims for sentimental fiction's middle-class affiliations (see Hansen 1991a, 1991b; Lewis 1987; Watt 1963). In particular, those who have followed in Watt's footsteps have avoided grappling with what it means to apply the phrase "middle-class novel" to fictions produced in a culture that still used class terminology only sparingly, and lacked a coherent "middle-class" to which that term might be applied (Blumin 1989, 19).

The key to solving this conundrum lies in Nancy Armstrong's analysis of the British sentimental novel. Viewed from Armstrong's perspective, sentimental fiction is a catalyst for, not a symptom of, middle-class development. Like their British counterparts, American sentimental novels did not address the needs of a pre-existing middle class, but instead "helped to generate the belief that there was such a thing as a middle class with clearly established affiliations

† From *Canadian Review of American Studies* 25.2 (1995): 41–62. Reprinted by permission of the Canadian Association for American Studies. I wish to thank Greg Eghigian, Kristie Hamilton, Gregory Jay, Patrice Petro, and Melissa Watts for comments on, or conversations about, innumerable drafts of this essay.
1. In *Revolution and the Word*, Cathy Davidson comments in her chapter on gothic fiction that "the American novel caught its society precisely at the moment . . . as the bourgeoisie was coming into power, and trained its sights upon that process of nascent empowerment" (1986, 218). However, Davidson evades the issue of class in her discussion of sentimental fiction. This weakness of *Revolution and the Word* notwithstanding, Davidson's book analyzes early American fiction with unprecedented rigour and sophistication. For an indication of how Davidson's work changed views on, and increased interest in, early American sentimental fiction see Cassuto (1994); Dalke (1988); Fabi (1990); Fizer (1993); Forcey (1991); Goldgeier (1990); Hamilton (1989); Hansen (1991b); Newton (1990); Pettengill (1992); Smith-Rosenberg (1988); Tassoni (1993); Waldstreicher (1992). With the exception of Forcey's article, all the abovementioned essays focus on Foster's *The Coquette*. For essays on sentimental novels written prior to the publication of *Revolution and the Word* see, *inter alia*, Davidson (1975, 1982); McDowell (1927); Shuffleton (1986); Wenska (1977). For earlier book length studies of the early American novel see H. R. Brown (1940) and Petter (1971).

before it actually existed" (1987, 66).[2] In a society that, much like eighteenth-century Britain, lacked either an easily identifiable or self-identified middle class, Brown, Foster, and Rowson suggest the need for that class to be invented by opposing the virtues of middle-class social models and norms to the vices of aristocratic codes of conduct.

Sentimental fiction was the most widely read genre in late eighteenth-century America (Davidson 1986; Hart 1950; Mott 1947). With a readership drawn largely from outside the post-revolutionary elite (Davidson 1986), sentimental novels were perfectly placed to contribute to the first steps of the middle class's gradual emergence from an alliance of artisans, retailers, small-business owners, "public officials . . . , clerks, . . . and genteel professionals" such as "school-teachers, doctors and lawyers with small practices, [and] ministers to congregations of ordinary people" (Blumin 1989, 37). Sentimental novels demonstrate both what this emergent class stands to lose from aping aristocratic manners and what it stands to gain from adopting middle-class values and behaviour patterns. For as they warn that a dramatic fall in class status inevitably awaits those seduced by the rake's promises of upward social mobility, they also reveal that self-interest demands an unstinting pursuit of middle-class repectability.

Brown, Foster, and Rowson represent the rake as both an aristocratic barrier to the practice of appropriately middle-class conduct, and as the embodiment of English and French threats to the new nation's stability and integrity. In an attempt to ward off the dangers posed by the rake, the first American sentimental novelists propose new models of patriarchal authority and womanhood. This new form of patriarchal authority depends on grounding male power in consent rather than coercion. What the new model woman who appears in these same novels consents to is a form of 'self-governance' by which she checks both sexual desire and the desire for social eminence. Women who consent to work in tandem with 'benign' patriarchs are conferred with a badge of superior moral righteousness that permits them a role, however limited, in shaping male conduct in both the private and public spheres. Women who fail to be convinced by the virtues of the newly benign patriarch, however, are condemned to seduction, ruin, and death.

2. My suggestion that early American sentimental novels help anticipate and create a middle-class social model also has some similarities with Richard Brodhead's investigation of how antebellum writing helped put into place a middle-class model of "disciplinary intimacy." However, while Brodhead suggests that "the antebellum decades were the period when the newly defined middle class began to establish its model as a social norm" (Brodhead 1991, 150), I argue that the American middle class's attempt to promote both its methods of regulating conduct and its versions of appropriate familial relations may be traced back at least as far as the 1790s. For useful accounts of the American middle class's emergence, see Blumin (1989), and Ryan (1981).

While Brown, Foster, and Rowson assert the advantages of adopting middle-class manners and mores, they simultaneously obscure the class dimension of the gender models they promote by cloaking them in a nationalist discourse of "liberal-republicanism" (Banning 1992, 101).[3] The middle-class project of rejecting aristocratic behaviour is thus made identical with, and indistinguishable from, the new nation's quest to rid itself of European influence. By conflating their attack on American practitioners of aristocratic manners with an assault on various kinds of European corruption, Brown, Foster, and Rowson nationalize bourgeois discourse by identifying the middle-class agenda not as that of a group or faction but as that of the nation.

Eighteenth-century sentimental fiction's role in creating middle-class consciousness is particularly evident when one examines how, in eighteenth-century terms, such fiction is sentimental.[4] Like the nineteenth-century women authors with whom they share a marked similarity of concerns,[5] Brown, Foster, and Rowson do not glorify all and any forms of feeling but suggest that the proper kinds of feeling need to be balanced by the proper amount of reason. Furthermore, those writers now termed sentimental often disagreed with one or more of sentimentalist philosophy's central tenets. Thus Brown, Foster, and Rowson show little faith either in sentimentalism's assumption that "the source of all knowledge and value is . . . individual human experience,"[6] or, as the rakes who people their pages suggest, in its belief that people were "innately benevolent" (Brissenden

3. My argument on the class affiliation of republicanism is influenced by Robert Gross's comment that "republican womanhood ought to be considered a reform movement that was essentially class based and served the interest of the emerging elite—a group that, in international terms, was broadly middle class" (Kerber *et al* 1989, 568). For a good introduction to debates on, and assessments of, republican ideology, see Shallhope (1982). For further studies of republicanism see, *inter alia* Appleby (1984, 1985, 1986); Banning (1992); Klein and Hench (1992); Wood (1992). On women and republicanism, see Bloch (1987); Kerber (1980); Lewis (1987); and Norton (1980).

I borrow the term "liberal-republican" from Lance Banning, who coined it to suggest that post-revolutionary Americans "blended and combined" liberal-capitalist and republican ideas (1992, 101, 93). For the strongest statement of the oft-made opposing argument that liberal-capitalist ideas wiped out the republican legacy, see Appleby (1984).

4. Stylistically, the novels of Brown, Foster, and Rowson contain such stocks in trade of sentimental fiction as seduction plots, deathbed scenes, copious tears, and floridly written asides to the reader.

5. Although recent critics have diametrically opposed views of the exact relationship between eighteenth- and nineteenth-century sentimental fiction, they agree that the two have little in common. In *Woman's Fiction*, Nina Baym argues that nineteenth-century women writers adapt the cult of domesticity to create a brand of middle-class "pragmatic feminism" that explicitly rejects eighteenth-century fiction as "a demoralized literature for women" (1978, 10, 51). Taking a view completely opposed to Baym's, Cathy Davidson suggests that eighteenth-century sentimental novels contain a faint but subversive "cry for female equality" that is "all but smothered in the early nineteenth-century" by the emergence of the middle-class cult of domesticity (1986, 135). Unlike Davidson and Baym, I see early national and antebellum sentimental novels as marked by a continuity of concerns. For more on this continuity see below.

6. For example, Eliza Wharton's remark that "experience is the preceptor of fools; but . . . the wise need not its instruction" suggests a dismissal of the value sentimentalism placed on experience as a source of knowledge (Foster [1794] 1986, 109).

1974, 24, 21). However, American sentimentalists' departures from
sentimentalist philosophy are not, as some critics have suggested,
a sign that their novels are "unsentimental" or "anti-sentimental"
(Hansen 1991a, 66; McDowell 1927, 401). For example, Brown, Foster, and Rowson all promote such forms of feeling as filial affection,
benevolence, and compassion. What one finds in early American
sentimental novels, then, is not "anti-sentimentalism" but rather an
attempt to distinguish the middle-class holders of appropriate and
effective moral sentiments from the aristocratic practitioners of
inappropriate, immoral, and affected sentimentality. Moreover, the
ultimate mark of the woman of sentiment is her ability to identify
and resist the affected sentimentality of the rake.[7]

For early American novelists, the rake is a threat to stable family
life and thus, by extension, to national well being.[8] The rakes in *The
Power of Sympathy*, *Charlotte Temple* and *The Coquette* end the marriage prospects of the women they seduce, ruin the lives of the
women they do marry, and prevent new families from forming. Thus,
in *The Power of Sympathy*, the elder Mr Harrington's illegitimate
daughter, Harriot, turns out to be the woman that his legitimately
conceived son wishes to marry. On discovering their marriage would
be incestuous, Harriot dies and the younger Harrington commits
suicide. While Harriot and Harrington at least live to early adulthood, in *The Coquette* the children born of Sanford's affair with
Eliza Wharton and of his marriage to his wife do not survive the first
weeks of infancy. Indeed, the many illicit couplings detailed in *The
Coquette*, *The Power of Sympathy*, and *Charlotte Temple* produce
only one child still alive at story's end. Significantly, the lone survivor
amidst this veritable deluge of dead babies and seduced women is the
daughter of Montraville and Charlotte Temple and she, at the end of
Rowson's novel, is taken back to England and safety by her grand-
father. Given the identification of family stability with national security in the early republic, it is tempting to conclude that the dead
babies in sentimental novels are evidence of a belief that the rake's

7. By suggesting that these novels differentiate between the man or woman of sentiment
and the sentimental woman or man, I am not confusing, or renaming, the distinction
eighteenth-century writers made between sentiment and sensibility. The rake figure
these novels warn against possesses neither strong moral sentiment, nor sensibility. For
a specific example of the way post-revolutionary writers sought to distinguish appropriate sentiment from affected sentimentality, see the comment of an anonymous critic
that "he must be strangely mistaken, who imagines that Richardson was what is vul-
garly called a *sentimentalist*" (quoted in H. R. Brown 1940, 33; original emphasis). It
seems to me that the distinction made between appropriate sentiment and affected
sentimentality develops into the nineteenth-century American middle-class mania for
sincerity and fear of hypocrisy studied so illuminatingly by Halttunen (1982). For useful discussions of the eighteenth-century meanings of sentiment and sensibility, see
Brissenden (1974); Hagstrum (1980); Todd (1986).

8. On the commonplace conflation of familial and national-political rhetoric and issues in
American revolutionary and post-revolutionary discourse, see Bloch (1987); Burrows
and Wallace (1972); Fliegelman (1982); Kerber (1980); Lewis (1987); Samuels (1987).

machinations could cause the nation conceived in the revolution to be stillborn.

Brown, Rowson, and Foster represent the rake as an un-American and unrepublican purveyor of the corrupt "European" morals that threaten to destroy America.[9] In *The Coquette*, for example, Sanford is described in terms that directly associate him with the English aristocracy. Thus, not only does Mrs Richman warn Eliza that Sanford is a "second Lovelace," but Julia Granby identifies him as "a Chesterfieldian" (Foster [1794] 1986, 38, 111). In branding Sanford as a follower of Lord Chesterfield's worldly philosophy, Foster informs her readers that his conduct is guided purely by reference to its likely impact on his position in society (Fliegelman 1982, 242). In particular, Foster thus explicitly criticizes Sanford's willingness to make a marriage based on the aristocratic preference for women of high birth rather than on republican standards of merit. Nor is the use of the term Chesterfieldian the only way in which Foster details Sanford's vices through the vocabulary republicans used to condemn aristocratic mores. Though debt ridden, Sanford, "lives in all the magnificence of a prince;" he is a "licentious . . . gallant" given over to "a life of dissipation and gaiety," and devoted to using "the syren voice of flattery" to seduce Eliza from the path of true virtue (Foster [1794] 1986, 86, 57, 31, 37, 38). Sanford is, in short, the very epitome of English aristocratic "libertinism" (163).

Foster's condemnation of Americans who imitate English aristocrats is strikingly paralleled by the anatomy of the rake offered in William Hill Brown's *The Power of Sympathy*. Much like Sanford, the elder Mr Harrington's days as a seducer were spent in "dissipation, . . . flattery [and] libertinism" (W. H. Brown [1789] 1969, 119, 134). Furthermore, Brown attacks Chesterfieldianism in even more explicit fashion than does Foster. Thus Mrs Holmes—Brown's figure for the virtuous republican woman—delivers a diatribe in which Chesterfieldians are depicted as "insidious gentlem[e]n" who cut a "ridiculous figure" because of "their ignorance or vanity in pretending to imitate those rules which were designed for an English nobleman" (89). As in *The Coquette*, the lesson of *The Power of Sympathy*'s attack on Americans who ape the English aristocracy is that "this affectation of fine breeding is destructive to morals" (89).

That Brown and Foster associate the rake with Lovelace and Lord Chesterfield comes as little surprise given the breadth and depth of anti-British and anti-aristocratic feeling in the early republic. Read alongside Foster and Brown, it comes as a shock when the bestselling

9. Jay Fliegelman points out that many late eighteenth-century American writers insisted that America distance itself from what they viewed as a "fatal European corruption" (1982, 63).

Charlotte Temple ends with the protagonist's daughter and father returning to the country that Americans had fought to win their independence from less than twenty years before. Given that Rowson was born in Britain and that *Charlotte Temple* was both written and first published there, the novel's designation of England as a place of safe haven suggests Rowson's loyalty to America co-existed with and was sometimes overwhelmed by her loyalty to Great Britain.[1] Furthermore, when placed in the context of 1790s British literature, the anti-French sentiment that runs through *Charlotte Temple* seems just one more example of the francophobia that consumed the British middle class during the French Revolution (Butler 1981, 53–56; Forcey 1991, 237).

Yet placing Rowson's novel in the context of British francophobia does little to explain how *Charlotte Temple* addressed the political situation in 1790s America. However, debates about the French revolution had a resonance in America as well as in Europe, and the relationship between the American and French Revolutions provided the focus for arguments on the "character of the American nation" (Fliegelman 1982, 251).[2] The American reaction to events in France was complicated by the support the French had given America in its fight against England. Thus, throughout the 1790s, American condemnation of the excesses of the French Revolution co-existed alongside praise of France's role as "Saviour of America" during the War of Independence (quoted in Fliegelman 1982, 234). It is in the context of such contradictory claims about America's proper relationship with France that *Charlotte Temple* is best read. In *Charlotte Temple*, Charlotte is persuaded to disregard the precepts inculcated by her fond and loving parents and, at the behest of a French schoolmistress, La Rue, and Charlotte's English but French named lover, Montraville, elopes to America. In America she becomes pregnant and, in part because of the machinations of Montraville's erstwhile friend Belcour, is abandoned by her lover for a wealthy heiress and descends into poverty and death.

That it is French named characters—Montraville, Belcour, and La Rue—who bring about Charlotte's downfall is almost too obvious to

---

1. Rowson described her dual allegiance to Britain and America in the preface to her *Trials of the Human Heart* (1795). Commenting on the war between the two nations Rowson writes:

   the unhappy dissensions affected me in the same manner as a person may be imagined to feel, who having a tender lover and an affectionate brother who are equally dear to her heart . . . sees them engaged in a quarrel with and fighting against each other, when let whichsoever party conquer, she cannot be supposed insensible to the fate of the vanquished. [See this NCE, p. 358.]

2. For a full account of American-French relations from 1789–1815, see Buel (1972).

mention.[3] However, as is often pointed out, Montraville receives more sympathetic treatment from Rowson than rakes usually received in seduction novels. Furthermore, one of the most sympathetic characters in *Charlotte Temple*, Mrs Beauchamp, has a French name. Yet Rowson's differentiation of her French named characters is only carried so far. While Rowson describes Montraville's woes in some detail, she also makes it clear that he is one of the main culprits in Charlotte's seduction. Moreover, though she offers Charlotte friendship, Mrs Beauchamp is powerless to prevent Charlotte's decline into poverty and death. Read against America's fluctuating relationship with France in the late eighteenth century, Rowson's depiction of Montraville stands as a symbolic representation of France as the purported fast friend who cajoles America with promises of friendship, only to betray her by destroying her reputation for morality. Similarly, Mrs Beauchamp, friendly but powerless to protect, stands for those former French friends of America who now stand and watch in horror as the Revolution, in the form of Belcour, Montraville, and La Rue, sweeps them from power.

In passing the Alien and Sedition Laws in 1798, the American government tried to put an end to what Secretary of the Navy George Cabot termed "the cursed foul contagion of French principles" (quoted in Samuels 1987, 188). The rakes who populate sentimental novels are unlike "real" aliens, however, because they go "[un]punished by the laws of the land" (Foster [1794] 1986, 63). To put a stop to the rake's seductions, sentimental novelists needed to develop a literary figure whose function was analagous to that of the Alien and Sedition Laws. Brown, Foster, and Rowson create just such an analogue in the figure of the good republican father whom dutiful daughters obey, not for fear of coercion, but out of respect. In the process, they once more equate national interests with middle-class interests and make middle-class conduct the key to both individual self-interest and national security.

As Jay Fliegelman points out, the good republican father is a stock figure in post-revolutionary American writing. However, Fliegelman views the praise of father figures in early American fiction and in the so-called "cult of Washington" as the final act in what he terms the "American revolution against patriarchal authority" (see Fliegelman 1982, passim). Thus he argues that, when late eighteenth-century Americans praise Washington as the father of the nation, "the point is not that [Washington] is being portrayed as America's father, but

---

3. The names of Rowson's villains—Montraville and La Rue—also have urban connotations, while Charlotte's one true friend, Mrs Beauchamp, has a name with rural connotations.

rather what kind of father he is described as being. He would at last
be the parent who would provide the forming example Britain had
failed to provide" (Fliegelman 1982, 199). Yet, as Cynthia Jordan
points out, the unexplored implication of Fliegelman's argument is
that pro-father rhetoric represents not a continuation of the American
revolution against patriarchal authority, but "the revolutionary generation's assumption of a new form of—a newly defined—patriarchy"
(1988, 509). Early American sentimental novels, while serving as a
critique of the 'old' autocratic form of patriarchy, create a new middle-
class republican patriarch who cuts such an exemplary figure in both
public and private spheres that he earns obedience from his offspring
without needing to resort to coercion.[4]

In *The Power of Sympathy*, Brown's tales of rakish men, bad
fathers, and seduced women are counterbalanced by his portrayal of
an exemplary republican family headed by a 'good' father, the "benevolent" and rural residing Mr Holmes, who earns respect through the
kind and gentle dispensation of wisdom to his domestic circle (W. H.
Brown [1789] 1969, 25). The Reverend Mr Holmes is the epitome of
the new good middle-class republican father:

> [he] is assiduous in the duties of his profession, and is the love
> and admiration of his flock. He prescribes for the health of the
> body as well as that of the soul, and settles all the little disputes
> of the parish. They are contented with his judgement, and he is
> at once their parson, their lawyer, and their physician. (25)

Praised for his work as a parson, Mr Holmes's actions as the good
father of his parish are merely an extension of his role in the home.
Mr Holmes's success in attending to the health of his family as well
as that of his parishioners is attested to by the behaviour of his
daughter-in-law, Mrs Holmes. Moreover, as if to testify to how the
idea of the benign patriarch was embraced by both men and women
of the post-revolutionary generation, it is chiefly Mrs Holmes and
Worthy—the other character in the *Power of Sympathy* who exemplifies Brown's idea of the republican new man—who chiefly speak for

---

4. While Washington is the historical model for the new good republican father, the fictional model is surely to be found in Samuel Richardson's *Sir Charles Grandison*. Both
James Hart and Frank Luther Mott suggest that *Grandison* had fewer American sales
than Richardson's other novels. Nevertheless, Mott lists the novel as one of the "better
sellers" in 1786 America (1947, 316), while Hart claims that contemporary American
readers thought "Grandison was a paragon of virtue" (1950, 56). Moreover, as Terry
Eagleton points out, "what is at stake in *Grandison* is nothing less than the production
of a new kind of male subject, . . . a womanly man, for whom tenderness and power are
compatible" (1982, 96). The seduction novels of Brown, Foster, and Rowson are hybrids
of *Clarissa* and *Sir Charles Grandison*. Packed with seduced and abandoned women,
they also set out to reestablish stability within the family and nation by creating the
figure of the good republican father as the representative man of a new "kinder, gentler" form of patriarchy.

and represent the new models of male and female conduct espoused in Brown's moral tale.

Brown described his novel, dedicated to "the Young Ladies of United Columbia," as one in which "the advantages of female education [are] set forth and recommended (iii, 5). Mrs Holmes is the model woman Brown wished his female readers to imitate. It is in her letters that Brown provides his critique of Chesterfieldianism, as well as many mini-lectures on the "importance of religion," and the need to cultivate both "contentment" and a "detestation of folly" (89, 91, 92). Mrs Holmes ascribes some of her own contentment at life in the family's rural retreat to "the improvements made here by my late husband who inherited the virtues of his parents, who still protect [her], and endeavor to console the anguish of his loss by the most tender affection" (19). Mrs Holmes's respect for the example set by both her father-in-law and late husband is matched by her praise of that other republican new man, Mr Worthy, whose "amiable character is adorned with modesty and a disposition to virtue and sobriety" (90). Writing to Worthy's future wife, Myra Harrington, Mrs Holmes advises her and, by extension, the novel's female readers, to "always distinguish the man of sense from the coxcomb" (90). The very image of a middle-class man in his republican virtues and values, Worthy, she writes, is "possessed of good understanding and an exact judgement. If you are united with him, let it be the study of your life to preserve his love and esteem" (90). By suggesting female readers aim to win and "preserve" the "love and esteem" of men like Worthy and Mr Holmes, Brown implies women should internalize and act on the codes of female propriety promoted and treasured by the republican new man. Furthermore, by lauding both Worthy and Mr Holmes as exemplary republican new men and simultaneously warning against the false pleasures offered by the rake, Brown uses Mrs Holmes as a mouthpiece to thump home the moral aim of his tale. That moral aim, in Mr Holmes's phrase, is "to impress the minds of females with a principle of self-correction" (40).

The lesson offered by *The Power of Sympathy* is that if men speak softly they will only occasionally need to carry a big stick. However, while sentimental novels are shaped by the gender of their authors, both male and female novelists played a role in creating the new patriarchal order. As Cathy Davidson points out, while Brown claimed to be addressing his novel to women readers, *The Power of Sympathy* is, on the level of style and diction, very different from the two early American novels, *Charlotte Temple* and *The Coquette*, most widely read by women (1986, 100). Nevertheless, the moral lesson Rowson and Foster offer women is little different from that offered by Brown. In *The Power of Sympathy* both Worthy and the Reverend Mr Holmes are portrayed as figures who by their presence guide the women in their families along the path of true virtue. In *The Coquette* and *Charlotte Temple* the protagonists have to prove they have internalized "the principle of self-correction" inculcated by fathers who are either absent or dead.

Arguing that women authors helped promote the new patriarchal order may seem tantamount to suggesting that such women had been duped into celebrating their own powerlessness. However, for ideas to become hegemonic they must win at least a measure of consent from, and seem to offer at least a semblance of power to, classes and/or genders other than those in which they originate. The middle class's rise depended on its ideas gaining just such a measure of consent from, and offering just such a semblance of power to, American middle-class women. Indeed, one might say that what distinguishes middle-class patriarchy from its aristocratic and autocratic forbears is that it recognizes middle-class power depends in unprecedented ways on gaining co-operation from, and therefore granting a limited supporting role to, women.[5] Rather than illustrating that women either resisted patriarchy at every step, or were utterly powerless before it, American sentimental novels show women how accommodation with the new form of patriarchy can secure them a supporting role in aiding middle-class development. Moreover, by holding out the threat of seduction and death as the alternative to internalizing the new patriarchy's codes, such novels suggest that women's best interests are served by heeding the advice of virtuous and soft-spoken men.

Rowson's Mr Temple is no less a representation of the republican new man than Brown's Worthy and Holmes. Before she embarks on the narrative of Charlotte's seduction and subsequent death, Rowson offers a counterpoint to the rakish behaviour of Montraville in her depiction of Mr Temple's model courtship and subsequent marriage of Charlotte's mother. The "youngest son" of a financially distressed "nobleman," Mr Temple turns his back on his aristocratic birth by disobeying his father's insistence that he marry for money (Rowson [1797] 1986, 11). Instead Mr Temple, determined "to marry where the feelings of his heart should direct him," weds a poor but virtuous woman whose family fortunes have been destroyed in a vendetta carried out by a rake whose attempted seduction she has thwarted (12). Mr Temple mortgages part of his own already limited fortune to remove his future wife and father-in-law from the debtor's prison

5. On the role women played in securing middle-class hegemony in Britain, see Armstrong (1987, 24, 26, and passim). See also the suggestion of Leonore Davidoff and Catherine Hall that the period between 1790 and 1850

> may well have been a time when there was more co-operation between articulate middle-class men and women, involved as they were in building up the material, social, and religious base of their identity, battling as a proselytizing minority for their place in the world and the rightness of their view of that world.

(1987, 454)

where they are held. Though disowned by his father, Mr Temple can still count on an inheritance of "three hundred a year" (25). Because both he and his wife lack "ambitious notions," Mr Temple's income is perfectly sufficient to purchase the "little cottage . . . [where] Plenty, and her handmaid Prudence, presided at their board, Hospitality stood at their gate, Peace smiled on each face, Content reigned in each heart, and Love and Health strewed roses on their pillows" (25–26). It is this blissful and quintessentially republican rural retreat in which Charlotte Temple grows up and to which Montraville's seduction prevents her return.

In *Charlotte Temple*, Mr Temple turns against the bad father in order to be a good father himself. Rowson thus projects the need for children to rebel against their fathers into the past. In Charlotte's present, and in the present of the novel's readers, obedience to parental instruction is the key to happiness. Thus, in the first of Rowson's many narratorial intrusions into the text, female readers are advised to "listen not to the voice of love, unless sanctioned by paternal approbation" (29). Furthermore, Rowson paints in lurid detail "the miseries that must rend the heart of a doating parent, when he sees the darling of his age at first seduced from his protection, and afterwards abandoned by the very wretch whose promises of love decoyed her from the paternal roof" (28–29). The seduced woman's suffering is represented as being no greater than that of her father: "every tear from her eye is numbered by drops from his bleeding heart" (29). Moreover, Rowson not only remarks on the suffering Charlotte causes her father, she also suggests that Charlotte's downfall is precipitated by her failure to "resist the impulse of inclination . . . [that] runs counter to the precepts of religion and virtue" embodied and inculcated by Mr Temple (29). Read thus, the moral of *Charlotte Temple* is that women should learn to discipline "inclination"—or, in Brown's terms, cultivate "the principle of self-correction"—by respecting the example offered by "benevolent" patriarchs such as Mr Temple.

After eloping with Montraville, Charlotte spends much of the rest of the novel writing letters to her parents in an attempt to regain the approbation she fears her actions have destroyed. All but one of Charlotte's letters are intercepted by Montraville and thus fail to arrive at their intended destination. Through Mrs Beauchamp's good offices, however, one letter finds its way to Charlotte's parents. At the end of the novel, Mr Temple finds Charlotte in New York and dispenses deathbed forgiveness before taking her daughter back to the safety and rural simplicity of the Temple family home. Rowson thus delivers Charlotte's daughter into the benevolent keeping of the father from whose protection and example Charlotte's insufficiently disciplined inclination led her to stray.

As in *Charlotte Temple*, the protagonist's downfall in Hannah Webster Foster's *The Coquette* cannot be traced to the actions of a cruel and tyrannical father. Indeed, Foster's novel begins shortly after the deaths of Eliza Wharton's father and of the man he had chosen for her husband. While both men are alive, Eliza performs the roles expected of a virtuous American middle-class woman (Smith-Rosenberg 1988, 171). In the novel's first two sentences, however, Eliza pronounces her "pleasure . . . on leaving the paternal roof" and thus announces her intention not to follow the precepts inculcated by her clergyman father (Foster [1794] 1986, 5). Freed of her obligation to marry the man of her father's choice, Eliza is pursued by two lovers: the virtuous but, in her eyes, dull Reverend Boyer and the rakish Peter Sanford. Only after over-delaying her acceptance of Boyer's proposals of marriage, does Eliza discover Sanford has no intention of marrying a woman with so few financial resources. After she has been abandoned by both men, Eliza writes to Boyer in an attempt to persuade him to renew his promise of marriage. Boyer's reply, however, both announces his impending marriage to another woman and recommends vigilant protection of virtue to Eliza. After receiving Boyer's letter, Eliza retires from New England society but again falls prey to the now married Sanford. Pregnant with Sanford's child, she again leaves the parental home and dies after giving birth to a stillborn child in a roadside inn.

Given *The Coquette*'s plot it seems unlikely Foster was calling the sentimental novel's conventional portrayal of seduced women into question. Moreover, it seems equally unlikely Foster is showing readers the choice between Boyer and Sanford is really no choice at all when what Eliza deems boring about Boyer are the characteristics Foster's contemporaries thought epitomized republican manhood (Hansen 1991*b*, 44). Even by Eliza's own reckoning, Boyer is a "gentleman of merit and respectability" whose conversation is "virtuous and refined" (Foster [1794] 1986, 39, 66). Moreover, to tell Foster's novel from Eliza's point of view, one has to ignore the fact that Sanford's description of Eliza and Eliza's description of herself are almost identical. While Eliza portrays herself as "naturally cheerful, volatile and unreflecting," Sanford finds her to be "gay, volatile, apparently thoughtless of everything but present enjoyment" (7, 18). Rejecting a marriage in which she will have to "sacrifice [her] fancy," Eliza is "exactly calculated to please the fancy" of Sanford (5, 18). Finally, by having Eliza inform readers she is attracted to Sanford's "wealth and equipage," Foster depicts Eliza's desire for Sanford as a female version of the "Chesterfieldian[ism]" her friend Julia Granby warns her against (53, 111).

Yet to interpret the novel from Eliza's point of view is not only to ignore the ways in which Foster draws parallels between Sanford and Eliza, it is also to dismiss the voices of the novel's other women characters, all of whom repeatedly tell Eliza that marrying Boyer and avoiding Sanford will enable her to unite virtue, happiness, freedom, independence and self-interest.[6] Eliza does not fall because she is "a venture-capitalist" in a society still ambivalent about its "new capitalist and individualist economy" (Smith-Rosenberg 1988, 178). Rather, Foster suggests that in such an economy the sure, modest yield from a country parson such as Boyer is a better bet than investment in Sanford's high-priced and valueless aristocratic stock. Thus, Lucy Freeman advises Eliza:

> you will not find a more excellent partner than Mr. Boyer. What-ever, you can reasonably expect in a lover, husband, or friend, you may perceive to be united in this worthy man. His taste is undebauched, his manners not vitiated, his morals uncorrupted. His situation in life, perhaps, as elevated as you have a right to claim.
>
> (Foster [1794] 1986, 27)

While Lucy Freeman advises Eliza that a safe investment is a wise investment, Mrs Richman counters Eliza's contention that marrying Boyer will compromise her freedom by telling her that she has "wrong ideas of freedom and matrimony" (30).[7] Moreover, Mrs Wharton, in an extended homily on the joys of life as a country par-son's wife, advises Eliza that such an existence is

> replete with happiness. No class of society has domestic enjoy-ment more at hand, than clergymen. . . . They are removed alike from the perplexing cares of want, and from the distracting parade of wealth. . . . With regard to its being a dependent situa-tion, what one is not so? . . . In whatever situation we are placed, our greater or lesser degree of happiness must be derived from ourselves. (41)

Her advisers' attempts to correct her understanding of "liberal-republican" concepts suggest that, both in declining Boyer until it is too late and in succumbing to Sanford, Eliza gives up virtue for vice, mistakenly equates self-interest and happiness with the pursuit and capture of social position, and refuses the "[un]abridge[d] . . . privileges" of a country parson's wife for the "libertinism" that

---

6. Carroll Smith-Rosenberg argues that *The Coquette* shows "virtue, independence, lib-erty, and happiness divided against themselves. Eliza would like to unite all. Her virtu-ous advisers advise her this is no longer possible" (1988, 174). But contrary to Smith-Rosenberg's claim, Eliza's advertisers tell her not that it "is no longer possible" to unite virtue, independence, liberty and happiness, but that she misinterprets the postrevolutionary meanings of all these republican keywords.
7. In similar vein, Lucy Freeman tells Eliza that "a man of Mr. Boyer's sense and honor will never abridge any privileges which virtue can claim" (Foster [1794] 1986, 31).

lurks behind Sanford's promise of liberty and independence (31, 163).

Rather, then, than imply that self-interest and virtue are at odds with each other, Foster suggests that both are served when one invests within one's means. She further seeks to persuade female readers that independence and self-interest are not to be equated with freedom and wealth-seeking, but are dependent on a form of self-governance that checks both sexual desire and the desire for material wealth. Independence and self-interest are achieved, Foster concludes, not through the pursuit of social eminence, but via an internalization of the precepts inculcated and expected by the figure-heads—Mr Holmes, Worthy, Mr Temple, Boyer—of a new middle-class patriarchal order.

The book Foster published one year after *The Coquette* offers an interesting gloss on her attitude to "fallen" women. Commenting on the Eliza Whartons of the world, a character in Foster's *The Boarding School* states:

> "I am generally an advocate for my own sex; but when they suf-fer themselves to fall prey to seducers, their pusillanimity admits no excuse. I am bold to affirm that every woman, by behaving with propriety on all occasions, may not only resist temptation, but repel the first attempts on her honor and virtue."
> (Foster 1798, 184; quoted in Newton 1990, 155)

Moreover, Foster makes it clear that educated women, above all, have no excuse for falling prey to seducers:

> Whatever allowance may be made for those, whose ignorance occasions their ruin, no excuse can be offered for others whose education, and opportunities for knowing the world and them-selves, have taught them a better lesson.
> (Foster 1798, 231; quoted in Newton 1990, 155)

Read through the lens of *The Boarding School Mistress*, Julia Granby emerges as the heroine of *The Coquette*; for, as Sanford describes her, she is "a girl . . . I should never attempt to seduce; yet she is a most alluring object I assure you. But the dignity of her manner forbids all assaults upon her honor" (Foster [1794] 1986, 140). Eliza Wharton, on the other hand, appears not as Foster's heroine but, because she is so well educated, as the very worst kind of fallen woman.

Writers in the early republic created a new role for women as republican mothers or wives who set standards of virtuous behaviour for their husbands and children (see Kerber 1980; Lewis 1987). In the novels of Rowson, Foster, and Brown, however, the exemplars of virtue are as often men as they are women. Furthermore, the republican woman's role as wife and/or mother is the role enjoined on her both by virtuous female friends and 'benevolent' republican men. The seduced woman in early American novels cannot play the role her culture ascribes her because she either fails to follow the path laid out by the republican father or because she fails to see the virtues of the potential model republican husband.

Far from valorizing seduced women, then, sentimental novels depict them as figures who ignore their own best interests by rejecting the supporting role assigned them within the middle class. The reward virtue holds out to women in the sentimental novel is not marriage to a wealthy landowner, but the possibility of acting as a moral authority in both private and public spheres. The sentimental novel thus teaches American middle-class women that the price of political influence is a constant effort to be politic. Moreover, by warning women against the corrupting influence of European aristocratic mores and recommending the more homely virtues of such men as Boyer, Mr Temple, Mr Worthy and Mr Holmes, early American sentimental novels argue for a model of womanly behaviour that is as definitively American in its tastes and preferences as it is definitively middle class.

Ultimately, perhaps the clearest sign of early American sentimental fiction's class affiliations lies in the concerns it shares with nineteenth-century American "woman's fiction" (see Baym 1978). I am not suggesting that early American sentimental novels and "woman's fiction" are identical. In particular, "woman's fiction" concentrates more on showing the benefits of female self-control and less on displaying the dangers of 'inclination' than do early American sentimental novels. However, such a change is not a sign that the sentimental novel's legacy has been abandoned. Rather, "woman's fiction" is a mutation of the early American sentimental novel which shows the American middle class becoming increasingly self-confident in the power of its models of conduct and familial relations. Thus, the coquettes of early American novels do not disappear but are relegated to the subplot of "woman's fiction" where they show up, still criticized by women authors, as "the 'belle'" who mistakenly thinks that "self-gratification is equivalent to power and influence" (Baym 1978, 28). While the coquette and the need to warn against her remain significant but now secondary concerns, women such as Foster's Julia Granby move from implicit heroines in an early sentimental novel's subplot to explicit heroines of the main plot in nineteenth-century "woman's fiction." Indeed, it is through the nineteenth-century daughters of Julia Granby that "woman's fiction" "shows [its] readers how to live" (26). Moreover, "woman's fiction" continued to use many of the other strategies early American sentimental novels used when showing readers not only how to live, but also how *not* to live. Thus, like "woman's fiction," early American sentimental novels set out to "reform a nation by correcting its manners," suggest heroines who are in thrall to their feelings set a bad example to female readers, praise men committed to the domestic virtues, criticize "acquisition and display," and portray ministers as ideal husbands (Baym, 47, 25, 27, 47, 41). Early American sentimental novels thus anticipate the concerns of woman's fiction and help the emerging American middle class begin its climb to power by "crystalliz[ing] its identity" as a class free of Europe's vices and political extremes (Kerber *et al* 1989, 574–75). Three decades before "woman's fiction" began to define the American middle class as a class in itself, male and female authored sentimental novels provide the preconditions for that development by portraying the American middle class as the representative class of a nation defined against European models of conduct.

WORKS CITED

Appleby, Joyce. 1984. *Capitalism and a New Social Order: The Republican Vision of the 1790s.* New York: New York University Press.

———. 1985. "Republicanism and Ideology," *American Quarterly* 37: 461–73.

———. 1986. "Republicanism in Old and New Contexts," *William and Mary Quarterly* 43: 20–34.

Armstrong, Nancy. 1987. *Desire and Domestic Fiction: A Political History of the Novel.* New York: Oxford University Press.

Banning, Lance. 1992. "The Republican Interpretation: Retrospect and Prospect, "*The Republican Synthesis Revisited: Essays in Honor of George Bilias,* edited by Milton M. Klein, Richard D. Brown, and John B. Hench. Worcester: American Antiquarian Society.

Baym, Nina. 1978. *Woman's Fiction: A Guide to Novels by and About Women in America, 1820–1870.* Ithaca: Cornell University Press.

Bloch, Ruth H. 1987. "The Gendered Meanings of Virtue in Revolutionary America," *Signs* 13: 36–58.

Blumin, Stuart. 1989. *The Emergence of the Middle Class: Social Experience in the American City, 1760–1900.* Cambridge: Cambridge University Press.

Brissenden, R. F. 1974. *Virtue in Distress: Studies in the Novel of Sentiment from Richardson to Sade.* London: Macmillan.

Brodhead, Richard. 1991. "Sparing the Rod: Discipline and Fiction in Antebellum America," *The New American Studies: Essays From Representations,* edited by Phillip Fisher. Berkeley: University of California Press.

Brown, Herbert Ross. 1940. *The Sentimental Novel in America, 1789–1860.* Durham, NC: Duke University Press.

Brown, William Hill. [1789] 1969. *The Power of Sympathy.* Edited by William S. Kable. Columbus: Ohio State University Press.

Buel, Richard. 1972. *Securing the Revolution: Ideology in American Politics, 1789–1815.* Ithaca: Cornell University Press.

Burrows, Edwin and Michael Wallace. 1972. "The American Revolution and the Psychology of National Liberation," *Perspectives in American History* 6: 167–306.

Butler, Marilyn. 1981. *Romantics, Rebels, and Reactionaries: English Literature and its Background, 1760–1830.* New York: Oxford University Press.

Cassuto, Leonard. 1994. "The Seduction of American Religious Discourse in Foster's *The Coquette,*" *Reform and Counter Reform: Dialectics of the Word in Western Christianity Since Luther,* edited by John C. Hawley. Berlin: Mouton De Gruyter.

Dalke, Anne. 1988. "Original Vice: The Political Implications of Incest in the Early American Novel," *Early American Literature* 23: 188–201.

Davidoff, Leonore and Catherine Hall. 1987. *Family Fortunes: Men and Women of the English Middle Class, 1780–1850.* Chicago: University of Chicago Press.

Davidson, Cathy N. 1975. "*The Power of Sympathy* Reconsidered: William Hill Brown As Literary Craftsman," *Early American Literature* 10: 14–29.

———. 1982. "Flirting with Destiny: Ambivalence and Form in the Early American Sentimental Novel," *Studies in American Fiction* 10: 17–39.

———. 1986. *Revolution and the Word: The Rise of the Novel in America.* New York: Oxford University Press.

Eagleton, Terry. 1982. *The Rape of Clarissa: Writing, Sexuality and Class Struggle in Samuel Richardson.* Oxford: Basil Blackwell.

Fabi, Maria Giulia. 1990. "*The Coquette* or The Ambiguities: On the Fiction and the Reality of Independence in the Early Republic," *Rivista di Studi Nord Americani* 1: 7–26.

Fizer, Irene. 1993. "Signing as Republican Daughters: The Letters of Eliza Southgate and *The Coquette,*" *The Eighteenth Century: Theory and Interpretation* 34: 243–63.

Fliegelman, Jay. 1982. *Prodigals and Pilgrims: The American Revolution Against Patriarchal Authority, 1750–1800.* London: Cambridge University Press.

Forcey, Blythe. 1991. "*Charlotte Temple* and the End of Epistolarity," *American Literature* 63: 225–41.

Foster, Hannah Webster. [1794] 1986. *The Coquette.* Edited and with an introduction by Cathy N. Davidson. New York: Oxford University Press.

———. 1798. *The Boarding School; or, Lessons of a Preceptress to Her Pupils.* Boston: Isaiah Thomas and E. T. Andrews.

Gilmore, Michael T. 1978. "Eulogy as Symbolic Biography: The Iconography of Revolutionary Leadership, 1776–1826," *Harvard English Studies* 8: 131–54.

Goldgeier, Adam. 1990. "*The Coquette* Composed," *Constructions* 1: 1–14.

Hagstrum, Jean H. 1980. *Sex and Sensibility: Ideal and Erotic Love From Milton to Mozart.* Chicago: University of Chicago Press.

Halttunen, Karen. 1982. *Confidence Men and Painted Women: A Study of Middle-Culture in America, 1830–1870.* New Haven: Yale University Press.

Hamilton, Kristie G. 1989. "An Assault on the Will: Republican Virtue and the City in Hannah Webster Foster's *The Coquette*," *Early American Literature* 24: 135–51.

Hansen, Klaus. 1991a. *Sin and Sympathy: Nathaniel Hawthorne's Sentimental Religion.* Frankfurt: Lang.

———. 1991b. "The Sentimental Novel and its Feminist Critique," *Early American Literature* 26: 39–54.

Hart, James D. 1950. *The Popular Book: A History of America's Literary Taste.* New York: Oxford University Press.

Jordan, Cynthia S. 1988. ""Old Words" in "New Circumstances": Language and Leadership in Post-Revolutionary America," *American Quarterly* 40: 491–513.

Kerber, Linda. 1980. *Women of the Republic: Intellect and Ideology in Revolutionary America.* Chapel Hill: University of North Carolina Press.

———. 1985. "The Republican Ideology of the Revolutionary Generation," *American Quarterly* 37: 474–95.

——— et al. 1989. "Beyond Roles, Beyond Spheres: Thinking About Gender in the Early Republic," *William and Mary Quarterly* 46: 565–85.

Klein, Milton M., Richard D. Brown, and John B. Hench, eds. 1992. *The Republican Synthesis Revisited: Essays in Honor of George Bilias.* Worcester: American Antiquarian Society.

Lewis, Jan. 1987. "The Republican Wife: Virtue and Seduction in the Early Republic," *William and Mary Quarterly* 44: 689–719.

McDowell, Tremaine. 1927. "Sensibility in the Eighteenth-Century American Novel," *Studies in Philology* 24: 383–402.

Mott, Frank Luther. 1947. *Golden Multitudes: The Story of Best Sellers in the United States.* New York: Macmillan.

Newton, Sarah Emily. 1990. "Wise and Foolish Virgins: "Usable Fiction" and the Early American Conduct Tradition," *Early American Literature* 25: 139–67.

Norton, Mary Beth. 1980. *Liberty's Daughters: The Revolutionary Experience of American Women, 1750–1800.* Boston: Little, Brown.

Parker, Patricia L. 1986. *Susanna Rowson.* Boston: G. K. Hall.

Pettengill, Claire C. 1992. "Sisterhood in a Separate Sphere: Female Friendship in Hannah Webster Foster's *The Coquette* and *The Boarding School*," *Early American Literature* 27: 185–203.

Petter, Henri. 1971. *The Early American Novel.* Columbus: Ohio State University Press.

Rowson, Susanna. [1797] 1986. *Charlotte Temple.* Edited and with an introduction by Cathy N. Davidson. New York: Oxford University Press.

Ryan, Mary. 1981. *Cradle of the Middle Class: The Family in Oneida County, New York, 1790–1865.* Cambridge: Cambridge University Press.

Samuels, Shirley. 1987. "Infidelity and Contagion: The Rhetoric of Revolution," *Early American Literature* 22: 183–91.

Shallhope, Robert E. 1982. "Republicanism and Early American Historiography," *William and Mary Quarterly* 39: 334–56.

Shuffleton, Frank. 1986. "Mrs. Foster's *Coquette* and the Decline of the Brotherly Watch," *Studies in Eighteenth Century Culture* 16: 211–24.

Smith-Rosenberg, Carroll. 1988. "Domesticating "Virtue": Coquettes and Revolutionaries in Young America," *Literature and the Body*, edited by Elaine Scarry. Baltimore, MD: Johns Hopkins University Press.

Tassoni, John Paul. 1993. "'I Can Step Out of Myself A Little': Feminine Virtue and Female Friendship in Hannah Foster's *The Coquette*," *Communication and Women's Friendships: Intersections in Literature and Life*, edited by Janet Doubler Ward and Joanna Stephens Mink. Bowling Green: Bowling Green University Press.

Todd, Janet. 1986. *Sensibility: An Introduction*. London: Methuen.

Waldstreicher, David. 1992. "'Fallen Under My Observation': Vision and Virtue in *The Coquette*," *Early American Literature* 27: 204–218.

Watt, Ian. 1963. *The Rise of the Novel: Studies in Defoe, Richardson, and Fielding*. Harmondsworth: Penguin.

Wenska, Walter P. 1977/78. "*The Coquette* and the American Dream of Freedom," *Early American Literature* 12: 243–55.

Wood, Gordon. 1992. *The Radicalism of the American Revolution*. New York: Knopf.

ELIZABETH BARNES

From Seductive Education and the Virtues of the Republic[†]

Midway through a protracted debate on the merits of narrative education, William Hill Brown's *The Power of Sympathy, or The Triumph of Nature* offers the following pithy comment by a discerning mother: "I conclude from your reasoning," said Mrs. Holmes, "and it is besides, my own opinion that many fine girls have been ruined by reading novels" (193). Implicit in her remark is the idea that all novels are not created equal. This was certainly the view of many critics troubled about the negative influence literary works might exert over their readers, but it was also the concern of novelists themselves. Such novelists went to great lengths to ensure that readers learned to discriminate between those dangerous romances that filled young women with fanciful notions about the future and their own "realistic" tales offering women valuable insights into the characters of men. Lessons of the first kind were considered seductive; lessons of the second were called education. The distinction between the harmful and the edifying is not necessarily an easy one to draw: in general, supporters of the early novel believed that the function of art—including fiction—was not to suppress but to arouse readers' emotions, because through their emotions an audience would be awakened to truths that logic alone could not impart.[1] The difference between education and seduction lay not in pedagogical practice, nor even in affective response, but in practical consequence—that is, how the organization of emotional stimuli caused an individual to *act*. Seduction could be distinguished from education only after the fact, depending on whether the protagonist—or reader—was led aright or astray (a determination itself subject to interpretation). Given these circumstances, it is no wonder that an author like Brown felt the need to include in the preface, the frontispiece, and even the body of his novel dedications to and examples of the "advantages of female education" and the "dangerous consequences of seduction." His success at anticipating and encoding reader response could well be all that distinguished his tuition from the lessons that had ruined many a fine girl.

Sentimental frameworks reinforce the congruity between education and seduction. The evocation of feeling becomes its own instrument of discipline, as readers' sympathies are employed in the service of modifying readers' behavior. As Brown's reference to "female education" indicates, sentimental pedagogy is gender-inflected. While the typical gentleman was schooled in situational discourse that allowed him to view the verbal arts as a means to an end, women and the middling and lower classes were specifically taught to accept their positions and to internalize rather than manipulate the information given them. The difference between these pedagogical premises can be said to reflect not only the difference between men and women, or the upper and lower classes, but the difference between performers of language and responders to it, that is, between seducers and seduced. Although educational experiences were necessarily different for women than for men, the designation of a specifically "female" education is somewhat misleading. For, in the novel of seduction, "female education" signifies the coding of the reader— whether female or male—as feminine and therefore as an appropriately affective respondent to the novel's rhetorical designs.

This chapter looks at some of the ways in which constructions of gender, marriage, patriotism, and especially education "seduce" audiences into intimate relationship with patriarchal authority after

---

1. See Janet Todd, *Sensibility: An Introduction* (London: Methuen, 1986), 30–31. [An excerpt from *Sensibility . . .* appears on p. 279 of this NCE.]

the Revolution. My readings suggest that sentimental literature and politics encourage a heteroerotic construction of the body politic, whereby both ideal readers and citizens are imagined as suggestible women—specifically, as the wives and daughters of a democratic paternalism.

*   *   *

The Authority of Representation: Charlotte Temple

Eighteenth-century seduction novels offer their own full-length "easy reading lessons" for feminine audiences, displaying and inculcating sympathetic attachments that will put narrative lessons (in)to effect. Women are not only construed as the target of the sentimental market, they become the central figures in these stories of seduction. One explanation for this has already been suggested: women's bodies and minds signified spaces that were singularly penetrable, thus constituting women as the logical emblems of a postrevolutionary culture's engagement with issues of influence and autonomy. Literary protagonists simultaneously evoking and expressing sympathy model an ideal readership for the literary market, one based on an economy of affective exchange.

The model of affective exchange informs political as well as literary structures. Both structures rely on modes of representation to engage the subject in acts of identification that affirm, simultaneously, personal and communal authority. As Christopher Newfield observes, in representative democracy a citizen "finds freedom in consenting to laws that he can claim were legislated, if not by him directly, then by others in his name."[2] Political representation has its premise in the flexible boundaries of subjectivity. Such a notion complicates traditional historical analyses, and even much eighteenth-century republican rhetoric, which posits disinterested benevolence as singularly fundamental to republican virtue. Popular sentimental ideology reveals republican virtue to be inseparable from the sympathetic mechanism that compels one to view others in light of one's own intellectual and affective position. The abstract concept of the Public Good shows itself grounded in the particulars of private desire, and civic disinterestedness in terms of the *self*-interest that underwrites it.

In *The Letters of the Republic*, Michael Warner contends that representation works via a "negative relation of private subject to the

2. Christopher Newfield, "Emerson's Corporate Individualism," *American Literary History* (Winter 1991), 3(4):660.

state and to the public discourse."[3] Personal or private desire is subsumed in the greater authority of the Public Good, which is itself an intangible concept fashioned from the material arts of a rising print culture. Citing the Constitution's "We, the People" as prime example, Warner persuasively argues that the success of representational polity hinges on the assurance that "the people" never be named, never be less than the whole, never, in effect, become personal. Disinterested republican virtue, embedded in the principle of public interest over private views or ends, finds its "voice" in the printed text that represents all men but is embodied by none.[4]

It is Warner's privileging of republican disinterestedness over liberalism that allows him to emphasize the generalized, impersonal, and public persona of "the People" in late eighteenth-century American culture. I suggest that representation works toward both republican *and* liberal ends, an idea we see most clearly presented in sentimental literature. Early fiction supports the republican cause of female education but effects this education through liberal strategies designed to conflate private and public authority and interest. Contrary to Warner's claim that the representation of letters denotes the depersonalization of authority for the greater glory of Union, sentimental literature confirms (and then often exploits) individual autonomy, authority, and desire through readers' sympathetic identification with the protagonist who represents them. Individuals are singularly affected in order to create a consensus of sensibility whereby the public is served through the modification of private desire, yet private liberty is affirmed by the attention to personal feeling.

At its most effective, sentimental representation obscures the distinctions between fiction and reality, heroine and reader, so that readers feel personally invested in the story's events. Susanna Rowson's purported "Tale of Truth," the seduction novel *Charlotte Temple* (1794), exemplifies sentimental representation at its best.[5] *Charlotte Temple* tells the story of a young woman at an English boarding school who is persuaded by a handsome soldier to leave home and family to cross the sea with him to America. The lover, Montraville, eventually abandons Charlotte and she, unmarried and alone, dies after giving birth to a baby girl. In her preface to the novel, Rowson requests that her "fair readers" consider the tale "not merely the effusion of Fancy, but as a reality" (5). Her readers apparently acceded to her request. A best-selling novel for over a

---

3. Warner, *The Letters of the Republic: Publication and the Public Sphere in Eighteenth-Century America* (Cambridge: Harvard University Press, 1990), 72.
4. Ibid., 73.
5. Rowson was born in England but spent much of her life in America. The setting of her story—moving between England and America—reflects the transatlantic nature of her career as well as the flexible boundaries of Anglo literary influence.

century and boasting over two hundred editions by 1964, *Charlotte Temple* is arguably the most popular novel in American literary history.[6] Its popularity is directly proportional to its power of representation: as Davidson points out, despite the lack of verifiable evidence, "for Rowson's readers Charlotte was real" (xv).[7]

* * *

The construction of readers as feminine, and the corresponding manipulation of "feminine" suggestibility intrinsic to the novel, becomes even clearer once we recognize the ways in which the seduction novel aligns itself with the classically educated gentleman-seducer it is attempting to denounce. Schooled in history and rhetoric, the typical upper-class male had the advantage of understanding both his own historical context and the significance of context in everyday discourse: "The gentry understood rhetoric not as the communication of definitive truth but as situational discourse aimed at persuading a clearly defined implied reader or auditor of the present worth of a present proposition for that particular audience."[8] Put another way— J. L. Austin's way—a gentleman views language as "performative" rather than "constantive."[9] Citing Austin for a similar purpose, Shoshana Felman argues that whereas the victim sees language as "an instrument for the transmission of *truth*" the seducer is "not susceptible to truth or falsity, but rather, very exactly, to felicity or infelicity, to success or failure."[1] In the seduction novel, the gentleman-seducer depends on his verbal skills to break down the woman's resistance. The novel itself does much the same thing. Each acts with intent— not to inform or to educate in and about context but to "modify the situation." In other words, to alter the woman's behavior.

Like the seducer it works simultaneously to undermine and emulate, the seduction novel exploits the suggestibility of its feminized audience by a performance of language designed to achieve

---

6. Cathy Davidson, introduction to *Charlotte Temple*, xi. I rely on Davidson's statistics and historical documentation throughout my discussion of this novel. All quotations come from Susanna Haswell Rowson, *Charlotte Temple*, ed. Cathy Davidson (Oxford: Oxford University Press, 1986). Citations hereafter will appear in parentheses following the quotation.

7. Terry Eagleton notes a similar phenomenon with regard to Samuel Richardson's novels, and argues that, though the characters are fictional, "nothing could be more insistently real than the ideological practices to which [the heroine's experiences] give rise. The national crisis which Clarissa's"—or in this case, Charlotte's—"death seems to have triggered is not to be ascribed to the heart-flutterings of gullible females; it is a measure of the material urgency of the themes which that death embodies." *The Rape of Clarissa* (Minneapolis: University of Minnesota Press, 1982), 17.

8. Davidson's summary of Gordon Wood's argument in "The Democratization of the American Mind." *Revolution and the Word*, 159.

9. J. L. Austin, *How to Do Things with Words*, ed. J. O. Urmson (Cambridge: Harvard University Press, 1962), 2–8.

1. Emphasis mine. Quoted and translated in John Lechte, *Julia Kristeva* (New York: Routledge, 1990), 24, 25.

a particular response.[2] In *Charlotte Temple*, the narrator secures readers through explicit and implicit moments of identification: "In affairs of love, a young heart is never in more danger than when attempted by a handsome young soldier. . . . When beauty of person, elegance of manner, and an easy method of paying compliments, are united to the scarlet coat, smart cockade, and military sash, ah! well-a-day for the poor girl who gazes on him." Following this sympathetic gesture on behalf of young women, the narrator changes tack to assume the father's jealous part: "When I think on the miseries that must rend the heart of a doating [sic] parent, when he sees the darling of his age at first seduced from his protection, and afterwards abandoned . . . my bosom glows with honest indignation, and I wish for power to extirpate those monsters of seduction from the earth" (22). The narrator's ability to take on a variety of different subject positions in these moments of sympathy establishes the free-floating nature of affective response: sympathetic identification may transcend conventional limitations such as age, experience, even gender. However, sympathy has a disciplinary function as well, one that blurs the distinction between theatricality and authenticity. For, in order to fulfill its pedagogical function, the novel of seduction must outperform the performer; it must win over its readers with the definitive show of sincerity. Only if the novel succeeds in this impersonation, this intimate and individualized representation of affection, will acts of seduction be translated into female education.[3]

* * *

JULIA A. STERN

From Working through the Frame: The Dream of Transparency in *Charlotte Temple*[†]

What is the significance of seduction and abandonment in the charged political atmosphere of the 1790s? What emotional ethos does such a phrase evoke? Literary genres speak to specific historical

---

2. See Austin, *How to Do Things with Words*. Austin himself excluded literary language from his analysis of speech acts, because "it cannot invoke conventions and accepted procedures, and because it does not link up with a situational context which can stabilize the meaning of its utterance." Wolfgang Iser, however, persuasively counters Austin's assumptions. See *The Act of Reading: A Theory of Aesthetic Response* (Baltimore: Johns Hopkins University Press, 1978), 60–62.

3. Davidson, on the other hand, writes that "the novelist's critique of illicit sexual behavior often had a feminist import and emphasized the unfortunate consequences of seduction for the individual woman, not the social mores (although these were in the novel, too) against which she had offended." *Revolution and the Word*, 116.

† Reprinted from *Arizona Quarterly* 49.4 (Winter 1993), by permission of the Regents of the University of Arizona.

moments with their attendant cultural and psychological needs. In the American eighteenth century, the novel of virtue in distress—maidenhood imperiled, ruined, and ultimately forsaken—exercises enormous appeal. Like the popular captivity narrative that provides the Puritans with a myth of acculturation into the new world wilderness and assuages their guilt over emigration, the sentimental, melodramatic, and gothic novel of seduction and abandonment also features a female victim and performs an important kind of cultural labor. The task of this literature is to address and work through the unprecedented sense of loss Americans experience in the wake of a Revolution that inscribes with fraternal blood the immutability of rupture from the mother country.

The sentimental *ur*text of this emerging American tradition is Susanna Rowson's *Charlotte Temple*—a work whose melancholic narrative unconscious will inscribe the most important novels of the period and against whose purported, if unrealized, affective politics *The Coquette, Wieland,* and *Ormond* will offer an increasingly gothic dissent. Rowson's novel languishes from neglect after it is published in England in 1791. Three years later, the book makes a spectacular literary "crossing" when it is reprinted and distributed by Mathew Carey in Philadelphia (1794). Thus transported, *Charlotte Temple* becomes a vital touchstone for Anglo-American cultural disjunction in the Federalist period, attempting, if ultimately failing, to afford its readers a transparent vision of social relations that would radically extend the boundaries of the national body imagined in master narratives of the Founding.

Set on the eve of the War of Independence, a phantasmagorical moment of political origin, *Charlotte Temple* articulates conflicting notions of social contract at work in the post-Revolutionary polity. The novel's strategy of retrospection evokes Rousseau's writings on the state of nature: like "The Discourse on Inequality," the "Letter To M. D'Alembert on the Theatre," and *The Social Contract* itself, *Charlotte Temple* is both backward looking—foregrounding the green world of the Temple's rural cottage in its nostalgic representation of the English past—and radically democratic—envisioning through its heterogeneous community of imagined and actual readers an American future that departs in startling ways from this protorepublican pastoral idyll.

In addition, *Charlotte Temple* represents, interrogates, and ultimately condemns the theatrical relations that continental aesthetic philosophers identify as distinguishing social intercourse in late-eighteenth-century culture. Against the background of Diderot and Rousseau's meditations on theatricality as a public problem with disturbing moral implications, Rowson's novel gains important cultural resonance. For Diderot, the danger of the drama lies in its propensity to make spectators forget the reality of authentic feelings, to mistake the world for the stage. For Rousseau, the social world is always already contaminated by theatrical relations: artifice and duplicity mark normative human exchange. Thus, the stage itself becomes a perverse mirror of the corruption of society, making doubly unnatural people's interactions in public.[1] Despite Rousseau's unease about the theater, he is not unequivocally hostile; he actually declares in a footnote embedded at the end of his "Letter To M. D'Alembert" that "I love the drama passionately," adding that he has "never willingly missed a performance of Molière." This ostensible endorsement comes nearly one hundred pages after an important earlier statement on the morality of the drama, strategically highlighted at the beginning of section four of the *Letter:* "But who can deny also that the theatre of this same Molière . . . is a school of vices and bad morals [manners] even more dangerous than the very books which profess to teach them?"[2]

Susanna Rowson's own career on the stage and as a playwright makes especially paradoxical—and Rousseauvian—the ambivalent deployment of dramatic spectacle in *Charlotte Temple*—particularly its equivocal incorporation of melodrama, a theatrical form less reliant on words than are its high-culture precursors, seventeenth-century tragedy and eighteenth-century comedy and farce. But in contrast to Rousseau's polemical rejection of contemporary society's corruption by artifice—duplicity that begins outside the playhouse and that is further amplified and perverted within it—Rowson's anxiety concerns the way theatrical relations displace compassionate exchange and thus enable a form of social dissimulation that victimizes the innocent. In that regard, her apprehensions echo Diderot's misgivings about dramatic representations: the notion that theatricality makes people incapable of deciphering authentic exhibitions of feeling rendered in a nondramatic mode; or the fear that theatrical expressions compel spectators to doubt the legitimacy of heightened displays of genuine emotion, causing them to misread real suffering as artful performance.[3]

Rowson shares some of Rousseau's more striking antitheatrical attitudes, which emerge when one compares the material practices of her career with the ideas she explores in *Charlotte Temple*.

1. My summary here is indebted to the extended discussion of eighteenth-century French writings on the ethics of the drama in David Marshall, *The Surprising Effects of Sympathy: Marivaux, Diderot, Rousseau, and Mary Shelley* (Chicago: University of Chicago Press, 1988), particularly 105–77. Jay Fliegelman explores the implications of "natural theatricality" in American culture during roughly the same period; see *Declaring Independence*, especially 79–93.
2. See "Letter to M. D'Alembert on the Theatre," in *Politics and the Arts: "Letter to M. D'Alembert on the Theatre,"* trans. and introd. Allan Bloom (1758; Ithaca: Cornell University Press, 1968), 34 and 131, note.
3. This discussion relies on Marshall's account of Diderot in *The Surprising Effects of Sympathy*, 133–34.

Between the years 1786, when she appears on the English stage, and 1797, four years after her permanent relocation to America when she joins Thomas Wignell's theatrical company in Philadelphia, the author of *Charlotte Temple* works as an actress and composes plays, patriotic songs, and odes celebrating the commercial vigor of the new republic and the emblematic lives of George Washington and John Adams, among other Federalist luminaries.[4]

Despite—or perhaps because of—her early professional life in the theater, Rowson's indictment of the way dramatic conventions structure and contaminate the most basic human associations evokes Rousseau's repudiation of the spectacular dynamics that underlie the social order. In contrast to such theatrical relations, *Charlotte Temple* offers an alternative form of communion through which the witnesses to the heroine's plight—characters within the novel and readers outside of it—come together and function as a unified corporate body. Rowson's plot shifts from the villainous La Rue's melodramatic rejection of the supplicating Charlotte, who appears on her treacherous French teacher's doorstep teetering on the verge of death, to a legendary account of the community's sorrow, an oral tradition about the suffering and death of the heroine that springs up within the novel world. Thus, the narrative swerves abruptly from a moment of heightened theatricality, in which a designated audience refuses to be moved, to an extended account of genuine emotion, in which the power of Charlotte's story to touch those who hear it creates a common emotional ground around the experience of loss. Based on a fantasy of unobstructed relations of sympathy—figured as the indivisible bond between an omnipotent maternal narrator and an audience whose constitution is infinitely expandable, unlimited by the distinctions of race, class, or gender that exclude the republic's "others" from the promises of the Founding—*Charlotte Temple* imagines, creates, and attempts to enfranchise a post-Revolutionary community linked by claims of universal compassion.

As the inaugural work in the fictive genealogy explored in *The Plight of Feeling, Charlotte Temple* stands at the end of a British sentimental legacy originating in Samuel Richardson's *Clarissa* (1747–48). Both English and American literary history make claims for Rowson's novel: this dispute over the native origins of *Charlotte Temple* eloquently attests to an incestuous intermingling of English and American cultures that begins after the events of the Revolution have become eclipsed by the struggle for national legitimation and that extends into the late-twentieth century. Viewed in the context of the American narrative tradition it historically instates, *Charlotte*

---

4. See Patricia L. Parker, *Susanna Rowson* (Boston: Twayne Publishers, 1986), "Chronology."

Temple plays the role of the favored eldest adopted child in a family of biological siblings (*The Coquette, Wieland,* and *Ormond*), all of which remain haunted by the legacy of their powerful Richardsonian progenitor.

In that epic novel of virtue assaulted and ultimately triumphant, representations of fractured familial relations become figures for the problem of female dissent from patriarchal authority. Jay Fliegelman takes up *Clarissa* in order to read the early American novel's own recurring images of domestic strife as a mode of social allegory in which the family stands for the state. Richardson's Clarissa, who functions as the fictional prototype for heroines of early American novels of the 1790s, emblematizes righteous filial rebellion against a brutally authoritarian patriarchy; Fliegelman points out that "the first American editions of *Clarissa* . . . virtually 'rewrite' the novel in such a way as to render it an unadulterated polemic against parental severity." He goes on to note that in the eighteenth-century American revisions and abridgements of Richardson's greatest work, "Clarissa is purely a victim caught between two tyrannies. Her rebellious spirit is not censured in these volumes."[5]

In contrast, literary critics studying *Charlotte Temple* identify Susanna Rowson's heroine as either child-victim or daughter-object of a paternal practice that is, perhaps, *too* liberal and egalitarian compared with that figured in *Clarissa.* In the Anglo-American version of the myth of seduced and abandoned maidenhood, benevolent and virtuous parental authority is righteous power that should command filial respect and obedience. Clarissa rejects unjust parental power and proves her father wrong, but children like Charlotte, unwittingly in conflict with rational benevolence, cannot be deemed rightful revolutionaries.[6]

Such scholars emphasize the novel's patriarchal and paternal plots, focusing on the framed narrative and its story of father, daughter, and seducer in the course of exploring *Charlotte Temple* for its political subtext. Omitted from any extended discussion of the parental politics operative in *Charlotte Temple* is the symbolic figure of the absent mother who occupies and directs the narrative frame. She is not to be confused with Charlotte's biological mother, Mrs. Lucy

5. Those two tyrannies are explicated in the subtitle of the nonepistolary American versions of the novel: *The Arts of a Designing Villain and The Rigours of Parental Authority.* Fliegelman identifies five surviving early American imprints of *Clarissa,* all of which were published in the 1790s and four of which were based on the Philadelphia edition of 1791. He postulates that a chapbook edition of 1772 and an abridged edition (1786) were literally "read to pieces"—neither version of the novel survives. See Jay Fliegelman, *Prodigals and Pilgrims: The American Revolution Against Patriarchal Authority, 1750–1800* (Cambridge: Cambridge University Press, 1982), 86–87.

6. For an extended meditation on the subject of rebellious children figuring revolution in the early American novel, see Fliegelman, *Prodigals and Pilgrims,* particularly 83–92 and 261–64. For a reading of Charlotte Temple's "sin" as a "betrayal of what she herself calls her 'filial duty,'" see Zwinger, *Fathers, Daughters and the Novel,* 52.

Temple, who receives critical attention for her role as forgiving parent, potential surrogate for Charlotte's orphaned infant. Mrs. Temple may be crucial to the "*felix culpa*" denouement of the novel, but her role in the narrative symbolic of *Charlotte Temple* is minimal.

Instead, it is the unnamed and overly present narrator who functions as the novel's absent emblem of maternal power and who does *Charlotte Temple*'s most important cultural work.[7] This symbolic mother stands in analogous relation to the "patriarchal authority" that Fliegelman identifies as central to these early American fictions of the family in distress. Fated to remain a disembodied figure, Rowson's narrator never achieves representational status as a dramatic character, but her parental prerogative needs no visual augmentation. In fact, such noncorporeality enhances the narrator's position in the novel's semiotic regime.

Perhaps the most fascinating, and certainly the most critically unexplored locus of *Charlotte Temple*, the narrator disrupts the unfolding story of Charlotte's decline and fall in important and unrecognized ways. If we are to recover the full narrative complexity and the cultural significance of *Charlotte Temple*, both in its own epoch and as the first American best-seller, which remains in print after nearly two hundred years, we must attend to the centrality of this symbolic absent mother and, specifically, to the narrative form in which and through which she does her work. At stake is a reading of *Charlotte Temple* that extends beyond a reductive decoding of Rowson's politics as patriarchal and conservative, as antirevolutionary.

Paradoxically, *Charlotte Temple*'s more utopian and egalitarian impulses are expressed through the autocratic eruptions of Rowson's maternal storyteller. At crucial moments the narrator breaks the frame of her account in order to regale the reader about the dangers of separation and independence and to argue that naive young women are easily lured by promises of economic, social, and romantic freedom. (In conventional readings of the novel such female innocents allegorize the fate of the new nation itself.) She exclaims, "Oh my dear girls—for to such only am I writing—listen not to the voice of love, unless sanctioned by paternal approbation: be assured, *it is now past the days of romance: no woman can be run away with contrary to her own inclination*" (22; emphasis added). Insisting that females are particularly vulnerable to the artful wiles and manipulations of social predators, the narrator brings to vivid life Rousseau's antitheatrical prejudice and anticipates Wollstonecraft's brief

---

7. This important phrase was coined by Jane Tompkins in her discussion of the antebellum American novel. See Tompkins, *Sensational Designs: The Cultural Work of American Fiction 1790–1860* (New York: Oxford University Press, 1985), xi–xix. The ongoing cultural power of *Charlotte Temple* may be attributed, in part, to its compelling representation of a fully rational speaking mother, the narrator of the frame.

for women's rationality one year before the publication of *Vindication of the Rights of Woman* (1792): she legislates for Enlightenment on sympathetic, rather than exclusionary, grounds. Had Charlotte been able to decode the dramatic performance underlying the concern the falsely maternal La Rue exhibited in conversations about her future; had the ingenuous virgin exercised reason and forethought instead of succumbing to her mentor's beguiling claims; and had she maintained her elective affinities for mother, father, and grandfather, her woeful seduction, piteous abandonment, and sorry death would have been unimaginable.

In fact, while Charlotte's imprudent rending of family ties—the breach that precipitates her suffering and demise—constitutes the novel's enabling political precondition, the devastating cost of self-government becomes its abiding subject. That such primal separation (what, according to the allegorical reading, we might characterize as the heroine's break with her "English family") cannot be undone is a crucial element in Rowson's radically democratic program. Such fracture allows the maternal narrator—whose own imperious temperament sometimes savors of a despotic will to power[8]—to transvaluate the operations of "independence" and extend the implications of "affiliation" in decidedly unconservative ways.

To argue that the traumas of "revolutionary" separation are remedied when Mr. Temple removes Charlotte's infant daughter from the American scene and restores the babe to the loving embrace of his grieving wife Lucy is to ignore the unique narrative form of *Charlotte Temple*. According to this conservative and plot-driven reading, Lucy Temple the elder (Charlotte's daughter is also, significantly, named Lucy) represents the English motherland mourning its erring colonial child who, though forever lost, has produced offspring worthy of redemption. While the ending of *Charlotte Temple* certainly supports such an interpretation, it stops short of explaining the political significance of the narrator's peculiar intrusive tendencies, which dominate and overtake the novel's form, ultimately obscuring the clarity of its ideological intentions.

If we focus instead on Rowson's maternal figuration of her narrator and explore the filial relationship this absent presence constructs with the audience, the democratic face of the novel comes into sharper focus. Charlotte cannot be restored, but the sorrow that her death provokes—in both narrator and reader alike—allows for the cohesion of an "imagined community" around the wound to the social body that her passing represents.[9] Thus, the fabric of narrative, rent by the death of Charlotte and rewoven by the audience's

8. Thanks to Jana Argersinger for this potent expression.
9. Benedict Anderson coins this phrase in his discussion of nationalism as a phenomena that begins affectively and, in a crucial sense, fictively. See *Imagined Communities: Reflections on the Origin and Spread of Nationalism* (1983; London: Verso, 1991), 6.

compassionate response both inside the novel and outside in the world of history becomes Rowson's abiding utopian figure for the new nation itself. Rather than viewing the trauma of post-Revolutionary separation as a condition from which to retreat in some kind of reactionary return-to-the-womb of mother country, Rowson crusades against the pain exacted by independence by transforming sorrow into an ostensibly enabling—because democratic—precondition for the future. The sacrifices exacted by the Revolution—symbolized by Charlotte Temple—and the work of mourning they inspire thus allow for the reimagining of the American polity as a body that is both more cohesive and more inclusive than its pre-Revolutionary avatar precisely because it is grounded in the sympathetic affective relations of its members.

* * *

To reconstruct *Charlotte Temple*'s cultural force, and particularly its utopian, Rousseauvian dimensions, we must consider not only the framed tale of seduction but the significance of the frame, not simply the narrative matter of *Charlotte Temple* but also its manner, expressed in disruptions and discontents. As we unpack the complexity of *Charlotte Temple*'s concentric narratives and explore the ways in which the outer story permeates the inner, we will come to a better understanding of Rowson's contribution to a subtle and important cultural conversation concerning gender and loss that was taking place in the post-Revolutionary context of the early American novel. The key to much that remains unexplained about both *Charlotte Temple* in particular and late-eighteenth-century American fiction in general is contained within the dynamics of narrative itself. Reading for the poetics of form will clarify both how and why *Charlotte Temple*, a novel predicated on the healing presence and plenitude of the female voice and underwritten by the attendant fantasy of women's *authorial* power, occupies a central place in the cultural and representational history of an affect: the feminization of loss that pervades late-eighteenth- and nineteenth-century American sentimental fiction.

At the heart of *Charlotte Temple*'s performance of such loss lies the narrator, a figure who rings a change on conventional eighteenth-century Anglo-American fictive depictions of women; Rowson creates a maternal voice notable for its extraordinary *rationality*, a pragmatic worldliness that stands in stark contrast to the tableau of female hysteria it frames. Speaking within the highly artificial context of a novelistic discourse, the narrator is fully aware that young female readers of fiction need to be grounded in the hard realities of the world in which they live. Her goal is to preempt what later would come to be termed "Bovaryism," girlish longings for "the days of romance" (22). In the social code of the eighteenth century, a zealous

enthusiasm for sensational novels was thought to debase the faculties of reason;[1] ever mindful of her culture's stereotype of female
sensibility, in which all women bear a latent propensity for hysterical
dissolution, Rowson's narrator will not dignify such identifications
for her community of readers.

But the narrator's rationality, which is crucial to rendering a persuasive case against seduction, represents only one level of her affective experience in *Charlotte Temple*; at the moment in which she
confidently registers her soundest judgments, she also inadvertently
gives voice to a melancholic grief.[2] Perhaps even more interesting
than the narrator's insistence that young women readers not be gulled
by fantasies of romantic rescue is her emphasis on proper and
improper ways in which to listen to the voice of love. Rowson's speaker
ostensibly promulgates "paternal approbation" as the value of choice,
offering an endogamous daughter-father dyad in the place of unrigh-
teous—if exogamous—heterosexual attachment, an arrangement
that leaves traditional, patriarchal structures of authority firmly in
place. But, against this explicit injunction, the narrator sets up an
alternative, maternal economy of feeling that substitutes reader and
storyteller for female child and male parent; displacing the law of the
father with the voice of the mother, *Charlotte Temple* reimagines the
gendering of power in decidedly antipatriarchal ways.

This female prerogative does not entirely escape the structures of
domination that inform patriarchal practice. Indeed, while the commitment the narrator offers to her audience is total, it is also virtually
autocratic: she is willing to lavish an unstinting flow of love, support,
and advice on the "young ladies" she identifies as her readers, but this
outpouring of generosity and concern is marked by a disturbing emotional extravagance. The narrator's insistence on her readers' approv-
ing response suggests that her investment goes beyond that of the
civic-minded woman who wishes to educate young girls in the meaning of true virtue; the intensity of the affect betrays the depth of the

1. The sexual downfall of the heroine of Hannah Foster's 1797 novel *The Coquette*, another
   tale of seduction, abandonment, and death based on the real life of Elizabeth Whitman,
   a woman poet from Connecticut, is also linked to excessive reading practices. In both the
   novel and the contemporary reports about Whitman herself, detractors attempting to
   trace the etiology of her ruin repeatedly point to the woman's overindulgence in certain
   (depraved) forms of reading; an imagination overworked and overheated by sensational
   novels has no defense against the seductive strains of the libertine.
2. The affective strata that organize *Charlotte Temple*—the way the novel's manifest narrative of rationality overlays its latent discourse of melancholy—are not unique to
   eighteenth-century American women's writing; in fact, they may be constitutive features of Enlightenment accounts of maternity and loss, found in both the fiction of
   sensibility and in biographical and autobiographical writings of the early Romantic
   period. Deployed in measured prose, William Godwin's extraordinary *Memoirs of the
   Author of the Rights of Woman* (1798), an agonized personal meditation on the brilliant
   life and untimely death of Mary Wollstonecraft, who succumbed to postpartum septic
   infection days after delivering their daughter Mary (Godwin Shelley), marks a fascinating case in point.

need. What she attempts to redress through her relationship with the reader is nothing less than a sense of loss that is so overwhelming that it blights every other idea in *Charlotte Temple*.

By asserting that the affective significance of *Charlotte Temple* inheres in the practices of Rowson's narrator, a figure who has at best been known for her intrusive preachiness, I am attempting to shift the ground of contemporary criticism of the early American novel to a cultural analysis of form. Scholars writing as recently as Susan K. Harris, who take the female narrator's frequent moralistic interruptions at face value, continue to identify the novel as a didactic fable warning against the dangers of seduction and advocating greater social tolerance for wayward girls.[3] Resting comfortably at the level of prescription, such critics accept that *Charlotte Temple* is a novel about ethics, but this line of inquiry stops short of questioning whether the narrator's didacticism may itself be symptomatic of an entirely other set of concerns, pertaining not to action but to feeling and its social implications. The didactic reading reduces to monologue the significantly more complicated and pluralized maneuvers of a narrator for whom female chastity is not, in fact, the last word.

To unravel the multiple voices that together constitute the text that is *Charlotte Temple* is to discover a feminist anatomy-*manqué* of eighteenth-century patriarchal culture. Punctuating the central tale of the virgin seduced and abandoned exists a less visible but perhaps even more powerful story: the tale of a narrator so haunted by the threat of loss that she generates the tightly controlled narrative universe to which we have alluded, a fictive world that encodes its own readership and modes of response in order to perform a preemptive and potentially reparative ritual of maternal mourning.

This powerful wish for control and restitution is acted out not only at the level of narratorial interruption but also through an obsessive retelling of Charlotte's story in the epistolary discourse, melodramatic spectacle, and oral tradition that are deployed *within* the novel's mimetic world.[4] Rowson's narrative economy functions according to a law of superlegibility: the more often the tale can be retold, the better. This strategy for storytelling insures that the affective core of

---

3. See Susan K. Harris, *Nineteenth-Century American Women's Novels: Interpretive Strategies* (New York: Oxford University Press, 1990), 39–50.
4. *Charlotte Temple*'s narrative functions textually through its embedded epistolarity, the inclusion and representation of multiple letters. The novel operates aurally in its employment of dialogue, in its use of narratorial interruption, and in its depiction of an oral tradition about Charlotte (the living legend) that springs up at the end of the novel and is passed from character to character by word of mouth. Finally, much of the power of *Charlotte Temple* is produced by the brilliant visual set pieces that punctuate the novel. Scenic tableaux proliferate: we see Charlotte swooning into the carriage at her elopement; we follow the pregnant and consumptive Charlotte, dressed in rags, as she makes her way through a blinding snowstorm to New York City; and we witness Montraville in the act of virtually throwing himself on Charlotte's open grave.

the novel—its horror over loss—will reach nearly transparent representation. If, as Freud argues in "Mourning and Melancholia," mourning is a process of recuperating the ego's investment of libido in the lost object through a *ritual of commemoration and farewell,*[5] the generic multiplicity at work within *Charlotte Temple* would seem to attest to the mournful nature of the narrator's psychopolitical enterprise.

And yet the narrator's framing discourse does not, ultimately, contain the grief unleashed by Charlotte's story. The moralistic interruptions, highly rational exhortations deployed to appeal to the mind as well as merely to the feelings of the reader, take us back to the scene of loss and replay it without allowing us to move on. The narrator's sorrow is unrequited by the end of the tale, her working-through incomplete, verging on the very sort of impasse that marks melancholia.[6] The frame does not close. Written during a period of renewed Anglo-American discussion about the place of women in republican culture, *Charlotte Temple,* with its multinational genealogy and its discourse of maternal loss and a mourning that remains unresolved, speaks to the unfinished business of post-Revolutionary American society. Understood in these terms, we can begin to recover the ongoing appeal of *Charlotte Temple,* which inheres in the staging of maternal grief as a kind of cultural work in progress.[7]

* * *

5. See Sigmund Freud, "Mourning and Melancholia," 1917, in *The Standard Edition of the Complete Psychological Works of Sigmund Freud,* trans. and ed. James Strachey, in collaboration with Anna Freud, assisted by Alix Strachey and Alan Tyson. 24 vols. (London: Hogarth Press, 1953–74), 14:237–58.
6. In "Mourning and Melancholia," Freud argues that the latter condition is a pathological disturbance of the mourning process in which the ego, unable to decathect from the lost object, introjects that object (incorporates the object cathexis) into the ego. The superego, enraged over the abandonment suffered in the external world, turns its fury against the encrypted lost object, which, by virtue of the process of introjection, has now become part of the survivor's self; melancholia is the process of internal self-devouring, the replaying of loss and punishment that occurs in the inner world of the mourner who cannot let go in order to carry on.
7. Kaja Silverman's theories about gender, the Oedipal phase, and melancholia are pertinent here. In *The Acoustic Mirror,* Silverman argues that, for females, the Oedipal phase, in which the girl child must relinquish her homosexual object cathexis to the mother in order to embrace a heterosexual identification, involves a melancholic form of loss. Since the girl must give up her connection to that which she also *is,* the loss constitutes a *loss of self* and thus never can be mourned fully. Instead, the loss is taken inside the self, incorporated as a central feature of female identity. For Silverman, to be a heterosexual female is to be, by definition, melancholic (155–59). While this hypothesis demands historicization, it nevertheless constitutes a compelling theoretical backdrop to my speculations about why the melancholic substrate of *Charlotte Temple* has appealed to readers across different historical eras. This is not to suggest that female melancholia is a transhistorical phenomena; rather, I am attempting to locate its particular social construction within the formation of the excluded American subject during the post-Revolutionary period. In that regard, women constitute the test case of melancholic subject formation as routed through "otherness," from which the cases of African Americans, Native Americans, and aliens would follow.

MARION RUST

What's Wrong with *Charlotte Temple?*[†]

Charlotte Temple, the eponymous heroine of Susanna Rowson's late eighteenth-century best-selling novel, is fond of "lying softly down," and her timing is terrible (p. 54). She faints into a chaise in Chichester; she crawls into the bed where her seducer, the dashing Lieutenant Montraville, already sleeps; and she takes an afternoon nap that allows his even less scrupulous "brother officer" in the British army, Belcour, to position himself beside her in time for her beloved to discover them together (p. 8). Given Charlotte's propensity for putting her feet up, it is no wonder that critics have taken the book bearing her name as an exemplar of the novel of seduction, a genre wherein the reader "is asked to deplore the very acts which provide his enjoyment." Some see the novel as evidence of "the appalling popularity of the seduction motif" in early American sentimental fiction, while others take a gentler view of how the genre "blended the histrionic and pedagogic modes." But whether they favor pleasure or instruction as the primary narrative impetus behind Charlotte's loss of virginity out of wedlock, most scholars take the centrality of the sex act—and with it, of Charlotte's presumed lust—for granted. A story of "the fatal consequence of . . . illicit sexuality," the novel is said to depict a woman "betrayed by her own naive passions" and thereby to provide an "example of virtue fallen through seduction and sexuality."[1]

A close look calls this emphasis on Charlotte's passion, and its ill-effects on her virtue, into question. The novel rarely mentions sex: there is no indication of how the "kindness and attention" that Montraville shows a seasick Charlotte during their voyage from Portsmouth, England, to New York leads, five chapters later, to the first allusion to her "visible situation" (pp. 45, 58). And while Charlotte's pregnancy attracts other euphemisms, such as "present condition," it receives little actual discussion beyond Charlotte's brief description of "an innocent witness of my guilt" in a letter to her mother and a

---

[†] Reprinted by permission of the Omohundro Institute of Early American History and Culture.

1. William C. Spengemann, *The Adventurous Muse: The Poetics of American Fiction, 1789–1900* (New Haven, 1977), 88; Herbert Ross Brown, *The Sentimental Novel in America, 1789–1860* (Durham, N.C., 1940), 44; John Seelye, "Charles Brockden Brown and Early American Fiction," in Emory Elliott, gen. ed., *Columbia Literary History of the United States* (New York, 1988), 168–86, 170; Cathy N. Davidson, "The Life and Times of *Charlotte Temple:* The Biography of a Book," in Davidson, ed., *Reading in America: Literature and Social History* (Baltimore, 1989), 170; Joseph Fichtelberg, "Early American Prose Fiction and the Anxieties of Affluence," in Carla Mulford, ed., *Teaching the Literatures of Early America* (New York, 1999), 200–12, 206; Maureen L. Woodard, "Female Captivity and the Deployment of Race in Three Early American Texts," *Papers on Language and Literature,* 32 (1996), 115–46, 127.

posthumous reference to a "poor girl . . . big with child" (pp. 69, 61, 88). This reticence cannot be attributed merely to a desire to spare the reader's feelings, since Rowson had no qualms about sensationalizing sexuality in other work. At the same time that the novel was taking off in America, Rowson was in Philadelphia writing stage comedies and patriotic drinking songs in which lust, albeit parodied, racially marked lust, played a central role. Her play *Slaves in Algiers,* first performed in 1794 in Philadelphia and Baltimore, makes much of the Algerian Dey's "huge scimitar" and includes a scene in which the cross-dressed heroine makes a "mighty pretty boy" in the eyes of her unknowing lover. The sailors drinking to their lasses in "America, Commerce and Freedom," Rowson's popular song of the same year, show "eager haste" to join the young women running across the beach to meet them over the "full flowing bowl." Even in the novel at hand, desire is given its due as long as it occurs within the sanctified bonds of marriage.[2] Mrs. Temple, Charlotte's mother, is the very picture of marital satisfaction, in continual possession of "the delightful sensation that dilated her heart . . . and heightened the vermillion on her cheeks" (p. 26) in the presence of her husband. The woman who speaks to Charlotte when no one else will and ministers to her in the hours before her family arrives (in opposition to Charlotte's female undoer, the malicious and cunning boarding school teacher Mademoiselle La Rue, this angel of mercy's name is "Mrs. Beauchamp") is similarly blessed, as "the most delightful sensations pervaded her heart" at the "encomiums bestowed upon her by a beloved husband" (p. 57). Clearly, Rowson is capable of alluding to heteroerotic attraction—it is just not what she is after in Charlotte's case.

Charlotte is "disappointed" in the only "pleasure" she does expect, that of the liberal provisions promised by Mademoiselle La Rue at the party to which she is lured early on, where she meets Montraville. Here, Charlotte experiences a rare instance of clear determination: she "heartily wished herself at home again in her own chamber" (p. 21). The narrator then acknowledges Charlotte's "gratitude" at Montraville's praises of her and, it must be admitted, a certain amount of satisfaction in his "agreeable person and martial appearance" (pp. 22). But her subsequent "blushes" are from shame, not pleasure, and her strongest sensation almost immediately becomes that of not knowing what to do. After Montraville gives her a letter, she turns

2. Rowson, *Slaves in Algiers, or, A Struggle for Freedom; A Play, Interspersed with Songs, in Three Acts* (Philadelphia, 1794), in *Plays by Early American Women, 1775–1850,* ed. Amelia Howe Kritzer (Ann Arbor, 1995), 59, 79; Rowson, "America, Commerce and Freedom," music by Mr. Reinagle (Philadelphia, 1794). On early American attitudes toward sexuality in marriage, see John D'Emilio and Estelle B. Freedman, *Intimate Matters: A History of Sexuality in America* (New York, 1988), esp. chap. 2; Ellen K. Rothman, *Hands and Hearts: A History of Courtship in America* (New York, 1984); and Richard Godbeer, *Sexual Revolution in Early America* (Baltimore, 2002).

to her teacher, asking, "What shall I do with it?" (p. 24). With every moment of indecision, La Rue steps in to direct Charlotte's path— "Read it, to be sure" (p. 24)—and it is thus and not through any over-whelming desire of her own that Charlotte is impregnated. She meets her lover to tell him she will see him no more, is persuaded by fits and starts to approach his carriage, and ends up literally fainting into it, whereby we are to assume that the fatal deed is done. The less Char-lotte credits her own instincts, the more her behavior is described as a form of collapse, in which her future direction is determined by nothing more deliberate than her center of gravity.

To seduce is to "induce (a woman) to surrender her chastity."[3] And yes, the reader anticipates Charlotte's defloration from her "blushes" and "sighs" and witnesses its effects in her subsequent condition. The word "passion" is even used a couple of times. But the sex itself exists only through its after-effects, and Charlotte's behavior in this regard is never explained. Not only, that is, do we fail to witness her "surren-der," being left to deduce it from subsequent irrefutable evidence, but we never learn just how she is "induced" to do so. In fact, Charlotte does not so much surrender her chastity—in the sense of giving up under duress something she values—as lose track of it altogether, along with every other aspect of her being. Thus, whereas to be seduced is to put "private and individual needs ahead of others" (by giving in to one's reciprocal lust), Charlotte loses her virginity only when she loses the ability to experience need altogether.[4] As the story develops, she becomes increasingly incapable of knowing what it is she feels, and she does what she feels she ought not, it turns out, not through an excessive respect for her desires, but rather through an increasing distrust of them. With "her ideas . . . confused," she is soon allowing herself to be "directed" not only by La Rue, but by her "betrayer" Montraville, rather than by her own self-appraisal, accord-ing to which she longs to remain loyal to her "forsaken parents" (p. 37). In sum, it is in relaxing her sensitivity to her own impulses, not in giv-ing in to them, that Charlotte loses her virginity and then her life.

Unlike her sister protagonist Eliza Wharton, who begins the novel *The Coquette* in constant appreciation of the effect she has on men, Charlotte rarely refers to her own ability to obtain power, or plea-sure, from erotically charged social interactions.[5] But she does spend

---

3. *The Compact Edition of the Oxford English Dictionary* (Oxford, 1971).
4. Michael T. Gilmore, "The Literature of the Revolutionary and Early National Periods," in *The Cambridge History of American Literature*, gen. ed. Sacvan Bercovitch, vol. 1: *1590–1820* (Cambridge, 1994), 539–694, 587.
5. *Charlotte Temple* may be unique among early American sentimental novels in its avoid-ance of sexually charged language. William Hill Brown's *The Power of Sympathy* (1798) capitalizes the word "seduction" in the dedication to its 1789 edition. Another popular novel from the 1790s, Hannah Foster's *The Coquette* (1797), also invokes Elizabeth Whitman's seduction, abandonment, and death, as first reported in the *Salem Mercury* in 1788. The *Coquette* goes even further than the *Power of Sympathy* in making passion

a great deal of time in contemplation of another aspect of her being, namely, its terrifying absence of self-direction. Just before collapsing into her lover's arms, Charlotte asks of her "torn heart": "How shall I act?" without receiving an answer (p. 37). It may be possible to explain her habit of prostrating herself as a manifestation of something other than sexual desire, for while fainting and napping share with more licentious behavior the tendency to take place lying down, they also possess another quality in common that is more important to understanding Charlotte than lust. They both entail the loss of consciousness and with it any capacity for self-direction. Asleep or passed out, Charlotte has virtually no say over how her life unfolds. Awake, she fares almost no better. *Charlotte Temple,* despite appearances to the contrary and decades of critical assumption, is *not* really a novel of seduction, in the sense of being a document that provides sexual titillation under cover of pedagogic censure. Instead, far from depicting Charlotte's overweening desire, the novel portrays the fatal consequences of a woman's inability to want anything enough to motivate decisive action. Charlotte falls into compromising positions not so much because she yearns to as because she does not, in the words of her evil counsel La Rue, "know [her] own mind two minutes at a time," and what she loses when she "falls" (p. 34) is not, or at least not importantly, her virginity, but rather her independent agency.

Disorientation, therefore, rather than passion, leads Charlotte from her British boarding school to her lover's arms and from there to a transatlantic crossing, the outskirts of New York, pregnancy, childbirth among strangers, temporary madness, and death in the redeeming presence of her father. This reading helps make sense of the observation that since Anglo-American women, far from being ostracized for having had premarital intercourse, were marrying after conception in record numbers by the late eighteenth century, the novel's extraordinary popular appeal in the new United States cannot be explained by its veracity as historical transcript.[6] As recent studies make clear, post-revolutionary Philadelphia, where the novel's first two American editions were published in 1794

---

its primary theme. "Sensation" appears twice in its first sentence and "pleasure" twice in its second, giving the astute reader notice that Eliza's destruction will be accompanied by plenty of sensual indulgence along the way. Eliza thrills in her "conquests" and admits to a pleasant "perturbation" at being so much "the taste of the other sex"; "letter 5" in Hannah W. Foster, *The Coquette* (New York, 1986), 8, 12; Brown, *The Power of Sympathy,* ed. William S. Kable (Columbus, Ohio, 1969).

6. Larzer Ziff, *Writing in the New Nation: Prose, Print, and Politics in the Early United States* (New Haven, 1991), 56. D'Emilio and Freedman, *Intimate Matters,* 43, provide the historical ground for Ziff's observation, noting that premarital pregnancy rates rose sharply in late 18th-century America, to as many as 1/3 of all brides in parts of New England. Summarizing the work of Joan Hoff Wilson, they claim this rise indicates "a breakdown of the traditional familial and community regulation of sexuality," as witnessed in "'a revolt of the young' against familial controls over marriage and sexuality." *Charlotte Temple* thus dramatizes the fate that more and more of its readers seemed to be avoiding: a young woman is impregnated by a man who then abandons her. See also Rothman, *Hands and Hearts,* 46.

shortly after the author's arrival from England the previous year, had a "sexual climate . . . remarkable for its lack of restraint. Casual sex, unmarried relationships, and adulterous affairs were commonplace," and although such activity highlighted the predicament of extramarital pregnancy for young women, it also featured a frank acknowledgment in popular print media of the sexuality of women outside the elite. Her contemporary urban readers may have found Charlotte's struggle to maintain her chastity most important not as a reflection on her ability to regulate sexual desire but rather class status. For while women outside the elite were often depicted as explicitly and even joyfully carnal, those who wished to claim the status of a lady needed to subdue lustful urges in order to lay claim to the virtue that was theirs to safeguard in the new republic. Attitudes toward sexuality were thus key indicators of social standing. As the daughter of a rural commoner and a father who had married beneath him, Charlotte bore a class status that was as indeterminate as that of many of her readers, and her control over her virginity would determine, for a fascinated young American urban female reader in a similarly volatile class hierarchy, whether the heroine descended into Philadelphia's "naturally lustful and licentious" lower class or qualified as an "exemplar[] of moral integrity." Furthermore, that she managed to reclaim her virtue, in the guise of her father's forgiveness, even after being seduced, suggested a way out for those who found the requirements of female gentility trying, while the high cost of reclamation (namely, imminent death) reminded them of the risks involved.[7]

The pressure to "assume responsibility for sexual propriety" in a culture dedicated to sexual transgression provides but one example of the myriad difficulties facing a young woman of the early national period hoping to "possess her soul in serenity," to borrow Judith Sargent Murray's polemic of a decade earlier on "Desultory Thoughts."[8] For even as certain valorized traits came to be associated

---

7. Godbeer, *Sexual Revolution in Early America*, 300, 306–07. On erotica in early America, see Peter Wagner, *Eros Revived: Erotica of the Enlightenment in England and America* (London, 1988). For an excellent summation of scholarly attitudes toward the history of sexuality in the 18th century, see Lynn Hunt and Margaret Jacob, "The Affective Revolution in 1790s Britain," *Eighteenth-Century Studies*, 34 (2001), esp. 496–97. Michel Foucault, *The History of Sexuality*, vol. 1: *An Introduction*, trans. Robert Hurley (New York, 1978), 15, 17, recounts "the repressive hypothesis" by which "an age of repression" intensified through the 19th century, only to turn the story on its head by performing a sort of word count. The more people condemned sex, he points out, the more certainly they inscribed it on their world in "a veritable discursive explosion"—the more certainly, that is, they produced it. Here, I reverse Foucault's gesture by noting how an apparent thematic presence (Charlotte's desire) is in fact more noteworthy as a discursive absence. On the relationship between the pursuit of gentility and the reading of sentimental novels, see Richard Bushman, *The Refinement of America: Persons, Houses, Cities* (New York, 1992), chap. 9.

8. Godbeer, *Sexual Revolution in Early America*, 306; Murray, "Desultory Thoughts . . ." (1784), in Sharon M. Harris, ed., *Selected Writings of Judith Sargent Murray* (New York, 1995), 47.

with post-revolutionary womanhood, ranging from a duty-bound notion of rights to a public, but no longer politically useful, conception of virtue, women's behavioral options were increasingly limited. Female rights, while not ignored, were conceived of according to Scottish common sense notions of societal obligation, while men alone, following the alternate trajectory of Lockean natural rights philosophy, possessed liberty, the ability "to choose one's destiny." At the same time, virtue in the previously male-oriented sense of active self-denial for the good of the polis was feminized in early national period precisely because, as a holdover from classical republicanism, it no longer served a nascent liberal political sphere premised on competition.[9]

The savage irony of a notion of female rights developing after the Revolution only to foster an increased sense of duty to outmoded notions of sexual virtue is made even more severe when one compares it with the ideology of perpetual opportunity facing young men of the period. Jay Fliegelman has written about the late eighteenth-century Anglo-American "adaptation and secularization of the Puritan narrative of the fortunate fall" by which "God had 'allowed' Adam and Eve to fall to permit them eventually to return to an even more intimate relationship with their Father than that they had originally lost." This dawning cultural emphasis on man's capacity to learn, and hence to benefit, from his mistakes is nowhere more evident than in the ultimate report of a prodigal son returned, Benjamin Franklin's *Autobiography*. By substituting the term "errata" for sin, Franklin turns moral trespasses into printer's errors that can, in the words of the epitaph Franklin wrote for himself, be "Corrected and amended." As Fliegelman suggests, the *Autobiography* exemplifies the belief that a prodigal son who has perfected himself is more valuable as a testament to self-improvement than would be one who had never failed.[1]

Franklin hardly mentions women in the *Autobiography*, and elsewhere he uses them mostly to illustrate lessons for men. This is because pregnancy gives the lie to Franklin's philosophy. Illicit sexual activity may, for a man, be simply another printer's mistake. A man who impregnates a woman bears no tangible mark of the experience, except possibly venereal disease (no slight possibility in post-

9. Rosemary Zagarri, "The Rights of Man and Woman in Post-Revolutionary America," *William and Mary Quarterly*, 3d Ser., 55 (1998), 203–30, 219; Ruth H. Bloch, "The Gendered Meanings of Virtue in Revolutionary America," *Signs*, 13 (1987), 37–58. For recent appraisals of the tensions between republican ideologies of "property and liberty" and liberal self-interest in the early United States, see Philip Gould, *Covenant and Republic: Historical Romance and the Politics of Puritanism* (Cambridge, 1996), esp. 25–26, and Nancy Isenberg, *Sex and Citizenship in Antebellum America* (Chapel Hill, 1998).

1. Fliegelman, *Prodigals and Pilgrims: The American Revolution against Patriarchal Authority* (Cambridge, 1982), 13, 83 (quotation), 111; Franklin, *Autobiography and Other Writings*, ed. Ormond Seavey (Oxford, 1993), esp. 227–28.

war Philadelphia). But an impregnated woman bears a mark that can only be erased at great physical and emotional cost, either through abortion or miscarriage. Pregnancy is a uniquely tangible sign of past activity, and it cannot be "corrected" without leaving record of itself. Unsanctioned pregnancy thus threatened the optimism of a newly developing moral and cultural system that emphasized man's capacity for self-determination. Prodigal daughters such as Charlotte were not offered the welcome their brothers received because it was impossible to reconcile their condition with the ideology of self-correctability that was reinforced by welcoming home a prodigal son. As exemplars of national virtue, women, like men, needed to learn, and learning required experimentation, but women's experiments were uniquely terrifying, since they did not possess the corollary privilege of having their mistakes expunged from the record. In such a climate, the secret wish to abdicate all decision-making must have had its appeal, even though, as Charlotte's story shows, it provided no real escape.[2]

The terrible consequences attendant on Charlotte's tendency to fall rather than step into events—her tragic indecisiveness, which made her a complete product of her surroundings, prey to nothing but circumstance—appealed to a female populace with increasingly limited capacity to experience themselves as independent, coherent beings in a post-revolutionary culture that made them the centerpiece of national identity even as it circumscribed their roles ever more closely. In her failure to become an agent, as opposed to an instrument of her destiny, Charlotte thematized, for the young American women who made her novel a household name, their difficulty in making contemporary theories of self-enfranchisement function in accord with equally powerful ideologies of womanhood that were an at best unwieldy fit with the mechanisms of agency in the new republic. Essentially, then, *Charlotte Temple* asks its American readers how women are to derive an integrated model of the self from the tortured cultural lexicon provided them.

In Charlotte, Rowson shows a woman who seems to fail at this task, only to commit, at the last minute of her life, a single decisive act: the handing over of her infant daughter to her father. This highly charged gesture suggests two contrary impulses. On the one hand, Charlotte literally makes her daughter the substance of her first autonomous act, investing her with a symbolic decisiveness unknown to her mother before this moment. On the other, that act is accompanied by a request for "protection" from the family patriarch, as if her

2. For an example of Franklin's textual use of women to illustrate lessons for men, see, for instance, his "Advice to a Friend on Choosing a Mistress," 1745 http://www.bibliomania.com/2/9/77/124/21473/1/frameset.html.

daughter were to pick up right where Charlotte left off, leaving her fate to others to determine. "'Protect her,' said she, 'and bless your dying . . .'" (p. 87). With this unfinished sentence, the reader is left hanging on the sounds of a wordless infant girl to find out how Charlotte would last have named herself. Will her daughter embody Charlotte's final courage and decisiveness or the meandering not-knowingness that led to her conception? Not until thirty-four years later would readers find out, in a posthumously published and similarly eponymous sequel, *Lucy Temple*. By that point, the young female readers asking this question of the early editions of *Charlotte Temple* would already have had to answer it for themselves, making the latter novel an exercise in nostalgia, whereas the original played a crucial role in the self-formation of a culture.

Whatever her legacy, Charlotte's final "ability to act" does suggest some "new knowledge": as La Rue would say, Charlotte does at last know her own mind, and as a result, she experiences agency, the "fortitude to put it in execution" (p. 36).[3] Of what exactly is the awareness that finally lets Charlotte take action composed? What kind of agency was available to a woman who had previously only seen herself as others saw her, or saw for her? And through what catalytic event could she come to experience it? Immediately before awaking to find her father at her side, Charlotte descends into a "phrenzy" that owes much to the evangelical tradition whose prioritization of affect as a means to understanding makes it an important precursor to American sentimentalism. Charlotte is no evangelical. Like Ellen in *The Wide, Wide World*, she loves her mother more than God, and her isolation is resolutely social, as opposed to spiritual, in nature. But she does proceed through something like conversion: the anxiety and alienation of a self distanced from its wished-for object drives her to a state Charles Chauncy would have been glad to label "enthusiasm," and her final return to her senses has all the earmarks of a work of grace, in that it seems impossible to explain without recourse to an intervening agent. Given the well-established historical links between evangelical and sentimentalist discourse and the

3. Susan Juster, "'In a Different Voice': Male and Female Narratives of Religious Conversion in Post-Revolutionary America," *American Quarterly*, 41 (1989), 53. See also Juster, *Disorderly Women: Sexual Politics and Evangelicalism in Revolutionary New England* (Ithaca, 1994). In viewing Charlotte's descent into madness through the lens of evangelical conversion, this essay expands on a field of inquiry linking 19th-century American sentimentalism to 18th-century evangelicalism initiated by Jane Tompkins, David S. Reynolds, Amanda Porterfield, Sandra Gustafson, and others. Tompkins, *Sensational Designs: The Cultural Work of American Fiction, 1790–1860* (New York, 1985), 149, claims that "sentimental fiction was perhaps the most influential expression of the beliefs that animated the revival movement." Reynolds, *Faith in Fiction: The Emergence of Religious Literature in America* (Cambridge, Mass., 1981); Porterfield, *Feminine Spirituality in America: From Sarah Edwards to Martha Graham* (Philadelphia, 1980); Gustafson, "Jonathan Edwards and the Reconstruction of 'Feminine' Speech," *American Literary History*, 6 (1994), 185–212.

almost uncanny way Charlotte's experience echoes accounts by female converts such as Sarah Pierpont, it seems useful to draw on one of the finest recent works on female conversion to come to an understanding of Charlotte's transformation. According to Susan Juster, published female evangelical conversion narratives from the late eighteenth-century United States reflected women's tendency to apprehend the world in terms of personal attachments, as opposed to men's relationship to an abstract order. For women, the challenge of conversion was to "disengage themselves from over-dependence on friends and family" enough to experience "individuation." Passing through the isolation of spiritual struggle, female converts emerged newly "empowered by recovering their sense of self through the assertion of independence from others." Certainly, Charlotte's progression from misplaced reliance on others, to being left "a prey to her own melancholy reflexions," to "the total deprivation of her reason," and to her final awakening makes sense in this frame, with the exception that most of the people Charlotte deemed friends turned out not to have her best interests at heart (pp. 71, 83). Moreover, in that the novel ends with Charlotte dictating terms to her father, however gently, it supports Juster's idea that evangelical women undergoing religious conversion obtained autonomy by passing through a period of alienation from those through whom they had formerly experienced life's significance. Torn from her country, her family, her schoolmates, her lover, and penultimately, any sense of her own reality (after giving birth, Charlotte "was totally insensible of everything. . . . She was not conscious of being a mother, nor took the least notice of her child except to ask whose it was, and why it was not carried to its parents"), Charlotte returns to familiar faces able for the first time to set the terms, albeit not of her own, but of her daughter's, future course (p. 84).[4]

But does the clarity of purpose this act portends, while obtained through isolation, necessarily derive from the forced rending of attachments that has characterized Charlotte's entire course in the novel? It would seem more likely that the new ability she demonstrates when she hands her daughter to her father is how to acknowledge her need for others. Before this decisive act, Charlotte turned

---

4. Juster, "In a Different Voice," 51, 53. Susan Warner, *The Wide, Wide World* (New York, 1987; orig. pub. 1851); Chauncy, "Enthusiasm Described and Caution'd Against," in Alan Heimert and Perry Miller, eds., *The Great Awakening: Documents Illustrating the Crisis and Its Consequences* (Indianapolis, 1967), 228–56. Sarah Pierpont Edwards's conversion narrative in Sereno Edwards Dwight, ed., *The Works of President Edwards: With a Memoir of His Life . . .* , 10 vols. (New York, 1830), 1:171–86. For a more punitive interpretation of Charlotte's delirium, according to which Rowson "reserves fits of insanity to identify and punish those guilty of sexual misbehavior," see Karen A. Weyler, "'The Fruit of Unlawful Embraces': Sexual Transgression and Madness in Early American Sentimental Fiction," in Merril D. Smith, ed., *Sex and Sexuality in Early America* (New York, 1998), 299.

away from love both licit and illicit, neither awaiting her grand-father's imminent arrival at her school nor actively defying her family in a spirited if socially disastrous adventure with her beseeching lieutenant. Far from experiencing herself as more distinct from others than she did before her period of "incoherence," Charlotte's final act may suggest that she has made her previously tenuous grasps at con-nection with them a fundamental aspect of her autonomy. In that case, she, like Franklin, has learned from her mistakes.

To suggest that Charlotte would have been better off had she acted on any form of preference, even sexual desire, than she was as a mere reflection of others' wishes for her is to see sexuality not only as a figure for agency but also as a potentially fundamental aspect of it. For Charlotte to move from being unable to act on any predilection, including that of a barely registered sexual yearning, to determining her daughter's guardian in the last moments of her life, suggests that the desire she once neither heeded nor subjugated underwent some form of transmutation in order to serve as the basis for a sophisti-cated moral agency. There is a tension in the novel, then, between understanding female desire as an impediment to autonomy (such that the seduction novel must warn against it in a fledgling democ-racy) and seeing desire as in some sense primary to autonomy (as I am suggesting Charlotte's final gesture should be read). The inten-sity of this struggle to understand the relationship between desire and independent action in the late eighteenth century can be seen in the first definition of "will" to appear in the fourth edition of Dr. Johnson's *Dictionary,* published in 1773, which does not appear in the first, published in 1755. Whereas previously Johnson was content to start off by calling will "choice," in the later edition he began by calling will "That power by which we desire, and purpose; velleity." "Velleity," in turn, is precisely what is left of will in the absence of subsequent action or choice; it is the "quality of merely willing, wish-ing, or desiring, without any effort or advance towards action or realization." Johnson's insertion of a definition of will that isolated desire from its execution demonstrates that he considered desire to be both will's fundamental impulse and insufficient to its exercise.[5]

This paradox, in turn, points to the difficulty of conceptualizing the self in a liberal polity. Locke defined the experience of selfhood as "perceiving that he does perceive," admitting the potentially infi-nitely regressive nature of self-awareness, given that each act of self-perception entails a new perceiving entity itself in need of witness for self-understanding to be complete. But because women were

---

5. Samuel Johnson, *A Dictionary of the English Language on CD-ROM,* ed. Anne McDer-mott (Cambridge, 1996); *Compact OED.* Johnson granted the novel a role in divesting will of its power, worrying that the desire inspired by fiction could "produce effects almost without the intervention of the will."

appointed guardians of features that threatened an ideology of male self-determination, post-revolutionary America had little use for what has been called "the constitutive disjunction of the self" into the perceiving "*I*" and the "*I*" as another object, perceived. Instead, self-possession was all: as the latter-day French *philosophe* Destutt de Tracy would exult, in a translation supervised by Thomas Jefferson for use in the United States, "individuality" is our "inalienable property."[6] Learning from one's mistakes was well and good, but the important thing was that one rest assured in the enabling fiction that one did in fact own oneself—that one existed in a fixed and commanding position over one's myriad psychic impulses. Self-formation thus entailed subjugating those aspects of mental experience that did not mesh with a forward-looking, self-promoting, property-obtaining citizenry. Authors such as Rowson and readers such as those who made *Charlotte Temple* a hit in its first years of American publication were toying with a notion of the self that found little favor in other cultural channels, one in which human errata, rather than needing to be corrected to fit a pre-existing order, could serve as constituent components of a changed order, much as Charlotte's daughter becomes part of her father's world after Charlotte herself is gone. In this environment, female error suggests not a fault on the part of the agent so much as an insufficiency in her surroundings, and female desire does not portend disaster, but rather independent action, a quality in short supply as young women learned elsewhere how not to want.

If one understands Charlotte's failure to direct her own life in its relation to the behavior of other characters in the novel, one sees these divergent modes of negotiating between impulse and action embodied in distinct characters. Lest there be any doubt that this is a book about the making of choices, its first words have to do with whether a character prefers to walk or drive. The central terms in the novel's discussion of agency are two, and they are used again and again in the text: "inclination" and "resolution." Both are considered modes of willing during the period (Johnson's definitions of the verb "to will" include "to be inclined or resolved to have"). Where they differ, not surprisingly, is in their relationship to desire. To be inclined is to experience "incipient desire" or "disposition of mind," while to be resolved is to possess "fixed determination." The latter category, though it does not deny desire outright, is differentiated from the former by a more explicit focus on subsequent action and, correspondingly, by an emphasis on the regulation of potentially inconsistent

6. Locke, *An Essay Concerning Human Understanding* (1690), ed. A. D. Woozley (Glasgow, 1980), 211. [Comte Antoine Louis Claude] Destutt de Tracy, "A Treatise on Political Economy" (1817), in *Psychology of Political Science*, ed. John M. Dorsey, trans. Jefferson (Detroit, 1973), 41–42, 47.

impulses to make such action possible as well as beneficial. In short, resolution directs will from "velleity" to "choice," from the passions to the understanding, and from proclivity to explicit action, with the latter's implications for self-mastery. The struggle between the two terms in the novel extends from the protagonist's coming to terms with her own propensities, to the interactions between characters, to the narrative mode itself, in which appeals to the reader's sympathetic identification based on benevolent inclination alternate with calls to disciplined detachment based on steely resolve.

Characters in *Charlotte Temple* tend to one of three ways of resolving these two terms, only one of which brings satisfaction. The most successful individuals, who end the book alive, well, and free from lasting inner torment, tend to experience simultaneity of inclination and resolve. Charlotte's father, Mr. Temple, wants Lucy Eldridge for his wife. He discerns that despite his father's objections and the resultant decline he can expect in his annual income, Lucy will bring him earthly felicity otherwise unattainable, and he pursues her without hesitation. Similarly, much later on, Lucy, now Mrs. Temple, wants to give her daughter a birthday party, and she knows to go to some lengths to persuade her reluctant husband to allow her to do so, because the party will make everybody happy (if only everyone, including her daughter, would attend). These are cases where inclinations based on affect (loving the woman, yearning to please the daughter) and resolutions directing understanding to satisfy inclination (defying the father, persuading the husband) go hand-in-hand. There is no real tension, no danger, no potential negative consequence, to giving into impulse. Moreover, on the rare occasions where resolution and inclination are in conflict, these individuals are also capable of self-regulation; when, for instance, Mrs. Temple learns of her daughter's elopement, she insists that "I will wear a smile on my face, though the thorn rankles in my heart," in order to make her husband feel better, and she proceeds immediately to "the execution of so laudable a resolution" (p. 43). Having somehow managed to cultivate a passion for duty, these characters embody what one critic considers the novel's mission to "instruct young ladies . . . in being content with one's lot in life," and while they lead peaceful lives, they make for extremely boring novels.[7]

Never fear, however, because these exemplars are inevitably paired with less benevolent twins who, while similarly inclined to follow their impulses, arrive at no such happy results for themselves or others. Their deleterious effects derive from two sources, rash-

<hr/>

7. Patricia Parker, cited in Devon White, "Contemporary Criticism of Five Early American Sentimental Novels, 1970–1994: An Annotated Bibliography," *Bulletin of Bibliography*, 52 (1995), 294.

ness or sheer sadism—or both. Like Mr. and Mrs. Temple, Lieutenant Montraville knows what he wants and acts on his wishes, but in his case, the effects on those he meets are disastrous. Thus "generous in his disposition, liberal in his opinions, and good-natured almost to a fault," Montraville is nevertheless "eager and impetuous in the pursuit of a favorite object," and "he staid not to reflect on the consequence which might follow the attainment of his wishes" (p. 29), even though he realizes that Charlotte is too poor to marry. Montraville learns too late the difference between "momentary passion" (p. 63) and lasting love; for him, inclination is all.

Finally, there are persons, such as La Rue and Belcour, who glory in the suffering of others. Ironically, these are beings capable of great resolve, happy to put off the satisfaction of a ruinous impulse as long as the ruination will be all the more dramatic. Thus La Rue can feign indifference as to whether Charlotte accompanies her on her nocturnal visit to the local regiment, and Belcour can (literally) lie in wait for Montraville's arrival, rather than accost Charlotte on the spot. Both know how to manipulate momentary impulse in the service of a greater end. It is significant, however, that Charlotte is finally undone not by these caricatures but by Montraville himself, who lifts her into the carriage at Chichester and leaves her alone among skeptical strangers outside New York. For pure evil, like pure good, is easy to recognize. It is those with good intentions but no capacity to regulate their outcome—those in whom inclination and resolve are at odds—that the novel trains its readers to detect, both outside and within themselves.

The problem is that even when, like Charlotte, the reader knows not to act on every impulse, disaster cannot necessarily be averted. Smart enough to doubt her inclinations but not strong enough either to defy or to indulge them, Charlotte ends up unable to form a resolution, and it is her fundamental inaction, rather than any particular inclination, that proves her undoing. Ironically, her strongest wish, had she merely obeyed it, was to rejoin her parents. Had she trusted to impulse, as Mr. and Mrs. Temple did before her, she would have been fine. Thus the novel presents contrary, and gendered, models of deportment. For young women such as Charlotte, it seems to suggest a surer grasp on benevolent impulse, a quickness to action that can prevent the reader from falling into vacuous indecision. For young men such as Montraville the call to action is tempered by another to reflection, because impulse itself in such cases seems less certainly altruistic. In a book addressed to "the young and thoughtless of the fair sex," Charlotte's indecisiveness takes precedence over Rowson's less detailed representation of the male subject.

Charlotte has several methods for forestalling choice. Unable to figure out her own preference, she tends to act according to whether she thinks her actions will make others think well of her. For this reason, La Rue, ever alert to the best ways to manipulate others to her own ends, can mock Charlotte's reticence to meet Montraville by pointing out that the whole school will laugh at her: "You will bear the odium of having formed the resolution of eloping, and every girl of spirit will laugh at your want of fortitude to put it in execution" (p. 36). Second, Charlotte possesses a fatal optimism regarding the possibility of remediable action: a faith most tragically misplaced in her misunderstanding of the nature of chastity, but nicely anticipated in her observation early in the novel that, because the wafer on a letter from Montraville is not dry (she has unknowingly wet it with her tears), she might "read it, and return it afterwards" (p. 25). In the context of her attempt to decide whether to see the lieutenant again, Charlotte's opening a letter from him with the idea that she can make the letter look as though it hasn't been read (since the wafer is wet, she won't have to break a seal) serves as a metonym for the event to which the letter invites her—the loss of her virginity—whose consequence, she also fails to anticipate, is ineradicable. Both these habits of mind get Charlotte into trouble. But by far her greatest failing is her over-great faith in her own "stability," as demonstrated in such passages as "Charlotte had, when she went out to meet Montraville, flattered herself that her resolution was not to be shaken, and that . . . she would never repeat the indiscretion" (p. 75–76) and "in her heart every meeting was resolved to be the last" (p. 32). At one point, she even exults: "How shall I rejoice . . . in this triumph of reason over inclination" (p. 36). Charlotte is good at resolving, or at least planning to resolve, but "resolutions will not execute themselves," and she is incapable of granting any single impetus to action enough sway to direct her once and for all.[8] Charlotte is not impetuous; she does not give in to inclinations once she senses that they might hurt her, but having come to the point of knowing not to do something, she is nonetheless incapable of doing something else, and this inability to come to any decision haunts her. At moments of great dramatic import, she is inflicted by a desire to be doing the opposite of whatever she is engaged in, such that "even in the moment when . . . I fled from you . . . even then I loved you most" (pp. 60), as she explains to her mother.

In a nation where individuality was seen as the ability to take action consistent with one's intent, for Charlotte not to know what she wants—or not to be able to act accordingly when she does know—is for her not to know who she is. And the novel brings the reader to a similar relationship to its words that Charlotte experiences in relation to her own fluctuating psychic processes. To the

8. Johnson, *The Rambler*, 1752, cited in *Compact OED*.

degree that incompatibilities between "inclination" and "resolve" operate in the book as a mode as well as a topic, with appeals to appetite and stern correctives occurring simultaneously on the page, the reader becomes an unwilling participant in the processes he or she might hope to have contemplated from a distance. Characteristic of the late eighteenth-century American sentimental novel as represented by its best-selling volume is not only its much-denigrated appeal to convention, its seemingly manipulative and paradoxically quite cold machinery for evoking emotion in its spectators both inside and outside the text, but another, more genuinely performative kind of energy.[9]

Many critics deny such a possibility in their assumption that Rowson's narrative persona is seamlessly controlling.[1] Such readings mistake a need for control with its achievement. That is, the very ostentation of the Rowsonian narrator's comforting asides might just as easily suggest an anticipation of loss such as that proposed by Julia Stern in her analysis of "the absent mother who occupies and directs the narrative frame."[2] This alternative is supported by an oscillation in the novel's narrative mode, which shifts between the self-monitoring impulse characteristic of the sentimental novel's didactic strand and a self-losing, almost ecstatic impulse of submission to forces outside the self.

The narrative is rent by opposing impulses and seems unable to decide on its own course of action. Instead, it swerves without seeming rhyme or reason between appeals to disciplined detachment and appeals to sympathetic identification. At the very moment, for instance, that Belcour is abandoning the dying Charlotte—a moment readers might be expected to empathize with her sad state—the description takes place at further and further removes:

> His visits became less frequent; he forgot the solemn charge given him by Montraville; he even forgot the money entrusted to his care; and, *the burning blush of indignation and shame tinges my cheek while I write it,* this disgrace to humanity and manhood at length forgot even the injured Charlotte; and, attracted

9. In reference to British novels of the same period, J. S. Tompkins, *The Popular Novel in England, 1770–1800* (Lincoln, Neb., 1961 [1932]), 107, describes the joining of mechanism to extravagance beautifully in the phrase "conventionalized extravagance of bearing."

1. Forcey, "Charlotte Temple and the End of Epistolarity," 231, 236, writes, "Rowson's narrative incursions provide an authoritative unifying voice which gives structure and guidance to the reader." She characterizes the novel's "narrative voice" as "unselfish, affectionate, gently admonitory, helpful, teacherly, and attentive," functioning primarily to "inform, improve and enrich the lives of [Rowson's] readers." See also Donna R. Bontatibus, *The Seduction Novel of the Early Nation: A Call for Socio-Political Reform* (East Lansing, Mich., 1999), esp. chap. 1 and conclusion.

2. Stern, *Plight of Feeling: Sympathy and Dissent in the Early American Novel* (Chicago, 1997), pp. 486 of this NCE.

> by the blooming health of a farmer's daughter . . . left the
> unhappy girl to sink unnoticed to the grave [pp. 74, emphasis
> added].

Why does the narrator feel compelled to interject her own cheek at
this moment? By doing so, she inserts another link in the perceptual
chain separating victim from reader, as we now must witness the
narrator watching Belcour watching (or failing to watch) Charlotte.
She thereby exacerbates the scene's already voyeuristic aspect, creating a spectacle now "dependent not only on the implied spectatorship of the reader/viewer," nor even "on the express spectatorship of
internal witnesses" alone, but on a third, explicitly embodied narrative presence.[3] Her comment thus distances us even further from the
events at hand and reinforces a sense of the remoteness of the events
taking place that is at odds with any sympathetic identification with
Charlotte. At the same time, the narrator provides the reader with an
extremely uncharacteristic reference to her own body. As such, it
mimics Charlotte's blush of shame and encourages the reader to
reflect on what she, too, might have to "blush" for, thereby creating a
sense of shared vulnerability with the protagonist. The Rowsonian
narrator is thus at her most confessional at the very moment she puts
us at the furthest remove from the details of her story. She appeals to
our sympathetic and our censorious tendencies simultaneously and
leaves us, like Charlotte, like the narrator herself, unable to do anything effective. Instead, we dwell in the kind of anxious self-doubt
that Charlotte found so painful.[4]

A similar entanglement occurs in the last paragraph of the novel,
when the dead Charlotte's father takes in the woman who could be
said to have murdered his daughter:

> Greatly as Mr. Temple had reason to detest Mrs. Crayton, he
> could not behold her in this distress without some emotions of

---

3. Karen Halttunen, "Humanitarianism and the Pornography of Pain in Anglo-American
   Culture," *American Historical Review*, 100 (1995), 317.
4. What Patricia Meyer Spacks, *Desire and Truth*, 121, calls the "incongruity between the
   benevolent human being's utter separation from the object of benevolence" and "the
   impulse toward merging implicit in the idea of 'sympathy'" has been central to discussions of 18th- and 19th-century sentimentalism for some time now. Halttunen,
   "Humanitarianism and the Pornography of Pain in Anglo-American Culture," 308,
   notes that "the convention of spectatorial sympathy . . . was deeply ambivalent in its
   treatment of the pain and suffering of other sentient beings. Sentimental sympathy
   was said to be . . . an emotional experience that liberally mingled pleasure with vicari-
   ous pain." The most incisive commentary on spectacle and sentimentalism in the
   American novel remains James Baldwin's attack on Harriet Beecher Stowe's *Uncle
   Tom's Cabin* and Richard Wright's *Native Son*: "Sentimentality, the ostentatious parad-
   ing of excessive and spurious emotion, is the mark of dishonesty, the inability to feel;
   the wet eyes of the sentimentalist betray his aversion to experience, his fear of life, his
   arid heart; and it is always, therefore, the signal of secret and violent inhumanity, the
   mask of cruelty"; Baldwin, "Everybody's Protest Novel," *Notes of a Native Son* (Boston,
   1984 [1955]), 14.

pity. He gave her shelter that night beneath his hospitable roof, and the next day got her admission into an hospital; where having lingered a few weeks, she died, *a striking example, that vice, however prosperous in the beginning, in the end leads only to misery and shame.* [p. 90, emphasis added].

Here the reader is treated to one last surrender to benevolent inclination ("he could not") over steely resolve ("had reason to"), only to be asked to relish it from a distance—to look not on Mr. Temple's kindness but on Mrs. Crayton's just deserts. The warmth of forgiveness is elicited, only to be trumped by the far more readily indulged satisfaction at the death of an enemy.

That American readers welcomed the opportunity to make Charlotte's struggle their own is indicated by the memorial they established for her in New York's Trinity Churchyard. Susanna Rowson could have asked for no surer testament that her "novel" had been received, at least in the United States, according to the plan laid out for it in her preface, as a template for the "conduct" of its readers, as opposed to a guilty pleasure meant to be forgotten as soon as finished (p. 5). It may have been the first American novel to take on antebellum sentimentalism's signature task: making imaginary engagement (reading) result in specific subsequent action (such as ending slavery). (In the most famous articulation of this ethos, President Lincoln is said to have credited Harriet Beecher Stowe with writing the book—*Uncle Tom's Cabin*—that started the Civil War.) In this sense at least, Rowson helped initiate American sentimentalism's most astounding accomplishment: causing the aesthetic to be re-conceived in implicitly political terms. Peering down at a presumably empty grave—or at least, we can assume, one that did not contain any fictional characters—also speaks to the ambivalence that lingers alongside Rowson's call to female action. Through its dissonant appeals to contrary readerly responses, the novel provides an instantiation, as well as an allegory, of the paradoxical nature of female subjectivity during a period in which women were expected to submit to codes limiting both pleasure and agency, and yet to conceive of their position as one they chose and from which they derived satisfaction.

Susanna Rowson: A Chronology

February 1762   Susanna is only child born to Susanna Musgrave Haswell and Royal Navy Lieutenant William Haswell, Portsmouth, England. Mother dies shortly after birth.

1763   Royal Navy sends Rowson's father, William, to Massachusetts as collector of Royal Customs; he leaves daughter with relatives in England.

1766   William, having settled in Nantasket and remarried Rachel Woodward, sails with his daughter to America, arriving in Boston Harbor in a severe storm.

1775–77   After William refuses to take an oath of allegiance to the revolutionary cause, the Haswell family is taken prisoner, moved inland, and kept under house arrest.

1778   The Haswell family is taken to Nova Scotia, exchanged for American prisoners of war, and sent to England. Susanna begins to frequent London's Drury Lane and Covent Garden theaters.

1786   Marries actor and musician William Rowson. *Victoria, A Novel . . . The Characters Taken from Real Life, and Calculated to Improve the Morals of the Female Sex, By Impressing Them with a Just Sense of the Merits of Filial Piety.*

1788   *A Trip to Parnassus; or, the Judgment of Apollo on Dramatic Authors and Performers. A Poem.* Also *The Inquisitor; or Invisible Rambler.* Also *Poems on Various Subjects.*

1789   *The Test of Honour. A Novel. By a Young Lady.*

1791   *Charlotte. A Tale of Truth* and *Mentoria; or the Young Lady's Friend.*

1792   Performs at the Edinburgh Theatre Royal. *Rebecca, or the Fille de Chambre.*

1793   In July, the Rowsons sail for America as members of Thomas Wignell's theater troupe. Their ship, the *George Barclay*, is unable to land in Philadelphia due to a yellow fever epidemic. The company opens in Annapolis.

1794   Wignell's company relocates to the New Theatre in Philadelphia. "America, Commerce and Freedom," with lyrics by Rowson and music by Alexander Reinagle, becomes a popular song, one of many collaborations between the two. Writes *Slaves in Algiers; or, a Struggle for Freedom: A Play Interspersed with Songs, in Three Acts* (published 1794); *The Volunteers* (published 1795); and *The Female Patriot; or, Nature's Rights*. American publication of *Charlotte*, *Mentoria*, and *Rebecca* (under its subtitle, *The Fille de Chambre*).

1795   *Trials of the Human Heart, A Novel*. Also *The Volunteers. A Musical Entertainment as performed at the New Theatre*.

1796   Susanna and William move to Boston to join the Federal Street Theatre. By July, she will have performed at least seventy-three roles. *Americans in England; or, Lessons for Daughters. A Comedy*.

1797   Mrs. Rowson's Young Ladies' Academy opens in Boston. *Charlotte* republished as *Charlotte Temple: A Tale of Truth*.

1798   *Reuben and Rachel; or, Tales of Old Times. A Novel*.

1799   London publication of *Reuben and Rachel*.

1800   Young Ladies' Academy moves to Medford.

1802   First student exhibition of the Young Ladies' Academy.

1803–04   Academy moves to Newton. *Sincerity* serialized in the *Boston Weekly Magazine*.

1804   *Miscellaneous Poems*.

1806   *An Abridgment of Universal Geography, Together with Sketches of History. Designed for the Use of Schools and Academies in the United States*.

1807   Academy returns to Boston. *A Spelling Dictionary, Divided into Short Lessons, for the Easier Committing to Memory by Children and Young Persons; and Calculated to Assist Youth in Comprehending What They Read*.

1811   Academy moves to permanent location on Hollis Street. *A Present for Young Ladies; Containing Poems, Dialogues, Addresses, & c. As Recited by the Pupils of Mrs. Rowson's Academy, at the Annual Exhibitions*.

1813   *Sarah, or The Exemplary Wife* (formerly published serially as *Sincerity*).

1814   Revised Boston edition of *Rebecca, or The Fille de Chambre*.

1818   *Youth's First Step in Geography. Being a Series of Exercises Making the Tour of the Habitable Globe. For the Use of Schools.*

1822   *Biblical Dialogues between a Father and his Family: Comprising Sacred History, from the Creation to the Death of Our Saviour Christ. The Lives of the Apostles, and the Promulgation of the Gospel; with a Sketch of the History of the Church down to the Reformation. The Whole Carried on in Conjunction with Profane History. Also Exercises in History, Chronology, and Biography, in Question and Answer. For the Use of Schools. Comprising Ancient History, Greece, Rome &c. Modern History, England, France, Spain, Portugal, &c. The Discovery of America, Rise, Progress and Final Independence of the United States.*

1821   Friend Catherine Graupner dies.

1822   Retires from the academy.

March 2, 1824   Dies.

1828   *Charlotte's Daughter: or, The Three Orphans. A Sequel to Charlotte Temple; To Which Is Prefixed a Memoir of the Author* (also known as *Lucy Temple*).

Selected Bibliography

• indicates items included or excerpted in this Norton Critical Edition.

• Armstrong, Nancy. "Why Daughters Die: The Racial Logic of American Sentimentalism." *Yale Journal of Criticism* 7.2 (1994): 1–24.
    In an exploration of "what happened to British sentimentalism when it came to this country," this essay illustrates the interdependence of gender and race in the construction of national identity.
• Barnes, Elizabeth. *States of Sympathy: Seduction and Democracy in the American Novel*. New York: Columbia University Press, 1997.
    Barnes argues that early American novels traded in the phenomena they warned readers against, seducing readers into an "intimate relationship" with postrevolutionary patriarchy.
Baym, Nina. *American Women Writers and the Work of History, 1790–1860*. New Brunswick, NJ: Rutgers University Press, 1995.
    This study foregrounds a neglected aspect of Rowson and other early American authors' *oeuvre*, which unlike fiction was highly recommended for female readers.
Bloch, Ruth. *Gender and Morality in Anglo-American Culture, 1650–1800*. Berkeley: University of California Press, 2003.
    In a study of the links between "American Protestantism, Scottish moral philosophy, and literary sentimentalism," Bloch shows how ideas about public virtue were feminized in the early republic.
Brandt, Ellen B. *Susanna Haswell Rowson: America's First Best-selling Novelist*. Chicago: Serbra Press, 1975.
    This neglected study provides a thorough, informative, and sophisticated overview of Rowson's literary career.
Brown, Herbert Ross. *The Sentimental Novel in America, 1789–1860*. Durham, NC: Duke University Press, 1940.
    Writing before the novels he studies attracted even minor critical attention, Brown apologizes for the paltry literary value of his subject before engaging in a detailed overview.
Bushman, Richard. *The Refinement of America; Persons, Houses, Cities*. New York: Vintage, 1993.
    Bushman's title might have added "and Novels," which he considers one of many objects nineteenth-century Americans used in a contradictory attempt to fashion a democratic gentility.
• Cott, Nancy. *The Bonds of Womanhood: "Woman's Sphere" in New England, 1780–1835*. New Haven, CT: Yale University Press, 1997. (Originally published 1977.)
    Sets the standard in early American women's history.
• Davidson, Cathy, ed. *Reading in America: Literature and Social History*. Baltimore: Johns Hopkins University Press, 1989.
    This fascinating collection of essays includes the textual history of *Charlotte Temple* reprinted here.

515

————. *Revolution and the Word: The Rise of the Novel in America.* Expanded ed. Oxford: Oxford University Press, 2004.

> This edition of the definitive study of the early American novel includes a new introduction by the author.

• Dobson, Joanne. "Reclaiming Sentimental Literature." *American Literature* 69.2 (June 1997): 263–88.

> Dobson uses formalist methods to argue for the literary merits of sentimental discourse.

Doody, Margaret. *The True Story of the Novel.* New Brunswick, NJ: Rutgers University Press, 1996.

> A sprawling, scintillating account of the novel's debt to classical literature.

Douty, Esther M. "Susanna Haswell Rowson, Writer-Patriot." In *Under the New Roof: Five Patriots of the Young Republic* (235–75). Chicago: Rand McNally, 1965.

> This imaginative reconstruction of Rowson's years in America, aimed at a young audience, is charming if a little dated.

Duyckinck, Evert A. "Susanna Rowson." *Cyclopaedia of American Literature.* New York: Scribner, 1856.

> An early and characteristically condescending account that has failed to garner much attention.

• Evans, Gareth. "Rakes, Coquettes and Republican Patriarchs: Class, Gender and Nation in Early American Sentimental Fiction." *Canadian Review of American Studies* 25.3 (Fall 1995): 41–63.

> Evans discusses three early American sentimental novels' attempts to consolidate middle-class identity by rejecting aristocratic behavior, personified in the figure of the seducing rake. Opposed to this figure stands a virtuous and benevolent father, symbolic of new forms of middle-class patriarchy.

Fiedler, Leslie A. *Love and Death in the American Novel.* Urbana-Champaign: Dalkey Archive Press, University of Illinois, 1998. (Originally published 1966.)

> Fiedler argues that *Charlotte Temple* begins the ruin of American literature by women.

Fliegelman, Jay. *Declaring Independence: Jefferson, Natural Language, & the Culture of Performance.* Stanford, CA: Stanford University Press, 1993.

————. *Prodigals and Pilgrims: The American Revolution against Patriarchal Authority.* Cambridge: Cambridge University Press, 1982.

> This scholar arguably influenced early American literary historians more than any other.

• Forcey, Blythe. "*Charlotte Temple* and the End of Epistolarity." *American Literature* 63.2 (June 1991): 225–41.

> This essay attributes *Charlotte Temple*'s popularity to its motherly narrative voice, which comforted a diverse and mobile population in a way that a novel without a narrator could not.

Franchot, Jenny. "Susanna Haswell Rowson." In *Dictionary of Literary Biography,* vol. 37: *American Writers of the Early Republic.* Ed. Emory Elliott. Detroit: Gale Press, 1985.

> An authoritative brief account by a late scholar.

• Gilmore, William J. *Reading Becomes a Necessity of Life: Material and Cultural Life in Rural New England, 1780–1835.* Knoxville: University of Tennessee Press, 1989.

> Gilmore documents the conservative bent behind early national practices of reading instruction, while allowing that they led women to a greater desire for social equity.

Halsey, Francis W. "Historical and Biographical Introduction." *Charlotte Temple, a Tale of Truth; Reprinted from the Rare First American Edition (1794), over Twelve Hundred Errors in Later Editions Being Corrected, and the Preface Restored.* New York: Funk & Wagnalls, 1905.

> The first scholarly edition of this text.

• Howard, June. "What Is Sentimentality?" *American Literary History* 11.1 (Spring 1999): 63–81.

  Drawing from sociology, psychology, and anthropology, this essay employs a transdisciplinary method in order to discuss the interdependence of thought and feeling.

• Kerber, Linda. *Women of the Republic: Intellect & Ideology in Revolutionary America.* Chapel Hill: University of North Carolina Press, 1997. (Originally published 1980.)

  This recent edition of a classic in women's history includes a new introduction by Kerber.

• Knapp, Samuel. *Charlotte's Daughter; or, The Three Orphans. A Sequel to Charlotte Temple. By Susannah Rowson. To Which Is Prefixed a Memoir of the Author.* Boston: Richardson & Lord, 1828.

  In the first published biographical account of Rowson, Knapp (the father of a former student of Rowson's) both describes and enacts her recuperation from unseemly public figure to model female citizen in terms oddly reminiscent of Charlotte's own transformation.

Kritzer, Amelia Howe, ed. *Plays by Early American Women, 1775–1850.* Ann Arbor: University of Michigan Press, 1995.

  Kritzer's anthology discusses Rowson's work as an actress, a playwright, and a lyricist.

Merish, Lori. *Sentimental Materialism: Gender, Commodity Culture, and Nineteenth-Century American Literature.* Durham, NC: Duke University Press, 2000.

  A materialist interpretation of the sentimental novel, which argues that it served to reinforce the illusion of self-determination among its nineteenth-century readers.

• Nason, Elias. *A Memoir of Mrs. Susanna Rowson.* Albany, NY: Joel Munsell, 1870.

  Nason praises *Charlotte Temple* for its appeal to a wide range of nineteenth-century Americans.

Noble, Marianne. *The Masochistic Pleasures of Sentimental Literature.* Princeton, NJ: Princeton University Press, 2000.

  Noble finds a crucial way to discuss the interdependence of choice and submission in the lives of sentimental heroines and their readers.

Parker, Patricia. *Susanna Rowson.* Boston: Twayne, 1986.

  Scholars rely on this biography for much of what we know about Rowson's career.

———. "Susanna Rowson (February 1762–2 March 1824)." In *Dictionary of Literary Biography*, vol. 200: *American Prose Writers to 1820* (313–25). Ed. Carla Mulford, Angela Vietto, and Amy Winans. Detroit: Gale Press, 1999.

  The most up-to-date account of its kind, this entry provides information not found in Parker's earlier study.

Rust, Marion. *Prodigal Daughters: Susanna Rowson's Early American Women.* Chapel Hill: University of North Carolina Press in association with the Omohundro Institute of Early American History and Culture, 2008.

  This study places *Charlotte Temple* in the context of Rowson's life and other writings, showing how an early form of American sentimentalism mediated the constantly shifting balance between autonomy and submission that is key to understanding both Rowson's work and the lives of early American women.

• ———. "What's Wrong with *Charlotte Temple*?" *William & Mary Quarterly* 60.1 (2003): 99–118.

  Rust challenges two prevailing interpretations of the novel, arguing that it should be read as a warning against neither unlicensed sex nor the perils of republicanism but rather the dangers inherent in female deference.

Ryals, Kay Ferguson. "America, Romance, and the Fate of the Wandering Woman: The Case of *Charlotte Temple*." In *Women, America, and Movement*:

Narratives of Relocation (81–105). Ed. Susan L. Roberson. Columbia: University of Missouri Press, 1998.

   Ryals reads *Charlotte Temple* as a quest romance in which a female character plays the hero.

Samuels, Shirley, ed. *The Culture of Sentiment: Race, Gender, and Sentimentality in 19th Century America*. New York and Oxford: Oxford University Press, 1992.

   This groundbreaking collection emphasizes sentimentalism's complicity in the institutional oppression of blacks and women.

Scheurmann, Mona. "The American Novel of Seduction: An Exploration of the Omission of the Sex Act in *The Scarlet Letter*." *The Nathaniel Hawthorne Journal* 78 (1978): 105–18.

   Hard to find but worth it, this study uses *Charlotte Temple* to explain *The Scarlet Letter*'s omission.

• Stern, Julia. *The Plight of Feeling: Sympathy and Dissent in the Early American Novel*. Chicago: University of Chicago Press, 1997.

   Stern argues that early American novels helped those betrayed by the American Revolution articulate a common plight.

• Todd, Janet. *Sensibility: An Introduction*. London and New York: Methuen, 1986.

   This overview of sentimentalism's roots in eighteenth-century theories of mind and emotion is especially useful for defining the relationship between sensibility and sentimentality.

Tompkins, Jane. *Sensational Designs: The Cultural Work of American Fiction, 1790–1860*. Oxford: Oxford University Press, 1986.

   This study put "cultural work" on the map, arguing that sentimental literature mattered because, and not in spite of, its reliance on convention, its concern with women, and its popular appeal.

• ———. "Susanna Rowson, Father of the American Novel." In *The (Other) American Traditions: Nineteenth-Century Women Writers* (29–38). Ed. Joyce W. Warren. Piscataway, NJ: Rutgers University Press, 1993.

   Making a case for Rowson's literary paternity, Tompkins compares the careers of Rowson and fellow author Charles Brockden Brown to show how women have been categorically excluded from the canon.

Vail, R. W. G. *Susanna Haswell Rowson, the Author of Charlotte Temple; A Bibliographical Study*. Reprinted from the *Proceedings of the American Antiquarian Society* for April, 1932. Worcester, MA: American Antiquarian Society, 1933.

   A classic study that provides the basis for much later work on the author.

Warner, Michael. *The Letters of the Republic: Publication and the Public Sphere in Eighteenth-Century America*. Cambridge, MA: Harvard University Press, 1990.

   Warner's last chapter takes on the early American novel, which he argues signals a decline in the nascent American public sphere.

Weil, Dorothy. *In Defense of Women: Susanna Rowson (1762–1824)*. University Park: Pennsylvania State University Press, 1976.

   With Brandt and Parker, this biography remains a crucial resource on the author.

Woodard, Maureen L. "Female Captivity and the Deployment of Race in Three Early American Texts." *Papers on Language & Literature* 32 (1996).

   Examines Mary Rowlandson, Charles Brockden Brown, and Rowson's treatment of female entrapment.

• Ziff, Larzer. *Writing in the New Nation: Prose, Print and Politics in the Early United States*. New Haven, CT: Yale University Press, 1991.

   To explain *Charlotte Temple*'s unprecedented appeal to American readers despite their historical tolerance of premarital sex, Ziff argues that the novel addressed anxieties latent in a geographically mobile Protestant society increasingly dependent on external signs to determine individual worth.